LOVE AT A CRUX

CAMERON CROSS

Love at a Crux

The New Persian Romance
in a Global Middle Ages

UNIVERSITY OF TORONTO PRESS
Toronto Buffalo London

© University of Toronto Press 2023
Toronto Buffalo London
utorontopress.com
Printed in the USA

ISBN 978-1-4875-4727-1 (cloth)
ISBN 978-1-4875-4728-8 (EPUB)
ISBN 978-1-4875-4729-5 (PDF)

Library and Archives Canada Cataloguing in Publication
Title: Love at a crux : the new Persian romance
in a global Middle Ages / Cameron Cross.
Names: Cross, Cameron, author.
Description: Includes bibliographical references and index.
Identifiers: Canadiana (print) 20230503152 |
Canadiana (ebook) 20230503179 | ISBN 9781487547271 (cloth) |
ISBN 9781487553128 (PDF-OA) | ISBN 9781487547295 (PDF) |
ISBN 9781487547288 (EPUB)
Subjects: LCSH: Fakhr al-Dīn Gurgānī, active 1048. Vīs va Rāmīn. |
LCSH: Romances, Persian – History and criticism. |
LCSH: Persian literature – 747–1500 – History and criticism. |
LCSH: Love in literature.
Classification: LCC PK6451.F28 Z78 2023 | DDC 398.22/0955–dc23

Cover design: EmDash

Calligraphy on page 1 adapted by Andrea LeJeune from the anonymous calligrapher
of Isl. Ms. 316, University of Michigan Library (Special Collections Research Center).
Translation by Geoffrey Squires in *Hafez* (Miami University Press, 2015). All sources
used with permission.

This book is freely available in an open access edition thanks to TOME (Toward
an Open Monograph Ecosystem) – a collaboration of the Association of American
Universities, the Association of University Presses, and the Association of Research
Libraries – and the generous support of the University of Michigan. Learn more at
the TOME website, available at: openmonographs.org.

We wish to acknowledge the land on which the University of Toronto Press
operates. This land is the traditional territory of the Wendat, the Anishnaabeg, the
Haudenosaunee, the Métis, and the Mississaugas of the Credit First Nation.

University of Toronto Press acknowledges the financial support of the Government
of Canada, the Canada Council for the Arts, and the Ontario Arts Council, an agency
of the Government of Ontario, for its publishing activities.

Canada Council
for the Arts

Conseil des Arts
du Canada

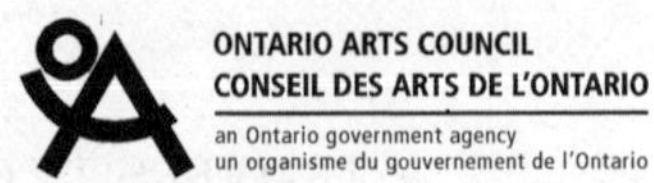

ONTARIO ARTS COUNCIL
CONSEIL DES ARTS DE L'ONTARIO

an Ontario government agency
un organisme du gouvernement de l'Ontario

Funded by the
Government
of Canada

Financé par le
gouvernement
du Canada

Canadä

To Andrea
For Frank

Contents

Reader's Notes

I have written this book to be accessible to a wide academic audience, not only specialists in Iranian studies. This goal has led me to adopt a few stylistic decisions that I outline below.

Dates. For simplicity's sake, I use only Common Era dates in this study; the bibliography, however, preserves solar and lunar *hijrī* dates as they appear in the publication, with the CE equivalent given in brackets.

Non-Roman Scripts. When transliterating Persian, I adapt the system used by the *Encyclopædia Iranica* with the following adjustments: the special characters š, č, ž, ḡ, and ḵ have been replaced with the digraphs *sh*, *ch*, *zh*, *gh*, and *kh*; ṯ is rendered as ś, and ḏ as ẕ (though I occasionally keep ḏ when it corresponds with the modern pronunciation *d*, as in *shavaḏ*). In addition, I write the unstressed indefinite marker as *-i* to disambiguate it from the stressed *yā-ye nesbat*; thus *mard-i* ("a man") vs. *mardi* ("manliness"). For Arabic and Turkish, I follow the system used in the *International Journal of Middle East Studies*; for Greek and Georgian, I refer to the Library of Congress and the American Library Association Romanization Tables; and for Middle Persian, I use D.N. MacKenzie's *A Concise Pahlavi Dictionary* (London, 1971).

Names. Names of places, individuals, dynasties, and texts follow established English spelling whenever possible. I also anglicize two important poetic forms, the qasida (*qaṣīda*) and the masnavi (using the modern Persian pronunciation of *mathnawī*); these complement the more well-established ghazal form (also "ghazel" in Merriam-Webster). When transliterating names and titles, I refer to the linguistic context they are most associated with: for example, al-Rāghib al-Iṣfahānī and Fakhr al-Din Gorgāni both lived and worked in Isfahan at around the same time, but as the former mostly wrote in Arabic and the latter in Persian, I render their personal names and the names of their works accordingly. To make this transition a bit less bumpy, I "fix" certain words – "Abu/Abi," "Ibn," and *Kalīla & Dimna* – to be consistent across languages. I hope this approach allows for an unobtrusive read.

Pronunciation. In pronouncing Persian words, readers can observe these guidelines:

- The unmarked consonants *b, d, f, g, h, j, k, l, m, n, p, s, t, v,* and *z* are pronounced as they are in English.
- Marked consonants – *ḏ, ḥ, ṡ, ṣ, ṭ, ẓ, ż,* and *ẓ* – are there for philological purposes only; they can be pronounced exactly as their unmarked counterparts.
- The digraphs *ch, sh,* and *zh* correspond to *church, shy,* and *azure* respectively.
- *R* is lightly trilled, as in Spanish and Italian *rosa, caro.*
- *Kh* sounds like "ch" in German "Bach."
- *Gh* (classical pronunciation) sounds like "r" in French "Paris."
- *Q* (classical pronunciation) is a voiceless uvular stop, like "k" but further back in the throat; the "c" in "caught" comes close to this sound.
- The characters ᶜ and ᵓ represent *ᶜayn* and *hamza* respectively; both can be pronounced as a glottal stop, as in "uh-oh."
- There is a clear distinction between short *a* ("dad") and long *ā* ("father").
- The other vowels *e, i, o,* and *u* are pronounced as they are in Italian and Spanish.
- The diphthongs *ay* and *ow* rhyme with *lay* and *low.*

To exemplify some of these rules, the names of the three major characters of *V&R* are pronounced as follows: Vis rhymes with "peace," Mobad with "nomad," and Rāmin with "raw mean."

Citations. When citing major primary sources, I include a locator in the body text for quick reference. The form of this locator depends on the nature of the book: (#) refers to line number(s); (#.#) indicates section.line; (#/#) indicates page/line; and (#:#/#) indicates volume:page/line. Note that the page number only points to that page where the cited passage begins, and not the entire range.

Editions. *Vis & Rāmin* has a long publication history: it was first printed by Lees and Ali (Calcutta, 1865), followed by the critical editions of Minovi (Tehran, 1314 [1935]), Maḥjub (Tehran, 1337 [1959]), the Iranian Culture Foundation (eds. T'odua, Gvakharia, and ᶜAyni; Tehran, 1349 [1970]), and Rowshan (Tehran, 1377 [1998]). In this monograph, I adhere to the Iranian Culture Foundation (ICF) edition, which I consider the best suited for scholarly research. A digital version of this edition is available at the TITUS (Thesaurus Indogermanischer Text-und Sprachmaterialien) Project: visit https://titus.uni-frankfurt.de/ and click on Text Database, then New Persian (accessed 1 June 2022). *V&R* has been twice translated into English, first by George Morrison (Columbia University Press, 1972) and then by Dick Davis (Penguin, 2008); to facilitate comparison, I frequently include the corresponding page number of the Davis translation in brackets. Thus, for example, the citation (136/110–11 [96]) means you will find the Persian text on page 136, lines 110–11 of the ICF edition, and the English on page 96 of Davis's translation. I use similar notation when cross-referencing other primary texts with their established translations, in which case I include the name of the translator: e.g., al-Nadīm, *al-Fihrist*, 2:327–31 (Dodge 719–24). Readers working with other editions or translations of *V&R* may refer to the concordance in appendix C of this book.

Translations. All translations from *Vis & Rāmin* are mine; while I greatly admire the work of Morrison and Davis, I felt it better to offer my own renditions for the sake of assuming full responsibility for how I read the Persian text. All other translations are also mine unless otherwise noted. Passages from the ancient Greek novels are from the anthology edited by Bryan Reardon (University of California Press, 1989), while those from the twelfth-century Greek romances are from *Four Byzantine Novels* (tr. Elizabeth Jeffreys, Liverpool University Press, 2014).

Geography. There are two main theatres of action in the story of *Vis & Rāmin*, described with an eclectic set of toponyms. To the west is the land of *Māh* (Old Pers. *Māda*, Gr. Media), also sometimes called *Kuhestān* (the Persian equivalent of the medieval Arabic name for the region, *al-Jibāl*); its capital is known as *Māh-ābād* (often *Māh* for short), as well as by its historical name *Hamadān* (ancient Ecbatana). This is where Vis and her family are based. The fiefdom of *Gurāb*, where Gol lives, is situated a little ways to the south. To the east is *Marv* (Old Pers. *Marguš*, Gr. Margiana, now Merv), often with its full name *Marv-e Shāhejān* (or *Shāyegān*), which provides the name of both the kingdom and its capital city; the text also uses the medieval name *Khorāsān* to describe the wider realm. This is the homeland of Mobad and his brother Rāmin. For the sake of clarity, I will regularize this range of terms and speak of Media and Khorasan as the regions, and Hamadan and Marv as their capital cities.

A few other places to note: The fortress of the "Devils' Grotto" (*eshkāft-e divān*), where Mobad imprisons Vis, might be placed in the Ghor province of modern Afghanistan, guessing from Shahru's malediction, "Perish Ghor Mountain, perish the Fortress of Ghor!" (*ma kuh-e*

Map: The Geography of Vis & Rāmin

ghur bādā ma dez-e ghur, 273/51 [238]). I have used the coordinates of the Ghorid capital, Firozkoh, to mark its approximate location – with the caveat that there is no necessary correlation between such place names in the imagined geography of *V&R* and the physical earth. *Khuzān*, where the Nurse is from, is also a bit of a mystery; Minorsky rules out any connection with the southwestern Iranian province of Khuzestan and suggests a number of tentative alternatives, possibly somewhere in the Koh-i-Baba mountain range in today's central Afghanistan. For a detailed discussion of *V&R*'s geography, see Minorsky, *Vīs u Rāmīn*, 167–75, and for more on the cities of Hamadan and Marv, see Bosworth, *Historic Cities of the Islamic World*, 151–3, 401–6.

Acknowledgments

This book took many years to write, and it could not have been accomplished without a veritable army of family, friends, and colleagues supporting me. It is my pleasure to recognize them now, and while I cannot fully express the extent of my appreciation to so many in so few words, the gist of my message is a world of thanks – *yek donyā mamnun* – to each and every one of you who have helped me on this journey.

I want to start with my amazing community at the University of Michigan, from staff to students to colleagues, who welcomed me to Ann Arbor with open arms and helped me to navigate a whirlwind of transitions, between settling into a new job at a new institution, developing classes, becoming a parent, and weathering a pandemic. My faculty mentors paid careful attention to my progress, read and discussed various chapters, supplied me with new concepts, terms, and scholarship to consider, and pushed me to rethink my paradigms and methods. Gottfried Hagen greatly expanded my range of knowledge about Islamic political theory and popular literature; Peggy McCracken always helped me see the big picture of what I was doing; Karla Mallette showed me how to think in multidisciplinary and multilingual frameworks; Paroma Chatterjee pointed out implications of my readings I didn't even realize were there; Samer Ali suggested the terms mythos and ethos for an alternative conceptual framework; and Maya Barzilai taught me how to communicate with an audience beyond my field. Above all, I owe an inexpressible debt of gratitude to Kathryn Babayan for her boundless hospitality, stimulating conversations, incisive critiques, unwavering support, and the constant mantra that has served me so well: think again, think more, think deeper. Here's to many more years of camaraderie and friendship.

In addition to these mentorships, I benefited tremendously from practically uncountable conversations with colleagues across multiple units

and departments, who heard about or read bits and pieces of my work
and shared their invaluable insights: the list includes Behrad Aghaei,
Gary Beckman, Erdem Çipa, Juan Cole, Jay Crisostomo, Aileen Das,
Katherine Davis, Kristin Dickinson, Christiane Gruber, Reginald Jack-
son, S.E. Kile, Alexander Knysh, Farina Mir, Ian Moyer, Ellen Muehl-
berger, Rafe Neis, Scotti Parrish, Christian de Pee, Michael Pifer, Shachar
Pinsker, Yopie Prins, Taymaz Pour Mohammad, Helmut Puff, Bryan
Roby, Cathy Sanok, Niloofar Sarlati, Celia Schultz, Anton Shammas,
William Stroebel, Ryan Szpiech, Kira Thurman, Antoine Traisnel, and
Rebecca Wollenberg. The wonderful admin team in Middle East Stud-
ies, including Alice Austin, May Jean Dong, Nikki Gastineau, Tammy
Kennedy, Kim Larrow, Patrice Whitney, and Ardella Williams, kept me
guided and on track throughout the many challenges of getting to know
a complex institution and stepping into a new phase of professional life.

Equally valued are the many undergraduate and graduate students
with whom I have had the privilege to work with over the years. Here,
too, the list would be too long to name everyone individually, but let
me just offer a blanket statement of thanks for taking my classes, for
involving me in your interests, for sharing your ideas and perspectives,
and for giving me the chance to learn and grow alongside you. I do
want to acknowledge a few people in particular: Marian Smith and Gol-
riz Farshi, who were my unofficial "welcome-to-Michigan" crew and
the backbone of our Iranian Studies community; Graham Liddell, with
whom I have had the pleasure of many years of mutual growth and
learning (not to mention the music!); Richard Hoffman Reinhardt and
Nadav Linial, for reading through chapters 3 and 4 with me, respectively; and especially Shahla Farghadani, from whom I have learned so
much: she generously helped me work through many difficult passages,
suggested many ways to expand my ideas, and much of my argument in
chapter 3 stems from an amazing close-reading session we had where
we looked carefully at the theme of sunlight in the opening scenes of
the text.

Beyond Michigan, I have had a great deal of assistance from friends
and colleagues both in my main field of Iranian Studies and related
disciplines. This includes those who have collaborated with me in the
Great Lakes Adiban Society, such as Aria Fani, Kaveh Hemmat, Aqsa
Ijaz, Alexander Jabbari, Hadi Jorati, Ayelet Kotler, Paul Losensky,
Shaahin Pishbin, and Nathan Tabor; the unforgettable moments strug-
gling through Georgian with Sergio La Porta, Michael Pifer, and Allison Vacca; the intellectual and moral support of Fatemeh Keshavarz
and Ahmet Karamustafa, who invited me, alongside other colleagues
such as Domenico Ingenito, Jane Mikkelson, and Fatemeh Shams, to

participate in the Yarshater Junior Scholars Workshop; and the community at the Centre for Medieval Literatures, including Paolo Borsa, Christian Høgel, Shazia Jagot, Lars Boje Mortensen, Nir Shafir, Elizabeth Tyler, and David Wacks. There are two colleagues in particular who have shown me tremendous encouragement, and whose scholarship has broadened my horizons beyond anything I could have attained on my own: Sharon Kinoshita and Panagiotis Agapitos. With them, every conversation is a pleasure, and every meeting an inspiration.

In addition to these networks, I was fortunate to have a number of smaller groups with whom I workshopped this book at regular intervals. At the top of the list is my long-standing reading group: Matthew Thomas Miller, Austin O'Malley, and Michael Pifer. They have been living with this book project as long as I have, and yet, if they ever experienced boredom or fatigue ("aren't you done with this already?!"), they never showed it, and always gave generously of their time, insights, and knowledge. Many of the fundamental aspects of this book, from its thematic organization, to technical details such as map creation and bibliography management, to its theoretical analysis and argument, are the direct product of these conversations, to the extent that I would gladly describe them as the book's unofficial co-authors, as long as they don't mind that association! My deepest thanks, gratitude, and appreciation to these dear friends.

In January 2020, my department generously sponsored a book-manuscript workshop, led by three scholars whose work I had admired and been inspired by for years: Suzanne Conklin Akbari, Peggy McCracken, and Julia Rubanovich. They read the manuscript with painstaking care, collectively providing me with comments to think about and suggestions to implement on virtually every page. Their feedback led to the entirety of the book's introduction and much of the first chapter being scrapped and rewritten, but in retrospect, I realize how many of the book's core ideas emerged only after this "molting" process; it was a true metamorphosis, and I'm deeply grateful for their role in making it happen. The pandemic broke out almost immediately after the workshop was over, and I am extremely grateful to my neighbourhood community – Erica, Juan, Chelsea, and others – with whose support I was able to keep working on the project during those long stretches of lockdown.

Another group of friends read the revised manuscript the following summer: Alexandra Hoffman, Allison Kanner-Botan, Samuel Lasman, and Rachel Schine. Their feedback, along with that of the two anonymous reviewers recruited by the University of Toronto Press, helped me tremendously in identifying lacunae and faulty assumptions, toning down and/or shoring up some of my more extravagant claims, and further integrating my discussion with pertinent examples from the primary and secondary literature. Implementing this feedback amounted to much more than a little spit-and-polish; in many cases, it once again helped me see more clearly the real argument I was trying to make, and the road I needed to take to get there. Theirs was a tremendous contribution, and I thank them for their generosity and support.

Having mentioned the University of Toronto Press, I want to issue a special word of appreciation to my editor, Suzanne Rancourt, for shepherding this project into existence. It's a daunting prospect, trying to pitch a book you haven't even entirely figured out for yourself, but the way that she saw the potential in what I was proposing, worked with me to make it come to life, and patiently supported me through my many delays, gave me hope that this might actually work out after all – and hope, I've learned, is an essential ingredient in my process. Thanks for believing in me. It was also a pleasure to work with my copy editor, Catherine Plear, who, with a keen eye and deft touch, fixed numerous errors and brought clarity to many a clunky passage. My dear friend Kevin Emery also read the final draft and offered additional helpful suggestions for style and readability. Any remaining mistakes or infelicities, needless to say, are entirely my own.

At the coda of this long list, I want to acknowledge my debt to three people who played a formative role in my growth as a scholar. First, to Julie Scott Meisami: I never once met her in person, but it was her translation of Nezāmi's *Haft paykar* and extensive scholarship on medieval Persian poetry that put me on the track I am now. Years later, I keep coming back to her work and find myself awed and humbled at the depth of her insight. If I have brought anything to the field that she has not already said or inferred, I will be pleasantly surprised.

Second, to Dick Davis: I don't think I ever would have discovered the treasures to be gleaned from a deep dive into *Vis & Rāmin* if his captivating translation had not shown me the way; similarly, it was his *Panthea's Children* that suggested to me the idea of looking into the Greek novels. His translations of the *Shāhnāma* and other masterpieces, past and present, have made teaching Persian literature possible in ways that simply could not have been envisaged before, and I firmly believe that they will transform anglophone university curricula as the years go by. I cannot express how much I owe to his labours, but I will at least offer my profound thanks and appreciation for all he has done for me and our community.

And finally, to my late advisor, Franklin Lewis, who tragically passed away shortly before this book went to press. Frank set a model of rigorous scholarship, intellectual curiosity, kindness and humility, and moral courage that will forever serve as one of my central guiding lights; more than a teacher, he was like a father to me. I never could have imagined how lucky I would be to have him in my life when I started graduate school, and even as I grieve his loss, I will treasure our friendship and times spent together to the end of my days. May this work serve as some small tribute to the tremendous legacy he has left behind, and may his memory be long and cherished.

My last and deepest debt of thanks goes to my lifelong friend and partner, Andrea LeJeune, who has made tremendous sacrifices so that this book could become a reality. Her support is there on every page, most visibly in the epigraph that she crafted from the model of a sixteenth-century manuscript. It is to her that I dedicate this book – with appreciation for the present, gratitude for the past, and all my hopes for a joyful and fulfilling future.

LOVE AT A CRUX

الا یا ایّها الساقی ادر کأساً و ناولها

که عشق آسان نمود اول ولی افتاد مشکلها

Boy   bring round the wine
and give me some

for love that at first seemed easy
turned difficult

                       —Ḥāfeẓ

Prologue | In Which Love Has Many a Tale

Yek-i bud, yek-i nabud
Zir-e gonbad-e kabud

It happened, and it didn't, too,
Below the dome of midnight blue.
> – Persian proverb, said at the beginning of a fairy tale

ONCE UPON A TIME, there was a king named Mobad Manikān, who ruled the land of Iran in peace and prosperity. But one fateful day, at the gathering of his nobles in celebration of the New Year, Mobad's eyes fell upon the lovely queen Shahru, and he was smitten then and there with desire for her. Although he promised her the world in exchange for her love, the queen protested that she was too old to accept. Undeterred, Mobad proposed a counter-offer: if not Shahru, let him wed her daughter – if she were to bear one – for she would surely inherit her mother's beauty. To this the royal pair agreed, sealing the deal with an exchange of oaths and a contract on painted silk.

Years later, the queen did indeed give birth to a daughter named Vis, who grew into the most beautiful woman the world had ever seen. But Shahru had forgotten her promise and instead betrothed Vis to her – Vis's – brother, Viru. Upon hearing this news, Mobad flew into a rage, marched his army into Shahru's domains, and brought Vis by force back to his palace, where he married her. It seemed that the king had secured his prize; but he did not count on the resistance of his new bride. Determined to preserve her virginity for the one she considered her rightful husband, Vis commanded her Nurse to curse the king with a spell of permanent impotence, then shut herself away in her chambers, waiting for the day her beloved Viru would come to the rescue.

But, much to Vis's dismay, that day never came.

Instead, the man to come knocking at her door was none other than Prince Rāmin, Mobad's younger brother. Rāmin and Vis had spent the first years of their lives together under the care of the same nurse, and, while escorting her back to the palace, the prince had fallen in love with his childhood friend. At first, Vis vehemently rejected his advances, but after much deliberation and soul-searching, she finally consented to the illicit union.

With this fateful decision, we find our three protagonists caught in a love triangle, and as befits this classic scenario, Vis and Rāmin will have many adventures as they plan their next tryst, while evading Mobad's attempts to catch and punish them. At times, these adventures end on happy and even humorous notes (at least for the lovers), but more often than not, they end badly for all parties involved – particularly Vis, who repeatedly suffers humiliation, abuse, exile, and imprisonment for her perceived violations of the social order. And here, something unusual happens: instead of steadfastly weathering these trials, the protago-nists' will to persevere gradually buckles and finally breaks, and Rāmin abandons Vis to marry another woman named Gol. This betrayal pre-cipitates an explosive confrontation between the erstwhile lovers, one that nearly results in their deaths. It is painfully clear to all at this point that Vis and Rāmin's story will never end successfully until Mobad is out of the way, and so, reconciled at last, the lovers launch a full-scale revolt against the king. Before their armies meet, however, Mobad is unexpectedly killed – gored by a wild boar. It is thus in the shadow of death that Vis and Rāmin finally wed and ascend the throne, in a happily-ever-after that cannot fully shake off the long years of personal suffering and political chaos that went into its making.

So goes, in brief, the story of *Vis & Rāmin* (*V&R*), one of the first romances of New Persian literature and the focal point of this book. As I hope to have shown in my summary of its plot, there is much in this tale that will register as familiar with scholars of romance. Its central themes of passionate love, obstacles and adventures, and the ongoing quest for union should likely "rhyme," so to speak, with memories of narratives we have heard and read before; those familiar with the love triangle between Tristan, Isolde, and Mark in particular may have experienced a moment of *déjà vu*.[1] Such familiarity would only emphasize some of the plot's more curious features: the persistent use of doubles (Shahru and Vis, Viru and Rāmin, Vis and Gol), the controversial matters (both then and now) of incest and adultery, and the protracted falling in and out of love in a genre that conventionally subscribes to the notion of true and enduring love at first sight. Perhaps most interesting of all is the way the

text seems to anticipate and then thwart the expectations of its readers –
and even its characters – at certain critical junctures: Viru appears well
poised to take up the role of the romance hero, but never does; Rāmin
breaks faith with his sworn beloved (while Mobad, ironically, remains
faithful); a bizarre accident takes the place of a climactic battle. It is
in this generic interplay of the conventional and the unfamiliar that I
situate my study. As I explain below, I see *Vis & Rāmin* as residing at
a crossroads of literary history – a radical renovation of older models
that anticipates later developments across the broad flank of southwestern Eurasia. By bringing these models together and connecting them
through *V&R*, I hope to offer one example of what we might discover
if we enter the "Global Middle Ages" – or, perhaps more appropriately
in this case, a *globally minded* Middle Ages – from the vantage point
of Persian: about the romance and its genealogy, about transregional
explorations of love, and about evolving notions around the links connecting language, the imagination, and truth.[2]

A Heterogeneous Text

Across the domains of history, language, modality, and genre, *Vis &
Rāmin* is a profoundly heterogeneous text, a quality that makes it particularly apt for approaching the Middle Ages as a network of diverse
but interconnected histories, deeply engaged with the legacies of the
ancient world. The tale's history is a textbook exemplar of these temporal and geographic connections: though written in New Persian verse
in 1054, its origins go back to the Parthian period, most likely the first
century CE, placing it in the same general milieu in which Greek prose
narratives about love, the so-called Greek novels, were being composed
in the eastern provinces of the Roman Empire.[3] It is not altogether
unsurprising, then, to find elements in common between *V&R* and the
Greek material, especially in terms of structure, motif, and theme.[4] Yet
at the same time, the story's medieval version draws heavily from the
conventions of Arabic literature and the hermeneutics of Islamic philosophy and theology. Tracing these linkages not only makes plain the
intersectional history of *V&R*, but also that of the romance genre more
broadly, a method of storytelling that spread and circulated across a
vast span of time and space.

The history of *V&R*'s transmission also tells a tale of hybrid modalities. The story was almost certainly performed orally, and while there is
no evidence of it being written down early on, it is possible to suppose,
as Abu Hilāl al-ᶜAskarī (d. after 1005) asserts, that "the [ancient] Persians, who had songs (*ashᶜār*) to propagate their deeds and memorialize

their wars, used to record and preserve [them] in their treasuries."[5] However it was transmitted in late antiquity, the occasional references to *V&R* found in medieval Arabic sources definitely indicate that it was known in the urban centres of Iraq and Iran, particularly Baghdad and Isfahan, in terms suggestive of both written and performed variations. For example, in one of his *fārisiyyāt* ("Persian poems"), the Abbasid poet Abu Nuwās (d. 813) mentions the *firjardāt* (> Mid. Pers. *fragard*, "book" or "chapter") of Vis and Rāmin in one of his verses; commenting on this line, Ḥamza al-Iṣfahānī (d. 971) explains that this is "a well-known fable among [the Persians]" (*uḥdūtha lahum maʿrūfa*) and glosses the word *firjardāt* as something "similar to odes" (*ka-l-qaṣāʾid*).[6] In that spirit, the critic and littérateur al-Rāghib al-Iṣfahānī (fl. before 1018) cites the following "Persian song" that, he claims, was popular among the urban elites of his day:

وتنكّبْ غناءلَ العربيّا   غننا يا غلاَمَنا وأمِهنا .

ـغرّ كرامٌ فغنّنا الفارسيّا   إنّنا مِعْشرٌ من العَربِ الـ

وبس دامِين بكْرَة وعشيّا   وأسقناها مدامةً نازعتها

> Sing us a song, O serving-boy, and sing it well –
>> enough with your singing in Arabic!
> For we are an honourable gathering of the noble Arabs,
>> so sing to us in Persian!
> And serve us an ancient vintage
>> that Vis took from Rāmin, morning and night.[7]

This little piece offers a helpful glimpse into a probable performance context of *Vis & Rāmin*, and presumably tales like it, within the courtly milieu of eleventh-century Isfahan: recited out loud, quite possibly sung, at the salons and gatherings of the city's upper crust. The appreciation for "local colour" in this poem is also notable: as Arabic was far and away the dominant language of educated discourse at this time, we can imagine how the collective "we" of al-Rāghib's circle might laughingly admonish their serving boy that they don't need to listen to his attempts at entertaining them in a language they know better than he.[8] We will see a similar interest in *V&R* as a distinctly regional tale when Fakhr al-Din Gorgāni, a near contemporary of al-Rāghib's who also lived in Isfahan, presents it to the city's governor as a popular yarn now made suitable, thanks to his poetic intervention, for courtly consumption.

Thus we arrive at the text at hand, a "cultural palimpsest," as Dick Davis nicely puts it, of the broad literary history of the Near East: heterogeneous and composite, encompassing performative and scribal

modalities, and accumulating aspects of diverse discursive legacies –
the Greek novel, Arabic lyric poetry, New Persian epic, Neoplatonic
metaphysics, and Islamicate political theory – across the *longue durée*
of the Parthian, Sasanian, and Islamic stages of its transmission.[9] This
internal diversity has afforded scholars a wealth of angles from which
to approach this text: philologists and linguists have long recognized
the value of *V&R* as an early testament of the New Persian language,
while historians have pored over its pages in the hopes of gleaning new
insights into the politics, culture, and society of ancient Iran, or indeed
of Iran in the eleventh century, when the poem was written.[10]

V&R plays a significant role in Persian literary history, too, although
here its reception is somewhat more chequered. While none deny
that it is one of the earliest Persian romances extant, it has often been
described as an odd and not altogether successful foray into the genre;
Davis again supplies the choice metaphor in calling it a "cul-de-sac"
in Persian literary history.[11] Quite a few modern critics have expressed
their dislike of the poem, most vituperatively Italo Pizzi, calling it "the
stupidest, clumsiest, and most tasteless poem to ever emerge from
the hands of a miserable poetaster," and even some medieval readers
found its contents scandalous.[12] The decisive vote, however, was cast by
Nezāmi Ganjavi, the most influential romancer in the history of Persian
poetry. He knew *Vis & Rāmin*, and composed his *Khosrow & Shirin* (w.
ca. 1180) on its model; and while it remains a point of debate whether
this reflects Nezāmi's admiration for or disapproval of his source, there
is no question over his spectacular success in supplanting it.[13] In the
following centuries, Nezāmi's collected works, known as the *Khamsa*
("Quintet"), became a literary touchstone, imitated time and again by
celebrated poets such as Amir Khosrow (d. 1325), Khwāju (d. 1352),
Jāmi (d. 1492), Navāʾi (d. 1501), and Hātefi (d. 1521). The story of Vis
and Rāmin, meanwhile, was never again told in Persian, and to this
day, it remains an obscure entry in the canon, rarely taught in Iranian
schools.[14]

The general study of *V&R*, with some important exceptions, has thus
acquired a distinctively hourglass shape, with much of the scholarship
looking *through* the text, as it were, to view what came before and after
it, much as one holds a paper to the light to discern its watermark.[15]
A significant factor that encourages this way of reading, I believe, is
the impact of institutional discipline. By and large, the academic frame
through which *Vis & Rāmin* has chiefly obtained its value and relevance
has been the study of Iran and of Persian literature more broadly – an
approach that tends to privilege the vertical over the horizontal, the diachronic over the synchronic, and the family tree over the neighbourhood

community. This framework, however, is not so well suited for handling the rather astonishing diversity of non-Iranian and non-Persian sources that went into the making of New Persian romance, evident not only in the composite history of *V&R* but also in other near-contemporaneous examples of poems that explicitly drew from Hellenistic and Arabic sources. From the standpoint of Persian literature, these texts certainly mark a significant moment – namely, the establishment of a new genre – but if we look beyond that frame, it is clear that they are participating in a much larger discursive practice, advancing a long-standing and transregional conversation about romance and romantic love: a beginning and a continuation at one and the same time. The singular aspect of *Vis & Rāmin* within this textual group, however, is its pronounced self-reflexivity, the way it and its characters seem to knowingly deviate from the expectations to which they hold themselves. This suggests a keen interest and sustained engagement with the idea of romance itself, perhaps to such a degree that, if we were to apply Sarah Kay's insights on parody, we could say that *V&R* plays a pivotal role in founding the genre in New Persian literature, even if its protagonists, and some of its more radical experiments, were never revisited.[16]

In short, I would like to present *Vis & Rāmin* not only as an early generic experiment in a nascent national literature, but as a reconstitution of and response to older traditions of narrating the affairs of lovers, now retooled to produce new kinds of meaning in the rapidly changing oikoumene of the early eleventh century. When approached from this angle, *V&R* emerges as a *crucial* text – in the literal sense of the word – in the history of romance. Appearing at a crux of intersecting literary traditions, it recasts elements from the ancient past and forges new possibilities for the genre at the dawn of the new millennium, anticipating many of the distinctive characteristics of the "medieval romance" as we have come to recognize it today. The purpose of this book, then, is to facilitate an awareness of these connections and explore their implications, hopefully to the benefit of Iranian studies and its neighbouring fields alike. Just as I assert that we cannot fully understand *Vis & Rāmin* without placing it within a multilingual and transregional history, I would also contend that *V&R*, and the New Persian romances in general, must form an integral part of that history. A globally minded study of *V&R* stands to tell us much about the spread, diffusion, and function of the romance from the largely unexplored vantage point of medieval Iran, providing a bird's-eye vista of what has been said and done before, and allowing us to take in a wider view of the many routes that this literary and intellectual endeavour has traversed.

Re-cognizing Romance

I have thus far been content to describe *Vis & Rāmin* as a romance, using the term both to indicate a distinctive field within Persian literature and to suggest possible lines of affinity with other literary traditions. This needs some clarification, however, given the notoriously broad valences of the word across time, place, and context. The Old French word *romanz*, from which "romance" derives, simply designates any text in the vernacular, without (too) much in the way of generic connotation.[17] This stands in sharp contrast with the romance in modern English, where it is highly generic – the adventure story, the high fantasy, the chivalric quest, the erotic thriller – and is almost always negatively compared against the novel.[18] The modern term also evokes a distinctive sense of affect, as in the way one "seeks romance" in the personal ads of a newspaper or dating app. Given the fluidity and fuzziness of the term, and the fact that there is no obvious analogue for it in ancient and medieval Greek, Arabic, or Persian, one might well be tempted to abandon romance altogether in favour of something more culturally specific.[19]

Indeed, recourse to the Persian offers a compelling alternative. *V&R* self-identifies as a *dāstān-e ᶜāsheqāna*, a phrase that has gone on to become the standard word for romance in contemporary usage. Loosely rendered as "love-story" (but see below), the *dāstān-e ᶜāsheqāna* captures in a nutshell the core premise of the narrative tradition I'm interested in: stories about love, and more specifically, about a love affair between two people. As I argue in chapter 1, when this motif appears at the centre of a narrative, it provides that narrative with a strong motivating force, moving it in certain anticipated directions and mobilizing it for particular purposes within its local context. This tight functional and etymological interplay of motif, motive, and motion gives the love-story a certain generic coherence that is quite a bit tighter and more traceable than the more open-ended domain of romance.

And yet, for the purposes of this study, romance still matters – indispensably so. For while I perceive certain tendencies, proclivities, and habits in my survey of stories about an amorous couple, they are always and necessarily imbricated with other generic aspects as well, and in that respect, a more capacious term is needed. This is especially visible when reading tales about lovers against tales about heroes, whose characters mingle and merge, whose topoi combine in ever-new arrangements, and whose horizons of expectation and preoccupation converge to form expansive vistas of possibility. Thus, if we situate the *dāstān-e ᶜāsheqāna* within a wider discursive spectrum that encompasses the two nodes of love and chivalric exploits – what Cesare Segre considers the "constitutive model" for most medieval romances – we have a dialectic to work with, a zoom-in lens on one hand and a panoramic view on the other, that allows us to place the local texts in conversation with their temporal and geographical neighbours.[20] Important theoretical contributions to (romance) genre studies, such as those of Patricia Parker, Jacques Derrida, and Barbara Fuchs, further help us to think beyond taxonomical structures and "to recognize romance within a variety of genres ... as a set of strategies that organize and animate narrative."[21] A comparative study of *Vis & Rāmin* cannot therefore dispense with romance, a term that offers tremendous analytical purchase precisely because of its diffuse, affective, and even inauthentic qualities. Exploring the productive yet irreducible tension that emerges between the *dāstān-e ʿāsheqāna* and the romance, terms that are clearly related yet not interchangeable, activates a networked reading of the Persian material that is not easily accomplished by emic labels alone.[22]

For the purposes of this book, then, the love-story is the topic; romance, the hermeneutic. It is eminently useful that romance, while being a familiar genre in English with a rich scholarly and critical tradition at its back, is a term that stubbornly resists absolute definitions and confounds any master narrative about origins or ontology. When I describe *Vis & Rāmin* as a romance, then, I mean it as a proposition: not that it "is" a romance, but that it is thinkable as romance – that it can be read romantically. This mode of engagement invites a *re-cognition* of the romance through *V&R*: by harnessing that sense of rhyme and resonance that it triggers in me (and presumably other readers), I aim to help us rethink the paradigms by which we define the cultural, geographical, and temporal borders of medieval Afro-Eurasia, especially in those moments of apparent but not necessarily "real" affinity across them.

But what does it mean to read romantically? My answer to this question is perhaps better shown by example than described in abstract. Here is the introduction to the love-story of Pyramus and Thisbe, as told by Ovid in his *Metamorphoses*: consider, as you read, the presentation of the characters, the architecture of the setting, and the crucial function of the wall.

> Pyramus et Thisbe, iuvenum pulcherrimus alter,
> altera, quas Oriens habuit, praelata puellis,
> contiguas tenuere domos, ubi dicitur altam
> coctilibus muris cinxisse Semiramis urbem.
> notitiam primosque gradus vicinia fecit,

> tempore crevit amor; taedae quoque iure coissent,
> sed vetuere patres ...
> fissus erat tenui rima, quam duxerat olim,
> cum fieret, paries domui communis utrique.
> id vitium nulli per saecula longa notatum –
> quid non sentit amor? – primi vidistis amantes
> et vocis fecistis iter, tutaeque per illud
> murmure blanditiae minimo transire solebant.

Pyramus and Thisbe – he, the most beautiful youth, and she, loveliest maid of all the East – dwelt in houses side by side, in the city which Semiramis is said to have surrounded with walls of brick. Their nearness made the first steps of their acquaintance. In time love grew, and they would have been joined in marriage, too, but their parents forbade ... There was a slender chink in the party-wall of the two houses, which it had at some former time received when it was building. This chink, which no one had ever discovered through all these years – but what does love not see? – you lovers first discovered and made it the channel of speech. Safe through this your loving words used to pass in tiny whispers. (*Metamorphoses* 4.55–61, 65–70)[23]

This scene lays out many of the elements that I recognize as prototypical in the structure of the love-story: the young and beautiful protagonists, the resistant parents, the instinctive rise of desire not *despite* but *because* of the lines that declare a state of separation. In foregrounding the mud-brick partitions of his setting, Ovid emphasizes their dual function as structures that join even as they divide: the shared wall between the two families is the very device that makes it possible for them to become neighbours, thus providing the medium by which Pyramus and Thisbe discover and declare their affection, setting the story of their love into motion, and producing their eventual metamorphosis. Love is not possible, in other words, without a barrier to overcome; affinity cannot be recognized except through the screen of difference, and radical transformation cannot be achieved unless one passes through that veil.

It is this kind of "romantic" modality I suggest we adopt when placing *Vis & Rāmin* and the New Persian tradition in which it takes part into a globally minded conversation about romance and romantic love, an encounter that elicits the (mis-)recognition of the Self in the Other, kindles the desire – the attraction – to better understand that Self-in-the-Other, and thus re-cognizes both entities in the process.[24] I expect the biggest danger with this mode of engagement "that is both close and distant, foreign but familiar," as Paul Zumthor puts it, lies in "the deceptive ease with which this *déjà vu* can be muffled as it comes in the door, and then become caught in our own systems of resemblances."[25] It would not do to hide the fact, therefore, that this book is (and must be) a highly personal narrative in the end, one in which my positionality (background, knowledge, expectations, values) plays a fundamental role in informing and shaping my encounter with the love stories of the past; I must proceed fully aware that whenever I "recognize romance" in *V&R*, I am likely to *mis*-recognize it at the same time. But, if we ultimately accept this hermeneutic, for all its pitfalls, as a form of re-cognition – of rethinking both the texts and the ways we draw relationships between them – it should still prove productive, especially in a moment when the concept of a global Middle Ages has seen increased interest and significance in the academy and beyond.

The Medieval Globe

One question the New Persian romance helps us reconsider is in what ways and to what extent we can (or should) place the rise of this literary genre within the temporal framework of "medieval" history, a term that is undeniably Eurocentric in its origins. Some scholars, Thomas Bauer for one, have strongly argued against the application of this framework to non-European contexts:

> Terms like "Islamic Middle Ages" and "Arabic postclassical literature" are not as harmless as they seem, but inevitably carry a strong political connotation. According to the Hegelian teleological worldview that is behind them, Islamic culture has to fulfill one single important task, that is, to bring classical thinking (here: science and philosophy of antiquity) to the West during the "dark" Middle Ages ... As has been realized repeatedly, the mentality of the people of these "Middle Ages" was anything but "medieval," rather more akin to the mentality of Renaissance and baroque Europe. The inevitable connotation of the construction of "Islamic Middle Ages" is to deny Islam's own history, and to derive its history exclusively from a European point of view.[26]

To circumvent the teleological bias that Bauer describes, some historians of Muslim or Islamicate civilization(s) avoid the term "medieval" altogether; Hodgson's "Middle Period" or Fromherz's "Second Axial Age" are notable examples.[27] Another common designation for this period, especially in the arenas of Arabic and Persian literature, is "classical," as we see in the work of Mahmoud Omidsalar, speaking here on the great poet Abu al-Qāsem Ferdowsi (d. 1020): "Being a contemporary of Europe's 'medieval period' does not make Ferdowsi a 'medieval' author, nor does it make other classical Muslim scholars of the Middle East 'medieval men.'"[28]

While I fully acknowledge the validity of these critiques, particularly as they highlight the importance of engaging with systems of thought on their own terms, I see a few compelling reasons for using, or rather repurposing, the term medieval – again, not as a definition but as a proposition – that I will now lay out. First of all, I intend the word in a way quite different from the quotations above, which seem to understand it less as a temporal and more as a social-cultural descriptor, with implicit (or for Omidsalar, explicit) connotations of stagnation and entropy, an indicator of a civilization's "distance from its former intellectual and artistic achievements," as he puts it.[29] However – apart from the natural objection that, even if it was only limited to western Europe, medieval cannot (or should not) imply a singular "mentality" that applies to every context – I worry that this insistence on separate timelines, so strongly founded on the assertion of cultural difference and vertical notions of progress and decline, obscures the fact that these societies *did* exist at the same time and *were* in close and continuous contact with each other. The medieval globe, as Valerie Hansen writes, was a highly connected world where "what happened in one place profoundly affected the residents of other distant regions," and to insist on some clean temporal-spatial break between neighbouring regions can produce odd results: "it seems rather artificial," Samuel Lasman observes, "to declare that Richard I Coeur de Lion is a medieval figure, while his opponent Ṣalāḥ ad-Dīn Yūsuf ibn Ayyūb is not."[30] This interconnection can be found in literary aspects as well; Emily Selove reminds us that "medieval European literature evolved in tandem with, even partly as a result of, contemporaneous Arabic literature, the authors of which, in turn, drew no less from classical texts for inspiration than did their European fellows."[31] Thus, if the term medieval can be repurposed "to look at larger global patterns during a particular period of history," then that for me justifies its use – at least for this endeavour.[32]

Naturally, a globally minded study does not need to be global in the literal sense, and thus I propose a term to both refine and deepen the connections I seek to make visible: the *Helleno-Abrahamic complex*, essentially a shorthand for what Michael Sells calls "the legacy of the encounter of Semitic prophetic traditions with the Graeco-Roman cultural world."[33] Hellenistic learning, particularly in areas like Galenic medicine, Aristotelian logic, and Neoplatonic metaphysics (although naturally received and conducted along diverse terms), played a critical role in the literary and intellectual cultures of medieval Christendom and Islamdom alike, including the many religious minorities that inhabited both zones.[34] Intertwined with this legacy is the equally significant element of Abrahamic monotheism: the fact that Judaism, Christianity, and Islam, despite their numerous internal disagreements and external competition with each other, all participate in a shared and mutually intelligible set of premises about a single God, a divine revelation conveyed by a mostly overlapping group of prophets, a similar eschatology, and so on. In this way, the threads of Athens and Jerusalem, to use the common metonym, weave a massive, if loosely connected, discursive network that enmeshes northwestern Europe, the Mediterranean basin, western Africa, the Levant and Mesopotamia, the Arabian peninsula and the Horn of Africa, Anatolia and the Caucuses, Iran and Afghanistan, Transoxania, and the northern Indian subcontinent within its fabric. When mediated through this "intellectual superstructure," as Christian Høgel puts it, referents like "Aristotle," "Alexander," and "Moses" gain meaning and significance for communities as distant and different from each other as Seville and Samarqand – a significance not so easily shared with, say, the "Sanskrit cosmopolis" or the cultural institutions of China – allowing for some baseline level of recognition between them.[35]

The advantage offered by this mode of engagement is that it forges a middle path between purely formal literary comparison on the one hand and the discipline of source research (*Quellenforschung*) on the other, allowing us to think both historically and dialectically: to quote again from Michael Sells, "Rather than focusing upon the textual 'borrowings' of one tradition from another, it seems more profitable to see these traditions as competing within a partially shared intellectual and symbolic world, defining themselves in conversation with one another and against one another."[36] Such a "conversational" approach, favouring routes over roots, speaks well to Karla Mallette's likening of the cosmopolitan languages of this complex – Latin, Arabic, and Greek – to the tribal rug: "it is fluid and flexible, yet at the same time it provides a structure for thought: the warp and woof of grammar; the lexicon of symbolic representation."[37] Though my study is more attuned to concepts and narrative types than to the languages themselves, the metaphor of the rug still works extremely well in setting up the Helleno-Abrahamic complex as a landscape that both resists notions of centre and periphery and accommodates multiple levels of comparative reading. This holds true not only at sites of intense interlinguistic and interconfessional exchange, such as Sicily or Andalus, but also between locales that had no direct or sustained contact with each other. By no means should this imply agreement or uniformity; it rather allows us to approach this space as "a broad and open system of distinct and yet interrelated regional cultures that come to display ... some highly marked common ways of artistically and intellectually expressing similar preoccupations and needs."[38] Engaging with the medieval globe in this manner allows us to study texts, ideas, and genres from a perspective that, while not omniscient, invites approaches that are more open-ended and inclusive than what is usually visible from within the frameworks of nation, language, or even civilization.[39]

This roundabout path brings us back to the romance as an extremely productive site for the comparative study of medieval Afro-Eurasia at a large scale. When looking at the texts and narratives that circulated most widely and successfully across (and beyond) this complex, they seem to fall into a type that I might call wisdom literature, a class that includes the writings of Plato, Aristotle, and Galen, tales of the prophets, the story of *Barlaam & Josaphat*, *Kalila & Dimna*, the *Sindbād* cycle, and the Alexander Romance.[40] (I mean "wisdom" in its most general sense here, in that all these examples purport to pass on useful knowledge of this world and/or the next in some way.) But alongside these texts, Daniel Selden argues that another kind of narrative experienced a similarly widespread expansion along the same pathways as Hellenistic thought and Abrahamic monotheism: the "Ancient Novel," by which he means the long-form love-story:

> Between 450 BCE and 1450 CE, readers across the Levant, North Africa, and Europe were united by complex networks of interrelated texts, attested in a multiplicity of languages, that contemporary scholars call the Ancient Novel. All available evidence points to the Afroasiatic origins of the narrative devices that typify these compositions, whose several types show a diffusional pattern from the Levant around the Mediterranean and into Europe, southward through the Ḥijāz and Yaman to Ethiopia as well as eastward across Īrān to India and central Asia.[41]

The reason why the romance is so well suited for exploring the global medieval stems from this intertwining of a distinctive set of novelistic narrative devices within the intellectual superstructures of Helleno-Abrahamic thought – facilitated, Selden adds, through a long train of multi-ethnic and transregional empires competing with and succeeding one another, including the Achaemenid, the Macedonian, the Roman, the Sasanian, and the Umayyad and early Abbasid caliphates. This is the general backdrop for my study, though the scope is much more limited: while Selden takes nearly two millennia of history into view, with a concept of the "novel" that is quite capacious (probably why he refers to its "several types"), I am specifically interested in the eleventh and twelfth centuries, when a particular "type" of love-story, mediated through Neoplatonic and Abrahamic hermeneutics, came to acquire a new degree of cultural capital in multiple locales across this complex, developing novel ways of talking about love in regard to the human and the divine. In this regard, transregional comparisons can be both enlightening and fruitful, allowing us, whatever our discipline, to recast our object of study in a broader field of horizons, and thus perceive with more clarity what might be distinctive, or not, about the specific texts and traditions we study.

As a final point, there is something distinct about the romance form itself, in terms of the ways it engages with difference, that make its study particularly useful for investigating the Middle Ages as a time of diverse meetings. An important pioneer in this regard is Geraldine Heng's *Empire of Magic*, where, casting the romance (like Selden) in extremely broad terms, with subgenres of chivalry, chronicle, travel, hagiography, and so on, she argues that its "re-beginning" in north-western Europe is in no small part due to the Frankish encounter with distant lands and foreign peoples during the Crusades, and whose recourse to pleasure and the fantastic allow its participants to "trans-act" the trauma of that encounter in a process of collective identity for-mation in a way that other genres such as history or chronicle could not manage.[42] Her account offers an interesting parallel with a line of schol-arship in Classics, from Tomas Hägg's *The Novel in Antiquity* to Tim Whitmarsh's *Dirty Love*, that similarly correlates the (re-)beginning of the ancient novel with the emergence of a heterogeneous and impe-rial Hellenistic world, probing and disrupting the boundaries of Self and Other.[43] The New Persian romances of the eleventh century both support and complicate this association. On one hand, they coincide with the rise and expansion of the Ghaznavid and then Seljuk empires (the latter, of course, bringing us to the same tumultuous encounter that Heng describes), suggesting in their range of sources a similarly global, or at least hemispheric, horizon of cultural engagement and aspiration. At the same time, they conceive of the Other on far more than ethnic or cultural grounds, and in this regard in particular, *Vis & Rāmin* has much to say.

The upshot of all this is that to place the New Persian romance within this framework offers an implicit but productive challenge to the idea of medieval romance itself, a chance not to expand the concept to include non-European representatives but instead to question, variegate, com-plicate, and even break it apart from within – as, I will argue, *V&R* actively does to the genre at its own moment in time. Thus, rather than acting as a site where modern white European-Christian identities have been retroactively located, the medieval romance can be repurposed as a tool for investigating the "polycentric and multivocal entanglements" that characterize not only the literal landscapes in which they were composed but also the literary landscapes they imagine – how they both arise from and construct the global.[44] It is in this light that the Persian material stands to enrich our understanding about what romance *means* as an idea and what it *does* as a widespread mode of writing – romance as a noun and romance as a verb – wherever we happen to position ourselves.

On Mythos and Ethos

To illustrate this notion of romance as a noun and a verb, let us look at a short but key passage in *Vis & Rāmin*, occurring at a charged moment in the story's plot. Vis has just directed her Nurse to use the charm of impotence on Mobad; meanwhile, Rāmin has fallen head over heels in love and is now wandering the palace gardens, reciting Vis's name in a trance-like litany. Their paths will join in the upcoming chapters, marking the start of the "official" romance. Perhaps it is no coincidence, then, that the narrator stops at this juncture to address us directly:

چه با دایه چه با رامین چه با شاه   بگویم با تو یک یک حال آن ماه

به درد دل ز دیده خون چکاند   به گفتاری که چون عاشق بخواند

بدو در عشق را چندین فسانه   بگویم داستان عاشقانه

Let me tell you about that Moon's every circumstance – with the Nurse, Rāmin, or the King – in a language that will spill bloody tears from the sympathetic eyes of lovers. Let me tell you a romance (*dāstān-e ᶜāsheqāna*) in which love has many a tale (*fasāna*). (112/68–70 [75])

This is where the term *dāstān-e ᶜāsheqāna* appears in the text; I glossed it as "love-story" above, but let me now further unpack its connotations. *Dāstān* establishes the work as a narrative of some sort, roughly equivalent with the Old French *conte* and *estoire*, the Arabic *qiṣṣa* and *ḥadīth*, and the Greek *diēgēsis* and *aphēgēsis*; but without further information, we could guess nothing about the narrative's content and contours.[45] That information is supplied by the second part of the term, *ᶜāsheqāna*, which tells us that this *dāstān* is deeply invested in the topic of love. This topical label is enough to invoke what Hans Robert Jauss calls a "horizon of expectations" in the minds of its readers, recalling other narratives about love and inviting a comparison between them: the recurring patterns of setup and denouement, themes and motifs, that encourage the mental formation of implicit links between a series of individual texts.[46]

The word *ᶜāsheqāna*, however, does more than simply announce the main topic of the narrative and invoke its associated expectations: it is formed by taking the word for "lover" (*ᶜāsheq*) and investing it with an intriguing adverbial force – a "lover-ly" story. Thus, the *dāstān-e ᶜāsheqāna* presents *Vis & Rāmin* as a tale in the *manner* of lovers, orienting its readers towards a certain modality of reading. To respond fully to the story, this term implies that the audience must engage with it as lovers themselves, identifying with its characters and shedding tears in sympathy with them; they enact and participate in love's story even as they read it. The term encodes, in other words, something of a user's manual: the invitation, and perhaps even the injunction, that readers must read its narrative *romantically*. In this way, the text articulates its identity not just as a thing but as a method – a noun and a verb.

This adverbial mode of reading love stories, I believe, plays as vital a factor in tracing the romance genre as the material topic itself. It produces what I might call a fellowship of discourse and praxis oriented around love, a fellowship that presumes on one hand an open community of lovers, wherever and whoever they may be, and a discursive affinity with like-minded texts. "Come, sit ye down, ye who have been born under the same fate [of love-sickness]," writes Shot'a Rust'aveli, the author of the Georgian tale *The Knight in the Panther Skin* (w. ca. 1220). The narrator of *Livistros & Rodamne*, a Byzantine romance written in the late 1200s, invites "every benevolent soul educated in love / and nobly graceful heart amorously disposed" to "listen to an amorous tale that I wish to recount," while the audience of the Old French tale of *Floire & Blancheflor* (w. ca. 1150) – "all those / who bear the burden of love's woes" – is promised, "if you will hear my tale, you may / learn many things about Love's way."[47] Across these assembled cases, love – more specifically, the state of being a lover and the ethical questions that accompany this commitment – offers a common place, or topos, where the fictional and historical participants of romance may gather and converse. In other words, while the characters of these stories inhabit different diegetic worlds, they nevertheless talk to each other – and readers talk to them – in the extra-textual imaginary of romance. To participate in this wider discourse gives the romance an intrinsic sociability, a sense of customs, codes, and norms by which noble people perform their love and know their own nobility through that practice: "The noble lover loves love-tales," as Gottfried von Strassburg writes.[48] All the more interesting, then, that the medium that helps create and perpetuate this social bond is not expressed as "truth," per se, but as *myth* – a "tale" (*fasāna*), as the narrator of *V&R* puts it.

The *dāstān-e ʿāsheqāna*, in sum, offers a way of thinking about romance as a dialectic of matter and manner: the *mythos* (or narrative) of the love-story itself, and the *ethos* (or ethics and customs) of loving romantically, whose interaction produces what we might call a genre, at least in John Frow's terms: "a schematic world, a limited piece of reality ... populated by specific players ... infused with a moral ethos which brings with it certain attitudes to these players."[49] I admit that my use of these Greek terms is a little unorthodox in this context, but I hope that their novelty might facilitate a fresh comparative engagement with the amorous narratives of the Helleno-Abrahamic complex, gesturing towards previous discussions of genre as "institution" and "ideology" without being too beholden to the theoretical paradigms on which they were founded.[50] This dialectic also helps me establish a more precise set of parameters for talking about romance, which, as we know, has the capacity for a practically infinite range of applications. The main prototype that emerges out of this method is what is commonly called the "idealistic" or "idyllic" love-story, a narrative whose basic myth is succinctly described by Stephen Trzaskoma as follows: "Boy and girl meet. Boy and girl fall for each other. Boy and girl become separated and face trials and tribulations. Boy and girl are reunited and live happily ever after."[51] It is this narrative kernel, as I explain in the next chapter, that informs my own horizon of expectations in this study.

Finally, there is a useful correspondence of mythos/myth and the Persian word *fasāna* (line 3 of the passage above, a variant of the word *afsāna*) that speaks to one of the overarching themes of this book: the complex relationship between story and history. While the *afsāna*, like the mythos, can technically denote any story about the past, it typically connotes a lingering ambivalence about the veracity of that story's contents.[52] The "lying" dynamic introduced by this term plays out on many levels. For us in the modern period, it strengthens the potential ties between the Persian tale and the generic label of romance, given the latter's long association with fiction and fantasy.[53] But in the milieu of *V&R*'s composition, it also conjures a rich philosophical conversation about the ability of the human mind to apprehend reality through the imagination – the mental production of believable images, or simply make-believe. I render this activity as "phantasy," a spelling meant to distinguish it from the modern connotations of "fantasy" and to recall its roots in the Greek verb of making something appear as an image, a concept quite close to the Arabic term *takhyīl*.[54] Finally, the problem of verisimilitude reminds us again of the likelihood of our own *mis*-recognition of what we see, warning us to be on guard against neat categories such as fact versus fiction, or simple equivalences such as the *dāstān-e ʿasheqana* with the romance. To think of narrative as myth, then, reminds us that all narratives must practice a kind of deception, presenting an inherently messy world as though it were orderly. The world of the *afsāna* is a world where the truth is forever debated and debatable – a quality that ironically makes the myth far more akin to the "real" world than its name would imply.

In a way that rivals its complicated relationship with reality, the romance mythos also raises challenging questions about time – relating the past to the present and vice versa. *Vis & Rāmin* was written at a moment in time when not only its pre-Islamic milieu was ancient history, but even the "classical" age of early Islamic history – the life of the Prophet, the Umayyads, the early Abbasids – was now removed from the present at a distance of some centuries. From that perspective, *V&R*'s readers would have observed a number of ruptures separating them from those multiple pasts: with the collapse of the Abbasid caliphate and the rise of new polities and political orders under the Ghaznavids and Seljuks, they could have seen themselves as inhabiting a temporal moment somewhere in between the foundational stories of their heroes and the impending, though unforeseeable, final era of the Eschaton. I would consequently argue that the term medieval, in its literal sense as "middle age" (*medium aevum*), again proves useful, not only in our modern frame of connected histories through romance, but also from the perspective of the texts themselves. The Iranian reassessment of myth in the tenth to twelfth centuries – that is, stories of the ancient past with less-than-absolute claims to positive historicity – can be understood as a medieval project in the sense that it displays an engagement with multiple chronological frameworks, multiple sources of authority, and multiple temporalities with different but no less valid claims to truth, setting "a horizon upon which various communities retroactively located moments of significant transition or becoming," and leading to a tension between exalting and regretting the present age.[55]

It is in this light that the theme of multiplicity – the "many" (*chandin*) tales of love within *Vis & Rāmin*'s pages – gains its significance. It is clear from this passage above that the story of Vis, the tale's luminous "moon," stands at the centre of the narrator's attention; but through her interactions with the Nurse (chapter 2), the King (chapter 3), and Rāmin (chapter 4), three additional accounts emerge about what it means to be a lover, each one conditioned by that character's personality, social position, and philosophy of love. Together, they form a multilayered, polyphonic discourse in which individual voices, and their associated world views, converse and intermingle, each telling us their side of the story, ready to contest and even refute the assertions of their interlocutors. In a manner akin to the novel, then – we might call it novelistic – *V&R* incorporates multiple discursive fields or genres within itself into a kind of heteroglossia. The implications of this discursive mixing are not insignificant; as Frow writes, "Genre theory is, or should be, about the ways in which different structures of meaning and truth are produced ... it is central to human meaning-making and to the social struggle over meanings."[56] Not only do genres organize discourse into recognizable patterns, they invest those patterns with an authority that in turn informs the way we read the world around us, projecting a distinct view of the world – a "reality" – and inscribing it with truth-value, significance, and meaning. Thus, by bringing many tales of love into deliberation, *V&R* demonstrates how the love tale becomes a site for interrogating multiple and sometimes incompatible ways of articulating the real.

These notions of polyphony and heteroglossia I mentioned above are, of course, key terms in Mikhail Bakhtin's theory of the novel, though it must be admitted that he would question their application to premodern examples.[57] Nonetheless, his emphasis on discourse is very helpful, for unlike the psychological orientation of the realist novel, with its interest in the subjective histories, experiences, and inner lives of its protagonists, *V&R* foregrounds the role of language in giving shape to the reality its characters perceive around them. If a character's discourse can produce "the position enabling [that] person to interpret and evaluate his own self and his surrounding reality" (and here we might note the same dynamic at work in the Arabic word *manṭiq*, simultaneously an "utterance" and a "logic" that both informs and is formed by that utterance), we can conceive of the story's three main characters not as flesh-and-blood people, but rather "images of language," avatars of discursive practices that converse and clash in the open landscape of romance.[58] In other words, we have in the text three distinctive theories (*theōria* being the Greek word for a "looking at," a "beholding," like the Arabic *naẓar*) of love that engage in the "project of approaching the truth," as Shadi Bartsch puts it, through the discursive eyes of Vis, Mobad, and Rāmin – a heteroglossia of ways of seeing, rather than of individual subjects.[59] Through this multiplicity of perspectives, *V&R* affords itself the critical distance necessary to produce a second order of analysis, attending not only to the plot but for how we are meant to understand it. It performs, I suggest, a meta-reading of itself and its generic framework: more than a story about lovers, it is a story about stories, particularly the stories that lovers tell about themselves, probing their various claims to truth and moral authority. Thus, the dynamics of compositeness, fragmentation, and indeterminacy that lie in the text's origins replicate themselves in the narrative arcs of its characters.

Love at a Crux

Earlier, I described *Vis & Rāmin* as a text that lies at the "crux" of a number of Late Antique traditions, now recast into the emergent New Persian idiom of the eleventh century and telegraphing developments characteristic of the romance in a number of other (often courtly) literary traditions within the Helleno-Abrahamic complex.[60] Hence the book's title – *love at a crux*. But this title also alludes to a darker side of the story, one in which *V&R*, quite graphically, places *love on the cross* as well: even as it elevates romance as a premier genre of writing, it simultaneously tortures the genre, twisting its norms to undo themselves, breaking it apart to reveal its blind spots, and splitting its main characters into various simulacra, broken and stymied by their own self-image as the literary embodiments of untenable discourse. The doubt and disorientation generated by this violence result in numerous instances of mis-recognition, false starts, and a pervasive uncertainty about what happens next; yet they also, in the long run, excavate new possibilities for the romance myth and raise nuanced insights about the nature of its ethos.

My account of how this happens begins with a retrospective look at the usual functions the love-story played in the centuries preceding *V&R*'s composition in 1054. As discussed above, the romance mythos stands at a certain distance from the authoritative referent of history; as such, critics held it in dubious esteem, at best a charming tale for an evening's entertainment, at worst a bunch of stuff and nonsense. But in the first chapter, I describe a literary movement that took place in the eleventh century that explored how the romance's connection with **Phantasy** could be used to produce truth for its readers, albeit in unconventional ways, and show how a particular attention to the measured, ordered, and ornamented word – poetry – played a key role in this process, giving the love-story a claim to prestige that it had not previously enjoyed. Through this complex enmeshing of history and imagination, the romance bends time, warps space, and creates alternatives that are unthinkable in the realm of the real, yet no less meaningful for it.

But what new meanings emerge out of this manipulation? In the following three chapters, I turn to a close analysis of *V&R*'s main protagonists, pulling out their distinctive and often conflicting theories about being a lover in the world, not in the sense of their personalities as in traditional character analysis, but rather through the literary matrices that establish the logical and moral universes in which they operate. As Tzvetan Todorov reminds us, "The point of view chosen by the observer redelimits and redefines his object"; each character thus offers a point of entry into a field of intertextual discourse in which the very means of establishing truth come into view, producing a complex literary text that rewards multiple readings from multiple angles.[61] To facilitate this dialogue, I pair each character with a set of interlocutors that strike me as productive, at times in sustained comparison, at others merely gesturing towards potential affinities, the goal being not to insist on the necessity of any one particular connection, but to highlight the range of insights that a variety of theoretical approaches might generate. By reading and conversing with these figures as "images of language" – discourse concatenated and embodied in literary entities – we can follow their journeys as they assess, and subsequently challenge, the logic of their own formation.

The story of Vis brings up the most immediately striking aspect of the text, namely its open treatment of adultery; hence the title of chapter 2, **Ethics**. Vis's decision to "abandon" her first husband and to "cheat" on her second has typically been read as a shocking divergence from the strict moral codes that characterize the Persian love-story, isolating her as an "anomaly" in the tradition.[62] But if we situate *V&R* within the romance's long-standing ethos of fidelity to the beloved, a more complex picture emerges: like the heroines of the Greek novel, who strive to act "within bounds of familiar and socially acceptable female behaviour," Vis's ostensible departure from the norms of fealty and chastity paradoxically stems from her desire to uphold those values at any cost.[63] The paradox of this treacherous fidelity shakes the romance to its core, undermining the moral authority of its central ethos and passing the power (and responsibility) of choice to Vis herself, who goes on to forge a radical ethics in which public scandal becomes the very proof of her inner virtue. Vis's actions thus no longer appear as a flippant disregard for the romance "contract," but a careful interrogation of that contract's ability to deliver on its promises.[64] In this regard, Vis sets a precedent in Persian literature in which the heroine not only plays the leading role but also raises the most challenging questions, making visible the cracks in the romance armature that neither her husband nor her lover can ignore.[65]

Chapter 3 turns to the fortunes of Vis's husband, Mobad, to assess the stakes of romantic love from the angle of **Politics**. Mobad's narrative provides a counterpoint and parallel to Vis: just as adultery produces a gap between Vis's current position and the self-image she desires, so too does it separate Mobad from a long-standing discursive tradition of divine kingship. According to this language, Mobad is the King of Kings, the Shadow of God on Earth, a position that vaults him to the top of a gendered and social hierarchy and endows him with both the might and right to dominate men (as king) and women (as man). Yet even as he exercises this authority, his power erodes and wastes away; it is as if, as the text eloquently puts it, he is a prisoner of his skin, a metaphor not only of his aging and impotent physical body, but also of the language of unlimited power that constitutes his social being and subjective identity. This chapter explores how kingship – the epitome of authority – contains within it the seeds of its own impotence, such that any man (un)fortunate enough to be exalted by this position must in the end be consumed and devoured by it. These themes resonate strongly with similar cases in medieval French and German romance, and I will turn to them frequently to explicate by comparison.

If Mobad cannot escape the political language of kingship, neither can Rāmin, the poem's minstrel, avoid his entanglement with the tradition of lyric. In chapter 4, **Affect**, I explore how Rāmin signals generic shift through in-text musical performances, endowing his character with a distinctive voice that heaves with sighs of unrequited love, personal abjection, and perpetual longing – tropes familiar to readers of troubadour *canso*s and Arabic *ghazal*s alike. But Rāmin has a problem: his signature mode has been transplanted into the heteroglossic setting of the romance, where love *is* (ideally) reciprocated and power relations *are* (supposedly) symmetrical. This gap thereby engenders a kind of showdown between multiple ways of seeing and speaking on the condition of love that refract and scatter any shared expectations about what it means to be a lover. Rāmin's sense of self, like that of Vis and Mobad before him, cannot emerge from this story unscathed: he too finds his persona threatened in fundamental ways, and over time, his performance as a devoted and selfless lover flickers and breaks apart, giving way to a suicidal rage and despair at a world that cannot support his self-image.

Across these three chapters, a common pattern emerges: while Vis, Mobad, and Rāmin are all guided to an extensive degree by the personae they inhabit, (in)formed by historical discursive practices that articulate a certain view of the world and theory of the self within it, they find themselves slowly forced into situations where the logic of that discourse no longer makes sense. This allows for a certain self-reflexivity: like Aegialeus the fisherman, who "stands both inside the story, living its fictions, and outside it, exposing them," the characters are split into the dual position of both performing the roles that constitute their personae and recognizing the limits of those roles at the same time.[66] Though their narrative arcs break down for differing reasons, they collectively point to a shared overarching failure: the failure of the romantic mythos itself, caught in a self-destructive loop, unable to arrive at its usual destination. In this way, *V&R* submits not only its characters but also its very generic identity to an extended ordeal that tests the limits of its capacity to make sense in a senseless world. The romance has arrived at its own moment of crux, no longer capable of pointing a clear way out for its characters without damaging its integrity. Eventually, the pressure becomes unbearable: the narrative creaks and groans under its own weight, its foundations crack, and the walls must soon come tumbling down.

This takes us to the final chapter, **History**, in which we confront the stunning fact that, perhaps for the first time in the genre's history, the titular protagonists of a romance *have fallen out of love*; their promised stories have failed to deliver, and with nothing left to cling to, their mutual ardour gives way to hatred. This leads to an explosive clash between Vis and Rāmin, first in written, then oral, then finally even physical form. In the first stage of this slow-burn climax, long regarded as the finest moment in the poem (especially by premodern critics), Vis mounts a blistering assault on Rāmin's conduct, denouncing his fixation on the affective condition of love at her expense; then, by recording this history as a document, with her physical wounds as its proof, she defends her memory in her readers' minds, laying claim to something that looks suspiciously like "real" history. In the final bout of this contest, against the backdrop of a freezing blizzard, Vis and Rāmin abandon each other to perish in the snow. Though they turn (or are turned) from this self-destructive course at the last second, rescuing the story from what would have been a shocking outcome, their brush with death is the catalyst that allows them to discover a new freedom to act, and thus a new kind of nobility (*āzādi*), for the very first time. Just as the lovers' relationship must be broken before it can be reforged, we might extend this metaphor to the genre itself: the death of one kind of romance and the birth of another.

Vis & Rāmin is thus a highly self-reflective text, turning the mirror on itself to re-cognize and critique the many discourses that inform its composition; in bringing these conventions to a point of logical yet irresolvable crisis, *V&R* helps instigate something of a paradigm shift in how the romance is viewed and the kinds of work it can do in society.[67] To end the book, then, I take a step back to consider what has been gained by this new style of romance, and whether that gain suggests a self-conception that invites us to look beyond the boundaries of genre itself. To judge from the story's ending, it seems that the conventions of romance, already broken down and reworked, are now being put towards ends that place the genre into conversation with ongoing attempts to make sense of the world through other means – history, philosophy, lyric poetry, theology, and so on – a world in which many a tale has love.

Although each chapter of this book is built around a particular theme or character, it also follows the chronology of the overall story, taking us from start to finish across *Vis & Rāmin*'s 127 episodes. In this way, those unfamiliar with the text will be able to follow a sometimes-convoluted plot without getting too lost (though readers can also consult appendix A for a quick synopsis). This linear arrangement also advances my claim that, across the many tales of love within its pages, *V&R* slowly performs a romantic reading of romance itself: for if we conceive of the romance as the affective encounter of Self and Other, the dynamic of affinity and difference between *Vis & Rāmin* and its informative codes produces both a fresh account of generic self-discovery and a vivid exploration of what it means to be in the world as a lover.

Chapter One

Phantasy | The Rise of Romance

It was the autumn of 1051, and another sleepless night for Fakhr al-Din Gorgāni. For seven months, the air of Isfahan, where Gorgāni lived and worked as a poet and courtier, had reverberated with the boom and blare of drum and trumpet as one embassy after the next marched down the city's streets, paying homage to its new sultan, Ṭughrıl Beg of the house of Seljuk. From the Caesar of Constantinople came prisoners and tribute; from the King of Syria, a glittering ruby; from the Qarakhanid prince of distant Kashgar, gifts and a pact of friendship; and above all, from the Abbasid caliph in Baghdad, the coveted robe, banner, and rescript of investiture that proclaimed Ṭughrıl's dominion over all the lands of Islam.[1] Change was afoot, the hubbub seemed to cry, and Gorgāni might well have whiled away his hours of insomnia wondering what the future held in store, both for him and for the new political order in which he played some small part.

In both scope and consequence, the changes wrought by the Seljuk Turks would indeed prove to be enormous. After overthrowing their former masters, the Ghaznavids, in what is now modern Afghanistan, the Seljuks began a highly successful campaign of westwards expansion, conquering the Iranian plateau, subduing the Islamic heartlands of Iraq and Syria, and eventually crushing the Byzantine army at the battle of Manzikert in 1071. This event marked a major turning point in the demographic and political history of the region, as it opened up Anatolia to Turkoman settlement on one hand and prompted the launch of the First Crusade on the other. One result of this domino effect was a massive shake-up of peoples and cultures: within a generation, Arabs, Greeks, Franks, Turks, Kurds, Persians, Georgians, and Armenians were intermingling in close and sustained contact, in the battlefield, the court, the bazaar, and the bedroom, engendering new forms of cultural production even as they struggled for political dominance.[2] In this light, the Seljuk conquest of Isfahan in the middle of the eleventh century stands as a convenient milestone in the history of the western half of the "Afro-Eurasian oikoumene," as the historian Marshall Hodgson calls it – the interlocking belt of urban settlements, cultural complexes, and agrarian empires running from China through India and the Middle East to the Mediterranean, north Africa, and Europe – an event heralding a political, demographical, and even literary sea change whose ripples would be felt across the region throughout the eleventh century and beyond.[3] In this context of political reordering, peoples on the move, intercultural encounters, and novel literary experiments, we might then imagine Gorgāni, and the poem he would go on to write, as standing at a crucial moment – a crux – of a wide and interregional history.

Gorgāni's poem, *Vis & Rāmin* (*V&R*), is generally recognized as one of the first major romances of New Persian literature, a work that helped establish the genre as a significant and prestigious one within the nascent literary language. More broadly, however, it figures in and presages a pattern of literary activity that took place over the following 150 years across the western oikoumene: the sudden resurgence of romance at the Byzantine court in the years 1130–60, for example, or the poems of Chrétien de Troyes and his many followers in the 1170s and beyond. It even proved directly influential at the Georgian court of Queen T'amar (r. 1184–1213), where it was translated as *Visramiani* and set the stage for Shot'a Rust'aveli's *Vep'xistqaosani* (*The Knight in the Panther Skin*). This general picture, as I discuss elsewhere, suggests that the "discoveries" of romance in Iran, Byzantium, or Western Europe are not isolated incidents but are at some level interrelated, part of a general trend that took place in various forms across Persianate, Hellenistic, and Latinate literary spheres over the eleventh and twelfth centuries.[4] To be clear, this proposition is not contingent on a paper trail of the transmission and translation of specific texts (although that certainly happened in some cases, such as the Persian-Georgian connection), but rather on the concurrent emergence of comparable habits of romantic writing and their associated patterns of thought – what I refer to in shorthand as shared patterns of mythos and ethos – in the wake of these massive sociopolitical upheavals: a growth of many trees that, taken together, constitute a forest. While it is not the intention of this book to offer a comprehensive account of this phenomenon, I begin with the premise that it is valid and indeed crucial to think of the Persian romance as part of this interconnected world, so that when we do see moments of similarity or convergence with neighbouring traditions, we might be able to appreciate the scope of these connections and better consider their ramifications.

So what might the history of romance look like, if we tell our story from the vantage point of Isfahan in the middle of the eleventh century? From this outlook, a few salient accounts suggest themselves to me. The first is a story about the literary elevation of legends, folklore, and fairy tales within elite circles, a move that reverses a long-standing scepticism about the place of such narratives within the field of serious discourse. As we shall see, the overwhelming majority of Islamic sources that mention this genre before the eleventh century describe it as a myth, fable, or fabrication – a narrative light on substance, usually frivolous in nature, with at best a tenuous grounding in worldly time. The second story, then, is about how Persian romance authors developed strategies for making the timeless timely for their audience, investing the fantastic and verisimilar landscapes of their tales with immediate significance. It was not a foregone conclusion that these strategies would emerge or prove successful; when tracing the fortunes of the love-story in Arabic and Persian writing, for example, we find them develop in markedly different directions. Thus, the last story this chapter will tell is a story about the power of poetry, the verbal technology through which the poets of the early eleventh century could spin narrative straw into gold.

The chief protagonist of this account, of course, is Fakhr al-Din Gorgāni, to whom I now return. Eventually, the fanfare and commotion that had so disturbed Gorgāni's repose died down, and the new sultan whom he served got to work. Isfahan had long been extolled as the greatest city of the Iranian west, the "second Baghdad" of "Persian Iraq" (al-ʿirāq al-ʿajamī), with a diverse yield of crops, a flourishing silk industry, and at least a hundred thousand people living within its circular walls.[5] But by the time Ṭughrıl passed through its gates, the city was in dire need of a "doctor," as Gorgāni puts it (23/32), having suffered badly from decades of drought and political strife. The daunting task of healing the city fell to one Abu al-Fatḥ Moẓaffar, a young bureaucrat from Nishapur who came to be well regarded for his competency and professionalism. His policies seem to have worked: a year later, the traveller Nāṣer-e Khosrow, passing through Isfahan in June of 1052, recorded that "everything in the city is flourishing, and I saw nothing in ruins."[6] While both Ṭughrıl and Nāṣer-e soon moved on to continue their adventures elsewhere, Gorgāni, for reasons known only to him – "I had some work to do in Isfahan" is all he divulges on the matter (27/10) – remained in the city and entered the service of Abu al-Fatḥ. Thus it is in Isfahan, perhaps on a fine spring afternoon in the early months of the year of 1054, that our story of the story begins.[7]

An Act of Creation

We know very little about the author of *Vis & Rāmin*, beyond contextual speculation and what we can glean from the poem itself.[8] His relational name (*nisba*) suggests that he or his family hailed from the land of Gorgan, a wide plain on the southeastern littoral of the Caspian Sea, and it is possible that he got his start at the court of the local Bavandid dynasty there.[9] If this is the case, he could very well have seized the opportunity and entered Ṭughrıl's retinue as the sultan passed through this region on his way to Isfahan. Gorgāni's profession can also be inferred with some confidence: given his career with the Seljuks, we can surmise that he was either a professional poet or a secretary with literary aspirations. The latter scenario seems to me the more likely. Professional poets, at least the ones who won the most approbation at court, earned their bread and butter by composing in the qasida form – the panegyric ode that was performed at public occasions to celebrate and immortalize the sovereign – and while it seems that Gorgāni did compose short poems under the pen name "Fakhri," we never hear him remembered for his encomiastic work, if indeed he wrote any. My guess, then, is that he was first and foremost a man of letters, what one would have called an *adib* in his time.

But lettered he was indeed. As one would expect of someone in his line of work, Gorgāni knew Arabic and was well versed in its literature, evidenced by his numerous references to and paraphrases of the Qur'an, hadith, Arabic proverbs, and lines by famous Arab poets such as Imruᵓ al-Qays, Abu Tammām, and especially al-Mutanabbī.[10] More remarkable, however, is Gorgāni's knowledge of astronomy. In his famous "description of the night" (*V&R* 87–91 [51–4]), he names all but two of the forty-eight constellations enumerated in Ptolemy's *Almagest*, of which several Arabic translations had been made by the tenth century; Paul Kunitzsch deems it probable that Gorgāni had recourse to a celestial globe or al-Bīrūnī's manual of astrology, *Kitāb al-tafhīm* (w. 1029), in composing this scene.[11] Gorgāni was also well acquainted with philosophy: this we can tell from his opening doxology, where he paraphrases, point by point, an account of God's creation of the universe written by Avicenna.[12] The great philosopher had resided in Isfahan from 1024 until his death in 1037 – only fourteen years before Gorgāni arrived – and so his access to this material is easily explained. This is perhaps the most significant detail of our poet's intellectual pedigree, for it allows us to put his work into conversation with Avicennan metaphysics and love theory.

There is one last facet of Gorgāni's learning, however, that has most captured the attention of modern scholars, and it is perhaps best introduced by turning to the poem itself. One day, we are told, Abu al-Fatḥ asked his poet if he knew anything about the tale of Vis and Rāmin. One can almost hear the curious tone of the Nishapuri governor, eager to learn about the local culture of this city under his care, some thousand kilometres removed from his own: "They say it's something truly fine, that everyone in this land loves it" (28/30). Here, in his own words, is Gorgāni's response:

ز گرد آوردهٔ شش مرد داناست   بگفتم کان حدیثی سخت زیباست

نماند جز به خرّم بوستانی   ندیدم زان نکوتر داستانی

نداند هر که برخواند بیانش   ولیکن پهلوی باشد زبانش

و گر خواند همه معنی نداند   نه هر کس آن زبان نیکو بخواند

چو بر خوانی بسی معنی ندارد   فراوان وصف هر چیزی شمارد

I said, "It is a very beautiful tale (ḥadiṡ), compiled by six wise men (*mard-e dānā*). I have never seen a fairer story (*dāstān*); it is like nothing but a garden in bloom. But its language is *pahlavi*, and not everyone who reads it out understands what it seeks to make clear (*bayān*). Not everyone knows that language well, and even those who do, do not fully grasp its substance (*maʿni*). It includes abundant descriptions of everything, [but] when you read it out, it doesn't have a lot of meaning (*maʿni*)." (28/31–4)

Little could Gorgāni have guessed how much his mention of *pahlavi* – a word notorious for its ambiguity, yet tantalizing in its implications – would impact the modern reception of his poem. The most common reading of *pahlavi* is "Middle Persian," a southwestern Iranian language, written in a modified Aramaic script, which served as the official *lingua franca* of the Sasanian Empire (224–651 CE). Knowledge of this language, and in particular its script, was in rapid decline among the Muslim population of Iran by Gorgāni's time; as the tenth-century geographer Abu Isḥāq al-Iṣṭakhrī writes, "Pahlavi" (*al-fahlawiyya*) is the language "in which are written books about the Persians of old and their exploits, and which Persians themselves cannot understand without it being interpreted."[13] Gorgāni's discussion of *V&R*'s *pahlavi* resonates with this assessment: following his comments that not everyone can read or understand the language well, he goes on to characterize his source as a "book" (*daftar*) that the people of "this land" (presumably Isfahan) use to study the "sweet speech" (*lafẓ-e shirin*) of *pahlavi* (28/39–40), and will later show off his philological chops in explaining the etymology of words such as Khorasan (176/1–4 [139]) and Rāmin's name (527/85 [491]). For scholars eager to learn more about the literary traditions of pre-Islamic Iran, about which we know so little, the suggestion that *V&R* was derived from such an antique source was an exciting prospect indeed.[14]

But *pahlavi* bears a number of additional valences that complicate this account. Ibn al-Muqaffaʿ uses *al-fahlawiyya* to indicate the northwestern Iranian dialect of Fahla, a region roughly commensurate with "Persian Iraq" (the ancient province of Media, and the medieval one of Jibal), while other writers use it in an even looser sense to denote anything temporally or culturally "Parthian"; that is, evocative of the heroic days of yore.[15] Gorgāni contributes to the ambivalence, moreover, by adding a second linguistic term to his introduction: *fārsi* (what both al-Iṣṭakhrī and Ibn al-Muqaffaʿ call *al-fārisiyya*), another toponymic designation that refers to the language of the people of Pars/Fars in southwestern Iran.

بگفتند آن سخندانان پیشین   کنون این داستان ویس و رامین

کجا در فارسی استاد بودند   هنر در فارسی گفتن نمودند

درو لفظ غریب از هر زبانی   بپیوستند ازین سان داستانی

برو زین هردوان زیور نکردند   به معنی و مثل رنجی نبردند

Now those previous masters of speech (*sakhon-dān*) told this story of *Vis & Rāmin*; they showed skill in speaking *fārsi*, for they were authorities in *fārsi*. In this way, they composed a story with strange words from every language in it. They took no trouble with motive (*maʿni*) or analogy (*maśal*): they did nothing to ornament it with these two [devices]. (29/50–2)

This turnaround is quite dramatic: in the matter of a few lines, we have shifted from *pahlavi*-literate "wise men," compiling a book that is beautiful but verbose and lacking in significance, to these "authorities in *fārsi*" who produce a strange concoction of linguistic hybridity and "words gone obsolete" (*lafẓ-hā mansukh gashta-st*, 29/59). This terminological scrambling makes Gorgāni's introduction an intriguing puzzle for philologists, who have published many a learned study in the search for the exact identity of his source(s), be they in prose or in verse, Pahlavi or Persian.[16] (My own best guess, for what it's worth, is that the "six wise men" would likely have hailed from the same class of landed nobility [*dehqāns*] and priests [*mobeds*] who are mentioned in the compilation of the *Shāhnāma*, while the "masters of speech" – literally "speech-knowers," but translated as "experts," "authorities," "eloquenti," "écrivains," and "poeti" by

Minorsky, Morrison, Gabrieli, Lazard, and Norozi respectively – are likely a different group of people who had produced some kind of prose New Persian rendition, analogous to the early prose translations of the *Shāhnāma*. Gorgāni probably worked from this latter text, and he could have made recourse to the former as well, in the event that it was indeed used as a primer for Middle Persian in Isfahan.)[17] However, if we set this matter to the side for a moment, an underlying pattern comes to light. Whether *fārsi* or *pahlavi*, Gorgāni's dissatisfaction with the tale's language, however "sweet" it may be, is quite evident, and this raises a more fundamental question: Why this focus on words, meanings, and expression? Why take such pains to describe the codex and evaluate its authors' linguistic and literary competence?

One line of explanation holds that the invocation of an "old book" is a common trope, found in many medieval literary traditions, that helps justify the story as an authoritative account from the past – an especially useful strategy when its contents appear on the surface to be fantastic, what we might today call fictional.[18] Given the prevailing attitude towards fanciful stories in Gorgāni's milieu, which I will discuss further below, this could well be a significant factor; however, it does not seem to be the primary one here.[19] Gorgāni's focus is rather trained upon *language*, particularly on the relationship of speech (*sakhon*) to wisdom (*dānesh*), terms that appear in his critique of both the "wise men" and the "masters" who preceded him. Marred by prolix description and archaic diction, he says, the language of his source(s) obfuscates the qualities of elucidation (*bayān*), analogy (*maśal*, a word that can also be glossed as "example," "simile," and "parable"), and meaning (*maʿni*) that are so important to good writing. This last term, *maʿni* (Ar. *maʿnā*), which I have purposefully rendered in my translations above with a variety of words – "substance," "meaning," "motive" – is perhaps the most significant locus for exploring the interplay of utterance and thought. Attempting to capture this range of meanings, as well as its relative untranslatability into English, Alexander Key glosses *maʿnā* as "mental content ... the content of our minds that can be expressed through speech"; as such, it plays a central epistemological role in the philosophical, theological, linguistic, and poetic theories of medieval Islamic cultures.[20] In highlighting these devices, Gorgāni announces his radical break from the old way of telling the story and the new one he is about to perform:

حکیمی چابک اندیشه نبودست   که آنگه شاعری پیشه نبودست

که اکنون چون سخن می‌آفرینند   کجااند آن حکیمان تا ببینند

معانی را چگونه بر گشادند   برو وزن و قوافی چون نهادند
فسانه گرچه باشد نغز و شیرین   به وزن و قافیه گردد نو آیین

> Back then, poetry was not a craft; there was no quick-witted sage. Where
> are those sages, that they might see how people create discourse now, how
> they have brought forth ideas (*maʿāni*) and imposed rhymes and metre
> upon them! ... However sweet and pleasing a fable may be, it becomes
> something new (*now-āyin*) with rhyme and metre. (28/36–8, 43)

This passage offers important insight into Gorgāni's attitude towards
his source, which he presents not as a memento of the ancient past, to
be cherished and preserved as though in a museum, nor as a fount of
wisdom and authority in its own right, but as a fable or myth (*fasāna*)
that through the art of discourse can be transformed into a modern
work of art, possessed of aesthetic beauty and intellectual substance.[21]
A telling resonance emerges here between Gorgāni's description of
poetry as a professional craft (*pisha*) and the treatise on the "craft of
speech" (*ṣanʿat al-kalām*) by Abu Hilāl al-ʿAskarī (d. 1010). As the latter writes, the vocal form (*lafẓ*) must suit the mental content (*maʿnā*)
as clothing suits the body, avoiding prolixity, disharmony, and the
use of rare, ugly, obsolete, or technical words – precisely the defects
that Gorgāni critiques – in order to hit the mark, a property that critics
describe as *iṣāba* (correctness) or *ḥaqīqa* (accuracy, truth).[22] There is
something powerful and provocative in this convergence of language
and truth in poetry, an act that Gorgāni describes as a kind of "creation," using a verb (*āfarinand*) that is typically reserved for God.[23] It is
clear that poetry, in Gorgāni's view, is far more than the arrangement of
rhyming words; it is a method of knowledge production, carried out by
the wise. "If a learned man (*dānanda*) took the trouble," he concludes,
"it would become as beautiful as a storehouse full of jewels" (29/54).[24]
Here, at the intersection of phantasy, discourse, and wisdom, treasure
may be wrought.

We thus find in this introduction a detailed manifesto, in a sense,
of the broader literary movement that took shape in the early eleventh century, in which Persian court poets recognized new possibilities in the popular stories, evening entertainments, and legends of the
distant past and embarked on a project of imbuing them with meaning in hitherto untried and unthinkable ways. This process entailed a
complex reappraisal of the relationship between elevated discourse
(*sakhon*, in some ways comparable to *logos*) and the production of
mental contents both rich and profound.[25] For unlike other textual

traditions inherited from the pagan past – philosophy, medicine, moral guidance, history, and so on – the love-story had no clear purchase on an inherent value or truthfulness to it; thus the act of refashioning this material into something valuable was not so much an act of discovering the diamond in the rough, as the saying goes, but of *creating* diamonds out of so much charcoal; the end result is of an entirely "new manner" (*now-āyin*) in relation to its source. As a result of these efforts, a distinctive literary genre, what we now retrospectively call the romance, emerged as a viable and prestigious kind of writing in New Persian and, as time went on, the Persianate world at large.[26] To explain how this happened, I will first discuss general classifications of and attitudes towards narrative in the Islamic middle ages, then show how the association of certain topics with certain temporalities could affect both the generic shape of various mythoi and their reception among the intellectual elite.

Legends and Legerdemain

As Northrop Frye remarks, "Any serious discussion of romance has to take into account its curiously proletarian status as a form generally disapproved of, in most ages, by the guardians of taste and learning, except when they use it for their own purposes."[27] This seems especially apt when looking at the literary theory of both Hellenistic and Islamicate tradition, for in neither case does the love-story receive much critical interest. Part of this neglect can simply be chalked up to accidents of timing and circumstance: the ancient Greek romances, for example, emerged centuries after the canonical genres had been established, and thus fell outside the purview of traditional criticism.[28] Similarly, in the Islamicate context, the lion's share of critical analysis was concentrated on the dissection and analysis on the qasida and its variants, which, due to its ancient pedigree and important role in the public sphere, had long held pride of place as the noblest poetic form and the highest register of speech (short of the Qur'an itself). Other poetic forms, such as the quatrain and masnavi, garnered scant attention in comparison.[29]

In addition to these external factors, however, there are aspects about the topic, content, and especially truth claims of romance that worked against its reception in educated and courtly circles. Famous among scholars of the ancient Greek romance are the words of the Roman emperor Julian (d. 363): "For us it will be appropriate to read such narratives as have been composed about deeds *that have actually been done*; but we must avoid all fictions (*plasmata*) in the shape of historical accounts (*en historias eidei*) such as were circulated among men in the past, for instance tales whose theme is love (*erōtikas hypotheseis*), and generally speaking everything of that sort" (my emphasis).[30] Another intellectual of late antiquity, Macrobius (fl. early fifth c.), writes that while philosophers could avail themselves of "fabulous narrative" (*narratio fabulosa*) to speak about certain "holy truths ... beneath a modest veil of allegory," they should shun "narratives about the imaginary fortunes of lovers" (*argumenta fictis casibus amatorum*), which in his view have no place but in the nursery.[31] In both cases, we see a general suspicion held towards the "shaped" or "made-up" narrative (*plasma, fictum*) that *imitates* reality without conveying it, diverting one's attention from what "actually" happened to what didn't. The verisimilar tale, known as the *argumentum* in medieval Latin, was perhaps the most untrustworthy kind of narrative one could encounter, an indeterminate third category of story that fell between those that claimed to possess truth (*historia*) and those that made no pretence of having it (*fabula*); as Morgan writes, "What makes them dangerous is that they blur an essential dividing line between truth and untruth, that they invite a confusion between what is and what is not real."[32]

We find similar attitudes towards "fictional" narrative in the vibrant literary milieu of Abbasid Iraq. Ibn Qutayba (d. 889), for instance, advises that anyone wishing to relate an amusing yarn (*mazḥ*) should ensure that "the story is true or nearly true, timely, and appropriate," a sentiment repeated by later writers such as Muḥammad al-Ghazālī (d. 1111) and Ibn al-Jawzī (d. 1201).[33] In an interesting metaphor, Abu Ḥayyān al-Tawḥīdī (d. 1023) compares fairy tales (*khurāfāt*), such as those found in the *1001 Nights*, to a kind of rust (*ṣadaʾ*) that darkens the lustre of eternal truths; while their appeal to the senses makes them attractive to women and children, he writes, those of mature intellect can (and should) polish the rust away and dispense with phantasy altogether.[34] The same convictions appear in an anecdote related by Abu Bakr al-Ṣūlī (d. ca. 946), in which an Abbasid prince boasts to his grandmother of the "books of tradition, jurisprudence, poetry, language, history, and the works of the learned" that adorn his library, "not like the books which you read excessively such as *The Wonders of the Sea*, *The Tale of Sindbad*, and *The Cat and the Mouse*."[35] This evident association of fantastic tales with women and children is a significant point: by naming the books he reads (or owns, at least), the young prince declares his entry into the privileged world of adult manhood, while implying an almost causal link between the stories that women allegedly enjoy and their inferior place in patriarchal society.

The distinction of narrative kinds along lines of utility, truth-value, and (male) nobility is on full display in the *Fihrist* (*Catalogue*) written by the Baghdadi bookseller Abu al-Faraj al-Nadīm (d. ca. 995), which provides a detailed snapshot of Abbasid book production and consumption at the turn of the millennium.[36] Of the *Fihrist*'s ten chapters, only two deal with narrative at all; the rest are concerned with scripture, exegesis, grammar, law, philosophy, and similar topics. The first, chapter 3, details the writings of rapporteurs (*akhbārūn*), genealogists (*nassābūn*), and scholars of transmitted sayings and customs (*aṣḥāb al-aḥdāth wa-l-ādāb*), categories that, by their very nomenclature, make an explicit claim to the historical past, to real people who really existed.[37] To be sure, this does not rule out the inclusion of stories that modern readers might consider fantastic, nor does this reduce them to "neutral" accounts of the "facts"; in al-Nadīm's list of the works attributed to the historian Ibn al-Kalbī (d. 819), for example, we find accounts of the Seven Sleepers of Ephesus, the reign of al-Ḍaḥḥāk (the notorious serpent-king), and the "language of the birds" (*manṭiq al-ṭayr*) – a Qur'anic story about Solomon (27:16) that became a prominent vehicle for allegory in the works of Avicenna, al-Ghazālī, Sohravardi, and ʿAṭṭār.[38] These stories, though, are gathered together as "Accounts of the Forefathers" (*akhbār al-awāʾil*) and thus presented as part of the collected lore of the Arabian tribes; as scholars like Tarif Khalidi, Tayeb El-Hibri, and Samer Ali argue, these discourses provided the raw material for the forging of communal memory, providing a field on which contemporary literati engaged with ongoing moral, political, and ethical debates in the pursuit of both figural and literal truths.[39]

Such pursuits, however, seem quite removed from the second category of narrative we find in the *Fihrist* (chapter 8), which is devoted to what al-Nadīm calls "evening tales" (*asmār*) and "fairy tales" (*khurāfāt*), along with books on "tricks" (*ḥiyal*) and "talismans" (*ṭilismāt*).[40] The etymology of these first two categories is quite revealing. The *khurāfāt* are supposedly named after a man named Khurāfa, a member of the Banu ʿUdhra (a tribe that lent its name to a whole ethos of chaste love, called ʿudhrī) who was abducted by the jinn. He returned to the human realm with incredible tales of what he had seen during his imprisonment, and thus the "sayings of Khurāfa" (*ḥadīth khurāfa*) became a shorthand term for anything difficult to believe or unprovable.[41] Even more interesting are the *asmār*. Derived from the verb *samara*, "to while away the night," these tales indicate first and foremost a particular performance setting, or more appropriately, performance time: stories told in the evening, within by association semi-private or private spaces like the symposium (*majlis*), the court's inner circle, the bedchamber, and so on. While there is no *a priori* relationship between the *asmār* and their contents, we see from their close association with the *khurāfāt* that they tend to gather about them the aura of the fantastic: *The Wonders of the Sea*, *The Tale of Sindbad*, and the like.[42] This helps us understand, furthermore, the rationale for their inclusion with tricks and talismans. Like other kinds of magic, the pleasure (and purpose) of the fairy tale lies precisely in the ruse of making the impossible seem possible.

It is here, under the broad heading of evening tales and fairy tales in the *Fihrist*, that we find the love stories – the narrative core of the amorous romance genre, as discussed in the prologue – gathered together in subgroupings such as "Those lovers who loved before and during Islam and had books composed about them," "Those lovers whose records entered the evening tales," "Names of humans who loved jinn and of jinn who loved humans," and so on.[43] There are two inferences we can make from this section. First, the number of titles (some 140 by my count) and proliferation of subgeneric labels suggest that narratives about love, though perhaps not prestigious, were certainly popular. At the same time, their collective placement under the broader heading of what we might call "legends and legerdemain" casts doubt on their value as sources of communal authority, thanks to a constellation of factors: their usual performance context, their association with women and children, the nature of their contents, and their ties with foreign (non-Arab) cultures. In this regard, the emerging picture of al-Nadīm's readership seems to resonate well with Morgan's description of the educated elites in the era of Julian and Macrobius: "Though people of some sophistication bought and enjoyed novels, they seem to have read them within a frame of cultural values which somehow consigned the pleasures of novel-reading to the categories of the insignificant or in some way ambivalent."[44] While accounts and reports of the past, however fluid and contested, afforded readers an opportunity to make sense of their present, contents deemed too unreliable or incredible were *by default* excluded from this discourse, relegated to what Miskawayh (fl. 950–83) described as "fanciful tales with no use but to bring on sleep and to entertain."[45]

I emphasize "default" because, as we shall see, being listed as a fairy tale or evening tale by no means excluded such stories from the patronage economy of "useful" discourse; the point is rather that they needed to employ a variety of legitimating strategies to get there. The *khurāfāt* (so called by al-Nadīm) of *Kalīla & Dimna* – a collection of animal fables originally stemming from the Sanskrit *Pañcatantra*, rendered into Arabic by Ibn al-Muqaffaᶜ (d. 757) – is a great example of this: while talking-animal stories would have had no obvious use-value in and of themselves, *Kalīla & Dimna*'s self-historicization, impeccable style, and diegetic performance setting as a dialogue between a king and his vizier all helped the text foreground its status as a book of practical philosophy, such that, as Ibn al-Muqaffaᶜ writes, "the animal is a diversion; what the animal says, wisdom and education" (*ṣāra al-ḥayawān lahwan wa-mā yanṭiq bihi ḥikmatan wa-adaban*).[46] Similarly, the *Maqāmāt* of Badīᶜ al-Zamān al-Hamadhānī (d. 1008), often singled out by modern scholars eager to locate the first openly fictitious work of Arabic literature, were admired by medieval readers not (only) for their creative phantasy but for their verbal elegance, and were thus regarded as a high achievement in the art of the epistle.[47] "True" evening tales about "real" people, to which I will return, also had a ready claim to the attention of elite audiences, who perceived themselves in the accounts of their forebears. Even the stories of the *1001 Nights*, as the chronicle of Ḥamza al-Iṣfahānī (w. 961) suggests, were known to move between the field of instruction and entertainment, depending on the manner of their presentation.[48]

The task at hand, then, is to follow the processes by which the love-story, another kind of narrative whose contents were understood to be of dubious intrinsic value, made its way into the prestigious circles of learned discourse. Our best route towards answering this, I think, is to attend to the crucial role of *topic* in medieval narrative, and observe how different subject matters lent themselves to different literary strategies, dominant thematics, performance settings, and audience receptions. In so doing, we stand to not only refine our understanding of narrative genre in the Islamic Middle Period, but also how genre itself makes certain claims upon time: on time's conception, emplotment, and veracity. As Mikhail Bakhtin noted with his famous notion of the chronotope, narrative space and time are closely intertwined: we will see the ramifications of this insight when we explore two topics closely associated with the modern concept of romance: refined ("courtly") love and exemplary ("chivalric") heroism, which might be boiled down to manifestations of inner and outer nobility.[49]

Heroic Lives and Amorous Tales

To explain why the notion of topic plays such a vital role in tracing the identification, function, and reception of various literary genres, we need to look back to the roots of Perso-Arabic genre criticism, which stem from engagements with the tradition's master form, the qasida. As the Abbasid critics understood it, the qasida was a polythematic performance that could be broken down along the lines of thematic content,

emotional tenor, and the rhetorical aims of its various motives: praise
(*madīḥ*), desire (*nasīb*), blame (*hijāʾ*), ridicule (*hajw*), eulogy (*thanāʾ*),
wisdom (*ḥikma*), and so on.[50] This attention to the interplay of theme,
mood, and intent also informed the critics' subsequent classification of
the "incidental" poems that emerged over the first centuries AH, often
as independent elaborations or spin-offs of qasida motifs. The ghazal,
whose name is derived from the Arabic verb *ghazala* – "He talked,
and acted in an amatory and enticing manner, with a woman, or with
women"[51] – is only the most famous example of this; in addition, labels
such as wine poem (*khamriyya*), hunting poem (*ṭardiyya*), renunciation
poem (*zuhdiyya*), garden poem (*rawḍiyya*), prison poem (*ḥabsiyya*), and
so on are readily found in anthologies and collected works.[52]

The usual Arabic word to describe these distinctions is *gharaḍ*, meaning the "aim" or "purpose" that informs the poem's composition.[53] For
comparative purposes, however, I find that the word *topic* is another
useful way to express this confluence of content and expression, especially thinking etymologically back to its Greek ancestor *topos*, namely
a "site" of communal discourse, a common-place around which and
over time develops a core of central ideas (*maʿānī*, also possibly glossed
as "themes" and "motifs") and ways of talking about them.[54] Curtius's
discussion of the classical *topoi* as "storehouses of trains of thought"
that "can serve a practical purpose" seems quite comparable.[55] In this
way, poetic topic aligns – or at least interacts – in meaningful ways not
only with the matters of rhetorical intent and social function expressed
by the *gharaḍ*, but with the notion of poetic style as it came to be articulated in Persian literary criticism. The poet Khāqāni (d. ca. 1195), for
example, uses topical markers to contrast his novel style (*shiva*) against
that of his predecessor ʿOnṣori, saying the latter "never declaimed
about philosophy, homily, or renunciation" (*na taḥqiq goft-o na vaʿẓ-o na
zohd*); this shows how we can think about subject matter as implying a
certain method and purpose, in addition to bare content.[56]

So far, I have been speaking only of relatively short poems as they were
discussed and classified by medieval critics; even the longest qasidas
rarely exceed two hundred lines. But what is interesting is that the lens
of topic seems to have guided the reception (and much later the critical
analysis) of larger units of discourse as well. Beyond the monorhyme
qasida and its derivatives, one of the few poetic forms that enjoyed
widespread success in Persian is the masnavi, a form that utilizes a system of rhyming half-lines (—A ● —A / —B ● —B / —C ● —C) and can
thus continue for thousands or even tens of thousands of verses, giving it a functional range similar to that of prose; as the critic Shams-
e Qays wrote, it is a form eminently suited for versifying "extended

stories and long tales" (*qeṣaṣ-e moṭavval va ḥekāyāt-e derāz*).[57] Perhaps because it was never formally theorized, the generic labels of masnavi poems tend to follow the same topical orientation as their short-form counterparts. Most of the New Persian narrative poems of the eleventh to thirteenth centuries describe themselves in literal terms as a "story" (*dāstān, qeṣṣa, ḥekāyat*), "report" (*ḥadis̱, khabar*), "fable" (*afsāna*), "evening tale" (*samar*), "book" (*daftar, nāma*), and so on, to which they would often append some descriptive or topical label(s) to better inform the reader of their theme and contents. For example, many works set in the *Shāhnāma* cycle describe themselves as "ancient" (*bāstān*), conjuring images of pre-Islamic kings and heroes, while accounts of Alexander emphasize the auspicious aspects of his legendary reign, such as Neẓāmi's "book of honour" (*Sharaf-nāma*) and "book of felicity" (*Eqbāl-nāma*), and Jāmi's "book of wisdom" (*Kherad-nāma*).[58] In comparison, amorous romances like Gorgāni's *Vis & Rāmin*, Neẓāmi's *Khosrow & Shirin*, and Jāmi's *Yusof & Zolaykhā* describe themselves as a "love-story" (*dāstān-e ᶜāsheqāna*), a "book of desire" (*havas-nāma*, albeit implicitly), and a "book of love" (*maḥabbat-nāma*) respectively.[59] In this basic strategy of self-identification through the rubric of *narrative + topic*, these Persian titles are quite similar to common naming conventions found throughout the western oikoumene of antiquity and the Middle Ages.[60]

These markers suggest that narrative genres did indeed exist for medieval writers and readers – not as a formal taxonomy, but as a practical nomenclature grounded in the loose affiliation of topics, themes, expectations, and features, akin to the way one might find books arranged in a public library (mysteries, thrillers, fantasy, etc.). The systematization of these genres seems to have begun in the early modern period, when critics and littérateurs again utilized topic as an analytical tool. As Pasha Khan has shown, the *Ṭirāz al-akhbār*, a manual of storytelling written circa 1631, lists four "particular narrative situations that called for a particular kind of text ... battle, courtly gatherings, beauty and love, and trickery" (*razm, bazm, ḥosn-o ᶜeshq*, and *ᶜayyāri*).[61] The first two of these topoi, the feast (*bazm*) and the battle (*razm*), lent their names to the eventual establishment of the *bazmiyya* ("court epic") and *razmiyya* ("war epic") genres in Indo-Persian literary scholarship.[62] Notably, the Iranian scholar Moḥammad-ᶜAli Tarbiyat, writing in the 1930s, calls *Vis & Rāmin* the oldest extant *"bazmi"* poem in Persian literature; he is clearly drawing from this older terminology that identifies the banquet as a foundational site in narrative poetry.[63]

It is important to stress that these critics did not think of these topical genres as independent, either/or categories – and neither should we. Just as contemporary audiences would expect a qasida to contain a number of thematic movements in its declamation, so too they would anticipate a long-form narrative to visit multiple topoi, from feasting and fighting to love and courtship and back again, including in its ambit other speech genres as well: homily, praise, exhortation, jokes. That said, however, it does seem to be the case that a particular topic will often assume a central enough position that it comes to (in)form the narrative as a whole, both in terms of the text's overarching structure and in the way readers were likely to engage with it. Roman Jakobson describes this as the "generic dominant," that is, "the focusing component" that "rules, determines, and transforms the remaining components."[64] By bringing this distinction to the corpus of medieval Persian narratives available to us, we can begin to distinguish certain conventions, "habits" so to speak, around the narration of particular topics, an approach that should bring us close to reading these works in something akin to their own terms, while gaining insight into how romances (in the broad sense of the word) unfold in various ways and prioritize different aspects of their thematic repertory.[65]

As I mentioned in the prologue, there is a particularly strong rapport between stories about lovers and stories about heroes, one that I would like now to explore further.[66] In terms of plot, both story types tend to frequent the core topoi of the romance in the broad sense of the word – love, adventure, feasting, and fighting – producing that generic interconnectivity and modulation discussed by Khan above. Yet as a dialectic, they also recall the themes of *amor* and *militia*, which scholars like Dennis Green and Cesare Segre have identified as the central dynamic at the heart of Western European romance.[67] As the pioneering work of Julie Scott Meisami has shown, the same themes are productive to consider in the Persian case too, as it is precisely these two aspects of noble male conduct that, when successfully aligned (she argues), result in the embodied image of the ideal king and perfect human (*al-insān al-kāmil*).[68] But beyond their value for literary analysis, the themes of love and heroism also allow me to suggest two focal points that have a significant impact on the structural features of the resulting narrative and on its social reception. When placed in the position of the generic dominant, these foci will tend to produce amorous love stories on the one hand and heroic life stories on the other, each with their distinctive features and implications.

Let me show what I mean first with a look at the conventional features of the Persian "heroic" narrative poems, in comparison with neighbouring traditions. They tend to name themselves via an established formula: the "book" (*nāma*) of the principal hero, such as the

Garshāsp-nāma, *Bahman-nāma*, *Farāmarz-nāma*, *ʿAli-nāma*, and many oth-ers (though there are of course exceptions, like the *Haft paykar*). Other family resemblances include the use of the "epic" *motaqāreb* metre, and the self-designation as *bāstān* ("ancient") – a label that, like the French *roman d'antiquité*, establishes some kind of association with the distant past. Because their focal point is the hero (typically male, but with nota-ble exceptions like the *Bānu-Goshasb-nāma*), these narratives generally assume a biographical framework, beginning with the circumstances of the protagonist's birth and childhood, elaborating his many deeds and adventures, and concluding with his death.[69] The story can be extended, of course, by relating the exploits of the hero's ancestors or descendants, or by combining multiple biographies into a broader account about the fortunes of a tribe, dynasty, or kingdom – what Malcolm Lyons, draw-ing from Viktor Shklovsky, dubs "linking."[70] In this light, these works compare well with stories that utilize terms like *archē* ("the beginning of [the account of]"), *vita* ("the life of"), *historia* ("the story of"), *sīra* ("the life story of"), *gestes* ("the deeds of"), *saga* ("the things said about"), and so on – all referring in some way to the life, deeds, or account of the titular protagonist or collective.[71] This biographical framework estab-lishes, in other words, the mythos of the heroic tale. To illustrate what this might look like in practice, here are the opening lines of the Byzan-tine tale of *Digenēs Akritēs*:

> Praises and trophies for the achievements
> of the thrice-blessed Basil the Frontiersman,
> the bravest and most noble,
> who possessed his strength from God as a gift
> and has overcome all of Syria,
> Babylon, and the whole of Charziane,
> Armenia and Cappadocia,
> and Amorion and Ikonion as well,
> and that famed and still great fortress,
> powerful and well-fortified,
> Ankyra I mean, and all Smyrna,
> and he subjugated the land by the sea.
> I shall now reveal to you the deeds
> which he performed in this present life ... (1.1–14)[72]

As this introduction makes clear, the life story of Basil the Border Lord will be the focal point of the narrative, and any amorous encounters that may occur will fall within the organizing structure of the heroic biography. To return to Shklovsky's terminology, the heroic biography can serve not only as a narrative "link," but as a "frame" as well, as H.T. Norris describes the Arabic *sīra*: "The main character is introduced and at the end bows and makes his exit; in between, a life-story is told or interest is sustained by a repetitive series of combats, amatory quests, fantastic escapades, poems and anecdotes."[73] *Digenēs Akritēs* is a great example of this, as the first episode that kicks the narrative off is an amorous tale – an account of how Basil's father, an Arab amir, fell in love with a Byzantine noblewoman, converted to Christianity, and settled in the Anatolian frontier. The *raison d'être* of this episode, however, is not the love-story itself, but rather to set the stage for the arrival of the central protagonist, a hero who is accepted by the story's community as both real and significant within their collective memory, giving him, as Panagiotis Agapitos writes, a "mythological-historical" character.[74]

I cite *Digenēs* because it, like some of the other Greek narratives, is particularly good at summarizing the plot at the outset, but there are many texts from Iranian sources that show a strong affinity to its model in terms of both mythos and ethos, ranging from the Middle Persian *Kār-nāmag ī Ardašīr ī Pāpagān* ("the book of the deeds of Ardashir, son of Bābak"), in which a love-story serves as the catalyst that launches the hero's rise to the throne, to the many "secondary epics" set in the world of the *Shāhnāma*.[75] The chapter introducing the topic of the *Garshāsp-nāma*, for example – notably titled "On Garshāsp's Manliness" (*dar mardānegi-ye garshāsb guyad*) – outlines for its audience the generic topoi that its protagonist will visit:

یکی نامه بد یادگار از مهان	ز کردار گرشاسب اندر جهان
هم از راز چرخ و هم از روزگار	پر از دانش و پند آموزگار
ز خوبی و زشتی و شادی و غم	ز فرهنگ و نیرنگ و داد و ستم
ز مهر دل و کین و شادی و بزم	ز نخجیر و گردنفرازی و رزم

There was a book (*nāma*) about Garshāsp's deeds in the world, a memorial of the great, full of wisdom and sage advice; of the secrets of the heavens and the times; of cleverness and trickery and justice and oppression; of good and evil, joy and sorrow; of hunting and nobility and fighting; of heart's love, vengeance, joy, and feasting. (19/11:1–4)

While the topic of love is not absent from this list of contents, we can see that the dominant themes of this narrative are heroic: feasting, fighting, vengeance, hunting, cleverness, trickery, and the noble struggle of good against evil. The poet, Asadi Ṭusi, goes on to describe how his Garshāsp is in fact a better exemplar of these virtues than the famous hero Rostam, and that the benefit of reading these exploits, as mentioned in the passage above, is that the reader will obtain a great deal of wisdom, advice, and knowledge of the world through following this biography.[76] The story itself, of course, follows the biographical model. It begins with Garshāsp's lineage, birth, and childhood, then follows his many travels and adventures (including a romance with the Caesar's daughter) until it reaches the end of his life. This compares fruitfully, by the way, with another work whose origins lie in the eleventh century, and whose story, like *Digenēs Akritēs*, is set in the Arabo-Byzantine wars of the early Islamic period: the Arabic *sīra* of the princess Dhāt al-Himma. Its compiler opens the work by delineating its subject and explaining its social function as follows: "The storytellers (*ruwāt*) have told this amazing tale (*sīra ʿajība*), and the marvellous accounts (*aḥādīth gharība*) [of the deeds] of the pre-eminent therein; and so I desired to assemble a tale (*sīra*) that would be a pleasure for its listeners, with something of benefit inside for all those who study it."[77] In all three texts, the heroic figure thus provides his or her tale with both its structural armature and dominant ethos: a celebration of chivalric and "manly" deeds (even when performed by women).[78] This is quite different from the amorous narratives – what I've been calling the love-story mythos – to which I now turn.

While heroic stories recount the life and deeds of a hero, amorous tales are concerned first and foremost with the love affair between two people, a topical orientation that bears immediate implications for the titling conventions, typical characters, narrative structure, anticipated topoi, and organization of time and space found in these works.[79] The protagonists of the amorous tale consist of a boy and a girl who are invariably young, noble, and exceedingly beautiful; both receive substantial (if not perfectly equal) narrative attention, and their names typically inform the title of the work; for example, *Vāmeq & ʿAzrā*, *Khosrow & Shirin*.[80] The topic of love also establishes the diegetic boundaries of the love-story, which typically begins with the onset of love and concludes with the lovers' eventual reunion, either happily in marriage or tragically in death (two major Persian romances, *Varqa & Golshāh* and *Layli & Majnun*, contain both endings).[81] While some of the most successful romances add little embellishment to this basic plot – Longus's *Daphnis & Chloe*, or Nezāmi's *Layli & Majnun* – others utilize a wide range of adventure motifs to expand the story to globe-trotting dimensions. Perhaps no one describes this repertoire better than Theodore Prodromos (fl. mid-twelfth c.), who begins his romance with a sneak peek of what his readers can look forward to:

> These [are the adventures] of the silvery girl Rhodanthe with the
>> lovely garland
>> and of the valiant and comely youth Dosikles,

> the flights and wanderings and tempests and billows, brigands,
> grievous eddies, sorrows that give rise to love,
> chains and indissoluble fetters and imprisonments in gloomy
> dungeons, grim sacrifices, bitter grief,
> poisoned cups and paralysis of joints,
> and then marriage and the marriage bed and passionate love.
>
> (20/1.17–24)[82]

As a Byzantine writer, Prodromos is consciously evoking a specific tradition of amorous narrative – what classicists usually now call the Greek novel – that dates back to the first centuries CE. But in general terms, and with some adjustments, this could be the synopsis of many a love-story in the broader region, stretching from the eastern Mediterranean to the Iranian plateau – namely, the contact zone between two major centres of multi-ethnic empire, the Hellenistic (then Roman) and the Persian (Achaemenid, Parthian, Sasanian).[83] We find elements of this narrative, for example, in the "Persian" tale (that is, attributed to Persian sources by Greek writers) of Odatis and Zariadres as related by Athenaeus of Naucratis, in which the lovers meet in a dream, and, after some travel, tricks, and adventure, meet in person and elope together.[84] Thanks to the wide geographic distribution that this imperial context made possible, it seems that the building blocks of this mythos were distributed across the Hellenistic, Islamicate, and Latinate cultural zones, adapted to local contexts and in conversation with local forms: examples include martyrologies told in early Christian communities, Arabic reports (*akhbār*) about chaste (*ʿudhrī*) lovers, the Komnenian and Palaiologan romances, and narratives like *Floire & Blancheflor* and *Aucassin & Nicolette* in western Europe. The love-stories coming out of eleventh- and twelfth-century Iran draw heavily from the same set of elements, and should therefore be considered as part of the same general literary ecosystem, not only in terms of narrative features (mythos), but also in their similar value systems and social norms (ethos). I emphasize here that I think of these two aspects, the mythos and the ethos, as interrelated but nonetheless distinct: even when two narratives might diverge in terms of their plot (*Kallirhoe* versus *Daphnis & Chloe*, for example, or *Khosrow & Shirin* versus *Layli & Majnun*), we can still discern strong affinities in their moral and ethical codes.

While the distinction of amorous and heroic tales allows us to draw clearer lines for comparison in the historical and cross-cultural study of romance, it also surfaces another element that seems to have carried more immediate relevance for medieval readers, especially in the Byzantine and Islamic milieux (although analogues with western Europe also suggest themselves): the tale's relationship with time, affecting thereby the timeliness of its telling. Bakhtin's notion of the chronotope is well suited for discussing this relationship: as he observes, time happens differently in particular kinds of literary space, and space works differently in particular kinds of literary time.[85] But in addition to this important insight, the chronotope also invites us to consider the ways that a narrative situates itself in the past and uses that setting to stake some kind of claim onto the present. In that regard, a simple but crucial distinction emerges between heroic and amorous narratives: since a hero, by definition, is a figure who, by collective consensus, *matters* to a particular community at a particular moment in time, stories about a community's past heroes obtain a self-evident relevance to the present. Another way of saying this is that the value of heroic narratives must partially be supplied by its historical readership, "the social acceptance of or response to literature," as Frye puts it.[86] While tales about Moses would be of intrinsic interest for readers brought up within Abrahamic sacred tradition, for example, they would have no such relevance in the Shinto milieu of medieval Japan. The love-story, by contrast, bundles its meaningfulness within its topical and temporal boundaries: by making its topic the story of a love affair, and following that affair from beginning to end within the confines of its narrative, it provides its own relevance; it "matters" in and of itself.[87] The upshot of all this is that a heroic story points to and relies on an external framework of the past, and is thereby *timely* for its intended audience, while a story about love is internally sufficient – it is, in a theoretical sense, *timeless*.

It is this distinction, I suggest, that helps us think about how different kinds of narrative interact with historical time in different ways and make differing claims on their audiences' attention, explaining why some would be readily picked up as relevant and meaningful histories, while others would be regarded as fairy tales of far less consequence. Navigating this issue of reception is by no means a clear-cut task of separating "fantasy" from "history" but rather invites an array of strategies by which the timelessness of the former can be brought into the timeliness of the latter. For example, Wen-chin Ouyang notes how the life story (*sīra*) of the hero ʿUmar al-Nuʿmān – a name that invokes both pre-Islamic and Islamic temporalities – "purports to have started in a time immemorial" and unfolds in a landscape that is "both historical and ahistorical," ultimately producing not a "factual" account of the past, but rather one that "imagines community as genealogy, here of the Muslims, and against the 'other,' in this case, the Christians."[88] In this way, as Thomas Herzog has shown, the *sīra* genre could make a convincing claim on its timeliness for contemporary audiences as "serious, truthfully transmitted, educational accounts of history," and indeed drew from the same literary strategies that characterized those of Arabic historiography.[89]

So much for heroes, those paragons of communal remembrance; but now, what about lovers, especially those who come across as purely invented figures, who come from foreign (non-communal) sources, or whose stories take place in the ambivalent era of "once upon a time," or, in its Arabic and Persian analogues, "it was and it wasn't" (*kān wa-mā kān; yek-i bud, yek-i nabud*)? As figures primarily defined by their private experiences of love rather than their exemplary public lives, lovers cannot necessarily avail themselves of the same strategies for their stories to be entered in the register of consequential writing. In the next section, I will explore this facet of the love-story in the context of the emergent New Persian literature of the tenth and eleventh centuries. This period marks a significant development, and perhaps – if we discard the advantage of hindsight – a surprising one. As the Iranian polymath al-Bīrūnī (d. ca. 1048) wrote at the time, all serious work should be done in Arabic; his native Persian, in contrast, "suits nothing but stories about kings and evening entertainments" (*lā taṣluḥ hādhihi al-lugha illā li-l-akhbār al-kisrawiyya wa-l-asmār al-layliyya*).[90] Such would prove to be the case, in a manner of speaking: although New Persian was firmly established on Arabic models, the fortunes of the love-story in the former language first followed and then sharply diverged from the trajectory set by the latter.

By Way of Symbol

The Abbasid era of the ninth and tenth centuries is often remembered – perhaps with a touch of romance – as a Golden Age of translation, a time when, as Dimitri Gutas writes, "almost *all* non-literary and non-historical secular Greek books that were available throughout the Eastern Byzantine Empire and the Near East were translated into Arabic."[91] Gutas's qualification is instructive here: while some narratives did make it through the "needle's eye" of the Christian Syriac community, ranging from the Alexander romance of Pseudo-Callisthenes, stories from the apocryphal New Testament, and some martyrologies, it seems from the paper trail that translators were almost exclusively concerned with the "useful" strands of Hellenistic writing – medicine, astronomy, philosophy, and ethics – while the likes of Homer and Euripides were left high and dry.[92]

On the Persian side, however, things get a little more complicated. There is no doubt that, in a manner similar to the translation of Greek into Arabic, many scientific, historical, and political works were also being translated into Arabic from Middle Persian, often by Iranian converts to Islam.[93] Yet the Persians were also closely associated with fantastic narratives; as al-Nadīm writes,

> The first people who composed fairy tales (*khurāfāt*), some of them in the speech of animals, were the ancient Persians (*al-furs al-uwal*), who put them down in writing and stored them in their libraries ... The Arabs translated this literature into Arabic, whereupon it was taken up by the masters of style and eloquence, who polished it, adorned it, and made their own compositions in its matter. (2:321 [Dodge 713])

The association of such "false" narratives with "foreign" elements is of course not unique to the Arabic case, and it perhaps serves as a good illustration of the cultural porousness (and concomitant anxiety) they represented, the love-story chief among them.[94] But when we explore further the kinds of tales al-Nadīm directly attributes to the Persians, an interesting distinction emerges. He assembles these books into two groups: the first, entitled "The evening tales of the Persians" (*asmār al-furs*), contains works like *The Bear and the Fox*, *Fairy Tale and Amusement*, *Rūzbih the Orphan*, *The Miserly King*, and other titles that evoke the fairy-tale world of the *1001 Nights*, which is of course also present under its Persian title of *Hazār dāstān* (*A Thousand Tales*). Worth a special note are a number of titles that follow the formula *Hero X & Hero Y* that is distinctive of romance, corroborating the description we find of these tales as a kind of evening tale in the Persian sources.

The second group, however, has a very interesting title indeed: *al-kutub allatī allafahā al-furs fī al-siyar wa-l-asmār al-ṣaḥīḥa li-mulūkihim*, which translates as "the books that the Persians composed for their kings on biographies and true evening tales" (or possibly "on true biographies and evening tales").[95] Either way, the title makes clear a close connection between truth and worthiness: we can infer that these stories were recognized as having value, and were told to kings and other nobility in the intimate settings of the evening. While they are distinct from the genealogies and accounts that al-Nadīm treats elsewhere, in that their authorship and/or transmission history is comparatively murky, these evening tales and biographies nonetheless purport to relate the stories of noteworthy men, with the additional claim of being "true" (*ṣaḥīḥ*, the same term used to describe authentic sayings of the Prophet) in their contents. The titles we find under this rubric corroborate this impression: we find tales of the heroes Rostam and Esfandiyār, the story of the rebellious general Bahrām Chubin, and the "book of deeds" (*kārnāmaj*) of King Anushirvān, alongside more general works on governance and kingly protocol, such as *The Book of Customs* (*Aʾīn nāma*) and *The Crown and the Good Omens Their Kings Gained from It* (*Kitāb al-tāj wa-mā tafāʾalat bihi mulūkuhum*). The most significant of the works listed in this section, from the standpoint of this study, is undoubtedly the *Book of Lords* (*Khudāy-nāma*), a Middle Persian chronicle whose contents (in translation) provided an important source for the *Shāhnāma*s written by Ferdowsi and other poets.[96] Such topics both invoke the aura of historical authenticity discussed in the "heroic" tales above – indeed, the Middle Persian *Xwadāy nāmag* was Arabized as *siyar al-mulūk* ("biographies of the kings") – and make clear their claim to immediate relevance for a ruling elite.[97]

This might explain, as far as the historical record shows, why these "biographical" evening tales, alongside other works of advice and protocol, stood as much stronger candidates for translation during the Abbasid period than their "fantastic" counterparts: we might think of them as functionally adjacent to the popular Middle Persian genre of wisdom literature (*andarz*).[98] This can be seen in the career of Ibn al-Muqaffaᶜ, who translated into Arabic a number of Middle Persian works on courtly etiquette and *savoir-faire*, including *Kalīla & Dimna*, the "great" and "small" *Books of Customs* (*al-Ādāb al-kabīr, al-Ādāb al-ṣaghīr*), the *Book of the Crown* (*Kitāb al-tāj*), the *Book of the Way* (*Āʾīn-nāma*), and the *Book of Lords* (*Khudāy-nāma*). The ninth century saw a development of great importance, when figures such as ᶜAlī b. Dāʾūd and Abān al-Lāhiqī experimented with casting these stories into a kind of verse called *muz-dawij*, formally identical to the masnavi; both authors used it to versify *Kalīla & Dimna*, and the latter may have tackled narratives such as the *Life of Ardashir*, the *Life of Anushirvān*, *Barlaam & Josaphat*, *Sendbād the Sage*, and other Sasanian works in like manner.[99] These choices show a consistent preference for narratives of biography, advice, and truth, whether in the figurative or literal sense. Yet, crucially, these versifications have not stood the test of time: they did not seem to supplant their prose sources (Ibn al-Muqaffaᶜ's *Kalīla* remains to this day a primer of literary Arabic), nor, judging from the total absence of extant copies, did they seem to have garnered much attention among the literati of their day.[100]

Thus, in the arabophone milieu of Baghdad, we do not find much interest in taking what would have been understood as fairy tales (*khurāfāt*) – love stories in particular – out of their intimate performance context and into the more public arena of "official" court poetry, dominated as ever by the qasida. There is no doubt, of course, that they were abundantly available, but they were not marketed as prestigious works of literature, and their versifications did not set any kind of major precedent. Where they do show some staying power are in various *adab* works, including biographical dictionaries of poets, theoretical and practical essays on love and refined behaviour, and thematic anthologies of prose and poetry, written over the course of the ninth and tenth centuries.[101] In an interesting coincidence, these various generic strands were gathered, not long after the composition of *Vis & Rāmin*, into a stand-alone work called the *Maṣāriᶜ al-ᶜushshāq* (*The Dying-Places of Lovers*, w. between 1063 and 1100) by the Hanbali traditionist al-Sarrāj al-Qāriᵓ. As the title suggests, this book was fully dedicated to recounting the exploits, poetry, and often tragic deaths of famous lovers of the past, and many similar works were later composed on its model.[102] It could be thus said that the mid-eleventh century saw some important steps in the institutionalization of narrative love literature as established genres in both Arabic and in Persian, yet these two institutions coalesced in markedly different ways. The Arabic narratives continued to take the form of collated short-form anecdotes (*akhbār*), usually organized under biographical or thematic rubrics – a form quite different from the Persian versified romance.

While all this activity was going on in Abbasid Baghdad, a new kind of literary Persian began to appear in the eastern Iranian lands, clad in Arabic script and infused with many Arabic elements.[103] This new idiom was actively patronized by local elites of Iranian and Turkic stock, most prominently the Samanids (819–1005) and Ghaznavids (977–1186), based in what is today Uzbekistan and Afghanistan; in a sense, it may be considered the first prestige vernacular to emerge in the territories under Muslim rule – one that would go on to become, in no small part thanks to the Seljuks, one of the major "imperial languages" of Eurasia in the second millennium.[104] Unsurprisingly, the most prominent field of literary activity in this new language was the qasida, thanks to its central role in court ceremony and encomium, but at the same time, Persian poets and writers were also experimenting with long-form narratives, both in prose and in verse. The prose examples before the year 1000 are fairly limited, and their titles cover the familiar topics of biography and advice: the Samanid official Abu Manṣur b. ᶜAbd al-Razzāq commissioned a prose *Shāhnāma* in 957, and around the same time Abu al-Fażl Balᶜami and his son ᶜAbu Ali respectively composed prose translations of Ibn al-Muqaffaᶜ's *Kalīla* and al-Ṭabarī's *History*. The works in poetry run a similar topical circuit: Rudaki (d. ca. 940) versified *Kalīla & Dimna* (and also *Sendbād the Sage*) on the basis of Balᶜami's translation, and Masʿudi Marvazi (ca. 912) and later Daqiqi (d. 976) did the same with Abu Manṣur's *Shāhnāma*. Other poets versified books of knowledge – the *Āfrin-nāma*, a collection of morals and aphorisms, the *Dānesh-nāma*, a *summa* of natural philosophy – and the lives of great and holy men: Farāmarz, son of Rostam, *Barlaam & Josaphat*, Zoroaster, Joseph.[105]

Taken together, these examples reflect the same general interest in practical knowledge that we observed in eighth- and ninth-century Baghdad, with similar topics and many of the same titles circulating in both contexts. While it is possible that tenth-century poets also versified independent love stories, there is no record of such works, suggesting that whatever might have been done in this vein did not receive much contemporary attention, and when episodes of love and adventure did (hypothetically) appear, it seems likely that it would have been through their inclusion within the overarching topical orientations of biography and wisdom. For example, the love-story of Yūsuf and Zulaykhā (Joseph and Potiphar's wife), a popular episode in the "tales of the prophets" (*qiṣaṣ al-anbiyāʾ*) genre, was versified at least twice in the tenth century, once by Abu al-Moʾayyad Balkhi and again by an otherwise unknown poet by the name of Bakhtiyāri; while we don't know whether these early versions employed the heroic-biographical framework used by Pseudo-Ferdowsi (Amāni?) in the eleventh century, or the amorous frame of the love affair that we see in Jāmi's 1483 rendition (though I strongly suspect the former), the fact that its male protagonist is a prophet makes the inclusion of this tale in the category of "true and important things that happened" unproblematic.[106] Another useful case in point is the *Shāhnāma*: while there has been a fair amount of debate among modern scholars about whether this compendium of stories is best understood as history, epic, or advice, the rubrification of its episodes under the reigns of its various kings suggests that contemporary readers understood the text as having some link to the "real" past, and in this way, the modern labels converge to an extent.[107] The preface to the prose *Shāhnāma* commissioned by Abu Manṣur describes these commitments in no uncertain terms:

> They called (the book) *Shāh-nāma*, – so that men of knowledge may look into it and find in it all about the wisdom (*farhang*) of the kings, noblemen and sages, the royal arrangements (*kār-u-sāz*), nature and behaviour, good institutions (*āyīn*), justice and judicial norms (*dād-u-dāvarī*), decisions and administration, the military organisation (*sipāh ārāstan*) (in) battles, storming of cities, punitive expeditions (*kīn khwāstan*) and night attacks,

> as well as about marriages (*khwāstarī*) and respecting honour (*āzarm*) ... everybody has some utility to derive from the book (*dārand tā az-ū fāʾida gīrand*).[108]

It is in the *Shāhnama*, however, that we can begin to observe the beginnings of a major shift taking place. The long-standing prestige of the *Book of Lords* ensured that it had already been translated into both Arabic and New Persian prose, as well as at least two tenth-century versifications by Masʿudi Marvazi and Daqiqi. After the latter poet died in 976, Abu al-Qāsem Ferdowsi, a member of the landed gentry of Tus (near modern-day Mashhad), took up the baton and completed his work in 1010, resulting in a *tour de force* of some forty thousand lines that is widely considered one of the finest works of New Persian literature, and certainly one of its foundational texts. Though it was not the first composition of its kind, Ferdowsi's *Shāhnāma* marks a significant turning point, not only in terms of era – marking the transition from the fourth/tenth to the fifth/eleventh centuries, and from the Samanid to the Ghaznavid dynasties – but in the fortunes of the love-story in Persian. The structure of the text, in which every chapter details the reign of a particular king, shows how closely the heroic biography aligned with historiography: yet within the framework of a grand chronicle, Ferdowsi was able to fold a great deal of material into his text that had long been confined to informal and oral settings, and might not otherwise have been deemed fit for independent versification: legends, folklore, and, of course, tales of love.[109]

This brings us to the first of two legitimating strategies that helped usher the New Persian romance into being, one that has an interesting analogue in western Europe. As Dennis Green has argued, the works of Virgil and Geoffrey of Monmouth (despite their many differences) both offer an account of the historical past to which its intended audience would have felt an immediate connection: the founding of Rome for one, the fortunes of the kings of Britain for the other. Within this temporal space, gaps begin to open up – intermissions, so to speak, between one event in the chronicle and the next – and it is in these narrative pauses that romance begins to appear. A famous example in the European context are the romances of Chrétien de Troyes, which take place at the time when Arthur has reached the apex of his power; one manuscript even embeds these tales in their appropriate place inside Wace's *Brut*, a verse rendition of Geoffrey's *Historia*.[110] Similarly, the love-story of Bizhan and Manizha takes place in the pause between the moment the king Kay Khosrow has defeated his adversaries and his dramatic abdication of the throne. In these "ecstatic" moments, standing outside (*ekstasis*) the historical account, the space emerges for stand-alone episodes of love, adventure, and derring-do that do nothing to advance the chronicle, but rather flesh out the heroic biographies with more (openly fanciful) material so as to enrich their value as *exempla* for the audience.[111]

This is not, however, a matter of covertly smuggling the love-story into elite discourse – for such cases exist in Arabic too, such as we see in the histories of al-Mas‘ūdī and al-Tha‘ālibī – but of proudly declaring its value even as it stands outside the flow of time, independent of its historical framework.[112] This takes us to our second legitimating strategy: the coexistence of literal and figurative truths, brought together by a knowingly complex use of language. Here, too, Ferdowsi serves as our oracle of times to come. Anticipating Gorgāni, he instructs his readers on how they are to approach and understand the manifold stories contained within his work:

تو این را دروغ و فَسانه مدان   به یکسان رَوِشنِ زمانه مدان

ازو هرچه اندرخورد با خرد   دگر بر رِه رمز معنی برد

> Don't suppose this to be lies and fairy tales! Don't consider time's passage in a single way! Everything in it accords with wisdom, or else procures meaning (*ma‘ni*) by way of symbol. (1:12/113–14)

There are two significant injunctions here. First, Ferdowsi's readers are not to consider his stories as falsehood (*dorugh*), nor as fables (*fasāna*) – that is, not to put them in the same categories as al-Nadīm's *khurāfāt* and *asmār*. Though they are already anchored within the past by means of their historical frame, they also carry within themselves, or rather within their telling, matters of substance and value. The second injunction in this passage is even more striking, for it suggests that time itself can happen, and be interpreted, in more than one way. As I speculated above, a distinguishing chronotope of the love-story, alongside other "fairy tales," is its internal sufficiency, its relative timelessness. What Ferdowsi might be suggesting, then, is that the historical past is not necessarily the only kind of time that makes things meaningful, and that other kinds of temporalities must be understood on their own terms. If the fables do not show an obvious connection with reason or wisdom, they can nevertheless produce mental content (*ma‘ni*) for its audience "by way of symbol." With this statement, Ferdowsi announces his crossing of the threshold into the figurative and multi-temporal world of poetry. Symbols demand a hermeneutic process far more involved than the straightforward *dos* and *don't*s of royal testament and books of protocol; they require the attentive and active engagement of the reader, a willingness to ponder and interpret the words on the page and glean their inner meaning. We arrive, in this way, at something akin to Geraldine Heng's understanding of romance "as a mode of narration in which history and fantasy jostle together and collide, vanishing each into the other, without apology or explanation, at precisely the junctures where both can be mined to best advantage."[113] Through their art, poets could recover narratives that, having "no history in themselves" (as Althusser puts it), had previously been downplayed or ignored in other genres of writing, and distil them "into a set of ideological propositions that ... allow the tale to circulate throughout the empire in its entirety as a parable, ubiquitously valid irrespective of time, ethnicity, or place."[114] It was this step, I believe, that helped produce the efflorescence of romance in New Persian at the dawn of the eleventh century.

A veritable epitome of this process plays out in Ferdowsi's introduction to the story of Bizhan and Manizha, one of the most prominent romances within the *Shāhnāma*'s pages. Like *Vis & Rāmin*, the tale of Bizhan likely has roots in the Parthian period, and indeed many scholars perceive a close relationship between the two legends.[115] It is also notable that the hero Bizhan appears in other chronicles that draw from the *Book of Lords*, such as those of al-Ṭabarī (d. 923) and Thaʿālibī (d. 1038), but only as a minor lord and exclusively in the contexts of politics and war (*razm*).[116] Only in Ferdowsi's account do we see these episodes paired with scenes of courtly gatherings (*bazm*) and amorous encounters (*ḥosn-o ʿeshq*), leading some scholars to speculate that the love of Bizhan and Manizha was not part of the *Khudāy-nāma* tradition, but rather "an isolated short romance" that Ferdowsi versified independently before eventually working it into his (much) larger poem.[117] The tale opens to a dramatic scene, a night so dark and ominous not even the stars dare appear; unable to sleep, the poet summons a "kind one" (*mehrbān*) who lived in his house and asks "her" (the gender is indeterminate, but there are conventional reasons to imagine a "she") to keep him company.[118]

مرا گفت شمعت چه باید همی   شب تیره خوابت نیاید همی

بپیمای می تا یکی داستان   ز دفترت برخوانم از باستان

پر از چاره و مهر و نیرنگ و جنگ   همه از درِ مردِ فرهنگ و سنگ

بدان سروبُن گفتم ای ماهروی   مرا امشب این داستان بازگوی

مرا گفت گر چون ز من بشنوی   به شعر آری از دفترِ پهلوی

همت گویم و هم پذیرم سپاس   کنون بشنو ای یارِ نیکیشناس

> She said to me, "Why do you always need your candle? Does sleep never
> come to you on a dark night? Serve the wine, and I'll read for you from the
> book a tale of yore, full of stratagem, love, tricks, and combat – all befit-
> ting a man of culture and consequence." I said to that cypress, "My moon,
> recite for me this tale tonight!" She replied, "If, while you listen, you bring
> what is in this *pahlavi* book into verse, I'll read for you and accept your
> thanks. Now listen, my discerning friend." (3:305/18–23)

This passage brings together many of the tell-tale elements of amorous
romance as we have tracked them in the Perso-Arabic milieu, and figuratively demonstrates the process by which it enters a new social register of learned and elite discourse. Ferdowsi emphasizes the "ancient"
(*bāstān*) provenance of this tale, an association reinforced by its *pahlavi*
character and/or language, while his description of its contents – love,
war, and adventure – presage the same situations as described in the
Ṭirāz al-akhbār. The setting of its performance confirms its status as an
"evening tale" (*samar*) read aloud from a book, the sort of thing people would tell each other as they waited for sleep to take them.[119] The
additional possibility that the narrator of this story is a woman, like
Scheherazade of the *1001 Nights*, would fit the gendered association
of these tales with the harem and the nursery.[120] It is this companion,
furthermore, who plants the hint that there may be something more to
this tale than what such associations would typically suggest: under the
right conditions, it becomes worthy of a cultured gentleman's consideration. For this to happen, not only verse is needed, but a good versifier:
a *niki-shenās*, which I render as "discerning," but more broadly connotes
a person who can recognize the *goodness* and *value* in a thing, perhaps
where others may not.

Why Read Romance?

Ferdowsi's *Shāhnāma* broke important ground by incorporating a huge
variety of genres, the love-story among them, within the overarching
framework of a historical chronicle, while urging its readers to seek
deeper meaning in the poetic language of their telling. This was but
the harbinger, however, of the literary movement to follow. Within a
decade after Ferdowsi's death in 1020, a cluster of texts emerged in the
court of Maḥmud of Ghazna that can be said to mark the advent of
the New Persian romance, utilizing a similar set of self-justifying strategies. ʿOnṣori, one of the pre-eminent poets of the Ghaznavid court,
versified three amorous stories from Greco-Bactrian lore; his contemporary, ʿAyyuqi, did the same with a well-known Arabian legend.[121] Then,

about twenty-five years later, under the aegis of the newly established Seljuk sultanate, Gorgāni composed *Vis & Rāmin* from his *pahlavi* book. The diversity of these sources speaks eloquently of the interconnectedness of the narrative traditions we find in this region, despite and across linguistic and political boundaries. As a group, though, they point to some notable trends. For one, these choices of source material reflect an invigorated attention to the ancient or pagan past (even the Arabian tale is set in the final days of the Jāhiliyya, the "age of ignorance" before Islam), showing a significant connection between "antiquarian interests" and romance that Agapitos has identified across the Persian, Byzantine, and Frankish cultural zones.[122] Equally important, all three poets took the novel step of shedding the historical scaffolding that had propped up the love stories found in the *Shāhnāma* and other accounts, such that they were no longer presented as episodes of a larger story but stand-alone narratives in their own right, producing a shift from the heroic-biographical framework of the chronicle to the amorous framework that sets the love between two people as its generic dominant.[123] Thus, for the first time, we see the production of long-form narratives that no longer leverage the historical past – that is, the communal Self – to justify their relevance for their elite patrons, but offer instead diverse and novel ways of romantically connecting their audience to Others across great distances of time, culture, and geography.

At this point, I would like to zoom in to look more closely at the specific language and self-presentation of these pioneering works, beginning with our best representative of the Hellenistic elements in this movement, Abu al-Qāsem ʿOnṣori (d. after 1031). As the poet laureate at the court of Maḥmud of Ghazna (r. 998–1030), ʿOnṣori is best remembered for his panegyric qasidas; however, as mentioned above, he also versified three long-form narratives that appear grounded in the heritage of the "Hellenistic Middle East," as Nikolaus Overtoom puts it.[124] Regrettably little of his *Shādbahr & ʿAyn al-Ḥayāt* (*Happy-Fortune & Spring-of-Life*) and *Kheng-bot & Sorkh-bot* (*White Idol & Red Idol*) remain;[125] but his *Vāmeq & ʿAẕrā* (*The Lover and the Virgin*), as Hägg and Utas have shown, is a close adaptation of the story of *Metiochos & Parthenopē*, a romance of some popularity that dates back to the first century CE.[126] Though we possess only fragments of the poem now, *Vāmeq & ʿAẕrā* clearly shows that the main features of the Greek novel were present as a romance prototype in the eleventh century and, in all probability, the preceding centuries as well.[127] Many of the common topoi of that genre occur in this text, including a love-at-first-sight scene in front of a goddess's temple, symposia on the nature of love, soliloquies on separation, blame, and self-remonstration, friends and guardians who act as the lovers' go-betweens, musical interludes, and so on. We can also surmise from a later prose summary of the story, embedded in the *Dārāb-nāma* – another narrative with strong resemblances to the Greek novel tradition – that a rival lover captures and enslaves ʿAẕrā (despite her fierce resistance), precipitating a series of adventures in which she performs the role of "chaste virgin" that her name declares.[128]

While ʿOnṣori's versification project, in and of itself, demonstrates an important connection between Greek and Persian love stories, it would be especially interesting to know why he embarked on this project to begin with. After all, there is no apparent reason to do so: the obviously pagan environment of the text, combined with the long-standing scepticism about the suitability of love tales for serious study, would make its acceptance as a work of any value or relevance an uphill battle from the get-go. We do know from al-Nadīm that *a* book by the name of *Vāmeq & ʿAẕrā* – though the title is too generic to be of much use – was in the possession of the court librarian, Sahl b. Hārūn (d. 860); but in that regard it is only one of the dozens of other like volumes that were written, collected, and eventually lost.[129] The anthologist Dowlatshāh Samarqandi, writing in the late fifteenth century, offers a further insight, if not for its historicity than for the point it illustrates. He relates that a book called *Vāmeq & ʿAẕrā* was brought before the Abbasid governor of Khorasan, ʿAbd Allāh b. Ṭāhir (d. 844). The bearer of the gift promised that it was a sweet and wonderful tale, but when the governor learned that it had been compiled by the "sages of King Anushirvān," he replied, "We read nothing but the Qurʾan and the prophetic traditions," and ordered the book thrown in the river, and all other books by Zoroastrians and the ancient Iranians burned.[130]

Set against this context, ʿOnṣori's handling of the foreign and non-Islamic elements of his source is quite remarkable. Situated on the island of Shāmis (Samos), populated by characters like Foluqrāṭ (Polykrates), Ifoqus (Ibykos), and Heghsefuli (Hegesipyle), the Greek environment of the tale is palpable and pervasive; even some proper names are direct translations of the Greek: *Metiochos* > *Vāmeq* ("Lover"), *Parthenopē* > *ʿAẕrāʾ* ("Virgin"), *Erōs* > *Dusti* (the god of love), and so on. Yet rather than minimize these elements as a domesticating strategy, ʿOnṣori instead draws analogous relations between them and his own milieu. For example, when the lovers first encounter each other at the temple, the narrator pauses the story to inform the reader, "Whenever you hear this '*haykal*' [lit., 'figure'], know that it is the Pahlavi name for 'idol-house'" (*chonān dān ke in haykal az pahlavi • bovad nām-e bot-khāna tā beshnavi*, 90/77); the latter term is a common trope in Persian love poetry, particularly in the setting of eastern Khorasan (modern-day Afghanistan) with its rich Buddhist heritage.[131] Later on, ʿOnṣori proposes a kind of cultural mapping between pagan and Islamic theology; when the minstrel begins singing the secret (*nohoft*) songs of Dionysos, the narrator aligns the latter with the figure of Hārūt (see Qur'an 2:102), one of two angels who taught magic to humankind: "Understand Diyānūs as the name of Hārūt – in Greek, [call] him Diyānūs" (*diyānush rā nām-e hārut dān • be yunāni u rā diyānus [khwān]*, 106/189).[132] By forging such relations between the distant (foreign) past and the modern (Islamic) present, ᶜOnṣori lays the groundwork for making the contents of this love-story productive and beneficial for his audience, despite its cultural difference. This didactic element could explain the function of some of the extended passages in the extant testimonia, such as the discourse on the invention of the lyre (106/198–235) and the symposium on love (100/151–78), in which ᶜAẕrā asserts the connection between love, youth, and similitude, motifs that echo contemporary philosophical writing on the topic (and directly pertain to the next two chapters of this book):

ازان پیکر دوستی پیر نیست   کزو مر دل پیر را تی[ـ]ر نیست]

همه رای او مرد برنا کند   ز گوهر هنر مهر [پیدا کند]

چه برنا ببرنا رسد دل بمهر   بیار آمده [تازه گردد بچهر]

کو همتا بود در خورآید همی   کی همت ب[ـ]همتا برآید همی]

زپیران نباید چنین گفت گوی   دل مرد برنا بود م[ـ]هر جوی]

همه چیز پیری پذیرد بدان   مگر دوستی کان بم[ـ]اند جوان]

The shape of Love [= Eros] is not old, for his arrows [are not intended] for the old heart. The young man follows all of Love's counsels; virtue, by its nature, [finds] love. Because the youth meets a youth with love in his heart, the one who's reached the beloved [blooms in the face]. Whoever has a match, it is always fitting that like and [like should come together].[133] Such words must not be said about the old; it is the young man's heart that [seeks love]. Know that everything grows old, save for Love, who remains [young]! (102/172–7)

Although we unfortunately lack the introduction to *Vāmeq & ᶜAẕrā*, scenes like the one above suggest that ᶜOnṣori was interested in exploring how narratives set in a context quite different from his own could still be harnessed for useful ends – an enterprise that recalls the multiple understandings of the past that Ferdowsi had invited his readers to adopt. Much as modern fantasy and science fiction do today, ᶜOnṣori seems to use the exotic setting of his story to fashion a parallel universe through which readers can gain practical wisdom, contemplate the nature of love, and possibly obtain other kinds of knowledge as well. The novelty of ᶜOnṣori's approach can be best appreciated by comparing

 Love at a Crux

it to that of his colleague al-Bīrūnī, who claims to have translated all three of ʿOnṣori's romances into Arabic prose, calling them, like the other stories about old kings and nightly tales that he associates with the Persian heritage, "silly and frivolous things to aid the digestion" (*mā yujrī majrā al-aḥmāḍ min al-hazl wa-l-sakhaf*).[134] In turning the story into New Persian verse, on the other hand, ʿOnṣori seems to have held that poetry can expand the accepted perimeters of what constitutes useful knowledge, and transform the phantasy of romance into something historically relevant.

This proposition gains much clearer explication in *Varqa & Golshāh* by ʿOnṣori's contemporary, ʿAyyuqi, who had chosen as his source the Arabian tale of ʿUrwa b. Ḥizām and his beloved ʿAfrā.[135] Like Ferdowsi before him, ʿAyyuqi includes a paean to *sakhon* ("discourse") in the opening of his work, a term that, as mentioned above, has some grounds for being equated with *logos* – "the pregnant, elevated, elaborated word" – a register of speech that lays claim to higher levels of meaning.[136] This is what he has to say on the matter:

سَخُن بهتر از نعمت و خُواسته   سَخُن بهتر از گنج آراسته
سَخُن مَر سَخُن گوی را مایَه بس   سَخُن بر تن مَرد پیرایَه بس
زِ دانا سَخُن بشنو و گوش کن   کی نامذ دگر ز آسمان جز سَخُن
سَخُن مرد را سر بگردون کشذ   سَخُن کوه را سوی هامون کشذ
سَخُن بر تو نیکو کنذ کار زشت   سَخُن ره نُمایذ بسونِ بَهِشت
بگفتم بشیرین سَخُن این سَمَر   که کس نیست گفته ازین پیشتر
چنین قصه یی را کس از خاص و عام   نگویذ بذین وزن و انشی تمام
سَخُن بی شک از نظم رنگین شوذ   عروس از مِشاطه بآیین شوذ
سَخُن را بیاراست خواهم همی   جمال از خرد خواست خواهم همی
بنظم آورم سرگذشتی عجب   ز اخبار تازی و کُثبِ عرب

Discourse is better than blessing, wealth, or treasure adorned; discourse is substance enough for the poet, and sufficient ornament for a man. Hearken to the sage's words and attend, for nothing but discourse comes from the heavens. Discourse turns mortal faces to the heavens, and pulls the peaks down to the plain. Discourse will turn your vile acts to mercies and show the path to paradise. I've told this evening tale (*samar*) in a sweet discourse that none before have uttered; none among the great and small have told the story in such faultless metre and composition ... Discourse, without doubt, gains colour when ordered; a bride becomes proper once arrayed by her attendant. So shall I ever array my discourse, seeking beauty from wisdom. I bring a tale into verse, an amazing event from the books (*kotb*) and chronicles (*akhbār*) of the Arabs! (4/9–15, 5/3–5)[137]

It is hard to miss the bold tenor of the poet's tone; despite having selected a story that al-Nadīm lists among the "fables" and "evening tales" concerning the affairs of lovers, ʿAyyuqi is confident that he can transform it into a work of high literature, drawing our attention not to the content of his material but to its language and the form in which it arranged.[138] There is an aesthetic pleasure behind ʿAyyuqi's description of *Varqa & Golshāh* as an "astonishing" (*ʿajab*) tale: the ability to produce wonder (*taʿjib, taʿajjob*) is one of the tell-tale signs that discourse has had its intended effect.[139] In other words, the fable cannot be simply distilled into didactic elements to be viable; it is poetry itself that transforms it into a work that will both serve and delight its audience. Not everyone can pull it off – indeed, ʿAyyuqi claims that none before him have ever done so – it requires one who is knowledgeable and skilled in the arts of the word.

Alongside the essential elements of rhyme and metre, ʿAyyuqi utilizes two narrative techniques to better impress his audience with the significance of his work: generic interplay and the manipulation of time. It is important to note that the tale had already been "romancified" by the time ʿAyyuqi got to it: like the more famous story of Laylā and Majnūn, the loves of ʿUrwa and ʿAfrā originally coalesced out of the assemblage of reports (*akhbār*) about the life of ʿUrwa and the ghazal poetry attributed to him, with versions appearing in the works of Ibn Qutayba (d. 889), al-Masʿūdī (d. ca. 956), and Abu al-Faraj al-Iṣbahānī (d. 972).[140] With each successive iteration, the tale became more elaborate and picked up the structure and motifs characteristic of the Greek novel, such that in Abu al-Faraj's account it begins with two perfectly matched cousins who grow up in proximity and discover their mutual love as they enter adolescence, followed by separation, false graves, tokens, disguises, go-betweens, and other common staples. ʿAyyuqi adds an epic twist to these elements by interspersing them with scenes of abduction, combat, and heroism. By combining the topoi of the feast (*bazm*) and the battlefield (*razm*) with lyric performances (*sheʿr goftan*), he thus reworks the story into a highly dramatic and generically sophisticated work of art.

As important as these aesthetic innovations, however, is the story's surprise second ending, which takes us back to the matter of time. In the Arabic versions, the lovers eventually die of broken hearts and are buried together, while all who knew them mourn the passing of two innocents, too pure for this world; this is the typical ending of *ʿudhrī* love stories. In *Varqa & Golshāh*, however, the Prophet Muḥammad suddenly appears on the scene, offering to revive the lovers on the condition that the Jews of the city convert to Islam. To this everyone readily agrees, and the story concludes with the usual marriage and happily-ever-after. This new ending tells us a lot about the generic expectations of ʿAyyuqi's audience and the literature fostered under Ghaznavid patronage; it seems that the tragic ending of the original tale did not sit well with this audience, who may have anticipated something a little more in line with the conventions we find in the Greek novels.[141] The added motifs of redemption and mass conversion also invest the story with a salvific character, which is not altogether surprising; Maḥmud of Ghazna, after all, actively cultivated a reputation as a *ghāzī* – a warrior in the service of Islam – in his propaganda.[142] Such would be the value, then, of a tale of love (and war) that takes place at a crucial moment in sacred history and transforms itself at the last second into a story of the victory of Islam over unbelievers.[143] In both ʿOnṣori's and ʿAyyuqi's work, then, we see the common goal of refashioning legendary material into a narrative medium that speaks to contemporary interests, demonstrating that truth and timeliness can be found in even the most fanciful of tales. An appreciation for different modalities of time, an openness to cultural difference as a site where learning can happen, and a careful attention to language are some of the key and underlying features of this enterprise.

Like Kingly Pearls

In this chapter, I have attempted to unpack the details of a process that Bo Utas summarizes in a single sentence: "On the whole, stories of various types (*dāstān, qiṣṣa, ḥikāyat, afsāna*) were held in low regard, unless they were adapted and integrated into literary works of high standing."[144] The roads to this outcome were many. One was to assert, in various ways, the historicity of the tale, as history was already accepted as a serious field of writing; another was to explicitly cast a manifest fiction (talking animals, for example) as a didactic tool, as Macrobius and al-Tawḥīdī recommend. So much for *historia* and *fabula*, to go back to the classical distinction. But the third and most challenging prospect was to deal with the verisimilar narratives of *argumentum*: the frivolous tales and pseudo-histories, the fables and legends of people who may have never existed and whose lives were of uncertain import for present communities. When setting Gorgāni's versification of *Vis & Rāmin* within this context, we can now understand it not as an isolated incident, but part of a broader literary movement that invited a new engagement with the fantastic and the foreign and that sought to incorporate those elements into the domain of intellectual inquiry – a new method of doing philosophy, so to speak. In this way, the rise of the New Persian love-story and its entry into the field of prestigious literature fits into the broader phenomenon of medieval romance as "a kind of thinking," as articulated by Little and McDonald: "a thinking, moreover, about things that other genres cannot or will not think about, as well as a thinking about genre itself."[145] Like the European romancers a century later, these Persian poets present their work as an unprecedented in(ter)vention in their communal past and present, an astonishing alchemy of the word that transforms the meaningless into the meaningful. "Throughout all I have said in verse, I have pierced pearls of meaning," writes the author of the *Homāy-nāma*, another romance tentatively dated to the middle of the eleventh century, "Who else has told such a story? Read it from end to end; study it."[146] Gorgāni describes the transformation he has wrought and the knowledge that can be gained from his *Vis & Rāmin* in very similar terms:

سخن را چون بود وزن و قوافی   نکوتر زانکه پیمودن گزافی

بخاصه چون درو یابی معانی   به کار آیدت روزی چون بخانی

معانی تابد از الفاظ بسیار   چو اندر زر نشانده دُرّ شهوار

نهاده جای جای اندر فسانه   فروزان چون ستاره زان میانه

مهان و زیرکان آن را بخوانند   بدان تا زان بسی معنی بدانند

همیدون مردم عام و میانه   فرو خوانند از بهر فسانه

Discourse is finer with metre and rhyme than in haphazard array [prose], especially as you discover meanings (*maʿāni*) therein that will one day benefit you when you read it ... Ideas (*maʿāni*) shine brilliantly from the words like kingly pearls set amid gold, placed here and there in the fable, blazing from within like stars.[147] The great and the wise read it to grasp many concepts (*maʿāni*), while the common and middling folk recite it for the sake of the fable. (28/41–2, 44–7)[148]

It is in Gorgāni's injunction that we be on the lookout for *maʿāni* – even in a story culled "from the evening tales (*samar-hā*) of events (*khabar-hā*) told by raconteurs" (31/1) – that I want to both situate *Vis & Rāmin* within the broad history of romance and frame my engagement with its many "fables" of love. Though it had never gone out of fashion, the mythos of a young couple who fell in love, were separated, and, after many adventures, came back together (or perished in their grief) was now being *re*-fashioned in radical ways: conveyed in a new language, deployed in new contexts, and directed towards new purposes. Remembering that, only a century earlier, Ḥamza al-Iṣfahānī had described *V&R* as a "fable" (*uḥdūtha*) – a word that, according to some medieval lexicographers, "peculiarly signifies *that [kind of story] in which there is no profit nor any truth; such as amatory stories ... a laughable and an absurd story*" – Gorgāni's project, and the New Persian romance more broadly, was made possible by a profound appreciation for the ability of well-crafted poetry, what Davis compares to the "jewelled style" of Greek and Roman rhetoric, to invest narrative with multiple layers of meaning.[149] In declaring its "doubled" nature, entertaining on the surface but inwardly instructive for a select readership, Gorgāni sets up his *V&R* to follow a similar path to success that had been taken by *Kalīla & Dimna* centuries before.

Following the work of Gorgāni, and the literary movement in which he participated, brings the mythos of the love-story to a crossroads in the history of Persian literature, pointing to a huge diversity of input sources and a wide horizon of possible outcomes. One way of exploring this crossroads would be to do a deep dive into the intersection of Greek, Arabic, and Iranian elements in the creation of the New Persian romance, with a chapter dedicated to the works of ᶜOnṣori, ᶜAyyuqi, and Gorgāni respectively. However, I have chosen to instead focus on *Vis & Rāmin* for the following reasons. First, there is too much to say about all three poets to cram into a single book; I would prefer to give the works of ᶜOnṣori and ᶜAyyuqi their due attention in separate projects. But secondly, Gorgāni's distinctive approach to making the love-story of Vis and Rāmin meaningful for his audience employs discursive techniques that are unprecedented for his time, introducing novel problems and complications to the genre that I do not see in its regional antecedents. As discussed in the prologue, *V&R* is distinguished by its vividly drawn characters, rich in their inner lives and embodying complex and conflicting models of being in the world. By focusing on this aspect of the poem, we can expand the scope of our consideration from a heterogeneity of sources to a heteroglossia of discourse; the latter, I believe, is ultimately the feature that gives *V&R* its historical importance, demonstrating at an early stage one of the key tools of "thinking romance" that made it such a successful genre, not only in Persian, but across the medieval Helleno-Abrahamic complex. For in contrast to Ibn al-Muqaffaᶜ's repeated insistence on the allegorical nature of his fables, Ferdowsi's idea of wisdom by means of symbol, ᶜOnṣori's antiquarianism, or ᶜAyyuqi's sacred history, Gorgāni's multivalent language exploits and amplifies the very "craftiness" that made Abbasid critics distrustful of the love-story – the verisimilitude that could "trick" the reader into believing its fantasy – in conveying its mental content. As the film-maker Abbas Kiarostami famously said, "We can never get close to the truth except through lying"; as we enter the unstable world of *Vis & Rāmin*, a landscape of fractured identities, mistaken personae, false starts, and ethical paradox, we might adopt this as our adage as we follow the twisting paths trod by its three protagonists: Vis, Mobad, and Rāmin.[150]

Chapter Two

Ethics | An Affair of Conscience

From the roof of her palace, with her Nurse standing by, a young woman named Vis silently watches as two noble houses engage in a game of polo. On one side of the field rides her brother, Viru, crown prince of the western land of Media; on the other, King Mobad and his younger brother Rāmin, sovereigns of Khorasan in the east. It is not the game itself that has so captured Vis's attention, however, but the champions at the head of the two teams, for her life is closely bound up with theirs. Viru is her former husband, Mobad her current one, and Rāmin her lover: a strange state of affairs brought about by an equally strange series of events. Vis had been betrothed to Mobad long before she was born, but when she came of age, she was married to Viru instead and rejected Mobad's claims when he tried to assert them. Frustrated, Mobad finally turned to war and stratagem to abduct Vis from her home in Hamadan and steal her away from Viru – only for Rāmin, in turn, to steal her away from him, inside his own residence in Marv to boot. The fallout of this affair, when the secret broke loose, was so bad that it drove the two houses to the brink of war for a second time, and though their rivalry is by no means resolved, the three lords have agreed to channel it, for the moment at least, into a less deadly contest on the polo grounds.

With the memory of these events fresh in her mind, Vis contemplates her brother and Rāmin as they ride up and down the field, "preferring them over so many men"; then suddenly, the colour drains from her face, her brow furrows, and her body begins to tremble (173/106–8 [137]). The Nurse, looking on, is nonplussed at this sudden loss of composure. "Why do you struggle so against yourself?" (174/111), she demands, proceeding to remind her charge of the many blessings she enjoys: Is not Vis queen of the East and the West, the most fortunate woman of Iran and Turan? Is not her husband the King of Kings, with two princes,

66 Love at a Crux

Viru and Rāmin, at her beck and call? How could she lament her fate, which has allotted her such a paradise on earth? Aghast at what these questions insinuate, Vis turns upon her Nurse with a furious rebuke; there is nothing joyful about her situation as far as she's concerned. Despite his wealth and power, Mobad is old and repulsive, while Viru is as beautiful as the moon – and just as remote and out of reach. And then there's Rāmin: a dashing fellow on the surface, but all lies and flattery underneath, a libertine who does not seek virtue in love (*najuyad rāsti dar mehrbāni*, 175/139). The Nurse has congratulated Vis on her multiple suitors, but it is this very abundance that lies at the root of her misery. Too many claim to be her lover, but none are up to the task; regardless of her choice, Vis will be stuck with a man who will prolong her personal hell, rather than deliver her from it.

منم با یار در صد کار بی کار   به گاه مهر با صد یار بی یار

همم یارست و هم شو هم برادر   من از هر سه همی سوزم بر آذر

With a lover, I am helpless in a hundred ways. At the time of love, I am loveless with a hundred lovers. I have a brother, lover, and husband; from all three, I ever burn in fire. (175/141–2 [138])

In this declaration, we can detect a familiar echo of the ethics of romantic love even as we know them today: quality over quantity, the superiority of a satisfying and enduring match over a train of unhappy affairs. The search for the one true love is a familiar trope in romance narratives, and when Vis wistfully remarks at the end of her plaint that if fortune had truly favoured her, her only lover would have been her first and lawful spouse Viru, we might expect her readers to nod their heads in approval. Yet this sentiment, perfectly apropos within the conventions of Vis's self-narrative, sets up a striking tension between the ethical worlds of the text and its audience. Vis's desire to reunite with her legitimate husband also implies a wish to commit incest with her brother, a twist that renders the normative solution as transgressive as the problem it seeks to resolve. The same taboo, in fact, hovers over Vis's relationship with Rāmin as well, for having shared the same wet nurse, they too count as siblings, according to Islamic law. Thus, the most and second-most preferable options for Vis become impermissible from the moral standpoint of Gorgāni's audience, while Mobad, "not merely the most appropriate partner, but the only possible one, from a legalistic Muslim point of view," is the only match that she and her literary ethos cannot countenance.[1] Thus we arrive again, now on the level of textual and social norms, at the same dilemma: a proliferation of bad options at the expense of anything good, a juncture at which every road leads to perdition.

This scene at the polo game provides a succinct illustration of the broad phenomena I am concerned with in this book: the dissolution of norms and expectations, the collapse of guiding principles, and the death of immanent resolution, experiences that alienate the story's actors from the moral and generic givens of their theoretical worlds. As I argued in the previous chapter, these processes pop into relief as soon as we read *Vis & Rāmin* from the standpoint of genre, looking for patterns of mythos and ethos across multiple traditions of amorous narrative, including the Greek novels and their Byzantine revival, ancient Iranian accounts of love and adventure, the "evening tales" (*asmār*) that boomed under the aegis of the Abbasid caliphate, and the chivalric romances of the Latinate west. What binds these literatures together is their participation in an ethos of love that, as a kind of shorthand, we can call *romantic*: a way of thinking, talking, and performing love that still persists in phrases such as "falling in love," "love at first sight," "you complete me," and so on. A fundamental premise of this ethos is that everyone has that special someone – the perfect match, the irreplaceable complement – and it acts within the mythos of romance with the force of a "simple truth," as Whitmarsh puts it, a force as persistent and inescapable as gravity.[2] It shapes the plot, conditions its characters, and, most importantly, establishes a certain range of actions as morally imperative, with especially strong ramifications for the codification of women's comportment and the regulation of female sexuality.

Embedded as they are in the logic of the text, these practices are rarely spelled out in any systematic or prescriptive fashion, but are rather most likely to emerge when the pressure to violate them increases. Vis is in good company in this regard, for a host of romance heroines have performed what it means to love romantically under severe duress. At the prospect of a second marriage, Kallirhoe declares, "To know no other husband – that is dearer to me than parents or country or child" (49/2.10); a thousand years later, we hear the echo of these words when Rhodanthe tells Dosikles, "May I be kept pure and preserved either for you / or for the sword, but not for [the rival lover] Gobryas" (66/3.521–2).[3] "A prayer towards two niches is not licit" (*ravā nabvad namāz-i dar do mehrāb*, 187/24.86), maintains Nezāmi's Shirin, while Fenice, the heroine of Chrétien's *Cligès*, promises her lover, "My heart is yours. My body is yours. No one will ever learn base behaviour from my example, for when my heart surrendered to you, it promised and gave you the body so that no one else would ever have part of it" (342/5234–9 [Staines 151]). Tormented at the prospect of her integrity broken, of her heart and body divided, Vis clearly shares in those values; but unlike her counterparts quoted above, she is denied any clear path towards implementing them. Caught in an impasse where no lover is the "right" choice, she is doomed to "fail" the moral expectations of her story; and when she finally does commit to a path, it unleashes a torrent of recrimination and vitriol that will dog her not only for the remainder of the story, but in the collective memory of New Persian literature.[4] Vis herself is not immune from the sense of having failed her obligations in some way. Though she stridently defends herself in public, she freely acknowledges her shame, frustration, and disappointment in private moments such as this one.

There is, however, a silver lining in this cloud. Though a source of incredible angst, the problem of multiple lovers also affords Vis a peculiar kind of freedom that is rarely available to the heroines of premodern romance. Caught in a situation in which there is no clear or pre-defined answer for what the right choice should be, Vis must choose whichever "bad" option makes the most sense within *her* world view, thereby acknowledging the emergent gap between her deliberative process – that is, her *theōria* or way of seeing things – and that of other characters and readers. (I should add that when I speak of "choice," I mean this in terms of performance models, rather than, say, a psychological analysis: I am tracking Vis against the established personae of romantic narratives and their typical trajectories.) By following her through this process, the text takes us into uncharted narrative territory that opens up complex questions about subjectivity, agency, and ethics, particularly as they pertain to her position as the story's female protagonist. As Vis struggles with her dilemmas, so too may we as readers, both then and now, find ourselves challenged to make sense of a romance that knowingly turns convention against itself, undercutting its internal logic and destabilizing its coherence. But in this critique and subsequent refashioning of romantic love, we stand to discover both new horizons of possibility in the romance and new understandings of what it means to be in the world as a lover.

The Ethos of Romantic Love

To begin my discussion, I will situate the ethos of romantic love within a broader historical context, not to give a full account of the notion (as that falls far beyond this book's purview) but to bring out a particular point that has significant implications for the first major act of the story: the tale of how Vis and Rāmin came to be together.[5] This point, in its most basic form, is the notion that erotic love (*erōs*, later *ʿishq* in Arabic) is the product of *the Self recognizing itself in beholding the Other*. One of the more famous early articulations of this idea occurs in a discourse embedded within Plato's *Symposium*, when the playwright Aristophanes recounts the following myth. Long ago, he says, humans were not the shape they are now, but were completely round, with four arms, four legs, and two identical faces (189e). These spherical humans were so powerful that Zeus, to limit their might, split them into two halves. "This," Aristophanes concludes, "is the source of our desire to love each other":

> Love is born into every human being; it calls back the halves of our origi-
> nal nature together; it tries to make one out of two and heal the wound
> of human nature ... When a person meets the half that is his very own,
> whatever his orientation, whether it's to young men or not, then some-
> thing wonderful happens: the two are struck from their senses by love, by
> a sense of belonging to one another, and by desire, and they don't want to
> be separated from one another, not even for a moment. (191d, 192b)[6]

This myth, although only one of many accounts of love offered in the *Symposium* (and possibly a satirical one at that), encapsulates some key elements that inform the driving ethos of many a love-story. Unlike other conceptions that depict love as a purely external force acting with impunity on its victims, Aristophanes balances that force with an equivalent inclination that stems from within, an interior drive that forever longs for an ancient wholeness lost in primordial time. Thus ingrained in the very core of the human subject, love does not require any active awareness, effort, or cultivation; the only external stimulus required is the presence or recognition of its long-lost mate, and then its seeds will burst into flower. Kleinias puts it well in the Greek novel *Leukippe & Kleitophon* when he compares this love to spiritual pregnancy: "When a young man feels the first stirrings of love within him, he needs no instruction in how to bring it to birth" (103/1.10).

Such is the nature of the force that arises when beings of similar attributes, kindred spirits, and like disposition are brought together and recognize themselves in each other. Plotinus (d. 270) refers to it as *suggeneia* ("same-kind-ness") in the *Enneads*, describing love as "the longing for beauty itself which was there before in men's souls, and their recognition of it and kinship with it and unreasoned awareness that it is something of their own" (III.5.1); the term was adopted into Arabic as *mujānasa* (from the same root word of *genos* > *jins*) or *mushākala* (sharing the same form, *shakl*).[7] Thus, for example, the philosopher al-Kindī (d. 873) writes that "whoever falls in love, falls in love only with the person to whom he was originally attached and of whose stuff (*ṭīna*) and substance (*jawhar*) he is," while the physician Muḥammad b. Aḥmad al-Tamīmī (d. 980) defines love as "the craving of every soul for its similar and kindred partner (*mushākilihā wa-mujānisihā*)."[8] In fact, though the *Symposium* was unknown by name in the Arabic tradition, the myth of Aristophanes resurfaces in multiple Arabic texts, from poetic anthologies (e.g., *Kitāb al-zahra*), philosophical treatises (e.g., *Rasāʾil Ikhwān al-Ṣafāʾ*), to this excerpt from a courtly *majlis* ("symposium") on love whose proceedings were related by al-Masʿūdī (d. ca. 956): "If certain philosophers are to believed, God, in his wisdom and great goodness, gave every soul at its creation a rounded form like a sphere. Then he divided them in half and placed each half in a different body. When one of these bodies meets that which encloses the other half of its own soul, love is of necessity born between them owing to the fact that they were once one."[9] Thus, as Joseph Norment Bell asserts, "by the late second/early ninth century at the latest, affinity or similarity (*munāsaba, mushākala, mujānasa, tashākul*, etc.), together with the corollary motif of the mingling of lovers' souls, seems to have become the most widely agreed upon element in Muslim definitions of love."[10]

Affinity, of course, can be recognized along many different lines, such as character, disposition, or physical appearance; as Plato writes in the *Symposium*, the best kind of love is found in the meeting of similar intellects (typically between two men), an intercourse that produces children of thought, rather than of flesh and bone (*Symp*. 208e–209e). It is striking, then, that in his comments on affinity in the *Kitāb mufākhirat al-jawārī wa-l-ghilmān* (*Book in Praise of Slave-girls and Boys*), the Basran essayist Abu ʿUthmān al-Jāḥiẓ (d. 868) stresses that "proper" or "correct" love – unlike the kinds of affection that one feels for, say, their possessions, children, or homeland – can only appear across the line of gender: "If complementarity (*mushākala*) is added to affection (*ḥubb*) and to passion (*hawā*) – I mean the similitude of nature, that is the affection of men for women, and women for men, which is ingrained in the males and females of all animals – then it becomes proper love (*fa-ṣāra dhālik ʿishqan ṣaḥīḥan*)."[11] This insistence on a kind of congruency and similitude that runs across (and despite?) the lines of gender is one of the most distinctive generic signals of the romance in the historical contexts of the Greek novels, Arabic love stories, and Persian romances alike. It is one of the strongest arguments for reading this mythos, to which I now turn, as a long-standing and intercultural narrative practice across the literary traditions of the ancient and medieval Middle East.[12]

The idea that love arose from the meeting of two perfectly matched souls provided the foundation for the ancient Greek novel, what R. Bracht

Branham calls "a new myth, that of *eros* in the cosmopolitan Greek world that surrounded the ancient Mediterranean"; the mythos, consequently, tends to commence at that decisive moment of encounter and recognition.[13] For instance, the *Ephesiaka* begins by introducing a young man and woman, Habrokomes and Anthia: children of the Ephesian upper crust, as beautiful as gods, and totally uninterested in matters of love. But then, on the day of the festival of Artemis, the two youths happen to lock eyes and fall into a lovesickness so powerful that they cannot recover until their parents agree to marry them (130/1.3–7). *Kallirhoe*, another early novel, follows the same pattern, introducing first the titular heroine, beautiful as Aphrodite, then Chaireas, handsome as Achilles, both of noble stock. Heading to the festival of Aphrodite, the two meet in a chance encounter: "At once they were both smitten with love ... beauty had met nobility" (22/1.1). These literary habits and conventions persist into the love stories of the Islamic world; if we fast-forward to the tale of Qamar al-Zamān and Budūr in the *1001 Nights*, we shall see the two protagonists – who, like Habrokomes and Anthia, had pooh-poohed any prospect of betrothal – fall desperately in love at first sight and desire nothing less than perpetual union.[14] The same fate will befall Vāmeq and ʿAẕrā, two noble cousins who bump into each other at the temple of Hera: "The hearts of the two youths began to seethe; it was as if all sense had left their souls. / From one glance all upheaval will arise, the sharp fire of love will enter the mind" (92/89–90). Time and again, the love is instant, all consuming, and irreversible, and the archetype of attraction-in-likeness, so well illustrated in the myth of Aristophanes, plays out as the normative relationship to exist between the protagonists of the romance mythos. As Massimo Fusillo writes,

> The narrative organization of the Greek novel seems almost to materialize this desire for symmetry, which is an internal reality to the subject: the two elements of the couple are represented as indistinguishable parts of a whole, insisting on their parallelism, which thus becomes the principle rhetorical figure upon which the entire story constructs itself.[15]

Indeed, the concept of symmetry is so fundamental that we often find it extended to the level of physical appearance. We find both elements at work in ʿAyyuqi's *Varqa & Golshāh* and Neẕāmi's *Layli & Majnun*: as in the Greek novels, the hero and heroine are born of noble families and exceedingly beautiful; in addition, they are paternal cousins, and grow up in the same household, with their mutual affection growing into erotic love as they come of age (a setup quite similar to that of the Greek novel *Daphnis & Chloe*). ʿAyyuqi reproduces this affinity on the level of language: by replacing the lovers' names with the ambiguous pronoun "one" (and taking advantage of the fact that Persian has no grammatical gender, including in its numbers and pronouns), he flattens them into interchangeable ideal figures whose only match is their mirror image:

چو دو سرو بوذند در بوستان   گُرازان بکام و دل دوستان

یکی ماه عارض یکی لاله خَدّ   یکی سیم ساعِد یکی سرو قَدّ

بیَکجای بوذند هر دُو بهم   کی این ابن عَمّ بوذ وآن بنت عَمّ

ز رَفتِ قضا وَز گذشتِ سپهر   هم از کوذکیشان بپیوست مهر

They were like two cypresses in the orchard, swaying to their beloved's delight: one with moon-like face, one with tulip cheeks, one with silver arms, one of cypress height. They lived together in one place, for this was the uncle's son, and that the uncle's daughter. By the passage of divine decree and the turning of the sphere, love took hold even in their childhood. (6/7–10)

The physical isomorphism of true lovers appears across a wide range of medieval romances, raising some interesting implications for the increasingly blurred distinction of Self and Other across the lines of kinship, ethnicity, and gender. For example, when Qamar al-Zamān (of the Khalidan Islands) and Budūr (of China) are laid side by side, they "looked as though they were twins (*taw²amān*) or full brother and sister (*akhawān munfaridān*)."[16] The protagonists of *Aucassin & Nicolette*, though hailing respectively from Christian and Saracen families, receive identical descriptions in which only the gendered pronouns are swapped: "S/He had blond, tightly curled hair, lively, laughing eyes, an oval face, a high, well-placed nose."[17] The similarity of Floire and Blancheflor, another Christian-Saracen couple, is so exact that it leads onlookers to repeatedly mistake them for siblings, and on one occasion, for two women.[18] Across these cases, we can see how the motif of the perfect match, once extended to the domain of the body, can produce suggestive moments of ontological slippage, resulting in doubles and duplicates (at one point, Budūr impersonates Qamar, then proceeds to seduce the "real" Qamar, as Qamar) and infusing even strongly exogamous relationships with the same incestuous overtones that underlie the myth of Aristophanes and, interestingly, Zoroastrian accounts of creation as well.[19] Both of these potentials will be exploited to powerful effect in *Vis & Rāmin*.

Even as the premise of "like unto like" encourages a tendency to flatten the hero and heroine into mirror images of each other, it also generates a new ethos that Michel Foucault dubbed a "new erotics," one whose paradigms of love and loving differ considerably from those that characterize classical antiquity.[20] If, in this new schema, love is understood to arise from a meeting of soulmates, to betray that bond would be an act of violence not only on the beloved, but on the self. Consequently, the obligations of love are redistributed along a reciprocal axis in which both sides of the equation are beholden to the other in similar ways. Chastity, virginity, and perseverance attain paramount importance in this system, attaining the rank of a "lofty form of existence" that demonstrates the lovers' self-control (*sōphrosynē*) and purity of spirit.[21] As David Konstan observes, the usual topoi of the Greek novel brings these virtues to the foreground; subjected to raids, captivity, enslavement, natural disasters, and a litany of other forces outside their control, the only thing the protagonists can manage through these trials is their inner constancy, their unflinching fixation upon their one and only. "What makes the heroes special," he concludes, "is not the nature of their love – as *eros* functions as a uniform force upon all – but the quality of their practice of it, especially in the face of adversity."[22]

While Konstan's (and Foucault's) observations are best understood as general, with many complications to be teased out in the fine details, their foregrounding of congruity, reciprocity, and fidelity helps us perceive an important thematic link between the Greek material and later Islamicate texts. One of the most famous dicta around love in the medieval Arabic tradition is found in the *Kitāb al-zahra*, an anthology of poetry compiled by Ibn Dāwūd al-Iṣbahānī (d. 910), which relates the following hadith: "He who loves, remains chaste, hides his love, and dies is a martyr" (*man ʿashiqa fa-ʿaffa fa-katama-hu fa-māta fa-huwa shahīd*); to this, Ibn Dāwūd adds a corollary: "And if the two lovers are not chaste and commit sin, it is incumbent on both of them that they abandon their love for each other."[23] Although scholars doubted this saying's authenticity, it was immensely popular in the medieval Islamic world as a pithy, if partial, vindication of erotic love. According to this premise, falling in love is involuntary, and therefore not un-Islamic, but the way lovers respond to their condition will reveal the base or refined quality of their spirits; love thus acts as a sort of litmus test, an opportunity for those afflicted by it to show their inner strength and nobility – essentially a revalidation of *sōphrosynē* in an Islamic context. Ibn Dāwūd found no shortage of examples from the Arabic poetic tradition to illustrate this position, and indeed the entirety of the first half of the *Zahra* is dedicated to naturalizing it through this corpus and exploring its manifold implications in the context of his own society.[24] One of the central figures in his canon is the poet Jamīl, who recites the following lines about his beloved Buthayna:

تعلَّق روحي روحَها قبلَ خَلْقِنا   وَمِن بعدِ ما كنَّا نِطافاً وفي المهدِ
فَزادَ كما زِدْنا فأصبَحَ نامياً   وليسَ إذا مُتنا بِمُنتَقِضِ العهدِ
ولكنَّهُ باقٍ على كل حالةٍ   وزائرُنا في ظُلمةِ القبرِ واللحدِ

My soul joined with hers before we were created,
    or a drop of sperm, or babes in the cradle.
As we grew, so did our love,
    and even in death, the covenant shall not be broken.
It remains eternal, visiting us in the darkness
    of our graves and tombs.[25]

These verses not only affirm the pre-eternal nature of Jamīl and Buthayna's love, something that existed long before they were born, but also emphasize – crucially – the *covenant* incumbent on them by dint of this connection. This covenant, as we will see, is often something of a two-edged sword: here, it offers the lovers access to a kind of immortality, but at the cost of their agency. By claiming Buthayna as his soulmate, Jamīl has prescribed everlasting fidelity from her *even before her birth*, effectively robbing her of any say in the matter. Deep beneath the mutual sighs and embraces is a restrictive pressure undergirded by the threat of violence, no better illustrated than in the following anecdote related by Abu al-Faraj al-Iṣbahānī:

ثم قال لها: يا بُثَينة، أرأيتِ وُدّي إيّاكِ وشَغَفي بكِ ألا تَجْزِينِيه؟ قالت: بماذا؟ قال: بما يكون بين المتحابّين. فقالت له: يا جميل، أهذا تَبْغي! والله لقد كنتَ عندي بعيداً منه، ولئن عاوَدْتَ تعريضاً بريبةٍ لا رأيتَ وجهي أبّداً. فضحك وقال: والله ما قلتُ لكِ هذا إلّا لأَعلمَ ما عندَك فيه، ولو علمتُ أنّك تُجيبينَني إليه لعلمتُ أنّك تُجيبين غيري، ولو رأيتُ منك مساعدةً عليه لضربتُك بسيفي هذا ما استَمْسَكَ في يدي.

Jamīl said, "Buthayna, having observed my fondness and passion for you, will you not reward it?" She replied, "With what?" He said, "With that which happens between two lovers." She said, "Jamīl, is this what you want (*a-hādhā tabghī*)?![26] By God, your feelings for me were far from it; for if you had requested even the hint of something suspicious you would never have seen my face." Jamīl then laughed and said, "By God, I only said that to know how you would react. If you had accepted my offer, I would know that you would accept it from someone else too, and if I had seen you in favour of the idea, I would have struck you down with this sword in my hand."[27]

This tale exemplifies the cautionary notes that Helen Morales and Simon Goldhill sound against Konstan's model of romantic love:

symmetry does not guarantee equality.[28] Although their "covenant" places similar obligations towards both lovers, the threat of violence facing Buthayna should she fail to meet those expectations – a threat she cannot hope to direct back at Jamīl – is impossible to miss. Because of this imbalance, it is often the female protagonist who takes centre stage in the Greek novels, at least insofar as these narratives are more interested in seeing how many assaults she can stave off (while fantasizing them in the process) then they are in the hero's parallel travails. After escaping numerous attempts at rape and seduction, Leukippe is forced to undergo a public ordeal to prove her virginity before she can be wedded to Kleitophon (280/8.13–14); Anthia remains chaste despite being married twice and working in a brothel, even killing one of her assailants (143/2.9, 2.13, 157/4.5, 163/5.7); so too will the Persian heroines Golshāh and Layli vigorously defend themselves from unwanted male attention.[29] The preservation of male virginity ("if one can speak of such a thing," quips Kleitophon, 271/8.5.7), on the other hand, tends to be presented along different lines: as an ideal (but non-essential) virtue in the Greek examples, or as a gesture of fidelity to another man in the Persian.[30]

The idea of love springing from affinity and complementarity is extremely widespread, found in many fields of discourse and in multiple Near Eastern languages, but it plays a particularly significant role in the love-story mythos as manifested in the Greek novels, Arabic *ᶜudhrī* tales, and Persian romances, providing it with a bedrock principle that informs (but cannot fully control) the genre's ethos, as Vis herself puts it: "It is because this heart of mine has a foundation of stone (*bonyād-e sang*) that loyalty abides in it" (367/13 [335]). The love-story, in other words, can be said to be built around the topos of love at first sight and the ethical imperative of fidelity at all costs. At the same time, the extension of similarity from the domain of the spirit to the realm of the body introduces a number of possible forms of slippage that make the *recognition* of love at first sight, and the *implementation* of its ethical imperatives, a much more difficult prospect than one might initially think. This backdrop is vital for understanding Vis and the choices she makes over the first third of her story: like her Greek and Arabic counterparts, Vis is committed to a theory of love that is simultaneously idealistic, restrictive, and unstable, in which the dual norms of amorous reciprocity and gender inequality – what we might describe as the intrinsic tension of a modality of seeing that both requires and erases the distinction of Self and Other – attempt to reinforce each other, while their inherent paradoxes and explosive consequences lie waiting in the shadows.

Conflicting Signals and False Starts

With characteristic insight, Dick Davis remarks that the beginning of
Vis & Rāmin is riddled with "conflicting signals" and "false starts" that
immediately preclude an unambiguous reading of the text.[31] This is
especially true when we read the poem against the backdrop of the first
encounter discussed in the previous section, which reveals an elaborate, almost methodical manipulation of the tropes that characterize
this moment. Such manoeuvres do not merely spice up the story with
additional intrigue, or delight the audience with unexpected twists;
they unsettle the convention of recognition itself, raising the disturbing
possibility that Mr. and Mrs. Right could misidentify each other, or even
worse, that such a couple may not exist at all. Were such a scenario to
occur, it would open the floodgates to a slew of unexpected questions
usually foreclosed by the ethos of romantic attachment.

These possibilities are introduced right at the get-go, in the story's
opening scene: a "joyous springtime festival" (*khorram jashn bud andar
bahārān*, 34/22 [1]), the celebration of Nowruz at Mobad's court. Both
the spring and the festival are suggestive elements: many of the Greek
novels, as well as *Vāmeq & ʿAzrā*, begin with a gathering of some kind,
such as a wedding or a deity's holy day. These occasions provide a
platform to introduce the story's protagonists, often along with their
parents, and provide the appropriate context for the love encounter
to take place, setting the story into motion.[32] The season, too, marks
an appropriate time for love, "the air being then temperate, springs
of water most abundant and the world indued with a pleasing countenance," as the author of the *Qābus-nāma* writes.[33] The heady sights,
sounds, tastes, and smells of this banquet make every promise of this
expectation: the amorous, nearly hungry glances exchanged between
the lords and ladies, likened to lions and gazelles; the wine-full gob-
lets, loosening tongues and opening hearts; the musky fragrance of
trees in bloom; the songs of birds and minstrels comingling in the air
(34/33–9). The moment seems clearly primed for an erotic encounter,
perhaps one that will identify the principal lovers of the story, like *Kallirhoe* or the *Ephesiaka*, or a marriage that will lead to the birth of the
protagonist(s), like *Vāmeq & ʿAzrā*. What happens next, however, does
both and neither of these things.

Here are the events in brief: as he presides over the banquet, Mobad's
eyes fall upon Shahru, the beautiful queen of Media; summoning her in
private, he invites her to be his consort, as "either wife or lover" (*yā joft yā
dust*, 39/6 [5]); Shahru, though expressing some interest in the proposition, turns it down on the grounds that she is too old; Mobad then requests

her daughter, if she were to bear one; Shahru agrees, and the two sign a contract to that effect. I discuss the politics and economics of this transaction in detail in chapter 3, so for now I will only focus on the implications it has for the story's narrative expectations. Rather than establishing the characters' functional roles through generic signals, this meeting splits and scrambles them into multiple possibilities. We see this in the ambiguity of the scene, thrumming with erotic energy and filled with flirtatious dialogue, yet unfulfilled with any of the conclusive signs of Love's arrows having hit their mark. The way in which Mobad first beholds Shahru suggests one modality, but his bargaining with her suggests another. Shahru's response implies that the desire for union is by no means one-sided, but that age might preclude them from following the script of young lovers. The indeterminate nature of their love is reinforced by the odd rationale of Mobad's counter-offer, in which he claims that Shahru's unborn daughter will be a suitable replacement for Shahru herself, "since the fruit will doubtless resemble the seed" (41/39). This is a strange (yet logical) twist on the convention of similitude: as we saw, the inner compatibility of two souls is usually reflected by their outward appearance, so it only stands to reason that the attraction Mobad feels towards Shahru will transfer perfectly onto her mirror image. The contract that emerges from this meeting, then, doubles Shahru into two figures: the powerful and desirable queen who says no, and the younger version of herself who, Mobad hopes, will say yes; through the latter, Mobad also attains the former and original source of his desire. He reiterates this rationale years later, when he tells Shahru, "Because I was a suitable *dāmād* for you, God gave you this daughter as my due" (*cho man budam torā shāyesta dāmād • be bakht-e man khodā in dokhtar-at dād*, 53/47 [21]). This line has an interesting ambiguity bound up in the word *dāmād*, which can mean either "bridegroom" or "son-in-law": by using this term, Mobad splits the objects of his desire into unstable and fungible roles, with Shahru as his prospective lover and/or mother-in-law, and her daughter/double Vis as his prospective lover and/ or daughter-in-law. As a result, and not incidentally, Mobad splits himself into two personae as well: that of Shahru's husband and Vis's father, and of Vis's husband and Shahru's son, all coexisting as possible modalities of engagement.

This is a revealing moment. By invoking the expected topoi of the love-story and then diverting them towards new and unexpected ends, the opening scene of *Vis & Rāmin* thus fulfils and denies its usual function. We have a love affair, but one that was negotiated and not instantly born; we have a wedding, but between an old man and an unborn girl. Although our story has introduced love as its primary theme, setting itself up as an amorous tale or what we might recognize as a kind of romance, it has split its initial characters into multiple personae, a move that destabilizes the default premise of love as a meeting of kindred spirits and raises some troubling ontological questions: What exactly is the thing loved? Where does it reside, how is it knowable, and can it be mis-/recognized? The theme of doubling, paired with the notion that love can be transferred from one identical body to another, is especially insidious, and a crucial means by which the "many tales of love" (112/70) of *V&R* disrupt and hijack one another. It is our first sign that both the common conventions of the love-story and its associated "rules" of romantic love are running off track in this story, a disruption, as our narrator predicts, that will come with severe consequences for Mobad and Shahru, and, by extension, for Vis and Rāmin: "Look at what hardship they fell into, when they gave an unborn child into marriage!" (*negar tā dar che sakhti uftādand • ke nā-zāda ᶜarusi rā bedādand*, 41/53 [8]).

This, however, is only the first of our many false starts. After the meeting of Mobad and Shahru, the romance resets, in a way, to present us with another opening scene, as familiar within the scope of its conventions as the previous one. Though Shahru, already advanced in years, might have signed the contract confident in the likelihood that she would never become pregnant, the improbable, as it is wont, comes to pass: "the withered tree once again turned green" (42/10), and Vis comes into the world.[34] She is sent to the province of Khuzan to be raised by the Nurse, and there we meet another child:

همیدون دایگان بر جانش لرزان   به دایه بود رامین هم به خوزان

چو در یک باغ آذرگون و نسرین   به هم بودند آنجا ویس و رامین

به هم بودند روز و شب به بازی   به هم رُستند آنجا دو نیازی

نه تخم هر دو در بوم اوفتاده   هنوز ایشان ز مادرشان نزاده

نبشته یک به یک کردار ایشان   قضا پَردَخته بود از کار ایشان

Rāmin was also with the Nurse in Khuzan, and she fretted over him the same way. Vis and Rāmin were there together, like poppy and wild rose in one garden. The two darlings grew up there together; day and night, they were together in play ... They had not yet been born of their mothers, nor even conceived, [but] fortune had settled their affairs and written out their deeds, one by one. (44/49–51, 54–5 [12])

This passage is loaded with suggestive cues. The repetition of the phrase "together" (*be ham*) and the simile of the garden recall the introductory scene of *Varqa & Golshāh*, whose protagonists "lived together in one place," "like two cypresses in the garden"; meanwhile, the allusion to their (love) affairs being written out even before they are born recalls the famous line of Jamīl: "My soul joined with hers before we were created." These cues prime the audience to expect and accept the love between the boy and the girl as the inevitable product of their natural affinity, placing their story within a similar horizon of expectations as those of the Greek novel and Arabic ʿudhrī tales. Yet there is some massaging of the details. For example, both ʿAyyuqi and Gorgāni include in this scene a nod towards the unchangeable will of destiny; but where the former is confident that the garden scene is indicative of divine approval, the latter is far more tentative about making this connection, speaking of his characters as though they are about to do things God would *not* approve of, even if He fated them to happen: "One mustn't blame them, for the road of God's decree (*ḥokm-e yazdān*) cannot be blocked" (45/58), he concludes. Equally striking is what goes unsaid. Though all signs point towards the children falling in love, Gorgāni does not follow ʿAyyuqi in explicitly confirming that it happened; on the contrary, Rāmin mysteriously disappears from the scene altogether (the Paris manuscript includes a line telling us that Mobad recalled him to his court at the age of ten), leaving us wondering what sort of affection ever did or could have blossomed between them.[35] We are thus left with another generic setup with no follow-through, blurring the identity of the "lover" still further in the process; Mobad and Rāmin have both been introduced as possible candidates for the role, but the authorial voice refrains from passing any final judgment.

At this point, now, the text has twice established the conditions for romance to begin, but without bearing fruit: two beginnings of a love-story without any love. Incredibly, this process is not yet complete. After what must have been a blissful childhood spent away from the court, Vis too comes of age, growing into a young woman of astonishing beauty, and her mother recalls her to Hamadan. Here, the story "begins" for a third time, giving its readers another chance to (re-)calibrate their expectations and determine who will ultimately be Vis's paramour. The latest candidate, I imagine, might have come as a bit of a surprise. After hosting an extravagant welcoming party for her daughter, Shahru immediately gets down to business, saying to Vis,

ترا خسرو پدر بانوت مادر   ندانم درخورت شویی به کشور

چو در گیتی ترا همسر ندانم   به ناهمسرت دادن چون توانم

درایران نیست جفتی باتوهمسر   مگر ویرو که هستت خود برادر

Your father's a king, your mother a noble lady; I don't know any husband in the realm who is worthy of you. Because I don't know anyone equal to you in the world, how could I give you to one not your equal? There is

no one in Iran worthy of marriage with you, save Viru, who is your own
brother. (49/3–5 [17])

Shahru's assessment invokes the long-standing principle of worthiness
and equality characteristic of romantic love: only one who can rival Vis
in beauty and nobility can claim to be her lover. We have already seen
this ideal produce couples of twin-like resemblance and/or make them
members of the same family; now, taking advantage of its Zoroastrian
setting, in which endogamy is a frequent feature, *V&R* pushes the latter tendency to its logical conclusion.[36] The text, in other words, utilizes
the norms of two "worlds" – the cultural milieu of the poem's dieg-
esis, and the generic logic of like unto like, especially when we recall
Aristophanes' myth of lovers having once shared the same body as
well as soul – to produce what must be the most suitable partner for
Vis's love-story: her brother. As we saw at the beginning of this chapter, Vis seems to accept this outcome without doubt or hesitation; on
hearing her mother's proposal, "love stirred within her heart, and she
silently indicated her consent" (*bejonbid-ash be del bar mehrbāni • nomud
az khāmoshi hamdāstāni*, 49/10 [18]). This wordless reaction, showing
that Vis has elected for the "way of silence" (*khāmoshi rāh*), meets with
Shahru's full approval (49/14–16) – and quite likely that of Gorgāni's
readers, too, given the widespread hadith that on a proposition of marriage, a woman's silence is her affirmation (*idhnuhā ṣumātuhā*).[37] It also
concords with a well-established trope in the love-story mythos: one
need only review Kallirhoe's embarrassed silence when she first sees
Chaireas (22/1.1), ʿAẕrā's attempt to conceal her feelings (94/103–4), or
Charikleia's bold (if ironic) statement that "silence becomes a woman"
(371/1.22) to find the literary precedents on which Vis models her
behaviour.[38] It is tempting, then, to guess that her shy but joyful reaction
evokes the innate, intuitive, and already-present love of kindred spirits
that provides the *sine qua non* of romantic love, and it is significant that
she agrees to this match without having yet seen Viru in the flesh, at
least as far as the text allows us to know. This will prove a crucial point
later in the story, when she looks on (adult) Rāmin for the first time.

One might well postulate, then, a reading of the tale in which, by
every indication, the best-suited match for Vis is her brother Viru, and
Shahru acts quickly to bring this narrative to its rightful conclusion:
after determining an auspicious date with her astrologers, she conducts
the wedding herself, saying, "There's no need for a document with the
priest's seal" (*be nāma mohr-e mobad ham nabāyad*, 50/30). This language
is a little suspicious. *Mobad*, of course, is also the name of the King of
Kings, and *mohr* ("seal") is iconographically identical to *mehr* ("love,

contract"). It would not be far-fetched to propose a double entendre here – "there's no need for a document of Mobad's love/contract" – suggesting that Shahru has not at all forgotten about the old contract and is acting swiftly to shore up her realm against the Great King's authority. Politics aside, this narrative trajectory seems to point in a direction quite different from the one indicated by its title, which is, after all, *Vis & Rāmin*, not *Vis & Viru*. Eventually, the power of the titling convention will prevail, pushing Viru to the sidelines as Rāmin steps in to replace him; but the fact remains that up to this point, *Vis & Rāmin* has done quite a lot to confuse the usual order of events. The contract betrothing Vis to Mobad, Rāmin's abrupt appearance and then disappearance during Vis's childhood, and now the marriage of Vis and Viru have fundamentally transformed the internal dynamics of the love-story that will ensue, destabilizing the mutual love of its protagonists from its usual protected status as an *a priori* given. The question of who will possess Vis's love is no longer a foregone conclusion; it has, on the contrary, transformed into a site of negotiation, persuasion, and violence – all practices that undermine the very integrity of that relationship.

Vis Unveiled

We can begin to dissect the vexed relationship between "natural" and negotiated love with the following scene in the Greek novel *Kallirhoe*. The protagonists have met, have instantly fallen in love, and are now married; fuming at this news, one of Kallirhoe's former suitors complains to his fellows,

> If one of us had married her, I should not have been angry; as in athletic competitions, only one contestant can win. But we have been passed over for a man *who made no effort to win the bride*, and I am not putting up with that insult. We have lain waking at the door of her house, we have curried favour with her nurses and maids, we have sent presents to the servants who brought her up ... And with kings competing for the prize, this nancy-boy, this worthless pauper carries it off *without lifting a finger*. (24/1.2, my emphasis)

Inadvertently, the suitor has hit the nail on the head: Chaireas, unlike the other suitors, did not need – and in fact *needed not to need* – to do any "work" to win Kallirhoe's affection. This is the fundamental premise of romantic love: it is *already there*, waiting to be awakened. Any form of persuasion, be it kind words, material gifts, or physical force, is not only unnecessary in this scheme, but self-defeating, for it would expose the bond as counterfeit, something that can be won, lost, and haggled over, and not the pre-eternal affinity of true lovers. Gottfried von Strassburg puts it well in his *Tristan*: "When anyone enters at Love's door who has not been admitted from within, it cannot be accounted Love, since it is either Deceit or Force."[39] The lover who seduces his beloved, in other words, is not a lover at all.

Despite this premise, or more likely because of it, the prospect of seduction and/or betrayal is never far from the consciousness of romance. Even those love stories that treat the effortless love of their protagonists as a self-evident fact often expend a great deal of effort attempting to disprove it, as if doubting it could really be so. The women, in particular, are thrown into situations of utmost duress and watched like hawks for the slightest lapse of behaviour (e.g., the anecdote of Jamīl and Buthayna cited earlier). It is precisely this landscape that colours their actions as heroic, even miraculous: the fact that they manage to come out on top, defying the odds stacked against them, makes them the exception that proves the rule. Writing on the context of medieval French literature, Howard Bloch calls this the "woman-as-riot" motif, in which "no position of innocence is possible"; the same motif is perfectly captured in the Arabo-Persian term *fitna*, which signifies both temptation (by, for, and of women) and civil strife.[40] As Fedwa Malti-Douglas, Afsaneh Najmabadi, Zahra Ayubi, and other scholars have documented, this trope appears across a wide range of texts and narratives, from the tale of Yūsuf and Zulaykhā (Joseph and Potiphar's Wife) to the queen's orgy in the opening of the *1001 Nights*, to the "wiles of women" premise of the *Sendbād-nāma*'s frame tale.[41] Vis herself articulates it numerous times, such as in her paraphrase of the well-known hadith describing women as "deficient in faith, endowment, and reason":[42]

زنان در آفرینش نا تمامند   ازیرا خویش کام و زشت نامند

دو گیهان گم کنند از بهر یک کام   چو کام آمد نجویند از خرد نام

Women are incomplete in their creation, for they are lustful and of ill repute. They'll lose two worlds for the sake of one desire; when desire comes upon them, they never seek honour in wisdom. (136/110–11 [96])

In this regard, *Vis & Rāmin* is no different from its generic neighbours in the Greek novel. Seduction attempts, both failed and successful – Mobad's on Shahru, and subsequently on Vis; Rāmin's on the Nurse; and finally the Nurse's on Vis, on Rāmin's behalf – proliferate in the opening act of the story, testing the moral fibre of its female characters. However, the outcome of these various probes turns the typical function of seduction, such as we see in a story like *Kallirhoe*, on its head: rather than serving as a litmus test that distinguishes true love from

false – the heroine falls for her beloved without any effort on his part
and stops at nothing to thwart the efforts of others to obtain her love –
it becomes the very process that brings the lovers together in *V&R*. By
flipping the script in this way, Gorgāni's narrative casts the authenticity
of its love affair into permanent doubt and brings a number of generic
unthinkables into play – the idea that Vis's love could transfer from one
person to another, or the shocking revelation at the polo game that she
would rather be with someone *other* than the titular hero – along with a
host of new ethical problems accompanying them.

The engine that makes this transformation happen is, again, a kind
of doubling. As noted above, the text went out of its way to comment
on the decorum and propriety that Vis displayed in her meeting with
Shahru; but in a scene prior to this, we are fed a very different image of
her. This comes in the form of a letter, written by the Nurse to Shahru,
in which we see a direct and causal relation forged between the girl's
sexual maturation and the "riot" of anxiety that follows:

که همبالای سرو بوستان شد   چو قدّ ویس بت پیکر چنان شد

چو یازنده کمند گیسوانش   شد آگنده بلورین بازوانش

به ناز دل نیازی را بپرورد   سر زلفش به گل بر سایه گسترد

ز دایه نامه‌ای شد نزد مامش   پراگنده شده در شهر نامش

که چون تو نیست بدمهری به گیهان   به نامه سرزنش کرده فراوان

سزای دخترت چیزی ندادی   به من دادی ورا آنگه که زادی

به پرواز اندر آمد بچهٔ باز   کنون بر رُست پیش من به صد ناز

به کام خود یک انباز گیرد   همی ترسم که گر پرواز گیرد

When statuesque Vis grew to such a height as to rival the garden's cypress,
her crystalline arms grew plump, and her locks became like a snatching
lasso; when the tips of her tresses cast shadows on the rose, when she
nurtured desire with her charms, her name spread throughout the land,
and the Nurse sent a letter to Vis's mother. She scolded her mightily in the
letter: "There are none in the world as unkind as you! ... You gave your
daughter to me when she was born, but provided nothing suitable for her.
Now that she's grown before me with a hundred graces, this fledgling fal-
con will soon fly off, and I fear that when she does, she'll find some mate
to her own liking." (46/1–5, 8–10 [13])

To bolster her case, the Nurse concludes the letter with a litany of damning
testimonials that portray her ward as proud, vain, and extravagant: never
satisfied with her clothing and accoutrements, demanding to accompanied by no less than eighty ladies in waiting wherever she goes, insisting
on the finest silk brocades for every occasion, and taking her meals in

golden dishes. These details, though often used as a sign of pre-Islamic excess, also promote the image of Vis as a moral degenerate in the eyes of her audience, as the use of gold and silver vessels (usually paired with the wearing of brocade) is forbidden in Islamic law.[43] The sum impact of this depiction is to immediately cast doubt on Vis's chastity and virtue; indeed, the Nurse takes it as given that if Vis were left to her own devices, her insatiable appetites would soon drive her to "fly off" and take whatever lover she desired. The only solution is for Shahru to take charge and get her married before she does something that would irreversibly disgrace the royal family.

Like many other opening scenes in the poem, the Nurse's letter seems calibrated to destabilize the typical figures of the love-story, in this case splitting Vis into two competing personae, the pure maiden on the one hand, the woman-as-riot on the other. This move is especially damaging to Vis's subsequent attempts to control her image, as the virtuous persona she cultivates can hardly survive even the suggestion of possible degeneracy: as Bloch writes of the precarious nature of virginity, "the mere thought of losing it is sufficient to its loss."[44] The Nurse continues to push her disparaging comments about Vis well into the story, telling Rāmin, for example, "You don't know how self-obsessed she is, how far she is from being tamed of her innate disposition" (*nadāni k-u cheguna khwish-kām ast* • *ze khu-ye khwad cheguna dir-rām ast*, 124/187 [86]), and it does not take long for Rāmin and Mobad to start repeating and perpetuating this narrative themselves. If Vis wishes to walk the path of the romance heroine, she has a steep climb ahead of her; the prerequisite aura of impeccable modesty has been compromised even before she enters the story, casting her under a cloud of perennial suspicion in which even the most righteous words or gestures can be used as further evidence of her fallen or fallible state.

The ramifications of this double bind begin to present themselves immediately after Vis's marriage to Viru. The wedding party is still in full swing when Zard, Mobad's half-brother and chief minister, appears with a letter from the king, requesting that Vis be brought to him in Marv immediately. While a wedding is the ideal moment, narratively speaking, to throw a wrench into the works, there is further significance in the timing of Zard's arrival. Mobad could not have dispatched the letter from far-off Khorasan knowing that Shahru would soon break her promise and marry Vis to Viru; indeed, the language of his missive conveys a confidence that she has been faithfully keeping his bride-to-be reserved for him until the proper time. But that time has apparently arrived, and to understand why, we may think back to a crucial development: "her name [had] spread throughout the land."[45] Word of Vis's beauty – and sexual availability – has gotten out, forcing Mobad's hand: he must seize his prize before another man snatches it from him.

کنون کان ماه را یزدان به من داد   نخواهم کاو بود در ماه آباد

که آنجا پیر و برنا شادخوارند   همه کنغالگی را جان سپارند

جوانان بیشتر زن باره باشند   در آن زن بارگی پر چاره باشند

همیشه زن فریبی پیشه دارند   ز رعنایی همین اندیشه دارند

مباد آن زن که بیند روی ایشان   که گیرد ناستوده خوی ایشان

زنان نازک دلند و سست رایند   بهر خو چون برآری‌شان برآیند

Now that God has given me the moon (*māh*), I do not wish her to be in Hamadan (*māh-ābād*), where the young and old alike are philanderers, wholly given to womanizing. The youth are the worst: full of tricks in their debauchery, constantly seducing women, always thinking of frivolity. May no woman see their faces, lest she adopt their contemptible natures! Women are fragile hearted and weak minded; they fall into any nature you bring to them. (54/51–6 [21])

Mobad then segues into a familiar refrain, asserting that no woman, however noble or austere she might be, can resist the honeyed words of rakes and dandies (which he mimics in an amusing parody at 54/60–4: "I am miserable and anxious on account of your love, I relinquish life in my pain and suffering for you," etc.). In this respect, Mobad echoes the sentiment expressed (or suggested by) other members of the older generation, namely that Vis cannot be trusted with the preservation of her virtue: "Although Vis is pure and unsullied," he concludes, "my heart is filled with anxiety on this account" (*agar che visa biāhu-vo pāk ast • marā z-in ruy del andishnāk ast*, 54/66). There is no small irony in these repeated expressions of the woman-as-riot motif, given the fact that, as the clamour around and about her intensifies, Vis herself has yet to utter a single word; it is her mere presence as an object of desire, and the concomitant *possibility* of her being seduced, that has generated the riot we see before us, a riot brought about by the presumption that Vis is incapable of rising to the standard set by the impossibly virtuous heroines of the romance mythos.[46] The solution to the dangers posed by and to Vis, as Mobad perceives them, is for the "moon" (*māh*) to be spirited away from its abode (*māh-ābād*) without delay, a grim pun foreshadowing the themes of exile and homelessness that will be such a dominant aspect of her story.

Although Vis had abstained from speaking up to this point, Mobad's letter, directly impugning her virtue and accusing her of a crime she might commit in the future, seems to strike a nerve: in a poignant

indication of events to come, her first vocalization in the story does
not take the form of intelligible speech, but emerges as a wordless cry
(*bāng*) of outrage (55/83). She then chastises her mother for making the
contract, sarcastically asks Zard if polyandry is a custom in Marv, and
sends a message of her own back to Mobad:

مرا چون دیده شایستست مادر   چو جان پاک بایسته برادر

بسازم با برادر چون می و شیر   نخواهم در غریبی موبد پیر

جوانی را به پیری چون کنم باز   ملا گویم ندارم در دل این راز

> My mother is as becoming to me as my eyes, my noble brother befits me
> as much as my pure soul. I mix with my brother like milk with wine; I
> don't want old Mobad in some foreign land! How could I exchange a
> young man for an old? I speak frankly; I keep no secrets in my heart.
> (58/123–5 [25])

This is the first time that Vis verbally expresses her feelings, and as we
can see, she makes no bones about her commitment to her brother, whatever the cost. That cost will indeed be high, if she insists on speaking so
"frankly" to the king; such public excoriations, standing in sharp contrast with Shahru's diplomatic language, are not only politically risky
but also undercut the narrative that Vis seeks to establish about her virtue. Even as she passionately declares her loyalty to Viru, she confirms
the Nurse's description of her as a proud and refractory woman who
disrespects the authority of her elders and superiors.

We can further appreciate the paradoxical effect of Vis's ethics in
another exchange that takes place a little later in the story. Having been
spurned once, and now stymied in his attempts to capture Vis by force,
Mobad sends another emissary to speak with her directly, promising
her the keys to his treasury if she will consent to the marriage. This new
bargain, with the unsubtle suggestion that her loyalty can be bought,
so enrages Vis that she responds with a wholly unconventional gesture,
tearing open her garments from neck to navel, "fearlessly" (*bi-bāk*, also
translatable as "shamelessly," 76/2) beating her breast, and firing back,
"See you don't ever think you'll bring me down from this fortress alive!"
(*negar tā to napendāri ke hargez • marā zenda be zir āri az in dez*, 76/12).
This striking combination of visual and verbal defiance instigates yet
another instance of doubling, one that hinges on the double entendre of
the imperative verb to look or behold (*negar*). While Vis's explicit message is that Mobad should "see" that he not misapprehend the plain
reality standing before him that she will never be his, her message is
mediated through the implicit command that he perceive this reality

through the act of beholding her partially disrobed body. As this image appears before Mobad's emissary, and by extension, Mobad's visualization of that image, the narrator's language, right on cue, shifts into the familiar tropes of the woman-as-riot: "a rush of love's sedition, a clamour, a body-melting catastrophe, a beguiler of hearts" (76/4 [41]). Thus, when Vis bids Mobad to behold the "naked" truth of his prospects, her body emerges as a site where both temptation and moral guidance can be found.

The intentionality behind this gesture deserves further consideration, as it speaks to what I will be describing further on as Vis's meta-knowledge of how her body is seen in her story, not only by its physical actors, but by the narrative tropes and expectations behind it. Vis seems to be fully aware of the destructive power of her beauty, yet instead of hiding it, she actively deploys it to destroy the desiring gaze altogether, calling on the beholder to apprehend *through* her a higher value system rooted in the ethics of romance and authorized by divine sanction. It is to this latter theme she now turns, continuing her reply to Mobad:

چه عذرآرم بدان سر پیش دادار و گر با او خورم در مهر زنهار

نترسی تو که پیر ناتوانی من از دادار ترسم با جوانی

کجا این ترس پیران را نکوتر بترس ار بخردی از داد داور

Were I to break faith in love with him [Viru], what excuse could I bring before the Creator, on the other side? I *fear* the Creator, though I am young; how do you, a feeble old man, not *fear* Him? If you are wise, *fear* the Lord's judgment, for this *fear* is better in the elderly. (77/27–9 [42], emphasis added)

Through this admonition, Vis brings together two separate bases for moral action and presents them as mutually compatible and interconnected systems: the law of like unto like that demands total fidelity to her other half, and her four-fold invocation of pious fear (*tars*). It goes without saying that this should, on the surface, render her a paragon of the virtues of steadfastness and loyalty so vaunted by the Greek and Arabic love-story traditions. It furthermore gestures towards the redemptive qualities of romantic love as they were understood in the literary heritage of Gorgāni's background, such as the famous dictum that he (or she) who pursued chastity in love would die a martyr. But the critical irony is that, in speaking frankly in defence of these norms, Vis steps outside their bounds and thus supplies endless ammunition for her critics to portray her as shameless and headstrong, the very traits that distance her from the ideal persona she seeks to inhabit. This irony calls attention to the impossibility of her innocence, the paradox of romantic virtue being placed squarely on the sexualized, immanently fallible female body and the political claims made upon it. In a poignant reflection later on, the narrator muses on how little control Vis has over her social reality, as all this clamour, shame, and subjective splitting is ultimately the product of a simple and unavoidable occurrence – the onset of puberty. "Look at how the world toyed with her! It raised her in joy and delight, brought her up in honour and esteem. But when her height became the bane of the straight cypress, and the full moon became enslaved to her face, and the tulips of her cheeks came into bloom, and two pomegranates ripened from her silver breast; the world turned from the path of kindness, and all her fortunes changed" (112/63–7 [75]).

Yet Vis's choice to respond to this reality through a distinctive practice of self-exposure, "unveiling" her mind and body alike to the public, raises important questions about the possibility and efficacy of pursuing such wilful actions in a world that is saturated with competing discursive pressures and set within the highly mediated environment of the court – a problem that Mobad and Rāmin will also confront in due course. If, as Foucault put it, the only meaningful action available to the protagonists of the Greek novel was to work upon the self, accepting one's inability to alter external forces and focusing instead on the preservation of inner integrity, it seems that Vis is pushing against this limitation in provocative ways. While some characters, such as Shahru, are quite adept at acting through the constraints of their situation, managing their speech and navigating the ins and outs of protocol to arrive at their desired outcome, Vis rejects such manoeuvres as incompatible with her persona; superficial propriety means nothing to her if it risks compromising her baseline ethics. By declaring her desire to walk in the footsteps of past romance heroines, then exposing the impossibility of doing so in her own story, Vis stands poised to reconfigure the orientation of the ethos of romantic love itself, from an inward-facing practice of self-discipline to an outward-facing struggle for a world in which her words and deeds can operate in transparent accord, ideally without bringing shame on herself in the process. In articulating this desire, Vis also expresses a kind of alienation from the narrative that has prevented her from realizing it, as though she were exiled in a land that refuses to see things her way. Her discursive sense of exile will soon be coupled with a physical one, brought about by a forcible relocation from Media to Khorasan – from Māh to Marv – in which her endogamous family unit will be broken and supplanted by an exogamous replica: the mirror image of the thing she wants, but not the thing itself.

From Māh to Marv: A Tale of Three Seductions

Vis's steadfast adherence to an ethics of fully aligned words, acts, and principles produces yet another form of doubling in the text, this time on the level of the poem's implicit narrative. As she has made clear, Vis identifies herself as the protagonist of a narrative whose title would be *Vis & Viru*; once separated from her husband-brother, her true love and perfect match, she repeatedly affirms her commitment to be faithful to him at all costs until their eventual reunion. (Indeed, Francesco Gabrieli suspects that Viru's role might have been much more prominent in other versions of the legend.)[47] But this, of course, is not the title of the present story – much to Vis's chagrin. How, then, are we to transition from the love-story we seem to be reading, *Vis & Viru*, to the "official" tale of *Vis & Rāmin*?

The shift will not be an easy one; after all, by the very fact of her self-identified role, Vis will never willingly consent to an affair with Rāmin. The imposition of *Vis & Rāmin* over *Vis & Viru* can only be brought about through non-consensual means: war, abduction, seduction, emotional blackmail, and other forms of physical and psychological coercion. To force the romance of Vis and Rāmin into being, however, has some significant ramifications for the romance itself. As noted above, the whole point of romantic love is that it emerges of its own accord; any "work" done to make it happen is proof of its inauthenticity. The introduction of coercion, then, as a necessary and constitutive element of the love-story of *Vis & Rāmin* is a move that will wreak havoc on the stability of the work's foundational ethos and the inner lives of its characters, ultimately casting into doubt the validity of any and all such attachments.

The violence is at first glance most visible in the public theatre of war between Khorasan and Media, in which many men – most notably Vis's father, Qāren – lose their lives. Generically speaking, however, this is but a trivial detail – raids, battles, and wars are standard elements of the love-story's narrative vocabulary and leave little impact on the protagonists' inner steadfastness: as Vis proudly asserts, the loss of her father has only strengthened her resolve to resist Mobad's overtures (78/32–3 [42–3]). Far more significant is the violence of seduction. It does not take long for both Mobad and Rāmin to realize that pursuing Vis directly is a lost cause; only by gaining mastery over her guardians, Shahru and the Nurse, can they hope to obtain their desire. The heroine's journey from Māh to Marv, from the endogamous *Vis & Viru* to the exogamous *Vis & Rāmin*, is thus the product of a complex chain of psychological violence, running along the line of the mother-daughter relationship: in their individual ways, Mobad and Rāmin "convert" Shahru and the Nurse respectively to their side, who then act as their proxies in inflicting the same coercion on Vis herself.

Vis & Rāmin is quite striking in the way it emphasizes the trauma of this journey: the inner struggles of Shahru, the Nurse, and especially Vis all receive sympathetic and nuanced exploration in the scenes that lie ahead. But on top of this quality, which is notable in and of itself, the violence does an interesting kind of work on the ethos of romantic love as well. It essentially smashes the code apart, studying its component parts, revealing its inner paradoxes, and showing how, as I postulated at the beginning of this chapter, it cannot ultimately guide its practitioners to felicity. If romantic love is to be rehabilitated, it must acquire a level of sophistication that would allow it to function in the complex and messy conditions of the "real" world. Leyla Rouhi emphasizes this point in her discussion of the Nurse, whose task, she writes, "consists of deciphering certain codes for the young girl, who hitherto has chosen to read the signs of honor and shame in more literal ways. It is thus no longer a question of employing ruses to facilitate a clandestine sexual encounter, but of a young woman's education within a system whose elaborate codes of conduct are prone to entirely contradictory inter-pretations."[48] As painful as it is, Vis's seduction also signals a riposte to the Greek and Arabic love-story models she so identifies with, with the takeaway lesson that simply being faithful may not be enough to survive.

The journey begins with Shahru, who had withdrawn with her daughter to the fortress of Gurab, while Viru counter-attacked and drove Mobad from the battlefield.[49] The victory is short-lived, however: a revolt in Daylam to the north calls Viru away, leaving Mobad free to devise another plan. The king is not the least bit dissuaded by Vis's rejection; he continues to see her as rightfully his, and hearing his emis-sary's report of her beautiful body has only inflamed his desire further (79/58, 74 [45]). Moreover, he learns that despite her marriage to Viru, Vis is still a virgin, a fact that he takes as sure proof that God has sanc-tioned his claim on her (he later says this explicitly at 85/14, 17). The narrator gives us a bit of backstory at this moment: although the astrol-ogers had chosen the most auspicious day for the wedding, Vis hap-pened to be menstruating at the time, making her ritually impure and unable to consummate the marriage, for "if the woman keeps this state hidden from her husband, she will become eternally forbidden to him" (*v-agar zan ḥāl az-u dārad nehāni • bar u gardad ḥarām-e jāvdani*, 80/67).[50] But because Vis will not budge in her commitment to Viru, Zard advises Mobad to target her mother instead, to first "give her abundant hope in your beneficence, and then instill the fear of God" (*be nikuyi omid-ash deh farāvān* • *pas āngāhi be yazdān-ash betarsān*, 83/58) – a variation of the classic carrot-and-stick manoeuvre.

Both lines of attack succeed in hitting their mark. The description of the king's gifts is one of the more sumptuous displays of material wealth in the poem, leaving Shahru astonished and dazzled. However, the *coup de grâce* seems to come not from the carrot but from the stick, delivered in the form of a long and bombastic letter that thunders with the vehemence of a popular preacher: "Think of your eternal shame when your soul sees the Judge," it reads, "Think of the Creator's judgement, the terror of Hell, and the end of things!" (84/5–6 [48]). Mobad forcefully reminds Shahru that she has sworn an oath (*sowgand*), given a pledge (*paymān*), and signed a contract (*ᶜahd*, 85/11–13, n5, cf. 41/49–51); and while oath-breaking is generally not a good thing in any case, it is especially serious in the Zoroastrian milieu of the story, where the covenant, deified as the sun god Mithra (*mehr*), counts among the most sacred and inviolate of undertakings.[51] With the fear of God freshly awakened within her (*ze yazdān niz āmad dar del-ash bim*, 87/49 [51]), Shahru opens the castle gates and surrenders her daughter to the king. As portended by the ominous writhing of the constellations above, this development will prove ill-fated, but it is worth noting how the narrative quietly absolves Shahru of any direct responsibility for bringing it about.[52] Twice, she has been placed in an impossible situation; had she reneged on her sacred oath, one wonders if the heavens would have been any less offended. Shahru therefore emerges as a woman who is forced to choose the best of two reprehensible options, rather than one who is easily diverted from the right path by treasure and trinkets.

This concludes the first seduction scene, which, I hope to have shown, has already deployed the motif in a way contrary to its usual function as a site to reaffirm the trope of women's susceptibility to material temptation; it instead portrays Shahru in a highly sympathetic light and sets the precedent for a similar moral crux that her daughter will face as well.[53] The second seduction scene is of no less importance, marking a pivotal juncture that not only brings Rāmin back into the flow of events, but also establishes the Nurse as one of its central actors, and no mere sidekick to Vis. Like many literary nannies, the Nurse is distinguished by a number of singular traits: her inferior social status relative to the rest of the cast; her pragmatic and down-to-earth attitude towards love and sex; her role as a mediator between the lover and beloved; and her association with the arts of witchcraft and enchantment.[54] All these aspects will come into play in the drama to unfold, revealing how the Nurse, though often acting behind the scenes, is possibly the most influential character in the story. While Shahru played a role in allowing Vis to be separated from Media, that does not necessarily diminish her daughter's emotional ties to her husband and homeland; the Nurse, in contrast, has a much more invasive surgery to perform. She will sever the emotional bond between Vis and Viru and replace it with one between Vis and Rāmin: a transfer of Vis's love from her blood-brother to her milk-brother, made possible by the careful manipulation of romantic norms and logic.[55]

This process is set into motion immediately following Vis's capture in Gurab. As Mobad and his company triumphantly march back to their capital, a chance breeze lifts the curtain over Vis's palanquin; Rāmin, riding alongside, catches a glimpse of her face and literally falls head over heels in love. But the feeling, for once, is not mutual: lost in her grief, Vis remains unaware of Rāmin's presence, and upon arriving in Marv, she immediately shuts herself away in her chambers. With no way of reaching her, the besotted Rāmin can only wander hopelessly through the palace gardens, until, to his surprise and joy, he runs across his old Nurse. He begs her to intercede on his behalf, but the Nurse, like Shahru, is not an easy nut to crack. Although she is moved by Rāmin's plight, she attempts to dissuade him from his obsession, insisting (truthfully) that Vis is far too proud and committed to heed his advances. Nothing that Rāmin can say will change her mind, and as his desperation grows, he turns to more drastic measures. "You know so many words (*sakhon*) at the time of speech, and have so many skills (*honar*) at the time of action," he cries, "Join well the two together, and lay a snare for Vis!" (127/233–4).

کشید و داد بوسی چند بر سر   بگفت این و پس او را تنگ در بر

بیامد دیو و رفت اندر تن اوی   وزان پس داد بوسش بر لب و روی

تو گفتی تخم مهر اندر دلش کاشت   ز دایه زود کام خویش بر داشت

چنان دان کش نهادی بر سر افسار   چو بر زن کام دل راندی یکی بار

He said this, and then drew her tightly to his chest. He kissed her head over and over, and then her lips and face; the demon came and entered her body.[56] He soon attained his desire from the Nurse; you'd say he planted a seed of love in her heart. Know that once you've taken pleasure of a woman, you've placed a bridle over her head. (128/237–40 [88])

Although Rāmin is often singled out in the story as the one with the silver tongue, in this scene we behold the limits of his power of persuasion:

after a series of useless entreaties, he can only resort to "seduction" in its most crude and physical form (the phrase "attained his desire" is as suggestive in Persian as it is in English) to get what he wants. Yet as the Nurse rises from his side, she praises him for the compelling power of his peculiar brand of rhetoric: "O you seductive speaker! You've beat us all in eloquence!" (*bedu goft ay faribanda sakhon-guy • bebordi az hama kas dar sakhon guy*, 128/243). This tongue-in-cheek assessment of Rāmin's verbal prowess, ironically juxtaposed against a moment in which he has both confessed his dire need of the Nurse's speech and demonstrated the impotence of his own, casts his eventual attachment to Vis in an even more ambiguous light. Rāmin's attempt to gain access to Vis by forcefully planting the "demon" of love in the Nurse essentially amounts to a kind of rape by proxy, a demonic act no less violent in its implications than Mobad's abduction of Vis from her home in Media. It also, as Nahid Norozi observes, effectively inverts the women-as-riot motif to identify Rāmin as the primary "corrupting force" in this process.[57]

It would be easy to forget, in moments like these, that Rāmin is the ostensible hero of the poem, and that even Mobad does not lack for redeeming qualities. The depiction of both brothers here as equally sinister and predatory figures shows that the narrative voice has aligned itself, to a degree, with Vis's perspective, telling the story in a way that she might tell it. It has adopted, in other words, the voice of a non-existent text, the love-story of *Vis & Viru*, in which Vis is expected to love and be loyal to Viru at all costs, and in which Mobad and Rāmin are the enemies, the illegitimate claimants to her love. The shift into this point of view also transforms the Nurse from helpful go-between to evil temptress, no longer facilitating the union of deserving lovers but instead posing an existential threat to Vis's moral and spiritual integrity.[58] Indeed, it is immediately after the appearance of the "demon" in this scene (whom we will soon meet again) that the narrator begins calling the Nurse a "sorceress" (*jādu*, 129/264, 130/1), an epithet never used for her before.

This change of perspective has important implications both for the theme of doubling I have been exploring throughout this chapter and my overarching argument about the use of heteroglossia in *Vis & Rāmin*, a love-story "in which love has many a tale." Vis's is not the only viewpoint the narrator will assume; as we will see in the following chapters, we will also be given a version of events from the eyes of Mobad and Rāmin, who each see themselves and the other characters in radically different lights. In that regard, it is important to emphasize that what we are witnessing is not the Nurse's transition from loving nanny to evil witch, or Rāmin's from romantic lover to sexual predator, but a doubling of these figures into both/and personae. It is precisely this fracturing of vision that allows Vis to start exploring the ethos of romance in multiple dimensions, rather than a black-and-white, two-dimensional space, such that she herself can ultimately step into the both/and persona of the faithful adulteress, seeing her choice as simultaneously licit and illicit and grappling with the moral problems that accompany such a stance.[59]

With this thought in mind, we are now set to track the last of our three seduction scenes, the seduction (*fariftan*) of Vis by the Nurse, a slow-burn process featuring a series of extended, and often explosive, dialogues between the two women. Though rich in evocative detail and insightful expressions, a blow-by-blow account of this conversation would require a great deal of space, more than what can be afforded here; but the following scene serves well as a representative example to observe which approaches fall flat and which eventually stick. Now fully "persuaded" to act as Rāmin's agent, the Nurse returns from the garden to find her charge weeping in bed. When asked what is the matter, Vis confesses she has just woken from an erotic dream of Viru (132/30–40). Seeing her opportunity, the Nurse responds,

نخواهی در جهان جستن جزاوکس   تو با تیمار ویرو مانده و بس

خدایت را چو ویرو نیست بنده   مرا گفتی که اندر مرو گنده

فرشته نیست پرورده به مینو   اگرچه شاه است و خودکام ویرو

دلیران جهان کشور ستانان   به مرو اندر بسی دیدم جوانان

کجا در هر هنر گویی جهانیست   وزیشان شیر مردی کامرانیست

ور ایشان عنبرند او مشك نابست   گر ایشان اخترند او آفتابست

به گوهر شاه موبد را برادر   به تخمه تا به آدم شاه و مهتر

فرشته بر زمین و دیو در زین   خجسته نام و فرخ بخت رامین

گروگان شد همه دلها به مهرش   به ویرو نیک ماند خوب چهرش

You're only destroying yourself for Viru; in all the world, you seek none but him. You told me that in "stinking Marv" there is no slave who could be your lord like Viru. Though Viru's a proud king, he's not an angel raised in the heavens! I've seen so many fine young men in Marv, world-heroes and kingdom-conquerors! … Among them is a lion among men, a propitious hero; you'd call him a world in every skill. If they are stars, he is the sun; if they are ambergris, he is pure musk. His line makes him a lord and king over other men, for Mobad is his brother: happy-named and fortune-bright Rāmin! An angel on earth, and a demon in the saddle!

> His handsome face is very much like Viru's, and all hearts are hostage to
> his love. (134/63–6, 70–4 [94])

This opening foray by the Nurse is deceptively sophisticated, for it challenges Vis to re-evaluate her choices on a number of levels. The first and most obvious level is her usual appeal to pragmatism, the admonition that Vis is pining away needlessly for an unobtainable beloved when there are many other fish in the sea. In this way, she is also appealing to Vis's self-acknowledged desire; we can almost see her wink as she calls Rāmin a "demon in the saddle." Finally, the Nurse offers a tempting reinterpretation of the laws of sexual symmetry, presenting Rāmin as a virtual clone of Vis's husband, a doppelgänger unto whom her desires can be diverted without any apparent loss of integrity. This proposed substitution recalls to mind Mobad's original plan of swapping out Vis for Shahru, and as noted then, it raises a lingering question about the ontology of love: as it is understood to be the image of the beloved that penetrates the eyes and brands itself upon the soul, one could say that the lover is technically infatuated with the beloved's *image* rather than the person him or herself. By this logic, Rāmin, like Viru, becomes a perfect match for Vis, forming "two halves of the same apple" (134/81), as the Nurse says. In a sense, the Nurse is not asking Vis to break the rules, but to hack them, treating the ethos of romantic love as a tool that expands her agency, rather than a code that limits it.[60]

Though initially taken aback by the Nurse's "upside-down speech" (*vāruna goftār*, 135/90), Vis quickly rallies. "Shame on you, for both my sake and Viru's" (135/96), she replies, before launching into a general diatribe oddly reminiscent of Mobad's earlier rant about the people of Hamadan, lamenting the weakness of women, the treachery of minstrels, and the horrible fate awaiting those who give in to temptation: "On this side, shame and dishonour, on that side, the fires of Hell, equally innumerable!" (*bedin sar nang-o rosvāyi-sh bi-mar • bedān sar ātash-e dozakh barābar*, 137/129). Undaunted, the Nurse presses her attack from a number of other angles, making various appeals to fate ("Fortune snatched you from Viru," 138/147), love ("When love comes to you, you must bear its burden," 139/172), health ("Don't cast your youth to the sea, or melt your silver body in burning toil," 143/62), and sex ("You haven't yet experienced this pleasure – you don't realize that life without it is joyless," 147/126). She concludes her monologue with a dose of peer pressure, in which she tries to convince her obstinate protégée that all high-born women, "while they each have noble husbands, secretly take another for their lovers" (*agar che shu-ye nām-bordār dārand ● nehāni digar-i rā yār dārand*, 147/130).[61]

These passages have often been cited as evidence that *Vis & Rāmin* imagines a "kinder" social world for women, where flings and affairs are taken with a tolerant shrug and the turning of a blind eye, as opposed to comparable discussions on love and marriage in medieval Iranian and Islamic contexts.[62] Perhaps – but if so, Vis's moral outrage during these conversations displays her continued alienation from this world; she does not espouse a liberal disregard for the conventional rules around women's behaviour, as is sometimes suggested, but a staunchly conservative desire to uphold them. Increasingly alone and isolated, she sees herself fighting a desperate battle to preserve her virtue against what seems to be an entire world aligned against her, trying to tempt her into betraying her original commitment: the basic paradigm of the love-story mythos, in other words, especially as we see it in the Greek novels. Thus, if we concur with Vis's self-identification as the heroine of (the non-existent romance of) *Vis & Viru*, then nothing less than a full paradigm shift is necessary before she is even willing to consider, let alone commence, an illicit affair with a man she appears to loathe with all her heart, breaking her vows to the man of her (literal) dreams. In that sense, this is not a kind world at all; though surreptitious, the levels of coercion required to force this shift will be as troubling as they are traumatic.

We must therefore turn to the moment of Vis's capitulation alert for clues that would explain what compelled her to make this self-damning choice. It begins as the Nurse returns to Rāmin and admits that even she cannot sway the queen: "Flattery, tricks, spells, deception – these, before her, are like philosophy before drunkards!" (*farib-o ḥila-vo nirang-o dastān ● bovad pish-ash cho ḥekmat nazd-e mastān*, 149/174). Frustrated, Rāmin once again resorts to violence, or at least its threat. He instructs the Nurse to deliver one more message to Vis, presenting her with a stark choice: either she give him a chance, or he will kill himself; should she choose the latter, he will hold her accountable "before the Judge who will mete out justice, who will give justice to the whole world" (151/204).[63] The threat of suicide has an electric impact on the Nurse, anxious for the well-being of her foster son; it also changes the nature of her discourse with Vis. In their subsequent conversation, she begins her plea on an entirely new note, revealing for the first time her own private fears:

بخواهم گفت با تو یک سخن راز   مرا شرمت فرو بستست آواز

همی ترسم ازین از شاه موبد   که ترسد هر کسی از مردم بد

ز ننگ و سرزنش پرهیز دارم   کزیشان تیره گردد روزگارم
ز دوزخ نیز ترسانم به فرجام   که در دوزخ شوم بد روز و بد نام
ولیکن چون بر اندیشم ز رامین   وز آن رخسار زرد و اشك خونین
همی ترسم که او ناگه بمیرد   به مرگ او مرا یزدان بگیرد
مکن ماها بدان مسکین ببخشای   به خون او و روانت را میالای

I'd like to confide one secret in you – shame before you has stopped my voice. I *fear* King Mobad in this, as all people *fear* the wicked; I *fear* shame and retribution, for through them my days grow dark; I also *fear* Hell in the end, that in Hell I'll be cursed and disgraced. But when I think of Rāmin, of his pale face and bloody tears ... I fear that he will suddenly perish, and that God will judge me for his death. O moon, do not so! Have mercy on that wretched one – do not stain your soul with his blood! (151/211–15, 223–4 [112], emphasis added)

The Nurse is finally speaking Vis's language: rather than belittling her ideals as naive or old-fashioned, she accepts her view (her *theōria*) and places herself within it, conspicuously echoing the four-fold expression of fear – fear of political blowback, public shame, and divine retribution – that Vis herself had articulated to Mobad. She then adds her own anxiety to the stakes, saying that she too fears for Rāmin's life and for her own damnation, if he follows through with his threat. Her request, then, is both a confirmation of Vis's values and a plea that she look beyond the most direct or superficial means of pursing them, to rethink love not as an act of withholding or forbearance, but rather of mercy, compassion, and self-sacrifice. The appeal works: as Vis listens to her Nurse's words, "mercy (*bakhshāyesh*) for Rāmin welled in her heart, and out of affection (*dusti*), Rāmin's adornments took hold" (152/233). As I mentioned in the prologue, the recognition of romantic love in others is a powerful force – perhaps one strong enough to be considered a fundamental element of romance writing – in producing individual change and group fellowship: it results in the conversions of Anthia's various suitors (*Ephesiaka* 143/2.9, 160/5.2, 5.4), Layli's husband Ibn Salām (*Layli & Majnun* 160/33.85–93 [Davis 103]), Asmat to Avtandil (*The Knight in the Panther Skin* 40/¶239–49), and the Emir in *Floire & Blancheflor* (164/3123–32 [Hubert 106/2864–76]), among other examples. Yet here, as before, the conversion is complicated by its mediation through the Nurse: Vis sympathizes with the Nurse's sympathy for Rāmin, just as Rāmin seduced the Nurse to seduce Vis (we might also note the absence of *ᶜeshq* or *mehr* in this passage, which are the two most common words in *V&R* to describe romantic love, and rather a set of emotions that seem to arise out of a sense of justice and compassion).[64] This may explain why Vis's conversion to Rāmin does not result in her gaining a clearer sense of purpose but rather obfuscates the one she had, casting her into a lasting condition of doubt and ambivalence.

Presented with a choice that cannot fit within the black-and-white schema of romantic attachment, Vis, for the first time, is unsure what to do: should she double down on her principles, gambling with the lives of those she has no desire to hurt (Rāmin, perhaps, but especially the Nurse, her surrogate mother), or should she compromise them? The text, with striking sensitivity, describes her experience of losing this moral clarity as a profound feeling of shame, as though she has let herself down: "From shame (*az sharm*), her face burned in two colours, sometimes flushed, sometimes pale. From shame, her body was like a spring of water, sweat dripping from her like lustrous pearls" (153/238–9). Vis's embarrassed silence – the same sign of her consent to marry Viru – is all the proof the Nurse requires to know that she has at last succeeded in changing her mind, not *despite* but *through* the ethical commitments of romantic love, now challenged and reconfigured. The ironic result is that Vis ultimately becomes the agent of her own seduction: rather than violate the rules of romance, she reconsiders them in such a way as to conceive of adultery as an act grounded in, not contrary to, the bedrock principles of her character. In learning to accommodate these new considerations in her self-view as a virtuous person, she will enter a long period of trial and tribulation, similar to – yet quite different from – those of her predecessors, in which the conventions that dictate proper action in a highly stratified social setting are destabilized and opened to question, breaking ground for new possibilities of action, even as the normative regiments of protocol are breaking down.

A New Covenant

Though she has now permitted herself to at least contemplate the possibility of an affair, Vis is no less determined to manage the terms of the liaison. So far, she has refused even to look upon Rāmin, let alone negotiate with him face to face. While this could be construed simply as a sign of Vis's pride, as we heard the Nurse complain above, it may reflect a more interesting meta-knowledge of the rules of her genre. In the mythos of romantic love, one of the most common routes to love is through the gaze, either through a direct encounter with the beloved, or through his or her mental image via a portrait, a dream, or a vivid description.[65] Rāmin experiences this first-hand when he beholds Vis atop her palanquin:

کجا چون دید رامین روی آن ماه   تو گفتی خورد بر دل تیر ناگاه

ز پشت اسپ که پیکر بیفتاد   چو برگی کز درختش بفگند باد

گرفته زاتش دل مغز سر جوش   هم از تن دل رمیده هم ز سر هوش

ز راه دیده شد عشقش فرو دل   ازان بستد به یک دیدار ازو دل

When Rāmin saw that moon's visage, you'd say he was suddenly struck by an arrow: he fell from the back of his mighty horse like a leaf blown off the tree. His brain began to boil from the fire in his heart; soul and reason fled from body and mind. Love for Vis entered his heart through his eyes, sealing his heart in a single glance. (94/17–20 [57])

This classic scene, loaded with familiar motifs (one might recall the scene where Arcite "cast his eye upon Emelya / And therwithal he bleynte and cride, 'A!'" in Chaucer's "The Knight's Tale," 40/1077–8), both links *Vis & Rāmin* to the broad network of romance narratives I discussed earlier and shows that the "physics" of this world are no different. By abstaining from any face-to-face encounter with Rāmin, Vis seems to be deliberately avoiding the chance that she might be struck by Cupid's arrow, circumventing the conventional route to love in this literature – that is, until she has been convinced of the moral value of her decision to do so. If Rāmin's moment of falling in love was a matter of chance, as it so often is, Vis is determined to have hers as a matter of choice. Thus, with Vis's consent, the Nurse finds an opportunity for her to look upon Rāmin from the roof of her pavilion:[66]

همی تا ویس رامین را همی دید   تو گفتی جان شیرین را همی دید

چو نیک اندر رخ رامین نگه کرد   وفا و مهرِ ویرو را تبه کرد

Vis stared at Rāmin long and hard; you'd say she beheld her own sweet soul in him. As she scrutinized his face, she laid waste to her love and loyalty to Viru. (154/21–2 [115])

The signs are incontrovertible, and her worst misgivings confirmed: in recognizing herself in Rāmin, Vis understands that he was her destined lover all along; she had been duped, so to speak, by the conflicting signals and false starts of the story's opening. And yet, even as love wells in her heart as she gazes on Rāmin, Vis's confidence in the authority or authenticity of that beholding, encapsulated in the litmus test of love at first sight, could well be shaken. After all, the Nurse was quite right about his appearance: "He's just as you said," Vis remarks, "He looks very much like auspicious Viru" (*be farrokhbakht-e viru nik mānad,*

155/30–1). But this visual congruity raises troubling questions: if Vis beholds herself in Rāmin, and if Rāmin in turn resembles Viru, then *what exactly is she seeing?* Is this love she feels truly instigated by Rāmin, or could it be her innate response to seeing Viru's *image* before her, just as she had desired his simulacrum in her dream? Has she fallen out of love with Viru, or could her love have simply been transferred to his alter-ego? The implications these questions have on the stability, even the viability, of romantic love are devastating: never again can she trust her eyes and heart to distinguish the real from the replica, to know beyond all doubt that the one she loves is the one she *thinks* she loves.[67] The notion of transferability, which she found so offensive in Mobad's contract with Shahru, has now reappeared in her own life, forcing her to question her presumption of love as a "final condition" and instead reconsider it as something vulnerable to change and evolution – a shift from an absolutist to a responsive understanding, in other words.[68] How Vis responds to these possibilities, both in thought and action, will tell us (and her) much about the basic question of who she is and how she understands herself through the practice of love, with significant implications for her self-conception as a figure who makes historical choices for which she is accountable, as we will see in chapter 5. Her focused gaze on Rāmin, as a result, reflects nothing less than a moment of intense *self*-scrutiny, a practice of coming to know the self through its mirror image that, as Shadi Bartsch has shown, is deeply rooted in classical thought and philosophy.[69]

Indeed, this act of beholding instigates a protracted battle within Vis's soul, in which the demon of love (*div-e mehr*) wrestles with her sense of shame (*sharm*) for mastery of her heart (155/37, 45).[70] The latter ultimately carries the day, and Vis departs the rooftop telling herself that she will never consent to a relationship with Rāmin. But on conveying her decision to the Nurse, Vis receives an unexpected shock. The Nurse is more committed than ever to seeing Vis and Rāmin together, and will not take no for an answer: "If you're going to be so unpleasant (*bad-khu*), it's not worth staying with you," she replies; "let the land of Marv with Mobad be yours, let the land of Māh with Shahru be mine" (158/18–19). For Vis, this is a bitter betrayal. Having been parted from her mother and husband-brother, the Nurse is the only family left to her, as they both know well. "How could I live here without you?" she responds. "You are just like my mother to me!" (*abi to chun tavānam bud idar • ke to hasti marā hamtā-ye mādar*, 159/27 [120]).[71] This comparison of the Nurse to Shahru not only expresses Vis's emotional attachment to both but also recalls her mother's decision to give her up to Mobad. The Nurse's threat to repeat this abandonment represents the worst emotional violence she knows she can inflict. Defeated, Vis accepts the Nurse's terms, with one last miserable rebuke: "The torment you've put me through weights heavy on my heart. Without it, I would harbour no desire there" (*marā āzār-e to sakht-ast bar del* • *v-agar na hich kām-am nist dar del*, 160/49). If there were any illusions of anything "romantic" in the story of how Vis and Rāmin got together, they are dispelled for good in the wake of this haunting conclusion.

The Vis that emerges out of this experience is a far more complex figure than the proud and defiant princess we met at the beginning of the story. Set up as a bargaining chip between two noble families before she was born, the constant object of scrutiny, plots, and counter-plots, abducted by a jealous king, and now threatened by her surrogate mother (who is pressured, in turn, by her surrogate son), Vis has shown herself capable of fierce and determined resistance against every new obstacle that has been thrown in her path; but the loss of clarity and shifting moral terrain of the story has made it impossible for her to stand her ground – at least not on the terms she had originally intended. The end result bears some resemblance to the love potion in the *Tristan & Isolde* cycle, which places two people in the unworkable situation of loving each other despite their own preference to the contrary. But in contrast to this, Vis's seduction is realized not by external magic but a combination of broken expectations, chimeric solutions, and physical and psychological violence, recasting the love of Vis and Rāmin not as the expression of an intuitive attachment, but as the outcome of a sequence of social and generic transgressions. This point must be emphasized especially in anticipation of the chapters to come, in which injustice becomes the central thematic of her later laments, letters, and attempts to reassert herself.

Although she has been pushed into a relationship she never desired, Vis is nonetheless careful to maintain control; if she must be with Rāmin, she will negotiate the tryst on her terms. She empties her quarters of all servants and grants Rāmin access through the roof. Upon beholding his beloved, regally sitting upon her throne, the happy lover springs into an impromptu encomium, until Vis cuts him off in a tone that leaves no guessing as to the seriousness of the situation. "I've sullied my pure body, I've annihilated loyalty and shame," she says bluntly. "Speak – what are your intentions with me, a friend's or an enemy's? You are like a bloom that fades in a single day, not like agate and turquoise" (163/46, 50–1 [126]). Chastened, Rāmin solemnly swears he will never break faith; only then does Vis return the oath, giving him a nosegay of violets (165/82, or as Hedāyat suspects, "forget-me-nots") as a token of their vow.[72] The story has come full circle: the disastrous pact between

102   Love at a Crux

Shahru and Mobad has been replaced with a new love/-covenant (*mehr*, a word whose valences I'll explore further in chapter 3) between Vis and Rāmin, though not without serious doubts and trepidation.

It is around here that the narrator makes the following remark: "Although there was no limit to her modesty, destiny stole shame from her eyes" (170/43 [133]). This is an interesting observation to make, especially at this critical juncture where Vis stands at the point of no return, violating both her personal vows to Viru and her public obligations towards Mobad; it seems to remind us that, despite crossing these lines, she has always been an ideal candidate for the role of romance heroine. Like many of the other characters we have put her in conversation with, Vis firmly adheres to the fairly conservative principles of shame, modesty, and total devotion to her male beloved, yet there is something "off" about the narrative frame guiding her (her "destiny") that sends her story awry. Indeed, I do not think it an exaggeration to say that the love-story of *Vis & Rāmin* was wrecked even before it got started, sabotaged by a series of false flags, doubled personae, visual replicas, and the total breakdown of trust. This is why the ceremony of the covenant is so important to Vis: if there is one thing left for her to stand on, it is the fundamental ethos of fidelity. While the trustworthiness of Rāmin as the object of her love may still be an open question, she has the ability, through her fidelity, to show that her love itself is beyond all doubt – not because of an accident of fate, but because she recognized and accepted it. Now, she is ready to demonstrate her love's reality, to make it real in fact, through the praxis of unwavering commitment, even at the risk of social disgrace and personal harm.

Her first test of this new praxis of romantic love is quick to appear on the horizon: Mobad overhears the Nurse whispering about the affair and launches a furious verbal assault on Vis, accusing her of what she had long feared: "You've abandoned righteousness and religion – you've become despicable in the eyes of all!" (*ze din-o rāsti bizār gashti • be cheshm-e har ke budi khwār gashti*, 169/30). But Vis, having grounded herself in the moral rectitude of her choice, is decisive in her response:

زتخت شاه چون شمشاد برجست   به کش کرده بلورین بازو و دست

مرو را گفت شاها کامگارا   چه ترسانی به پادافراه ما را

سخنها راست گفتی هر چه گفتی   نکو کردی که آهو نا نهفتی

کنون خواهی بکش خواهی برانم   وگر خواهی بر آور دیدگانم

وگر خواهی ببند جاودان دار   وگر خواهی برهنه کن به بازار

که رامینم گزین دو جهانست   تنم را جان و جانم را روانست

چراغ چشم و آرام دلم اوست   خداوندست و یار و دلبر و دوست

چه باشد گر به مهرش جان سپارم   که من خود جان برای مهر دارم

من از رامین وفا و مهربانی   نبرم تا نبرد زندگانی

وگر تیغ تو از من جان ستاند   مرا این نام جاویدان بماند
که جان بسپرد ویس از بهر رامین   به صد جان می خرم من نام چنین

She leapt from the king's throne like a tall boxwood, crossed her crystal arms, and said, "O mighty king! Why do you threaten us with retribution? All you have said is true; you've done well not to hide our faults. Now, if you wish, kill me! Drive me away! Gouge out my eyes! Keep me forever in bonds! Strip me naked, and parade me in the market! Over both worlds, I choose Rāmin: the life in my body, the soul in my life, the light of my eyes, the ease of my heart, my lord, lover, friend, and darling. So what if I give up my life for his love? I live only for love's sake! I shall never cut off love and loyalty from Rāmin until they are cut off by death ... And if your sword takes away my life, this name of mine will forever remain: 'Vis gave up her life for the sake of Rāmin!' I'd give up a hundred lives for such a reputation!" (170/44–52, 60–1 [133]))

With these words, Vis appears to have taken full ownership of her affair with Rāmin: even as she acknowledges its transgressive appearance, she proudly accepts it as her legacy in the world, even her key to immortality, as a testament to her virtue and steadfastness. Moreover, by openly declaring this love-based commitment for all to hear, she seeks "to make their mutual answerability *authoritative* for others," as Paul Kottman writes on Romeo and Juliet, thus pointing to the newly public-facing dimension of her ethical project.[73]

Such bold proclamations, however, cannot entirely mask the fragility of Vis's position. As her earlier conversation with Rāmin implies, Vis seems inclined to suspect that he is not capable of upholding the high expectations she has of him (and of herself), despite his promises and protests to the contrary. Though founded on vows that uphold the fundamental ethos of romantic love, the affair remains an uneasy arrangement at best: structurally faulty, stretched to the limit, and prone to collapse. With her new love-story raised over such a weak foundation, it is no wonder that she is unconvinced that this is or will be the right choice for her; as a result, she will be beset with episodes of doubt, anxiety, and self-remonstration for all but the last pages of her story. Indeed, in the very next scene, we arrive back at the polo game where we began this chapter, in which Vis, her eyes lingering over Mobad, Rāmin, and Viru below, confesses to her Nurse with a wistful sigh:

اگر بختم مرا یاری نمودی   دلارامم بجز ویرو نبودی
نه موبد جفت من بودی نه رامین   نبهره دوستان دشمن آیین

> If my fortune had aided me, my beloved would be none but Viru. Neither
> Mobad nor Rāmin would have been my mate, those contemptible friends
> who behave as foes. (176/147–8 [139])

There, in a nutshell, lies the ambiguity of *Vis & Rāmin*: though presented
as a love-story that invokes a familiar narrative structure and metaphysics of desire and attraction, the love of its protagonists is destabilized by
the introduction of a seemingly more-perfect match – Viru, whom Vis
will lose and never regain – twisting the instinctual and mutually con-
sensual love that makes up the bread and butter of the romance mythos
into an unwilling relationship forged through coercion, calculation,
and compromise. Vis's nostalgia for the simplicity and moral clarity of
that first relationship, hovering over her world like the moon in the sky,
beautiful yet unattainable (175/137), speaks meta-volumes about the
degree to which the ethos of romantic love has lost its innocence.

The world we have entered is a world where a clear-sighted and
unveiled ethics is no longer possible. As Vis has discovered, to simply
proclaim her commitment to the ideal practice of total fidelity to the
perfect match, while chiding the older generation for not recognizing
that ideal – speaking truth to power, as it were – does not and cannot resolve her story in the happily-ever-after of union or martyrdom
that is so often forthcoming in the romance tradition; on the contrary,
it only sabotages the very virtues she hopes to embody. To meet this
challenge, she must therefore complicate the ideals she once embraced
with such devotion, blindly repeating commonplace tropes about
women's weakness and imitating the archetypes of previous literary
lovers; her discourse, like the myth of romance itself, must acquire a
lying dimension as it seeks to uncover and articulate (the) truth. Thus
we are left with the paradox of Vis: the faithful adulteress, a woman
roundly condemned as a creature of loose morals and unbridled passion by the people around her (both diegetic characters and historical
readerships), yet whose actions, when we look closely, are motivated
above all by an unflinching dedication to the *possibility* of righteousness, even when it seems impossible, and the courage to look for it in
the most unlikely of places. Despite her "official" status as a sinner and
an outcast, Vis remains an exemplary figure in the story, for she has
discovered the paradoxical lesson that, as Sufi poets would later like
to say, a deep commitment to inner principles may necessitate actions
that appear to run against their outer implementation. This self-damning choice complicates and critiques the ideal of romantic love and the
ethical codes that it mandates.

Chapter Three

Politics | The Prisoner of His Skin

IT IS A SAD IRONY that Vis, having claimed she would "give up a hundred lives" to be remembered as one who died for her loyalty in love, would soon become notorious for her infidelity to her husband, King Mobad. Our first extant response to *Vis & Rāmin*, found in the *Bahman-nāma*, a narrative poem written between 1108–11 in the region of Azerbaijan by the poet Irānshāh ibn Abi al-Khayr, attests to this early reception. Although the *Bahman-nāma* follows the usual biographical path of a heroic tale – the life and adventures of Bahman, son of Esfandiyār – the first major episode in the story recounts how the young prince fell in love with and married a woman who eventually betrays him. This event calls to Irānshāh's mind the versification of *Vis & Rāmin* done by his predecessor Fakhr al-Din Gorgāni, and he does not mince his words in sharing his opinion of it:

که دلها ز مهر زنان کرد سرد   یکی داستان گفت گوینده مرد

ز آغاز شادی سرانجام کام   ز رامین و از ویسهٔ زشت نام

همان ویسه کزرام شد ناشکیب   نگارین سخنهای بند و فریب

که دایه ببستش ز نیرنگ و بند   چنان تنگ دل موبدِ مستمند

The poet [Gorgāni] told a story that froze men's hearts towards women: of Rāmin and infamous Vis; of joy at the beginning and pleasure at the end, with elaborate talk of shackles and shenanigans, when Vis could no longer wait for Rāmin; of sad and helpless Mobad, when the Nurse "bound" him with tricks and spells. (179/2847–50)[1]

Irānshāh's depiction of Vis as a wanton woman will probably not come as a surprise, even though it disregards the complex ethical dilemmas she faced; the fact that her choices ultimately result in an extramarital affair – humiliating the man who, as noted last chapter, is legally speaking the only possible match for Vis – is enough to earn his censure.[2] Mobad, on the other hand, elicits his pity: he describes him as aggrieved (*del-tang*) and helpless (*mostmand*), a victim of the Nurse's sorcery in particular and the wiles of women in general.

Passages like this suggest that a sympathetic reading of Mobad – positing him as a hero whose tragic story provides its presumably mature, male, and courtly audience with a cautionary *exemplum* against over-associating with women – was one of the possible and indeed prominent ways medieval readers engaged with the poem over the thousand-year course of its reception history.[3] Nor was this limited to premodern or Middle Eastern contexts. In the first assessment of the poem in Western scholarship, a 1869 article by Karl Heinrich Graf, we hear the echo of Irānshāh's sentiments: "The only noble characters present, as we see it, are the king, who is constantly denied, betrayed, and ultimately killed by sheer bad luck, and his stepbrother and vizier Zard, who is treacherously murdered. Not so Rāmin or Vis, despite all the exuberant praise and musk-scented descriptions of [their] beauty."[4] Some thirty years later, Baron R. von Stackelberg also expressed his disappointment at the poem's denouement, one that "does not coincide with our view about the issue of the tragic crime and its expiating."[5] That "tragic crime," in his view, was Mobad's marriage to an unborn girl, an opinion shared by Henri Massé in his 1959 translation of *V&R*: if not for this one "unthinking act" (*acte irréfléchi*), Massé writes, the king would have ended his days in joy and prosperity.[6] In these readings, Mobad's personal and political collapse, wreaked by those who should have been closest to him, stood out as one of the more memorable plots within the story, a tale about the precariousness of kingship and the perfidy of the heavens.

It is a testament to the power of shifting cultural attitudes that, as Vis's star rose, Mobad's declined. Even in the 1950s, scholars like Vladimir Minorsky and Jan Rypka had soured on the king, the former calling him "brutal" and "weak," the latter "ridiculous" and "pitiful."[7] Similar characterizations appear in studies by Minoo Southgate, Julie Scott Meisami, and J.-C. Bürgel, all published in the late 70s and 80s, who saw Mobad as the counter-foil to the lovers: where Vis and Rāmin give themselves to love, Mobad is the "cold moralist," interested only in law and contracts (Bürgel); where Rāmin realizes the error of his ways, Mobad falls victim to his own concupiscence (Meisami).[8] Scholars exploring the ancient Iranian background to the tale, furthermore, have produced readings of Mobad that establish him as nothing less than a sorcerer-king, a perversion of the priesthood he embodies in his violation of the sacred laws of family relations and bonds, both between brothers (Mobad–Rāmin) and between brother and sister (Viru–Vis).[9]

In addition to reflecting shifts in contemporary mores, these differing perspectives may also tell us something about the role of genre: what kind of story is *Vis & Rāmin?* In that regard, the distinction of heroic and amorous orientations of romance, as discussed in chapter 1, can be helpful in sorting out the various responses that readers have brought to that question. For those steeped in Aristotelian literary theory, he is a perfect example of the tragic *hero*, brought down by a single yet fatal flaw. But for readers who foreground the *love-story* within the text, Mobad easily falls into the role of the "Villain," the figure who, according to Propp's terminology, "disturb[s] the peace of a happy family"; Sādeq Hedāyat, writing in 1945, invoked the same narratological view in describing Mobad (along with Viru!) as the "great Obstacle" (*mānec-e bozorg*) of the plot, the agent who keeps the lovers apart and prevents the resolution of their love-story.[10]

This split decision among the critics, feeding Mobad into multiple possible personae, is further enabled by the machinations of the text itself. In a manner very similar to what I discussed in chapter 2, *V&R* deploys convincing narratological cues to suggest both readings as plausible. This ambiguity, in Dick Davis's opinion, places Mobad alongside Vis as one of the most complex characters in the story, "whose hopeless psychological situation flickers wearily from patience to self-assertion to fury and back again."[11] Recent studies have sought to engage with this complexity; Christine van Ruymbeke suggested that Mobad should be read as the protagonist of both the heroic and the amorous readings of the tale, such that he becomes its tragic lover/hero; while I explored how his multiple personae drive him down paths that are mutually anathema to each other, undoing the assumed harmony that is presumed to exist between lover, ruler, and the "perfect man" (*al-insān al-kāmil*) in Islamic philosophy.[12] Although I will revisit some of the points made in that study, my proposition here is a little bit different: where before I read Mobad as containing multitudes, here I want to delve further into the underlying unicity of those multiple performances. Regardless of whether we read Mobad as hero or villain, lover or legalist, the various roles that assign him a central and authoritative position in society uniformly limit and undercut that authority, pushing him to the margins of acceptable action and leading to his experience of self-entrapment, self-alienation, and self-destruction. The apparent disharmony of superficial obligations belies an underlying harmony of the same fundamental problem: the discursive forces that make Mobad who he is unmake him in the same motion.

Mobad is uncannily similar to Vis in this regard. Both characters appear as "images of language" who "long to be embodied," to use

Mikhail Bakhtin's terms, by attaching themselves to external and well-established plots – Vis as the faithful romance heroine, Mobad as the glorious king – and in making that attachment, both stake a claim in the sublime, the transcendent, and the immortal. Both outwardly possess an abundance of choice – Vis has her pick of lovers, Mobad's word is law – yet both come to recognize the poverty of their plenty; Mobad even repeats Vis's exact words to describe his own situation, saying "I ever burn in fire" (*hami suzam bar āzar*, 235/33, cf. 175/42), as he too laments the way the stars have apparently forced him to violate the mandates of his literary and political role. Though narrated from differing perspectives of gender and power, my accounts of Vis and Mobad are in a sense two versions of the same story: both figures are forced to confront the aporias inherent within their mythic characters, disrupting the respective practices (ethos) that first promised and then denied them coherence and autonomy.

In developing these themes of dissociation and self-alienation, Mobad takes us further into the murky topic of the "self" in *Vis & Rāmin* and the discursive networks in which it participates. Navigating these waters is a tricky business, as the gap between modern and medieval modes of subjectivity is so wide that any attempt to translate the latter into a contemporary episteme is highly fraught; as Paul Zumthor asserts, "When a reader of our century confronts a twelfth-century work, the time span separating them distorts and even destroys the relationship that is normally produced by the text's mediation between author and reader."[13] Nevertheless, our focus on the love-story might allow us at least to approach subjectivity from an oblique angle, reading it from the outer position, if not the inner perspective, of the desiring self. As I postulated in the previous chapter, romantic love is contingent on two acts, the *recognition* of the Self in the Other, followed by the *desire* for union with that Self-in-the-Other, a being both part of and exterior to the lover: it is through this process that the heroes of the romance mythos represent themselves to others and come to know themselves. (I want to add here that, while I analyse this dynamic through the medieval concepts of *mushākala* and *munāsaba* – similitude and affinity – I see intriguing resonances with Lacan's theory of the mirror stage, and so I will occasionally invoke Lacanian terms to gesture towards directions for possible inquiry.)[14] But as we have seen, *V&R* raises the real possibility of *mis*-recognition within this literary field; through Mobad, we can consider the implications of this possibility when brought to the domains of patriarchy, sovereignty, and the kinship networks that form the basis of dynastic power.

As Gorgāni tells us, his composition is a love tale that tells many tales of love, some of them written between the lines of its explicit account of *Vis & Rāmin*. Having explored the unnamed romance of *Vis & Viru*, I now follow another implicit tale, the love-story of *Mobad & Vis* – or perhaps more fundamentally *Mobad & Shahru* – to discover the nature of his recognition, the source of his desire, and the way these enwrap a set of transcendental discursive codes that simultaneously produce and dismantle his power and authority. This account of Mobad Manikān, with its connotations of a man driven against his will towards his own destruction as if under the control of some malignant spell, produces one of the more troubling and uncanny stories of *Vis & Rāmin*.[15]

"All Kings Were His Slaves"

Its title notwithstanding, it is easy to see why Mobad could be (mis?-) taken as the hero of *Vis & Rāmin*. Witness the opening lines of the story:

نوشته یافتم اندر سمرها   ز گفتِ راویان اندر خبرها

که بود اندر زمانه شهریاری   به شاهی کامگاری بختیاری

همه شاهان مرو را بنده بودند   ز بهرِ او به گیتی زنده بودند

I have found, written amongst the evening stories of events told by raconteurs, that once upon a time there was a king, blessed and auspicious in kingship. All kings were his slaves; they lived in the world for his sake. (31/1–3 [1])

This introit places Mobad at the front and centre of the emergent narrative, and all but one of the surviving manuscripts of *V&R* go on to flesh out his character with a litany of royal attributes: a rain cloud of generosity, a shining sun at the feast, a raging lion in battle, the master of the world from east to west, a man favoured by the celestial bodies above, whose every day was a victorious Nowruz, and so on and so forth (31/4–21). These descriptions are significant not only in their abundance (with the Istanbul manuscript piling on another fifty lines in this vein) but especially in their semiotics.[16] "Power," as Aziz al-Azmeh writes, "is by nature enunciative"; by fixing Mobad in a particular spatial and ritual setting, adorning him with meaningful emblems and accoutrements, and investing him with established figurative qualities, the opening lines of *V&R* "speak" him into, and consequently allow him to embody, the role of an easily recognized ideal figure in Gorgāni's milieu: the *shāhanshāh*, or King of Kings.[17] Although versions of this title date back to ancient Assyria, it came to be particularly associated with the Persianate tradition of kingship, thanks to the aggressive propaganda of the Achaemenid and Sasanian empires (550–330 BCE and 224–651 CE).[18] It fell out of use for a time after the Muslim conquest of Iran, but the late Umayyad (early eighth c.) and especially the Abbasid caliphs (eighth and ninth c.) revived many of the old Sasanian protocols and ceremonies as part of their enunciative vocabulary of imperial power – occasions in which the recitation of poetry played no small role.[19] In this way, the performative presence of the universal sovereign remained in play, and by the tenth and eleventh centuries, regional Iranian dynasts adopted the role, and even the King of Kings title, for themselves.[20]

One of the central rituals that was used to re-present this ideal figure was the celebration of Nowruz, the "new day" of the Spring equinox that announced the end of Winter and the return of life and prosperity. The Sasanian custom of holding coronation ceremonies on this day was continued, in a more limited fashion, by the Abbasids, Buyids (tenth c.), and the Ghaznavids (eleventh c.), who marked the occasion through the ritual exchange of gifts.[21] Being such a key signifier of universal kingship, and an occasion to reassert and reforge the bonds of authority and fealty between the king and his subjects, it is no surprise to find Mobad demonstrating the magnitude of his dominion with a Nowruz feast of his own:

به جشن اندر سراسر نامداران   چه خرم جشن بود اندر بهاران

ز هر مرزی پری رویی و ماهی   ز هر شهری سپهداری و شاهی

از آذربایگان وز ری و گرگان   گزیده هرچه در ایران بزرگان

ز شیراز و صفاهان و دهستان   همیدون از خراسان و کهستان

چنان کاندر میانِ اختران ماه   نشسته در میانِ مهتران شاه

به تن بر زیور مهترِ خدایان   به سر بر افسرِ کشور گشایان

چو خورشیدِ جهان فرِّ خدایی   ز دیدارش دمنده روشنایی

What a joyous springtime festival, with the great and famous assembled throughout! A king and commander from every city, a moon and fairy-face from every march; the cream of the nobles, whether from Iran, Azerbaijan, Ray, Gorgan, Khorasan, Kuhestan, Shiraz, Isfahan, and Dehestan ... The king sat amidst them, as the moon sits among stars, the crown of conquerors upon his head, the ornament of the Lord of Lords upon his body. Light shone from his countenance: the royal *farr*, like the world-illuminating sun. (34/22–5, 29–31 [1–2])

For historians of ancient Iran, this scene might call to mind the famous reliefs of the Apadana Stairs in Persepolis, on which delegations from the Achaemenid Empire's far-flung territories line up to present the

Figure 1: Persepolis, Iran, Apadana: Procession of Tribute-Bearers, Syrian Delegation, Eastern Stairway. University of Chicago, Oriental Institute, ORINST P 29002.

King of Kings with the choice products of their native lands (figure 1).[22] While Gorgāni, like his peers, would have had only limited (and fairly distorted) knowledge of the historical dynasty, the symbolism of this ceremonial tribute would have been quite familiar to him; he even depicts the Seljuk sultan, Ṭughrıl Beg, receiving gifts from his vassals in a similar manner (13/63–81).[23] Mobad's visual appearance in this passage is also evocative of ancient Iranian iconography and mythology. The Achaemenids depicted themselves wearing solar crowns that figured their bodies as the bridge between heaven and earth, a visual motif that lived on in the flames and haloes that illuminated the faces of saints. It appears here as the *farr*, the radiant light shining from Mobad's sun-like countenance; in this way, he joins – or at least appears to join – the ranks of the great sovereigns of the past.[24]

Comparing the king to the sun is far more than poetic flourish; it provided a powerful metaphor for articulating the nature of universal kingship. We see this in the *Kutadgu Bilig*, a mirror for princes written in 1066 that sought to incorporate "Irano-Islamic ideals of statecraft ... as part of an Inner Asian Turkish literary heritage."[25] In this passage, the sovereign, "Rising Sun," explains the significance of his name:

The sun, you see, never wanes but is always full, its brightness is constant and excellent. That is how I am too: full of justice, and with no deficiency.

> Second, when the sun rises, it sheds its light on all creation without being in
> any way diminished thereby. This justice of mine is likewise undiminishing;
> my deeds and words are for all creatures unvarying and constant. Third,
> when the sun rises and warms the earth, myriad flowers bloom. Similarly,
> when my law extends over a land, that land prospers, though it be stones
> and rock ... Finally, the sun's abode is stable, its foundation firm: the constel-
> lation of the sun is Leo; its house never moves and so it never falls to ruin.[26]

In this account, the king is nothing less than a beacon of perfect justice and the source of life and prosperity – firm, unwavering, and
eternal.[27] His connection with the sun marks him not only as the best
of men but also as an icon of divinity, reflecting celestial power and
enforcing its will at one and the same time. This singular role implies
a perfect union of sacral and temporal authority, a concept strongly
articulated in Sasanian theories of kingship with manifest carry-
over into the Islamic period.[28] The founder of the Sasanian empire,
Ardashir I (d. 242), proclaimed himself the "image [also seed] of the
gods" (*čihr az yazdān*), a term with conceptual echoes in the Islamic
royal title *ẓill allāh fī al-arḍ*, "the Shadow of God on Earth."[29] New Persian renderings of Sasanian political treatises, such as the Testament
of Ardashir in the *Shāhnāma*, or the Letter of Tansar in the *History
of Tabaristan*, declare religion (*din*) and dominion (*shahriyāri, molk*)
to be born of the same womb, a proverb that appears across Arabic, Persian, and Turkish works by the Ikhwān al-Ṣafāʾ, Muḥammad
al-Ghazālī, Neẓām al-Molk, and Yūsuf Khāṣṣ Ḥājib.[30] Mobad's very
name invokes and reinforces these ideal convergences: as the narrator
of *V&R* says, "The world called him 'Shāh Mobad,' for he was both
priest (*mobad*) and wise sage" (*jahān-ash nām karda shāh mobad • ke
ham mobad bod-o ham be-khrad rad*, 32/16). This pun is deeply meaningful; while it is possible that an ancient form of Mobad's name may
point to a different etymology, the link between the Priest and the
King established in this line would not only evoke the general concept
of divine kingship for contemporary readers, but also invite comparison with the prototypical exemplars of that tradition.[31]

Within this context, the Priest-King *par excellence* is none other than
the mythical figure of Jamshid, whose story had been recently been
given a vivid retelling in the *Shāhnāma*. Here, the etymology can indeed
be instructive: *Jam* is the ancient Indo-Iranian god Yama (or Yima), the
lord of the dead in Vedic tradition (his name also means "twin" – more
on that in a moment!), while *shid*, from Avestan *xšaēta*, means "radiant" or "shining" (the same epithet as the sun, *khwar-shid*).[32] These two
aspects tie Jamshid to both the concept of solar-celestial kingship and the

prospect of immortality – a *sol invictus*, as it were. He is remembered in the Avesta as the "the sunlike-one of men," who "made from his authority both herds and people free from dying" (Yasna 9.4); the *Shāhnāma* repeats this tale, affirming that for three hundred years, no one experienced sickness, old age, or death (1:44/56 [Davis 7]).[33] He goes on play a pivotal role in the foundation of human civilization, gaining mastery over all living things (including animals, demons, and other non-humans), introducing advanced technologies (weaving, building, mining, and sailing), dividing society into the four canonical castes (priests, warriors, farmers, and artisans), and establishing Nowruz to mark the triumph of Summer over Winter, of light over dark, and of life over death.[34] Through these acts, many Muslim historians saw Jamshid as the Iranian analogue to Solomon, the great prophet-king of Abrahamic tradition. The analogy is especially visible when both kings command the demons (or the jinn) to lift their thrones into the air, symbolically placing themselves at the meeting point of heaven and earth; it is at this moment, al-Bīrūnī adds, that Jamshid's throne shone as bright in the sky as a second sun.[35]

Through the simple dual meaning of his name, Mobad activates this living tradition that binds secular and spiritual authority into a single figure, a connection that Jamshid himself articulates as he ascends the throne in the *Shāhnāma*: "I am endowed with divine *farr*, and I possess both kingship (*shahriyāri*) and priesthood" (*mobadi*, 1:41/8 [Davis 6]). This semantic slippage fuses Mobad into the horizon of expectations set by his mythical predecessor; if there is was any doubt about the intentionality of this coincidence, it would likely be dispelled when Gorgāni credits him with the founding of Nowruz (*yek-i jashn-e now-āyin karda bod shāh*, 33/20), a celebration traditionally attributed to Jamshid instead.[36] While to be so closely associated with the greatest world sovereign in history might not seem like bad publicity on the part of our king, it does raise some significant warning signs; after all, Jamshid, for all his glory, does not come to a good end. In most accounts, the god-like power to ascend to the heavens and ward off death goes to his head, and he begins to boast that it is he, and not God, who adorns the world with his beneficence and blessings.[37] The instant he articulates this hubris, expressing his desire for power beyond his purview, the *farr* vanishes from his countenance, leaving him vulnerable to the onslaught of the serpent-king Żahhāk, a monstrous hybrid whose insatiable appetites call to mind not only the destructive toxicity of the snake (*aži*), but the demonic force of concupiscence (*āzi*, *āz*).[38] Żahhāk eventually overthrows the king, hunts him down, and has him sawn in half, bringing the "twin" – or "doubled" – ontology encoded in Jamshid's name to its literal fulfilment (figure 2).

Figure 2: The execution of Jamshîd by the order of Zahhâk (detail from
Shâhnâmah, Spencer Collection, Pers. ms. 3). Courtesy of The New York
Public Library.

Thus, as Mobad appears on the stage of *Vis & Rāmin*, sparkling with Jamshidian splendour, he summons the memory of a myth that anticipates both the heights and perils of divine sovereignty: the undying sun, cloven in twain by the demon of desire. Though neither Jamshid nor Żahhāk are physically present in *V&R*, they are still "there" in both symbolic and even material ways, hovering over the characters like unquiet ghosts, particularly during Mobad's fateful meeting with Shahru. This encounter demonstrates how the Jamshid-Mobad connection is far more than an analogy or a case of parallel accounts: it is a spilling over of one story into another, the stubborn persistence of a past that has never quite passed. Desire lies at the heart of this ever-unfolding history, evident in both the fortunes of Mobad the man and in the mythos of divine kingship that he embodies.

Beholding *Mehr*

True to the rhetorical tradition of *barā'at-e estehlāl* ("ingenuity in the opening"), the introductory scene of *Vis & Rāmin* captures a complex entanglement of politics and erotics that will carry on through the entirety of the work and dominate Mobad's fortunes within it.[39] While the Nowruz banquet is a standard set piece for the enunciation of a vertical hierarchy of political authority, particularly in the qasida genre, its appearance in the romantic framework set by *Vis & Rāmin* also creates the perfect *locus amoenus* for love, introducing a horizontal counter-force through which that hierarchy can be turned on its side and renegotiated. We can detect these two vectors at play in the visual "camera work" of the scene: as it enumerates the kings, princes, and heroes who have assembled at Mobad's court, the narrative gaze is compelled to pull back from the figure of the king himself to take in the full panorama of the occasion. Not just Mobad, but "everyone" (*hama kas*, 35/43) has gone out to celebrate, all wearing "crowns" (*afsar*, 35/46), though made of tulips, of their own: "A group taking joy in horse-riding, a group in music and dance, a group drinking wine in the orchard, a group picking flowers in the garden, a group by the river, a group in the tulip-field" (35/47–9). As the scene before us widens in scale, the once-towering figure of Mobad gets lost in the crowd, reduced to merely one of the many revellers at the feast: "the King of Kings had *also* gone out for this purpose" (*shahanshah niz ham rafta bedin kār*, 35/51). This momentary glimpse of an alternative order, flattening the established political hierarchy into a new economy of play and desire, could well serve as a premonition of events to come.

The full integration of love into politics immediately follows suit, with a long list of the beautiful queens, princesses, and noble ladies that parallels the previous catalogue of noblemen, adding weft to the warp as it were: "the idols of China, Turkestan, Byzantium, and Barbary, of violet locks, rosy face, and jasmine-white breast" (*botān-e chin-o tork-o rum-o barbar • banafsha-zolf-o golruy-o saman-bar*, 37/76). As in Hellenistic culture, gazing at beautiful figures – "a kind of copulation at a distance," as *Leukippe & Kleitophon* puts it (183/1.9.4) – was counted a highly erotic activity in medieval Islamic society: "the eyes fornicate" (*al-ʿaynān tazīnān*), writes Hojviri in his *Kashf al-maḥjub* (w. ca. 1065), citing a prophetic hadith.[40] Thus, as the women in this procession strut across the page like models on a catwalk, both the diegetic and extra-diegetic participants in this scene are drawn into a voyeuristic position that borders on the illicit.[41] When Shahru, the queen of Media and fairest of them all (*nekutar bud-o khwashtar*, 37/81), appears at the end of the procession, she outshines her peers with a vivid description of her grace and elegance, just as Mobad shone above his; the king, it seems, has met his match. As such, he immediately takes an interest in her:

به تنهایی مرُو را پیش خود خواند   به سان ماه نو بر گاه بنشاند

به رنگ روی آن حور پری زاد   گل صد برگ یک دسته بدو داد

به ناز و خنده و بازی و خوشّی   بدو گفت ای همه خوبی و گشّی

به گیتی کام راندن با تو نیکوست   تو بایی در برم یا جفت یا دوست

He summoned her to meet him in private, sat her upon the throne like the new moon, gave her a bouquet of roses that matched the colour of that fairy-born houri's face, and said with a smile and a wink, "May you always be gay and joyful! You ought to join my embrace, as wife or as lover, for it would be good to take pleasure in the world with you." (38/3–6 [5])

In this passage, the first thing that may strike the reader attuned to the conventional signs of romantic love is their total absence: Mobad does not cry out as the arrow of love pierces his heart, nor does he fall ill with melancholy as desire disturbs his inner equilibrium. The controlled manner of his proposition instead bespeaks an assured confidence in his position of power; the terms of his offer reinforce its appearance as a contractual exchange of love, objectified and commodified in the currency of beautiful bodies. Yet despite this practised ease, the stakes of this negotiation are suspiciously high. In return for Shahru's partnership – notably with no stipulation of marriage – Mobad will make her the effective power behind the throne: "I shall always be yours to command, just as the world is at my beck and call" (39/8). The material aspect of this offer shines through in subsequent lines as he promises to choose her over all that he has, bequeathing to her his heart, soul, and *property* (*māl*, 39/10). It is a "kingly" offer indeed, one that may appear an overpayment for sex or companionship, no matter how pleasant, especially for a man who presumably has an entire harem at his disposal.

Shahru's response shows that she, too, is perfectly capable of playing the game Mobad has initiated. "O you who obtain all your desires in the world," she protests, "How could I join with a husband, having borne so many children – all of them warriors, captains, and kings?" (39/13, 15–16). Her deferential tone and playful reference to her mature age (while pointedly silent on her marital status) do not fully disguise the underlying message of this rejoinder, a subtle reminder to her audience that she is the matriarch of a large and powerful family, not some small fry to be gobbled up by the king. Nonetheless, we may not be amiss if we also detect a note of desire in Shahru's voice as she veers down memory lane, reminiscing over the many sleepless eyes and broken hearts she left behind in her youth: "My beauty made slaves out of kings," she recalls, perhaps with a wink of her own, "my perfume revived the dead!" (40/24).[42] This flirtatious exchange, unfolding against the established backdrop of the two monarchs' near equivalence, surfaces the interplay of erotics and politics in the world of *Vis & Rāmin*. Within the amatory milieu of the Nowruz banquet, Mobad and Shahru can negotiate power and pleasure alike, forming political bonds through their enjoyment and appreciation of a shared aesthetic sensibility. In this light, the implications of Shahru's desirability to Mobad – and even of Mobad's to Shahru – will come into focus.

To further explore the nature of this complex attraction, negotiated by a subtle thrust-and-parry of words, we might, as we have with Mobad, consider the symbolic implications of Shahru's name. On the surface, it is merely a contraction of her full name, *Shahr-bānu* ("lady of the realm," 37/81), but the shortened form *Shah-ru* ("king-face") introduces a wide range of suggestive connotations. As discussed in the previous chapter, the advent of desire was often thought to occur at the moment of recognition, of seeing something of the self, a "same-kind-ness," within the other, leading to the simultaneous experience of self-alienation, brought about by the realization that the "self" is no longer whole (and indeed never was) and by the obsessive longing for union – for healing the wound – at any cost. Given that Mobad's entire identity has been wrapped in the powerful discursive tradition of universal kingship, his encounter with Shahru suggests that a similar moment of crisis, though in a manner quite different from the codes of romantic love, is now taking place. Mobad knows himself as the bearer of divine authority (the *farr*), yet he nevertheless perceives that same aspect in Shahru's radiant, kingly face, and thereby desires it as his own. As a result, he too experiences – perhaps for the first time – a sensation of *lack*, the loss of self-sufficiency: the thing that he thought was his, and his alone, turns out to be already there, external to his person. It is as though, Jamshid-like, a second sun has risen in the sky.

The meeting of Shahru and Mobad, then, brings out many of the same elements of mutual recognition discussed in the previous chapter, and as I also mentioned, all the narrative cues are in place for the blossoming of love to ensue. However, there is one decisive factor that makes this impossible. Shahru is the one to express it: alas, those halcyon days of her youth are long gone, and to pursue love now, she maintains, would only court disaster; "The world will heap shame and disgrace on anyone old who plays at being young" (*har ān pir-i ke bornāyi nomāyad* • *jahān-ash nang-o rosvāyi fazāyad*, 40/28). This argument, it is worth noting, is in perfect accord with the literary and political wisdom of Gorgāni's day: *Vāmeq & ʿAẕrā*, for example, declares that "the heart of the young man is [the seeker of] love; such talk does not concern the old"; the *Qābus-nāma* concurs, "That a prince in old age should indulge in his passion is a matter of grave concern."[43] By invoking this sage advice, Shahru not only extricates herself from a delicate position, but reaffirms her status as a member of the ruling class, conducting her affairs according to the same standards that her male counterparts should hold themselves to.[44] It is a good reply, a *javāb-e niku* as the narrator says (39/12), and Mobad is rightly pleased with her verbal acumen (40/30).

The implications of this defence, however, are far from innocuous. This is the first hint we are given – and an oblique one at that – that Mobad may be in anything other than the prime of his youth. This little detail severely undercuts the image of Mobad we were fed in the opening pages of *V&R*, which painted for us a classic portrait of the universal sovereign, not merely vigorous but practically *ageless*, in the mould of Jamshid; given the verbosity of the poem's introduction, it is almost as if the text has gone out of its way to bury the issue of Mobad's age before it could surface. While Shahru has suggested, in her diplomatic way, that this might be something of a sticking point, it will take the far more outspoken Vis, upon being summoned to Mobad's court, to state the matter plainly: "Your mind has gone defective in old age" (*ze piri maghz-at āhumand gasht-ast*), she replies, "how could I let go of a young man for one who is old?" (*javān-i rā be pir-i chun konam bāz*, 57/115, 125; she later gives him the unflattering epithet *fartut*, 76/9, which roughly translates as "dotard"). This development introduces a worrying twist to the conventional dynamics of love: for if, returning to Propp, the Villain of the typical love-story is *external* to the lovers – tempests, bandits, recalcitrant parents, and so on – that dynamic gets inverted in the case of Mobad, for whom the only obstacle to his desire turns out to be *himself*, in his aging physical body. This possibility introduced, Mobad finds himself on the brink of turning into his own Villain.

All of these connotations, unarticulated except through the subtle hints of courtly exchange, might help us understand why Mobad proves so insistent on pursuing this relationship, one way or another. Even as he congratulates Shahru for finding so elegant an excuse, he fires back with a surprising counter-offer: if he cannot have her, then he must have her daughter.

کنون گر تو نباشی جفت و یارم   نیارایی به شادی روزگارم

زتخم خویش یک دختر به من ده   به کام دل صنوبر با سمن به

کجا چون تخم باشد بی گمان بر   بود دخت تو مثل تو سمن بر

به نیکی و به شادی در فزایم   که باشد آفتاب اندر سرایم

چو یابم آفتاب مهربانی   نخواهم آفتاب آسمانی

Now if you won't be my mate and lover, and fill my days with joy, give me a daughter of your seed, for it is good for the pine and jasmine to be united in joy. Since the fruit will doubtless resemble the seed, your daughter, like you, will be of jasmine breast. I shall flourish in joy and success when the sunlight is in my abode. When I gain the sunlight of [your] love, I shall not desire the sunlight of the heavens. (40/37–41 [7])

In the previous chapter, I discussed how Mobad's request manipulates, in a seemingly cynical way, the romantic principle of like unto like, in the way it implies that the *image* of the beloved is the real site where the recognition of inner affinity takes place, such that, in this case, Shahru could be swapped with her mirror image with no impact on the relationship. But there is something striking about Mobad's choice of words that suggests that gaming the system is not his final, or only, intention. Three times he refers to Shahru's "sunlight" (*āftāb*) as a beneficial presence that, when brought into his "abode," will sustain and nourish him. The sun, as we know, is strongly associated with the institution of universal monarchy in general, and in particular with its prototypical avatar, Jamshid. The allusion is no accident, for it will later be revealed that Shahru is indeed the direct descendant of the sun king himself.[45] Thus, the thing that Mobad desires in Shahru will also be present in Vis: her royal lineage, the divine light of Jamshid's house that may one day illuminate his own.

This gesture is profoundly unsettling, both for Mobad's public position and his inner psychology. He entered the narrative essentially as the reincarnation of Jamshid, the universal Priest-King/Perfect Man of unbounded dominion.[46] Yet his encounter with Shahru splits that inner self apart: as he beholds the Jamshidian presence in her radiant countenance, he apprehends the reality that he is not actually his self-image and must now struggle, in the manner of a romance lover, to close the gap, to get that image back through union with it. The problem with this, and what makes it different from a romantic encounter, is that the whole point of the universal monarch is that there can be only one, not two; recognizing himself in another destabilizes the fundamental core of that identity. This upset instigates some potentially radical renegotiations of both power and gender between the two monarchs, some of which are suggested even in this initial passage. Mobad's request for Shahru's sunlight places her in an elevated position as the "sun" above him, anticipating the way she will later scoff at the need for a priest (*mobad*) to officiate the marriage of Vis and Viru (50/25–35 [19]) and threaten to overthrow Mobad after he has apparently killed her daughter (273/51–121 [238–41]). His expressed desire for her "seed" (*tokhm*), furthermore, subtly casts him in the passive role as the seed's recipient, the soil in which it will be planted – a role that was typically associated with the female in Aristotelian and Avicennan theory.[47] These are only hints, of course, but they seem to foreshadow Mobad's physical impotence and, more importantly, to underscore the many complaints of helplessness and emasculation (e.g., "What man am I, who cannot overcome a woman?" 290/27) he will express throughout *Vis & Rāmin*.

The main takeaway, in the end, is this: the exchange between Shahru and Mobad, though depicted in a way intended to declare Mobad's royal authority over all others, simultaneously makes visible the tenuousness of that authority. He emerges from this encounter far less in control of the scene than he would like his vassals – or his readers – to believe: less a master of, and rather subject to, a range of external discursive forces that both make and unmake his kingly persona. It also places him in the middle of a paradox: the scene shows how kingship constitutes itself as an embodiment of *mehr* – bringing together the Persian word's superficially disparate meanings of "sun," "covenant," and "desire" – such that it is no longer a static "thing" within the sovereign but rather external to and desired by him, even while insisting that he must refrain from desiring, at least (and especially) as he enters old age. Mobad's claim to Jamshidian power thus puts him at the edge of a precipice from which the slightest slip could send him tumbling; indeed, if he were to most faithfully follow the footsteps of his mythic counterpart, that slip would be self-inflicted: a product of his own desire.

The Sacred Bond

I would like to explore this theme further through the mechanism of the covenant (*paymān*) between Mobad and Shahru, sealed by an exchange of solemn oaths (*sowgand*) and a contract (*ʿahd*) on painted silk (41/49–51). The narrator strongly reacts to this artifact, describing it as a "trap" (*dām*) set by the faithless world to ensnare the unsuspecting king: "Wisdom did not reveal to him the secret that his doom would be born from the mother" (42/3–5). There is, however, a profound irony in this depiction, given that the contract is, in its own way, the very thing that gives Mobad his authority in the first place.

We can explore this paradox by considering the relationship the text sets up between the contract, the trap, and the motif of the *band* (cognate to the English words "bond," "band," and "bound") that dominates Mobad's story. The bond is a device that both empowers and limits: while the bonds of friendship join people together, and the bonds of loyalty ensure communal and political stability, these benefits come with the loss of a certain amount of individual freedom.[48] Such give-and-take dynamics pervade any kind of social relation, but they play an especially vital role in Mobad's case, due to the unique relationship between kingship and justice in Persianate political theory. We see this connection succinctly illustrated in the *Kutadgu Bilig*, when King Rising Sun informs his vizier, "Know then that I am Justice ... for justice is the foundation-stone of sovereignty."[49] The King, in other words, is Justice embodied; for him to break his word (his bond) would countermand his social function and disrupt his claim to rule.[50] The contract is thus a symptom of Mobad's desire to be obeyed; it announces his entry into the symbolic order of kingship. Through the exchange, he claims the authority to rule as King, but he also gives up his autonomy, being now ruled by the sublime Kingly body he claims for himself (but which is not, in fact, his). It is exactly along these lines that Mobad, in entering a contract with Shahru, both claims his authority over Vis and becomes subject to that authority.

Let me elaborate on this further, taking into account the dual position of the king as both servant and embodiment of divine justice. When Mobad sends his emissary Zard to fetch Vis from her mother, he includes in his message an emphatic exhortation to righteousness (*rāsti*), couched in a conspicuous invocation of God and His will.

سر نامه به نام دادگر بود   خدایی کاو همیشه داد فرمود

دو گیتی را نهاد از راستی کرد   به یک موی اندران کژّی نیاورد

چنان کز راستی گیتی بیاراست   ز مردم نیز داد و راستی خواست

کسی کز راستی جوید فزونی   کند پیروزی او را رهنمونی

به گیتی کیمیا جز راستی نیست   که عزّ راستی را کاستی نیست

من از تو راستی خواهم که جویی   همیشه راستی ورزی و گویی

The name of the Judge was at the head of the letter, the Lord who always
ordains justice: "He made righteousness the foundation of the two worlds,
bringing in not a hair of crookedness. Just as he adorned the world in
justice, so too he sought justice and righteousness from mankind. He who
seeks excess in righteousness will have success as his guide. There is no
alchemy in the world save righteousness, for there is no deficiency in the
glory of righteousness. It is righteousness that I ask you to seek; that righteousness you always practice and speak." (53/37–42 [21])

The steady repetition of the terms "justice" and "righteousness" in this
passage points to the united roles of Priest and King envisioned in the
myth of universal kingship, insisting that to obey the king and honour the terms of the contract is to follow the righteous path that God
demands of His followers. Indeed, Mobad opines that the miraculous
birth of Vis, thirty years after the compact was made, is a clear sign of
his divine support: "God has upheld my hopes; with this contract, he
has made my desire licit" (*kojā yazdān omid-am rā vafā kard* • *bedin pay-
vand kām-am rā ravā kard*, 53/50, cf. also 85/14). He will frequently refer
to the contract's authority in this manner to validate his actions, posi-
tioning himself as the wronged party who is bound – not by his will,
but by God's – to seek and execute redress on behalf of the divine: "you
cannot escape the bonds of the heavens, the fate that God has spun for
you" (*ke natvāni ze band-e charkh jastan* • *ze taqdir-i ke yazdān kard rastan*,
75/19 [40]), or later, "remember the Judge's court, the terror of Hell, the
recompense of God" (*be yād āvar ze dāvargāh-e dādār* • *ze howl-e dozakh-o
farjām-e kerdār*, 84/6 [48]).

Thus we behold the king's entry into the symbolic. He has poured his
authority into the agreement, such that it is now an extension or pros-
thesis of himself: an attack on the contract is an attack on the king.[51] But
this symbolic objectification of the self, turning it into a kind of material commodity, comes with interesting and perhaps unexpected consequences. Even as the contract grants Mobad authority over Shahru,
it externalizes that authority and subjects him to its rule at the same
time. That is to say, the extent of Mobad's power will now be measured
by his ability to uphold and defend the contract, making him entirely

dependent on its enforcement; as King Rising Sun puts it, "What kind of ruler would I be if my wish went unfulfilled and if none of my commands were carried out?"[52] This places the ruler on a slippery slope: as Ernst Kantorowicz has shown, the symbolic authority invested into institutional mechanisms of kingship, such as oaths, treaties, and ritual practice, could become so powerful that they allowed a king's foes to claim that they were in fact defending the symbolic King from his human representative – "the king body natural becomes a traitor to the king body politic" – saving him from himself, so to speak, by removing him from power.[53]

The symbolic extension of power is not limited to the contract alone, for the object of that contract, by proximity, will also receive a share of that infusion of kingly authority. In this case, it is the person of Vis: now that Mobad has invested his power into the right to claim and possess her, she too becomes a signifier of that power and a manifestation of its triumph (or failure). If she abides by the contract and marries him, she will visibly display the efficacy of his authority; but if she refuses or defies him, that will carry the opposite effect, manifesting the limits of his power in the visible world. Mobad has thus incorporated Vis into the apparatus of his kingship and made her its most critical cornerstone. As king, he *must* pursue Vis's love – the very act that, as an old man, he should *not* be doing.

This unhappy misalignment of Mobad's physical and symbolic bodies sets off an explosive chain reaction. Zard speeds back to Marv, bursting into the court in a cloud of dust, an entrance so dramatic one might suppose that some army has descended upon the capital. And, in a way, it has: after the usual benedictions upon his liege (including the conspicuous prayer that he "bind the demons, like Jamshid," 60/152 [27]), Zard cuts right to the chase, informing Mobad that Shahru has broken the covenant and given Vis to Viru instead, an act he portrays as nothing less than open rebellion, saying that the people of Media now recognize only Viru as their king (61/170–4). Hearing this, the noblemen in attendance join in the outrage, gnashing their teeth and promising each other that Mobad's retribution will be swift and terrible: "Fate has rung the death-knell upon all who live there, now that the property of one is now another's!" (64/31). The king, meanwhile, remains pointedly silent, "bent and burning in the fires of anxious thought" (*shāhanshah zamān-i bud pichān • del andar ātash-e andisha suzān*, 64/34). He may well have realized that he, the king, has been stripped of all choice: he must either act as his nobles expect him to or lose their loyalty and thence his kingship. And so, like it or not, he marches his army to Media, facing the highly unlikely gamble that waging war on Vis's family will somehow win her over to him.

This new reality receives dramatic illustration when the armies of
Khorasan and Media collide on the plains of Dinavar. The battle scene
teems with references to the original Nowruz banquet where Mobad
declared his universal kingship, a once-bounteous land now stricken
with blight. The munificent rain clouds thunder with the promise of
war, while the joyful tunes of the minstrels and nightingales give way to
the blare of fife and trumpet; the musky incense that filled the air is now
ash and smoke; the season is no longer the time of love and rebirth but
instead the age of war and destruction. The gruesome metamorphosis
continues as men die in the embrace of the defiled earth:

خدنگ چارپر همچون درختان   برُسته از دو چشم شوربختان
درخت زندگانی رسته از تن   به پیشش پرده گشته خود و جوشن
چو خنجر پرده را بر تن بدرّید   درخت زندگانی را ببرّید
هوا از نیزه گشته چون نیستان   زمین از خون مردم چون میستان

> Four-feathered arrows of white poplar sprouted like trees out of luck-
> less eyes; the tree of life grew from the body, cloaked by helmet and mail.
> When the dagger rent the cloak from the body, it felled the tree of life. The
> air became a reed-bed of spears; the earth became a wine-cellar of men's
> blood. (71/84–7 [35])[54]

In her analysis of this scene, Meisami is quite right to read these images
as a signal that Mobad's legitimacy is on the wane, a consequence of
Mobad's "unjust war" against the ostensibly vassal kingdom of Media.[55]
Unjust is undoubtedly how the Medes perceive his actions, and so too
the world at large, it seems, having collectively "lost hope of his *farr*"
(*jahān az farr-e u bobrid ommid*, 72/93). But it is crucial to stress that this
injustice is, at one and the same time, an expression of *justice*. As we have
seen, the text has gone to great lengths to show how Mobad understands
himself within the discursive system of divine sovereignty, in which
he stands as the bearer of a sacred office and executor of God's justice
upon the land. From that standpoint, the contract has been violated,
his authority has been challenged, and the only "right" thing to do, as
Mobad's nobles so forcefully expressed, is to bring the oath breakers
to justice. Paradoxically, then, Mobad's loss of authority is a product of
that very authority: rather than "use it or lose it," as the saying goes,
the exercise of kingly power here seems to effect its own disintegration.
Something doesn't add up here; we are left with a sense that the king is
a patsy somehow, that the text has rushed to declare him guilty of injustice before we can realize the underlying illogic of his situation. When
carefully examined, the simple narrative that Mobad has brought ruin

to the garden of kingship may not prove so tenable; the blight, perhaps, was there all along.

The Iron Band

So far, I have concentrated on the way Mobad's symbolic personhood – his performative persona as universal king, in the mould of Jamshid – gains control over his personal agency, jerking him about like a marionette on invisible strings. (Gabrieli's comparison of *V&R*'s characters to "puppets" is quite germane in that regard, though not in the way he meant it.)[56] I now turn to the physical constraints that block him from his desire, in what is perhaps one of the most famous aspects of his character: the iron band that "binds" (*bandad*) his "manhood" (*mardi*, 110/16). According to Meisami, this is a symbol that "figures his moral incapacity, as it identifies his confusion of love, and of the lover's goal, with concupiscence: the physical possession of the beloved."[57] While I am fully on board for taking both the material and semiotic aspects of the talisman into consideration, I might suggest a slight rephrasing of this interpretation, so that it is not so much about his "moral incapacity" (which I do not perceive, at least not when reading the story from his perspective), but rather the *moral questions that arise in the face of incapacity*: the confrontation, in other words, with the limits of the physical body, with old age, and with death.

The critical scene takes place shortly after Mobad has captured Vis from Gurab and brought her to his palace. Although, as Vis acknowledges, he has made no sexual advances towards her, she cannot afford to let him change his mind, and so orders her Nurse to "do some trick" (*yek-i nayrang sāz*, 110/16) to keep things that way; else, she will commit suicide on the spot. Muttering that the army of some "demon sorcerer" (*div-e jādu*, 110/28) must have invaded Vis's heart, the Nurse fashions a charm of copper and brass, binds it with an iron clasp, and buries it by the side of the Murghab River, leaving a mark at the site. (The Georgian *Visramiani*, by the way, adds some interesting details about the Nurse's talisman, which are worth a look: "Then the nurse took copper and bone, and with some sort of enchantment made a talisman; two in the likeness of Moabad, and one of Vis; she uttered some charm, firmly welded them one upon another with iron ... These two bonds were made in such a manner that as long as they were welded together, Moabad should be bound with regard to Vis, and if anyone undid these, at that moment he [Moabad] would be unbound."[58] Though it is not found within the Persian text, I am struck by the theme of doubling in this passage, in the way the talisman explicitly represents two kingly figures, the mortal and the symbolic, such that the "binding" of the latter to Vis simultaneously "binds" the former from her.)[59] "I've done what you ordered," the Nurse announces on her return, "on the condition that when a month has passed, your evil fortune comes to an end" (111/40–1); at that time, she plans to destroy the talisman, rekindle the king's desire, and ensure that the married couple will finally have joy of each other.

But such was not meant to be. In a bizarre twist of fortune, the river suddenly rises in a great flood, washing away the bank, the mark, and the talisman itself, leaving Mobad forever bound in a state of magically induced impotence. The narrator comments on this newfound condition with a good deal of sympathy, comparing Mobad to a beggar watching wealthy people walk by, or a chained lion observing prey it cannot catch, but it is the final phrase of this aside – "You'd say his skin was a prison on his body" (*cho zendān bud gofti bar tan-ash pust*, 112/60 [75]) – that is the most poignant. Mobad's self-entrapment captures the unsettling recognition that we are all, in a sense, prisoners of the bodies we are born into – bodies that drive a wedge between us and our self-image, even as they make our image visible – recasting the Nurse's talisman into a powerful metaphor about the rupture between physical and symbolic selves that, I would contend, is a driving thematic in *Vis & Rāmin* as a whole. While forms of bodily alienation can occur around many aspects of identity, Mobad's struggle revolves around two points that lie at the extremes of human particularity and universality: his status as the King of Kings, ostensibly marking him as one of a kind, and his status as an old man, placing him under the same process of aging and death that all must undergo. Reconciling these two positions generates an exceptional amount of tension within his character: for a man whose entire identity is constituted by the timeless imagery of the universal king, as the sun that "never wanes but is always full," whose house "never falls to ruin," to realize its impossibility – that it is, essentially, a *myth* – produces a profound moment of reckoning with a selfhood whose integrity, even as (and possibly *because*) he contemplates it, starts to unravel before his very eyes.

The motif of self-entrapment that runs through Mobad's story casts the mythos of kingship in a very different light than its more celebratory accounts; for an instructive comparison, we can return again to the *Bahman-nāma*. Much like Mobad, Bahman discovers that his wife, Katāyun, has hatched a plot to overthrow him in concert with her lover, Loʾloʾ, who, like Rāmin to Vis, is also her milk-brother. Bahman meets this threat head-on, waging war against the rebellious army and exiling its leader; he reserves his worst punishment, though, for his treacherous wife, whom he has stripped, drawn, and quartered, throwing the remains of her corpse to the dogs (179/2840–5). Mobad makes an interesting contrast to Bahman: though he seems eager to project himself as adhering to a similar ethics, he consistently pulls back from its most violent implications. When he first learns of the affair, for example, his first move is not to directly punish Vis, but to ask Viru to discipline (*befarhang*) her on his behalf, framing it as an act of mercy: "Were I forced to discipline them," he explains, "I would do damage beyond measure: I would burn Vis's eyes with fire, crucify the Nurse, and drive Rāmin from my city, never to speak his name again!" (169/36–40 [133]). This is virtually the same course of action Bahman carried out, suggesting that there is a shared ethos between the two texts around the kingly, or manly, way to respond to adultery; yet Mobad, while saying he would follow it, rarely does so in practice.[60]

Why this hesitation? It may signal Mobad's love for Vis, such that he cannot bear the thought of punishing her as protocol demands. Or it might evince a more cynical view that Vis, as the scion of the line of Jamshid, is only useful to him alive and in one piece: while he might assuage his wounded honour by maiming or killing her, he would ultimately deprive himself of the sublime kingship he seeks for his own. But on top of these equally plausible explanations falls a crushing, if mundane, reality: where Bahman was young, Mobad is old, and impotent to boot. The stark implications of this fact emerge in a conversation between Mobad and his mother, in which, having admitted that Rāmin will continue to cuckold him under his nose, the king concludes that he must kill the two lovers if he is ever to salvage his kingship:

نگه کن تا پسند هیچ هشیار   مرو را گفت نیکو باشد این کار

کند بدنام بر من گاه شاهی   که رامین با زنم جوید تباهی

چه باشد در جهان زین ننگ بدتر   یکی زن چون بود با دو برادر

ازیرا کردم این راز آشکارا   دلم یکباره بر گشت از مدارا

چو بیچاره شدم با تو بگفتم   من این ننگ از تو بسیاری نهفتم

He said to her, "Can this be right? What sensible man could allow Rāmin to court destruction with my wife and dishonour my royal position? How can two brothers share one woman? What shame could be worse? My heart has completely turned away from leniency, which is why I am revealing this secret. I've long hidden this shame from you, but now that I have no choice, I'm telling you." (189/7–11 [151])

As Mobad is careful to emphasize, this is a matter in which he has "no choice"; regardless of his personal feelings towards Rāmin, his "royal position" (*gāh-e shāhi*) must call the shots, thereby turning the odious crime of fratricide into a legitimate and indeed the only "sensible" course of action open to him.[61] But his mother, appalled at the prospect, quickly supplies a counter-argument. "No sensible man would cut off his own two hands!" (189/16), she retorts, reminding Mobad that he is old, infertile, and childless; if the royal line is to survive, Rāmin must live. The king thus finds himself caught between a rock and a hard place, in which the "sensible" demands of kingship point in contrary but equally self-destructive directions: either he kills Rāmin and terminates the dynasty, or lets Rāmin live at the cost of his office (and most likely his life).[62] Either way, he commits a kind of suicide – a "senseless" act that is, at the same time, the only "sane" thing to do.

This troubling paradox stems from what Kantorowicz has theorized as the "doubled" body, or *gemina persona*, of the king: a mortal man who embodies immortality; the image (simile) and the servant (executive) of God; the binder of the Law and the one bound to it.[63] The problem for Mobad is that his symbolic authority is now too far invested in Vis, who categorically dissociates herself from his mortal body by dint of his old age: in this process, he has not been doubled so much as split, the two aspects of his identity fundamentally estranged from one another. These inherent tensions, however, are invisible to the naked eye, especially Mobad's. Too deeply buried within – or constructed by – the common-sense tautology of kingship, which holds that a king *should* be in a position to do what he likes, Mobad can only sense the presence of these conflicting pressures; but it would be absurd, from his perspective, to suggest that there is something about his power that makes him powerless. All he knows is that he has been wronged, but every effort to do his job and implement justice circles round like a boomerang and hits him instead.[64] His attempts to make sense of this impasse raise questions about the nature of power, probe the categories of truth and falsehood that supposedly allow his justice to function, and conclude with a dramatic crisis brought about by the loss of that clarity.

Un/knowing the Truth

The question of "knowing" the truth, and the repercussions that it has for decisive action, receives detailed treatment in two stories I would like to mention by way of comparison. In a famous episode of the *Shāhnāma*, the king Kay Kāvus faces a tough decision when his wife Sudāba comes to him claiming she was raped by his son, Siyāvash, while his son protests that this is a false accusation in revenge for his rejection of her advances – a version of the famous Joseph and Potiphar's Wife motif.[65] These contrary assertions put the king in a position similar to Mobad's, for if Sudāba's accusation is true, he must kill his son, and if it is false, he must kill his wife (2:225/340, 368). Given the seriousness of the matter, Kāvus is under enormous pressure to do *something*, yet any action he takes will necessarily entail the loss of something precious to him; as one of his advisors warns him, "If you want to find [the source of] this talk, you'll have to smash the jug with a stone" (*cho khwāhi ke payda koni goft-o guy • bebāyad zadan sang rā bar sabuy*, 2:232/451). Eventually, Kāvus decides to subject his son to an ordeal by fire, in a half-hearted attempt to deflect the responsibility of judgment onto another entity.

A similar dilemma appears in the tale of *Tristan & Isolde*. When King Mark is confronted with the seemingly damning evidence of Tristan's blood on his bedclothes, he struggles to accept it as the final proof of his nephew's affair with Isolde, retreating instead into a state of wilful uncertainty that receives eloquent description by Gottfried von Strassburg:

> He believed one thing, he believed another. He did not know what he wanted or what he should believe. He had just found Love's guilty traces in his bed, though not before it, and was thus told the truth and denied it. With these two, truth and untruth, he was deceived. He suspected both alternatives, yet both eluded him. He neither wished the two of them guilty, nor wished them free of guilt. (15250–70 [Hatto 242])[66]

Such self-imposed ignorance, of course, cannot fix the structural fault at work in both cases, but merely provides both kings with the temporary survival technique of delayed judgment. (Mark, too, resorts to subjecting Isolde to an ordeal that, thanks to an ingenious trick on her part, buys them both some time.) Although Siyāvash survives the ordeal, Kāvus's subjects nevertheless curse Kāvus as an unjust tyrant for arranging it (2:236/498 [Davis 226]). King Mark, this time in Béroul's account, faces a similar crisis: he knows there will be "serious trouble" (*grant luite*, 54/1118) if he punishes Tristan and Isolde for their affair, but, as one man tells him, "if you do not now take cruel vengeance, you have no rightful claim on this land" (90/1903–4), and the barons who currently support him will revolt (29/583–8, 619–24). This leaves him with only one other exit, and an ironic one at that: "Unless I drive them out of my land, the villains [i.e., his own barons] will no longer fear my power" (150/3189–90). Both kings thus find themselves in the paradoxical position in which they must undermine or destroy their power to prove they ever had it – to "smash the jug," as it were – and although they opt for different solutions, they arrive at the same self-destructive result.

These examples demonstrate how the aura of sovereign power is in some ways susceptible to the same "observer effect" described in physics: as soon as it is measured, tested, or otherwise probed, it changes and risks falling apart. They expose, in other words, the lying dimension of the kingship myth. Like other mythoi studied in this book, the story of the universal king is very good at hiding its own counterfeits, at presenting an image of the world *as though* it were natural and real; yet, as Slavoj Žižek puts it, "if we come to 'know too much,' to pierce the true functioning of social reality, this reality would dissolve itself."[67] Mobad's existence is so bound up with this false reality that he can neither escape nor confront it – for both would be a form of suicide – yet he can sense, like Kāvus and Mark do, that any exercise of his power will paradoxically result in its loss. His only hope, then, lies in maintaining the dual practice of un/knowing the world around him: of seeing and suppressing what he sees, of miming the decisive actions that certainty requires. Examples of this practice are scattered across *V&R*, especially in Mobad's dealings with his wife and brother: the way he overhears – but pretends he didn't – their secretive whispers during his drinking party (221/50 [183]), or when he symbolically cuts off a lock of Vis's hair in his garden instead of killing her as he originally swore to do (297/141 [262]). However, there are two cases that are especially useful for unpacking the political and personal ramifications of un/knowing that I will explore below.

The first case occurs in the immediate aftermath of Mobad's conversation with his mother. After convincing the king that killing Rāmin will not resolve his problem, she redirects his ire towards the exogenous Others in his life, Vis and Viru, claiming that it is they who have rebelled against his authority. Presented with this easy out, Mobad leaps into action, writing a ferocious letter to Viru in which he threatens to invade Media again if he doesn't give up his claim on Vis once and for all. Conspiratorial language pervades the letter's opening: "Who commanded you to pursue injustice (*bidād*) and seek power over me? Who's your refuge? Who's behind you?" (191/48–9 [154]). This flurry of accusations leaves Viru nonplussed; he puts down the letter and asks aloud, "Who is he angry with? He placed my sister within his harem, then kicked her out in the middle of winter. It was he who struck, then he who cried foul: indeed, he's the one who's shown two kinds of injustice!" (194/98–100). Significant here in this confused pointing of fingers is the lack of clarity: Mobad seems unable to believe that Viru could really be the leader of this imagined rebellion, while Viru perceives a deranged monarch injuring himself and then pinning the blame on his subjects. Both sides go back on high alert, and war nearly breaks out again, until Mobad, realizing the mortal danger that this puts him in, finally backpedals and – fulfilling Viru's perception – blames his advisors for misleading him, again with the telling keyword: "I did not know they were committing injustice!" (*bidād*, 197/48).[68] Ironically, as a result of his attempt to locate and then to crush the source of his injustice, Mobad nearly instigates an actual revolt, and throws his own partisans under the bus in the process; every attempt to clarify the picture only seems to drag him down further. As a result, we may begin to speculate that the "enemy" that Mobad faces cannot be externalized as an outside threat: the maleficent forces working against him seem to originate from within the very institution that he embodies.

The consequences of knowing too much are not limited to the political domain, but spill over into Mobad's sense of self. After mending fences with Viru, but still stinging from his embarrassing retraction, the king privately admonishes Vis with the complaint that if it weren't for his brother, she'd have no cause to leave him. Of course, as we know from chapter 2, this is not at all true, and Vis counters his admonishment by bringing back the "twins" motif that played such a crucial role in her story. Describing Rāmin and Viru as brothers, with Shahru as their mother (199/19), Vis splits the identity of her lover into two near-identical figures and challenges Mobad to determine once and for all which one is the source of his displeasure: "Sometimes you say, 'Viru was with you,' and fault me for having seen him, while sometimes you say, 'Rāmin was with you'; why do you blame me so?" (199/7–8). Having once again shaken Mobad's confidence in his knowledge, Vis volunteers to swear an oath before the sacred fire attesting to her innocence, to which the king, still longing to "release his heart from the bonds of doubt" (*band-e gomāni*, 208/168), readily agrees.

This is the famous ordeal episode that many scholars have compared with the story of Tristan and Isolde, and although the motif is found beyond that one pairing, the comparison here is apt in that the kings in both tales organize the ritual in the hope that it will restore their authority.[69] True to form, Mobad's attempt produces the opposite of its intended effect. On the appointed evening, he assembles the priests, officials, and officers of his court to witness the event, but even as he does so, Vis, Rāmin, and the Nurse flee the city, leaving him alone – the pyre burning but no one to pass through it – and more humiliated than ever. This drives the king into a frenzy: handing his entire kingship (*shāhi sarāsar*, 208/2) over to Zard, he takes to the wilderness, hunting high and low for Vis, chanting her name as though it were a mantra. (Such a total withdrawal from politics for the sake of love, as the tale of Bahrām Gur in the *Shāhnāma* reminds us, is seldom an appropriate

move.)[70] As he roams the landscape, Mobad blames love for dragging
him to these depths:

همی گفتی دریغا روزگارم   سپاه و گنج و رخت بی شمارم

ز بهر دل سراسر برفشاندم   کنون بی شاهی و بی دل بماندم

به پیری گر نبودی عشق شایست   مرا این عشق با این غم چه بایست

بدین غم طفل گردد پیر دلگیر   نگر چون زار گردد مردم پیر

بهشتی را ز گیتی برگزیدم   که با هجران او دوزخ بدیدم

ز پیش عاشقی بودم توانا   به کار خویشتن بینا و دانا

کنون در عاشقی بس ناتوانم   چنان گشتم که گر بینم ندانم

He said, "Alas for my fate! I have scattered my innumerable soldiers, treasures, and belongings to the winds for the sake of my heart, and now I've
lost both my heart and my kingship ... Even if love in old age is not a
seemly thing, why must this love of mine come with this pain? This duress
would turn a child into a dejected old man; look, then, at how wretched
it's made an old man! I chose a creature of Paradise from the world, such
that in her absence, I see only Hell ... Before I became I lover, I was capable, both wise and perceptive in my affairs. Now, as a lover, I have become
totally incapable, such that even if I see, I do not perceive." (209/19–20,
27–9, 33–4 [172])

Mobad's self-diagnosis certainly accords with the common-sense
understanding of love as a destructive force that addles the brain
and turns kings into slaves, and as such, it provides him with a last
resort in his ongoing search to know the source of his failure: as
Rāmin and Viru have both been tried and discarded, he can at least
accept the dignity of being laid low by a force too powerful for any
man, even the King of Kings, to conquer. The story of losing it all for
the sake of love is indeed a mythos that offers some kind of redemption for its protagonists, most famously in the figure of Majnun, the
"madman" persona that Mobad is now taking on with his obsessive
wandering.

And yet beyond the apparent similarities of these two characters –
at least for this moment in the story of *V&R* – there lies a fundamental difference. Majnun's desire is directed towards an external object,
and ostensibly, Mobad's is too; just as Majnun fell abject and eventually disintegrated in his love for Laylā, Mobad seems to be doing
the same in his love for Vis. But Vis, as we have seen, was theorized
("beheld") by Mobad as a double of Shahru, who, as the descendant
of Jamshid, is in turn a reflection of his *image of himself*. Therefore,
while an initial reading of this scene might suggest that Mobad is so

stricken by love that he no longer cares about his kingship, I would argue that the distinction of love and kingship here is itself a false one: Vis *is* his kingship, the substance of his sublime authority and the mirror that makes it manifest.[71] His abandonment of the material trappings of authority suggests that he is once again experiencing something of a gap between its mundane aspects and the sublime reality behind it, such that Vis is the only thing "real" about his power – all else is temporary, ephemeral, and ultimately meaningless. This possibility may help us consider Mobad's obsession with Vis as something beyond the concupiscent force of passionate desire; it emerges out of his very sense of self and expresses an ongoing search for the "Real-Truth" (as Shahab Ahmed glosses the word *ḥaqīqa*) that is simultaneously part of and external to his divinely invested body.[72]

It is precisely here that the self becomes its own adversary. Returning to the passage above, we can see that a central theme of Mobad's lament is his old age, a condition that automatically forecloses any possibility of union with Vis, and thereby the consummation of his kingship: she is as unattainable as eternal youth. Thus, Mobad's search for the transcendent and undying Jamshidian sovereignty that he apprehends in her angelic features inevitably instigates and then exacerbates his separation from it, and he experiences instead a sense of imprisonment by and from within his own skin – to revisit the narrator's phrase – that both bars him from Paradise and traps him in Hell. Yet although he has confronted the source of his problems (the self), he cannot ultimately "know" it, as knowledge entails action, and any action, for him, entails suicide (self-destruction). His state of perpetual un/knowledge, such that "even if I see, I do not perceive," is thus not only a strategy for continued political existence but is also expressive of a fundamental limit in his capacity for self-knowledge – a kind of existential blind spot, as it were.

I suggest that desire resides at the heart of this blind spot. As we have already seen, sovereignty is not something Mobad simply "has," as though it were part of his body; it is acquired and maintained through an act of will. Yet it must present itself *as if* it were innate and inherent, blinding itself to its own founding impulse, for how else could it retain its transcendental claims? Mobad's confrontation with his aging body as the chief obstacle of his self-fulfilment has already brought him to the verge of exposing the myth of his authority, but it is his mother, understandably concerned at her son's relentless decline, who gets to the heart of the problem in the following exchange:

به پیری هر کسی نیکی فزایند   کجا از خواب برنایی در آیند
دگر بر راه ناخوبی نپویند   ز پیری کام برنایی نجویند

کجا پیریش باشد سخترین بند   همان موی سپیدش بهترین پند
ترا تا پیر گشتی آز بیش است   دلم زین آز تو بسیار ریش است

Goodness increases for everyone in their old age, for they have emerged
from the slumber of youth. They pursue no longer this evil road, and seek
not the joys of youth in old age, for old age is their strongest constraint,
and white hair their best guidance. Your desire (*āz*) has grown since
you've become old; my heart is quite wounded by this greed (*āz*) of yours.
(214/53–6 [176])

What distresses Mobad's mother here is that the normative relationship
between age and desire has been somehow flipped in Mobad, resulting in a trajectory diametrically opposed to the "natural" process. She
tellingly describes old age as a kind of constraint – a *band*, the same
word that describes Mobad's impotence – as a *positive* influence that
directs people towards the good. By restraining, reducing, and ultimately destroying worldly desires, the constraint of old age ideally acts
as a device that both liberates and ennobles: in freeing people from the
world, it confers a form of sovereignty.[73] But what she fails to recognize
in this account is the inseparable link between power and desire, such
that Mobad's love for Vis is concurrently the articulation of his kingship
and the expression of his very self. Old age cannot stymie this desire,
and actually seems to increase it, for the further Mobad sees himself
pulled away from his self-image, the more his longing for it intensifies.
Mobad's bondage, then, is not liberating but crucifying, keeping him
simultaneously and irreconcilably bound *to* Vis by his desire for kingship, materialized in the sacred bond, and bounded *from* her by the
iron band, the curse of impotence that, in the end, seems to signify the
inexorable reality of aging and death.

To read Mobad's desire as one originating from and expressive of
the self bears important implications for the use of the word *āz* in this
passage, a word that, as discussed earlier, both invokes the name of the
ancient demon of insatiable desire and evokes the rapacious greed of
the serpent-king Żaḥḥāk. By reconfiguring *āz* from an external force
to an internal and even self-generated presence, *V&R* grants it a conceptual correspondence with the Islamic notion of the "commanding
soul" (*al-nafs al-ʿammāra*, cf. Qur'an 12:53), comparable to the "animal
soul" (*al-nafs al-ḥayawāniyya*) in Avicenna's terminology.[74] This animate faculty, in contradistinction to Avicenna's "articulate soul" (*al-
nafs al-nāṭiqa*) – which Gorgāni describes as both the "speaking soul"
(*nafs-e guyā*) and the "holy spirit" (*ruḥ-e qodsā*, 6/80) that God bestowed
on humankind – is notorious for its ability to mis-recognize worldly

pleasures as the ultimate good, standing in the way of attaining what it truly desires.[75] This new conceptualization of *āz*, which I think has analogues in the *Shahnāma*, thus produces in the tale of Mobad a much more radical version of the Jamshid myth: no longer a warning against kingly hubris, but against the hubris of kingship itself.[76] It also offers an account of desire that unfolds along the opposite trajectory of the classical model: instead of love entering from outside and disturbing the mind, the mind projects its desire outwards and is disturbed by what it sees. We will observe the grim consequences of this destabilization in the climactic scene that follows.

Smashing the Mirror

One of the most striking features about Mobad's character throughout *V&R* is that, for the most part, he abstains from exercising the violence that is the prerogative of his kingship. This stands in stark contrast not only with comparable examples in epics such as the *Bahman-nāma*, but even with *V&R* itself, whose story is framed by an extensive panegyric to the ascendant king of Gorgāni's era, the Seljuk sultan Ṭughrıl Beg. Like Mobad, Gorgāni presents Ṭughrıl in the familiar role of the universal sovereign, whose unification of religious and political authority is emphasized by his Muslim name, Muḥammad: "He appeared out of the east, just like the sun; he obtained the dominion of the King of Kings, just like Jamshid" (10/11–12). As such, Ṭughrıl and Mobad provide useful parallel performances for comparison and contrast.[77]

Especially informative is Ṭughrıl's exercise of power and violence, which gets a strikingly detailed exposition during his conquest of Isfahan. Gorgāni begins his account with the declaration that, had the sultan not been "exceptionally just" (*sakht ʿādel*), he would have not left a brick of Isfahan standing (18/4–5), backing this with a citation from the Qur'an (27:34, on the story of Solomon, no less) that claims that when kings enter a city, they despoil it (19/10). Instead, Ṭughrıl instituted a "better way" (*rasm-i nekutar*, 19/12), favouring his former enemies with gifts, lands, and high positions. These munificent acts, however, are couched in language thick with violent overtones: even as he rewarded those who submitted to his rule, Ṭughrıl "ground their crimes under his foot, so that none would complain of his anger" (18/7), and "cleansed the city of ill-wishers" (19/17). In one instance,

گروهی را به مردم می سپردند رعیت را به دیوان غمز کردند

به فرمانش زبانهاشان بریدند به دیده میل سوزان درکشیدند

پس آنگه رنج خویش از شهر برداشت   برفت و شهر بی آشوب بگذاشت
بدان تا رنج او بر کس نباشد   که با آن رنج مردم بس نباشد

There was a group treading over the people, libelling the populace in the
tax records. On his order, their tongues were cut out and their eyes pierced
with red-hot needles. After that, he removed his molestation (*ranj*) from
the city, leaving it in peace, so that his *ranj* would afflict no one: it would
have been too much for the people [to withstand]. (19/18–21)

The main point to extract from this episode is that violence, when
wielded by a king, is not only *justified* but indeed *required* as an expression of the king's justice. In the domestic sphere, it is easily compared
with Bahman's brutal dismembering of his wife, or with the way the
king Nushin-Ravān executes one of the women of his harem by hang-
ing both her and her lover upside down, covered in blood (*Shāhnāma*
7:175/1064 [Davis 801]). The idea(l) consistently on display in these
examples is that the wrath of a king is both terrible and unbearable,
and Mobad gives voice to it himself when he warns that his punishment
of Vis "would do damage beyond measure" were he to inflict it; his
request that Viru do it for him is thus meant to be construed as a sign
of kingly magnanimity. But as the foundations of Mobad's legitimacy
begin to crack, we can observe how quickly and easily the discourse can
change around him: when he forbears from inflicting harm, it is now
a sign of weakness, while his acts of war and violence now affirm his
injustice and tyranny. It is almost like the lifting of an illusion: the act is
one and the same, but the mythology surrounding it has dissipated, the
Shadow of God on Earth giving way to reveal a mere man, desperate
and terrified. It is thus with the final exposure of the lie that Mobad's
kingship hits rock bottom, dragging the king down with it; and like the
rest of his misfortunes, it is curiously – and necessarily – self-inflicted.

The episode begins with yet another assault on Mobad's kingdom.
The Caesar has invaded the western frontier, and Mobad – perhaps
relieved to face at last an enemy of flesh and bone – readies his army
for war. But then he hesitates: What to do about Vis, who seems to be
a liability wherever she goes? After some deliberation, he imprisons
her in a remote fortress known as the "Devils' Grotto" (*eshkaft-e divān*)
and takes Rāmin along on his campaign for good measure. At first, the
plan seems to work; after winning a decisive victory over the Romans,
Mobad returns to his capital confident that his suzerainty over all other
kings has been restored (260/8 [224]). But the victory proves illusory;
no sooner does he reach Marv than he learns that Rāmin had long ago
slipped away to be with his lover.

Learning this news sends the king over the edge. He orders his army, still weary from the campaign, to march on the Devils' Grotto, leading the rank and file to openly grumble at his leadership for the first time (260/18–23). But such trifles are now beyond Mobad's consideration; roaring like an animal (261/28), he bursts into Vis's bedchamber, where he comes face to face with the scene he had both longed and dreaded to behold: there is Vis, weeping in the middle of the room; there is the improvised rope ladder that afforded Rāmin a hasty retreat. Transfixed before this image of his wife, only one degree short of *in flagrante delicto*, Mobad can no longer seek refuge behind doubt and dissimulation but must take in the full view of his fundamental powerlessness. No matter how well he plays the part of king, Vis, and the sublime kingship that she embodies, will never be his; he will always be met by her persistent question, "How could I let go of a young man for one who is old?"

Neither Mobad nor his kingship can survive this knowledge. Everything he thought he had achieved has gone up in smoke, and in a final irony, he finds himself, the King of Kings, now asking his wife what he should do with her (*naguyi tā che bāyad kard bā to*, 267/138). Brought to this state, the only recourse left to him is violence, no longer rationalized in the rhetoric of justice and order, but a raw unbridled anger at the futility of the entire system. "You fear neither God nor man," he complains to Vis, "Neither wounds nor fetters nor admonitions, nor contracts nor oaths have any effect" (267/136, 141). With all his options exhausted, Mobad makes a new promise – to break his own:

کنم کردار با تو چون تو کردی	خورم زنهار با تو چون تو خوردی
چنان سیرت کنم از جان شیرین	کجا هرگز نیندیشی ز رامین
نه رامین هرگز از تو شاد باشد	نه هرگز در دلت زو یاد باشد
نه او پیش تو گیرد چنگ و طنبور	نه تو با او نشینی مست و مخمور
نه او با تو نماید رود سازی	نه تو او را نمایی دل نوازی
به جان چندان نهیب آرم شما را	که بر هر دو بنالد سنگ خارا
شما تا دوستی با هم نمایید	مرا دشمنترین دشمن شمایید
هر آن گاهی که با هم عشق بازید	بجز تدبیر جان من نسازید
من اکنون بر شما گردانم این کار	دل از دشمن بپردازم به یک بار

I'll do to you what you've done to me; I'll break my oaths as you've broken yours. You'll be so sick of your sweet soul, you'll never again think of Rāmin, nor will he ever delight in you, nor will you ever hold him in your heart, nor will he play the harp and tambour before you, nor will you sit drunkenly with him, nor will he play the lute for you, nor will you make eyes at him. I'll bring such ruin upon you two that it would make a granite boulder weep. As long as you are lovers, you are the worst of my enemies,

> and every time that you make love, you do naught but wreck my soul.
> Now I will turn this deed upon you, and rid my heart of this enemy once
> and for all. (268/160–8 [232])

The anaphora of Mobad's oath recalls to my mind the dying words of
King Lear, "Never, never, never, never, never" (V.3): below its primal
anger, it expresses a profound mourning, the realization that his dream
of kingship – and with it, his self-image as a beneficent king – has been
irretrievably lost. Perhaps goaded by the knowledge of the futility of it
all, Mobad finally snaps, declaring he will turn "this deed" upon Vis –
analogically her betrayal, but syntactically her lovemaking – in what is
doubtless the most violent passage in the story. Seizing Vis by the hair,
Mobad drags her along the ground, binds her limbs "like a thief," and
whips her, "over and over, upon her back, her haunches, her breasts
and thighs, until her frame split open like a pomegranate, and blood
dripped from it like pomegranate seeds; her blood flowed from her
silvery limbs like wine spilling from a crystal goblet" (269/175–7).
He then turns on Vis's Nurse with even more fury (*z-ān bishtar zad*,
269/181), continuing his assault until both women lose consciousness.
Mobad slams the door behind him and leaves them to die.

Beyond what this scene tells us about Mobad's relationship with
Vis, it reveals even more about his relationship with himself. In finally
witnessing Vis's refusal to love him – the very *impossibility* of her love,
in fact, due to his aged body – Mobad comprehends the lie of his sublime authority, brought out by his mortality. Perhaps this is why, in
his fury and despair, he targets the sexualized areas of Vis's body in
his attempt to do the same "deed" to her that she has been doing with
Rāmin. This is the only way he can obtain his desire: the virginal blood
of Vis in his bed chamber, announcing the union of the two houses
and the integration of Jamshid's line into his own. At the same time,
his conscious act of breaking the covenant – the network of symbolic
bonds that held his kingship together – signals an attack on the institution itself. Mobad has finally made good on his repeated threats
of doing "damage beyond measure" to those who betray him; he is
finally acting the part of the king. Yet the kingship dies even as he con-
summates it; his sublime body is no more, his claims to transcendence
are denied. No longer able to close his eyes at the reality Vis forces
him to perceive, he smashes it, and her: the mirror of his self, the icon
of his sovereignty.

We thus arrive at a turning point, both in Mobad's textual presentation and his self-understanding. Until now, as Massé notes, the king's
repeated efforts to maintain public order and his personal dignity

were conveyed with a certain amount of pathos, given the inherent impossibility of his situation, and his many monologues in which he wonders out loud what on earth he can do to deliver himself from his predicament are some of the most profound ruminations on choice and agency in the story as a whole.[78] But his futile act of violence, like all his other efforts, only further transforms his kingly justice into the worst form of oppression – even when similarly violent retributions are tolerated and even celebrated in kings such as Bahman and Ṭughrıl Beg. (Rostam's pitiless murder of Sudāba after the death of Siyāvash also comes to mind.) Mobad, for his part, seems more shocked than anyone in beholding this image of himself, stripped of justice and even reason. "I have done that which I never have done nor will never do," he later laments to Shahru; "I have destroyed my glory and your reputation" (*bekardam ān che pish-o pas nakardam • shokuh-e khwish-o āb-e to bebordam*, 271/17 [236]). In the culmination of the suicidal trajectory we have observed developing across his story, the king has inflicted the mortal blow on himself, effecting the collapse of his moral authority.

This new reality receives ample treatment in the aftermath of Mobad's attack. When Shahru learns what he has done, she reveals the extent to which Mobad is in fact subject to her, and not the other way around. "From west to east, men will gird themselves to avenge the blood of Vis!" (274/62), she declares, describing – in a nearly perfect inversion of the threats Mobad's courtiers had once made against the Medes – the "storm of destruction" that will rain on the land of Khorasan (273/57–61). She ends her denunciation by calling on God to witness that the king to whom justice has been entrusted has turned to tyranny:

خدایا تو حکیم و بردباری که بر موبد همی آتش نباری

جهان دادی به دست این ستمگر که هست اندر بدی هر روز بدتر

نبخشاید همی بر بندگانت به بیدادی همی سوزد جهانت

O Lord, you are wise and forbearing indeed, that you do not rain fire upon Mobad! You put the world in the hand of this tyrant, whose evil gets worse every day. He is not kind to Your servants; he scorches Your world with his injustice. (277/116–18 [241])

As the theory goes, an unjust king is no king at all, and with Shahru now declaring him tyrant, Mobad's fall from power is both inevitable and justified. Ironically, the only one who can save him now is Vis, and so Mobad, dejected and listless, restores her to his side at court; in this concession, he at last gives up the struggle and accepts his impending doom: "As long as Vis is my mate and beloved, my only business will be suffering" (278/139). By this means, the narrative architecture finally falls into place along the axis of Lover – Beloved – Villain that it needs to resolve itself, yet through a method that severely undercuts the sense of it all.

The final blow to Mobad's symbolic authority comes shortly thereafter, back in the royal garden in spring, the *locus amoenus* where our discussion began.[79] The narrator lays out the scene in such detail that it could be staged: Mobad sits at the head of the assembly, with Vis at his side; to his right is Prince Viru, to his left, Queen Shahru. Rāmin sits opposite (in opposition to) the king, and before him stands a *gosān*, a kind of professional minstrel (300/12). This arrangement suggests that the *gosān* is a mouthpiece for Rāmin, who – as we will discuss at length in the next chapter – is a singer himself.[80] With all our *dramatis personae* assembled, the *gosān* performs a lay "in which he hid the state of Vis and Rāmin" (300/15): he sings of a tree grown atop a mountain, a crystalline stream flowing by its base and a "Gilani bull" champing at the flowers. If the significance of this image is a little opaque to modern readers, it was probably more apparent in Gorgāni's time, for in the *Shāhnāma*, the king Nushin-Ravān has a similar dream, which Bozorj-Mehr correctly interprets to signify a strange man living in his harem.[81] But for those who might have missed the connection, some manuscripts of *V&R* include a reprise of the song that fully spells out its meaning. Vis commands the *gosān* to "pull back the curtain of our love" with another performance in the mode of *rāst* (an established mode in Persian music, but also the word for "right," "true"); the obliging musician repeats his tale, explaining that the tree, lofty but immobile, represents Mobad, who watches helplessly as Rāmin the bull despoils the garden and muddies Vis's limpid waters (301/24–40).[82] He concludes both songs with a parody of the benediction (*doʿā*) that typically closes the qasida: "May the water of this spring be ever-flowing, and from it, the Gilāni bull ever-grazing!" (301/39, also 301/23). If the garden was once a site where Mobad ritualized his authority, now it has become a carnival, an anti-ritual in which the minstrel (and behind him, Rāmin) can twist the conventions of courtly panegyric to mock the king to his face.[83]

Mobad responds to this open challenge much in the same way he did to Vis: in a last-ditch effort to keep his authority alive, he turns to physical violence, leaping at Rāmin with his dagger. But here, as with Vis, his old age betrays him; with a nimble feint, Rāmin disarms his brother and casts him off the dais. In this symbolic deposition, the king is essentially incapacitated – "his comprehension broken, his power gone" (*gosasta āgahi-o rafta niru-sh*, 302/53) – and he makes only incidental appearances as the text moves on to the last major obstacle separating the lovers: their own deteriorating relationship. Commenting on this poignant image, the narrator remarks that love (*ʿeshq*) and drunkenness (*masti*) had brought the king to this wretched state (302/55–6); given the symbolically charged context of this scene, however, it seems clear that we should look for meaning in these words beyond their literal valence. Interpreting them through the framework of this chapter, I would suggest it is not a carnal passion that has ensnared Mobad, but rather desire as a self-constituting act, a reaching out for the Self through its (mis-) recognition in the Other. The product of this encounter is a story – a myth – about the self, whose image of reality gains authority as if it were real. Mobad's drunkenness – his state of being able to see, but not to perceive – speaks to his unknowing participation in that myth, a discursive imprisonment from which he can never break free.

"The World Is a Dream"

These scenes above show how Mobad plays a vital role in developing *Vis & Rāmin*'s underlying interest in the relationship between discourse, desire, and the real. With devastating precision, the text dismantles the mythos and ethos of universal kingship, just as it had done for Vis in its takedown of romantic love, narrativizing the breakdown through the eyes of the theory's avatar. Mobad enters the story secure in his belief that divine authority emanates from him as surely as the sun radiates light; but after experiencing his body animated by this power, compelled to act in ways seldom of his choosing, he comes to realize that he is little more than a slave to the discursive forces that crowned him. The hierarchy, in a sense, has been doubled: not only does he embody kingship, but kingship embodies him. Thus the normative social world that his position projects, with him as the master of other men and women, is simultaneously flipped into its inverse, such that his kingship and even his life are entirely dependent on the young woman he once claimed as the sign of his authority. As Zard puts it, any attack on Vis is an attack on himself: "If you plunge your dagger into lovely Vis, your pain from that wound would only increase" (297/139). It is very much as Kantorowicz writes on Shakespeare's *Richard II*: "Instead of being unaffected 'by Nonage or Old Age and other natural Defects and Imbecilities,' kingship itself comes to mean Death, and nothing but Death."[84] We can only imagine the epistemic horror this revelation might entail, as Mobad gazes into the void of his own irrelevance; as this new and terrifying self-knowledge sinks in, it provokes a fascinating glimpse into the phenomenology of betrayal, no longer by Vis per se but rather the very discourses that constitute his sense of self and the world.

One of the masterful strokes in the execution of Mobad's character is that the dynamic interplay of power that both creates and destroys plays out along multiple axes of interpretation. This solves, in one way, the initial problem I posed in this chapter about how we are to read this text: its many tales in this case tell different versions of the same story. For example, if we read *V&R* as a mythos of romantic love, Mobad adopts the functional role as the Villain, the "key" who starts and stops the narrative: the intrigue begins the moment he claims Vis for himself, standing between her and her preferred option(s), and it cannot come to an end until that claim is somehow neutralized. By virtue of this function, Mobad both writes the tale and writes himself out of it. The same suicidal trajectory holds if we approach *V&R* from another vantage point (*thēoria*) that takes him for the story's Hero, the mythos of universal kingship. In stepping into the persona of King of Kings, he gains tremendous authority, yet at the same time surrenders himself to its tyranny and must in the end sacrifice himself at its altar. Villainy destroys the villain; kingship devours the king.

Crucially, this self-generated collapse is not a foregone conclusion, but rather unique to Mobad's case; other kings (or nobility) who fall in love, such as Dionysios in *Kallirhoe*, the Emir of *Floire & Blancheflor*, and the King in *Varqa & Golshāh*, rescue themselves (and their rule) by relinquishing their claim and assuming a paternalistic relationship with the united lovers, converted from foe to ally.[85] But the difference between them and Mobad is that their stories understand desire as fundamentally extrinsic, and often inimical, to their royal position. By that account, a king, and really any mature man in full control of his faculties, can and should control his desire and dispense with it when need be, especially as he eases into old age. Mobad's authority, however, is so deeply bound up with the fortunes of Vis and Rāmin that he can in no way dispense with them, neither by letting go of his love or letting go of them: the only dispensable figure in the equation is ultimately Mobad himself. By challenging the conventional narrative in this way, Gorgāni puts a new model of kingship on the table, a theory in which the very act of performing "king" is in itself an act of desire; thus the seeds of the king's demise are built into his (self-)creation.

Mobad's story thus proposes a far deeper and more problematic interrogation of the desiring self than what first meets the eye. The initial "moral" that one might take away from his story was that he fell victim to love: had he been more circumspect in managing his gaze (per Cyrus's recommendation in the *Cyropaedia*, later reiterated in the *Qābus-nāma*), or made sure not to let women mix with politics (as Neẓām al-Molk advises), he could have avoided his evil fate.[86] Mobad himself expresses the latter diagnosis on more than one occasion, blaming his woes first and foremost on his own mother: "My mother threw me into this disaster, for she warmed my heart towards Rāmin. It's only just that I am stuck in misfortune, for I bound my affairs to the words of women!" (516/16–17). This statement is a classic example of the misrecognition that has plagued Mobad throughout his story: while pitying himself as a man ruled by women, he fails to perceive how this relationship is itself a symptom of the self-image to which he has subjected himself. That is to say, if Mobad is drawn to Shahru because it is in her that he recognizes his own ideal self, then it places his desire for her/himself as the agent of his simultaneous self-fashioning and self-destruction. The author of the *Qābus-nāma* illustrates this paradox beautifully in his chapter on love (*ʿeshq*), where, we might recall, he reminds his son that an elderly king should never ever fall in love. But shortly after pronouncing this advice, he admits, "However much I may tell you this tale, I know that, if love falls upon you, you will not implement what I have said. I myself recite the following verses to old men (*pirān-sar*) on the condition of love":

بایدکه چو عذرا و چو وامق باشد   هرآدمیی که حیّ و ناطق باشد

مؤمن نبوَد که او نه عاشق باشد   هرکونه چنین بُوَد منافق باشد

> Any human who is alive and in possession of their mind (*nāṭeq*) must be
>   like [the lovers] Vāmeq and ʿAẕrā;
> Anyone who is not like this is among the hypocrites: there is no believer
>   who is not a lover.

"But however much I have spoken in this way," concludes the author, in a delicious self-subterfuge, "you must not act on this poem."[87] The message, in other words, is that the ideal king must, and can never, free himself from desire, no more than he could free himself from himself. Indeed, one variant of the second verse replaces the word "believer" (*moʾmen*), with its strongly Qurʾanic overtones, with the more universal word "person" (*mardom*), such that it becomes an almost perfect echo of a proverb the narrator of *V&R* quotes when speaking of Mobad and his desire for Vis: "A person who does not love is not a person" (*har ānk u nist ʿāsheq nist mardom*, 83/52).[88] In these cases, the paradox of desire ceases to be an issue unique to kings or believers but pertinent to humanity at large: to be alive and to possess *noṭq* (the faculty that allows for thought and speech, like Aristotle's *logos*) necessarily constitutes humans as not just speaking, but desiring animals.[89] Desire, then, lies at the heart of the properties that give life to humankind, by which humans know themselves and make their humanity known; yet at the same time, it is the force that drives all people to ruin.

The paradox lying at the heart of Mobad's identity might help us begin to grapple with, if not make sense of, the seemingly senseless manner of his death, which takes place in the final pages of the story. Vis and Rāmin have joined forces and launched a coup against the king; now pushed to make a final, desperate stand, Mobad marches to join Rāmin in battle. But before the two armies can meet, Mobad's camp is suddenly set upon by a ravening boar. Showing none of his characteristic hesitation, the king leaps on his horse and charges "like a lion" at the beast; but his javelin, to his dismay, misses the mark (518/33–4 [485]). The enraged boar knocks Mobad to the ground and gores him open from navel to chest: "The light of love dead in his heart; the fire of vengeance likewise extinguished" (*cherāgh-e mehr shod dar del-ash morda • hamidun ātash-e kina fesorda*, 519/39). As sudden and brutal as it may be, perhaps the most disturbing after-effect of this scene is its punishing humiliation. Mobad seemed on the verge of a small moral victory, riding out to meet the enemy in a final blaze of glory. But he is even denied the satisfaction of taking down the boar; the image we are handed instead is rather that of a man, already defeated and broken, now ignominiously crushed as though under the heel of some spiteful god.

There is no doubt that the scene bears the hallmarks of divine retribution: one is reminded of an incident in the *Shāhnāma*, when a wild stallion appears out of the blue, kills the wicked King Yazdgerd with a kick to the head, and then vanishes; the *Bahman-nāma*, too, ends with its unjust protagonist getting devoured by a dragon.[90] Given the originally Zoroastrian context of the story, and the (possible) ancient identity of Mobad as a sorcerer-king, there may be some symbolic significance to the boar itself, for in the *Mehr Yašt* of the Avesta, the god Mithra (*mehr*) assumes the shape of "a sharp-toothed he-boar" (18.70) to punish those who have broken sacred oaths: "He cuts all the limbs to pieces, and mingles, together with the earth, the bones, hair, brains, and blood of the men who have lied unto Mithra" (18.72).[91] More immediately, the image of Mobad's cloven body recalls the death scene of the great Jamshid, sawn in half by Żaḥḥāk.[92] Considering Mobad's ontological bonds with both *mehr* and Jamshid – the (broken) contract of love, the fall of the royal sun – these symbolic and intertextual elements produce a convincing case that the king got nothing less than what he deserved.

The narrative seems eager, in fact, to insist this was the case: as Rāmin enters Marv following the king's demise, we are told that its inhabitants "had suffered under Mobad for years" (524/49 [489]). Perhaps justice has finally been served.

But even as it tells this tale, the story seems unwilling to fully embrace its self-justification; having followed the embedded paradoxes of Mobad's life, we now know too much. This is evident in this scene's framing: rather than moralize about what Mobad should or should not have done in the domain of politics, the text instead uses his death as an occasion to meditate on the strange and senseless ways of the world, a place where time marches on with little regard for those it crushes in its path. The narrator opens the episode with a poignant question about our inability to understand – "Although we experience much of the world, how can we open the hidden lock (*band*) of its secrets?" (517/1) – then develops that theme in a tone of personal distress:

مرا باری به چشم این بس شگفتست   وزین اندیشه ام سودا گرفتست

ندانم چیست این گشتِ زمانه   وزو بر جانِ ما چندین بهانه

جهانداری شهانشاهی چو موبد   جهان را زو بسی نیک و بسی بد

بدین خواریش باشد روزِ فرجام   بماند در دل و چشمش همه کام

This is truly astonishing in my view, and I am gripped by the melancholy of these thoughts. I don't understand this turning fate and the many pretexts it makes on our lives, such that a world-king like Mobad, who did much good and evil in the world, would end his days in such wretchedness, with every desire in his heart and eye unfulfilled. (518/19–22 [484])

This outburst of illicit rage, a literary technique that also occurs in the *Shāhnāma*, profoundly challenges the legitimacy of any interpretive attempt to rationalize, or even fully understand, the question of what went wrong for Mobad.[93] That may well be the fundamental point: time, as the narrator puts it, does not *deserve* to be understood, nor even its name to be pronounced (*kojā dahr ān nayarzad k-ash bedānand* ● *va yā khwad bar zabān nām-ash berānand*, 520/57). Thus Mobad, whose aged body manifests a visual icon of time and its passage, offers far more than a negative *exemplum* on the conduct of kings; the "universal king" myth simply creates the discursive field for this inquiry to unfold. Rather, he provides, alongside Vis and Rāmin, a study on how humans use discourse in their ongoing desire to make sense of the senseless. The self-defeating trajectory of his narrative, however, tempers the transcendent quest for meaning with the ultimately illusory nature of the effort. "The world is a dream," the narrator remarks, "and we are [but] phantoms within it" (*jahān khwāb-ast-o mā dar vay khayāl-im*, 517/3). If the other protagonists in the story seek life beyond death, Mobad balances this with a story of death within life, showing how desire produces what is perhaps a uniquely human experience of mortality. To be human is to desire; to desire is to die.

Chapter Four

AFFECT | The Limits of Lyric

FOR ALL THE PAIN AND HEARTACHE its characters endure, *Vis & Rāmin* has its fair share of tender, joyful, and even funny moments. Take, for example, the scene after Vis has gone public about her affair with Rāmin, and Mobad has asked Viru to discipline her accordingly. But when Viru takes his sister to the side, complaining about the dishonour she has brought upon him and their mother, the bulk of his chagrin appears to be directed at her choice of lover. "If you had to do it," he seems to say, "did it *have* to be with a minstrel?"

چرا او را ز هر کس بر گزیدی   نگویی تا تو از رامین چه دیدی

بجز رود و سرود و چنگ و طنبور   به گنجش در چه دارد مرد گنجور

بر او راهی و دستانی نوازد   همین داند که طنبوری بسازد

نهاده جامه نزد می فروشان   نبینندش مگر مست و خروشان

Will you not tell me what you saw in Rāmin? Why choose him, of all people? What treasure does that treasurer possess, save for lute and song, harp and tambour? All he knows is how to string up a tambour, and strum some melody on it in some mode. No one sees him except roaring drunk, pawning his clothes to the wine-sellers. (172/73–6 [135])

These misgivings raise intriguing questions about Rāmin's character and role. One would assume, on the basis of the story's title, that Rāmin is supposed to be the male counterpart to Vis, her perfect mate; according to the love-story convention of sexual symmetry, as discussed in chapter 2, the two protagonists should be basically identical in terms of their youth, beauty, noble lineage, and inner virtue. While Rāmin certainly meets the first three of these criteria, the characterization of his lifestyle we get here may yet cast some doubts on his credentials for the job. At the same time, the two particulars singled out in this passage – his skill at music and his love of wine – link Rāmin to themes strongly associated with Persian and Arabic lyric poetry. We would do well, then, to begin our study of Rāmin by investigating the various personae he might bring into play in *V&R*. This journey will lead us through the boundaries of genre and into the hinterlands where literary systems mingle, break down, and challenge established practice – a process that mirrors the events of the narrative that contains them.

Some valuable work has already been done to excavate the various "Rāmins" present within this narrative, offering us a number of options for how we might read this character against a broader network of literary types and tropes. T'odua suspects that in some now-lost versions of the *Vis & Rāmin* cycle, Rāmin was not a prince of good breeding, but a "roguish, vagabond minstrel" (*navāzanda-ye qalandar-o velgard*), perhaps a popular hero akin to Samak-e ʿAyyār or Robin Hood – not a bad fellow, but certainly not one bound to the mores and niceties of the ruling elite.[1] Conversely, Meisami contends that Rāmin is meant to evoke the courtly lover *par excellence*, "weeping, sighing, and wasting away with love."[2] This persona, whose apotheosis was often located in the desolate lover Majnun, was enormously widespread and productive in early Islamic and particularly Abbasid literature, with striking parallels observable with the personae cultivated in Occitan and Catalan lyric forms centuries later.[3] Putting these readings together, Rāmin comes across as something of a composite figure, simultaneously multiple and indeterminate, with one foot in the court and one foot outside it.

This fuzziness around Rāmin's identity is explicitly supported by the rather odd way(s) by which he enters the text. He first appears, alongside Viru, among the heroes in Mobad's entourage during the New Year celebrations (34/27 [2]); but the next time we see him, he is but a babe, raised alongside Vis under the Nurse's care (44/49 [12]). Then, after a mysterious absence for a number of chapters, he pops up again at the siege of Gurab, where we learn that "ever since childhood, Rāmin's heart had secretly harboured desire for Vis" (80/77 [45]); but then, on catching a glimpse of her face on the return trip to Marv, he falls (literally) head over heels in love (94/14–33 [57–8]). As any account that manages to accommodate all these details would strain the bounds of credulity, Ḥamid ʿAbd-Allāhiyān believes that Gorgāni's work must actually be a synthesis of two discrete storylines, one about the rivalry between two princes, the other about a queen's affair with a court minstrel of low birth, producing in Rāmin a doubled persona who cannot fully reside in either role.[4]

Despite these narrative and typological bifurcations, our multiple Rāmins do share a common ground, and that is in their association with the ghazal, a "lyric" poem (I'll explain the scare quotes below) that takes love as its central theme. Formally, the ghazal is quite distinct from the masnavi – being short in length, closely associated with music, and structured around monorhyme – and it has a long history going back to the Abbasid period in Arabic poetry that I will discuss further on. As Meisami observes, because of its basic orientation around the theme of love, the most prominent speaking voices of the ghazal are all lovers of some kind, such that both its "courtly" and "roguish" personae express their love along similar, if not identical, lines: they venerate the beloved above all else, they have little concern for social propriety, and they mingle metaphoric and literal drunkenness in their speech-acts; J.-C. Bürgel sees Rāmin as the figurative embodiment of this underlying ethos.[5] As the story's minstrel, Rāmin inculcates and develops a distinctive voice that is not only mediated through song but also grounded in the thought patterns of that medium. The ghazal thus provides a net of sorts that allows us to hold and work with his many personae.

This internal multiplicity produces a very complex set of discursive relationships when brought to the romance, however. We start with a figure cast as the co-protagonist of a long-form narrative about love, with all the expectations that accompany that mythos; but at the same time, that figure's speech-acts evoke another kind of protagonist who is closely tied to the lyric "I" of the ghazal and its various modes of expression. Rāmin, like the author of *Guillaume de Dole* (c. 1209–28), thus "plays on the parameters of two textual traditions (romance and lyric), but in incorporating one type of text into another he troubles these parameters as he evokes them."[6] With multiple backstories, inhabiting multiple personae, and projecting multiple expectations of behaviour, he will inevitably overflow the boundaries of his character, regardless of how we choose to read him. Not only a hybrid creation, Rāmin is also a figure whose actions hybridize the textual fabric of his story; in a variation of my earlier phrase, he stands with one foot in the romance and one foot outside it.

This intertextual and genre-minded approach to Rāmin's character will help us consider what happens when he evokes the persona(e) of the ghazal, an established poetic tradition with its own distinct history, and "posits another language" (Maureen Boulton's phrase) that disrupts the norms and best practices that usually hold fast in the love-story universe.[7] I will expand on the qualities of this "other language" later, but for now let's note that it shifts the emphasis from *reciprocity* to the *yearning for reciprocation* – an affective stance with significant ramifications for the narratives it invokes and projects. By introducing a discursive heterogeneity that will ultimately lead to love's collapse in the overarching story, Rāmin plays a crucial role in realizing the text's broader investigation into the ways that discourse can fashion subjective experience and connect it with the real, transforming the phantasy of *Vis & Rāmin* into an imagined experiential history, as I discuss further in chapter 5. The story of how this unfolds will not only prove relevant to this particular text, but should also help us develop our account of the complex interactions possible between "lyric" and "romance" in Persian and other medieval literary traditions.

Lyrics, Episodes, and Adventure-Time

As Patricia Parker and Barbara Fuchs have argued, some of the distinctive features of romance – as a modality of narration, rather than as a historical genre – are found in its handling of time and space: its inclination towards delay and digression, its open landscapes and meandering plot lines.[8] Even as these strategies stall the story's forward momentum, they can also provide room for the incorporation of multiple kinds of speech into the textual fabric, shifting their formal and generic contexts. In this process, the codes that inform and structure discourse are defamiliarized and brought into the open as constructs to be evaluated against others, producing a degree of critical distance and self-reflexivity, a mode that Mikhail Bakhtin describes as "novelistic" in the way it is "always criticizing itself."[9] This is especially evident, as scholars of romance in Old French have observed, with the insertion or intercalation of lyric performances in the narrative.[10] Just as we might look for tragic or comedic models of reality in texts that are not, strictly speaking, comedies or tragedies, we can discover through Rāmin and his performances distinctively "lyrical" ways of engaging with the world that put him at odds with the other major characters of *V&R*.

Rāmin's entry into *V&R* as an active character produces significant transformations in the structure, pacing, and rhythm of the story's narrative. As noted above, he is largely absent from the opening chapters of the book, which are devoted to the story of Vis's birth, first marriage to Viru, abduction, and second marriage to Mobad. Even after the affair begins, the narrative focus turns not to Rāmin but to the king, who must battle his own demons in the face of this crisis. Up to this point, one might sense that Rāmin is something of a functional character, a place holder and not the focal point of the story; he is there to be loved by his lover and envied by his rival, with little of his own to contribute besides the conventional gestures of the ardent suitor. But as the mists of doubt and confusion that cloud the early chapters of *V&R* dissipate, a new reality comes into

Table 1: The Four Episodes

Episode	Description
1. The Ordeal	Mobad asks Vis to undergo an ordeal by fire to prove her innocence; on the day of the trial, she escapes Marv along with Rāmin and the Nurse and takes refuge in Ray; the brothers are eventually reconciled through the mediation of their mother.
2. The Bed Trick	After a drinking party, Mobad takes Vis to bed with him, but Vis has the Nurse take her place so that she may join Rāmin on the palace roof; when dawn arrives, she hastily returns to bed and convinces Mobad she was there the whole time.
3. The Devils' Grotto	Before marching off to fight the Roman emperor, Mobad sequesters Vis in a remote castle called the Devils' Grotto; Rāmin deserts the army and joins Vis; when Mobad returns from his campaign, he discovers the treachery and beats Vis but restores her to favour after Shahru's intervention.
4. The Garden	Mobad leaves town for a hunting trip; Rāmin again deserts camp, but cannot gain access to Vis's chambers; Vis climbs out her window and joins him in the palace garden; when Mobad returns the next day, she explains she had been carried there by an angel.

view: it is finally clear that Vis and Rāmin are madly in love and will go to any lengths to be together, while Mobad, admitting but not accepting this state of affairs, must keep them apart to the extent he can. So – what next? Where will this love triangle take our protagonists?

In a word: nowhere. Caught in a situation in which no side will back down, the characters can only spin their wheels in frustration, while the focus and momentum of the first quarter of *V&R* gives way to a series of episodes that repeat what is essentially the same story over and over again: the king tries to separate the lovers, the lovers outsmart him for a while, the king comes to his senses and/or realizes the trick, and the lovers must once again part ways. Like episodes in a sitcom, the love-story has entered a "floating timeline" of stasis, destabilization, and restoration – a temporal loop from which there is no seeming escape (see table 1).[11]

This change in the story's trajectory maps remarkably well onto Bakhtin's concept of "adventure-time," which he used to analyse the Greek romance (or novel) against other novelistic works. Adventure-time, Bakhtin proposed, is part of the chronotope – "the intrinsic connectedness of temporal and spatial relationships" – distinctive to this genre, which constructs its stories around two basic moments in time: the moment when the lovers meet and fall in love, and the moment when they consummate that love in marriage.[12] Between these two nodes lies a timeless void, an "extratemporal hiatus" that can expand or contract *ad infinitum* to accommodate however many episodes the storyteller desires to include, with no repercussions on the overarching plot. "In this kind of time," Bakhtin writes, "nothing changes: the world remains as it was, the biographical life of the heroes does not change, their feelings do not change, people do not even age. This empty time leaves no traces anywhere, no indications of its passing."[13] Although his object of study was the "ideal" Greek novel of the Imperial period, this description certainly applies to *Vis & Rāmin* as well, whose protagonists will pass through thousands of lines of text and *ten years* of diegetic time, with no fundamental change to their lives or relationship.[14]

Interestingly, Francesco Gabrieli, a contemporary of Bakhtin (though probably unaware of his theories), arrived at the same conclusion in his study of *V&R*, in which he observes that the basic intrigue – the meeting of the lovers, the point at which Bakhtin's adventure-time is activated – is established barely a quarter of the way into the narrative, leaving us with a new *status quo* that will not easily be resolved:

> With the aid of the Nurse, Rāmin has subdued Vis, who is at first resist-ant to his ardour, [and] the adultery is consummated; the remaining three quarters of the work should have been filled with adventures, such as in the story of the sorceress of Ireland [Isolde, I presume?], in which the narra-tor's creative genius would have introduced novel and interesting episodes to add variety to a uniform situation that is, at its root, always the same.[15]

Notable is the ready familiarity with which Gabrieli spells out the rules of this literary game as though they were common knowledge, a telling indication of the degree to which these conventions had been estab-lished and internalized over centuries of repetition.[16] Though he is not aware of the chronotope as a theoretical concept, he clearly expects Gorgāni to take advantage of this time-space and give his readers some-thing to enjoy as the plot turns about itself in the meandering manner discussed by Fuchs and Parker. The problem, in other words, is not the circularity of the episodes, but that they are "as monotonous and clum-sily told as one can imagine," filled with "interminable laments" and "melodramatic declamations" that are devoid of "real storytelling."[17]

It is precisely at this juncture that Rāmin leaps into the spotlight. Though he has a monologue or two prior to this, they are nothing in comparison to the dense accumulation of songs we are about to encounter. In the episodes that follow, Rāmin will sing paeans to love in Mobad's court, bellow out ballads while riding on horseback, serenade the wind on the eve of separation, and intone silent melodies as he wrestles with his heart. In total, Rāmin has some thirty performances to his name, with a complete monopoly over the *in situ* songs and the lion's share of the poem's interior monologues (see appendix B). These performances reach their highest rate of frequency in these cyclical episodes, this adventure-time where "nothing changes," fundamentally altering the feel and flow of this section of *Vis & Rāmin*.

What are we to make of this? Why is it that Rāmin comes to life at a moment when everything else is in stagnation? In historical terms, the shift may substantiate the hypothesis that this section of *V&R* is an amalgamation of discrete episodes that utilize the same *status quo* as their point of departure and return, stories in which Rāmin played the leading role. Generically, too, Rāmin's poems bolster his (self-)image as a classic romance hero, helplessly caught in love's embrace. Many are the romance lovers who, unable to "do" anything for themselves, occupy their stage time with laments, soliloquies, and expositions about their inner state.[18] Both explanations are perfectly adequate, but I suspect that more insight can be gained by taking up Boulton's observations on the Old French material: "However marked a disruption the lyric insertions cause, they nevertheless form part of a greater whole. If they alter the meaning of a work, they also help to create that meaning."[19] Below their elegant surface, a forceful current runs throughout Rāmin's lyrics; they do a kind of work, despite their appearing not to, that will transform the text that houses them and advance a distinctive argument about discourse, power, and love.

For starters, we might consider the phenomenological experience of reading through one of these episodes, in which the narration is interrupted time and again by Rāmin's songs. The constant digressions naturally affect the story's pacing: we lose the thread of the plot, time slows to a snail's pace, and our attention is drawn away from what's happening to what's being said about it; as Gabrieli puts it, the action "seems reduced to simply an introductory or concluding caption to the rhetorical declamation."[20] The songs thus reproduce the narrative stasis of adventure-time on the level of perception and diction. This is probably no coincidence: as Meisami argues, this "timeless" quality is part and parcel of the ghazal repertory, whose speakers exemplify "the various states and stages of a fictionalized, idealized experience of love, an underlying narrative from whose episodes the poet selects his topic."[21] She posits a mythos, in other words, implicitly encoded inside the ghazal's poetics, that resists or stands outside the "normal" flow of time.[22] As Rāmin embraces his role as the story's minstrel, challenging and at times drowning out the voice of its narrator, he consequently introduces an alternative narrative, one that unfolds not so much between the lines as between the minutes.

This bifurcation of the narrative into two parallel lines raises important questions about authorial power, narrative control, and violence. Although Rāmin repeatedly uses his songs to declare his powerlessness in the face of Love and Destiny – the default position of lovers in the mythos of romantic love – we must not forget that there is one crucial moment in which he proactively intervenes in the story's development. As we saw in chapter 2, Vis did not fall in love with Rāmin in her childhood or by a chance encounter as an adult, as is the usual case; rather, Rāmin had to win her over by having the Nurse act as his proxy, and the only way he could win over the Nurse was by physically forcing himself on her. This violent intervention remains embedded in the core of his relationship with Vis, no matter how much he might try to bury it under the verbiage of his lyrics. By competing with the narratorial account and imposing their own report of what happened, Rāmin's songs manifest this unresolved tension: just as the romance was brought into being by a violent act, so do the songs echo and indeed amplify the violence, extending it from the level of the body to the level of discourse. They re-enact and perpetuate the initial transgression that was required to make the affair possible in the first place.

In this way, Rāmin is both like and unlike Vis and Mobad. In the two previous chapters, I sought to demonstrate how the latter characters invoke, by virtue of their emblematic or typological status, a particular narrative world (mythos) and its associated practices (ethos) through which they see, understand, and conduct themselves. In a basic sense, they manifest the contract motif we have seen running through the story, for as they invoke these discourses to give their lives identity and purpose, they thereby submit themselves to that discursive power, which limits their range of choices in any given scenario and sometimes backs them into a corner. The same process holds true for Rāmin, but with an important complication: while the personae of romance hero/ine and universal sovereign are relatively stable, their fundamental norms and expectations visibly consistent across the *longue durée*, Rāmin is anchored in a repertory of affective postures – not a single "code" but a dialectic tradition, steeped in the language of lyric – that invoke in turn a variety of latent narrative worlds and practices. This makes his character something of a chameleon, shifting across courtly, libertine, and even homiletic modalities of lyrical speech as need and circumstance require. Thus, while Vis and Mobad are largely judged (and judge themselves) along the conformity of their acts with their speech, Rāmin foregrounds the notion of speech *as* act – the manipulation of discourse as a means of shaping and even controlling the time-space in which life happens – both in its successes and, more importantly, in its failures. In the sections below, I will conduct four case studies, following the four episodes in succession, to explore the interaction of song and story that Rāmin brings to *V&R* and unpack its long-term consequences.

Episode 1: Mode Switching

Now is an appropriate time to clarify my use of "lyric" in this discussion, as it is a term, like romance, that we cannot apply to a medieval Persian or Arabic literary context without some reflection on what we mean by it, especially when writing in English. In the tradition of Anglo-American literary criticism, lyric has generally come to be understood as an expression of interior feeling, "utterance overheard," in John Stuart Mill's famous phrase, when the poet (as Northrop Frye later put it) "turns his back on his listeners."[23] This notion of the lyric as a private and personal expression of the poet's interior state has a discrete history that cannot be automatically applied to a context like Gorgāni's.[24] At the same time, there is still a semantic distinctiveness to the lyric that is grounded in the "I" of its first-person speaker, which, "although frequently no more than a grammatical cipher, nonetheless fixes the plane and modalities of discourse to the exclusion of any narrative element," Paul Zumthor writes.[25] From this standpoint, we might re-envision the lyric as turning its back not on the audience but on diegetic time: it interjects a pause, so to speak, that produces in Peter Haidu's words "not so much the absence of narrative, as the continual negation of a narrativity insistently invoked."[26]

Both understandings of the ghazal-as-lyric are on display in Robert Dankoff's pioneering study of *Varqa & Golshāh* (w. ca. 1030), the first romance in Persian literature (as far as we know) to intercalate ghazals, in their formal aspect, within its narrative.[27] Dankoff writes,

> The ghazals serve to give the reader or listener an occasional glimpse into the character's inner state at various points in the story, whether critical or not; and the characters often seem to be reflecting aloud, rather like an "aside" in drama, not caring whether anyone else hears their laments.[28]

To his credit, Dankoff does not universalize this temporal stasis as a uniform feature of the ghazal writ large – indeed, he notes that the intercalated lyrics in the poem's Turkish adaptation (w. 1342) are much more engaged with the plot, even moving it forward at times.[29] His point is rather that the ghazals of ᶜAyyuqi's *Varqa & Golshāh* introduce a *shift* in the narrative, a distinctiveness of sound, voice, space, and time that we might recognize through the contemporary notion of lyric. This shift is made possible, in part, by the text's use of formal and paratextual markers. When a character in *V&G* pauses to recite a poem, the rhyme scheme changes from the masnavi's rhyming hemistichs to the monorhyme of the ghazal; when the monorhyme ends, we can be sure that we have re-entered the narrative. The performances, moreover, are visually identified in the manuscript with the heading *sheᶜr goftan* ("the recitation of a poem"), followed by the name of the poem's reciter. These explicit cues mark the poems as discrete discursive units, open to being declaimed (perhaps even sung) in a manner that distinguishes them from the surrounding masnavi.[30] Akin to a prosimetrum, *Varqa & Golshāh* thus maintains a clear division between story and song, two discursive modalities with their own conventions and expectations.[31]

In comparison, the lyric performances found in *Vis & Rāmin* are quite different. The text rarely makes use of headings to announce a soliloquy, the rhyme scheme does not change, and the speech events are considerably longer than those of *V&G*, often running at thirty lines or more. Rāmin's songs, in other words, are devoid of sharp boundaries to offset them from the surrounding text. They are rather narrativized, woven into the story through diegetic phrases – such as "He said to his heart" (*bā del goft*), "He sang a song" (*sorud-i goft*), or just "he said/sang" (*goft*), and so on – all using the verb *goftan*, a word whose range of connotations include regular speech, the declamation of poetry, and the singing of songs.[32] The lines between these categories are rarely discrete and often intersect, and with the exception of a few moments in which the text makes the performance context explicit – "Playing the tambour, [Rāmin] sang a sweet song" (*sorud-i goft khwash bar rud-e ṭanbur*, 254/130), for example – it is up to the reader to decide how to "hear" these performances, whether as poems, songs, monologues, or even interior thought. My discussion of Rāmin's "lyrics," therefore, must be understood within the boundaries of air quotes, not *as* but rather *as if* they were ghazals, producing what Bakhtin calls "the novelistic image of lyrics (and of the poet as lyricist)."[33] We might think of this as a kind of *abstraction* of the lyric, in that the lyricality of Rāmin's speech-acts is obtained not through explicit markers but by the reader's cultural and intertextual literacy. It is the language of these passages (their tone, motifs, and images), as well as their diegetic setting (banquets, bedchambers, the open plain), that invites a lyrical reading of their contents – a reading that invokes the ghazal tradition and relies on its conventions in making itself meaningful.

This shift from a "formal" to a "modal" way of reading lyric presents an interesting conceptual opportunity. Although we lose the security of knowing what these passages "are," in the sense that their final status as "song" or "story" is always open to debate, we can divorce our concept of the "lyric" from the ghazal form and reconfigure it in more general terms as a modality – a way of thinking, speaking, and acting around love – that can be abstracted and translated from the ghazal into other literary forms through linguistic and performative cues. In the analysis below, I will call this, to play off the linguistic term of code switching, a kind of *mode switching*. As a method that capitalizes on the space between the poet, narrator, characters, and audience to produce narrative through a multiplicity of discursive modes, mode switching highlights the work's self-consciousness as a heteroglossic composition, a written text that adopts the speaking voice of the oral storyteller, who conveys in turn the speech-acts – spoken, written, thought, and sung – of many different figures in a variety of discursive stances and registers.[34] To follow these shifts in mode requires us to imagine the text not as a stand-alone medium but rather a component in a larger network of media, including elements of body, sound, and space, that come together in the production of a story.

The first episode, which relates Vis's ordeal by fire, is an ideal place to demonstrate the mechanics of this mode switching and to observe how certain passages call attention to themselves as song-like through sonic and diegetical cues. It begins with a common if crucial marker of time – "one day" (*ruz-i*, 198/3), that is, once upon a time – signalling to the audience that we have entered the episodic cycle of adventure-time, opening with the stasis of Mobad and Vis sitting together at court, while Rāmin lurks on the sidelines, waiting for his chance. Unhappy with the swirling rumours of his wife's infidelity, Mobad asks Vis if she would swear an oath to the contrary before the court and the sacred fire. To this Vis readily agrees, but when the flames are lit, she prepares to turn the tables on her accuser:

همان که ویس در رامین نگه کرد   مرو را گفت بنگر حال این مرد

که آتش چون بلند افروخت ما را   بدین آتش بخواهد سوخت ما را

بیا تا هر دو بگریزیم از ایدر   بسوزانیم او را هم به آذر

Vis turned to Rāmin at that moment and said, "Look at this man, who's built a great fire, hoping to roast us on it. Come, let's away from here; we'll burn him instead upon those flames!" (202/59–61 [164])

As we can see, the Vis of this episode, a trickster who delights in hood-winking her husband, is a far cry from the austere maiden we came to know in the first third of the story, another clue that this and other epi-sodes could well have come from a variety of sources. With the Nurse's aid, the three conspirators loot the royal treasury, scramble through a secret passageway in the bathhouse, scale the garden walls using Rāmin's turban as a rope, and flee the palace dressed in women's cloth-ing, "hiding their faces like demons" (203/85). In the mounting excite-ment, the narrator gains prominence as an active storyteller, directly addressing the audience in a manner comparable to Béroul's *Tristran*, with phrases such as "Look how she pulled off her trick!" (*negar z-ānjā cheguna sākht dastān*, 203/78) and punctuating the story with didactic asides that reflect on and interpret the narrative as it unfolds.[35] Once they have found refuge in the city of Ray, the lovers settle in for a long sojourn of drinking and dalliance, a period that affords Rāmin ample opportunity to serenade his lover. The transition from story to song, and from the narrator's voice to Rāmin's, is announced by a diegetic event:

نشسته پیش او رامین دلبر   گهی طنبور و گاهی چنگ دربر

همی گفتی سرود مهربازان   به دستان و نوای دلنوازان

At times with harp, at times with tambour, charming Rāmin sat before Vis, and sang the song of lovers in the mode and melody of "Lovers." (205/126–7 [168])[36]

This transition is an excellent example of the "as-if lyrical" reading dis-cussed above. On one level, it explicitly identifies the performance as a "song" (*sorud*); it adorns this "fact," furthermore, with additional details that draw us into the imaginary soundscape of the world, allowing us to "hear" how it might have been played and the mood it would have con-jured. Yet at the same time, the performance that follows complicates our ability to treat it literally as a song text: it does not transition to monorhyme, and at thirty-seven lines it extends far beyond the typical length of the early ghazal form, which tends to hit its upper limit at around twenty.[37] But despite not adhering to the formal features of a ghazal, it still manages to capture the ghazal's feel by virtue of its performance setting, literary topoi, and sonority. Consider how the song begins, in which five of the six opening lines end with the rhyme /-im/ (breaking with my standard practice, I render the Persian here in transliteration so that all can follow):

hami gofti ke mā do nik yār-im ● *be yāri yek-digar rā jānsepār-im*
be hangām-e vafā ganj-e vafā-im ● *be chashm-e doshmanān tir-e jafā-im*
cho mā rā khorrami-o shādkhwāri-st ● *bad-andishān-e mā rā ranj-o zāri-st*

be ranj az dusti siri nayābim • ze rāh-e mehrbāni rokh natābim
*be mehr andar cho do rowshan cherāgh-**im** • be nāz andar cho do beshkofta*
    *bāgh-**im***
*ze mehr-e khwish joz shādi nabin**im** • ke az piruzi arzāni bedin-**im***

"We are two dear lovers," he sang, "the other's sacrifice in love.
We are loyalty's treasure at the time of loyalty; we are merciless ar-
    rows in the eyes of our foes.
As we enjoy delight and merriment, our enemies suffer trouble and
    misery.
No toil makes us tire of love, our heads never turn from love's way.
We're like two shining lights in love, like two gardens in bloom in
    dalliance.
We experience nothing but joy in our love, for we deserve this joy in
    our success."

(205/128–33 [168])

The high frequency of the same rhyme throughout this opening passage, especially in the context of a wine song, suggests an aural kinship
with the ghazal form; one might think of it as an extended *maṭla*[c], the
opening line that sets the tone of the piece and utilizes the same double
rhyme as we hear above. Its distinctive sonority, furthermore, suggests
that this section of *V&R* is a very singable one. Following this introduction, Rāmin's song changes tactics and begins a series of blessings and
benedictions, first on Vis, then Rāmin, then Media and its people:

khwashā visā neshasta pish-e rāmin • chonān kabg-e dari dar pish-e shāhin
khwashā visā neshasta jām bar dast • ham az bāda ham az khubi shoda mast
khwashā visā be kām-e del neshasta • omid andar del-e mobad shekasta
khwashā visā be khanda lab goshāda • lab āngah bar lab-e rāmin nehāda
khwashā visā be masti pish-e rāmin • ze [c]eshq-ash kish hamchun kish-e rāmin
zehi rāmin neku tadbir kardi • ke chun visa yek-i nakhchir kardi
zehi rāmin be kām-e del hami nāz • ke dāri kām-e del rā nik anbāz
zehi rāmin ke dar bāgh-e beheshti • hamisha bā gol-e ordibeheshti
zehi rāmin ke joft-e āftāb-i • be farr-ash harche to khwāhi biyābi
hazārān āfarin bar keshvar-e māh • ke chun vis āmada-st az vay yek-i māh
hazārān āfarin bar jān-e shahru • ke dokht-ash visa bud-o pur viru
hazārān āfarin bar jān-e qāran • ke az posht āmad-ash in māh-e rowshan
hazārān āfarin bar khanda-ye vis • ke karda-st in jahān rā banda-ye vis

O happy Vis, seated before Rāmin, like the graceful partridge
    before the falcon.[38]
O happy Vis, seated with wine-cup in hand, drunk from wine and
    beauty both.

O happy Vis, seated in heart's delight, while hope in Mobad's heart
   is dashed.
O happy Vis, her lips parted in smile, then pressed against Rāmin's lips.
O happy Vis, drunk before Rāmin: her religion is love, like that of
   Rāmin.
Well done, Rāmin! – you planned it well, having captured a prey
   such as Vis!
Well done, Rāmin! – glory in your heart's delight, for in heart's
   delight you have a good mate.
Well done, Rāmin! – in a heavenly garden, forever with the May-time rose.
Well done, Rāmin! – you're paired with the sunlight, you'll gain all
   you desire from its radiance (*farr*).
Thousands of praises on the land of Media (*māh*)! For a moon
   (*māh*) such as Vis has come from it.
Thousands of praises on the life of Shahru! For her daughter was
   Vis and her son was Viru.
Thousands of praises on the life of Qāren! For from his loins came
   this radiant moon.
Thousands of praises on the smile of Vis! For it's made this world
   the slave of Vis!

(206/134–46 [168])

Probably the most impressive aspect of this song for most listeners is its
insistent repetition of the phrases *khwashā visā* ("O happy Vis"), *zehi rāmin*
("Well done, Rāmin"), and *hazārān āfarin* ("thousands of praises"), which
bundles the lines into self-referential units akin to the turns of a rondo.
There is a good deal of internal repetition and rhyme within these groups
as well, such as *neshasta*, *k/pish-e rāmin*, *jān*, and the relative pronoun *ke*
that follows every benediction. Following this passage, we "hear" another
eighteen lines that draw heavily, as do most of Rāmin's songs, from the
conventional tropes and iconography of the ghazal (206/147–64). There
are also some important bits of information conveyed in these lines, such
as Rāmin's suggestion that, having "captured" Vis, he now receives royal
charisma (*farr*) from her radiance, just as Mobad had hoped to do – but
we'll return to the implications of this self-image later. "Every time Rāmin
drank wine," concludes the narrator, "he brought up this kind of talk"
(207/165); with this transition, the language shifts out of Rāmin's lyrical
mode and back to the default narrative voice.

As a whole, this "song" utilizes a wide array of cues, from tropes
to sonic features to mise-en-scène, to produce a discrete textual space
that recalls the ghazal and invites the reader to experience this performance from within the genre's discursive horizons. While I can only
speculate on this point, it seems to me that this moment would mark the

emotional climax of the episode: having drawn us in through a series of dramatic scenes and colourful adventures, interwoven with asides of admonition and advice, the narrator now invites us to vicariously take part in the lovers' joy by giving the microphone to Rāmin, so to speak, that we may bask in the aesthetic pleasure and affective power of his lyrical language. Following the song's conclusion, the adventure needs to return its characters to their stasis, and the narrating voice resumes its straightforward presentation of events: Mobad's despair and retreat to the desert, followed by his mother's reconciliation of the two brothers. The episode ends with an eye-catching reference to its own cyclicity, describing how, after their trials and tribulations, Vis, Rāmin, and Mobad "once again" (*degar bāra*) resumed their merrymaking at court: "In joy they sat, contented at heart, and watered the fields of pleasure with wine" (218/126–7 [180]).[39]

As we turn our attention to the next episode, the main point to linger on is the way Rāmin's performances produce a mode switch in the narrative. By abstracting the ghazal into a distinctive mode or way of speaking, the text presents Rāmin's songs and monologues as imagined performance events that claim affinity with the songs sung by court minstrels or the ghazals penned by professional poets. But like an organism brought to a new habitat, the literary tradition embodied by our minstrel here cannot hope to remain unaffected by its surroundings.

Episode 2: Lyrical Reality

For our next episode, I will consider another aspect of the lyric-in-the-romance: its interaction with the surrounding text, that is, its diegetic "reality." If Rāmin performs a song or soliloquy, what significance, if any, does it have for the story? To clarify the stakes of this question, I cite the following passage by Gian Biagio Conte, who asserts that "every literary genre is obliged to manifest itself by [the] reduction of the world to a partial field of vision."[40] If we think of the ghazal as a genre – that is, a "specific organisation of texts with thematic, rhetoric, and formal dimensions"[41] – then we might consider the ways it sees (and thereby creates) the world through the lens of its own rhetorical position:

> As a language, this rhetoric is partial, in both senses of the word, because it is neither "complete" nor "impartial": it is only one part of the world, but it is indifferent to its own relativity; it claims to be completed and total; it believes in its own absoluteness. It is a limited perspective, but it reduces everything to itself, turns everything into an image of itself. Modeling the world on its own language, it prohibits the belief that there might be anything else outside of the image of that world it knows how to give.[42]

With this proposition in mind, I am interested in exploring the extent to which the particular vision of the world (the *theōria*) summoned by and manifested in Rāmin's speech-acts can engage with, disrupt, or challenge the world view of his fellow characters. Investigating these moments should shed light on if and how the text's multiple voices mingle into a polyvocalic discourse in which the very truth and meaning of the story's events become a matter of debate.

It is admittedly common in *Vis & Rāmin* for speech-acts to occur as if in a vacuum, running in parallel channels with little interaction. The song we just heard above, for example, passes by without remark or acknowledgment from its diegetic audience, Vis. Nor does it leave any discernible impact on the storyline: song or no song, the lovers would have still escaped the bonfire, enjoyed their time together, and rejoined Mobad months later. Rāmin's performance, therefore, seems to be devoid of narrative force; it is "unreal," so to speak, somehow separate and disengaged from the world in which it was performed. Such observations could reinforce the common tendency in literary criticism to think of the lyric and the dramatic as ontologically distinct modalities: if the drama unfolds across time, the lyric is a break from that temporality, a timeless moment forever held in the "now" of the speaker's thoughts. We might consider how, in a Broadway musical, the action can be put on pause at the beginning of a song, only to start back up when the song is over.[43] (Of course, many Broadway numbers do move the action forward, although still in a distinctive modality.) It is the change in mode that makes such defiance of "reality" (time's constant flow) possible and palatable for modern audiences, precisely because the new mode brings along with it its own reality (a suspended time in which people spontaneously burst into song). Such a "lyric" modality often seems applicable to Rāmin (who, narratively speaking, does not "do" much in these pieces) and to the static adventure-time in which he plays such a prominent role.

The songs we will hear in this upcoming episode, however, rupture the theoretical boundary that separates lyrical and narrative modes into disconnected worlds. Here, Rāmin's songs communicate with other characters, elicit responses, and move the narrative forward.[44] Furthermore, they acquire additional meaning from the story that surrounds them, infusing the common tropes of his language with valences specific to his setting and character. Through their intercourse with their narrative context, Rāmin's songs subtly interrogate the conventional logic of their own mode, generating new questions and complications in their presentation of love. They also invite us to reconsider the mode's relationship with time: if the lyrics are "real" in a narrative sense, can they also impart trajectories of motion into the cycles themselves? Can they serve as an index of change in Rāmin's story, despite its apparent stasis?

To explore these questions, let us dive into the second episode, the (in)famous story of the bed trick. As before, it opens with a formula that announces its episodic nature: Vis, Rāmin, and Mobad have reconciled and forgiven past sins, when "one day" (*yek-i ruz*, 219/3 [181]), the king, drinking wine with Vis, summons Rāmin to join them. This effectively sets the stage for a symposium (Ar. *majlis*), a setting that carries strong associations with intimate discourse, often on the theme of love.[45] In this setting, Rāmin's songs not only articulate a vision of love that stands at odds with those of his interlocutors, but they also carry perlocutionary force – the power to affect, divulge, negotiate, and transform.

Rāmin's first performance – "a sweet song about his state" (*be ḥāl-e khwad sorud-e khwash*, 219/8) – shows how he can leverage his diegetic environment to bring new layers of meaning to his language. Isolated from this context, this song would come across as a fairly conventional appeal to patience and endurance, in which the speaker urges himself to calm the torment that rages within him, keeping faith that the heavens will one day reward him with his due (219/13). This message, however, seems tailor made for Rāmin at this point in the narrative. His self-assurance that things must change advances the sub-textual implication that Mobad's turn with Vis must eventually come to an end, and when that happens, Rāmin will be next in line. The same idea seems to have occurred to Mobad as he listened: when the song is finished, he grows melancholy and requests another piece, "one about love, sweeter than the last one" (219/17). Rāmin obeys and sings a tune "from the despair long held within his heart" (*az del bar gereft anduh-e dirin*, 219/18):

رونده سرو دیدم بوستانی — سخنور ماه دیدم آسمانی

شکفته باغ دیدم نوبهاری — سزای آنکه در وی مهر کاری

گلی دیدم درو اردیبهشتی — نسیم و رنگ او هر دو بهشتی

به گاه غم سزای غمگساری — گه شادی سزای شاد خواری

سپردم دل به مهرش جاودانی — ز هر کاری گزیدم باغبانی

همی گردم میان لاله زارش — همی بینم شکفته نو بهارش

من اندر باغ روز و شب مجاور — بد اندیشم چو حلقه مانده بر در

حسودان را حسد بردن چه باید — به هر کس آن دهد یزدان که شاید

سزاوارست با مه چرخ گردان — ازیرا مه بدو دادست یزدان

I saw a strutting cypress – itself a garden. I saw an eloquent moon – itself the sky.

I saw a blooming garden – a new Spring, a worthy bed for sowing love.

And there I saw a rose that held the month of May, a paradise in both scent and hue,

dispelling grief in times of sorrow, a delight to behold in times of joy.

I gave my heart to its love forever, I chose to be a gardener above all other trades.

And now I walk among its tulip beds, and gaze upon its springtime blossoms.

I sequestered myself in the garden, day and night, while my ill-wisher hangs by the door like a knob.

Why must the jealous ones persist in their envy? God bestows each one his due.

The turning sky deserves the moon, for God conferred the moon to him.

(219/19–27 [182])[46]

Again, we see Rāmin describe himself in vocabulary steeped in the tropes and imagery of the ghazal: the cypress, the garden, the moon, the springtime, the rival. The latent and possible meanings of these stock images, however, begin to multiply when read within the narrative context: who does Rāmin mean when he states that the moon is best matched with the sky? In relation to the song that preceded it, we might read this as a continuation of Rāmin's coded claims on Vis; his decision to nurture the May-time rose in the garden will ensure his future access to the moon in the sky, anticipating his eventual triumph over Mobad. This time, however, the king seems to have reached a different conclusion, for on hearing the song, "love became new in his heart for joy" (*ze shādi gasht ʿeshq andar del-ash now*, 220/28); perhaps he heard its closing lines as a concession from Rāmin, an admission that, however much the speaker may desire it, the moon is by rights the sky's (the king's) alone, while the speaker-as-gardener must content himself with earth. In "releasing" his poems into the narrative, and by extension, the public space of *V&R*'s readership, Rāmin no longer gets the final word; the discursive framework that makes his speech-acts meaningful to him does not automatically govern the way his interlocutors will understand them. The interweaving of song and story, in other words, makes possible the conditions for debate and negotiation.

Thus, behind the formal etiquette of the symposium and the conventional language of Rāmin's songs, we can perceive a fierce power struggle unfold: the players, as in a game of chess, begin to make their moves. Vis tells the Nurse to take Rāmin's spot in the room, allowing the minstrel to approach her and arrange that evening's tryst (220/38–47);

perceiving the ruse, Mobad breaks up their conversation by ordering Rāmin to sing another song. Rāmin obeys, but this time, his choice of tune backfires. Ostensibly an ode to wine, the theme of his next song is secrecy: it is wine that will restore the lover's pallid colour and keep his secret desire under wraps. Yet the wine, paradoxically, is also the vehicle of disclosure; just as a drunkard cannot hold back his tongue, so too Rāmin's ode to wine adopts a manner of speaking that cannot but reveal his inner state.[47] ("And who would be surprised?" remarks the narrator, "A young man in love, drunk, with a harp at his side?" 222/71–2). This faux pas brings the banquet to an end: the furious king sweeps Vis away to his bedroom, leaving the minstrel alone and dejected.

These examples show how Rāmin's lyrics, when placed within a fictional performance context and informed by the concerns of the overarching story, acquire new significances they could never have possessed without this larger framework, and in so doing, become part of the framework itself; no longer an aside from the plot, they provide the very material through which the plot unfolds. We see an especially interesting allusion to this spill-over effect after the symposium has ended, when Mobad, now alone with Vis, angrily reprimands her for her brazen flirting with Rāmin: "Sitting right in front of me, you two act as if you think you're alone!" (*neshasta rāst pish-e man chonān-id • ke pendārid tanhā har dovān-id*, 223/85). This phrase underlines the abiding tension between lyric and narrative modalities as *V&R* unfolds. When Rāmin performs his songs "as if" his back were turned to the audience, or "as if" they occurred outside diegetic time, Mobad reminds us that they can in fact be "real" and have real consequences.

In fact, bringing in the likely performance context of *Vis & Rāmin* itself, these songs might become the most "real" part of the story altogether, not only spilling *over* into the narrative but also spilling *out* of the text and into the world. We can conduct this thought experiment with Rāmin's song at the bed-trick episode's climax. Vis lies awake next to her slumbering husband, thoughts of Mobad and Rāmin turning in her mind, while Rāmin, drunk and restless, ascends the palace roof. Framed by this backdrop, the winter snow swirling about him (something to note for chapter 5), he sings a lament of separation, calling on the wind to "bring my wretched plaint to her ears" (226/150 [189]). Generically, this is a classic trope in Arabic love poetry, an apostrophe in which the wind functions as an abstract interlocutor for the poet.[48] But the scene's vivid setting, combined with the likelihood that *V&R* was read aloud, imbues the performance event with a distinctly dramatic flavour.[49] When placed into the mouth of the text's reciter, who performs the narrator, who performs Rāmin, the song produces a moment

166	Love at a Crux

of *mise-en-abyme*, extending the performance out of the text and into the court of Abu al-Fatḥ Moẓaffar. Through his embodiment by the reciter, the audience can no longer see Rāmin as a purely fictional character who lives and acts only in the mind's eye: there he is in the flesh, singing the lament of his love and begging the wind to wake Vis and bring her to him.[50]

The rising presence of two authorial voices – Rāmin's and the narrator's – and their possible embodiment through oral recitation, draws our attention to an emerging struggle over the representation of reality itself. This marks a new development in the text; while there are extensive passages of reported speech coming from Vis, Mobad, and the Nurse, they tend to sit comfortably within the she-said-he-said mode of third-person narration. But here, as we imagine the reciter of the poem oscillating with increasing frequency between the "I" of the narrator and the "I" of Rāmin, a certain bifurcation of the account into two competing stories becomes visible. Let us return to Rāmin's lament to see this in action.

Unlike the ghazal form, which necessarily ends when the speaker stops speaking, Rāmin's song on the roof flows back into the narrative after its utterance, with lingering effects. Picking up the sound of his voice, Vis realizes that Rāmin is nearby, and this in turn precipitates the bed trick, in which she commands the Nurse to take her place in Mobad's bed while she joins her lover on the roof (another moment that has inspired many comparisons between *V&R* and *Tristan*). Had she heard his words, though, and not merely his voice, her ardour to reach him might have been dampened, for this is how his song begins:

تو در خانه من اندر برف و باران   نگارینا روا داری بدین سان

میانِ قاقم و سنجاب خفته   تو دیگر دوست را در بر گرفته

دو پای اندر گلِ تیمار مانده   من اینجا بی کس و بی یار مانده

که عاشق چون همی گرید به زاری   تو در خوابی و آگاهی نداری

Do you think it right, my idol, that you're at home, while I'm in the snow
and rain,
having taken your other lover in your embrace, snuggled between furs of
mink and ermine?
I'm left out here, friendless, loveless, my two feet helpless in the mud of
anguish,
while you're asleep and cannot know the bitter tears your lover sheds.

(226/142–5 [189])

Like the invocation of the wind, these lines are also rather conventional for their genre; it is a commonplace in ghazal poetry for the lover-poet to complain of solitude and loneliness, while accusing the beloved of scorn, indifference, or preferring the company of another, in tones that can range from truculent to playful. But when placed within the narrative context, a small but significant disjuncture emerges. Only some twenty lines prior, the narrator has explicitly told us that Vis is not asleep, showing that the content of Rāmin's lyrics is not reliable; more important, however, is the implicit accusation of infidelity, an accusation that not only diverges from the narrator's account but would also surely annoy Vis to no end.

At this point in the game, such disagreements in the details may appear relatively trivial, especially if one reads Rāmin's song as a set piece, disconnected from the surrounding narrative: from this perspective, his lyric "I" simply adopts a familiar range of postures, none of which need advance an account of the "truth." However, as we have seen, the presumed separation of lyric and narrative domains can no longer be taken for granted. Rāmin's songs *can* and *do* interact with the narrative world and form part of its reality, and yet, even as they harness the diegetic winds to reach Vis's ears, they project a reality that does not always align with the one that contains them. It is thus not the disconnect between lyric and narrative that's important here but the increasingly unstable dynamic between them, their simultaneous engagement and disengagement from each other, their boundaries blurring and reforming, their horizons alternating between states of fusion and rift. This interaction stands to split the diegetic world of *V&R* into two versions, or indeed visions (theories) of reality, which not only dispute the question of "what happened" but also compete for the authority to represent it.

The quick juxtaposition of these two accounts thus introduces a moment of friction that, in time, will grow in stakes and intensity to become the central driver of the plot as it continues its cyclical iterations. It has shown, returning to Conte's discussion of genre, how Rāmin operates within a world view that is "indifferent to its own relativity" and "turns everything into an image of itself." In the following section, we will watch this play out in Rāmin's deteriorating relationship with Vis, as he grows increasingly isolated from her version of events, captivated by the self-image that frames his vision of the world and constitutes himself as that world's hero. This emerging gap sets the stage for a sustained inquiry into the discursive mechanisms of the lyric as well as an exposure of its limits and blind spots: "The 'model of the world' that is thereby proposed," Conte continues, "if confronted with reality, will turn out to be partial and will clearly reveal its ideological lines of force."[51] In this way, the never-stable interaction of song and story contributes to the overarching didactic aim of *V&R* to interrogate the dis/empowering affects of discourse.

Episode 3: The Mirror of the Self

To explore how this happens, let me briefly revisit the concept of lyrical abstraction. As I suggested earlier, Rāmin's lyrical performances effect a kind of translation, a literary moving-across from a source genre to a target genre, from the short-form ghazal to the long-form romance. Through this process, a certain amount of abstraction occurs, in that the conventions of an independent genre are distilled into a more general sense and feel in the new literary vessel. Once divorced from its formal constraints, this ghazal-in-the-abstract must be summoned through other cues: these may include the setting of its performance, its dominant tropes and topoi, and even its distinctive diction and sonority, all signs that invite us to read the text lyrically, if not as "lyric" per se. The poems we have studied thus far have made liberal use of these cues, and as a result, are fairly easy to distinguish from the narrative.

These diegetically "real" songs constitute only the minority of Rāmin's performances, however, and as the story proceeds, their supporting cues begin to fall away, making it increasingly difficult to distinguish between words privately thought or articulated aloud, or between what is "said" and what is "sung" (intensified by the fact that both modalities of speech are conveyed in the verb *goftan*). As a result, the mechanics of mode switching that enabled us to read and interpret Rāmin's songs as belonging to a particular genre, and thus intelligible on their own terms, begins to break down. We might call such a process the *lyricization* of speech, such that *all* Rāmin's speech-acts, regardless of their formal presentation, can be seen as expressive of a world view that is grounded in the lyric.

A prominent example of this abstraction and lyricization occurs at the beginning of our next episode, the story of the Devils' Grotto (*eshkaft-e dīvān*). We have already visited this episode in the previous chapter from the perspective of Mobad, but let us now observe Rāmin as he laments his impending departure from Marv to fight the Romans, while Vis has been locked away in the Grotto. His songs, poems, and soliloquies now run thick and fast, with four such speech-acts occurring in rapid succession. But, unlike the *in situ* songs we heard at the wine party, the form of delivery here is ambiguous and varied. The first of Rāmin's performances is introduced with the words, "He secretly spoke to his heart" (*hami gofti nehāni bā del-e khwish*, 239/21), and with no formal features or performance context to guide us, we might be tempted to construe it as a kind of inner monologue. But upon finishing, "He then began another 'song' in his heart" (*be del kardi sorud-i digar āghāz*, 240/33), suggesting that both this speech and the one that preceded it could have been sung or at least experienced as though they were. The final two poems of this cluster grow more obviously vocal: when Rāmin learns of Vis's imprisonment in the Devils' Grotto, he says (or sings) some "heart-wrenching words" (*hami gofti sakhonhā-ye del-angiz*, 240/47) – though to no one in particular – then leaps on his horse and gallops away, singing (*sorāyān*, 242/81) another poem to himself as he goes.

With the loss of clear diegetic or narratorial cues, this blurring of song and speech suggests that a new mechanism for mode switching has emerged: not Rāmin with a tambour in hand or Rāmin singing at a party, but simply Rāmin. His words and songs have coalesced into a general way of speaking, producing a composite and totalizing modality now embodied by its speaker: composite because it lyricizes his spoken words, while giving his lyrics power and presence beyond the limits of their enunciation; totalizing because it encompasses not only his manner of speech, but his habits of thought and action as well. In other words, Rāmin need not really sing to invoke the ghazal: his mere presence instigates the switch to a modality informed and inflected by its conventions. The whole world, in a sense, becomes a part of his lyrical performance.

In this light, the hyper-conventional content of Rāmin's speech is all the more significant, for it both illustrates and enacts the way his discourse gradually isolates and alienates him from the world around him. In his first monologue, for example, he addresses an imaginary comrade, asking him, "Do you know a state (*ḥāl*) worse than this, that death to me seems sweeter than life?" (239/29 [203]).[52] In the speech-acts that follow, Rāmin will invoke a number of other conventional addressees: he explains to his heart why it is right for him to weep in the beloved's absence; he implores the breeze to convey news of his suffering to Vis; galloping towards the Devils' Grotto, he tells his absent beloved that nothing shall deter him in his love; and on his arrival, he sings to the abode (*sarāy*) itself, lamenting its lost brilliance:

نه آنی آنکه من دیدم نه آنی   کزین گیتی به رامین خود تو مانی

جهان جادو و خودسازست و خودکام   ستم کردست بر تو همچو بر رام

ز تو بردست روز شادمانی   ز رامین برده روز کامرانی

دریغا آن گذشته روزگارا   که چندان کام و شادی بود مارا

نپندارم که روزی باز بینم   ترا شادان و بر تخت نشینم

You're not that which I once saw, you're not! Out of [all in] this world,
  you're exactly like Rāmin!

> The world is a sorcerer, arranging its affairs to its own pleasure: it has
>   oppressed you, just as it has Rāmin!
> From you, it's snatched the days of joy, from Rāmin, the days of pleasure;
>   alas for those bygone days, when such pleasure and joy were ours!
> I doubt I'll ever see again a day when you are joyful and I sit upon your
>   throne.
>
> (248/18–22 [211])

Despite the diversity of these addressees – the companion, the heart, the wind, the beloved, the fortress – we can see that they fall into the same pattern and perform the same function: they hold up absent, inanimate, or unresponsive interlocutors as a mirror for Rāmin to regard himself in monological fashion.[53] With repetition, they reveal that the hero of Rāmin's world is none other than Rāmin.

There are a number of ways we can understand the implications of this pattern. As modern readers, we might be tempted to chalk up Rāmin's self-obsession to his narcissistic personality, though this may rely overmuch on an anachronistically modern notion of character as having a coherent inner psychology and consciousness. The notion of Rāmin as a "type" is more plausible in Gorgāni's context, especially since he often evokes the stance of the "manly" lover who weeps on separation, endures unendurable pain, and is willing to sacrifice himself on the path of love. But further insight still can be gained, I think, by considering the vision of the world that is created by Rāmin's discourse, which has a significant impact on the way it shapes his self-image in relation to the other characters. Imagining Rāmin as the product of generic abstraction brought into the polyphonic landscape of the love-story, we may gain further insight into the way the text explores competing modalities of love, and alternative visions for its fulfilment, by overlaying multiple discursive traditions on top of one another.

To do this, I'd like to briefly step away from Rāmin and visit the poetic models that (in)form his character, to offer a clearer sense of what I mean by "the" ghazal in this context. The ghazal form, and the myriad genres and subgenres it developed over time, is far too vast to be reduced to a single modality of speaking; but, as Meisami has noted, there are clear lines of affinity between Rāmin's speech and a lyric style, one that I will call "courtly," that gained popularity in Abbasid Baghdad, epitomized by the poet al-ʿAbbās b. al-Aḥnaf (d. ca. 808).[54] In the ghazals of al-ʿAbbās, we can detect the cultivation of a certain type of erotics, one that would receive further elaboration in essays, anthologies, manuals of conduct, and even philosophical treatises as al-ʿishq al-ẓarīf, "refined" or "elegant" love.[55] In many ways, both the love stories and love lyrics of this period commit to similar values, reaffirming a basic relationship between love, fidelity, and nobility. Despite this shared ethos, however, the courtly ghazals of al-ʿAbbās – and of many subsequent court poets, such as Saʿdi – rely on a distinctive relationship between lover and beloved that sets the ghazal apart from the love-story. The difference is evident, as Domenico Ingenito explains, in the principle of *mushākala*, or similitude, of romance protagonists:

> The physical similarities in the depiction of the two lovers attests to an ideal of love as a mutually reciprocated attraction that does not apply to the dynamics of power embedded in the lyricism of the qasida and the ghazal ... The lover of the ghazal *hopes* to be reciprocated, *wishes* to be as young and attractive as the beloved, and longs for the interchangeability that turns the two desirous subjects into each other's beloveds. The constant frustration of this ideal of amorous beatitude (or its temporary validity) is what provides the ghazal with its dramatic ethos, which calls for the continuous reiteration of the lamentation.[56]

Thus, although Bürgel is right in pointing to the close thematic connections between the two literary forms – "the spirit of the *ghazal* has its flesh and blood in the romantic epics," as he puts it – we can see how differing configurations of power can produce markedly different dramatics, or what we might call (implied) narratives, in the languages produced.[57] As the ongoing or imminent separation of lover and beloved provides one of the central topoi of the Abbasid courtly ghazal, one of its most standard scenes is to feature the lyric "I" as a loner, suffering in the absence of his (or her) inaccessible, haughty, or unfaithful beloved.[58] The following passage from a poem by al-ʿAbbās conveys well the kind of story one often hears in this tradition:

شكتْ ما بها نفسي من الشوق والهوى   فقلتُ: لقد طالبتِ وُدَّ مُمَنَّع
وما كان منكِ ٱلعشقُ إلّا لَجاجَةً   ولو شئتِ لم تَهْوَى ولم تتطلَّعى
وما هو إلّا ما تَرَينَ ، وذو الهوى   يُعالج ثِقلاً فأصبِرى أو تقطَّعى
عسى الله أنْ يرتاحَ يوماً بِرحمةٍ   فيُنصفَنى من فاضِحِى ومُرَوِّعى
لَعَمْرى لَشتَّى بين حَرَّانَ هائِم   وبين رَخِيّ بالُهُ مُتَودِّع
كتمتُ أسمَها كِتمان من صان عِرْضَه   وحاذَرَ أنْ يفشو قبِيحُ التسمُّع
فسمَّيتُها «فوزاً» ولو بُحثُ بِأسمها   لَسمَّيتُ بِأسم هائِل الذِكر أشنَع
فَواحسرتِى إنْ نحتُ لم تُقضَ نَهمَتى   ولم يُغنِ عنّى طُولُ هذا الَتضرُّع
وهبتُ لها نفسى فضنَّتْ بِوصلِها   فَيا لَكَ مِن مُعْطٍ ومن مُتَمنِّع!

My soul complained of its longing and desire, so I said to it: you demanded an unattainable love.
Your love was nothing but stubbornness; if you had willed, you would have neither lusted nor pursued.

It [the matter] is nothing but what you see: a [true] lover undergoes bur-
    dens, so ride it out or get cut off!
Perhaps God in his mercy will be see it fit to give me my due from the one
    who disgraces and frightens me.
By my life, what a difference between the one burning and baffled and one
    cosy and comfortable, his mind at ease.
I concealed her name as one who protects his honour, wary that an evil
    eavesdropper might divulge [it],
so I called her "Fawz"; were I to reveal her name, I'd give her an ignomini-
    ous name too repugnant to mention.
Alas! Were I to wail, it would not bring an end to my desire, nor would this
    long supplication avail me.
I gave her my soul and she begrudged our union – what a gift, and what
    a repayment![59]

When reading this ghazal against the speech-acts we've heard from
Rāmin, many thematic parallels will be apparent. As al-ᶜAbbās con-
trasts his distress and suffering to his beloved's tranquil contentment,
we might hear the echo of Rāmin's rhetorical question, "Do you think it
right, my idol, that you're at home, while I'm in the snow and rain?"; or
again, as he seeks refuge from scandalmongers, we may recall Rāmin's
complaint, "my ill-wisher hangs by the door like a knob." Despite their
(perceived) ill treatment at the hand of their lovers, both poets declare
their determination to remain loyal nonetheless: "As long as my sweet
soul aids me, my job will be to keep faith with Vis" (*marā tā jān-e shirin
yār bāshad • vafā-ye vis jostan kār bāshad*, 251/70). In addition to these
shared motifs, al-ᶜAbbās's poem announces a significant theme that will
find its parallel in Rāmin's lyrics: the notion of reward. Al-ᶜAbbās takes
it as a given that his beloved will not repay the poet for the suffering he
endures; this recompense may only come from God, who might, perhaps, "equalize" (*yunṣif*) the poet's fidelity by rewarding him with *her*.
The strange admixture of veneration of and contempt for the beloved
implied by this equation can be sensed as well in the poet's refusal speak
her name, lest he utter a four-letter word; indeed, the other pseudonym
he uses for her is *Ẓalūm*, "Tyranny."[60]

As we return to Rāmin at the gate of the Devils' Grotto, we can see
this same language and its associated mode of thinking persist even
at the moment of union. Unable to penetrate the fortress walls, Rāmin
shoots an arrow into Vis's chamber. Vis and the Nurse discover the
arrow, realize that Rāmin is outside, and open the great doors of the
bathhouse, giving him light enough to scale the wall; Vis then lowers
a rope fashioned of her silk garments to haul him up to her bedroom.

Although these scenes emphasize the collaborative labour of both partners in achieving their union, Rāmin contests this point with the following song, sung in the aftermath of their lovemaking. Ironically, although Vis is this time directly in his presence, the object of Rāmin's address is, once again, himself:

بلا بردی و ناکامی کشیدی   چه باشد عاشقا گر رنج دیدی

به بی رنجی نیابی نیکنامی   به آسانی نیابی شادکامی

ز وصل دوست بر گوهر رسیدی   به هجر دوست گر دریا بریدی

ز رنج خویش اکنون بر بخوردی   دلا گر در جدایی رنج بردی

که نزدیکی بود فرجام دوری   ترا گفتم به جا آور صبوری

چنان چون تیره شب را عاقبت روز   زمستان را بود فرجام نوروز

ز وصلت بیش باشد شادمانی   چو در دست جدایی بیش مانی

چو کام دل بیابی بیش نازی   هر آن کاری که چارش بیش سازی

بهشتی گشته با حوران نشسته   منم از آتش دوزخ برسته

به دی مه از رخانت گلفشانست   مرا خانه ز رویت بوستانست

مه تابان به مهرم سر در آورد   وفا کشتم مرا شادی بر آورد

ازیرا شد جهان با من وفادار   وفاداری پسندیدم به هر کار

O Lover, what does it matter that you've suffered toil, calamity, and frustrated desire?

Desires are not easily attained, nor is a good name won without effort.

Though you swam a sea in separation, you've acquired a pearl in union with your love.

O Heart, though you suffered in separation, you now see the reward for your troubles.

I urged you to have patience, for after separation comes union.

New Year's spring lies at the end of winter, just as day follows night's darkness.

The longer you remain in separation's grip, your joy will be all the more at the time of union,

and for every deed you do for its sake, you'll find even more delight when you've acquired your desire.

The flames of Hell that roasted me have changed into Paradise with houris around me:

I have a home in your face, a springtime garden that scatters flowers in the winter.

There I planted fidelity, and it bore me joyous fruit; the months of burning have delivered me my love.

I kept myself faithful in every deed, and thus the world has been faithful to me.

(254/131–42 [218])

This song vividly demonstrates how Rāmin's lyrical performances not only develop a certain kind of persona for him within *V&R*, but also project an image of Vis into the story that appears disengaged from the physical Vis in front of him. As in al-ʿAbbās's poem earlier, Rāmin assigns himself both the burden of loverhood and the joy of its fruits. It is to his credit that he endured the pains of separation, mastered his impatient heart, and traversed fire and water to reach his beloved; now that he has overcome these obstacles, he has acquired the pearl-like prize that is his due. His use of the words "fidelity" (*vafā*) and "faithful" (*vafā-dār*) in this context is striking: fidelity to the beloved is like sowing a seed, and the reward lies in plucking the fruit that grows after the patience and labour that goes into its nurturing (reminiscent of his claim to be a "gardener" in a prior poem). In such a scheme, Vis has little to say in the matter, for in the end it is not *she* who rewards him for his fidelity but the *world* itself.

The gendered and political implications of this language are significant: by embodying and enacting the conventions of the courtly ghazal, Rāmin is propounding a mythos that effectively writes Vis out of *Vis & Rāmin*, depriving her of agency, autonomy, and even mutability. It is an attempt, in other words, to remake the world of *V&R* through the mirror of his poetry, in which the primary interlocutor for Rāmin is his own heart. (There is one song where he speaks to Vis in her presence, at 257/179–89 [221], but this the sole exception.) More than just a product of Rāmin's self-regard, this world view seems to emerge out of the structure and grammar of Rāmin's speech, which paradoxically casts him as the subject of a world that he himself has created. As Zumthor observes, speaking of the I-thou relationship of the courtly love lyric in troubadour poetry, "*My* glance, at the same time as the word uttered by *I*, thus gives *you* life and the only sort of reality possible."[61] And as long as the worlds generated by Rāmin's speech-acts come into being and then disappear in tandem with his utterance, no significant challenge to that creative power is forthcoming. The end result is an image of the world in which Rāmin's male privilege and authorial control are unquestioned and absolute.

But the problem for Rāmin is that we are no longer in the ghazal; the story continues after the song is concluded, and now, Vis can speak back. She responds to his song in an interesting way, pouring him a cup of wine and praising him as one faith keeping, faith seeking, and faith seeing (*vafā-dār-o vafā-juy-o vafā-bin*, 255/145). Her three-fold repetition of the word *vafā* ("fidelity") emphasizes its conceptual importance for Vis as well as for Rāmin, recalling the nominally shared ethos between lyric and romantic articulations of noble or courtly love. Yet as Vis continues her praise, we can see that this is not quite the same idea of faith as what Rāmin has proposed: "Until death, I will be caught in his love, and honour his fidelity" (*bovam tā marg dar mehr-ash gereftār* • *vafā-dāri-sh rā bāsham parastār*, 255/148).[62] The distinction here is minute but vital: she is not promising Rāmin her eternal love with no strings attached but is linking it to his constancy (*vafā-dāri*); that is, the understanding that he is, has been, and will be faithful to her. With this implicit condition in place, Vis recalibrates the conditions of Rāmin's reward in such a way that she, and not the world, has the final say. This alternative notion of *vafā* not only restores her ability to choose but also puts forth the possibility that she, and her love, may not be so like a timeless pearl as Rāmin would have it. It emerges that Vis *is* capable of change, and that her love for him is not inertly "there," like a fruit for the picking, but contingent on his own choices.

Even as it exposes a subtle rift opening up between the lovers, this dissent over the meaning and practice of *vafā* – the ethos of fidelity – drives home Graham Allen's point that the "clash of ideologies and past utterances within language is not simply to do with a dialogic clash between distinct, separate 'languages' but often exists within individual utterances and even within the same word."[63] Vis, as we have seen, constructs her concept of fidelity out of the conventions of the love-story, a mythos that anticipates the strict fidelity of *both* partners as its normative practice. Unpacking Rāmin's expectations of himself and others, however, proves to be a little more complicated, due to his linguistic hybridity. On one hand, he is a romance hero and operates in dialogue with the normative ethos of this genre, articulated by Vis; yet because so much of his self-fashioning happens through lyrical performance, it suggests that his primary interlocutor is an *extra-textual* community of like-minded poets – the ghazal tradition of courtly love – who reside outside the space-time of the romance proper.

Rāmin's final performance in this episode is especially jarring in the way it exhibits a growing divergence between Vis and Rāmin's expectations of themselves and each other, even as they claim to value the same key principles. When Rāmin learns of Mobad's imminent return to the Devils' Grotto, he beats a hasty retreat from the castle, descending the walls using the same silken ropes that had granted him access in the first place. Once safe in the wilderness, he recites a lament that begins, "You cannot know my state, my love; how bitter my life is without you" – all while Vis is being beaten within an inch of her life by her furious husband (265/104). The irony of this juxtaposition is hard to ignore, or to forget.

Episode 4: A Crisis of Authority

As the cyclical narrative continues its revolutions, it becomes difficult
to shake the impression that the former concord between the lovers is
rapidly disintegrating. We sense it in the increasingly blatant ways in
which Rāmin's depictions of his beloved contradict the account given
us by the story's narrator; we feel its presence as Vis and Rāmin declare
slightly discordant understandings of who owes what to whom in their
practice of fidelity. But while the divergence of thought worlds is interesting in its own right, showing an innovative use of generic norms in
the development of interiority, it is more serious than a mere difference
of opinion: it bespeaks the gritty negotiation of power, not just the relative power of one person over another, but the power to control the narrative (world) itself. As I have argued, Rāmin has been slowly crafting
a story in his verse that fashions him as the chief protagonist of *V&R*,
while abstracting Vis into the haughty, absent beloved that his songs
require her to be. This story stands at total odds, of course, with the
one that Vis wishes to tell, and here the shift from the formal ghazal-as-
performance to the abstracted ghazal-as-character plays a crucial role.
In the final episode of this four-part sequence, we will see Vis respond
to the contents of Rāmin's songs in ways that would have been impossible to develop in the short-form lyric. Her pushback, building on the
precedents set above, grows much more visible and vigorous in this
scene, in which she adopts the conventions of his poetry to challenge his
authority over her narrative and to redirect his accusations onto himself.

In its broad strokes, the fourth episode is quite similar to its predecessor, perhaps suggesting that they are variations of the same scenario:
Mobad again goes to war and locks Vis in his palace while he's gone,
charging the Nurse (instead of Zard) to be her warden. But there is an
important difference: although the fabula is the same, it is told from a
different perspective. Rāmin has only one poem in this cycle; otherwise,
it is Vis who takes the initiative, does the talking, and controls the story.
Here is the relevant scene: Rāmin has deserted the army and doubled
back to Marv, and he soon arrives at the palace gate. With his usual
agility, he scales the wall and jumps into the garden, but at this point
he cannot get any further. As he paces the garden, he recites a familiar
refrain: his enemies delight in his misery, he's drowning in the unjust
sea of love, and his beloved is both absent and oblivious – "For what do
I weep so wretchedly, when you have no awareness of my state?" (*che
sud ar man hami geryam be rāzi* ● *ke az ḥāl-am to āgāhi nadāri*, 281/34). Having finished his piece, and with nothing left to do, Rāmin falls asleep
amidst the flowers.

Her intrepid lover thus stalled, Vis takes matters into her own hands, in a feat of dexterity to match Rāmin's acrobatics: scrambling up the ropes of a nearby pavilion, she leaps to the palace roof, fastens her chador to a fissure in the wall, and uses it to rappel down to the garden below. On one level, this scene performs an interesting reversal of roles, such as we find in *Varqa & Golshāh*, where the heroine slays her own abductor and rescues her would-be rescuer; or, further afield, the moment when Nicolette ties her clothes into a rope and climbs from her tower window to save her lover Aucassin, who is weeping abjectly in his father's dungeon.[64] On a deeper level, however, it goes beyond a simple swapping of hero and heroine in a way that would present the identities of Vis and Rāmin as analogous or interchangeable; the switch rather occurs in such a way as to bring out an irreducible difference between the two. This is achieved by the narrator's fixed visual attention to Vis's body, which, during the course of her escape, is gradually and almost methodically stripped naked by her surroundings: first her shoes, then her veil, then her necklace and earrings (285/84–7), and finally her clothes.

قبا شد بر تنش بر پاره پاره   گرفتش دامن اندر خشت پاره

به درد آمد ز جستن هر دو پایش   اگرچه نرم و آسان بود جایش

چو شلوارش دریده بر دو رانش   گسسته بند کستی بر میانش

دریده بود یا افتاده یکسر   نه جامه بر تنش مانده نه زیور

به هر مرزی دوان و دوست جویان   برهنه پای گرد باغ گردان

The hem [of her chador] snagged on a piece of brick, and the robe upon her body was torn to pieces. Although the place [of her landing] was soft and spacious, her two feet were pained by the jump [she had made]. The girdle about her waist was broken; the trousers upon her thighs were torn. Neither clothing nor ornament remained on her body; it was all either shredded or lost. With bare feet, she circled the garden, running from end to end and calling for her beloved. (285/90–4 [249])

The disrobing of Vis in the course of her "trick" suggests something distinct from the usual motif of role reversal, which is typically accomplished by putting clothes on, rather than taking them off. For example, Rāmin twice disguises himself as a woman, in both cases to pull some subterfuge against Mobad (the ordeal by fire and the coup, 203/84–5, 509/45).[65] Likewise, there are many examples of women in Islamicate literature, such as the *Shāhnāma*, the *Dārāb-nāma*, *Samak-e ʿAyyār*, the *Abu Moslem-nāma*, *Dhāt al-Ḥimma*, and the *1001 Nights*, who shift their gender by wearing male clothing, riding into battle, and marrying other women.[66] In contrast, the voyeuristic imagery here is meant to expose rather than conceal, to titillate the audience and humiliate Vis: a round-about fulfilment of Mobad's threat to parade her before his army "without shoes or veil, like a dog" (193/86). While such scenes are quite common in the tradition of Hellenistic romance, it is significant that here the narrative destabilizes the very premise of sexual symmetry that so often guides the genre's structure and ethos.[67] Rather than flatten Vis and Rāmin into an (almost) interchangeable pair – such as we see in ꜥAyyuqi's *Varqa & Golshāh*, for example, and a technique we *have* seen used elsewhere in *V&R* – it emphasizes their pointed difference, throwing he who falls asleep to the music of his own songs into sharp relief against she who suffers every indignity in the struggle for union.

This widening gap is further established in the lyrical interlude that follows. As we know, Rāmin's preferred mode of delivery is the song (*sorud*), a form that is exclusive to him and other minstrels, like the *gosān* at Mobad's banquet; Vis's discourse, meanwhile, takes the form of spoken conversation, written letters, or lamentation.[68] Nevertheless, she can deftly adopt lyrical language into these settings, taking advantage of the same process of genre abstraction that Rāmin has employed. When she arrives at the garden, Rāmin is still asleep amidst the flowers and nowhere to be found; thinking herself alone and abandoned, Vis recites a long lament – literally, a "cry of woe" (*vāy*) – as blood flows, both figuratively and literally, from her eyes and feet (*ham az chashm-ash ravān khun-o ham az pāy*, 285/95). Poised in this declamatory stance, she turns to address the wind – a classic cue for entering "lyric mode," one we have seen Rāmin perform many times – to send a message of her own to her apparently absent beloved.

به حق دوستی ای باد شبگیر　　　برای من زمانی رنج بر گیر

اگر با بی دلان هستی نکورای　　　منم بی دل یکی بر من ببخشای

که پایت گر جهانی بر نوردد　　　چو نازک پای من خونین نگردد

نه راهی دور می بایدت رفتن　　　نه رنجی سخت ناخوش بر گرفتن

گذر کن بر دو نسرین شکفته　　　یکی پیدا یکی از من نهفته

نگه کن تا کجا یابی کسی را　　　که رسوا کرد همچون من بسی را

هزاران پردگی را پرده برداشت　　　ببرد و در میان راه بگذاشت

هزاران دل بخشم از جای بر کند　　　به هجران داد تا بر آتش افگند

ببین حال مرا در مهر کاری　　　بدین سختی و رسوایی و زاری

For the sake of love, O wind of morning's light, spare a moment's trouble
　for me,
　if you look kindly on the lovelorn; I am such a one, have mercy!
For though your feet may tread the world, they do not bleed as do mine.

You need not travel far, nor take up unpleasant burdens;
just pass over two white rose blossoms, one in plain sight and the other
 hidden from me,
and see where you can find someone who has dishonoured many like me,
who tore the veil from thousands of virgins, stole them away, and left them
 by the wayside,
who stirred a thousand hearts in hatred, left them, and cast them in the
 fire.
Look at me in my pursuit of love, in this hardship, shame, and misery!

(285/98–106 [250])

Although Vis has moved into the same modality of speaking as her lover's signature style, she repurposes its motifs and conventions to tell a different story.[69] Where Rāmin has frequently followed convention to complain, even in this very episode, that Vis is heedless of his state, Vis's plaint enumerates the potentially disastrous consequences that his brand of "courtly" love might entail for women, delivered in a voice that could only have come out of the experiences of his disgraced mistress, whose humiliation was put on visual display only moments before. The violent implications of Vis's broken belt, scattered pearls, shredded garments, and bleeding feet gain figurative importance as she works them into her account of Rāmin's cruel transgressions. Her demand that the wind (and by extension, her readers) behold and acknowledge the utter wretchedness of her position – stripped, wounded, and abandoned, robbed of both her first husband and her dignity – could not be a more apt response to Rāmin's speech; not only does it remind us that the stakes and consequences of her love cannot be conflated with Rāmin's, but it also foregrounds the physical harm and social exposure she has repeatedly undergone for his sake. Vis thus articulates herself in a way that is both specific to her personal experience and expressive of the female voice that is generally controlled by or excluded from the normatively male "I" of the courtly ghazal, directly challenging its authority to speak on her behalf. Indeed, in one stinging rebuke, she hurls his accusation back at him:

مرا گفتی چرا ایدر نیایی   من اینک آمدستم تو کجایی
بدا بخت منا امشب کجایی   چرا ببریدی از من آشنایی
ببخشاید به من بر دوست و دشمن   چرا هرگز نبخشایی تو بر من
کجایی ای مه تابان کجایی   چرا از باختر بر می نیایی

You said to me, 'Why do you not come here?' Well, here I am! – And where
 are you?

> ... O my evil fortune! Where are you tonight? Why have you deprived me
>   of your company?
> My friends and enemies have pity on me; why do you never show
>   mercy?
> Where are you, O shining moon, where are you? Why do you not appear
>   to me from the eastern horizon?
>
> (286/117, 126–8 [251–2])

Such ripostes not only undercut Rāmin's attempts to vindicate himself
at Vis's expense, but even begin to actualize the possibility of infidelity,
not (yet) in the form of physical action, but through speech *as* act. Has
Rāmin, in repeatedly describing Vis as distant and unfaithful, spoken
this rift into existence, and thereby betrayed her?

Vis's lament in this episode tells us two important things about the
lyrical passages in *V&R* and their relationship with the narrative that
surrounds them. First, it makes it clear that Vis and Rāmin are using the
same words to tell different stories about themselves and each other:
although they often utilize the same repertory of tropes, images, and
conventions, the way they integrate these speech-acts with the narrative context either confirms or undermines their moral authority. Second, the characters' lyrics retain perlocutionary force even after their
utterance, contributing to the overarching development of the story; in
that light, they are not superfluous at all, but the very site where the
differentials of ideology (as Conte puts it) and the struggle for power
between the lovers makes itself most apparent.

As a result, the story that seems to be unfolding does not bode well
for their long-term prospects. If Vis's anger at Rāmin suggests that her
patience may have limits after all, her rejection of his claim over her
story – her demand to speak back and be heard – will come as something of a shock to our minstrel, who inhabits a discursive world view
in which both his gender and his poetic persona grant him full normative authority. The episode backs away from this impending crisis
before it can play itself out – Vis eventually discovers Rāmin sleeping
amidst the violets (an important moment of foreshadowing, as we'll
see below), leading to a night of passion and Rāmin's escape the next
morning – but the widening rift between the lovers has been laid bare
for all to see.

Breakdown and Break-up

Given the generic background of the text, for *Vis & Rāmin* to even raise
the possibility of love breaking down is something of a landmark event,

certainly unusual and perhaps unprecedented within its regional tradition.[70] As Bakhtin asserted, on the basis of his extensive reading, the guiding principle of romance is the unspoken rule that the protagonists' love must remain intact *no matter what*: "The hammer of events shatters nothing and forges nothing – it merely tries the durability of an already finished product."[71] Yet in *V&R*, the reliability of that "product" has been fatally compromised. The source of this problem, I would argue, is the fact that Rāmin had to actively (and violently) divert the story towards a course that would bring him and Vis together, disrupting one of the basic structural and ethical premises of the romantic-love mythos. Like the grain of sand at the heart of a pearl, the memento of this act is then wrapped up, smoothed over, and made beautiful by the numerous songs and lyrics he performs, which ultimately produce an alternative narrative in which that originating violence never happened. His voice thus contributes to the disturbance of the "monologic plane" of the narrative, joining the speech-acts of Vis, Mobad, and the narrator such that they interrupt and disrupt one another, bleed into each other's horizons, and lay claim to the same territory from different perspectives.[72] This heteroglossic friction produces the conditions necessary for romantic love to lose its former stability: it transforms the function of narrative time, generates individuated viewpoints with conflicting interests, and instigates a struggle for authority between the eponymous protagonists.

This outcome allows us to reassess the notion of adventure-time and its function within the narrative. On first impression, the cyclical episodes discussed in this chapter seem to support Bakhtin's model, for after every adventure, the trio of Vis, Mobad, and Rāmin reconcile with one another, and the cycle begins anew with the next episode. In terms of raw plot, these episodes seem to have no visible impact; one could feasibly shuffle their order, or take them out altogether, without bringing us any closer to resolving the basic intrigue. After a long slog through four episodes and thousands of lines, the love triangle is still in place, the affair remains illicit, and no road to resolution is in sight. Such repetition can come across as monotonous and even infuriating; it has long been characterized as a strike against the poem's legacy.

But what if that is the point? As Gabrieli noted long ago, there is a striking correlation between these repetitive episodes and the frequency of lyrical passages: the latter amplifies the former, dragging down the plot and forcing everyone (characters and readers alike) to experience and acknowledge the fatigue of this stasis. The many songs, laments, and asides make it clear that change is indeed taking place, if not on the level of plot than on that of character, not *despite* but *because* the lovers remain stuck in a destructive loop that is gradually taking its toll on them. They are by now more apt to dwell on their misery than on their happiness, and the monologues of the fourth episode consist entirely of mutual recrimination and expressions of exhaustion. One can almost hear the weariness in Vis's voice as she tells Rāmin, upon learning of Mobad's approach, "It's time for you to escape; it's time for me to take his blows" (*torā bāyad ke bāshad rastegāri* • *marā shāyad ke bāshad zakhm-khwāri*, 292/54 [257]) – just the latest iteration of a routine, wretched existence in which "I have become a byword for affliction: a hundred lashes for every kiss" (292/58). Arriving on the scene, Mobad kicks her, almost robotically, as she lies on the ground; she does not stir.

Lyrical amplification not only produces this fatigue but also allows us to track its impact on the characters across time, restoring temporality to an atemporal world. In other words, it does not simply fill the void of adventure-time, but rather mobilizes that time in a way that becomes both emblematic and productive of a critical problem that will drive the lovers apart if it cannot be resolved. As a result, the chronotope's function has been turned on its head: once meant to demonstrate the durability of the lovers' bond, it now makes manifest that bond's inherent weakness, the reality that the love of Vis and Rāmin may not ultimately withstand the "hammer of events" unless it undergoes some kind of radical transformation.

The cause of this structural weakness may be traced in part to the lyrical passages, which individuate the characters as inhabiting discrete and not entirely compatible thought worlds. As I discussed in chapter 2, one of the central presumptions of romance narrative is that the lovers must share a uniform and mutually compatible vision of love, one that glorifies chastity and demands reciprocal fidelity. This is certainly the *modus operandi* of Vis, who strives in all she does to remain loyal to the recipient of her love, despite her less-than-ideal circumstances; but the introduction of another set of norms, grounded in the conventions of the ghazal and personified by Rāmin, disrupts the prerequisite uniformity of feeling in the romance genre. It is a subtle distinction, as it is mostly the same vocabulary they trade back and forth – a word like "loyalty" being a prime example – but it is their conception and enactment of these terms by which the lovers drift apart: they may be speaking the same words, but not the same language.

This generic admixture produces a complex and, at times, highly damaging matrix for the lovers' interaction, visible in the way Rāmin builds his expectations of the possible through his songs. Drawing from the thought world of ghazal poetry, he frequently portrays his beloved as fickle, distant, and passive; yet even as he complains of her neglect, he does so in a narrative world where she will always be there to open the window, shimmy down the rope, pull off a bed trick, or suffer beatings for his sake. Rāmin thus gets to have his cake and eat it too, benefiting from the privileges afforded him by both his persona and gender. As we have seen, the focal point of Rāmin's words is Rāmin himself, specifically his affective "state" or "condition" (*ḥāl*) – a word that, if we review the songs discussed in this chapter, appears time and time again – while he seems unable to see or remember the myriad ways in which Vis has proven his version of reality to be a false one.[73] It stages a conflict, as I will discuss in the next chapter, between Rāmin's presentist focus on affect and Vis's historical memory of the past.

The combined implications of these points come to a head – and with astonishing speed – at the conclusion of the fourth and final episode. The next scene to come is the disastrous spring party, during which the host Mobad is first mocked by the *gosān* and then cast from his dais by his brother; at this breakdown of basic protocol, it seems that the two lovers realize that something has got to change. In a private conversation with the sage Behguy ("Speak-well"), Rāmin complains, "The hearts of men are not of stone or iron; how long can a body manage? How long can a heart endure?" (304/18–19 [269]). Meanwhile, Vis turns to Mobad as her confessor: "Why should I love in this way, which only brings pain and eternal shame?" (314/32 [279]). Both the sage and the king have the same advice for their confidants: move on from this joyless lust and find true happiness in lawful marriage. Though it is not the first time the lovers have heard such counsel, they accept it now, concluding independently of each other that they must break off the affair.

Like so many break-ups, mutuality does not guarantee amicability. Rāmin goes to Vis and takes a seat on Mobad's throne, intending to tell her he's leaving, but before he can open his mouth, she chides him for impudently sitting above his station – a not-so-subtle warning against taking what is by rights the king's. This short rebuke is the straw that breaks the camel's back; with his long-standing narrative about his beloved's cruelty seemingly vindicated, Rāmin storms off, chiding his heart in another lyric-like passage for having squandered his youth on a woman who cannot appreciate him (317/25–42 [282]). Vis tracks Rāmin down and apologizes for her harsh words, but her lover is now resolved to go; to console her, he promises to seek no love but hers during his absence (323/119 [287]). But immediately upon arriving in Gurab – the same place where Mobad abducted Vis many years before – he happens upon a local noblewoman of great beauty named Gol ("Rose"); he is smitten on the spot and proposes marriage then and there. Just as Tristan abandons Isolde for Isolde of the White Hands, Rāmin has left Vis to pursue her "double," the same external form without – he hopes – the old messy baggage.[74]

Thus, in a matter of some 150 lines – after literally thousands of lines of speeches, songs, and suffering – the strained relationship of Vis and Rāmin comes crashing down like a house of cards, an inevitable collapse perhaps, but none the less stunning for it. This is not the end of the story, but it prefigures in dramatic fashion the death of love (and its subsequent rebirth) that will be our topic for the next chapter.

The Final Word

To bring this one to a conclusion, however, I would like to briefly discuss the aftermath of Rāmin's separation from Vis, and the consequences it has on his power and authority. According to Behguy's diagnosis, Rāmin is miserable because he is a slave to love; to restore his dignity and honour, he needs to step up and "practice manliness" (*mardi koni*, 307/69 [272]): he must get hold of his emotions (307/67–90), realize there are plenty of fish in the sea (308/91–104), and prepare himself to be king himself one day (309/105–10).[75] While this is all common advice in the mirrors-for-princes literature – even the narrator stops to commend it (305/35) – it does not, in this case, work out.[76] Rāmin can implement Behguy's instructions as far as dropping the affair and marrying a respectable woman from a noble family, but he cannot fully forget his old passion. This much becomes clear when he turns to Gol one day and blurts out, "You well resemble heart-ravishing Vis" (*vis-e del-setān rā nik māni*, 337/75), which, to no one's surprise, quickly sours the honeymoon. In a manner similar to Mobad's relationship with Vis, Rāmin's attempts to clear up his name only compound his predicament; he can no more give up his attachment to her than can his brother. Furious and humiliated, both by this evidence of his own dependency and by the dressing-down he receives from Gol, Rāmin writes back to Vis, blaming her for all his woes:

که چند آمد مرا از تو زیانی	به نامه گفت ویسا نیک دانی
همه کس در جهانم سرزنش کرد	خدا و جز خدا از من بیازرد
شدم از عشق در گیتی علامت	شنیدم گه نصیحت گه ملامت
یکی کس را که کار من پسندید	چه بودی گر دو چشمم در جهان دید
که مرد و زن برو کردند نفرین	تو گفتی مهر من بودای عجب کین

He said in the letter: "O Vis, you know well how much damage has come
upon me from you: both God and [His] creation are offended by me; everyone in the world has berated me. I've sometimes heard advice, sometimes
blame; I've become a byword for love in the world. How [nice] would it be
if my eyes searched the world and found one person who approved of my
actions! How strange! It's as though my love is hatred, for men and women
alike curse it!" (338/5–9 [305])

A notable feature of this vindictive overture is its singular focus on
discourse – on what everyone is saying. This seems to suggest that something important is happening in regards to Rāmin's ability to control
the narrative. As Bakhtin contends, the novelistic hero "eavesdrops on
every word someone else says about him," yet ultimately knows "that
he has the *final word*, and he seeks at whatever cost to retain for himself this final word about himself, the word of his self-consciousness, in
order to become in it that which he is not."[77] In a similar way, Rāmin has
utilized his lyrical speech to allocate enormous power and privilege to
himself: the liberty to absolve himself of his many offences against the
king, as well as the authority to portray his lover as both exalted and
haughty. But the events of the four cycles, culminating in his marriage
to Gol, have turned the narrative around such that Rāmin ultimately
falls short of the very personae he sought to embody: he can neither
stay loyal to his first love (nor to his second), nor can he be counted
on to uphold his political and familial commitments. The many stories
of Rāmin portrayed in his speech-acts – Rāmin the faithful, Rāmin the
clever, Rāmin the valiant – has given way to a single, ugly reality: Rāmin
the oath breaker, a figure in whom the practice of love, to his astonishment, is in the end indistinguishable from hatred (*kin*).[78] Therein lies
the letter's furious tone, for it is in the figure of Vis that the gap between
his discourse and his actions – the limits of lyric – becomes apparent for
all to see.

Rāmin's rage and disorientation at the "damage," as he put it, wrought
by this exposure receives dramatic visual testimony in the subsequent
scene. After receiving his letter, Vis sends the Nurse out to treat with
him in person, hoping that she might soften his stance. But when the
Nurse arrives, she is shocked to find Rāmin in the midst of a hunt, the
plain strewn with broken carcasses, the mountainsides stained with
blood (350/4–9 [316]). Although the slaughter may not be too far from
the way actual hunts were conducted in Gorgāni's milieu, "her heart
was filled with arrows at his cruelty" (350/10), a reaction that seems
fully intended to convey a negative message about the hunter. Rāmin's

ferocity is no less vivid in the way he reacts to the Nurse's presence, excoriating her and Vis with the same hurtful language of his letter, such that the Nurse "saw no warmth in his words, nor goodness in his visage" (352/49).[79] Meisami understands this scene as conveying a message about the moral equivalence of Rāmin and Mobad, who both resort to violence when their desires are thwarted.[80] Building on that insight, these moments of unbridled rage also correspond with crises within their own personae (with which Vis is deeply imbricated): just as Mobad found himself blocked and undone by his role as king, Rāmin encounters the same aporia through his performance of the courtly lover, who, it turns out, is no less a tyrant, despite his claims to the contrary. The faces of "king" and "lover" emerge as merely two sides of the same coin, founded in shared assumptions of masculinity and privilege, with the only difference between them lying in their discursive claims to authority.

The remainder of Rāmin's songs – all but the final two, sung much later near the end of the text – articulate this new-found self-alienation. One day, while riding in the country, one of the maidens in his company hands him a posy of violets (403/14 [371]), the same flowers that Vis had given him as a token of their pledge (165/82 [128]). As memories of that compact come flooding back to him, he launches into an interior monologue in which he castigates his heart, likening it to a drunk man who cannot distinguish between good and evil (404/36 [373]). This war against the self is a central trope in the case of Mobad as well, and places Rāmin's crisis of identity within the much larger pattern of internal fragmentation we have seen unfold for all the major characters in the story. However, the rhetorical tactics of his monologue reveal an aspect of Rāmin's inner conflict that distinguishes him from his brother: while Mobad digs into his role and discovers paradox at the bottom, Rāmin's amorphous ghazal persona allows him to inhabit conflicting stances and experience it as a cogent performance. In other words, while the ideal king should never be at war with himself, the ideal lover as played by Rāmin is assumed to be in a state of perpetual estrangement (*ghorbat*, 406/66); it is part and parcel of the identity. Thus, by shifting across these various stances, Rāmin can confess his guilt and absolve himself of it at the same time, at times placing the burden of infidelity on the "bad" Rāmin who is misled by his fickle heart, while the "good" Rāmin professes an undying loyalty that was never truly compromised: "I'm ashamed – why did I follow your orders? Why did I put my reins into your hands?" (405/51), he says to himself.

As a result, Rāmin can continue to hang onto a both/and modality that always allows him to remain the hero of his story. This is the engine that drives the romance to the point of no return, as it perpetuates an alternative, timeless account of *affect* that is incompatible with Vis's historical reckoning of *deed*, of who did what to whom. The final poem in this episode confirms Rāmin's refusal to alter the heroic mythos of his poetry, setting the stage for the final clash between the two lovers and the breakdown of their romance. As he sits gloomily at the evening's banquet, Rāmin speculates, rehashing his prior performances, that Vis must have no idea of his state, that she misunderstands him, and that she must believe that he is happy here with his wife (410/27–34 [379]); once again, we are seeing the conventions of the ghazal, which assumes the beloved is totally ignorant of the lover's suffering, controlling Rāmin's train of thought. At the end of this reverie, he comes to a sudden decision:

هم اکنون راه شهر دوست گیرم   که گر میرم به راه دوست میرم

نهندم گور باری بر سر راه   همه گیتی شوند از حالم آگاه

غریبانی که خاکم را ببینند   زمانی بر سر گورم نشینند

ببخشایند چون حالم بدانند   به نیکی بر زبان نامم برانند

غریبی بود کشته شد ز هجران   روانش را بیامرزاد یزدان

غریبان را غریبان یاد آرند   که ایشان یکدگر را یادگارند

همه جایی غریبان خوار باشند   ازیرا یکدگر را یار باشند

I'll take the road, here and now, to the city of my beloved, so that if I die, I'll die on the path to the beloved. They'll place a grave for me at the side of the road, and the whole world will know my story. Strangers, seeing the mound, will sit for a while by my tomb; they'll pity me when they learn of my situation, and will utter my name with approval, saying, "He was a stranger, killed by separation in love – God have mercy on his soul!" Strangers remember strangers, for they are the ones who memorialize one another. Strangers are abject wherever they are; it's because of this that they befriend one another. (412/50–6 [381])

As before, Rāmin's fascination with discourse speaks volumes in this passage. Rather than seeing himself as the suicidal victim of his self-image, as Mobad does, Rāmin eagerly commits himself to his own martyrdom in (or to) love, a narrative of the self that vindicates his persona and immortalizes his name, while conveniently sweeping his past deeds under the rug. In so doing, he declares his loyalty not to the diegetic actors in the romance, but to the intertextual and diachronic brotherhood of "strangers" (*gharibān*), the many lovelorn "I"s of the ghazal tradition, who are and always have been his chief interlocutors.[81] This choice of word is significant: on one level, it declares his status as a lover, whose commitment to the path to (or of) the beloved (*rāh-e dust*) necessitates a certain detachment from society – a wholly romantic ethos, especially prominent in the story of Majnun – yet on another level, it may also express his alienation from the romance itself, which has so complicated and disrupted his attempts at self-representation. As Michael Pifer writes, "The *gharīb* provides us with an affective grammar of estrangement, or a manner of being paradoxically foreign and native at the same time, that challenges conventional notions of what belongs within and without any given culture"; applied to this context, Rāmin's simultaneous belonging to and estrangement from *V&R* signals the text's broader interest in raising questions around what "belongs" in the praxis of love by exploring multiple experiences, exposing their partiality, and questioning their authority.[82] Ever the liminal figure, with one foot in the romance and one foot out of it, Rāmin seems most concerned about the reception of his story, rather than its outcome; his final wish is ultimately not union with Vis but that "the whole world will know my story." He continues in this vein a few verses later:

همی گویند بر حالم سرودی   چو بنیوشی زهر دشتی و رودی

همم بر دشت خواننده شبانان   همم در شهر داننده جوانان

سرود من همی گویند هموار   زنان در خانه و مردان به بازار

When you listen, they're all singing a song about me, from every river and plain. The youth in the city know it, the shepherds in the field sing it; women in the home, men in the market-place – everyone's singing my song! (412/94–6 [383])

This resolution makes it clear that Rāmin is now on a mission to save his *story*, even at the cost of his own life; indeed, to die a martyr to love would be the perfect ending for him, a sure-fire way to salvage this travesty of a love-story. Yet in seeking this heroic sacrifice, Rāmin again falls into the trap that has plagued him from the outset. His thoughts remain firmly anchored on himself and the character he sees himself playing; his road to redemption only circles back to the hall of mirrors that constitutes his generic self. Vis, not even mentioned by name in this passage, is only relevant insofar as she is the "beloved" for whom he dies; his chief concern is not her welfare but the fact that his side of the story will be remembered.

As we shall see in the next chapter, this is the one point that Vis will never concede, for she is as determined as Rāmin to make sure that her audience – both in the text and outside it – will witness the pain she has suffered and acknowledge the legitimacy of her actions. And thus, as Rāmin flees the scandal he has created in Gurab "as a coward flees a battle" (416/125 [385]), we arrive at the explosive climax of *Vis & Rāmin*: a contest that will decide not only the story's ending but also the terms by which we read it.

Chapter Five

History | The Death of Romantic Love

"It is the nature and custom of the world," announces the narrator of *Vis & Rāmin*, "that its own elements are in conflict with one another" (233/1):

هر آن کس را که او خواند براند   هر آن چیزی که او بخشد ستاند

بود تلخش همیشه جفت شیرین   چنان چون آفرینش جفت نفرین

شبش با روز باشد ناز با رنج   بلا با خرمی بدخواه با گنج

نباشد شادمانی بی نژندی   نه پیروزی بود بی مستمندی

بخوان این داستان ویس و رامین   بدو در گونه گون کار جهان بین

Every one whom it summons, it drives off; every thing that it gives, it snatches away. Its bitter is forever coupled with sweet, such that its blessing is coupled with [its] curse. Its night and its day mingle burden with play, disaster with delight, malice with riches. There is no joy without sorrow, no success without privation. Read this story of *Vis & Rāmin*: behold therein the mottled affairs of the world. (233/2–6 [197])

This simple statement, coming at the beginning of Mobad's disastrous campaign against the Romans (not for the campaign itself, but for what follows in its wake), provides an important premise for making sense of the story's relationship with the "real" world. If the balancing of every element with its opposite suggests an underlying order to creation, that order is paradoxically manifested by the visible disorder of a world that operates in a perpetual state of internal war. Thus, as the bonds of love and loyalty bend and give way in the diegetic space of the story, casting the protagonists into mutual strife, we are invited to read this collapse as a mirror of the world we inhabit.

The alignment of the imaginal world "in here" and the experiential world "out there" is more than a static reflection of space, however. It also presents this disharmonious state of affairs as the outcome of time, offering us what we might call a history to aid in its reckoning. This is indeed how the *Shāhnāma* frames itself to its readers, as an act of one curious man asking the learned sages of his day, "How did they [the great kings and heroes] keep the world at the beginning, such that they left it to us now in such a wretched state?" (*ke giti be āghāz chun dāshtand* • *ke idun be mā khwār bogzāshtand*, 1:12/121). In this way, we arrive at the convergence of history and phantasy. Although it describes itself as a fable or fairy tale (*afsāna*), *V&R* enacts the processes of worldly time on its characters, subjecting them to its curse even as it sustains them: the word "its blessing" (*āfarin-ash*), after all, is orthographically identical to the word for "creation" (*āfarinesh*), allowing for a secondary reading of the passage above that implies that every act of creation is also a form of malediction. It is time, as much as space, that establishes a connection between the textual denizens of *V&R* and its flesh-and-blood readers – not time in the sense of a linear continuity linking "then" with "now," but rather the experience of time itself and the consequent imperative to make sense of it in some way. In other words, the challenge and opportunity *V&R* poses to its readers is to engage with the reality of death: not merely the corporeal death of individuals, but the knowledge that *all* things – even love itself – are historical entities, subject to the laws of entropy, and ultimately doomed to annihilation by the relentless passage of time.

As markers of beginnings, endings, and temporal change, the radicals of life and death thus provide a valuable key for reading Gorgāni's literary project and gauging its success in renovating the romance, making it matter to elite audiences and creating new possibilities for meaning-making within the tradition. The story begins and ends on Nowruz (34/22 [1], 530/1 [495]), suggesting that it has taken us through the passage of a metaphorical year, wherein we observe the lives of its characters passing by as so many seasons.[1] Across this temporal journey, each character experiences paradox, aporia, and breakdown in the discursive systems that form them and inform their view on the world. Vis experiences a radical transformation by giving up her old commitment to Viru for the sake of a new one with Rāmin, a move that nearly effects her dis-integration; although she manages to bounce back and reconstitute herself, we have seen that their relationship is mortally wounded by its violent and coercive origins. Mobad discovers, to his shock and horror, that the authority he considered intrinsic to his status as king was actually an external power, such that the only agency he appears to have is materialized in the self-inflicted murder of his sublime body. And Rāmin, unable or unwilling to give up the affective privilege his songs afford him, withdraws into a grotesque parody of the courtly lover he so wishes to embody, a nihilistic path in which death is the only desirable outcome. In all three cases, the resulting story is a movement from order to disorder, from purity to adulteration, and from innocence to knowledge.

This master narrative not only drives *Vis & Rāmin* to its unusual conclusion but also guides the meta-account of Gorgāni's project: the destruction and renovation of romance for a new era. Underlying these three individual manifestations of breakdown is the crumbling foundation of the romance chronotope – the mechanics of space and time in the genre's world – now too deeply disturbed by its entangled polyphonic tensions to function as it should. Such a disturbance deeply complicates the temporal physics of romance in Mikhail Bakhtin's account, in which time is essentially redeemable and reversible, and the moment of restitution promises a return to the harmony of the status quo: "There is a sharp hiatus between two moments of biographical time, a hiatus that leaves no *trace* in the life of the heroes," he writes, such that "nothing that takes place, nothing they see or undergo, can be utilized as life experience that alters and shapes them."[2] Just as this pronouncement cannot be taken for granted in the case of the Greek novel, we have seen how time *does* leave its traces in *V&R*, to the extent that love itself becomes temporal: with each repetition of a theoretically infinite cycle, the romantic relationship grows increasingly strained and distorted, and the possibility of restitution diminishes.[3] The breakdown of romantic love in this text produces two major effects: one, the need for some kind of intervention – a little help, as it were, to put things back on track – and two, the integration of romance into a discursive mode whose temporal orientation is, in some way, historical.

We can track this breakdown by observing the traces, both bodily and discursive, that the events of the story leave on its characters. To begin this chapter, I will explore how the scars and wounds on Vis's body, along with the strokes and dots of her written words, produce a material legacy (*asar*, the Arabo-Persian word for both "trace" and "[literary] work") that cannot be forgotten or obliterated: as the narrator says, "Her stony heart did not soften to Rāmin, for an etching on adamant is not quickly scraped off" (*nashod sangin del-ash bar rām khoshnud • ke naqsh az sang-khārā nastorad zud*, 448/2 [416]). These traces are not only a visual monument but also a verbal testament, a preserved word for Vis's readers to ponder. By curating her textual legacy, in no small part out of the material of her physical suffering, Vis claims for herself the same remembrance that historical actors could possess after their deaths, a kind of "soul" that bears the same posthumous impact as other "real" humans in a community's historical memory. The testament, as the literary trace of a time-bound bodily experience, effects and performs the romance's integration into the flow of history and the meaningful etchings of the past.

The weight of this paradigmatic shift well justifies the urgency and high emotions of the story's explosive denouement, when Vis and Rāmin confront each other face to face in a whirling blizzard. Time, again, cannot be denied; the characters cannot forget the broken promises and frustrated expectations that have brought them to this crisis, leading them to the realization that the expected deliverance of the romance mythos, in the end, might not be available to them. Rather, it appears that death offers the only escape from their living hell; blood must be shed before any resolution can be obtained. This is of course taken to the literal extreme with Mobad's gory demise, but it also applies in a more subtle but radical way between Vis and Rāmin, who are locked in a struggle to assert a narrative corresponding with their self-image (or to produce their self-image through that narrative) that writes their counterpart out of it. Vis *must* be to blame somehow for Rāmin's narrative to work, and Rāmin *must* be in the wrong for Vis's image of herself to hold; thus, in an inversion of the motif of dying in love – *Liebestod* – Vis and Rāmin must silence, negate, and effectively "kill" the other if they are ever to recuperate their stolen life stories. I read this as signalling the symbolic death of not only the characters but also of romantic love itself, a paradigm that is no longer sufficient, at least in its current form, to provide a cogent or satisfying account of self-reckoning.

This is not the final word, however: in a spin on the classic romance topos of the false death – *Scheintod* – we can witness new possibilities for being-in-the-world arise from the rubble of paradigms lost. To guide my reading of this transition, I draw from a previous study on beauty's transformative power in *Vis & Rāmin* by Claude-Claire Kappler and triangulate it with a recent book by Paul Kottman that posits romantic love as a historically evolving practice of making sense of the world, particularly in response to its most unintelligible threats, and discovering in the face of those threats new forms of human freedom. (The centrality of love to meaning-making, as we will see, is equally valid in Avicenna's metaphysics.) Some version of this process is evident in *Vis & Rāmin*. As their relationship enters its death throes, the lovers begin to make curious allusions to their newfound freedom, an agency that allows them to recommit to each another on terms that are only now, in this state of being-in-death, available to them; and after making this recommitment, they find themselves capable of breaking free of the love triangle that had imprisoned them for so long, producing a final ending that weaves together personal satisfaction, political triumph, and spiritual redemption. This consolidates a vision of romance as a genre with the same relevance to the temporal concerns of the "real" world as any other account that purports to benefit its historical readership.

The distinctive manner in which *Vis & Rāmin* presents and manages time thus brings it into a tight orbit with another landmark text of the eleventh century, Ferdowsi's *Shāhnāma*. Such a relationship may seem unexpected at first, considering that one text is typically classified as "romance" and the other as "epic," yet for all their generic differences, as Eslāmi-Nodushan puts it, "there is no book in the Persian language that is both so close to and so distant from the *Shāhnāma* as *Vis & Rāmin*."[4] Though they are not woven into the same kind of historical framework that the *Shāhnāma* employs, Gorgāni's characters nonetheless gain in reality through their prolonged experience of time, transforming their love-story from phantasy to a kind of history. And like the *Shāhnāma*, which repeatedly pits the mortality of the World with the immortality of the Word, *V&R* deploys two lines of tension within its temporal flow: the narrative of decline and collapse on one hand, leading to inevitable death, pitted against the redemptive impulse of romantic love on the other, which purports to see its characters finally united either under the sanctity of lawful marriage or in the salvation of their martyrdom to love. The romance's promise of redemption is not altogether lost, but its paradigms must be fundamentally altered before the rejuvenating light of a Nowruz ("new-day") sun can crest the horizon.

Transcribing the Soul

As I have shown in previous chapters, both Vis and Rāmin harbour an abiding concern for their legacies beyond the text, the enduring presence of their "name" (*nām*) even after their tale has come to an end. We see it, for example, when Vis describes the account she would like to hear told of her: "'Vis gave up her life for the sake of Rāmin!' I'd give up a hundred lives for such a reputation!" (171/61 [133]). Likewise, Rāmin dictates his own eulogy as he rides towards Marv: "'He was a stranger, killed by separation in love – God have mercy on his soul!'" (412/54 [381]). That said, Vis and Rāmin elect remarkably different methods for curating their afterlife: while Rāmin, as we have seen, leaves behind a large volume of "traces" or "works" (*āsār*) in the form of songs and lyrics – an oral *divān*, so to speak, that establishes an affinity between him and other famous lover-poets – Vis is more inclined towards a written testament, a cache of material evidence that corroborates her version of the story. While the most obvious aspect of this testament lies in her famous ten-part letter, she also invokes her physical body, whose manifest wounds and scars provide another and less flattering account of her former lover's works and traces.[5] These diverging strategies reproduce the tension of word versus deed discussed in the previous chapter, while posing new questions about their value: if the world is as treacherous and ever changing as the narrator tells us, what ultimately matters, and what ultimately endures?

It is probably no coincidence that Vis begins to compare her body to a text in the same scenes where her relationship with Rāmin is visibly deteriorating. During a lament in the "Devils' Grotto" episode, she declares, "My heart is like a book (*nāma*), filled with pain and toil, with this sallow face at its heading; behold what suffering is in that book, whose title is a sea of blood" (245/30–1 [209]). A similar passage occurs in the subsequent episode, when Vis, standing naked and wounded in the garden, repeatedly commands her addressee – ostensibly the wind, but by implication anyone else within earshot – to "look" (*negah kon*) and "see" her (*bebin*) "in this hardship, shame, and misery!" (285/103, 106 [250]). Coupled with the stark visual imagery of sexual violence just described, this command imbues Vis with an iconicity of sorts: her testament of Rāmin's betrayal, a man she charges with having violated "thousands" of women before her, is conveyed through both verbal and visual language, such that the truth of her words is manifest on the body of their speaker. In this way, Vis becomes her own witness.

Vis's meta-textual appeals to the audience, imploring them to "see" her body and "read" her story as an embodied account, show an interesting contrast with the Greek novels, which are replete with images of bodily harm yet tend to elide this violence by submitting the heroine to various scenes of scrutiny, oath, or ordeal to ensure that nothing "happened" to her during the course of the narrative. At the ending of the *Ephesiaka*, for example, Anthia declares to her beloved Habrokomes that despite suffering "insults, chains, trenches, fetters, poisons, and tombs," she is "the same as when I first left you," this "same" not only implying chastity preserved and love undiminished, but even projecting a fantasy in which none of these troubling events ever occurred in the first place; as the narrator wryly concludes, "They made these protestations of innocence all night and easily persuaded each other, since that was what they wanted" (169/5.14–15).[6] With this, the protagonists knowingly buy into the mythos of their love-story, an account that often inclines towards, though rarely with complete success, as Jennifer Ballengee points out, "erasing the transgressive body in the process of reincorporating the hero and heroine as socially acceptable or comprehensible individuals."[7] By declaring the material permanence

196   Love at a Crux

of her physical body, in contrast, Vis claims a different sort of ontology
for herself, one that both exists within the story and endures beyond its
limits.

Vis's efforts to position herself in this way pick up speed and urgency
the moment she learns of Rāmin's marriage with Gol. After lamenting
her misplaced faith, and praying that her erstwhile lover will one day
experience the same heartbreak and hardship that she is suffering now
(a nice bit of foreshadowing), Vis turns directly to her readers with a bit
of free advice (*naṣiḥat kard khwāham rāyegāni*), as she puts it:

الا ای عاشقان مهرپرور مرا بینید حال من نیوشید مرا بینید و خود هشیار باشید نهال عاشقی در دل مکارید اگر چونانکه حال من ندانید منم بر عاشقان امروز مهتر دگر در عشق ورزیدن مکوشید ز مهر ناکسان بیزار باشید و گر کارید جان او را سپارید به خون بر رخ نوشتستم بخوانید

O lovers who practice love! Today I am the greatest of lovers! ... Look at
me! Hear my story! And strive no more to practice love! Look at me! Take
heed! And beware of loving base people! Do not plant the sapling of love
in your hearts, for if you do, you'll give up your lives! If you don't know
what happened to me, I have written the tale in blood on my face – read it
there! (346/77, 80–3 [313])

As I discussed in the prologue, many romances invoke a specific readership of lovers and ask to be read in a "lover-ly" way; as a *dāstān-e
ᶜāsheqāna*, a story in the mode of lovers, *V&R* is no exception. But here
is it not the narrator but Vis herself who reaches out to this ideal audience; then, by declaring herself to be a member of that extra-textual
readership, and indeed its greatest exemplar, she breaks the fourth
wall, joining that community as an observer of the tale and commenting on it as it unfolds, simultaneously the actor and interpreter of her
story. Crucially, this entire process is contingent on her readers' willingness to engage with her on this level, to *recognize* themselves in her –
hence her repeated requests to be "seen" – a transaction that instils in
her some amount of the same historical "substance" that they themselves possess. Thus, in speaking from this position of "real" experience and "real" injustice, it is no longer possible to discount the many
inequities she has suffered as so much water under the bridge, or to
make-believe that they never happened in the first place. By making
this extra-textual connection, Vis establishes a new set of conditions by
which her story must end: not by mere reunion, but by justice, and the
restitution of past wrongs.

The call for justice lies at the heart of Vis's textual self-fashioning, most famously represented in her long letter to Rāmin, a discrete unit of about 625 lines that has long been admired for its compositional harmony and rhetorical brilliance.[8] Although it is generally known as the *Dah-nāma* or "Ten Letters" (perhaps better glossed as a "decalogue," i.e., a volume of ten discourses), Vis gives it another and more pointed name: the *Jafā-nāma*, or the "Book of Iniquity" (388/5 [355]), a testament of the many wrongs her lover has committed. Crucially, this letter is not her direct speech, nor even her authorial composition; she rather commands her scribe, Moshkin, to compose this account in her voice and on her behalf. The work, then, should not be read as an unmediated expression of subjectivity, but rather her attempt to write herself into history, producing a document in which she builds solidarity with her readers, asking them repeatedly to heed her words and bear witness to the injustices she has received (354/16, 18, 20 [320]). Rāmin's betrayal, in her view, is nothing short of metaphorical murder: "His cruel sword has severed my head; the lance of his separation has skewered my heart. How can I tolerate my own beheading? How can I stay silent at my own impalement?" (356/49–50 [322]). The purpose of this document, then, is to set the record straight against the contesting narrative put forward by Rāmin; as such, it marks a major escalation in the (ex-)lovers' bitter struggle to establish the truth about what really happened in the story of *Vis & Rāmin*.

To realize this goal, Vis utilizes a number of strategies that set up her letter as a meta-textual document, interposed between text, reader, and character. The most immediately arresting aspect of the *Jafā-nāma*, as noted above, lies in its unforgettable use of rhetoric. Like Rāmin's songs, which also break down the line between ghazal and masnavi, many of the individual sections of Vis's letter address established topoi of the ghazal tradition and treat them in an exceptionally fine manner: the beloved's image (*khayāl*) visiting the lover (part 2), the lover's reaffirmed fidelity in the face of blamers (parts 3, 7, 8), elaborating the beloved's cruelty (part 5), finding strength in hope (parts 4, 6), and turning to God, sometimes for love renewed, sometimes with love renounced (parts 3, 9, 10). This sustained study of the ghazal universe, juggling multiple and often contradictory stances and emotions, not only produces a complex psychology of love for Vis's character, but asserts her identity as an ideal lover. In addition, just as Rāmin did in his songs, Vis uses her extended time in the spotlight to assume the role of the piece's narrator, speaking directly to her ex and her extra-diegetic audience at one and the same time. For example, in the opening passages of the letter, she reminds

her readers that the world is a volatile place: "Sometimes toil, sometimes joy, sometimes death, sometimes life" (360/37 [327]). This
nearly direct citation of the narratorial aside discussed at the head
of this chapter has the effect of placing Vis and the narrator on equal
footing as meta-diegetic characters, a blurring effect that continues
with the following lines: "All that remains of us in the world is a fairy
tale (*fasāna*); let the whole world read our tale (*fasān*), and know our
every virtue and fault" (360/39–40). This is a highly self-reflexive
passage; it is as if Vis has stepped out of the mists of "once upon a
time" to observe her story in the year 1054, fully aware of her fictionality while contending that it makes her no less a "real" part of
that historical community. Through these strategies, Vis seeks to both
unravel Rāmin's discursive claims and establish a presence that will
outlive her diegetic life and linger beyond the narrative itself – her
lifeline to literary immortality.

Given the high stakes of this project, it is worth reading Vis's letter
carefully to examine how it produces a durable reality, perhaps even
(after-)life, through its language. Its exordium opens with a remarkable sequence of anaphora, clearly meant to grab the reader's attention
and set the stage for Vis's self-presentation, while also providing an
outstanding example of Gorgāni's use of language to mode switch into
the distinctive voices of his characters and to project an imagined world
in which that voice gains intelligibility. These are the first five lines, with
the Persian in transliteration:

> *ze sarv-i sukhta v-az bon gosasta* • *be sarv-i az chaman shādāb rosta*
> *ze māh-i dar mohāq-e mehr penhān* • *be māh-i dar sepehr-e kām tābān*
> *ze bāgh-i sar be sar āfat gerefta* • *be bāgh-i sar be sar khorram shekofta*
> *ze shākh-i khoshk gashta hāmvāra* • *be shākh-i bār-e u māh-o setāra*
> *ze kān-i kanda va bi-bar bemānda* • *be kān-i dar jahān gowhar feshānda*

> From a cypress burned, its roots ripped out,
>   to a cypress verdant, flourishing in the field;
> from a moon unseen as love wanes to a crescent,
>   to a moon shining bright in the heavens of pleasure;
> from a garden in blight from end to end,
>   to a garden in bloom through and through;
> from a branch that has forever dried out,
>   to a branch whose fruit is the moon and stars;
> from a mine dug out and depleted,
>   to a mine casting jewels to all the world.
>   (358/10–14 [326])

The strong syntactic rhythm and striking parallel imagery of this opening easily translates into English without losing any of its effectiveness.
What's more, this *from-to* pattern continues on for a total of nineteen
consecutive lines, ratcheting up the intensity of its force with each reit-
eration; it's as though Vis, who has repeatedly complained of Rāmin's
slights against her, is now prepared to enumerate them individually.
An even longer performance in the same vein is found in the *Jafā-nāma*'s
peroration: there, the phrase "Greetings from me to that [one] who"
(*dorud az man bedān ... ke*) repeats across twenty-five consecutive lines,
increases the anaphoric tempo by doubling up the first clause (*dorud az
man*) for another four lines, and closes with the repetition of the phrase
"more than" (*fozun az*) twelve times in rapid succession (392/34–70
[360]).[9] Such rhythmic patterns are striking enough on the page (see
figure 3), but they are even more effective when read out loud – as *V&R*
probably was.[10] Like the act of reading out the individual names of a
group of people killed in a disaster, the cumulative effect of time and
repetition conveys a sense of impact and magnitude that a single word
such as "hundreds" or "thousands" cannot easily capture; in this way,
the letter impresses Vis's voice, and the memory of her version of the
story, into the minds of her audience.

Indeed, the rhetorical arrangement of the *Jafā-nāma* unfolds very
much like the arguments of a court scene: having softened her readers with this show-stopping overture, she now lays down her formal
charges against Rāmin: (1) he seduced another man's wife; (2) he broke
his word; (3) he abandoned his faithful lover; (4) he spoke unjustly to
her (361/58–61 [328]). It is important to note that these accusations are
articulated as breaches of the codes of honour that regulate male-male
relations in a courtly setting: Rāmin's failings in love, in other words,
are only a symptom of his general lack of chivalry (*javānmardi*, 387/42
[354]), for which Vis holds him accountable. Moreover, Vis turns to
the most conventional and I daresay conservative manifestations of
the romance ethos in defending her record: she stresses her fidelity
to Rāmin even after his betrayal (377/34 [344]), reminds him of their
mutual likeness and suitability (371/27 [338]), and declares that the
true beloved has no substitute (370/16–18 [337]), all statements that
contribute to her image as a lover of impeccable credentials who has
been unjustly wronged. These gestures to a shared courtly ethos of
honour and love would situate Vis as part of the same milieu to which
Gorgāni's work is addressed, affirming that she is one of them, so to
speak, in terms of their moral and religious sensibilities, such that they
must support her in her castigation of Rāmin. It is extremely telling
that the *Jafā-nāma* marks the only time that the most explicitly Islamic

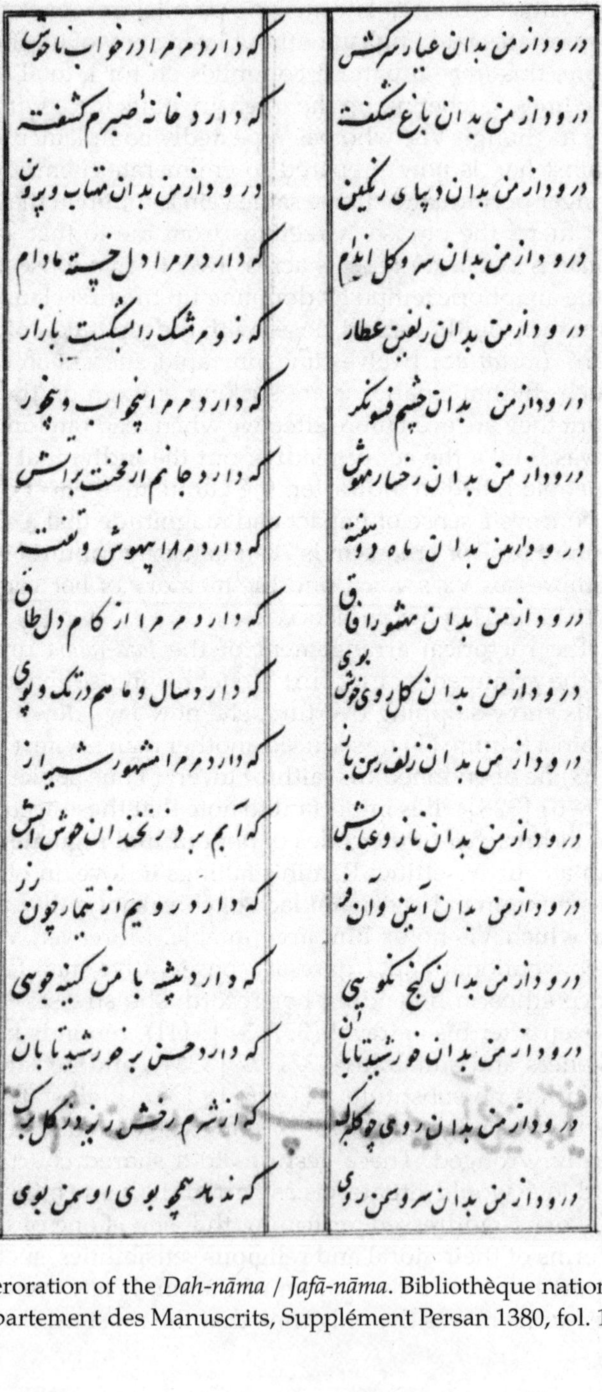
درود از من بدان عیار سرکش — که دارد مرا در خواب ناخوش
درود از من بدان باغ شکفته — که دارد خانهٔ صبرم کشفته
درود از من بدان دیبای رنگین — درود از من بدان مهتاب و پروین
درود از من بدان سرو گل اندام — که دارد مر مرا دل خسته مادام
درود از من بدان زلفین عطار — که زو مر مشک را بشکست بازار
درود از من بدان چشم فسونگر — که دارد مر مرا بیخواب و بیخور
درود از من بدان رخسار مهوش — که دارد جانم از محنت بر آتش
درود از من بدان ماه دوهفته — که دارد مر مرا بیهوش و تفته
درود از من بدان مشهور آفاق — که دارد مر مرا از کام دل طاق
درود از من بدان گلروی خوشبوی — که دارد سال و ماهم در تک و پوی
درود از من بدان زلف رسن باز — که دارد مر مرا مشهور شیراز
درود از من بدان ناز و عتابش — که آبم برد زنخدان خوش آبش
درود از من بدان آئین و آن فر — که دارد رویم از تیمار چون زر
درود از من بدان کبک نکو پی — که دارد پیشه با من کینه جویی
درود از من بدان خورشید تابان — که دارد حسن بر خورشید تابان
درود از من بدان روی چو گلبرگ — که از شرم رخش ریزد ز گل برگ
درود از من بدان سرو سمن روی — که ندهد هیچ بوی او سمن بوی

Figure 3: Peroration of the *Dah-nāma / Jafā-nāma*. Bibliothèque nationale de France, Département des Manuscrits, Supplément Persan 1380, fol. 191a.

name for God, Allāh, appears in *V&R* instead of the more neutral terms *khodā* and *yazdān*:[11]

چگوید هر که این نامه بخواند   وزین نامه نهان ما بداند

مرا گوید عفا الله ای وفادار   که چندین جست مهر بی وفا یار

ترا گوید جزا الله ای جفا جوی   که خود در تو نبود از مردمی بوی

What will they say, when they have read this letter and understood our natures from it? To me: "God reward you, O faithful one, who sought love from a faithless lover!" To you: "God punish you, O oppressor, who has not a whiff of humanity about him!" (389/37–9 [357])

In light of passages like these, it does not seem to me an exaggeration to suggest that the ultimate purpose of the *Jafā-nāma* is to establish Vis's "soul" – a lifetime of experience, memory, and discourse that may survive beyond the boundaries of the narrative within the minds and hearts of her readership. If she can persuade this audience of her virtue and Rāmin's degeneracy, Vis will enjoy a blessed textual afterlife, while Rāmin will face eternal condemnation. References to this theme abound. In one example, Vis turns one of Rāmin's favourite accusations, that she is stony-hearted, into a badge of honour: "I *am* stony-hearted in love; [my] loyalty to him is like an everlasting engraving" (*man-am sangina-del dar mehrbāni • vafā dar vay cho naqsh-e jāvedāni*, 367/12 [334]). In another, she alludes to her desire for a good name to outlast her – "So what if I stay awake for a hundred years, if I am famous in the world for my fidelity?" (*che bāshad gar bovam ṣad sāl bidār • cho dar giti bovad nām-am vafā-dār*, 369/45 [336]) – presumably indicating the world of *V&R*'s readers as much as the world of the text. Her hope that fidelity will be rewarded, whether by Rāmin's return, divine blessing, or the sympathy of her readers, both defines her and gives her a certain self-sufficiency: "I hope, I hope, and I hope ... and by this hope, my soul remains" (*be omid-am be omid-am be omid ... bedin omid jān-e man bemānda-st*, 375/46, 48 [342]). And as long as this hope lives on, "I see one benefit in separation, that as long as I am in this state, I am *safe from death*" (*be hejr andar hamin yek ṣud binam • ke az marg iman-am tā man chonin-am* (365/21 [332]). These and similar passages throughout the *Jafā-nama* help figure Vis as a "self," one that in a literary fashion possesses the same social weight and claim to life after death as its analogues preserved in the historical memory of her extra-textual readership.

This is an important element when we consider the way the document handles the notions of witness, testament, and truth, which requires the existence of stable selves that are both knowable and enduring beyond

the temporal boundaries of a single moment. The letter insists that such
a continuation of the mind, even for literary beings, is possible: "I am that
same one who was so dear to you" (*man ān yār-am chonan bar to gerāmi*,
389/30), Vis claims, while confirming elsewhere that Rāmin "is exactly as
I have seen him, stone-hearted and faithless" (*hamān ast u ke man didam
hamān ast • hamān sang-del nā-mehrabān ast*, 386/19). In a longer passage, she
juxtaposes the self she once was (and still is) with the change she perceives
in Rāmin, using the alternating pattern "Am I not the one who…?/Are you
not the one who…?" (*na man ān-am ke, na to ān-i ke*) to highlight the contrast in a striking visual acrostic; the passage ends with the pointed question, "How is it that I am still that person, while you are not?" (*cherā aknun
man ān-am to na ān-i*, 379/17–23 [347]). The synthesis of these arguments
receives its most striking articulation in the letter's exordium, which again
applies a thick layer of anaphora to emphasize Vis's continuous existence,
making the case that her name and her name alone is enough to define her
person and assert her intrinsic value. Here is it is in transliteration:

> *man ān vis-am ke ruy-am āftāb ast • man ān vis-am ke muy-am moshk-e nāb ast*
> *man ān vis-am ke chehr-am now-bahār ast • man ān vis-am ke mehr-am*
>   *pāydār ast*
> *man ān vis-am ke māh-e nikvān-am • man ān vis-am ke shāh-e jāvdān-am*
> *man ān vis-am ke māh-am bar rokhān ast • man ān vis-am ke nush-am dar*
>   *labān ast*
> *man ān vis-am man ān vis-am man ān vis • ke budi to solaymān man cho belqis*

> I am that Vis whose face is the sun!
> I am that Vis whose hair is pure musk!
> I am that Vis whose face is the spring!
> I am that Vis whose love lasts eternal!
> I am that Vis, the moon of all beauties!
> I am that Vis, the queen of enchantresses!
> I am that Vis whose cheeks are the moon!
> I am that Vis whose lips are ambrosia!
> I am that Vis, I am that Vis, I am Vis,
> who was to your Solomon the queen Bilqis!
>
> (361/62–6 [329])

In this bold declaration, Vis transforms her letter into a symbolically
charged act of self-creation: her discourse, circling around her name as
though it were a sculpture in the round, visits the question of *who she is*
from a variety of angles, and finally settles upon the name itself, to the
exclusion of all external descriptors, in a thrice-spoken phrase: "I am that

Vis" – that is, *I am myself*, whom the world knows and recognizes by name alone. This claim is quite extraordinary, considering that it comes out of a context in which the main actors in "serious" narrative are typically drawn from the ranks of the "real" men of the historical and sacred past – kings, heroes, prophets, and so on – while the significance of the women in such accounts is usually contingent on their connections with these men. That her chosen analogue is Bilqis, held by the hagiographers to be half-jinn and possessed of a power and wisdom that could only be bested by Solomon himself (an association that perhaps reinforces her ancestral ties to Jamshid), shows Vis claiming a subject position for herself that far transcends the "phantasy" of her love-story.[12] She is staking a claim in history, in other words, if not literally than analogically, furthering the argument that truth may reside as much in the fairy tale as in any other narrative kind, and that it can come from the mouths of "fictional" women.

Vis's literary self-fashioning raises two further implications about the role of love in the human subject. The first is the element of knowledge. Through the interweaving of body and text, Vis presents her story as an intelligible document that we can know and understand, as long as we are willing to read it on its own terms. In Kottman's account, this is precisely where the possibilities of love begin: love signals the desire to "really" know a person, not on the basis of what they did (loving the dead) but in the ongoing curiosity to grasp *who they are* (loving the living). Romantic love, then, is a project of getting to know the Other in a way that holds ourselves and each other accountable for the knowledge we gain from that inquiry.[13] By writing herself into the world, Vis establishes a framework in which we might not only get to know her, but she might better understand herself in the bargain.

This, in turn, raises the secondary element of freedom: through her knowledge gained, Vis can produce an experience of time in which she is the originator and the owner of her actions, obtaining a degree of autonomous selfhood that is quite different from the usual story of lovers utterly subject to the whims of fate. Her testament, in other words, gives her purchase into the symbolic order of the real, the space where meanings are made, judgments are passed, and right and wrong are made concrete: "If you read this letter and do not come back [to me]," she promises, "I will bear witness to your cruelty" (*gar in nāma bekhwāni bāz nāyi • be bi-raḥmi deham bar to govāyi*, 366/50 [334]). By asserting her ability to bear witness, Vis gains a lasting presence of the kind that is readily ascribed to historical figures; her letter parallels the famous testaments (*ʿahd-nāma*) left behind by the mythological-historical kings of yore, such as Ardashir and Anushirvān.[14] The emergence of the "real" Vis through the act of giving witness and written testimony takes us back to the meta-textuality of her *Jafā-nāma*, which functions as a supplicant (*khwāhesh-gar*, 389/21 [356]) not only between herself and Rāmin, but between the narrative and its audience. The *Jafā-nāma*, Vis insists, is a textual extension of herself that bears the traces of her bodily experiences:

ببین این حرفهای پژمریده   همه نقطه بریشان خون دیده

خط نامه چو بخت من سیاهست   همان نونش چو پشت من دوتاهست

جهان حلقه شده بر من چو میمش   امید من شکسته همچو جیمش

Behold these drooping letters, all these scattered dots of blood from my eyes, the lines are as black as my fortune, its *nun* (ن) bent in two like my back. The world encircles me like its *mim* (م); my hope is broken just like its *jim* (ج). (388/10–12 [355])

Thus, the fusion of body and text that we have been exploring in this section does important work in making the romance a part of history, and vice versa. Having begun with the premise that all living creatures must eventually perish and fade from the world, Vis's *Jafā-nāma* demonstrates how it is ultimately the stories – and only the stories – that people tell each other that confer any kind of lingering presence, the ability to affect life even after death. To borrow from Kottman's discussion of Shakespeare's Desdemona, Vis records not just what happened, but her *experience of what happened*, leaving behind a testimony that "gives that subjective experience an objective, clamorous, undeniable reality" outside of the text.[15] In this way, regardless of whether she exists within the realm of phantasy or of history, Vis produces a past, and perhaps even a soul, that can become as meaningful to subsequent generations as any of the kings or heroes of al-Nadīm's "true" evening stories. She gains a life, in other words, that matters beyond the limits of its temporal enclosure.

These gains in self-knowledge, autonomy, and personhood do not only add meaning to Vis's life, however. They also add weight to her death, as well as to that of Rāmin, producing an experience of mortality that the available paradigms of romantic love will struggle to explain.

Love-Death (*Liebestod*)

The next major episode in *Vis & Rāmin* brings the intersection of selfhood, story, and death to a dramatic conclusion. I use "dramatic" intentionally here, for this scene, alongside a few others, like the *gosān*'s allegory or Rāmin's soliloquy on Mobad's roof, is one of the most stageable moments in the text: two figures, one on horseback looking up, the other at her palace window looking down, locked in heated debate against the imposing backdrop of a blustering winter storm. Traditional Persian literary criticism would label this episode a "debate" (*monāẓara*), a compositional mode "commonly used in didactic/pedagogical texts" that was certainly well known in Gorgāni's time, thanks to the work of his contemporary Asadi Ṭusi (d. 1073), and which may draw from models dating as far back as the Parthian era.[16] But the scene here bears two elements that are absent in most examples of the medieval genre. The first is the setting, which not only complements the dialogue between the characters, but indeed has an agency of its own in mediating the characters' interaction and setting the stakes of the debate. In this regard, it shows some interesting parallels with the *paraklausithyron*, a topos developed in New Comedy and continued by Latin poets, in which the lover is locked out from (or by) his beloved.[17] In this example, the poet Tibullus addresses the barrier itself:

> Ianua difficilis domini, te uerberet imber,
> te Iouis imperio fulmina missa petant.
> ianua, iam pateas uni mihi, uicta querelis,
> neu furtim uerso cardine aperta sones;
> et mala siqua tibi dixit dementia nostra,
> ignoscas: capiti sint precor illa meo.
> te meminisse decet quae plurima uoce peregi
> supplice, cum posti florida serta darem.
>
> O door, stubborn as your master, may the rainstorm lash you
> and launched at Jove's command may flash of lightning blast you!
> Please, door – open just for me, moved by my complaining.
> But silence, as you swing on slowly turning hinge!
> Forgive me if I cursed you in my infatuation.
> Let the curses light on my own head.
> It's right you should remember all my prayers and promises
> When I hung those garlands of flowers on your post.
>
> (*Elegiae* 1.2.7–14)[18]

This apostrophe to the locked door is reminiscent of Rāmin's song to the Devils' Grotto, discussed in the previous chapter, in that both poets use the closed edifice as a topos to describe their inner state.[19] But the topos itself establishes a certain architecture of power, one that Rāmin alludes to as he reminds the Grotto of "the warlike lions at your gate, the feasting onagers in your palace" (*be dargāh-e to bar shirān-e razmi • bar ayvān-e to bar gurān-e bazmi*, 248/15 [211]): namely, a structure that places the "onagers" above (*bar*) the "lions" and prevents the latter from feasting with (or on?) them inside. The power dynamics that the debate is about to expose are thus reflected and indeed materialized by the backdrop on which it takes place.

The second dramatic element to consider in this scene is the characters, who are far more like "people" than what we typically find in the *monāzara* tradition. The debates in Asadi Ṭusi's poems, for example, are between archetypal figures or personified inanimates, judging the pros and cons between the two sides they represent: Arab versus Persian, Mazdean versus Muslim, Day versus Night, Sky versus Land.[20] While Vis and Rāmin are also deeply entrenched in the stylistic and generic codes that inform their speech, actions, and ideology, their debate spills over into the historical realm; it has to take account of the lived experiences we have witnessed over the course of the poem. Vis's letter to Rāmin, which shows history being written and makes the case for literary personae to be the objects of that history, sets both the stakes and the terms of this reading. If the battle to be fought is one of historiography – that is, which narrative of the poem's events will prevail – the parameters of engagement revolve around the words and deeds of individual subjects and the essential question of *who they are*, not as abstracted "images of language," but as individuated actors in time.

If we read this episode, then, as a dramatic contest between two literary creations attempting to "know" each other in the historical sense of a life path, some valuable gains come into reach. On a general level, it helps push against an old and yet still influential presumption, dating back to Hegel and Goethe, that drama does not really exist in Persian and other Islamicate literatures.[21] The analysis below will contribute to the literature challenging this presumption by showing how various elements of drama (if we wish to employ Aristotelian terms like character, speech, thought, and visuals) play a significant role in *V&R*'s literary project.[22] Through the production of characters who not only represent ideas but (hi)story, that is, the effects of individual choices on individual lives over the long passage of time, Gorgāni's work raises an important question. Do the traditional paradigms of the love-story provide an adequate framework for its characters to know and thereby to love each other as "historical" entities – that is, as people who experience time and must take its inevitably destructive forces into account? This question marks a significant innovation for the romance, a topical genre that had been largely disassociated from the flow of "real" time, both in terms of its historical reception (e.g., al-Nadīm) and its internal structure as a series of seemingly timeless episodes. The admission of the inadequacies of the romance mythos to produce "real" love stands poised to deliver a potentially devastating blow to the genre's basic premises.

With these thoughts in mind, let us turn to the debate itself. As Rāmin returns his homeland of Marv, it seems to him that he has entered paradise (426/8–11 [394]), while Vis, learning of his arrival, takes a seat by a small embrasure (*surākh-e rowzan*) in her palace to greet him as the snow begins to fall. These details set up a number of themes that will play a prominent role in what follows: the imminent transformation of the landscape, Edenic on first sight, into a frozen wasteland where no life can survive, and the establishment of Vis, looking down at Rāmin while she herself is hidden from his view, as the judge presiding over his trial, just as kings would mete out judgment from elevated heights, sometimes obscured by curtains.[23] It is no coincidence that this handling of space recalls the way Vis carefully managed her first (adult) face-to-face encounter with Rāmin, discussed in chapter 2, when they first exchanged vows of fidelity; her determination to maintain control, now that she must punish him for breaking that vow, is emphasized by the narrator's comment that, upon beholding Rāmin's arrival, "the flower of love blossomed in her heart, but she exercised patience and kept her heart suppressed, showing no sign of the turmoil she held therein" (428/40–1). Like a chess player opening with an unconventional gambit, she begins by addressing not Rāmin but his horse, reprimanding it for seeking shelter in another stable. "To whom dates do not suit, thorns," she concludes, citing a proverb with an ominous subtext about the consequences of Rāmin's treachery, "to whom the dais does not suit, the gallows" (429/49).[24]

This unorthodox welcome leaves Rāmin reeling and off balance. Astonished at Vis's refusal even to acknowledge him (which she will do again, 438/3 [407]), he begins to protest:

توی ویسه مرا از جان فزونتر	منم رامین ترا با جان برابر
توئی ویسه مرا بایسته مهتر	منم رامین ترا شایسته کهتر
ز مهر تو به گیتی داستانم	منم رامین که شاه بی دلانم
به چشم و زلف شاه جاودانی	توی ویسه که ماه نیکوانی
همان شایسته یار مهربانم	همانم من که تو دیدی همانم
چرا بر من نمایی دل گرانی	همانم من که بودم تو نه آنی

I am Rāmin, as dear to you as life! You are Vis, more [dear] to me than life! I am Rāmin, your worthy servant! You are Vis, my requisite mistress! I am Rāmin, the king of the love-lorn: I am a story in the world from my love for you! You are Vis, the moon of beauties, eternal sovereign by your eyes and curls. I am he whom you saw, I am he, I am that same lover, kind and worthy: I am the same as I was, but you are not: why do you show me displeasure? (429/8–13 [397])

In terms of their rhythm and syntax, these lines are a clear echo of that memorable passage in the exordium of Vis's letter discussed above, where Vis declares her value on the basis of her name alone. However, Rāmin's self-presentation is strikingly different, revealing the same problematic patterns we saw in chapter 4. He (correctly) identifies himself as a "story in the world," the protagonist in the account of the romantic love of Vis and Rāmin; this self-view, though, brings him to see their relationship in pre-determined absolutes that fail to recognize the history Vis is holding him accountable for. He presumes that he *must be* as dear to Vis as her own life, that she *must be* his mistress; his use of the words *shāyesta* and *bāyesta*, which invoke the sense of worthiness, suitability, and necessity, confirm his view of a love attachment over which neither he nor Vis have any control.

This vision, consistent with the conventional understanding of romantic love in which "a man under its sway is beneath criticism" (*ṣāḥibuhu adhallu min al-naqd*), absolves Rāmin of any durable consequences for his actions, so long as his love for Vis remains.[25] Thus, he can adopt multiple responses to Vis in the same speech, reversing the accusation ("The sin was yours from the start, my love, but I got caught up in it," 432/52), tearfully confessing ("I'm a sinner, a sinner, a sinner ... I'm penitent, penitent, penitent," 432/56–7), growing defiant ("So what if I sinned once? Am I the only sinner in the world?" 432/64), and assuming the passive voice, as though he were as surprised by what happened as anybody else: "If a mistake (*khatā-i*) came from me unexpectedly, don't brand me for every wicked act!" (433/67).[26] These vacillations suggest an inability to apprehend the root of the problem, given Rāmin's baseline assumption that love and forgiveness must flow out from Vis as a matter of natural order; in such a universe, it is almost inconceivable that the prince could ride up to the tower only to hear that his fair lady has changed her mind and would like him to please go away. As far as he is concerned, Vis is *obliged* to let him in; were she to refuse, it would be nothing short of murder.

کسی کاو را وفا با جان سرشتست   به برف اندر بکشتن سخت زشتست

گمان بردم که از آتش رهانی   ندانستم که در برفم نشانی

منم مهمانت ای ماه دو هفته   به دو هفته دو ماهه راه رفته

به مهمانان همه خوبی پسندند   نه زین سان در میان برف بندند

اگر شد کشتنم بر چشمت آسان   به برف اندر مکش باری بدین سان

> It is a terrible crime to kill in the snow a man whose soul is infused with
> loyalty! I thought you'd free me from fire; I didn't know you'd throw me
> into the snow. O full ["two-week"] moon, I am your guest – I've made a
> two-month journey in the space of two weeks. People lavish every kind-
> ness upon their guests – they don't trap them in the middle of the snow
> like this! If killing me has become easy in your eyes, at least don't kill
> me like this in the snow! (434/84–8 [402])

In speaking of his imminent death, Rāmin's repeated allusions to the
snowstorm around him are quite conspicuous. Two possible connections could be made: one with the topos of the *paraklausithyron*, which
often places the lover "shivering ... where storms their watches keep"
(Horace, *Odes* 3.10), the other with the Zoroastrian image of perdition,
where we find "driving snow and severe cold" listed among its many
tortures.[27] I consider both connections intriguing but tentative at best,
and at any rate so buried within the history of the *Vis & Rāmin* narrative that they were probably not evident to Gorgāni or his readers.
The Islamic idea that one of the regions or punishments of Hell was
a bitter cold (*zamharīr*) may have had more purchase; above all, however, the motif of dying in a snowstorm suggests a clear allusion to a
famous moment in the *Shāhnāma* tradition, the so-called occultation of
Kay Khosrow.[28]

This episode merits a brief digression, not least because of its extreme
ambivalence. The good king, obsessed with the knowledge that he, as
a fallible mortal, must fall from justice into tyranny, embarks on an
Oedipus-like quest to avoid this evil fate and so fulfils it. He retires
from court life, abdicates the throne, and then, oblivious to the entreaties of his ministers and subjects, withdraws from the world altogether:
accompanied by a small coterie of his greatest heroes, he absconds to
the top of a mountain, where he mysteriously vanishes. His followers,
searching for their lost king, are overcome by a sudden snowstorm and
perish, effectively decapitating Iran of its leadership and setting the
stage for the last tragic chapters of the Kiyanid dynasty, the fatal battle
between Rostam and Esfandiyār and the invasion of Iran by Alexander.[29]
The motif of death in the snow, then, simultaneously delivers two contrary narratives: the narrative of beating or transcending death, as Kay
Khosrow seems to have accomplished, coupled with the corresponding
breakdown of the existing sociopolitical order. Both narratives come to
a head in *Vis & Rāmin*.

Having taken on the role of Rāmin's judge, Vis is determined that she
will not be fooled again by his glib excuses (434/4 [402]) and orders
him to quit Marv and return to his loveless marriage in Gurab. She then

withdraws from the embrasure, leaving Rāmin stunned at this unimaginable turn of events, and with nothing but his dejected thoughts and his horse to keep him company. On the heels of the lovers' furious exchange, the eerie quiet of the dark night seems all the more ominous, the snow falling silently around the prince, as white as the camphor that the Persian kings used to embalm their dead.[30] It was only moments before that Rāmin had begged Vis not to kill him in the snow, and now it seems that the deed has been done. True to form, he responds to this realization with a soliloquy, first with a prayer to God for aid, followed by a vow to stay put, "for if I go back in despair, I am not a man" (436/44):

بمانده تا به زانو رخش در گل   همی گفت این سخن رامین بیدل
هوا بر رخش او کافور بیزان   همه شب چشم رامین اشک ریزان
به برف اندر سوار از رخش بدتر   همه شب رخش در باران شده تر
همه شب باد پیچان در بر رام   همه شب ابر گریان بر سر رام
ز سر تا پای بفسرده چو آهن   قبا و موزه و رانینش بر تن

Lovesick Rāmin spoke these words, while his horse sank up to its knees in the mud. All night, Rāmin's eyes shed tears, and the air sifted camphor upon his mount. All night, his horse grew soaked in the rain, and its rider's state was worse in the snow. All night, the clouds wept over Rāmin's head; all night, the wind swirled around his body. From head to toe, the cloak, boots, and leggings upon his body froze like iron. (437/55–9 [405])

Both language and imagery reinforce the hopelessness and desolation that pervade this scene: the four-fold repetition of "all night" (*hama shab*), invoking a backdrop of endless, utter darkness; the likening of Rāmin's frozen clothes to iron, chaining him to the ground as the chill drains him of life; the sight of Rāmin's unfortunate mount, sinking up to his knees into the mire. In this hellish landscape of snow, mud, wind, and rain, it seems certain that something is coming to an end, a premonition that seems to strike Vis as well. As she turns away from the window, she wonders aloud, "What is this snow and cold, from whence Vis's resurrection (*rastakhiz*) has appeared?" (437/61). While one could read this word *rastakhiz* in the figurative sense of extreme duress, I am intrigued by its literal connotations: could it not be that Vis sees the winter storm as the harbinger of a new spring – that not despite but through this death, she may live anew? For this to be possible, the notion of romantic love, the obligations and commitments it places on lovers, and in short the story of what it means to be a lover in the world – the *dāstān-e ʿāsheqāna* – must be broken down, rethought, and reworked from the ground up.

The debate resumes at the first light of dawn. Despite his ordeal, Rāmin does not seem to have changed his tune; he continues to interweave profuse apologies (442/23–30 [410]) with various attempts to excuse his behaviour, including some rather inventive ploys: "I sinned in order to test you, to see how you'd be at forgiveness" (442/29); "My dear, I'm just a man, how could I escape the clutches of lust?" (446/26 [414]); and "If I looked joyful on the outside, I was still weeping at your absence on the inside" (448/50 [415]). Vis shows no such wavering, even if her heart still burns for Rāmin on the inside (448/3); to each new excuse, she counters by referring back to the history they share:

سمن برویس گفت ای بی خرد رام   نداری از خردمندی بجز نام

جفا بر دل زند خشت گرانش   بماند جاودان بر دل نشانش

تو خود دانی که من با تو چه کردم   به اومید وفا چه رنج بردم

پس آنگه تو بجای من چه کردی   بکشتی وانچه کشتی خود بخوردی

Vis of jasmine breast spoke: "Rāmin, you fool, you have nothing of wisdom but a name! When iniquity scores the heart with its heavy stone, the scar remains forever ... You know well how I was with you, how much I suffered in the hope of your fidelity; and what did you do, in my place? You killed, and then ate of your kill!" (443/1–2, 6–7 [411])

Vis has now turned Rāmin's accusation of murder back upon him, driving home the theme of double death, both in and of the love-story, brought about by its protagonists' fundamental incompatibility. Rāmin has "killed," as Vis puts it, and the fact that she does not specify what or whom leaves the door open for multiple readings, each one more macabre than the last. Our first impression might be that, just as Vis devoted herself to the hope of Rāmin's fidelity, Rāmin killed and consumed that hope. Yet it might also be Vis herself who has been murdered and cannibalized by Rāmin's treachery, leaving her not only dead (a state where redemption is still possible), but hollowed out and defiled. Or, in light of this study, it might be the romance itself that has died: in failing to live up to the expectations of his role, Rāmin has killed off the genre's viability. But in any of these readings, something venerable, practically sacred, has been irretrievably lost – even a miraculous resurrection, like that of ᶜAyyuqi's *Varqa & Golshāh*, is no longer possible after the corpse has been desecrated. This both resonates with and marks a strong divergence from the death-drive motif in Kottman's account, in which he argues that the outcome of a world in which lovemaking has no social authority is "a world in which killing one's lover, being killed by one's lover, is perhaps the only way to prove that one loves truly."[31] Vis and Rāmin have come to see each other as anathema to the stories they seek to tell; it is this anger that drives them to embrace their mutual deaths, not out of love like Pyramus and Thisbe or Laylā and Majnun, but rather to kill each other in despair and desperation.

It takes some time for this new reality to sink in, partially because it reflects the long history between the lovers that needs to be undone, but also, I suspect, because this undoing opens new and unexplored horizons of relational affect for the text to explore. But Vis's patience is not endless; when Rāmin complains again that he is dying in the snow and that his death will be on Vis's shoulders (451/18 [419]) – a strategy he had once successfully used before – she bids him again to depart, effectively issuing an edict of banishment ("Now you are homeless in Marv," 452/4), and adding, in a significant phrase, "For God's sake, *free me!*" (*marā āzād kon ze bahr-e yazdān*, 453/26 [421]). This initiates the argument's closure. Rāmin must finally face the reality that the woman he had expected would always be waiting for him with open arms has declared her independence – "God did not create me wholly for you" (459/16), as she says – and with the premise of innate and instinctual affection between soulmates irreparably ruptured, he gallops off, swearing to his heart that he, as a free and noble man (*āzād*), will never again submit to the fetters of love (464/41–2).

Thus, the nearly unthinkable – within the mythos of romantic love – has happened: given an opportunity to reunite, the lovers have instead rejected, and symbolically killed, each other in favour of their personal freedom, nobility, and self-regard. The protagonists' inner worth is no longer demonstrated by their practice of love but by renouncing love altogether: as Vis says in a notable line, "Everyone repents of iniquity (*jafā*), whereas I regret my loyalty" (*vafā*, 459/20 [426]). The landscape itself seems to recoil at this breach of custom; as Vis turns away from her window, she warns her Nurse to be on guard, "For tonight's a night so dreadful, that the blizzard threatens the world with oblivion," making (in some manuscripts) apocalyptic comparisons with the Flood and the Day of Judgment (463/28–31+n8–9 [429]). Gorgāni, too, seems to have recognized the gravity of this moment, for his narrator breaks away from the story to express amazement at what has transpired: "O wonder! O deceitful world!" (465/1). Such astonishment at the world, as a fairly common trope throughout *V&R*, is in itself not particularly conspicuous here; but then, after the usual reflections about the wheel-like turns of fortune, the narrator veers into a provocative meditation on what the collapse of Vis and Rāmin's love might teach us:

وگر چونین نبودی خود نشایست   مگر ما را جزین بهره نبایست

نگفتی از گشی با هیچ کس راز   تن ما گر نبودی بستهٔ آز

نه باری زین جهان بر تن نهادی   نه کس را در جهان گردن نهادی

نجستی از بزرگی جز جدایی   ز بند مردمی جُستی رهایی

به که کردی جهان افسوس و بازی   چو بودی در گهرمان بی نیازی

بگسترد از پس مهر آن همه کین   چنان کاندر میان ویس و رامین

Perhaps we need nothing other than this fate; if it wasn't like this, it wouldn't be right. If our bodies were not bound to desire (*āz*), we would never joyfully share our secrets with another. No one would bow their necks, no weight of the world would burden their bodies. We would have sought to escape our humanity; we would have sought nothing of greatness save solitude. If the lack of need (*bi-niyāzi*) was in our nature, whom would the world trick and bewitch? Thus, in the wake of love, all hatred enveloped Vis and Rāmin. (465/4–9 [431])[32]

These speculations on desire (*āz*) and need (*niyāz*) might indicate one of the most unexpected and significant moral turnarounds in *Vis & Rāmin*. *Āz* is an almost universally negative concept in early Persian literature; one of the great demons of Zoroastrian cosmology, it appears in the *Shāhnāma* and other texts as the force that destroys kinship relations, upsets political order, and blinds people from recognizing the evil of their actions.[33] And so, the question arises: what would happen if we did *not* desire? The superficial answer this passage implies is that we would all be better off, no longer slaves to the world and its innumerable snares and burdens. Yet, despite acknowledging this apparent gain in independence, the text also suggests that we would lose something critical to our human essence (*gohar*) in the process: we would lose the act of submission, of "bowing the neck." The fact that the narrator refrains from telling us the object of this act maintains a crucial ambivalence, for while submission to a tyrant is one thing, submission to God quite another; the beloved, perhaps, is a little bit of both. Thus, as we saw in the case of Mobad (chapter 3), the text posits the intriguing possibility that this "demon" is in fact necessary and appropriate to the human experience: it is only *through* the encounter with *āz* that humanity can aspire towards any kind of greatness. Desire, in the end, may prove itself the saviour of humanity as well as its scourge.[34]

As I have argued across the last three chapters, the protagonists of *Vis & Rāmin* come to know themselves through their desire to inhabit various "images of language," discursive traditions of mythos and ethos so powerful that they animate its speakers, in the literal sense of giving them life (*anima*). Through these linguistic mirrors, the characters make the world around them intelligible, invest their actions with meaning, and evaluate themselves as individuals with agency, choice, and ownership of their lives. To put it simply, through discourse (*manṭiq*), they find reason (*manṭiq*); through *logos*, they find logic. But as the mirrors break apart, the characters experience the loss of that faculty whereby they are aware of themselves as acting sensibly in the world: they experience death, not of the body but of the soul, as the lifeless setting of the debate suggests. Thus, the reflections on desire above cast the scenes that follow into a comprehensive reconsideration of the link between desire and humanity; after all, as we heard in the story of Mobad, *har ānk u nist ᶜāsheq nist mardom* – a person who does not love is not a person (83/52). Love (*ᶜeshq*), as a form of passionate desire that cannot disentangle itself from carnal appetites (*āz*), provides Vis and Rāmin the matrix through which they come to grips with how they will relate to one another and know themselves through that relationship, producing a portrait of the human being whose status as a thinking animal is ultimately secondary to and contingent upon its success as a loving animal.

False Death (*Scheintod*)

The narrator's reflections on desire as a paradoxical interlacing of autonomy and submission, such that one happens through the other and vice versa, suggests a dialectic that may help us make sense of the ending of the debate, and of *Vis & Rāmin* itself. This dialectic can be further unpacked by bringing in Kottman's thesis on the connections between romantic love and human freedom, which shows remarkable resonances with the passage on *āz* above. Kottman avers that love is "one way we teach ourselves that we are free and rational – capable of leading lives for which we are at least provisionally answerable and whose possibilities we open for ourselves"; he understands the experience of choosing one's actions as one's own, above and beyond the social obligations imposed by one's family or kinship group, as an experience that enacts and tests a self-conscious effort to make sense of the world and the self through one's commitment to another.[35] The declaration of that commitment thus weaves the themes of independence and self-ownership (the declaration) and subjugation and answerability (the commitment) into a single cloth, held together in part by their perpendicular tension. This produces a hermeneutical framework in which both our being-in-life ("who we are") and our being-in-death ("what we did") matter equally in our self-evaluation.[36]

In many ways, Gorgāni's romance suggests such an ontological reconfiguration of love at work. As we have seen in the previous chapters, the pressures of their literary-social personae force Vis, Mobad, and Rāmin into unique crises of self from which there is no apparent escape. Now, at this moment of crux, it is only in the act of "killing" their partner, and experiencing their own "death" in the process, that the lovers can discover a new agency in themselves: not necessarily the power to control their destinies, but at least to understand themselves in terms of their own choosing. Subtle shifts in diction suggest this transformation at work: while the three characters have, for the majority of the poem, repeatedly complained of feeling "bound" or "enslaved" by their desire, the words *āzād* and *āzādi*, with their primary denotations of nobility and freedom, begin in this section to take on a certain thematic prominence. At the same time, however, this freedom is not independently discovered by the story's protagonists but is rather given to them by – to use another dramatic term – a *deus ex machina*; and in their reconstitution of themselves, they do not destroy the old order, but recreate it on a more perfect level. Unlike Kottman's lovers, then, who in various ways escape their old paradigms to discover a life *outside* the meaning-making framework of death, Vis and Rāmin tell a story of life *within* death and of freedom *within* submission, showing how apparent falsehoods provide a gateway for the apprehension of inner truths.

This dance of antitheses brings two of the hallmark motifs of the romance – the love-death and the false death – together into a novel synthesis. The love-death occurs in stories as far-flung as *Pyramus & Thisbe*, the Arabic *ʿudhrī* narratives (most famously Laylā and Majnun), and *Romeo & Juliet*; its presence is also felt in the competitive *thanatos* of Floire and Blancheflor, who strive to beat each other to the finish line of dying on behalf of their beloved (156/2978–90 [Hubert 102/2737–61]). False deaths are a mainstay of the ancient Greek novels, such as Chaireas's accidental "murder" of Kallirhoe (27/1.5) or Leukippe's apparent disembowelment (216/3.15); false graves appear in *Varqa & Golshāh* (79/1–4) and *Floire & Blanchefor* (32/543–660 [Hubert 38/538–653]), and of course it is the misidentified false deaths of Thisbe and Juliet that instigate their lovers' suicides. Thus, to explore how *Vis & Rāmin* works with these two elements highlights both its place within a widespread and enduring tradition of amorous narrative and its distinctive features as a medieval Persian poem coming out of the Islamic milieu of Seljukid Isfahan. By combining the love-death and the false death into a double ending, *V&R* produces an account of death and rebirth that comes remarkably close to that of its predecessor, *Varqa & Golshāh*. Both texts perform with this fusion what I might call a *ta'wīl*, an exposition of the hidden but "true" meaning of the mythos of romantic love. But in this process, the mythos itself undergoes a conversion of its own.

For Vis and Rāmin alike, this experience of conversion appears to be ecstatic and traumatic in equal parts. As Vis rejects Rāmin's entreaties, "washing my heart of useless hope," she begins to speak, almost in awe, of a newfound "contentment" (*khorsandi*) rising in her soul (439/19–21 [407]); now "freed" from the shackles of love, she claims to have undergone a spiritual metamorphosis: "My heart was a fox, now it's a lion" (455/11–12 [423]). Yet even as she sends Rāmin away, "having extinguished [lit., 'killed'] my lantern with my own hand" (*cherāgh-e khwad be dast-e khwish koshta*, 466/26 [432]), as she puts it, she suddenly experiences a surge of regret, and rushes out of her fortress to catch up. On reaching him, Vis exhibits the same verbal flailing that we previously witnessed in Rāmin: she first asserts her right to punish him for his infidelity, stressing that she herself has done nothing wrong ("Your sin is not mine," 469/42 [435]), but then begins to downplay her reprimands ("I just meant to flirt with you," 476/16 [442]), and by the end of the scene, she is in a pitiable state, clutching Rāmin's hands, weeping and shivering in the cold, and apologizing profusely for her actions ("I hurt you, and I did you wrong," 480/6 [445]). The parallel this establishes between the two characters suggests that they both – first Rāmin and now Vis – have been forced to experience an extreme kind of mortification, what Kappler describes as "a state of interior nudity, the complete abandonment of herself: she is in the darkest moment of the night, alone."[37]

Accordingly, the power dynamic between the two is turned on its head: just as Rāmin had supplicated Vis from below, he now towers over her on his horse as she pleads her case, and like Vis before him, he remains unmoved. "How shameless you are, how faithless, that you hold the death of lovers in contempt," we can almost hear him snarl, "now that I know who you are, I hate your stony heart!" (474/55, 60 [440]). The word choice here is significant; we have seen a lot of back-and-forth between the couple about *who they are*, and with this, it seems that Rāmin can no more accept the "real" Vis than Vis can accept the "real" Rāmin. The notion of reality, however, recalls one of Vis's most suggestive lines in this section of the debate: "Your iniquity was real, in deeds; mine was metaphorical, in words" (*jafā-ye to ḥaqiqat bod be kerdār • jafā-ye man majāzi bod be goftār*, 466/31 [433]). As Matthew Thomas Miller has discussed, the "metaphor" (*majāz*) was not merely understood as figure of speech, but in the literal sense as a site of passage or transfer, akin to its Greek meaning of "carrying across," furnishing its audience with a "bridge to the Real" (*qantarat al-ḥaqīqa*) beyond immediate or superficial appearances.[38] If we take up Miller's suggestion to consider the *majāz* as somehow embodying the thing it points to, then, we might perceive in Vis (and her apparent iniquity) new ways of seeing – new theories, as it were – entering the realm of possibility. This recalibrated vision seems to emerge in real time, for even as Rāmin berates his ex-lover, a strangely euphoric tranquillity begins to creep into his voice. He begins to describe himself as "free" (*āzād*, 478/7), not only of Vis's love but of the world itself:

تو گویی بنده بودم شاه گشتم   زمین بودم سپهر و ماه گشتم

چنان بی رنج و بی غم گشت جانم   که گویی من کنون نی زین جهانم

من از مستی چنان هشیار گشته   ز خواب ابلهی بیدار گشته

نه بینا بختم اکنون گشت بینا   چو نادان جانم اکنون گشت دانا

چو پای از بند خواری رسته کردم   نیابد هیچ گور امروز گردم

You'd say I was a slave, I've become a king; I was the earth, and now I'm the moon and sky. My life is so free of pain and distress, you'd say I'm not of this world now. I've sobered up from drunkenness, I've woken from a silly dream; my blind fate gained vision as my ignorant soul became wise. Since freeing my feet from the fetters of abasement, my dust today will never find any grave. (478/20–4 [444])

There are some strongly Neoplatonic overtones to this passage, evident in the transition from slavery to kingship, from delusion to reality, from the terrestrial to the celestial, and from death to immortality. These thematics, coupled with Rāmin's epithet in this passage as "world-illuminating" (*jahān-afruz*, 477/1), suggest a certain resonance with philosophical accounts of the soul's felicity (*saʿāda*) on its escape from the material world, as well as the Sufi understanding of the experience of extinction (*fanāʾ*) – that is, the "death" of the self in the apprehension of God – commonly allegorized as the flight of a bird to its source, such as in Avicenna's *Epistle of the Birds* (*Risālat al-ṭayr*), treatises by Muḥammad al-Ghazālī and Sohravardi of the same name, and ʿAṭṭār's *Speech of the Birds* (*Manṭeq al-ṭayr*).[39] With this associative context in mind, it seems clear that *Vis & Rāmin* has brought its characters to an inflection point, a moment of conversion. In coming to know the other for who s/he "really" is, both Vis and Rāmin act on that knowledge by destroying that image, breaking their former idols; by the same token, as they are humiliated and symbolically killed at the hands of their beloved, they come to know their own lowliness and contingency. Situated within this newly gained knowledge, they

can now see in ways that they never before could: if before they could
accuse each other of acting blindly ("You too do not see your own
faults," 473/39 [440]), they can now recognize how their love, mis-
matched and untenable, was holding them back from their full potential. Caught in the spell of his euphoria, Rāmin even thanks Vis for
making him realize his ignorance (*nādāni*) and encourages her to take
the same road: "Go back and renounce your love for me, just as you
said" (472/20 [438]).

In short, concupiscence has been tamed, and freedom achieved; this
could have made a fine and instructive ending to the story. But we are
still not quite there. As Kappler writes, "This liberation is the fruit of a
decisive *reaction* against [their] humiliation" (my emphasis), a perceptive observation that indicates the protagonists have yet to move into
the realm of free choice and action.[40] Thus, it is precisely at this moment
that the poem launches a second ending that will suggest an alternative
resolution, achieved not by escaping from but by re-engaging with the
destructive power of desire.

As Rāmin departs, the already cataclysmic storm morphs into a bel-
lowing "dragon" (*damanda azhdahā*), driving snow upon him with a
fury that would stupefy an elephant, blinding his eyes and sucking the
breath from his lungs (482/1–5 [448]).[41] This is a conspicuous intervention; while Fate is often described as a powerful force in the story,
it rarely makes its influence known in such direct and dramatic fashion.[42] The tempest's draconian form, moreover, evokes the twin themes
of death and desire (*āz*) that Rāmin must now confront face to face,
forcing him to pause and reflect on the choices that brought him to this
point: "His body was in snow and his heart on fire – why he had become
rash and rebellious with his beloved?" (483/6). It is a question of significant depth despite its brevity, and uncharacteristically, we are given
no access to Rāmin's thoughts as he silently contemplates its answer,
falling into a mental position that is both a hallmark of Neoplatonic
writing (e.g., Augustine) and would later be thematized by Sufi poets
such as Rumi as the state of *khāmushi*.[43] If we consider how, throughout
this book, our protagonists have found themselves controlled by and
at odds with institutional structures that regulate every aspect of their
lives, from speech (genre) to power to desire, almost all of their choices
up to this point have been framed not as action but as *reaction*, of strug-
gling to survive in a world that doesn't work out along the lines promised by its ordering logics. But now, with those frameworks destroyed,
Rāmin is presented with an opportunity to take a fresh look at himself:
in the face of death and desire, who is he, and how will he act on that
knowledge?

While we are not privy to Rāmin's thoughts, the outward form of his conclusion could not be more dramatic. "Suddenly, a cry was freed (*rahā shod*) from him, such that you'd say his soul had left his body"; he turns the reins and gallops back to Vis, and then "fell senseless from his horse like a drunkard" (483/8–10). Begging her forgiveness, he proposes a different ending to their story: if they are fated to die in this storm, they should at least perish in union:

بگیرم من ترا در برف دامن　　　　بدارم تا نه تو مانی و نه من
مراکس نیست جز تو در جهان نیز　　چو من مانده نباشم تو ممان نیز
اگر شاید که من پیشت بمیرم　　　چرا در مرگ دامانت نگیرم
به گاه مرگ جویم چون تو یاری　　در آن گیتی به هم خیزیم باری

Let me grasp your hem in the snow, and hold it neither you nor I remain. I've no one save you in the world, too, so when I'm no longer here, you must not stay either. If it's right that I die before you, why should I not clutch your hem in death? Dying, it's you I'll seek as a lover, and we'll rise together in the next world somehow. (484/23–6 [449])

This sequence of events vividly illustrates the themes of death and resurrection: Rāmin first undergoes a symbolic death ("his soul had left his body"), returns to Vis, re-enacts the scene in which he first fell in love with her, and then chooses to die with her in the hope that they might yet "rise again together" in another world. The prescriptive logic ("when I'm no longer here, you must not stay either") and salvific overtones of this passage recall the double ending of ʿAyyuqi's *Varqa & Golshāh*, in which the lovers first perish in the grief of their separation and are then brought back to life through the intercession of the Prophet Muḥammad. There is a key difference between these two accounts, however. While the miraculous resurrection in *V&G* is manifestly something that happens *to* the lovers, a reward from above for their steadfastness and purity, the supernatural intervention in *V&R* instigates a change *within* them, with first Vis and now Rāmin offered the chance to make a radical break with their past selves and consciously alter their stance towards the other. Vis has abandoned her high place in the tower, relinquishing her authority over Rāmin as his "judge," while Rāmin, in an analogous motion, falls off his horse, a sign of defeat and submission.[44] The implications of this break are well captured in Kappler's analysis:

Love passes the heart through fire, the crucible of separation, and, furthermore, that of *deception*: Rāmin must forgive Vis's "mistake" and

Vis must forgive Rāmin's; each one will be obliged to give up the *ideal image that they had of the other*, in exchange for a more human reality, which makes an appeal to the finest qualities of the heart ... They have passed from the immaturity of passion to the maturity of unconditional love; each entirely submits to the beloved (*l'être aimé*) and completely renounces obtaining what they wanted from the other to consolidate a *glorious image of the self*.[45]

As I emphasized in my translation, Kappler identifies the *image* – both of the Self and of the Other – as the main currency of this transformative exchange. If their initial pledge of love was meant to "fix" their respective roles according to the expectations of their discursive worlds (which, as we have seen, do not ultimately line up), this new one professes a commitment to the person rather than to the discourse. Thus, to emend an earlier point, it is not technically the world itself that doesn't "work out," as I put it, but the *visions* that Vis and Rāmin bring to it, their *theōrias*, that have proven to be deceptive and self-limiting. To compare, then, if the story of *Varqa & Golshāh* foregrounds the struggle for *social* recognition through an agreed-on world view, *Vis & Rāmin* instead follows the search for *self* re-cognition through the active questioning of such norms, a cognitive process that Kottman describes as "the struggle of individuals to recognize themselves as the *protagonists* of their life, as actively leading a life rather than merely suffering whatever happens."[46] It is no longer sufficient, in other words, for love to function as a commitment to an external ethos that regulates the lover's behaviour and infuses it with institutionally approved value. It must be reconfigured into an exchange that recognizes the desires of the Other and willingly situates the Self within that framework, replicating the paradoxical synthesis of freedom and submission that lies at the core of a new kind of subjecthood, one that operates beyond the limits of conventional discourse and its images (idols).

One of the most striking outcomes of this shift can be observed in the reconciliation process that follows. In contrast to the ending of the *Ephesiaka*, whose lovers "easily persuaded each other, since that was what they wanted," the anxieties and traumas of the past are not so quickly forgotten. Seemingly oblivious to the swirling snow around them, Vis and Rāmin start again into their conversation:

سخنهایی که صد باره بگفتند   دگر باره همان از سر گرفتند

جفاهای کهن را تازه کردند   دگر باره یکایک بر شمردند

بگفتند آن جفا کز هم بدیدند   سخنهای جفا کز هم شنیدند

دراز آهنگ شد گفتار ایشان   جهان مانده شگفت از کار ایشان

دل ویسه چو کوهی بود سنگین   رخش همچون بهاری بود رنگین
نه از گفتار رامین نرم شد سنگ   نه از سرما بهارش گشت بی رنگ
چو بام آمد سخنها گشت کوتاه   دل گمراهشان آمد سوی راه

They resumed speaking words they had spoken a hundred times before; they renewed the old cruelties, and counted them again, one by one. They spoke of the inequities they had seen from each other, and the unkind words they had heard. Their talk lasted a long time, and the world was amazed at their work. Vis's heart was like a stony mountain, her face as colourful as the Spring. The stone did not soften from Rāmin's words, nor the spring lose its colour from the cold ... When dawn broke, cutting short their talk, their lost hearts had found the way. (484/31–6, 40 [450])

With this, the happy ending that seemed so doomed for so long finally materializes; joining hands, the lovers return to the palace, united at last. But when read against other love stories in Greek, Persian and Arabic, the pathways leading to this moment stray rather far off the beaten track: the lovers have come together not through patience and fortitude, but through an act of *reckoning*, by taking stock of the things they had said and done and holding each other to account. By far the closest comparison in this regard is the ancient novel *Kallirhoe*, whose similarities with *V&R* run so deep they border on the uncanny. As Steven Smith observes, the reunited protagonists of that story also prioritize storytelling over love-making: "Chariton's romantic couple is especially anxious to *tell themselves*, to reconstitute their identities for one another despite the changes that they have undergone."[47] Time, in the end, does seem to move in the two tales; the lovers cannot simply bounce back to their old selves and pick up where they left off. With love broken, and broken by love, their only way forward is to revisit their stories, where they might discover a narrative in which they can both own their choices and know each other through them. Vis's heart – once again compared to a stone that has been indelibly etched with the deeds of the past – refuses to "soften," and even during the lovemaking scene that follows, the narrator reminds us that this joyful reunion can never erase the memory of the past: "Although their hearts were still full of pain, with kisses, they begged each other's forgiveness" (*agar che bud delhā-shān por āzār* • *be busa khwāstand-ash ᶜozr besyār*, 485/54). The admixture of pleasure and pain in this scene speaks well to the "doubled" power of love to kill and revive, to humiliate and ennoble, that makes such an ending possible, one that ultimately reflects Gorgāni's vision of the world itself: "Its bitter is forever coupled with sweet, such that its blessing is coupled with [its] curse."

Thus, in the norm-shattering act of reciprocal murder, and the subsequent rebuilding that follows, both characters discover a mode of "being a lover in the world" (*ʿāsheqi*) that is, necessarily, a worldly one, establishing the self as a historical experience of the past and giving that self access to modes of free and self-expressive action in the present. On a superficial level, it might seem that the reunion of Vis and Rāmin merely recreates the dynamic of sexual symmetry; but thanks to the passage of time and the writing of the self that we have seen achieved, the implications of what it means to love now run far deeper than they could ever have before. It is only after falling out of love, the dangerous possibility suggested by the suspicious circumstances of their initial union, that the lovers are free to reforge their connection on something like a kind of mutual recognition, not of their sameness, but of their irreducible difference, a process that both Kappler and Kottman, in their distinctive ways, theorize as a gain in human self-consciousness.[48] Even as they reconstitute what appears to be the normative relationship of romantic love, it is not a reboot of the original paradigm but a full renovation of its conditions and mechanics from the inside out – not unlike what Gorgāni achieved with the romance mythos itself.

Endings and Beginnings

With the collapse and reconstitution of Vis and Rāmin's love, the narrative is at last primed to snap back into motion. In an action-packed finale, coming on the heels of thousands of lines of discourse and debate, the lovers will rise up in unison against Mobad, topple him from power, and rule over the united realms of Māh and Marv for many years in joy and contentment.[49] So sharp and sudden is the transition that it can induce a sense of whiplash (my first impression on reading was one of a hasty "That's all, folks!"), as if the text is intentionally diverting our attention away from the messy circumstances leading up to its conclusion. This in itself is an interesting literary strategy, as it would remind its readers that they, no less than Vis and Rāmin, should simply empty their memory of all the iniquitous and confounding events they have so recently witnessed. But from another perspective, the pivot contains a message of its own: it is in the swift transition from the resolution of love to the restoration of political order under a new generation of leadership that *Vis & Rāmin* steps out of the temporally self-contained framework of the love-story and announces its relevance within a broad intertextual discourse, one that transcends the borders of narrative genres. With the romance having created its own "history" – a time frame different from that of biography or chronicle to be sure, but none the less "real" for it – it is now the task of the ending to stitch this alternate temporality into the world of eleventh-century Isfahan, thus fulfilling Gorgāni's promise to his patron, Abu al-Fath, that the story "will one day benefit you when you read it" (28/42).

This chronotopic shift, however, comes at a considerable cost, with most of the *dramatis personae* experiencing some kind of verbal suppression or physical violence. Soon after the debate in the snowstorm, Vis and her Nurse fade into the background, joining Shahru, Viru, Gol, and Mobad's mother, while Mobad and Zard are abruptly killed off. As the dust settles, only Rāmin remains standing, as far as the narrative focus is concerned, and this strangely lonely image – a single, solitary voice concluding the work after its deafening cacophony – raises the question of what has been lost in the transition from phantasy to history, asking us to reflect on the (self-)sacrifices necessary for the (re-)establishment of a normative and ideal order.

First, let us say farewell to Vis. After she and Rāmin have reconciled, they return to Mobad's court and fall back into their usual routine of paying lip service to the king while cavorting behind his back. But with the arrival of spring, the inevitable threat of separation again rears its head: Mobad organizes a hunting party, and when he sees Rāmin wavering, he immediately whisks him away before the couple can cook up any new scheme to fool him. At this juncture, Vis confronts a choice of no return; as she laments to her Nurse, either she can step back into the suicidal loop of adventure-time or she must find some way to escape it once and for all. It is perhaps only after experiencing the trauma of the snowstorm that she is prepared to consider the possibility of outright revolt, an option that the Nurse, perhaps seeing her own political moment, now places on the table: "God has given you kingship" (*torā dāda-st yazdān pādshāyi*, 498/32 [465]), she reminds her charge, and all she has to do is wield it. With Mobad gone on the hunt, far from his palace and treasury, it is the perfect time to checkmate the king – and Rāmin the perfect pawn to do it.

This prompts one last letter from Vis to Rāmin, and, coming on the heels of her lament, marks the final time that Vis will "speak" in the narrative. In terms of its eloquence, the letter does not disappoint: opening with a refrain on the *from–to* rhythm of the *Jafā-nāma*'s peroration, it speaks on the agonies of separation and reminds Rāmin of Vis's commitment to him. With this established, she concludes with a series of lines commanding him to come (*biyā*), which, through its repetition of the word, gains the tone and character of a summoning spell (503/60–5 [470]). If poetry is a form of "licit magic," this is the moment when Vis "activates" Rāmin, transforming him from a help-less lover to a man of action.[50] But like many spells, this one demands a sacrifice:

خدایا جان من بگذار چندان　　که بینم روی او آنگاه بستان

که با این داغ گر جانم بر آید　　ز دود جان من گیتی سر آید

O God, keep my life long enough for me to see Rāmin – then take it! For if my soul were to rise up in this burning pain, the world would be consumed by its smoke. (504/74–5 [471])

And with these words, Vis bows out. It is a strangely self-aware progno-sis: in calling on Rāmin to rise up and seize the crown, simultaneously with and from her, her job appears to be finished. As she anticipates, her "life," in a narrative sense, will be sacrificed for Rāmin's success, and the world in which she played such a dynamic and powerful role will give way to a new order in which she need never "speak frankly" (58/25 [25]) again.[51] And such proves to be the case: though she is around for the events to come next, she will produce no more speech of any kind, dissolving instead into the general backdrop of Rāmin's political triumph. This transition offers a sobering counterbalance to the narrative of personal emancipation and agency that distinguishes Vis's character for much of the story. While the drama of *V&R* emerges out of the disruption and even inversion of established social hierarchies, the lovers' reconstitution of their vows clears the space for a norma-tive ideal order to reassert itself, one in which the affairs of court are an exclusively male domain and from which women are expected (as advice manuals such as Yūsuf Khāṣṣ Ḥājib's *Kutadgu Bilig* and Neẓām al-Molk's *Siyar al-moluk* make amply clear) to keep a wide berth.[52] As a result, Vis resumes the silent, modest, and obedient persona she pre-sented to us in our first meeting with her, following the fate of many of her predecessors (and successors, if we look ahead to figures like Guenevere).[53] Davis's description of Gordiya, one of the many dynamic noblewomen of the *Shāhnāma*, seems quite apropos to her case: "The system she defends takes her to its bosom as it were, but in so doing obliterates her individuality."[54]

And yet, this final gesture consolidates Vis's centrality to the politics of *V&R* in interesting ways. Her acts of self-fashioning and legacy mak-ing throughout the poem, though rooted in a world of legend and fairy tale, mingle with the visible realities of Gorgāni's historical moment, in which women *did* play prominent and public roles in the highest echelons of power, however much Neẓām al-Molk might have wished otherwise. We know, moreover, that the Seljuk courts of the twelfth century "produced educational literature not just for princes but also for princesses," suggesting that it is by no means inconceivable to posit a female readership for *V&R*, and to bring that consideration to bear in ways similar to what has been explored in the study of Greek and French romance.[55] In that light, Vis's role within the poem's allegorical denouement becomes extremely intriguing. As the Nurse points out, it is she, and only she, who gets to designate the king of Iran; it is out of her own volition that, having selected Rāmin as her preferred partner (now that he's made amends), she will "set the golden crown upon his head" (*be sar bar neh mar u rā tāj-e zarrin*, 499/44 [466]). This act puts her in quite a different position from most of the royal women in the *Shāhnāma*, who, when and if they rule, usually do so as regents – "crown-holders," so to speak – providing a bridge of sorts between two male members of the line.[56] Vis, in contrast, performs a function quite close to that of the "crown-bestower" (*tāj-bakhsh*), a role that falls squarely on the shoulders of male warriors like Zāl and Rostam in the *Shāhnāma*. The closest equivalents to a female *tāj-bakhsh* in the latter text might be found in Arnavāz and Shahrnavāz (Jamshid's sister-wives) and Farānak (the mother of Feraydun), who actively resist and conspire against Żaḥḥāk to ensure his overthrow – an overlap that might not be so surprising, when we consider Vis's own close associations with Jamshid.[57] In both cases, we are given a story not so much of the continuation of sovereignty but its reconstitution, a process in which the female characters do not bridge the gap between two mortal men, but rather establish a passage, a *majāz*, from the secular to the sublime – not through their abstraction but through their embodiment as historical subjects. This legacy cannot be easily overlooked, and I will return to its implications below.

But for now, with Vis serving as the "pivot," as Meisami puts it, between the ambitions of "two opposing contestants" for the throne, the juxtaposition of the two brothers assumes the narrative's attention, throwing into relief the aspects and qualities of Rāmin's success against those of Mobad's failure.[58] Upon reading Vis's letter, Rāmin challenges himself to give up his usual state (*ḥāl*, 505/85 [472]) of wailing and lamenting, declaring that "now I must either break open these bonds, or submit entirely [to them]" (505/95). Explicit in this call is the performance of a fuller, freer, and more capable ideal of masculinity – "I am not a man if I tolerate this any longer" (505/97) – hardly a coincidence, considering the extensive amount of time that *V&R* has spent exploring the inherent limits of Mobad's ability to act. Rāmin's new course will not be an easy one; as he reminds himself, no success comes without struggle (*ze bi-ranji nayābi kāmrāni*, 506/103), an allusion to the Qur'anic consolation that "with [every] difficulty comes ease" (*maᶜ al-ᶜusri yusrā*, 94:5–6). This line frames Rāmin's conversion into a new ideal of manhood within a narrative of eschatological hope and triumph. In choosing to act, Rāmin muses, perhaps the days of tribulation (*balā*) will come to an end, and a "new day" (*ruz-e digar*) will begin: the hardship of winter will soon pass, with an auspicious spring just around the corner (506/112–13).

Girded with this quasi-apocalyptic zeal, Rāmin plots and executes his coup, drawing a sharp contrast between the delicate affectations of courtly love and the brisk, unsentimental world of *realpolitik*. On the pretext of making a sacrifice at the temple, Vis leaves the palace with her ladies in waiting, exchanging places with Rāmin and his men, disguised in women's clothing. Once inside, the soldiers massacre the palace guard, and Rāmin kills their leader, Zard, in single combat. Burdened by the guilt of this latest offence, he weeps over his half-brother's mangled body, but the narrative voice appears to have little sympathy. It's time for Rāmin to "grow up," it seems to say, remarking in an almost admonishing tone that lamentation and mourning have no place when it comes to war and securing a legacy (512/29 [479]). In that light, the scene seems to be offering a bit of hard advice to its audience, presenting Rāmin's deeds as a kind of initiation by blood into the business of rule: if he wants to be king, Rāmin must be willing to strike down anyone who might stand in his way, even members of his own family – something Mobad could never bring himself to do. This detached, even cold tone continues to resound as Vis and Rāmin seize Mobad's treasure and make off for Daylam, the mountainous land south of the Caspian Sea whose indomitable warriors no king can subdue (aside from Ṭughrıl Beg, of course! [13/56–60]). Rāmin is no exception to this rule; although he assembles a coalition of lords and nations to back his bid for the throne, the narrator is surprisingly candid about their reasons for supporting him: "The whole world flocked to him, not for Rāmin, but rather for the dinars beyond count" (*jahān yekbāra gerd āmad bar u bar • na bar rāmin ke bar dinār-e bi-mar*, 515/26 [481]). In making such remarks, the text maintains a critical distance from the events it relates: this is no account of good triumphing over evil, but simply the messy realities of the internecine struggle for power, a phenomenon all too familiar for readers in Gorgāni's courtly world.[59] With the brothers' armies drawn up and ready for a bloodbath, it seems as though we have fully departed from the lofty ideals of romance and divine kingship alike.

It is nothing short of a miracle, then, when news arrives that Mobad has been unexpectedly killed by a wild boar on his way to confront his brother. Through this second *deus* (or perhaps *monstrum*) *ex machina*, the impending civil war gives way to a vacant throne and a widowed queen, both of which Rāmin can now claim without any offence. As Rāmin knows well, his revolt had already set him towards the unequivocally bad moral territory of fratricide, parricide, and regicide: indeed, he had confided to Vis, as they planned their rebellion, "I should not look on Mobad's face after this, and if I do, I deserve every evil" (*nashāyad did az in pas ruy-e mobad* ● *v-agar binam sazāvār-am be har bad*, 507/11 [474]). It is thus a great relief to him to learn of his brother's "accident":

که او فرجام موبد را چنان کرد   نهانی شکر دادار جهان کرد

نه خونی ریخته شد در میانه   نه جنگی بود مرگش را بهانه

نبوده هیچ رامین را گناهی   سرآمد روز چونان پادشاهی

Secretly Rāmin thanked the world's Creator that He had finally done this to Mobad. There was no war to blame for his death, no spilled blood between them. The days of such a king had come to an end, and no guilt was on Rāmin. (521/3–5 [487])

By emphasizing that God has all along been at the lovers' backs (despite the fact that almost every law of the poem's social order was at some time or another violated in the process), this passage brings *Vis & Rāmin* to its triumphant conclusion: the restoration of ideal rule, the coming of spring after a long winter. Although one can see in this the typical resolution of a Hellenistic romance, with the lovers' reunion and happily-ever-after, the text's persistent focus on Rāmin and his reign suggests a broader generic metamorphosis at work. Virtually overnight, Rāmin blossoms into a just and pious ruler who "liberates" the inhabitants of Marv from Mobad's oppression: "You'd say they had all escaped Hell, and found respite under the shade of Ṭubā [the tree of Paradise]" (524/51 [489]) – a Qur'anic allusion that once again evokes images of divine providence.[60] This description of Mobad as a tyrannical despot confirms a number of previously seeded hints about his deteriorating relationship with both the army (260/18–23 [225], 516/12 [482]) and the aristocracy (274/61–3 [238], 499/48 [466]); and while it is perhaps disappointing to watch the text paper over the complex portrait of the king it had so carefully painted, replacing him with a stock villain whose overthrow can be easily welcomed and celebrated by all, his marginalization, like that of Vis, is part of the process through which *V&R* establishes Rāmin as the new embodiment of an idealized sovereignty. Hence the heavy overtones of salvation and deliverance, and the moralistic warning to the (courtly) audience that they should avoid the road of injustice, lest a similar fate befall them (524/53). In this light, one can argue that *V&R* activates the romance structure to produce a treatise on kingship, thus ushering itself into the same discursive field as its close predecessor, the *Shāhnāma*.[61]

Indeed, Rāmin's subsequent career, though briefly recounted, offers a comprehensive snapshot of what the perfect kingdom should look like: roads and villages rebuilt, wisdom nurtured and religion fostered, and justice rendered to the downtrodden and oppressed, a legacy that stamps the sovereign's name on the enduring material of his realm, from the designation of cities ("Rām-shahr") to the make of the harp he played so well (526/83–8 [491]). Amidst all these indications of Rāmin's ascent to an ideal archetype, perhaps the most significant appears as he and his queen reach the end of their lives, after eighty-one prosperous years. Vis is the first to fail and die, and while Rāmin bitterly regrets her passing, he observes that it would not be proper for him to rend his clothes or smear dust upon his face: "For I am old, and you" – addressing his now-deceased beloved – "know that it is shameful for the elderly to behave in such a manner" (529/27 [494]). These words stand in pointed contrast to Mobad, recalling in particular the warning that Shahru had given him so long ago: "The world will heap shame and disgrace on anyone old who plays at being young" (40/28 [7]). In electing the path of forbearance, Rāmin both corrects his brother's fundamental mistake and sheds his former persona as the lovestruck bard, his once-effusive tongue now bound to silence.

This juxtaposition of the two kings and the consequences of their decisions gains greater significance as the text brings its narrative to a close. The final chapter begins, like the first, on Nowruz; but instead of celebrating his rule, Rāmin decides the time has come to let it go. In his final act as king, he instructs his son, Khwarshid-e Mahān ("Sun of the Moons" – an interesting fusion of Rāmin's representation as the kingly, light-bestowing "sun" that rises in Khorasan [*khwar-āsān*, 176/4] and Vis's association with *māh*, meaning both "Media" and "moon"), on the dos and don'ts of proper governance, a testament scene that also marks the end of successful reigns in the *Shāhnāma*, such as those of Ardashir and Nushin-Ravān. Then, descending from the royal throne (*takht-e khosrovāni*) of the court, Rāmin mounts the "other-worldly" throne (*takht-e ān-jāhāni*) of the Zoroastrian ossuary (*dakhma*) and fire temple (531/16). This move places another bookend against the opening of *V&R*, where Vis had told Mobad that if he had any wisdom, he would have sought provisions for "that" world (*tusha josti ān jahān rā*, 57/117 [25]); it also reinforces the implicit comparison with Kay Khosrow we saw above, in that Rāmin does a far better job than his counterpart in leaving the kingdom in good hands. Now freed from his temporal duties, he wages his final war: the defeat of desire itself.

که خرسندی گزید و پارسایی   خدای آن روز دادش پادشایی

همیشه آز را چون کهتری بود   اگرچه پیش ازان او مهتری بود

ز بهر کام دل فرمانبر آز   جهان فرمان او بردی و او باز

تن از آز و دل از انده بری ساخت   چو زآزاین جهان دل را بپرداخت

چنان دان کز بلای جاودان رست   دلی کز شغل وآزاین جهان رست

God granted him sovereignty that day, for he chose piety and contentment. Although he had been a noble before then, he had always been like an underling before desire (*āz*). The world bore his command, while he, for the sake of his heart's pleasure, bore the commands of desire (*āz*). When he expelled desire (*āz*) for the world from his heart, he freed his body of desire (*āz*) and his mind of grief. Know that a heart that escapes the affairs and desires (*āz*) of this world has escaped everlasting calamity. (531/18–22 [496])

This passage makes clear that a key element in Rāmin's ascension to "true" sovereignty is the expulsion of desire (*āz*), and given the striking reappearance of this word at the end of the poem, we are well justified to consider it one of the central issues of *V&R* as a whole. Desire lies at the heart of the many story arcs we have followed, from Vis's determination to control it, to Mobad's initial encounter with Shahru, to the collapse and restitution of Vis and Rāmin's relationship; and in every case, it serves as a kind of catalyst that disrupts and potentially dissolves the authority of temporal institutions, opening the space for a new epistemology of self-knowledge to emerge. It is through this process, the text maintains, that our very humanity can be realized (or destroyed), thus situating *āz* at the core of the human experience. What, then, are we to make of Rāmin's final excision of this element?

My initial answer to this takes us back to the medieval notion of the metaphor (*majāz*) as a bridge that provides some kind of mental access to the Real-Truth (*ḥaqīqa*). If Vis presents her speech – which, we should recall, she insists is a material extension of her body – as possessing this metaphorical quality, then this might allow us to understand Rāmin's symbolic death at her hands, his subsequent reconversion and reunion with her, and finally his attainment of temporal and then spiritual success as a way of instantiating a theory in which bodily desire enables a being-in-the-world that ultimately transcends the body. We might imagine this as a kind of scaffolding: though we must use desire to ascend to the heavens, once arrived at the top, that ladder is the only thing tying us to the ground below. This may help explain Vis's shift in the narrative, for although she is the agent of Rāmin's transformation and makes possible his newfound connection with the divine realm, it is no surprise that the text would take the position that she is no substitute for God. As Meisami observes, one of the meta-narratives of *V&R* is the story of how Rāmin attained felicity through his love for Vis, succeeding where his brother Mobad had failed; he thus models the life story of an ideal king, one who, despite his many flaws and transgressions, "delivered to God a soul washed pure" (*be yazdān dād jān-e pāk shosta*, 532/32).[62] The final scene, when Rāmin and Vis meet again in Heaven, delivers the final union of amorous, political, and spiritual success that both wraps up the love-story mythos and integrates it with a broader tradition of wisdom literature and sacred history, a convergence that Gorgāni now sees manifest before him, as he dedicates his poem to Abu al-Fath:

از آفتهای گردون دور گشته   جهان بینم همه پر نور گشته

مگر نو کرد یزدان گیتی از سر   جهان دیگر شدست و حال دیگر

I see the world entirely filled with light, and taken far away from the afflictions of fortune ... The world has changed, as has its state; perhaps God has recreated the earth! (535/6, 10)

This final synthesis invites us, along with Gorgāni's contemporary readers, to reconceptualize the boundaries of history and phantasy alike, presenting the former as something far greater than an account of verifiable truth and demonstrating how truth can be obtained through the speculative exercise of the latter.[63] Vis's *Jafā-nāma* proposes a way of writing a life story (*sīra*) – and the creation of a "life" behind it that can do things such as bear witness, leave testimony, and talk to audiences far beyond its diegetic space and time – that does not require some kind of basis in the agreed-on record of "what happened" to be meaningful. Instead of validating itself in and through the past, it contends that the emotional and ethical lives of imaginal people can be just as valid as their historical counterparts; it shifts the focus, in other words, from *lives* that matter to *experiences of life* that matter, a conjoining of time and subjectivity with analogues in western European romances as well.[64] Thus, the existential threats our protagonists face leading up to the letter's composition, and the moments of despair, death, intercession, conversion, and felicity that follow, gain in meaning and value, simply because those "lived examples," real or imagined, have something to teach us in and of themselves.[65]

With this hypothesis in mind, we may finally go back to a question posed early on in this study: Why read romance? What place does it have amidst the "books of tradition, jurisprudence, poetry, language, history, and the works of the learned," as our Abbasid prince once said?[66] Having explored the passage, traces, and experiences of time in *Vis & Rāmin* and on its characters, Gorgāni's answer to this question should now be more revealing: "When someone reads out this story, they will understand the faults of the world" (*cho bar khwānad kas-i in dāstān rā* • *bedānad ʿaybhā-ye in jahān rā*, 45/57 [12]). The imaginal realm of phantasy does not take us away from reality; on the contrary, in subjecting both the lovers and the love-story that contains them to an experience of dead ends, death, and discovery, it provides us with a threshold into a deeper and more profound knowledge of its workings.

Epilogue | In Which Many a Tale Has Love

To bring this study to a close, I would like to repeat the formula invoked at its beginning. *Yek-i bud, yek-i nabud*: "There was one, there wasn't one," or in a more colloquial idiom, "It happened, and it didn't." Traditionally recited at the beginning of a fairy tale, this formula speaks beautifully to the liminal status of the romance within the broader arena of discursive activity in medieval Helleno-Abrahamic cultures. Did Vis, Mobad, and Rāmin really exist? How does our answer to this question change the way we read their stories, and what can we learn from them, given these multiple possible perspectives?

In embracing these ambiguous questions and leveraging them to propose complex answers, *Vis & Rāmin* represents a landmark text, not only in the history of a genre, but in a wider set of formative developments of the early eleventh century, which included a new fascination with the ancient past, new ideas about the function of poetry and the imagination, and new ways of grappling with the perennial issue of desire. This is not the place for such a comprehensive intellectual history, but I will endeavour at least to connect the findings of this book with other recent advances in scholarship, suggesting some of the questions they might raise when placed in an interdisciplinary context. *V&R* is not only a text in which love has many a tale (*bedu dar ʿeshq rā chandin fasāna*, 112/70 [75]), as its author claims; it also points to an emerging world beyond its diegetic borders: a world in which many a tale has love.

An intriguing place to start is to consider the concurrence of the rise of romance with the life of Avicenna (d. 1037). Avicenna's life itinerary dovetails in striking ways with the westwards expansion of Persian court poetry: his professional career began in Samanid Bukhara in the court of Nuḥ b. Manṣur (d. 976), the same dynasty under whose patronage Ferdowsi began writing the *Shāhnāma*, and, after a stint in Hamadan, ended up in Isfahan, the very city where Gorgāni would compose his *Vis &*

Rāmin some seventeen years later. It seems likely, moreover, that the latter poet was aware of or had access to some of Avicenna's writings, as the first chapter of *V&R* closely follows the account of the world's creation as laid out in the philosopher's "sublime sermon" (*al-khuṭba al-gharrāʾ*).[1] Both passages end with a short discussion of the hierarchy of souls, from the mineral to the vegetable to the animal to the human (Avicenna: *jamād, nabāt, ḥayawān, insān*; Gorgāni: *gohar, nabāt, ḥayvān, mardom*, 5/72–4), postulating that only the latter, "if purified through knowledge and good deeds," in Avicenna's words, "becomes like the Substances of the First Causes (i.e., angels)"; or, as Gorgāni writes,

به چشمش خوار گردد شاه و شاهی زدوده گردد از زنگ تباهی

ولیک از قدر و عز جاودانی بلندی جوید آنجا نه مکانی

شود آنجا که او را هست میعاد چو رسته گردد از چنگال اضداد

کزیشان مایه آمد این جهان را شود ماننده آن پیشینگان را

It [the human soul] is scoured of the rust of decay, and kings and kingship become contemptible in its view ... It seeks loftiness there – not [just] a high social standing, but rather from the power and glory of the eternal. When it is freed from the grip of contraries, it goes to that place that is its origin. It resembles those primordial [souls] from which came the substance of this world. (6/83, 86–8)

The upward return of the human soul from the multiple to the unitary, freeing it from the "grip of contraries," closely aligns with Rāmin's discovery of "true" nobility and freedom (*āzādi*) discussed in chapter 5; situating this final outcome within its Avicennian frame suggests that Gorgāni conceived of the romance as a productive site for philosophical inquiry – a proposition that was firmly established by the time Jāmi wrote his *Yusof & Zolaykhā* in 1483 – with significant ramifications for the ways we can understand desire. In his "Treatise on Love" (*al-Risāla fī al-ʿishq*), Avicenna postulates that all motion, even that of inanimate objects, is an effect of the innate desire in all creation to return to the Creator. Desire is thus hardwired within the human soul, but its function is complicated by the presence of the intellect, which, though capable of discerning higher truths, is also more prone to *mis*-recognizing the Good than its vegetable and animal counterparts. Paradoxically, then, desire "is one of the causes of corruption, but it is necessary in the general desired order which is good."[2] The finest possible human response to desire, recognizing its potential as a sword that cuts both ways, is thus not to repress but to wield it, activating it as a bridge to gain approximation to the Pure Object of love, veiled, as it were, by its material manifestations. As Domenico Ingenito has recently discussed, Avicenna's psychology became hugely influential in the work of later poets such as Saʿdi of Shiraz (d. 1291), and given Gorgāni's clear knowledge of at least some aspects of the philosopher's works, an Avicennian reading of *V&R* may show how far back this genealogy runs.[3]

Yet, at the same time, I do not mean to suggest a story of cause and effect – that Gorgāni simply read Avicenna and worked the latter's theories into *Vis & Rāmin*. Indeed, the rise of romance strongly complicates any such single-point genesis narrative, for as we have seen, this development took place *alongside* Avicenna's career in the first decades of the eleventh century, and in rather different locales (Ghazna in the east, Hamadan in the west); the lines only converge, so to speak, with Gorgāni's arrival in Isfahan as it fell to the Seljuks in 1051. What seems to be happening instead, therefore, is a much broader conversation about fundamental topics – why do we desire, and how do we make sense of ourselves in a divinely ordered world as desiring animals – that receives significant advances in multiple discursive fields and landmark texts in this transitional moment.

Let me offer another example by turning to another contemporary figure (and resident of Gorgan), the celebrated theorist ʿAbd al-Qāhir al-Jurjānī (d. 1078 or 1081), recently described by Lara Harb as one of the major pioneers of a "new school" of literary criticism, established at the turn of the eleventh century. One of the significant ways al-Jurjānī diverged from his predecessors, Harb writes, was in his attitude towards truth and make-believe: while the old school used "truthfulness" (*ṣidq* or *ḥaqīqa*) – comprising "the accurateness and correctness of the language on a literal level, the plausibility of the ideas, and adherence to conventional imagery" – as one of the main criteria for assessing the quality of a poetic image, the new school grounded its analysis on the internal cogency of the images produced, rather than measuring them against extrinsic or empirical considerations. In this way, "what was previously treated as untruthful in the old school of criticism, such as figurative language and imaginary comparisons, becomes part of the realm of truthfulness because they do not require their acceptance as an actual truth and remain accurate on the literal level."[4] The ability of the image itself to produce insight through phantasy (*takhyīl*) was the paramount issue at stake, a perspective that would imbue "fanciful tales with no use but to bring on sleep and to entertain" with a whole new range of possible uses.[5]

Again, as in the case of Avicenna, I do not mean to propose a direct link between al-Jurjānī's work and the New Persian romances. But there are intriguing correlations. Harb's identification of a shift from extrinsic to intrinsic modes of literary analysis resonates with the move from the external frame of reference, typical of heroic biographies, to the internal and self-sufficient architecture of the amorous tale discussed in chapter 1. Furthermore, many of the ninth- and tenth-century critics surveyed in that chapter seem to operate within a similar "old school" paradigm of truthfulness, relegating narratives with no obvious basis in the authoritative accounts of the past to the domain of fables (*khurāfāt*, *afsāna*); that is, tales suitable for evening entertainment (*asmār*), but not to be confused with "real" history. But when we arrive at Ferdowsi's claim that truth may still be found by way of symbol (*ramz*), or Gorgāni's argument that the techniques of poetry can fill an otherwise meaningless story with valuable mental content (*māʿāni*), it seems that new ideas about the potential benefit of apparently fantastic images and topics were starting to gain traction. Thus, the romances may be participating in broader developments, also evinced by figures like al-Jurjānī, that Harb describes as "a general shift in paradigm that is evident (a) across the critical treatment of the various aspects of poetic language that concerned Arabic criticism, (b) beyond al-Jurjānī in the science of eloquence, and (c) across disciplines, including philosophy."[6]

One possible manifestation of this paradigm shift may also be found in the rising attention given to narratives set in the antique, "pagan" past. "There was a huge surge of interest in national history in a very short period in mid- to late tenth-century Iran," Jaakko Hämeen-Anttila observes, with a proliferation of texts drawing from the *Book of Lords* (*Khudāy-nāma*) and the Sistani epic tradition during this time.[7] As we enter the eleventh century, the parameters of this interest seem to expand even further across time, locale, and topic, encompassing the Hellenistic romances of ʿOnṣori, the Jāhiliyya-era love-story of ʿAyyuqi, the indeterminate but "ancient" (*bāstān*) setting of the *Homāy-nāma*, and, of course, the archaic Iranian milieu of *Vis & Rāmin*. In that regard, the rise of versified epic and then romance represents a significant innovation of this period, a refurbishing of old tales in a "new manner" (*now-āyin*, as Gorgāni puts it) by which contemporary audiences could make these stories meaningful to their own times. In his recent dissertation, Samuel Lasman describes this manner as a "speculative" mode of engaging with the past:

> Advocating for the literary value of the speculative represents a critique of narrowly euhemerist (or, perhaps, more generally positivist) views of how the past should be understood. Classical Persian verse epic re-enchanted history without rendering it inconsequential; indeed, the *Shāhnāmeh* came

to be considered fully on-par with al-Ṭabarī's masterpiece across the medieval Islamic world.[8]

This notion of the speculative strongly resonates with Travis Zadeh's work on the "wonders" or "mirabilia" (*ʿajāʾib*) literature of the medieval Islamic period, where it was understood that "speculation (*naẓar*) ultimately bears a theological dimension," bringing "both pleasure in this world (*al-ladhdhāt al-dunyawiyya*) and happiness in the next (*al-saʿādāt al-ukhrawiyya*)."[9] The "re-enchantment" of history thus allowed eleventh-century readers to experience wonder (*ʿajab*) and find truth (*ḥaqīqa*) in the most unlikely of places, whether a symposium on love set in idolatrous Greece (*Vāmeq & ʿAẕrā*, w. early 11th c.), or an epic biography featuring an elephant-tusked demon as its protagonist (the *Kush-nāma*, w. 1108–11), described by its author as a "useful" (*sudmand*) book, but deceptively so: "a spring, but made gloomy from the rain; a beautiful image, but one that has experienced injustice" (*bahār-i valikan ze bārān dozham • negār-i valikan resida setam*, 152/134–5). *Vis & Rāmin*, a tale no less scandalous in its depictions of incest, adultery, and regicide, nevertheless offers its readership a similar packaging of aesthetic pleasure with mental and spiritual training, excavating the various "views" (*naẓar* or *theōria*) its characters bring to the table, breaking down their premises, exposing their contradictions, testing their limits, and proposing new paradigms for its readers to discover – all strategies that help bring forth a "novel emergent" of perception.[10]

Taken together, these various examples suggest that the "new manner" of romance makes a lot of sense when placed into a larger context in which conversations about desire, poetry, history, and phantasy were in a state of rapid flux. The love-story was an active participant in shaping the discourse of this milieu, engaging with a wide range of interlocutors and contributing to other fields of writing, the theological and the philosophical chief among them. To be sure, this shift did not happen overnight, nor was it entirely unprecedented; but in the grand scheme of things, *Vis & Rāmin* marks an important milestone in the formulation of what Ingela Nilsson calls a "theology of erotics," a literary undertaking that, by narrating the adventures of lovers in ways that allowed for multiple levels of interpretation, explored the links between "physical, spiritual and, not least, rhetorical desire."[11]

Let me draw a quick contrast to explain what I mean. One of the most successful vessels for conveying the affairs of lovers in Arabic "high" literature, outside the biographies of poets and the manuals of customs and advice, was the genre commonly known as "deliverance after hardship" (*al-faraj baʿd al-shidda*). An allusion to the Qurʾanic verse cited in the previous chapter – "with [every] difficulty comes ease" (94:5–6) – this phrase supplied the title for a number of anecdote collections, including those of al-Madāʾinī (d. 849), Ibn Abi al-Dunyā (d. 894), Abu al-Ḥusayn b. Yūsuf (d. 939), and al-Tanūkhī (d. 994), organized around the basic message that those who display perseverance and steadfastness in the face of adversity will at last see their virtue rewarded.[12] This message accords with the dominant ethos of the Hellenistic romance, in which the lovers, on the brink of losing all hope, suddenly find themselves reunited through a serendipitous cascade of events; indeed, one anecdote related by al-Tanūkhī, featuring two separated lovers who presume each other to be dead until their miraculous reunion, retreads the plot of the ancient novel in all its major features.[13] When presented through this framework, such tales can be appreciated as much as devotional reading as they can for their entertainment value; as Ibn al-Dāya writes, they are a kind of "medicine" for the soul.[14]

There is no doubt that the earliest extant romances in Persian, *Varqa & Golshāh* and *Vis & Rāmin*, retain this didactic and devotional aspect. Both stories conclude with a (false) death, resurrection, and then a pivot that both sublimates and integrates the love affair into an account of conversion and deliverance: in this way, they break down the love-story and reconstitute it into something that transcends its original scope. (Regrettably, we do not know how ʿOnṣori's *Vāmeq & ʿAzrā* concluded, but Hägg and Utas note some contextual indications that point to apparent deaths and trials by fire, so there may be some thematic consistency.[15]) On one level, then, we could see the rise of the romance as an expansion of the *faraj* genre, in which ʿAyyuqi and Gorgāni assume its rhetorical goals and incorporate them into long-form narratives, a technique that likely informed the use of amorous tales by later Sufi poets like ʿAṭṭār and Rumi.[16]

And yet at the same time, some key differences arise as well, particularly with *Vis & Rāmin*. As this book has shown, *V&R* is deeply concerned with the relationship between language and the mind, tracing how the stories we use to order the world both enable and hamper our ability to make sense of it. From the start, the text seems to know that its ending must necessarily be an ambivalent one, in the sense that what is wrong in one framework is proven to be right in another; in this regard, it produces in narrative form something akin to Avicenna's insights on desire and the human soul. As a result, *Vis & Rāmin* resists any easy form of closure, calling its readers to seek an evermore robust hermeneutics in their interpretation of the tale.[17] They must recognize that the common-sense and self-evident world of the empirical faculties

is not to be fully trusted, leaving them with the challenge of making
meaningful a tale of two lovers who broke all the rules and yet had God
on their side:

نبشته یک به یک کردارِ ایشان   قضا پَردَخته بود از کارِ ایشان

به زورو چاره زیشان بر نشگتی   قضای آسمان دیگر نگشتی

بداند عیبهای این جهان را   چو بر خوانَد کسی این داستان را

که راهِ حکمِ یزدان بست نتوان   نباید سرزنش کردن بدیشان

> Fate had settled their affairs, written their deeds out one by one. The will
> of the heavens would never change; whether by trickery or force, it would
> not turn away from them. When someone reads out this story, they will
> understand the faults of the world. One cannot condemn them, for the
> road of God's will cannot be blocked. (45/55–8 [12])

In this way, I am left with the impression that *V&R* presents its ideal
reader's engagement with this problem as not only a devotional but also
a speculative exercise, an activation of the imagination by which wisdom is not acquired from the text as a simple transfer of knowledge, but
generated from within via the reader's entanglement with uncertainty.
In other words, in a way resonant with Matthew Keegan's discussion
of the "hermeneutical dramas" in the *Maqāmāt* of al-Ḥarīrī (d. 1122),
the many tales of *V&R* "are not spoons of sugar that help the medicine
go down," but "potentially *constitutive* of Islamic ʿ*ilm* [knowledge]."[18]
The "new manner" of love-story, in this light, can be understood as a
significant contribution to the wider phenomenon of making meaning
through ambiguity that scholars of premodern Islamic societies have
been recently examining.[19] It was in the recognition that complex language and sophisticated storytelling – even if the material has little
intrinsic value in terms of its recognized historicity or veracity – "will
one day benefit you when you read" (28/42) that the romance emerged
as a viable genre in New Persian literature; a recognition that Neẓāmi
shared when he prepared to commit the amorous adventures of Majnun, Shirin, and Bahrām Gur to verse a century later (even as he dis-
tanced himself from Gorgāni's work). Standing at the threshold of the
possible and impossible, the romance allows its readers to look at both
realms from the other side and reconsider the assumptions we bring to
them, travelling in our thoughts between the realms of what is, what
was, and what could be.

Vis & Rāmin falls at a crux of this movement, showing how the
mythoi of love can play a central role in the formation of an intellectually mature, spiritually inquisitive, and, perhaps in an ideal case,

emotionally generous personhood in the interconnected world of the medieval eastern hemisphere. In the grand scheme of things, it is this final point that may be the most significant thing to take away from this book; after all, *V&R* has long been recognized as a foundational (if divisive) text in the history of Persian romance. But what new ways of seeing present themselves, what opportunities arise, when we strike out that qualifying term, "Persian"? This is not to erase the linguistic and cultural specificities of the text – indeed, it visually draws our eye to the word, inviting us to reflect on how its presence or absence might impact our subsequent engagement – but to shape the conversation in ways that encourage us to look beyond its boundaries. By considering how *Vis & Rāmin* – alongside *Varqa & Golshāh*, *Vāmeq & ʿAzrā*, and other ~~Persian~~ love stories – participates in and contributes to a much larger ecosystem of intellectual histories and literary habits, scholars from a wide array of fields can bring their diverse perspectives and proficiencies to the same table. In a manner similar to the goals of New Mediterranean Studies, these exchanges should furnish "a productive way both of reframing familiar texts in a new light and of bringing new material into focus," as Sharon Kinoshita writes, "that unsettles or reshuffles the 'self-evident' categories – notably nation and religion – into which our discourses on the Middle Ages are so often poured."[20]

There are some small examples of what can arise from this conceptual exercise that this book may have helped illuminate. One is the proposition of *a* framework – by no means the only possible one, as alluded to in the book's subtitle, "*a* Global Middle Ages" – in which Abrahamic and Hellenistic traditions come together to produce a distinctive "grammar" of meaning-making that highlights the connections between antiquity and the medieval period, spanning across a wide patchwork of cultural zones from Andalus to Afghanistan: a sort of temporal-spatial warp and weft, as it were. This framework allows us to compare particular narrative types (mythos) and their associated conventions and values (ethos) across this broad complex without shoehorning the inquiry into the search for genetic relations and lines of influence; it also allows us to consider how these various communities utilized such narratives to situate themselves within this shared past and interconnected present. From this perspective, it is clear that love stories in Greek, Persian, Arabic, Hebrew, Georgian, Armenian, the Romance vernaculars, and so on have quite a lot to say to each other.

In addition, this study has examined some of the ways that the early Persian romances made bold forays into the creation of discursively heterogeneous texts that could deliver profound insights into matters of ethics, politics, and poetics, "rhyming" with similar strategies and concerns visible in neighbouring traditions. *Vis & Rāmin*'s keen interest in that very plurality of discourse makes it an exemplary model for this kind of comparative work. In telling a story in which love has many a tale, it teaches its audience that those love stories contain lessons that apply to all aspects of human life: *a person who does not love is not a person*. In this recursive way, fusing the horizons of love and personhood together in the manner of a Möbius strip, *V&R* spins itself into a ~~love~~ story about stories, about the desire to have our stories heard and to hear the stories of others, both in making sense of our lives and in understanding the lives of those around us, whether on the other side of a wall or across huge distances of space and time. Perhaps the pursuit of this fusion, in the end, is what romance is all about: the closing lines of *Vis & Rāmin* offer a poignant image of humanity itself as nothing more than the net sum of the stories we tell, producing a discursive network that, by its open-ended nature, is available to all, but only if we are willing to engage with it – in the manner of lovers.

چو ما از رفتگان گیریم اخبار   ز ما فردا خبر گیرند ناچار

خبر گردیم و ما بوده خبرجوی   سمر گردیم و خود بوده سمرگوی

> Just as we take tidings from those who have passed,
> tomorrow they will certainly take them from us.
> In seeking a story, we become one ourselves;
> in telling a tale, we pass into legend. (533/52–3 [498])

APPENDICES

Appendix A: Summary of *Vis & Rāmin*

Following the practice of the rest of this book, this summary is keyed to the page numbers of the ICF edition of *Vis & Rāmin*; page numbers in brackets refer to Dick Davis's 2009 translation. Readers using other editions can refer to the concordance (appendix C) to locate specific passages.

Exordium

Doxology. Praise of God, account of the creation of the world (1); praise of the Prophet Muḥammad, and the story of his feats and exploits (7).

   Panegyrics. Praise of Sultan Ṭughrıl Beg and account of his conquests (10); praise of the Seljuk vizier Abu Naṣr al-Kondori (16); on Ṭughrıl's conquest of Isfahan and appointment of Abu al-Fatḥ Moẓaffar as its governor (18); praise of Abu al-Fatḥ (21).

   On the story's composition. Description of *Vis & Rāmin*'s origins and discursus on the *ars poetica* (26).

From Media to Marv

The Nowruz feast. Mobad celebrates the new year with a great banquet (32 [1]). He asks Shahru to be his consort; she refuses, but promises him her daughter, should she have one (38 [5]).

   Vis and Viru. Vis is born many years later and is raised by the Nurse in Khuzan (42 [9]). As Vis matures, the Nurse complains of her vanity to Shahru, who brings her daughter back to Media (46 [13]) and marries her to Viru (48 [17]). Mobad's brother, Zard, appears with a letter from the king, summoning Vis (51 [19]); Vis ridicules Zard and rejects the summons (56 [23]), and Zard returns to Marv with the news (58 [26]).

War. Humiliated, Mobad prepares for war (62 [28]). Viru learns of Mobad's approach and musters his forces (64 [30]). The armies join in battle; Vis's father Qāren is killed, but Viru rallies his troops and drives Mobad from the field (66 [32]). But then, Viru is diverted by an uprising in Daylam (72 [36]).

Abduction. With Viru distracted, Mobad moves on Gurab, where Vis is lamenting her separation from her husband (74 [39]). Mobad sends Vis another proposition (75 [40]), which Vis again rejects (76 [41]), revealing that she is still a virgin. Mobad's ardour is only inflamed by this news (79 [44]), and he consults with his brothers; Rāmin advises him to give up, while Zard suggests persuading Shahru with presents and threats (80 [45]). Mobad follows Zard's advice, with a letter of admonishment (84 [48]) and rich treasures (86 [50]). Shahru submits and opens the castle gates; a description of the night sky (87 [51]). Mobad enters the castle and captures Vis (91 [54]); Viru learns of his mother's surrender and mourns his loss, while Mobad revels in his victory (92 [55]).

Resistance. On the journey home, Rāmin espies Vis inside her litter and falls in love (93 [56]). Mobad brings Vis to Marv with much pomp and fanfare, but Vis withdraws to her quarters (97 [60]). The Nurse joins Vis and advises her to accept her new circumstances (99 [62]), but Vis replies that she will accept no man save Viru (103 [66]). The Nurse convinces Vis to at least leave her seclusion for the sake of her honour (104 [66]) and arrays her, while Mobad plays polo (106 [69]). At Vis's request, the Nurse curses Mobad with a charm of impotence (109 [72]).

Vis and Rāmin. Rāmin walks in the garden, lamenting his love for Vis (113 [76]). He meets the Nurse and convinces her to intercede on his behalf (115 [78]). Vis vehemently rejects the Nurse's match-making efforts (130 [90]), and only after numerous attempts does she agree to even look at Rāmin (140 [100]); when she does, she falls in love (153 [114]). Vis chastises the Nurse, but consents to a meeting with Rāmin (157 [118]). Rāmin enters Vis's quarters through the roof, and Vis presses him to swear eternal fidelity, giving him a token of violets; they become lovers (160 [123]).

A King's Collapse

Discipline. Mobad summons Rāmin and Vis to his court in Media (166 [129]). There, he learns of their secret and tells Viru to "discipline" his sister; the three men play a game of polo, while Vis looks on and laments her situation (168 [130]). Upon his return to Marv, Mobad tries to woo Vis, but she swears she will never be faithful to him; furious, he banishes her to Media (176 [139]).

Bluster. Anxious to rejoin Vis, Rāmin asks permission to hunt in Media; Mobad sees through the ploy, but lets him go with a warning that no betrayal will go unpunished (180 [143]). Vis welcomes Rāmin into her castle, where they spend seven months together (186 [148]). Mobad swears he will kill Rāmin, but his mother convinces him that the real traitors are Vis and Viru, and Mobad writes the latter a letter promising vengeance (188 [151]). Viru is astonished at the letter and writes a scathing reply; Mobad is ashamed and calls off the war (193 [156]).

Madness. Now reunited with Vis, Mobad asks her to prove her chastity by undergoing a trial by fire (198 [161]); he goes to the fire temple to make the preparations, while the Nurse, Vis, and Rāmin (disguised as a woman) flee the city and take refuge with their friend Behruz in Ray (201 [163]). In a frenzy of grief, Mobad abandons his kingdom and wanders the world for six months searching for Vis, before he finally comes to his senses and returns to Marv (208 [171]).

Duplicity. Rāmin informs his mother that he will remain in hiding until Mobad has died (211 [174]), but she reveals his whereabouts to Mobad on the condition that he not harm either Vis or Rāmin; Mobad agrees to this, and the lovers return to Marv (213 [176]). After a riotous banquet, Mobad goes to bed drunk, taking Vis with him; Vis convinces her Nurse to take her place in bed while she steals off to sleep with Rāmin in the garden; when Mobad awakens, he realizes something is amiss and begins to shout, but Vis returns in time to resume her place in the bed before Mobad is altogether cogent (218 [181]).

Betrayal. Mobad is forced into a war against Rome (233 [197]) and locks Vis in the Devils' Grotto, with Zard as her jailor; heartbroken, Rāmin falls ill and is allowed to remain behind (238 [201]). Vis laments her separation from Rāmin (243 [207]). Rāmin arrives at the fortress and shoots an arrow to the roof to signal his presence, then scales the walls and spends nine months with Vis (247 [210]). Mobad returns victorious from the war, but learns of Rāmin's betrayal and presses on to the fortress, while Vis and her Nurse lower Rāmin down the wall; Mobad bursts in, sees the rope, and savagely beats Vis and the Nurse (259 [223]). When Shahru learns that Vis might be dead, she threatens to destroy Mobad's kingdom in revenge (270 [235]). Mobad reassures Shahru that Vis is alive and has her returned to his court in Marv (277 [241]).

Humiliation. Before embarking on another campaign, Mobad bars all the entrances to his palace and charges the Nurse to guard Vis; that night, Rāmin deserts the King but cannot gain access to the palace, instead falling asleep in the garden; Vis uses her own clothes to rappel down the wall and joins him (279 [245]). Mobad turns the army around to go back to Marv; Rāmin escapes over the wall, and Mobad finds Vis naked and alone in the garden; although he is ready to kill her, she persuades him she had been transported there by an angel (289 [254]). The next day, Mobad holds a banquet, and a minstrel (*gosān*) lampoons him as a cuckold; humiliated, Mobad tries to kill Rāmin, but Rāmin throws him off his throne and onto the floor (299 [264]).

Vis and Rāmin Separate

Break-up. Rāmin, exhausted by his struggle with Mobad, takes counsel with Behguy, who advises him to give up love and seek a new life in other lands (303 [268]); meanwhile, Mobad attempts a rapprochement with Vis (310 [275]), which Vis accepts (312 [277]). Vis and Rāmin have an altercation, and Rāmin resolves to go; before he leaves, however, the two renew their vows of loyalty, though Vis doubts Rāmin's strength of will (316 [280]).

Rāmin and Gol. Rāmin travels west to Gurab, where he beholds Gol, daughter of the margrave of Azerbaijan, and falls in love with her; Gol is at first hesitant to accept his proposal to marry (Rāmin's reputation has preceded him), but after many promises, she finally consents (324 [289]), and the couple get married (332 [299]). Rāmin slips and tells Gol that he loves her because she looks like Vis (336 [302]), and after a thorough dressing-down, he writes an angry letter to Vis, blaming her for his troubles and repudiating his love for her (337 [304]).

Vis's Letter. Vis is devastated and responds with a letter of her own, begging Rāmin not to relinquish his love (342 [308]). The Nurse attempts to deliver the letter, but he turns her away, saying he will pursue Vis only if he has a legitimate claim to her as King (349 [316]). At this news, Vis falls ill and summons her scribe (353 [319]), who writes the *Dah-nāma* ("Decalogue"), also called the "Book of Iniquity" (357 [325]). Vis sends her slave to deliver the letter (394 [363]), while lamenting her separation from Rāmin (397 [366]).

Remorse. Rāmin grows tired of Gol and longs to return to Vis (402 [371]). Gol's father is none too pleased to hear this and informs his daughter of Rāmin's wavering. That evening, while sitting at banquet (and ignoring Gol), Rāmin broods over his situation, then abruptly rushes out the hall, mounts his horse, and rides towards Khorasan (409 [378]).

Death and Deliverance

Debate in the Snowstorm. On his way back, Rāmin meets Vis's messenger, who gives him the *Dah-nāma* (417 [385]). Rāmin composes his own letter promising his return (419 [387]). Vis is both happy and apprehensive at the news (422 [390]). Rāmin comes to Marv in the midst of a whirling blizzard; Vis refuses him entry, leaving Rāmin in the snow (426 [394]). The next morning she returns to the portico and tells him to let her go (438 [406]). A bitter debate ensues, concluding with Vis again turning Rāmin away; stunned at her rejection, Rāmin departs, declaring himself finally free of love (463 [429]). Vis repents (465 [431]) and sends the Nurse after Rāmin; she then goes out herself to track him down (467 [433]). Rāmin now rejects Vis, who turns back to her castle in despair (471 [437]); at that moment, a dragon-like storm drives Rāmin back to her, where they reconcile and return to the castle (482 [448]).

Rebellion. Rāmin returns to Mobad's court (486 [453]); but when Mobad declares his next hunting expedition (489 [456]), making it clear that he expects Rāmin to go with him, the lovers are doomed to be separated again (493 [460]). The Nurse advises Vis that the time has come to overthrow Mobad (496 [463]). Vis sends a message to Rāmin informing him of the plot (500 [467]), and after a soliloquy (504 [471]), Rāmin and his followers enter Mobad's citadel in disguise and join forces with Vis's men (507 [474]); Rāmin kills Zard in the fighting (510 [477]). The lovers seize Mobad's treasure and flee to Daylam, where they recruit an army to overthrow the king (513 [479]). Mobad rides out to meet them (515 [481]) but is killed by a mysterious boar before battle can be joined (517 [483]).

Conclusion. Rāmin takes his brother's place on the throne; he and Vis bear two sons and rule Iran for eighty-one years (520 [487]). Vis dies in old age (528 [492]); Rāmin hands over the kingship to his son, retreats to the fire temple, and lives the remainder of his life in penitence, so that he and Vis reunite in heaven (530 [495]). Gorgāni dedicates *V&R* to Abu al-Fatḥ Moẓaffar and invokes God's blessing on him and his three sons (534).

Appendix B: Rāmin's Songs

"Real" songs – that is, lyrics explicitly marked as songs (*sorud*) in the text performed before an audience – are in small caps, while the internal monologues (*bā del hami goft*, etc.) are in italics; some of these monologues are also called "songs," and these are both small caps and italics.

Rāmin Falls in Love

- *How Would It Be?* (95/38–48 [58]): Falls in love with Vis, and wonders if she would love him in return
- *O Heart, What's Wrong With You?* (96/51–72 [59]): Chides his heart for these foolish notions, for Vis is aloof, unattainable, and unkind

Rāmin Woos Vis

- *Why Do You Grieve?* (114/28–33 [77]): Reproaches the nightingales as he wanders lovelorn in the palace garden, for they sing to their lovers, while his laments fall on deaf ears
- *O Heart, What Do You Want of My Life?* (182/34–59 [145]): Curses his heart and the cruelty of Fate when Vis is exiled from Marv; prepares for a life of pain and suffering before his death

Episode 1: The Ordeal

- WE ARE TWO DEAR LOVERS (205/128–65 [168]): Sung in victory after their escape; a praise to wine and call to enjoy the good times

Episode 2: The Bed Trick

- O WOUNDED HEART, DON'T WORRY SO (219/9–15 [181]): A *carpe diem* wine song, the first of a series at Mobad's banquet

- I Saw A Gliding Garden Cypress (219/18–27 [182]): Recounts the story of his love for Vis
- My Face Is Blanched (221/55–65 [184]): A lament of separation
- *Do You Think It Right?*: (226/142–53 [189]): Complains to the storm that Vis sleeps indoors while he suffers on the roof
- *O Idol, O Moon-face, O Quickly Sated* (227/158–80 [190]): A message to Vis complaining of her neglect
- *O Night So Fair And Fetching* (230/219–31 [193]): An *alba* poem lamenting the end of their night together

Episode 3: The Devils' Grotto

- *What Is This Love?* (239/22–32 [203]): The first of three laments Rāmin sings when Vis is imprisoned
- *Sigh, O Heart, If You're a Lover* (240/34–43 [203]): A second lament
- *I'm That Broken-Hearted One* (240/48–56 [204]): A third lament, addressing the breeze and exhorting it to bear his message to Vis
- Without You, My Love, I Don't Desire Life (242/82–93 [206]): A final song in which he pledges to find her
- *O Dwelling, You're That Happy Place* (247/10–21 [211]): Sings to the fortress as a stand-in for Vis
- *O My Heart, Give Up Your Life* (250/58–73 [214]): Summons his courage in an address to his heart
- O Lover, What Does It Matter (254/131–42 [218]): Celebrates their love when they are united
- Wine Scours Rust from the Heart (256/161–77 [220]): A song of love and wine as they winter together
- *O Moon, Bring the Cup of Rose-Red Wine!* (257/179–89 [221]): Another wine song, addressing Vis while she is present
- *O Fate, What Do You Want of Me?* (264/83–96 [228]): After escaping Mobad, he curses his fate and laments his broken heart
- *You Cannot Know My State* (265/104–14 [229]): Rebukes Vis in her absence

Episode 4: The Garden

- *Since They Sundered Me from You* (281/28–42 [247]): Scales the garden wall and calls out to Vis, lamenting her absence

The Break-up

- *You Foolish, Misguided Heart!* (317/25–42 [282]): Rāmin curses his heart and resolves to abandon Vis

- *How Long, My Heart?* (404/35–67 [373]): Remorseful, he censures his heart
- *What Could Be Sweeter?* (410/26–122 [379]): Resolves to die a martyr to love

The Coup

- *I Saw a Night Like Last Night* (495/104–12 [462]): A lament of separation, reflecting on the vagaries of time
- *O Heart, Till When Will You Allow This State?* (505/75–114 [472]): Addressing his heart, resolves to overthrow Mobad

Appendix C: Concordance

All plain numbers refer to pages; numbers in brackets indicate chapter numbers. The ICF edition of *V&R* does not actually number its chapters, but those referring to its digital version at https://titus.uni-frankfurt.de/ will need these to pull up the appropriate passage.

Chapter	ICF	Davis	Rowshan	Morrison	Massé
Praise of God	1 [1]	—	19 [1]	1	—
Praise of the Prophet	7 [2]	—	22 [2]	4	—
Praise of Ṭughrıl Beg	10 [3]	—	24 [3]	6	—
Praise of Abu Naṣr al-Kondori	16 [4]	—	29 [4]	10	—
Ṭughrıl seizes Isfahan	18 [5]	—	30 [5]	12	—
Praise of Abu al-Fatḥ Moẓaffar	21 [6]	—	33 [6]	14	—
On the composition of the story	26 [7]	—	36 [7]	16	—
Beginning of the story	31 [8]	1	41 [8]	19	25
The beauties of Mobad's banquet	36	3	43 [9]	21	27
Mobad and Shahru make a pact	38 [9]	5	45 [10]	23	29
The birth of Vis	42 [10]	9	47 [11]	25	32
Vis and Rāmin are raised by the Nurse	44	12	49 [12]	27	34
The Nurse's letter to Shahru	46 [11]	13	50 [13]	27	45
Marriage of Vis and Viru	48 [12]	17	52 [14]	29	38
Zard comes before Shahru	51 [13]	19	53 [15]	31	40
Vis questions Zard	56	23	56 [16]	35	44
Zard returns to Mobad	58	26	58 [17]	36	47
Mobad prepares for war against Viru	62 [14]	28	60 [18]	38	49

(Continued)

Continued

Chapter	ICF	Davis	Rowshan	Morrison	Massé
Viru learns of Mobad's plans	64 [15]	30	62 [19]	40	52
Description of the battle	66 [16]	32	63 [20]	41	53
Mobad is defeated by Viru	72	36	67 [21]	45	58
Mobad goes to Gurab	74 [17]	39	68 [22]	46	60
Mobad sends an envoy to Vis	75	40	69 [23]	47	61
Vis responds to Mobad's envoy	76 [18]	41	69 [24]	48	62
The envoy returns	79	44	72 [25]	50	65
Mobad consults with his brothers	80	45	72 [26]	51	66
Mobad sends a letter to Shahru	84 [19]	48	75 [27]	53	69
Description of Mobad's gifts	86	50	76 [28]	55	71
Description of the night	87	51	77 [29]	56	72
Mobad captures Vis	91	54	79 [30]	58	76
Viru learns of Vis's abduction	92 [20]	55	80 [31]	59	77
Rāmin sees Vis and falls in love	93 [21]	56	81 [32]	60	78
Vis and Mobad are married in Marv	97 [22]	60	84 [33]	63	82
The Nurse travels to Marv	99 [23]	62	85 [34]	64	84
Vis's reply to the Nurse	103	66	88 [35]	67	87
The Nurse again advises Vis	104	66	88 [36]	67	88
The Nurse adorns Vis	106	69	90 [37]	69	90
The Nurse binds Mobad	109 [24]	72	92 [38]	70	93
Rāmin's love for Vis comes to a head	113 [25]	76	95 [39]	73	96
Rāmin sees the Nurse in the garden	115	78	96 [40]	75	98
The Nurse beguiles Vis	130 [26]	90	105 [41]	85	113
The Nurse returns to Rāmin	140 [27]	100	112 [42]	92	123
Vis sees Rāmin and falls in love	153 [28]	114	121 [43]	102	135
The Nurse returns to Vis	157 [29]	118	124 [44]	105	139
Vis and Rāmin come together	160 [30]	123	126 [45]	107	142
Vis and Rāmin go to Kuhestān	166	129	130 [46]	111	148
Mobad learns of the affair	168 [31]	130	131 [47]	112	149
Mobad returns to Khorasan	176 [32]	139	137 [48]	117	157
Vis goes to Kuhestan	180 [33]	143	139 [49]	120	160

Chapter	ICF	Davis	Rowshan	Morrison	Massé
Rāmin joins her	186 [34]	148	143 [50]	124	165
Mobad learns of Rāmin's departure	188 [35]	151	144 [51]	125	167
Mobad marches on Hamadan	193	156	148 [52]	129	172
Viru responds to Mobad's letter	195 [36]	158	149 [53]	130	173
Mobad reprimands Vis	198 [37]	161	151 [54]	132	176
The ordeal by fire	201	163	153 [55]	134	179
Mobad searches the world for Vis	208 [38]	171	158 [56]	139	186
Rāmin writes a letter to his mother	211 [39]	174	160 [57]	141	189
The mother intervenes	213	176	162 [58]	142	191
Mobad's banquet (the bed trick)	218 [40]	181	165 [59]	146	195
Mobad prepares for war against Rome	233 [41]	197	175 [60]	156	210
Mobad imprisons Vis in the Devils' Grotto	238 [42]	201	179 [61]	160	214
Vis laments Rāmin's departure	243 [43]	207	182 [62]	164	219
Rāmin comes to the Devils' Grotto	247 [44]	210	185 [63]	166	222
Mobad returns from Rome	259 [45]	223	193 [64]	174	232
Shahru's lament	270 [46]	235	201 [65]	182	243
Mobad responds to Shahru	277	241	205 [66]	187	249
Mobad entrusts Vis to the Nurse	279 [47]	245	207 [67]	189	251
Mobad finds Vis in the garden	289 [48]	254	213 [68]	195	259
Mobad and the minstrel	299 [49]	264	220 [69]	202	269
Behguy's advice to Rāmin	303 [50]	268	222 [70]	204	271
Mobad's advice to Vis	310 [51]	275	227 [71]	209	277
Vis's answer	312 [52]	277	228 [72]	210	279
Rāmin leaves Vis and travels to Gurab	316 [53]	280	231 [73]	212	282
Rāmin sees Gol and falls in love	324 [54]	289	236 [74]	218	290
Marriage of Rāmin and Gol	332 [55]	299	242 [75]	224	297
Gol gets angry at Rāmin	336	302	244 [76]	226	300
Rāmin's letter to Vis	337 [56]	304	245 [77]	227	301
Vis receives the letter	342 [57]	308	248 [78]	230	305
The Nurse visits Rāmin in Gurab	349 [58]	316	253 [79]	235	311
Vis becomes ill	353 [59]	319	255 [80]	237	314

(Continued)

Continued

Chapter	ICF	Davis	Rowshan	Morrison	Massé
Vis's letter to Rāmin	357 [60]	325	257 [81]	240	318
Part 1: On longing and separation	363 [61]	331	261	243	323
Part 2: On dreams and remembrance	366 [62]	334	263	245	325
Part 3: On seeking alternatives	369 [63]	336	265	247	328
Part 4: On forbearance and hope	372 [64]	340	267	249	331
Part 5: On the lover's tyranny	375 [65]	343	269	251	334
Part 6: On caressing and calling	378 [66]	346	271	253	336
Part 7: On weeping and wailing	382 [67]	349	273	255	339
Part 8: On seeking news of the beloved	385 [68]	352	275	257	342
Part 9: On describing one's grief	387 [69]	335	277	258	344
Part 10: On supplication	390 [70]	358	279	260	347
Peroration	392 [71]	360	280	261	349
Vis sends Āzin to deliver the ten letters	394	363	282 [82]	263	351
Vis's lament	397 [72]	366	284 [83]	265	354
Rāmin grows weary of Gol	402 [73]	371	287 [84]	268	358
Rafidā tells Gol of Rāmin's state	409 [74]	378	291 [85]	273	364
Āzin comes to Rāmin	417 [75]	385	296 [86]	278	371
Rāmin responds to the letter	419 [76]	387	298 [87]	279	373
Vis learns of Rāmin's arrival	422 [77]	390	300 [88]	281	375
Rāmin comes to Vis in Marv	426 [78]	394	302 [89]	283	379
Rāmin answers Vis	429 [79]	397	304 [90]	285	381
Vis answers Rāmin	434 [80]	402	307 [91]	289	386
Vis returns and addresses Rāmin's horse	438 [81]	406	310 [92]	291	390
Rāmin's reply	440 [82]	409	312 [93]	293	392
Vis's reply	443 [83]	411	313 [94]	294	394
Rāmin's reply	445 [84]	413	315 [95]	296	395
Vis's reply	448 [85]	416	317 [96]	298	399
Rāmin's reply	450 [86]	418	318 [97]	299	400
Vis's reply	452 [87]	419	319 [98]	300	402
Rāmin's reply	453 [88]	421	321 [99]	301	403
Vis's reply	455 [89]	422	321 [100]	302	404
Rāmin's reply	456 [90]	423	322 [101]	303	406
Vis's reply	458 [91]	425	323 [102]	304	407

Chapter	ICF	Davis	Rowshan	Morrison	Massé
Rāmin's reply	459 [92]	426	325 [103]	305	408
Vis's reply	461 [93]	428	326 [104]	306	410
Vis grows angry and shuts Rāmin out	463	429	327 [105]	307	411
Vis regrets her actions	465 [94]	431	328 [106]	308	413
Vis sends the Nurse after Rāmin	467 [95]	433	330 [107]	309	415
Rāmin's reply and complaint	471 [96]	437	333 [108]	312	419
Vis's reply and excuse	475 [97]	441	335 [109]	315	422
Rāmin's reply	477 [98]	443	337 [110]	316	424
Vis's reply	479 [99]	445	338 [111]	317	426
Rāmin regrets his actions	482 [100]	448	340 [112]	319	428
Rāmin appears before Mobad	486 [101]	453	343 [113]	322	432
Mobad goes hunting	489 [102]	456	345 [114]	324	434
Mobad takes Rāmin with him	493	460	347 [115]	326	438
Vis asks the Nurse for a solution	496 [103]	463	350 [116]	329	441
Vis writes a letter to Rāmin	500 [104]	467	352 [117]	331	444
Rāmin receives the letter	504	471	355 [118]	334	448
Rāmin steals to the castle	507 [105]	474	357 [119]	335	450
Rāmin kills Zard	510 [106]	477	359 [120]	338	453
Rāmin takes Mobad's treasure and flees	513 [107]	479	361 [121]	339	455
Mobad learns of Rāmin's betrayal	515 [108]	481	362 [122]	341	457
Mobad is killed by a boar	517 [109]	483	363 [123]	342	458
Rāmin assumes the throne	520 [110]	487	365 [124]	344	461
Death of Vis	528 [111]	492	369 [125]	348	467
Rāmin retires from rule	530 [112]	495	371 [126]	349	469
On the completion of the story	534 [113]	—	373 [127]	352	—

Notes

Prologue

1 I owe this idea of "memories that rhyme" to a podcast I listened to in the summer of 2021 entitled *Dolly Parton's America*, hosted by Jad Abumrad and Shima Oliaee. The phrase came from Episode 4, "Neon Moss," and the transcript reads, "And bears aside, the whole time I couldn't shake this feeling like I had been here before. Like, it was something like deja vu but not quite. Maybe more like a rhyme, the way that one memory rhymes with another." See https://www.wnycstudios.org/podcasts/dolly-partons -america/episodes/neon-moss (accessed 1 June 2022).

2 Alex J. West persuasively argues for a "Hemispheric Middle Ages" as a framework for comparative historical study, adding that this is best accomplished by working from the understanding that "medieval greater Afro-Eurasia was ultimately one place." See https://indomedieval .medium.com/the-hemispheric-middle-ages-part-i-173779f237f6 and https://indomedieval.medium.com/the-hemispheric-middle-ages-part -ii-7f1630e00e12 (accessed 1 June 2022).

3 The dating of *Vis & Rāmin* to the Parthian period was achieved by Minorsky's painstaking research, published in a series of articles for the *Bulletin of the School of Oriental and African Studies* (1946, 1947, 1954, and 1962), then consolidated, lightly revised, and re-published in his *Iranica* (1964). The medieval histories *Tārikh-e gozida* (w. 1330) and *Mojmal al-tavārikh* (w. 1126) set the tale in the reigns of the Parthians (Gotarzes I, r. 91–80 BCE) and Sasanians (Shapur I, r. 240–70 CE), respectively; see Mostowfi Qazvini, *Tārikh-e gozida*, 101; Najmābādi and Weber, *Mujmal al-tavārīkh*, 74. Interestingly, the name of Gotarzes's son and successor, Orodes/Wērōd, aligns with the name of Vis's brother, Viru.

 4 Some valuable studies that have investigated the connections between
    Greek, Arabic, and Persian love narratives are von Grunebaum, "Greek
    Form Elements in the Arabian Nights"; von Grunebaum, *Medieval Islam*,
    294–319; Hägg, "The Oriental Reception"; Davis, *Panthea's Children*;
    Whitmarsh and Thompson, *The Romance between Greece and the East*; and
    Whitmarsh, *Dirty Love*.
 5 al-ʿAskarī, *Risāla fī al-tafḍīl*, 89. For more on the Iranian tradition of
    minstrelsy and its relation with storytelling, see Boyce, "The Parthian
    Gōsān"; de Bruijn, "Poets and Minstrels." Boyce ("The Parthian *Gōsān*,"
    34–7) doubts that stories such as *V&R* would have been deemed worthy
    of being written down, and while this accords with the impression we
    have from the Abbasid and Samanid periods, so little survives from the
    Sasanian context that I prefer to be agnostic on that matter.
 6 Abu Nuwās's poem and Ḥamza's commentary can be found in Abu
    Nuwās, *Dīwān*, 143–6. See also Minovi, "Yek-i az fāresiyāt," 67, 69; de Blois,
    Persian Literature, 141–2. On the semantic connotations of *uḥdūtha* as a
    "fable," see chapter 1.
 7 See Rāghib al-Iṣfahānī, *Muḥāḍarāt al-udabāʾ*, 1:820. Note the corruption of
    Vis as DBS and Rāmin as DMYN, rectified in Minovi, "Yek-i az fāresiyāt,"
    77, and Norozi, *Esordi del romanzo*, 42. For a full survey of these references,
    see Minovi, "Vis-o Rāmin," 19–21.
 8 One of the requirements of entry into the elite society of eleventh-century
    Isfahan was a mastery of Arabic: "It served as a distinguishing mark, on
    the one hand distancing them [the elites] from the common people who
    only spoke the local Persian dialect, and on the other hand linking them to
    Baghdad, the absolute cultural model." Durand-Guédy, *Iranian Elites and
    Turkish Rulers*, 43.
 9 Davis, "Introduction," xii. There are a number of studies that consider
    V&R as a composite work, particularly T'odua, "Yek do sokhan," xxiv–
    xxv; ʿAbd-Allāhiyān, "Az farādast"; and van Ruymbeke, "Wretched King
    Mobad," 82n7.
10 For a survey of this literature, see Cross, "The Lives and Afterlives," 533–4.
11 Davis, "Introduction," xxxii.
12 Pizzi, *Storia*, 2:87. For a fuller discussion of the poem's medieval and
    modern reception, see Cross, "The Poetics of Romantic Love," 48–52, 57–9;
    Cross, "The Lives and Afterlives," 523–32.
13 For two perspectives into Neẓāmi's reception of *V&R*, see Eslāmi-
    Nodushan, "Āyā 'Vis-o Rāmin'," 353, and Zolfaqāri, *Yekṣad manẓuma*, 952;
    for a broader summary, see Cross, "The Lives and Afterlives," 523–4, 535,
    and footnote 109.
14 For a review of *Khosrow & Shirin* and its major imitations, see Orsatti,
    "Ḵosrow o Širin"; and for an exhaustive survey of poetic imitations of

Nezāmi's *Khamsa*, see Rādfar, *Ketābshenāsī*. While *V&R* was never retold in Persian, it was translated into Ottoman Turkish (with substantially altered content) by the court poet Lāmeʿi (d. 1531); see Cross, "The Lives and Afterlives," 525–6, for further discussion. On its place in the modern canon, see Eslāmi-Nodushan, "Āyā 'Vis-o Rāmin,'" 346.

15 The last decade has seen an uptick in literary scholarship on *V&R*, including studies by Kahduni and Bohrani, "Tahlil-e shakhsiyat-e Mobad"; Hākemi and Zavāriyān, "Barrasi-ye jāygāh-e zan"; Khorāsāni and Dāvudi-Moqaddam, "Tahlil-e dahnāma-hā"; ʿAbdi and Ṣayyādkuh, "Barrasi-ye do shakhsiyat"; ʿEshqi-Sardehi, Amir-Ahmadi, and Kiyāni, "Naqd-e shakhsiyat-e Vis"; Cross, "A Tree Atop the Mountain"; van Ruymbeke, "Wretched King Mobad"; and the new monograph by Nahid Norozi, *Esordi del romanzo*. I regret that I had more or less finished my own manuscript before this book came into my hands, else I would have engaged with it more substantially, but I indicate important connections between our two works where I can.

16 See Kay, "Genre, Parody, and Spectacle," esp. 173–4.

17 On the literal meaning of *romanz*, see Bruckner, "The Shape of Romance in Medieval France," 13–14; Gaunt, "Romance and Other Genres," 45; and Kinoshita, "Romance in/and the Medieval Mediterranean," 187–9. Sullivan suggests, however, that the term was more aligned with the modern understanding of romance than might have been previously thought, as it usually described some kind of secular adventure narrative set in the past (*Roman de Troie, Roman d'Eneas*), later expanding to include satirical and allegorical narratives (*Roman de Renart, Roman de la Rose*). See Sullivan, *The Danger of Romance*, 2–8, 28–30.

18 For more on the relative prestige accorded to "novel" versus "romance," see Doody, *The True Story*, 1–4; Fuchs, *Romance*, 9–11; Khan, *The Broken Spell*, 8–20; Goldhill, "Genre," 191–3.

19 For an assessment of the nominalist approach, see Orlemanski, "Genre," 208–10. I will note that, while there have been many critiques of the term "medieval" in Islamic studies, I have not encountered any comparable resistance to the application of generic terms such as "epic" and "romance" to Persian poetry.

20 Segre, "What Bakhtin Left Unsaid," 36.

21 Fuchs, *Romance*, 35–6. For romance as a poetics of delay, see Parker, *Inescapable Romance*. Derrida ("The Law of Genre," 59) discusses genre in general as "a sort of participation without belonging."

22 A helpful interlocutor on this point is Pasha Khan, whose recent book on the Persian and Urdu *dāstān*s and *qiṣṣa*s of early modern South Asia, which he cautiously glosses as "romance," deftly explores the fraught terrain of genre terminology. See Khan, *The Broken Spell*, 10–16.

23 Critical text and translation by Frank Justus Miller in Ovid, *Metamorphoses*,
    1:182–5.

24 Recent scholarship has taken the theory of romance as a Self-Other
    entanglement in different directions. For example, Tim Whitmarsh writes,
    "Novelistic erotic stories were from late classical times onwards much
    more culturally fluid and flexible, and allowed for transfer between
    ancient traditions. More than this, they reflected on this very process of
    transfer: 'dirty love' became a narrative expression of the idea of cultural
    combination encapsulated in the very form of the novel"; see Whitmarsh,
    Dirty Love, 8. In Saeed Honarmand's account, the Persian romance (like
    the Persian epic) is aimed at eliminating the Other, but "instead of the
    elimination of the body of the other [in the epic], it is the elimination of
    otherness itself [in the romance]." Honarmand, "Between the Water and the
    Wall," 59.

25 Zumthor, *Speaking of the Middle Ages*, 29–30. Although his focus lies on
    a different time and place from my own, I believe Zumthor's reminder
    that we must assume a basically unbridgeable gap between medieval and
    modern ways of encountering and reading texts (*Toward a Medieval Poetics*,
    3–6; "The Text and the Voice," 70) applies as well to the case of eleventh-
    century Isfahan as it does to twelfth-century Paris.

26 Bauer, "In Search of 'Post-Classical Literature,'" 141–3.

27 Hodgson, *The Venture of Islam*, 2:3–11; Fromherz, *The Near West*, 209–25.

28 Omidsalar, *Poetics and Politics*, 31.

29 Omidsalar, ibid., 18. Agapitos and Mullett note a similar prejudice in the
    scholarship on medieval Greek; see Agapitos, "Contesting Conceptual
    Boundaries," 66–7; Mullett, "No Drama, No Poetry, No Fiction, No
    Readership, No Literature." For further discussion of the "medieval"
    debate, see Lasman, "Dragons, Fairies, and Time," 3–12.

30 Hansen, *The Year 1000*, 3; Lasman, "Dragons, Fairies, and Time," 5.

31 Khaṭīb al-Baghdādī, *The Art of Party-Crashing*, x.

32 Davis and Puett, "Periodization and 'the Medieval Globe,'" 6.

33 Sells, *Mystical Languages of Unsaying*, 4.

34 The term "Islamdom" was coined by Marshall Hodgson; to learn more
    about his justification for this term, and its relative "Islamicate," see
    Hodgson, *The Venture of Islam*, 1:56–60. A recent appeal for this kind of
    interconnected historiography is found in Bulliet, *The Case for Islamo-
    Christian Civilization*, 1–45, with a response and follow-up in Tolan,
    "Forging New Paradigms."

35 See Høgel, "World Literature Is Trans-Imperial," 14; Pollock, *The Language
    of the Gods*, 11–12. See also Akbari, "Modeling Medieval World Literature,"
    14, who describes geography as a "crucial common ground" that could

inform the composition of diverse travel narratives, such as Ibn Baṭṭuṭa's *Riḥla* and *The Book of John Mandeville*.

36 Sells, *Mystical Languages of Unsaying*, 5.

37 Mallette, *Lives of the Great Languages*, 82. I borrow the juxtaposition of "roots" versus "routes" from Kinoshita, "Romance in/and the Medieval Mediterranean," 192, 202.

38 Agapitos and Mortensen, "Introduction," 6–7. It is worth noting that the authors are specifically referring to medieval Europe in this sentence, but they go on to discuss how the Islamic lands fit into this complex in the following paragraph.

39 The field of New Mediterranean Studies offers a helpful model for this kind of scholarship; see Akbari, "Modeling Medieval World Literature"; Mallette, "Translation in the Pre-Modern World"; Kinoshita, "Romance in/ and the Medieval Mediterranean." Another highly productive circle for me has been the push to recognize the supralocal role of "imperial" languages in making possible the transregional circulation of stories and texts: see Gaunt, "French Literature Abroad"; Agapitos, "Contesting Conceptual Boundaries"; Høgel, "World Literature Is Trans-Imperial"; Mallette, *Lives of the Great Languages*.

40 Many of these cycles stem from Sanskrit sources, a reminder that the Helleno-Abrahmic complex is only one of many possible ways of framing literary globality in the medieval period. Some useful studies that situate transregional narratives such as *Barlaam & Josaphat*, *Kalīla & Dimna*, the Alexander romance, and the *Seven Sages* within globally minded frameworks include Lopez and McCracken, *In Search of the Christian Buddha*; de Blois, *Burzōy's Voyage to India*; Stoneman, Nawotka, and Wojciechowska, *The Alexander Romance*; Hoffmann, "Cats and Dogs, Manliness, and Misogyny."

41 Selden, "Mapping the Alexander Romance," 19.

42 See Heng, *Empire of Magic*, 2–4, and of course the rest of the book. Similarly, Samuel Lasman's recent dissertation explores, in a comparative manner, the role of fantastic and imaginative narratives about the past, what he calls "speculative fiction," in parallel processes of identity formations in the medieval period; for his theoretical framing of how the project speaks to and indeed requires a "Global Middle Ages," see Lasman, "Dragons, Fairies, and Time," 3–43.

43 Hägg, *The Novel in Antiquity*, 82–90; Whitmarsh, *Dirty Love*.

44 Keene, "Introduction," 31. On the relationship between medieval studies and white nationalism, see the collected essays in Albin et al., *Whose Middle Ages?*; Heng and Ramey, "Early Globalities, Global Literatures," 392; Heng, *The Invention of Race*, esp. 1–5 and 15–24; Lomuto, "Becoming

Postmedieval," 503–5 (and associated references); Phillips, *Craft Beer Culture*, 97–135.

45 See Krueger, "Introduction," 1; Gaunt, "Romance and Other Genres," 45; Fuchs, *Romance*, 37; Agapitos, "Genre, Structure and Poetics," 20–2.

46 Jauss, *Toward an Aesthetic of Reception*, 23–4.

47 See, respectively, Rust'aveli, *The Man in the Panther's Skin*, 2/¶7; Agapitos, *The Tale of Livistros and Rodamne*, 55/6–9; Hubert, *Floire and Blanchefleur*, 23/1–6. As Matilda Bruckner succinctly observes, "That romance speaks to lovers is a staple of the genre"; see Bruckner, "The Shape of Romance in Medieval France," 17.

48 Gottfried von Strassburg, *Tristan* (tr. Hatto), 42.

49 Frow, *Genre*, 7–8.

50 For genres as "institutions" and "ideologies," see respectively Todorov, "The Origin of Genres," 162; Jameson, "Magical Narratives," 135. Jameson argues that every text necessarily encodes and embodies some kind of ideological formation (*The Political Unconscious*, 79), a point that Simon Gaunt develops in the context of Old French literature (see Gaunt, "Romance and Other Genres"; Gaunt, *Gender and Genre*, 10). Bakhtin's use of ideology – a "system of ideas" in which "every speaker is thus an ideologue and every utterance an ideologeme" (*Speech Genres and Other Late Essays*, 101n3) – seems to me the most appropriate way to discuss ideology in my context; but ultimately, the premodern Greek term *ethos*, as a "custom" or "way" of doing things, provides by far the closest conceptual match with the Persian material, a discourse that is saturated with discussions of various "paths" or "manners" (*mazhab*, *tariqa*, *āyin*, *ravesh*, etc.) of thought and action.

51 Trzaskoma, *Two Novels from Ancient Greece*, xix. For the use of the words "idealistic" and "idyllic" to describe this mythos, see Holzberg, *The Ancient Novel*, 9–10; Hubert, *Floire and Blanchefleur*, 13–16.

52 The lexicographer Dehkhodā defines the *afsāna* as a story about those who lived in the past (*ḥekāyāt-e gozashtagān*), but then adds that it is "baseless and false" (*bi-aṣl va dorugh*), fabricated (*sākhta*) for either didactic or entertainment purposes. Dehkhoda, *Loghat-nāma*, s.v. *afsāna* at https://dehkhoda.ut.ac.ir/fa/dictionary/ (accessed 1 June 2022). The Middle Persian *afsān* carries a similar connotation, as does the ancient Greek *mythos*; see MacKenzie, *A Concise Pahlavi Dictionary*, 5, s.v. *afsān*; *The Brill Dictionary of Ancient Greek*, ed. Franco Montanari, s.v. μῦθος (accessed 1 June 2022 at https://dictionaries.brillonline.com/search#dictionary=montanari&id=78221).

53 See, for example, Walter Scott's definition of romance in 1834 as "a fictitious narrative in prose or verse; the interest of which turns upon

marvellous and uncommon incidents." Scott, *Essays on Chivalry, Romance, and the Drama*, 129.

54 An excellent introductory work on image-making in Arabic philosophy and aesthetics, including discussions of how it interfaces with the Greek notion of *phantasia*, is the edited volume by van Gelder and Hammond, *Takhyil*. For applied studies of this topic to the context of Arabic and Persian poetry, some important recent works include Harb, *Arabic Poetics*; Ingenito, *Beholding Beauty*; Landau, "Naṣīr al-Dīn Ṭūsī and Poetic Imagination."

55 Lasman, "Dragons, Fairies, and Time," 12. As Samuel Lasman pointed out to me, this ambivalent stance towards the present age is palpable not only in the *Shāhnāma*, but also in coeval Zoroastrian texts such as the *Ayādgār ī Jāmāspīg*; on the latter, see Boyce, "Ayādgār ī Jāmāspīg."

56 Frow, *Genre*, 10.

57 See Bakhtin, *Problems of Dostoevsky's Poetics*, 6–7; also Morson and Emerson, *Mikhail Bakhtin*, 231–2. Though Bakhtin attributes "true" polyphony to the modern novel, he allows that the ancient Greek novels and Dostoevsky both inhabit "one and the same generic world," though the "heteroglossia from above" in the former remains controlled by an overarching monology. See Bakhtin, *Problems of Dostoevsky's Poetics*, 121–2, also Bakhtin, *The Dialogic Imagination*, 400. Steven Smith, however, disputes this assessment, and Massimo Fusillo discusses ancient polyphony at length: see Smith, "Bakhtin and Chariton," 183–4; Fusillo, *Il romanzo greco*, esp. 111–78. Simon Gaunt, too, points to the "plurality of perspectives" distinctive to medieval European romance, which "leads to an interest in individual psychology and identity"; see Gaunt, "Romance and Other Genres," 47.

58 Bakhtin, *Problems of Dostoevsky's Poetics*, 47; Bakhtin, *The Dialogic Imagination*, 336. Bakhtin further develops the idea of "images of language" (though the exact term is never used) in Bakhtin, *Problems of Dostoevsky's Poetics*, 51–7, 79.

59 Bartsch, *The Mirror of the Self*, 46. On *theōria*, see *The Brill Dictionary of Ancient Greek*, ed. Franco Montanari, s.v. θεωρία (accessed 1 June 2022 at https://dictionaries.brillonline.com/search#dictionary=montanari& id=53775). For more on the relationship between character and viewing in the Greek novel, see Morales, *Vision and Narrative*, 77–95.

60 For a more extensive discussion of this movement, see Cross, "Poetic Alchemy."

61 Todorov, "The Origin of Genres," 161.

62 Two salient publications in this vein are by Minoo Southgate ("Conflict between Islamic Mores"; "Vīs and Rāmīn: An Anomaly"), but virtually no

study of *Vis & Rāmin* fails to comment on the text's apparently iconoclastic nature.

63 Wiersma, "The Ancient Greek Novel and Its Heroines," 109.

64 My diction here is informed by Jameson's discussion of genres as "essentially contracts between a writer and his readers"; see Jameson, "Magical Narratives," 135. While I do not utilize Jameson's analytical methods, I find this metaphor an extremely effective way to describe how generic discourse creates a collectively agreed-upon space in which certain "rules" (the "contract") are expected to hold; I visit versions of this argument in chapters 2, 3, and 4 of this book.

65 After Vis, we might cite the famous examples of Neẓāmi's Shirin and Jāmi's Zolaykhā, along with the broader practice in which women serve as guides to their male counterparts: see Meisami, "Fitnah or Azadah"; Talattof, "Nizami's Unlikely Heroines"; Merguerian and Najmabadi, "Zulaykha and Yusuf"; Alam and Subrahmanyam, "Love, Passion and Reason"; Gabbay, "Love Gone Wrong, Then Right Again." The case for a similar shift in Old French is made by Krause, "Gender and Paradigm Shift."

66 This description of Aegialeus comes from Whitmarsh, *Narrative and Identity*, 3.

67 Although "paradigm shift," in the manner theorized by Thomas Kuhn, might be too strong a term here, I do find Albrecht Classen's description of taking a model and pushing it to its breaking point an apt descriptor of what I see *Vis & Rāmin* doing with the generic conventions it had inherited: "All paradigm shifts are accompanied or determined by crisis insofar as the old set of explanations no longer helps to cope with the world and its phenomena. A shift is about to occur when the old parameters explaining the world we are living in or allowing us to survive in it *no longer work properly* and when a new set of concepts is required for a rational explanation of our environment." Classen, "Introduction," xxii, emphasis mine.

1 Phantasy: The Rise of Romance

1 This admittedly poetic reconstruction of Gorgāni's circumstances is derived from *V&R* 13/63–88, analysed in detail in Foruzānfar, *Sokhan*, 374–6. I provide a more prosaic account of this period in Cross, "The Poetics of Romantic Love," 22–4, and for more discussion of the caliphal rescript, see Crone, *God's Rule*, 234.

2 For a meditation on how the war zone can paradoxically also become "an arena of exuberant cultural exchange and meaning making," see Ouyang, "War and the Worlding of Story."

3 Hodgson, *The Venture of Islam*, 1:144.

4 See Cross, "Poetic Alchemy."

5 The distinctly Arabic cultural-linguistic orientation and "Iraqi" identity of
Isfahani elites before the Seljuk conquest is discussed in detail in Durand-
Guédy, *Iranian Elites and Turkish Rulers*, 32–49. For more on Isfahan's
size, industries, buildings, and commerce in the eleventh century, see
Bosworth, *Historic Cities*, 167–72; Durand-Guédy, *Iranian Elites and Turkish
Rulers*, 23–32; and Peacock, *Early Seljūq History*, 89–94.

6 Nāṣer-e Khosrow, *Safarnāma*, 166 (Thackston 125). Nāṣer's description
of Abu al-Fatḥ's governorship largely corroborates the details provided
in *V&R* 25/59–65. For more on this figure, see Minorsky, "Vīs u Rāmīn,"
152, 198; also Ephrat, *A Learned Society*, 24.

7 The likelihood of *V&R*'s composition in or shortly after 446/1054 has
been convincingly argued in Foruzānfar, *Sokhan*, 374–6; see also Maḥjub,
"Moqaddema," 16–17.

8 For a concise summary of what we know about Gorgāni, see Massé,
"Gurgānī"; more detailed accounts can be found in Cross, "The Poetics of
Romantic Love," 7–20; Norozi, *Esordi del romanzo*, 27–33.

9 Gorgāni's time at the Bavandid court is surmised from a piece of invective
attributed to him, quoted in ʿOwfi, *Lubábu 'l-albáb*, 2:240, entry no. 98; for
further discussion, see Minorsky, "Vīs u Rāmīn," 154–5, 196.

10 Gorgāni's allusions to Arabic literature are documented in Moḥaqqeq,
"Yāddāsht-hā-i," 462–4; see also Foruzānfar, *Sokhan*, 371.

11 Gorgāni's knowledge of astronomy is discussed in Kunitzsch,
"Description of the Night," 77–9; Neugebauer, "The Date of the
'Horoscope.'"

12 Gorgāni's familiarity with Avicenna is briefly mentioned in Foruzānfar,
Sokhan, 370; Maḥjub, "Moqaddema," 12; and Gorgāni, *V&R* (tr.
Morrison), 1n1; with more discussion in Cross, "The Poetics of Romantic
Love," 11–17. For an English translation of Avicenna's treatise on God's
creation of the world (known as *al-khuṭba al-gharrāʾ*, "the sublime
sermon"), see Akhtar, "A Tract of Avicenna," 220–2.

13 Quoted in Perry, "The Origin and Development," 47. Other current
scholarship supports the notion that, while both Middle and New Persian
were productive languages in the eleventh century, their use, with the
one being written in a "Zoroastrian" script and the other in a "Muslim"
one, largely broke down along confessional lines: see de Blois, "Pre-
Islamic Iranian and Indian Influences," 334; Vevaina, "The Ground Well
Trodden," 172.

14 The excitement around *V&R*'s antiquity is especially palpable in the
earliest recorded reactions. Alois Sprenger, who first brought the tale to
European attention in 1854, writes, "I have discovered a most important

Persian poem ... a translation from the Pahlavi, beyond any doubt."
Eleven years later, the cover of the first published edition of *V&R* by
William Nassau Lees and Ahmad Ali (Calcutta, 1865) advertises the
story as "A Romance of Ancient Persia, Translated from the Pahlawi"; and
when Oliver Wardrop translated the Georgian *Visramiani* into English in
1914, he introduced it to his readers as "one of the oldest novels in the
world." See Sprenger, "Bibliographische Anzeigen," 608; Gorgāni, *V&R*
(ed. Lees/Ali); T'mogveli, *Visramiani*, v.

15 al-Nadīm, *Fihrist*, 1:31–2 (Dodge 24). The many possible valences
of *pahlavi* are discussed further in Frye, "Development of Persian
Literature," 71; Lazard, "Pahlavi, Pârsi, Dari," 364–9; Lazard, "La source
en 'farsi,'" 35–6; Lazard, "Dari"; Omidsalar, "Unburdening Ferdowsi,"
238; Perry, "The Origin and Development," 51; Pourshariati, "The
Parthians and the Production," 376–7; Shahbazi, *Ferdowsī*, 40; Tafażżoli,
"Fahlavīyāt."

16 There is quite a lot of scholarship on the topic of *V&R*'s sources, the most
detailed found in de Blois, *Persian Literature*, 55, 141–2; Lazard, "La source
en 'farsi'"; Maḥjub, "Moqaddema," 18–22; Norozi, *Esordi del romanzo*,
37–50. I provide a broader survey of the literature in Cross, "The Poetics
of Romantic Love," 26–36 and Cross, "The Lives and Afterlives," 540n5.

17 Ferdowsi discusses the *mobad-dehqān* class responsible for compiling his
source in the *Shāhnāma*, 1:12/115–25; cf. the Abu Manṣuri introduction,
translated in Minorsky, "The Older Preface," 168–9. To compare different
translations of this passage, see Gabrieli, "Note sul *Vīs u Rāmīn*," 170;
Gorgāni, *V&R* (tr. Morrison), 18; Lazard, "La source en 'farsi,'" 34;
Minorsky, "Vīs u Rāmīn," 153; and Norozi, *Esordi del romanzo*, 45–7; the
latter scholar and I reach similar conclusions about how to interpret
Gorgāni's discussion of his sources.

18 See Norozi, *Esordi del romanzo*, 39n37. Some well-known examples of
the "old book" motif in European romance include Chrétien's *Cligès*,
62/18–32 (Staines 87), and Gottfried's *Tristan*, 5/155–66 (Hatto 43), and
for further discussion in a broader comparative fashion, see Agapitos,
"Rhomaian, Persian and Frankish Lands," 254–7, 261–3. The "old book"
in the *Shāhnāma* is discussed further in Davidson, *Poet and Hero*, 29–53;
Davis, "The Problem of Ferdowsi's Sources," 49; Omidsalar, *Poetics and
Politics*; and most recently, Hämeen-Anttila, *Khwadāynāmag*, 152–8. Other
examples of the "old book" appearing in eleventh-century Persian are
found in Arberry, *Homāy-nāma*, 4/58, and Asadi Ṭusi, *Garshāsb-nāma*,
14/9.21; but see the next note.

19 I am not sure the "old book" appears with enough frequency and
predictability for it to be called a motif in the Persian case. ʿAyyuqi
rightly attributes his source to "the lore and books of the Arabs" (*akhbār-e*

tāzi-o kotb-e ᶜarab, 5/5); but these aren't "old" in the same way, and it's not impossible that his contemporary readers could have guessed what specific texts he might be alluding to. Irānshāh, for another example, says that his *Bahman-nāma* is his rendition of the "old tale" (*gofta-ye bāstān*, 12/210) of Bahman, and that he based his *Kush-nāma* on a book (*nāma*) that his friend gave to him about the king of China (152/132–3); neither of these seem to invoke the "old book" as a source of *auctoritas*. Neẓāmi explicitly refers to his predecessor Ferdowsi in his *Haft paykar* and *Eskandar-nāma* (and claims to have consulted other books on the biography of Alexander); in contrast, he describes the love stories of *Khosrow & Shirin* and *Layli & Majnun* as "tales" (*hadiś*, *dāstān*) and makes no mention of a source, reaffirming their status as light entertainment relative to books of history. Consequentially, when I see a Persian poet mention an old book, I am inclined to take it seriously.

20 Key, *Language between God and the Poets*, 74. Two useful illustrations of *maᶜnā* in the context of poetic theory, preceding Gorgāni by only a generation or so, are the *Dīwān al-maᶜānī* by Abu Hilāl al-ᶜAskarī, which catalogues and analyses poetry on the basis of motival "ideas," and the *Majmaᶜ al-balāgha* (*The Confluence of Eloquence*) by al-Rāghib al-Iṣfahānī, which provides writers of Arabic with a kind of thesaurus of finely tuned combinations of thought and expression. See, respectively, Gruendler, "Motif vs. Genre"; Sadan, "Maidens' Hair and Starry Skies," 70–4, 84–8.

21 It is not a little ironic to think that *Vis & Rāmin*, celebrated by modern scholars as a precious artefact of the pre-Islamic Iranian heritage, was written by a poet who could not be more eager to jettison its archaic elements and cleanse it of those "meaningless words" (*alfāẓ-e bi-maᶜni*, 29/58)! For further commentary on this aspect, see Hedāyat, "Chand nokta," 490–1.

22 See Kanazi, "The Literary Theory," 23–8; also Athamina, "*Lafẓ* in Classical Poetry," 49. For *lafẓ* as "vocal form," see Key, *Language between God and the Poets*, 38; on *iṣāba* and *ḥaqīqa*, see respectively Kanazi, "The Literary Theory," 26–7 and Key, *Language between God and the Poets*, 65.

23 See the examples provided in Dehkhoda's *Loghat-nāma*, s.v. *āfaridan* at https://dehkhoda.ut.ac.ir/fa/dictionary/ (accessed 1 June 2022).

24 Writing about a century and a half later, Neẓāmi likewise describes his *Haft Paykar* as a box of pearls, a treasury inside each one. See Neẓāmi Ganjavi, *Heft Peiker*, 300/53.23–43 (Meisami 266–7).

25 For more on the concept of *sakhon*, particularly in the work of Neẓāmi, see Talattof, "Nizāmī Ganjavī, the Wordsmith"; Talattof, "The Wordsmith," 142–7.

26 The "Persianate world," or alternatively the "Persophone ecumene," derives from the "Persianate zone," a term coined by Marshall Hodgson

to describe "cultural traditions, carried in Persian or reflecting Persian inspiration." The boundaries of this zone naturally shifted over time: in Gorgāni's day, the Seljuks were instrumental in bringing this culture into western Iran, the Caucuses, and Anatolia, but centuries later, it would encompass most of the Islamic(ate) communities of Eurasia, what Shahab Ahmed calls the "Balkans-to-Bengal complex." See Hodgson, *The Venture of Islam*, 2:293; Ahmed, *What Is Islam?*, 32. As an object of study, the Persianate has seen a surge of scholarly interest in recent years; for an excellent synthesis and review of this literature, see Hemmat, "Completing the Persianate Turn."

27 Frye, *The Secular Scripture*, 23.

28 For discussions of the various ways the ancient Greek novels defined themselves, and were defined by their readers, see Goldhill, "Genre," 190–3; Hägg, *The Novel in Antiquity*, 2–4; Morgan, "Make-Believe and Make Believe," 176–93; Reardon, *The Form of Greek Romance*, 7–8, 46–53; Ruiz-Montero, "The Rise of the Greek Novel," 32–7.

29 The literature on the qasida and its criticism is vast and cannot be fully reviewed here, but the essays by Abdulla el Tayyib and Salma K. Jayyusi in *The Cambridge History of Arabic Literature: Arabic Literature to the End of the Umayyad Period* offer a good introduction to the form. For a short article on the cultural significance and global reach of the qasida, see Talib, "Qasida Poetry"; more expansive studies of these features are found in the essays presented in Sperl and Shackle, *Qasida Poetry in Islamic Asia and Africa*.

30 Julian, Emperor of Rome, "Fragment of a Letter to a Priest," 326/301b, translation slightly modified. For discussions of this passage, see Reardon, *The Form of Greek Romance*, 48; Morgan, "Make-Believe and Make Believe," 178; Ruiz-Montero, "The Rise of the Greek Novel," 17–18.

31 Macrobius, *Commentaire au Songe de Scipion*, 1.2.7–11 (Stahl 84–5). For discussions of this passage, see the following note.

32 Morgan, "Make-Believe and Make Believe," 177–8; cf. Holzberg, "The Genre," 15–18. For a discussion of the *argumentum* and the "double game of belief and disbelief" it fosters between readers and writers alike, see Green, *Beginnings*, 1–17.

33 Bonebakker, "Some Medieval Views," 30; for an interesting comparison with Boccaccio in this regard, see ibid., 32.

34 Tawḥīdī, *Imtāʿ*, 1:22–3; cf. Abbott, "A Ninth-Century Fragment," 156; Irwin, "The Arabic Beast Fable," 37.

35 Abbott, "A Ninth-Century Fragment," 155.

36 Regarding this author's name, both "al-Nadīm" and "Ibn al-Nadīm" are common usages. Here I follow the convention set by Bayard Dodge in al-Nadīm, *The Fihrist of al-Nadīm*, 1:xv.

37 Al-Nadīm, *Fihrist*, 1:277 (Dodge 192).
38 Ibid., 1:303 (Dodge 208).
39 See Khalidi, *Arabic Historical Thought*, esp. ch. 3; El-Hibri, *Reinterpreting Islamic Historiography*, 13–15; and Ali, *Arabic Literary Salons*, 57–64. A similar parabolic engagement with mythical, legendary, and historical anecdotes in the Persian tradition is discussed in de Bruijn, "Fiction i. Traditional Forms."
40 It is worth adding that al-Nadīm's chapter on fables and fairy tales concludes with a summary of other "one-off books" (*kutub mufradāt*) that seem to defy easy classification, including topics such as buffoonery, freckles, twitching, coitus, veterinary surgery, perfume, weapons, dreams, poisons, and so on. This leads me to guess that part of the reason why the "evening tales" (*asmār*) ended up in this chapter is because there wasn't any other obvious place to put them. Cf. Irwin, "The Arabic Beast Fable," 37, who notes that the animal fables fell "somewhat randomly" into the "broader category of secular entertainment and instruction." But, as Matthew Keegan rightly notes, this may also reflect the lack of generic stability and the ongoing contestation over how to categorize certain texts; see Keegan, "'Elsewhere Lies Its Meaning,'" 15.
41 Bonebakker, "Some Medieval Views," 24. The root of *khurāfa* also suggests other interesting etymological links with the concepts of senility, nonsense, and the act of "plucking" choice fruits for entertainment; see Lane, *Arabic-English Lexicon*, 1:725–7, s.v. *kh-r-f*. Al-Masʿūdī directly links the *khurāfa* with the Persian *afsāna* (*al-khurāfa bi-l-fārisiyya yuqāl lahā afsāna*); see al-Masʿūdī, *Murūj al-dhahab*, 2:406/¶1416.
42 For more discussion of the *khurāfāt* and the *asmār* in Baghdadi literary culture, see Toorawa, *Ibn Abī Ṭāhir Ṭayfūr*, 46–50.
43 al-Nadīm, *Fihrist*, 2:327–31 (Dodge 719–24).
44 Morgan, "Make-Believe and Make Believe," 178.
45 Meisami, "The Past in Service of the Present," 264.
46 Ibn al-Muqaffaʿ, *Kitāb Kalīla wa-Dimna*, 39 (Knatchbull 30). The prefatory comments in this book revisit time and again the theme of extracting wisdom from the amusing fables; for another example, see Ibn al-Muqaffaʿ, ibid., 72–3 (Knatchbull 63): "It behoves the reader of our book not to linger over its adornments, but to observe those parables (*amthāl*) contained therein, that he may absorb them, lingering over every parable, deliberating over every word." For more discussion of this topic, see Bonebakker, "Some Medieval Views," 31; Irwin, "The Arabic Beast Fable," 37; Keegan, "'Elsewhere Lies Its Meaning,'" 26–8, 34–6; London, "How to Do Things with Fables." For a comparable example in Western Europe, cf. the Latin beast epic *Ecbasis captivi*, which defines itself as a "lying book"

(*mendosam cartam*) that nonetheless bears "great utility" (*utilita multa*) to its readers, discussed in Green, *Beginnings*, 7–8.

47 Hämeen-Anttila, *Maqama*, 360–4; see also Irwin, "The Arabic Beast Fable," 40.

48 See Hoyland, *The "History of the Kings of the Persians" in Three Arabic Chronicles*, 56, discussed in MacDonald, "The Earlier History," 361–2.

49 I use "chivalric" in a fairly general sense here: while there is no doubt that the sociopolitical context is quite different between western Europe and the Middle East (see Irwin, "Futuwwa"; Ridgeon, *Javanmardi*; Zakeri, "Javānmardi"), the ideal values and ethos of young manhood, particularly in regards to faith and fighting, show a great many shared features across the spectrum of terms like *futuwwa* and *muruwwa* (Arabic), *javānmardi* and *ᶜayyāri* (Persian), *neaniskeia* and *andreia* (Greek), *juventās* and *virtūs* (Latin), and *bachelerie* (Old French); for a survey of these values, see Flatt, "Martial Skills," 271–6; Mahjub, "Chivalry"; Tor, *Violent Order*, 231–51.

50 For an illustrated discussion of Arabic genre theory, see Eksell, "Genre," 163–7, 170–7; Meisami and Starkey, *Encyclopedia of Arabic Literature*, 243–4, s.v. *genres, poetic*. For the continuing relevance of these terms in the Persian context, see Meisami, "Genres," 233–4.

51 Lightly adapted from Lane, *Arabic-English Lexicon*, 6:2255, col. 1, s.v. *gh-z-l*.

52 Two excellent examples of this "topological" orientation at work are found in the *Ḥamāsa*s of Abu Tammām (d. ca. 845) and al-Buḥturī (d. 897), both anthologies of poetry that include headings such as "Elegies," "Invective," "Praise and guests," "Travel and sleep," and "Blaming women" (Abu Tammām, *Ḥamāsa*, 37), and "On preparing for war and turning down women," "The advantages of gratitude," "The separation of brothers," and "Youth and old age" (al-Buḥturī, *Ḥamāsa*, 1–8). The arrangement of Abu Hilāl's *Dīwān al-maᶜānī* and al-Sarī al-Raffā's *al-Muḥibb wa-l-maḥbūb* demonstrate a similar clustering of topic and motif; see Gruendler, "Motif vs. Genre," 83–5, and Sadan, "Maidens' Hair and Starry Skies," 74–84, for a description of their respective contents. On the Persian side, some illustrative examples can be found in the *Qābus-nāma*, which lists poems of "praise and love and elegy and renunciation"; ᶜAṭṭār's *Mokhtār-nāma*, which gathers its poems under titles such as "Censure of the World," "Descriptions of Weeping," "Hopefulness," "The Lover's Pain," "The Candle's Speech," and so on; and Shams-e Qays's *al-Moᶜjam*, which speaks of diverse "arts" (*afānin*) and "methods" (*asālib*) of poetry, such as flirtation, praise, blame, grievance, rejection, humility, and forgiveness. See respectively Kay-Kāʾus, *Qābus-nāma* (ed. Yusofi), 189–92 (Levy 182–8); ᶜAṭṭār, *Mokhtār-*

nāma, 5–7; Shams-e Qays, *Moᶜjam*, 331; for more on these categories, see Browne, *A Literary History of Persia*, 2:44–5; Lewis, "Reading, Writing, and Recitation," 50–4; Miller, "Poetics of the Sufi Carnival," 1–21, 373–91; Utas, "Genres," 200–3, 210–14.

53 See Meisami, "Genres," 234.

54 For *maᶜnā* as "theme" and "motif," see Gruendler, "Motif vs. Genre"; Kanazi, "The Literary Theory," 26; Sadan, "Maidens' Hair and Starry Skies," 64–6.

55 See Curtius, *European Literature and the Latin Middle Ages*, 70; in the same paragraph, he brings up the evolving relationship between ethos and topos, resonating with some of the central terms of this study.

56 Khāqāni, *Divān*, 2:1248; for a detailed discussion of this passage and the broader notion of style, see Farghadani, "A History of Style." In a similar vein, we see the poet Saᶜdi (d. 1291) mocking the words of an imaginary critic: "His thought is eloquent and profound in this style (*shiva*) of renunciation, devotion, and advice / [but] not in the lance, club, and heavy mace"; see Saᶜdi, *Bustān*, 136/5.2504–5 (Wickens 153).

57 Shams-e Qays, *Moᶜjam*, 308. For more discussion of the masnavi form and its origins, see de Bruijn, Flemming, and Rahman, "Mathnawī."

58 For the adjective *bāstān* ("ancient") in early Persian masnavi, see Ferdowsi, *Shāhnāma*, 1:12/115, 1:164/41, 2:118/7, 3:289/16 (among other occurrences); Asadi Ṭusi, *Garshāsb-nāma*, 13/9.16, 14/9.21, 43/15.21; Arberry, *Homāy-nāma*, ii, 4/58; Irānshāh b. Abi al-Khayr, *Kush-nāma*, 199/906, 641/9309.

59 See *V&R* 112/70; Neẓāmi Ganjavi, *Khosrow-o Shirin*, 136/11.32–5; Jāmi, *Haft owrang*, 2:40/416. While these terms could all be glossed in English as "love-story," it is important to note the fine differences between these three forms of love: *ᶜeshq* for *erōs*, *havas* for caprice or fancy, and *mohabbat* for something akin to *philia* or *agapē*; for more on these distinctions, see Ernst, "The Stages of Love"; Lumbard, "From Ḥubb to ᶜIshq"; Chittick, "Love in Islamic Thought"; Cross, "The Many Colors of Love."

60 For just two examples of the *narrative* + *topic* nomenclature at work, we can first look at ancient Greek novels, which described themselves or were described with terms like "narrative" (*diēgēma*), "action" (*drama*), "plot" (*hypothesis*) "history" (*historia*), and "fiction" (*plasma*); Chariton calls his *Kallirhoe* an "amorous disaster" (*pathos erōtikon*, 1.1.1), while the narrator of *Leukippe & Klitophon* speaks of the "amorous fable" (*mythōn erōtikōn*, 1.2.3) that awaits his reader. See Holzberg, *The Ancient Novel*, 8–9; Goldhill, "Genre," 190–1; Ruiz-Montero, "The Rise of the Greek Novel," 33–6; Whitmarsh, *Dirty Love*, 16. Writers in Old French likewise described their "romances" as a tale (*conte*, *estoire*) in the vernacular (*romanz*) that was further distinguished by its subject matter (*matiere*), such that,

between the "matters" of France, Britain, and Rome, the likely generic features of the text at hand could well be anticipated. See Fuchs, *Romance*, 37; Gaunt, "Romance and Other Genres," 45; Sullivan, *The Danger of Romance*, 28.

61　Khan, *The Broken Spell*, 111; cf. Rubanovich, "Aspects of Medieval Intertextuality," 250.

62　For examples of this nomenclature, see Āftābi, *Tarif-i-Husain Shah, Badshah Dakhan*, 12, 15; Ahmad, "Epic and Counter-Epic in Medieval India," 471; also Khan, *The Broken Spell*, 111–12.

63　Tarbiyat, "Maśnavi va maśnavi-guyān-e Irāni," 433.

64　Jakobson, "The Dominant," 82. See also Cairns, *Generic Composition*, 158–76; Jauss, *Toward an Aesthetic of Reception*, 81–3.

65　For more on the notion of genre as a set of norms and habits, see Pavel, "Literary Genres."

66　Love and heroism, of course, are not the only significant topical nodes in Persian narrative; they are just the ones most directly pertinent to theorizing romance in the Persian context. A third topic that I think is quite impactful is that of wisdom, which tends to manifest as collections of parables and homilies within an allegorical frame tale, leading to the "didactic-homiletic-mystic" masnavi, in Bo Utas's words, or what Matthew Melvin-Koushki calls the "philosophical romance"; see Utas, "Genres," 239; Melvin-Koushki, "Imperial Talismanic Love."

67　See Green, *Beginnings*, 156–63, 190–1; Segre, "What Bakhtin Left Unsaid," 35. Peter Heath makes a similar distinction between the themes of "Love Story" and "Heroic Service" within the Arabic epic (*sīra*) in Heath, *The Thirsty Sword*, 68–9; but crucially, these themes are enclosed within the overarching heroic-biographical frame that begins with the hero's birth and ends with his death, as I discuss later in this chapter.

68　See Meisami, *Medieval Persian Court Poetry*, chs. 3–5; Meisami, "Kings and Lovers"; Meisami, "The Theme of the Journey."

69　For more on the *Bānu-Goshasb-nāma*, see Khaleghi-Motlagh, "Gošasb Bānu"; van Zutphen, *Farāmarz*, 105–9. There is also an interesting subgenre of "anti-heroic" narratives, named after their brigand or demonic protagonists: the *Kush-nāma*, the *Shabrang-nāma*, and the *dāstān* of Kok-e Kuhzād are some prominent examples.

70　Lyons, *The Arabian Epic*, 1:73; cf. Heath, *The Thirsty Sword*, xvi.

71　For more on these "biographical" naming conventions, see Agapitos, "Genre, Structure and Poetics," 22–3; Herzog, "What They Saw," 31; Krueger, "Introduction," 10; Whitmarsh, "The Greek Novel."

72　Translated from the Grottaferrata version of the text by Jeffreys, *Digenes Akritis*, 3.

73　Norris, "Fables and Legends," 145.

74 Agapitos, "Genre, Structure and Poetics," 23. See also Davis's perceptive observation that, "with the single exception of *Bizhan o Manizheh*, the point of the love stories of the legendary section of the *Shāhnāmeh* is the future birth of a hero"; Davis, *Panthea's Children*, 38.

75 For more on the "secondary" Persian epics, see van Zutphen, *Farāmarz*; Gazerani, *The Sistani Cycle*.

76 For a comparable example of the immediate link between martial exploits and instruction in medieval Greek literature, see the *Chronicle of the Morea*: "If you desire to hear of the deeds of good soldiers, to learn and be instructed ... sit down by me and listen. And I hope, if you are sensible, that you will profit, since many of those who have come after them have made great progress because of the stories of those great men of old." Translated in Jeffreys and Jeffreys, "The Oral Background of Byzantine Popular Poetry," 507/1349–55.

77 Manāqibī, *Sīrat al-amīra Dhāt al-Himma*, 1:5. For an abridged English translation of this work, see Magidow, *The Tale of Princess Fatima*.

78 In his introduction to Rust'aveli's *Knight in the Panther Skin*, Robert Stevenson makes the interesting observation that, while the Georgian poet clearly shows a deep familiarity with Persian romances like *V&R* and Nezāmi's *Layli & Majnun*, it is with the Arabic *sīra* of ꜤAntar that he finds the closest "kinship in ethos"; see Rust'aveli, *The Lord of the Panther-Skin*, xvii. That "ethic kinship," in my view, could be expanded to include stories like the *Digenēs*, *Samak-e ꜤAyyār*, and the *Homāy-nāma*. In a similar vein, Geraldine Heng offers a productive comparison of ꜤAntar with Middle English romances: see Heng, "A Global Middle Ages," 417–19.

79 One of the most useful discussions of this generative dynamic between topic and narrative that I have found is in Fusillo, *Il romanzo greco*, where, after positing that the chief innovation of the Greek novel is giving love "an absolutely central position" in the story (180), he goes on to enumerate the major features that emerge from this premise, including a distinctive theory of love, symmetry, love-sickness, monomania, a distinctive use of space and time, and the drive towards triumph or transcendence (179–234). I will visit many of these themes in the following chapters.

80 See Meisami, "Genres," 253; Rubanovich, "In the Mood of Love," 67 (for titles, and the rest of the article for characteristics). These features of the Persian love-story show distinctive similarities with those of the ancient Greek novel, particularly its five so-called "ideal" exemplars; see, for example, Bakhtin, *The Dialogic Imagination*, 87–9; Bowersock et al., "The Literature of the Empire," 684–5; Holzberg, *The Ancient Novel*, 9–10; Reardon, *Collected Ancient Greek Novels*, 2. On the titling conventions of the Greek stories, see Agapitos, "Genre, Structure and Poetics," 22–3;

Whitmarsh, "The Greek Novel"; cf. the overview of the *roman idyllique* in Kinoshita, "Romance in/and the Medieval Mediterranean," 191–2.

81 The idea that the lovers' union is ultimately attained, be it in this world or the next, offers a useful way to situate the Greek novels and the Arabic *ʿudhrī* tales within the broader mythos and ethos of romantic love, despite their apparently diametrically opposed endings; for more on the imbrication of felicity and death in the Greek material, see Greene, "(Un)happily Ever After"; Perkins, *The Suffering Self*, 15–40.

82 Translated in Jeffreys, *Four Byzantine Novels*, 20.

83 Studies that engage with this long-standing contact zone and its literary implications include Davis, *Panthea's Children*; Selden, "Mapping the Alexander Romance"; Whitmarsh, *Dirty Love*; and the essays in the edited volume by Whitmarsh and Thompson, *The Romance between Greece and the East*.

84 See Athenaeus, *The Learned Banqueters*, 328–3/13.575b–575f. Other "Persian" narratives from antiquity that show some affinity with the Greek novel are the stories of Stryangaeus and Zarinaea in Ctesias and Panthea and Abradatas in Xenophon, which both feature the motif of suicide when union with the beloved is no longer possible. For discussion of these works, see Davis, *Panthea's Children*, 26–9, 61–5; Reichel, "Xenophon's Cyropaedia and the Hellenistic Novel"; Stoneman, "Persian Aspects of the Romance Tradition," 7–9. The latter article notes additional thematic correspondences in the Book of Esther and the Sasanian story of Ardashir and Zijanak/Golnār.

85 For Bakhtin's introduction of the chronotope, see Bakhtin, *The Dialogic Imagination*, 84–5.

86 Frye, *The Secular Scripture*, 17.

87 For a parallel discussion of external and internal referentiality, see Green, "The Rise of Medieval Fiction in the Twelfth Century," 60: "The antique romance remains externally referential (its events were regarded as historically true) while the narrative of the Arthurian romance is self-referential. The former was seen as history, but with fictional insertions, while the latter is fiction with the possible addition of historical touches." The relationship between epic (a term that I think fits fairly well with the heroic-biography model I discuss here) and history in a number of premodern contexts is further discussed in Konstan and Raaflaub, *Epic and History*.

88 Ouyang, "Romancing the Epic," 11.

89 Herzog, "What They Saw," 31; see also Reynolds, "Epic and History in the Arabic Tradition"; Ghazoul, *The Arabian Nights*, 72–3; Magidow, *The Tale of Princess Fatima*, xi–xiv.

90 al-Bīrūnī, *Book on Pharmacy*, 1:12 (Arabic), cf. Hägg and Utas, *The Virgin and Her Lover*, 195; for other translations of this passage, see Bausani, "Muhammad or Darius?" 56; Meisami, "The Past in Service of the Present," 264. While I follow these scholars in interpreting *al-akhbār al-kisrawiyya* and *al-asmār al-layliyya* as royal biographies and evening tales, the editor of al-Bīrūnī's text translates it as "the tales of Khusraw and the romance of Laylá" (1:8 [English]); this intriguing interpretation would suggest a much more explicit singling out of love stories in particular, if we understand the first phrase as an allusion to the amours of Khosrow and Shirin.

91 Gutas, *Greek Thought, Arabic Culture*, 1, also 137, 152, 194. See also Hägg, "The Oriental Reception," 101–6.

92 On the "needle's eye" of Greek-to-Syriac translation, see Hägg, "The Oriental Reception," 102–3; for a general survey of the kinds of Hellenistic works that were translated or integrated into Persian literature, see van Ruymbeke, "Hellenistic Influences," 361: "In spite of the great variety of Greek works translated into Arabic, hardly any Greek *belles lettres* were included." The *Fihrist* more or less corroborates this account; in his short list of Greek evening tales, histories, fables, and proverbs, al-Nadīm names versions of the *1001 Nights* and *Kalīla & Dimna* (which are Indo-Persian in origin), some books about "society" (*adab*), proverbs, a treatise on reason and beauty (*al-ʿaql wa-l-jamāl*), and five books about kings – nothing that would suggest any of the distinctively Greek traditions of drama or poetry. See al-Nadīm, *Fihrist*, 2:327 (Dodge 718).

93 For more on the history of Greek-to-Middle Persian translation, see van Bladel, *The Arabic Hermes*, esp. ch. 2; Gutas, *Greek Thought, Arabic Culture*, 25–7, 34–45; Nallino, "Tracce di opere greche"; Pingree, "Classical and Byzantine Astrology in Sasanian Persia."

94 Irwin writes that the tenth-century Abbasid writers seemed "too ready" to associate the fictional with the foreign; Boyce and Meisami also ascribe this habit to the Iranian case, noting the Greek and Indian origins of much of the Middle and New Persian material. See Irwin, "The Arabic Beast Fable," 38; Boyce, "The Parthian *Gōsān*," 35; Meisami, "Genres," 253.

95 al-Nadīm, *Fihrist*, 2:325 (Dodge 715–16). For a detailed discussion of this section of the *Fihrist*, see Cross, "Poetic Alchemy."

96 al-Nadīm, *Fihrist*, 2:325 (Dodge 716). For more on the Middle Persian *Book of Lords*, see Hämeen-Anttila, *Khwadāynāmag*.

97 For more on the Arabic translations of the *Book of Lords*, see Shahbazi, *Ferdowsī*, 34–5.

98 For more on Middle Persian wisdom-literature (*andarz*), see Macuch, "Pahlavi Literature," 160–72; Shaked and Ṣafā, "Andarz."

99 For more on Ibn al-Muqaffaᶜ and his translation project, see Latham,
    "Ebn al-Moqaffaᶜ"; for Middle Persian-to-Arabic translations more
    generally, see de Blois, "Pre-Islamic Iranian and Indian Influences," 339;
    Latham, "Ebn al-Moqaffaᶜ"; Ṣafā, "Sharāyeṭ-e ejtemāᶜi"; Toorawa, *Ibn
    Abī Ṭāhir Ṭayfūr*, 79–82; Zakeri, "ᶜAlī ibn ᶜUbaida ar-Raihānī," esp. 89–93.
    Discussions of figures who translated from Middle Persian to Arabic
    are found in al-Nadīm, *Fihrist*, 1:369–70, 1:516, 2:326, 2:331 (Dodge 260,
    359, 716, 724). The use of *muzdawij* at this early stage raises a number of
    intriguing possibilities about the history of the masnavi form that are
    discussed in Cross, "Poetic Alchemy."
100 This is admittedly an unresolved question for me: why did the Arabic
    muzdawij never gain the same formal prestige as the Persian masnavi? I
    give my best answer for now in the body text – that it may have sounded
    foreign or unpoetic for Arabic speakers, who had a rich tradition of
    monorhyme poetry behind them (this is sometimes also used to explain
    the lack of interest in Greek poets such as Homer) – but it is worth noting
    that Turkic poets had no qualms about adapting the form into their
    literature, as is evidenced by, among others, the *Kutadgu Bilig* (w. ca.
    1070) and the masnavis of ᶜAli-Shir Navāʾi (d. 1501).
101 To name a few examples of short love stories in *adab* literature: Ibn
    Qutayba's *al-Shiᶜr wa-l-shuᶜarāʾ* and Abu al-Faraj al-Iṣbahānī's *Kitāb al-
    aghānī* (biographical dictionaries); al-Jāḥiẓ's *Risālat al-qiyān*, al-Washshāʾ's
    Kitāb al-muwashshā, and Ibn Ḥazm's *Ṭawq al-ḥamāma* (essays); Ibn
    Qutayba's *ᶜUyūn al-akhbār*, Ibn Dāwūd's *Kitāb al-zahra*, and al-Tanūkhī's
    al-Faraj baᶜd al-shidda (thematic anthologies). The latter work contains
    an episode that follows the Greek novel formula of union – separation –
    reunion quite closely, discussed in Bray, "Isnāds and Models of Heroes,"
    12–14; for a much more extensive survey of this literature, see Giffen,
    Theory of Profane Love.
102 For discussions of the *Maṣāriᶜ al-ᶜushshāq*, see Bell, *Love Theory*, 9–10;
    Bell, "Al-Sarrāj's *Maṣāriᶜ al-ᶜushshāq*"; Giffen, *Theory of Profane Love*, 25–7;
    Vadet, *L'Esprit courtois*, 379–430.
103 For two accounts of the rise and development of New Persian, see
    Lazard, "The Rise of the New Persian Language"; Perry, "The Origin and
    Development."
104 Høgel, in dialogue with Beecroft and Pollock, suggests the term
    "imperial" as a more precise label for the kinds of literary languages that
    tend to circulate on a global, or at least transregional, scale; see Høgel,
    "World Literature Is Trans-Imperial"; Pollock, *The Language of the Gods*;
    Beecroft, *An Ecology of World Literature*.
105 For discussions of these works, see the following pages from de Blois,
    Persian Literature: 64–5 (Abu al-Moʾayyad Balkhi's *Yusof & Zoleykha*, w. ca.

976); 70 (the *Āfrin-nāma* of Abu Shakur Balkhi, fl. 947); 150–2 (*Mawlud-e Zartosht*, w. ca. 978 by Kay Kaᵓus of Ray); 160 (Maysari's *Dānesh-nāma*, w. 980); 469 (*Barlaam & Josaphat*, w. early ninth c.); 472–3 (the *Farāmarz-nāma* of Āzād Sarv, d. before 919).

106 For a discussion and assessment of these early *Yusof & Zolaykhā* poems, particularly the one by pseudo-Ferdowsi, see de Blois, ibid., 476–82.

107 For a survey of the debate over the *Shāhnāma*'s genre, see Askari, *The Medieval Reception*, 6–7.

108 Minorsky, "The Older Preface," 169.

109 We don't know, of course, whether Ferdowsi was the *first* versifier of the *Shāhnāma* to include fables and love tales within its historical framework, as earlier renditions, such as that of Masᶜudi Marvazi, have regrettably not survived; see de Blois, *Persian Literature*, 166. But in any case, Ferdowsi's work was so impactful that it probably does mark a turning point.

110 See Green, "The Rise of Medieval Fiction in the Twelfth Century," 59, with further and more detailed discussion in Huot, *From Song to Book*, 27–35.

111 I thank Suzanne Conklin Akbari for pointing out the term ekstasis to me.

112 To give a few examples of short love stories worked into historiography, al-Masᶜūdī (d. ca. 956) relates the accounts of ᶜUrwa and ᶜAfrāᵓ (the source of ᶜAyyuqi's *Varqa & Golshāh*) and of Laylā and Majnūn in his *Murūj al-dhahab*, while al-Thaᶜālibī (d. 1038) includes the romance of Zāl and Rudāba in his *Ghurar al-mulūk*; see al-Masᶜūdī, *The Meadows of Gold*, 285–7, and van Zutphen, *Farāmarz*, 235, respectively.

113 Heng, "A Global Middle Ages," 420.

114 Selden, "Mapping the Alexander Romance," 26, who quotes Althusser.

115 For a detailed comparison of *Bizhan & Manizha* with *V&R*, see Khaleghi-Motlagh, "Bizhan-o Manizha," 274–84. Minorsky also makes an intriguing connection between Manizha and Mobad Manikān (Manēkān > Manēč > Manizha) in Minorsky, "Vīs u Rāmīn," 185–6.

116 For Bizhan in *Book of Lords*–inflected historiography, see al-Ṭabarī, *The Ancient Kingdoms*, 12; al-Thaᶜālibī, *Histoire*, 238.

117 Shahbazi, *Ferdowsī*, 65. Like Shahbazi, Khaleghi-Motlaq suspects that *Bizhan & Manizha* was an independent love-story, very much like *V&R*, that "had to lose many ingredients unsuited to the heroic world before it was admitted into the epic literature"; if that is the case, Ferdowsi would count among the first Persian poets that we know of to produce a stand-alone romance, though he shied away from presenting it as such. See Khaleghi-Motlagh, "Bīžan"; and for more on the autonomy of the *Shāhnāma*'s episodes, see Krasnowolska, "Ferdowsi's *Dastan*."

118	The identity of Ferdowsi's "kind companion" (*mehrbān*) is an interesting, and potentially quite important, point. While modern scholarship has tended to assume this companion to be female, even his wife (Khaleghi-Motlagh, "Ferdowsi, Abu'l-Qāsem i. Life"; Shahbazi, *Ferdowsī*, 65), Hamid Dabashi rightly points out that there is no basis in the text for this assumption, noting that al-Bundarī's Arabic translation of the *Shāhnāma* (w. ca. 1230) in fact genders this figure male; see Dabashi, *The Shahnameh*, 80–4. Acknowledging the speculative nature of my reading, I lean towards calling this companion a "she," mostly on some contextual clues. The line "I had a *mehrbān* in [my] house" (*yek-i mehrbān bud-am andar sarāy*, 3:304/15) suggests a domestic affiliation and a position of social inferiority, such as a wife, a concubine, or a male slave (*gholām*); but given the common, if cliché, association of evening tales with women (e.g., the *1001 Nights*), I guess that one of the former is implied.

119	Evening-time storytelling was a long-established practice among courtly elites. Al-Masʿūdī, for example, describes how the caliph Muʿāwiya would "spend the first third of the night [listening] to tales about the 'days' of the Arabs and the kings of the Persians" (*yasmur thulth al-layl fī akhbār al-ʿarab wa-ayyāmihā wa-l-ʿajam wa-mulūkihim*); see al-Masʿūdī, *Murūj al-dhahab*, 3:222/¶1836. The *History of Bayhaqi* mentions professional storytellers – occasionally with some contempt – in the Ghaznavid court a number of times, who entertain their masters at hunts and soirées and soothe them to sleep in the wee hours of the morning; see Bayhaqi, *Tārikh-e Bayhaqi*, 1:117, 1:124, 1:502 (Bosworth and Ashtiany 1:212, 1:219–20, 2:172), with further discussion in Omidsalar, *Poetics and Politics*, 27–30. Parallel cases of storytelling as soporific are abundant, from the Book of Esther 6.1 ("That night the king could not sleep; so he ordered the book of the chronicles, the record of his reign, to be brought in and read to him," NIV translation) to the sleepless narrator of Chaucer's *The Book of the Duchess*, who requests a "romaunce" to "rede and drive the night away" (331/48–9). For more on this topic, see de Bruijn, "Poets and Minstrels," 16–18; de Bruijn, "Classical Persian Literature as a Tradition," 24; Lewis, "Reading, Writing, and Recitation," 84–5; Omidsalar, "Unburdening Ferdowsi," 238; Stoneman, "Persian Aspects of the Romance Tradition," 6–7.

120	I have already discussed the association between evening tales and women made by writers like al-Ṣūlī and al-Tawḥīdī; to compare this with similar associations made in Greek and Old French contexts, see Whitmarsh, *Dirty Love*, 3–4, and Sullivan, *The Danger of Romance*, 26–8, respectively. An interesting example in the latter context is the story of *Floire & Blancheflor*, which presents itself as a tale read out of a book by a woman to her younger sister in 4/33–56 (Hubert 24/33–56); the generic implications of this staging are discussed in Gaunt, *Gender and Genre*, 85–7; Krueger, *Women Readers*, 7–9.

121 By "Greco-Bactrian," I mean (in an admittedly vague way) the synthesis of Greek and Bactrian (eastern Iranian) cultural traditions that took place after Alexander of Macedon's conquest of the region, under the aegis of the Greco-Bactrian kingdom, the Indo-Greek kingdom, and the Parthians. For some useful studies of this synthesis, see Bernard, "The Greek Kingdoms of Central Asia"; Overtoom, *Reign of Arrows*.

122 Agapitos, "Rhomaian, Persian and Frankish Lands," 261, 288–92.

123 A similar shift has been noted in other contexts, too: on *Floire & Blancheflor*, Simon Gaunt describes how "the world of the *chansons de geste* needs to be evoked only to be discarded"; William Ker (with obvious distaste) writes how the matter of the "fictitious stories" in the Icelandic saga tradition "is taken from the adventures of the heroic age ... the substance was eliminated, and the romantic *eidolon* left to walk about by itself." See Gaunt, "Romance and Other Genres," 52; Ker, *Epic and Romance*, 321.

124 See Overtoom, *Reign of Arrows*, 1–26.

125 References to both *Shādbahr & ʿAyn al-Ḥayāt* and *Kheng-bot sorkh-bot* occur in the Persian *Eskandar-nāma*, which describes them as famous works. For the text, see Afshār, *Eskandar-nāma*, 288–9; for a translation and discussion, see Hägg and Utas, *The Virgin and Her Lover*, 197–9.

126 See Hägg, "The *Parthenope Romance* Decapitated?"; Hägg, "Metiochus at Polycrates' Court"; Utas, "Did ʿAdhrā Remain a Virgin?"; Utas, "The Ardent Lover and the Virgin"; and their joint efforts, Hägg and Utas, *The Virgin and Her Lover*, esp. 193–203 and 251–3; Hägg and Utas, "Eros Goes East."

127 The Greek novel model would later be continued by Persian poets like Farid al-Din ʿAṭṭār and Khwāju Kermāni: see de Bruijn, "Ḵⱽāju Kermāni"; Norozi, "The Verse Romance *Homāy o Homāyūn*," 24–5; O'Malley, "An Unexpected Romance."

128 For the text and translation of this passage of the *Dārāb-nāma*, see Hägg and Utas, *The Virgin and Her Lover*, 144–9. On the tale's Hellenistic roots, see Rubanovich, "In the Mood of Love," 69n9; on ʿAẕrā as a "chaste virgin" character, see Davis, *Panthea's Children*, 83–109; cf. the figure of Parthenopē, "so named because she preserved her virginity in spite of falling into the hands of many men," in Hägg and Utas, *The Virgin and Her Lover*, 243. More discussion of this character type in other Islamicate sources can be found in Lewis, "One Chaste Muslim Maiden and a Persian in a Pear Tree," 164–80.

129 See al-Nadīm, *Fihrist*, 1:373–4 (Dodge 262–3). Hägg and Utas note seventeen narrative poems in Persian and Turkish with this title, with

various degrees of affinity with what we know of ᶜOnṣori's text; see Hägg
and Utas, *The Virgin and Her Lover*, 203–12.

130 Dowlatshāh Samarqandi, *Tadhkiratu 'sh-Shuᶜará*, 30; cf. Hägg and Utas,
The Virgin and Her Lover, 194–5.

131 The word *tā* appears in the Shafi manuscript, but many of the other
testimonia replace it with *gar*. See Hägg and Utas, *The Virgin and Her
Lover*, 90–1, 183. This didactic gesture is a distinctive feature of *Vis &
Rāmin* as well, where the poet periodically stops to tell his readers about
the Pahlavi etymology of various words. For more on Eastern Iranian
Buddhism during the Indo-Greek, Sasanian, and Abbasid periods, see
respectively Bernard, "The Greek Kingdoms of Central Asia," 117, 128;
Rezakhani, *ReOrienting the Sasanians*, 61–4, 154–5; Bulliet, "Naw Bahār
and the Survival of Iranian Buddhism."

132 Hārūt and his counterpart Mārūt, mentioned in the Qur'an 2:102, were
generally understood by the tenth century to be two "fallen angels" who
brought sorcery to humanity; for more details, see Tottoli, "Hārūt and
Mārūt." A similar conflation of pagan and Islamic knowledge occurs in
Floire & Blancheflor; see Kinoshita, *Medieval Boundaries*, 84–6.

133 In this citation, I'm following the words *che* and *ku* as they are recorded
in the manuscript. To compare this passage against the Greek *Metiochos &
Parthenopē*, see Hägg and Utas, *The Virgin and Her Lover*, 28–9.

134 al-Bīrūnī, *al-Āthār al-bāqiya*, xxxxiv; cf. Hägg and Utas, *The Virgin and Her
Lover*, 195; Rubanovich, "In the Mood of Love," 69n6. In this passage,
al-Bīrūnī is specifically speaking of a number of love stories he himself
wrote, likely his Arabic translations of ᶜOnṣori's romances (though
perhaps these were ᶜOnṣori's sources). The gastronomical image
resonates with al-Nadīm's dismissal of the *1001 Nights* (*Hazār afsān*) as a
"meagre" or "mangy" book, "frigid" in its storytelling (*kitāb ghathth bārid
al-ḥadīth*), as though it were an unsatisfying dish; see al-Nadīm, *Fihrist*,
3:322 (Dodge 714). For a discussion of how a good story ought to be told,
see Tawḥīdī, *Imtāᶜ*, 1:22–3.

135 We know little about this poet's life and career; he twice identifies himself
with the pen-name ᶜAyyuqi, and, based on the "manifest influence" of
Ferdowsi in this poem, the archaic vocabulary, and the fact that it was
dedicated to Sultan Maḥmud of Ghazna, Khaleghi-Motlagh surmises that
it was written sometime after the *Shāhnāma* was completed and before
the death of Maḥmud, most probably in the 1020s. See ᶜAyyuqi, *Varqa-vo
Golshāh*, 3, 122; Khaleghi-Motlagh, "ᶜAyyūqī."

136 Utas, "Genres," 200.

137 ᶜAyyuqi, *Varqa-vo Golshāh*, 4–5. I reproduce the text exactly as it appears
in this edition, including the possible typo of *shavad* for *shavaḏ* on 5/3.
For other translations of this passage, see Meisami, *Medieval Persian Court*

Poetry, 89n19, and Melikian-Chirvani, "Le roman de Varqe et Golšâh," 102. The word *enshā*, which Ṣafā emends from the manuscript's *aᶜshā*, is a little obscure, and, if Ṣafā's emendation is correct, could suggest a misspelled rendition of the Arabic word *inshāʾ*, meaning "construction," "composition," or "recitation"; Melikian-Chirvani renders it as "mots" and Meisami as "style."

138 Al-Nadīm, *Fihrist*, 2:328 (Dodge 719).

139 For more on the aesthetic pleasure and cognitive power of wonder, see Yarshater, "The Indian or Safavid Style," 268; Utas, "The Aesthetic Use of New Persian," 4; Harb, *Arabic Poetics*, 5–12. The author of the *Homāy-nāma* makes a similar if very brief statement along these lines: "My greatest passion is in poetry, for I am amazed by it" (*marā āz bish-ast dar shāᶜeri • ke hastam shoda khira bar shāᶜeri*); see Arberry, *Homāy-nāma*, 3/57.

140 Ibn Qutayba, *al-Shiᶜr wa-al-shuᶜarāʾ*, 622–7; al-Masᶜūdī, *Les prairies d'or*, 7:349–55 (Lunde and Stone 285–7); al-Iṣbahānī, *Aghānī*, 24:80–90, no. 534.

141 In a similar example, we might consider the temptation of later scribes, or perhaps Neẓāmi himself, to add the happy ending to the otherwise tragic tale of *Layli & Majnun* about a century later in Ganja. For a discussion of this "expanded version," see Chelkowski, *Mirror of the Invisible World*, 68.

142 On Maḥmud's lasting reputation as a solider of Islam, and the role of the *ghāzī* class in his army, see Bosworth, "The Early Ghaznavids," 169–70, 182–6.

143 The literary strategy of using love as effecting a kind of conversion has analogues in other traditions as well. As Wen-chin Ouyang discusses, the love stories found within the life story (*sīra*) of ᶜUmar al-Nuᶜmān in the *1001 Nights* help the hero "convert" his downward trajectory from misfortune (romance) to success (epic), restoring him to the history from which he had been expelled; see Ouyang, "The Epical Turn of Romance." Further abroad, the introduction of *Floire & Blancheflor* frames the love-story as a genealogy of Charlemagne's birth – a sort of prequel to the *Chanson de Roland* – and closes with a scene of mass conversion. See d'Orbigny, *Floire et Blanchefleur*, 174/3323–8 (Hubert 110/3016–20), discussed further in Delcourt, "Swords and Flowers."

144 Utas, "Genres," 203.

145 Little and McDonald, "Introduction," 4. Similarly, Karen Sullivan explores how the Arthurian romances of western Europe self-consciously assert their ability to express forms of truth that are not accessible in "realist" genres of writing – a movement that I think parallels what we see in the New Persian context. See Sullivan, *The Danger of Romance*.

146 For the original passage, see Arberry, *Homāy-nāma*, 193/4327–8: *sarāsar be sheᶜr ānchenān gofta-am • ke dorr-e maᶜāni dar u softa-am / chonin dāstān kist gofta degar • sarāsar bekhwān-o bedu dar negar.*

147 There is another reading of this line that points the verb as *bāyad*, not *tābad*, which is used by the translations in Gorgāni, *V&R* (tr. Morrison), 18, and Minorsky, "Vīs u Rāmīn," 153. I also differ from these translations (and also Lazard, "La source en 'farsi,'" 38) in that I read *alfāẓ* without *eżāfa*, such that the word *besyār* is no longer attached to it ("abundant words"), but rather as an adverb ("very much"), which I render as "brilliantly."

148 The notion of "unmeasured" (*gazāfi*) speech is an interesting concept for comparative study. For example, one finds a similar term (*ametroepēs*) in the *Iliad*, 2.212, to describe the impolitic oration of Theristes; see Kahane, "Epic, Novel, Genre," 62–3.

149 Quoted from Lane, *Arabic-English Lexicon*, 1:529, col. 1, s.v. *ḥ-d-th*, emphasis original. For Davis's comments on the "jewelled style" in *Vis & Rāmin*, see Davis, "Introduction," xxii–xxix.

150 Perez, *The Material Ghost*, 267; also cited in https://bombmagazine.org /articles/abbas-kiarostami/ (accessed 1 June 2022).

2 Ethics: An Affair of Conscience

1 Van Gelder, *Close Relationships*, 184–5.

2 See Whitmarsh, *Narrative and Identity*, 3.

3 Jeffreys, *Four Byzantine Novels*, 66. All other citations and translations from *Rhodanthe & Dosikles* are from this volume.

4 As Saeed Honarmand notes, Vis's infidelity to Mobad has rendered her "*bad nām* (having a bad reputation) throughout classical Persian literature"; see Honarmand, "Between the Water and the Wall," 77. For an overview of this reception, see Cross, "The Lives and Afterlives," 523–9; Norozi, *Esordi del romanzo*, 231–79.

5 One recent attempt to sketch out a broad history of romantic or "courtly" love, by comparing its modalities in medieval Europe, India, and Japan is found in Reddy, *The Making of Romantic Love*; regrettably (though I don't hold it against the author – one can't do it all!), Byzantine, Islamic, and Chinese contexts are largely absent from this study.

6 All translations from the *Symposium* are from *Plato on Love*, edited by C.D.C. Reeve.

7 Plotinus, *Ennead, Volume III*, 167. For a thorough discussion of the reception of Plotinus and Porphyry in Arabic philosophy, particularly in the thought of al-Kindī, see Adamson, *The Arabic Plotinus*.

8 Gutas, "Plato's *Symposion* in the Arabic Tradition," 37, 40.

9 al-Masʿūdī, *The Meadows of Gold*, 112–13, discussed in von Grunebaum, "Avicenna's *Risâla*," 235–6. For similar passages, see Ibn Dāwūd, *Zahra*, 21; Ikhwān al-Ṣafāʾ, *Rasāʾil*, 3:272; Tawḥīdī and Miskawayh, "On Why People Take Pleasure," 217.

10 Bell, *Love Theory*, 108. As Domenico Ingenito observes, the recognition of affinity (*munāsaba*) was also central to vertical configurations of love, such as in the relationship between the human (rational) and divine (celestial) realms as discussed by Avicenna, Muḥammad al-Ghazālī, and Saʿdi; see Ingenito, *Beholding Beauty*, 375–6.

11 al-Jāḥiẓ, *Rasāʾil*, 2:168; cf. the translations by Beeston, *Epistle on Singing-Girls*, 29, and Pellat, *Life and Works*, 264. Describing the many degrees and kinds of love was a favourite topic in this genre; for a survey of the most popular terms, see Giffen, *Theory of Profane Love*, 83–96.

12 For the presumption of asymmetry in the Greek context, see Halperin, *One Hundred Years*, 30–6; Konstan, *Sexual Symmetry*, 7–8, 36. For its analogue in medieval Muslim societies of the eastern Mediterranean region, see Bauer, "Male-Male Love in Classical Arabic Poetry," 113–14; El-Rouayheb, *Before Homosexuality*, 13–33; Lewis, *Rumi*, 321–4. This backdrop underscores the "radical innovation," as Tim Whitmarsh puts it, of the ideal Greek novels in narrating "the emotional, sexual, and psychological lives of young men and (most shockingly of all) young women, even παρθένοι [virgins]"; see Whitmarsh, "The Greek Novel," 608; cf. Fusillo, *Il romanzo greco*, 188–9. For more discussion of how the love-relations in the Greek novels differ from their predecessors, see Muchow, "Passionate Love," 1–21.

13 Branham, "The Poetics of Genre," 27.

14 Lyons and Lyons, *The Arabian Nights*, 1:712–16. For an analysis of the Qamar-Budūr encounter, and for more examples of the motif of love in similitude in the *1001 Nights*, see Antrim, "Qamarayn." Finally, for a useful survey of the habits and conventions shared between Hellenistic and Islamic love literature, see von Grunebaum, *Medieval Islam*, 305–19.

15 Fusillo, *Il romanzo greco*, 187.

16 Macnaghten, *Alf layla wa-layla*, 1:828 (Lyons and Lyons 1:708). The "twins" motif in the story of Qamar and Budūr, and its striking impacts on the interplay of gender, race, and desire, is explored in Doniger, "The Rings of Budur and Qamar al-Zaman," 114–19; Epps, "Comparison, Competition, and Cross-Dressing," 114–21.

17 Sturges, *Aucassin and Nicolette*, 6–7, 30–1. The French syntax leaves no doubt about the two lovers' identical visage: "Il/Ele avoit les caviaus/x blons et menus recercelés, et les ex vairs et rians, et le face traitice, et le nés haut et bien assis ... "

18 For all occurrences of the twins motif in *F&B*, see d'Orbigny, *Floire et Blanchefleur*, 62/1291–6 (Hubert 54/1096–1101), 76/1545–6 (Hubert 62/1355–6), 86/1733–40 (Hubert 67/1541–8), and 134/2591–2664 (Hubert 92/2376–2443).

19 In an account that offers interesting conceptual points of comparison with the myth of Aristophanes, Gayōmard, the Zoroastrian "first man,"

is described in the *Bundahishn* as being as wide as he is tall; after his destruction at the hands of Angra Mainyu, Gayōmard's seed gives rise to the twins Mashya and Mashyanag, who go on to populate the world with humanity. See Cereti, "Gayōmard"; Curtis, *Persian Myths*, 20.

20 Foucault, *History of Sexuality*, 3:228–32.

21 Ibid., 3:230.

22 Konstan, *Sexual Symmetry*, 58.

23 Ibn Dāwūd, *Zahra*, 66; for a translation and discussion of this hadith as it was treated by subsequent writers, see Giffen, *Theory of Profane Love*, 99–115.

24 For a recent contribution to our understanding of Ibn Dāwūd's ethics of love, as illustrated through his poetic contributions to the *Kitāb al-zahra*, see Tobkin, "A Man of Our Times."

25 Ibn Dāwūd, *Zahra*, 15. This poem also appears in al-Mas'ūdī, *Les prairies d'or*, 6:381 (Lunde and Stone 113).

26 Buthayna's question "Is this what you want" (*a-hādhā tabghī*) is a bit of a pun. In addition to indicating wishing, desiring, and seeking, the verb *baghā* also means to oppress, to act haughtily, and, in the case of women, to commit adultery; perhaps she is chiding him the way a male lover might chide his female beloved? See Lane, *Arabic-English Lexicon*, 1:231, cols. 2–3, s.v. *b-gh-y*.

27 al-Iṣbahānī, *Aghānī*, 8:76–7, cf. Irwin, *Night and Horses*, 57. A very similar anecdote about Jamīl and Buthayna appears in al-Jāhiẓ, *Epistle on Singing-Girls*, 16.

28 See Goldhill, *Foucault's Virginity*, 160, and Morales, "The History of Sexuality," 48, contra Konstan, *Sexual Symmetry*, 55.

29 'Ayyuqi, *Varqa-vo Golshāh*, 14/6–17, 35/7–36/14; Neẓāmi Ganjavi, *Layli-o Majnun*, 160/33.81–4 (Gelpke 112, Davis 102). The motif of the virgin female warrior, reminiscent of Athena, also appears in 'Onṣori's 'Aẕrā (see Hägg and Utas, *The Virgin and Her Lover*, 84/31–9); similar characters can be found in the *Shāhnāma* (Gordāfarid), the *Homāy-nāma* (Gol-e Kāmkār), the *Bahman-nāma* (Bānu-Goshasb and Zar-Bānu), the *Bānu-Goshasb-nāma*, and the *Dārāb-nāma* (Homāy and Burāndokht) – although in these "heroic" narratives the emphasis is less on chastity and more on martial exploits. See Davis, "Women in the *Shahnameh*," 74–5.

30 In a subtle but interesting juxtaposition, Anthia asks Habrokomes to keep his desiring eyes away from other people, while Habrokomes asks Anthia to "live and die with [me] a chaste wife" (*Ephesiaka*, 113/1.9); for more on Kleitophon's male virginity (despite his short fling with Melite, an act that he says "could no longer be considered precisely a marital one but was rather a remedy for an ailing soul," 249/5.27), see Zeitlin, "Gendered Ambiguities," 111–12, 119–20. For examples of male-male fidelity via the

female beloved in Arabic, see Ibn Qutayba, *al-Shiᶜr wa-al-shuᶜarāʾ*, 625, and al-Iṣbahānī, *Aghānī*, 24:83, both translated in Cross, "The Poetics of Romantic Love," 420, 427; and in Persian, see ᶜAyyuqi, *Varqa-vo Golshāh*, 106/3–6, and Arberry, *Homāy-nāma*, 435–40.

31 Davis, *Panthea's Children*, 42–3.

32 The springtime festival as the *locus amoenus* for the onset of love in the Greek novel is discussed at length in Muchow, "Passionate Love," 106–23. So too will Chaucer begin his *Troilus & Crysede* in "Aperil, whan clothed is the mede / With newe grene, of lusty Ver the pryme, / And swote smellen floures whyte and rede" (475/1.156–8), and then have Troilus fall in love with Crysede upon beholding her in the temple (476/1.267–73).

33 Kay-Kāʾus, *Qābus-nāma* (ed. Yusofi), 87 (Levy 77–8).

34 The miraculous reversal of menopause has a significant place in the story of Abraham and Sarah (Genesis 18:11–15, Qur'an 11:70–3), and the motif also occurs in the Arabic *sīra* literature as well; see Schine, "On Blackness in Arabic Popular Literature," 126–7.

35 See *V&R* 45n1.

36 Endogamous marriage (*xwēdōdah*) was a common practice among the Sasanian nobility, sometimes endorsed as the best kind of marriage by the Zoroastrian clergy (see, e.g., *Dinkard*, ed. Sunjana, 2:91–6/3.80); it was also a common theme for anti-Zoroastrian polemic among Muslim writers, as discussed in van Gelder, *Close Relationships*. For a detailed treatment of the subject, see Sadeghi, *The Sin of the Woman*, 74–7; Skjærvø, "Marriage ii. Next of Kin Marriage in Zoroastrianism"; and for a discussion of its importance as it pertains to *V&R*, see Kappler, "*Vîs et Râmîn*," 58–62; Norozi, *Esordi del romanzo*, 98.

37 The hadith that "her consent is her silence" is attested, for example, in Malik's *Muwaṭṭaʾ* (28:1097), the *Ṣaḥīḥ*s of Bukhārī (6971) and Muslim (1421a), the *Jāmiᶜ* of al-Tirmidhī (1108), and many additional sources as well; one can easily find them by going to https://sunnah.com/ (accessed 1 June 2022) and running a search with the keywords "consent" and "silence," or *idhnuhā ṣumātuhā* in Arabic script.

38 For a discussion of women's silence in the context of the ancient Greek novel, see Wiersma, "The Ancient Greek Novel and Its Heroines," 121.

39 Gottfried von Strassburg, *Tristan* (tr. Hatto), 265.

40 For "women-as-riot," see Bloch, *Medieval Misogyny*, 17. The same position, which Fatemeh Sadeghi calls "the Pandora image of women," is also an established trope in pre-Islamic Iranian sources as well; see Sadeghi, *The Sin of the Woman*, 43.

41 Malti-Douglas, *Woman's Body*, 44, 85–92; Najmabadi, "Reading – and Enjoying," 207; Merguerian and Najmabadi, "Zulaykha and Yusuf," 487; Ayubi, *Gendered Morality*, 132–38. Such tropes, of course, do not stop there;

some examples from the European context, by way of comparison, include the tirade against women in the third book of Andreas Capellanus's *De amore*, or the jealous husband in *Le roman de la rose*, who claims that women "will never be so walled in that they do not hate Chastity so strongly that they all aspire to shame her." See, respectively, Andreas Capellanus, *The Art of Courtly Love*, 187–212; Lorris and Meun, *The Romance of the Rose*, 163/9013–62.

42 *Inna al-nisāʾ nawāqiṣ al-īmān nawāqiṣ al-ḥuẓūẓ nawāqiṣ al-ʿuqūl*, in ʿAlī ibn Abi Ṭālib, *Nahj al-balāgha*, 105–6, no. 80; cf. Moḥaqqeq, "Yāddāsht-hā-i," 462. For further discussion of Vis as simultaneously a "proto-feminist" and champion of patriarchal values, see Norozi, *Esordi del romanzo*, 95–6, 106–7.

43 In the *Shāhnāma*, golden vessels appear inside the palaces of Kabul (77), among the gifts of the Greeks (562, 891), and in the hands of Rostam (155, 489) and Bahrām Gur (738); near the end of the story (946), the decadent opulence of the Sasanian court is thrown into stark contrast with the poor but pious Arabs (all page numbers refer to Davis's 2016 translation). Prohibitions against the wearing of brocade and the use of gold and silver vessels can be found in the hadith collections of Bukhārī (5837), Muslim (2065c, 2067g), and al-Tirmidhī (2809); for these and more examples, visit https://sunnah.com/ (accessed 1 June 2022) and search for "gold vessel."

44 Bloch, "The Arthurian Fabliau," 243.

45 The trope about a beautiful woman's uncontrollable fame (and thereby potential shame) appears in the romance of *Varqa & Golshāh*, where the narrator writes tells us that, as the heroine reaches fifteen years of age, "her secret spread among the Arabs" (*begostarda andar ʿarab rāz-e uy*, 8/14).

46 For a comparable scene in ancient Greek novel, see *Kallirhoe* 77/5.2–3. Interestingly, it is a rampant motif in both *Kallirhoe* and the *Ephesiaka* for the heroines to blame their own beautiful bodies for throwing them into misfortune, e.g., "My beauty, my treacherous beauty, you are the cause of all my troubles" (*Kallirhoe* 96/6.6) or "My beauty conspires against me; my charms are fatal!" (*Ephesiaka* 162/5.5). Other examples are found in *Kallirhoe* 37/1.14, 81/5.5, 106/7.5; *Ephesiaka* 144/2.11.

47 Gabrieli, "Note sul *Vīs u Rāmīn*," 172–3.

48 Rouhi, *Mediation and Love*, 178–9.

49 In his research on *V&R*, Minorksy notes the location of the ruined fortress and includes a photograph taken by his colleague, A.C. Edwards; see Minorsky, "Vīs u Rāmīn," 193–4, and the map in the frontmatter.

50 For more on Zoroastrian purity rules surrounding menstruation, see Sadeghi, *The Sin of the Woman*, 90–100. Vis's menstruation on her wedding-day is an interesting twist on a common technique by which romance heroines defend their virginity; when Golshāh is captured by Rabiʿ b. ʿAdnān, for example, she buys herself some time by telling him

that she cannot wait to take him into her embrace – "but I have the excuse of women, and you must give me a week" (*valikan marā hast ᶜozr-e zanān* • *yek-i hafta-am dād bāyad zamān*, 14/12). This is similar to Charikleia's argument that she has consecrated her body to Artemis and must set aside her religious duties before consummating her marriage with Thyamis (*Aithiopika* 372/1.22); see also *Ephesiaka* 146/2.13, 153/3.11, 161/5.4, 163/5.7.

51 See, for example, the *Mihr yašt* ("Hymn to Mithra"), which begins with the statement: "The ruffian who lies unto Mithra (*miθra-druj*) brings death unto the whole country, injuring as much the faithful world as a hundred evil-doers could do"; Müller, *The Zend-Avesta, Part II*, 120. For the many punishments that await those who break their oaths, see chapter 4 of the *Wīdēwdād* in Moazami, *Wrestling with the Demons*, 102–7, 118–21. In prior occasions, too, we see Shahru deeply troubled when she is challenged with the crime of oath breaking (55/76–80 [23]).

52 I feel sorry not to discuss this famous passage in detail, but it would be something of a tangent here. See, instead, the excellent studies of this scene in Meisami, *Medieval Persian Court Poetry*, 103–7, and Kunitzsch, "Description of the Night."

53 The contrast between Shahru and Golshāh's mother in *Varqa & Golshāh*, for example, could not be starker. From the beginning, she is against Varqa marrying her daughter on the grounds that he is too poor, and when the king of Syria's petition to wed Golshāh is turned down by her father, he turns to her avaricious mother and easily wins her over with his promises of untold wealth. The wife, then, tongue-lashes her husband into submission, a favourite topos of misogynist polemic. See ᶜAyyuqi, *Varqa-vo Golshāh*, 72–4 (Melikian-Chirvani 166–7).

54 Pinning down the Nurse's social rank is a somewhat speculative task. The repeated insults from Mobad notwithstanding, it is possible that she owns a bit of property in her native land, for after Vis is born, we are told that "her Nurse brought her to Khuzan, where she had space, home, and abode" (*be khuzān bord u rā dāyegān-ash* • *ke ānjā bud jāy-o khān-o mān-ash*, 43/18 [10]). But in any case, it is safe to say that the Nurse is socially inferior to Shahru, Vis, and the other characters. A general discussion of her role in the story is found in Morrison, "Flowers and Witchcraft," and Davis, "Vis o Rāmin"; some valuable studies on the "nanny" figure more broadly include Milani, "The Mediatory Guile of the Nanny"; Robinson, "Going Between"; Rouhi, *Mediation and Love*; and Southgate, "Vīs and Rāmīn: An Anomaly."

55 For an in-depth discussion of this reconstitution of a "blood-family" (Shahru-Vis-Viru) into a "milk-family" (Nurse-Vis-Rāmin), see Kappler, "*Vîs et Râmîn*," 62–73.

56 There being no grammatical gender inflection in Persian, this phrase *tan-e uy* could describe the demon entering either Rāmin's or the Nurse's body. From the context, however, I think the Nurse is the likely referent.

57 Norozi, *Esordi del romanzo*, 101; for further discussion of the Rāmin-Nurse encounter and its implications, see ibid., 102–4.

58 *Pace* Minoo Southgate, who argues that *Vis & Rāmin* provides a window into a time in pre-Islamic Iran when women of the aristocracy were autonomous and could freely marry and have affairs without fear of reprisal, a notion that Fatemeh Sadeghi calls "entirely ahistorical," the prospect of an extramarital affair was, generally speaking, no laughing matter in the Zoroastrian context either. See Southgate, "Conflict between Islamic Mores," 21–2; Southgate, "Vīs and Rāmīn: An Anomaly," 44–6; Sadeghi, *The Sin of the Woman*, 10. For scenes that detail the many ghastly tortures that adulterers will undergo in Hell, see Asa, Haug, and West, *The Book of Arda Viraf*, chaps. 24, 60, 62, 69, 71, 78, 81, 85, 86, 88 (English translation in 171–98); for a broader review of how attitudes towards adultery shifted in Sasanian and post-Sasanian Zoroastrian writings, see Sadeghi, *The Sin of the Woman*, 120–5.

59 An interesting analogue to Vis's "faithful adultery," though drastically different in its circumstances and consequences, is found in Kallirhoe's "affair" with Dionysius; see Wiersma, "The Ancient Greek Novel and Its Heroines," 117–19.

60 For more on how the Nurse "educates" Vis in the "rules" of love, see the excellent discussion in Rouhi, *Mediation and Love*, 177–9.

61 For discussions of this passage, see Davis, "Introduction," xviii; Southgate, "Vīs and Rāmīn: An Anomaly," 43. This depiction of amorous liberties may be a reflection of Zoroastrian rules around the "self-governing woman" (*xudsarāy*), a specific class who were permitted to have lovers with no legal consequences; Sadeghi suggests this "astonishing" development may have emerged "in the last years of the Sasanian era perhaps due to social pressures and domestic turbulences." See Sadeghi, *The Sin of the Woman*, 79. On a comparative note, the passage also reminds me of the *Mantel Mautaillié* and the *Lai du Corn*, where it is revealed that all the women of Arthur's court, and not just Guenevere, are guilty of adultery; see Bloch, *Medieval Misogyny*, 95–7, and McCracken, *The Romance of Adultery*, 54–65.

62 See, for example, Davis, "Introduction," xviii; Kobidze, "Antecedents," 89; Southgate, "Conflict between Islamic Mores," 21–2; Southgate, "Vīs and Rāmīn: An Anomaly," 43–5.

63 Rāmin's threat to commit suicide if Vis will not accept him as her lover is comparable to Aucassin, who warns he will kill himself if Nicolette leaves him. In both cases, the suicide threat, which is usually directed towards a

hostile world by the lovers in solidarity (e.g., *Pyramus & Thisbe, Floire & Blancheflor*) is here used to manipulate the other member of the loving couple. See Sturges, *Aucassin and Nicolette*, 34–5; and for further discussion, Pensom, *Aucassin et Nicolete*, 57.

64 Leyla Rouhi offers a useful note on the function of the go-between in this context: "It is not so much what the go-between says or does, but the younger party's reactions to it, that defines the definition of seduction in the art of love. Despite the texts' efforts to endow the old woman in particular with an impression of power and skill, her words and actions never gain the status of a paradigm to follow in love: rather they serve to reveal aspects of the lovers' capacity to handle mediation as a concrete act." I take this to mean that the Nurse's standing between Vis and Rāmin affords both characters the space necessary for discovering the complex depths of *themselves* in the course of their negotiations, by proxy, with one another. See Rouhi, *Mediation and Love*, 131; for an example of how *V&R* often treats *mehr* and *ᶜeshq* as a close and possibly interchangeable pair, see *V&R* 117/71–2.

65 For examples of falling in love on sight in Persian love stories, see *Vāmeq & ᶜAẕrā*, 90/84–90, and the tales of Sudāba (217), Manizha (337), Golnār (642), and Maleka (688) in the *Shāhnāma* (page numbers refer to Davis's 2016 translation). Ferdowsi also uses the motif of description in the stories of Zāl and Rudāba (70–3), Kāvus (176), and Tahmina (189). Dreams provide the site for lovers to meet in the stories of Odatis and Zariadres, Neẕāmi's *Khosrow & Shirin*, and Jāmi's *Yusof & Zolaykhā*; for a discussion of this theme in Persian romance, see Davis, *Panthea's Children*, 61–5; in the *1001 Nights*, Gerhardt, *The Art of Story-Telling*, 122–3, and Antrim, "Qamarayn," 8–13; and in the Greek novel, Montiglio, *Love & Providence*, 58, and Morales, *Vision and Narrative*, 156–65.

66 The motif of viewing the beloved from an elevated height, such as from a window, tower, or roof, is well attested in Persian love stories; for a detailed survey of its appearance in the works of Ferdowsi, Gorgāni, Neẕāmi, ᶜAṭṭār, and Khwāju, see Norozi, *Esordi del romanzo*, 280–328.

67 These same implications are beautifully drawn in the "Hall of Statues" scene in Thomas's *Tristran*, where the hero, separated from his beloved Isolde, both marries another Isolde and builds a statue of the original Isolde that he venerates in secret, only adding to the "double pain, double sorrow" (*duble painne, doble dolur*) of possessing two eidolons of Isolde while separated from Isolde herself; see Thomas of Britain, *Tristran*, 54/1050, cf. Gottfried von Strassburg, *Tristan* (tr. Hatto), 317.

68 Quoting Gerhardt, *The Art of Story-Telling*, 129, in her description of the prevailing ethos of the *ᶜudhrī* love-tales in the *1001 Nights*: "Exemplary tales like the specimens just outlined illustrate a very remarkable,

one might say absolutist conception. Love, thus understood, is a final condition, a 'state', admitting neither of change nor of evolution."

69 Bartsch, *The Mirror of the Self*, first introduced in 16–28.

70 Vis's debate with herself is reminiscent of a similar scene in *Kallirhoe*: having been forced into another marriage, the heroine has resolved to commit suicide rather than betray her husband, but she is swayed from this course of action by the knowledge that her unborn son will be the spitting image of Chaireas, and so to die would also constitute betrayal. Thus the rules that demand she die also demand she live, and she can only acquiesce to the latter diktat by channelling her husband's presence: "I call you to witness, Chaireas – it is you who are giving me to Dionysius as his bride" (49/2.11). Another interesting point of comparison is found in Gottfried's description of the battle between "anger" and "womanhood" that takes place in Isolde's heart on realizing the identity of Tristan; see Gottfried von Strassburg, *Tristan* (tr. Hatto), 176.

71 The themes of exile and homelessness are common ones in the love-story mythos, whether in the broad wanderings of Greek novel characters like Habrokomes and Anthia or in the social banishment experienced by ʿudhrī lovers like Majnun. However, Vis's exile rings most strongly (for me) with Gottfried's depiction of Isolde, sailing off to Cornwall to be wedded to Mark: "she wept and lamented amid her tears that she was leaving her homeland, whose people she knew, and all her friends in this fashion, and was sailing away with strangers, she neither knew whither nor how." See Gottfried von Strassburg, ibid., 193.

72 See Hedāyat, "Chand nokta," 518. Michael Muchow discusses how the swearing of oaths, not as a social contract but as a private and personal agreement, is a cornerstone feature in the Greek novels and a mechanism that enforces the themes of parity and reciprocal responsibility between the two lovers; see Muchow, "Passionate Love," 16–20, 140–51.

73 Kottman, *Love as Human Freedom*, 63, emphasis original.

3 Politics: The Prisoner of His Skin

1 For an English translation of this full passage from the *Bahman-nāma*, see Cross, "The Lives and Afterlives," 523.

2 Norozi, *Esordi del romanzo*, 266–7, reaches similar conclusions about Irānshāh's reaction to Vis and Mobad, which she describes as squarely based on the juridical categories of *ḥalāl* and *ḥarām*; see also Norozi, "Il *Vis e Rāmin* di Gorgāni e il *Bahman-nāmé* di Irānshāh," 216.

3 The admonition that princes should limit their interactions with women lest they be dominated by them is a very common topos, found in, e.g.: Ferdowsi, *Shāhnāma*, 2:213/161 (Davis 218); Kay-Kāʾus, *Qābus-nāma* (ed.

Yusofi), 131 (Levy 119); Nezām al-Molk, *The Book of Government*, 185; Ṭusi, *Akhlāq-e nāṣeri*, 319 (Wickens 164). For further discussion, see Southgate, "Conflict between Islamic Mores," 22–6.

4 Graf, "Wîs und Râmîn," 378. My thanks to Rodrigo Adem for his assistance with this translation.

5 My summary is cited from the translations made by Minorsky, "Vīs u Rāmīn," 190–2, and Kaladze, "The Georgian Translation," 139; for the Russian original, see von Stackelberg, "Neskol'ko slov o persidskom epose 'Visa i Ramin.'"

6 Massé, "Introduction," 15–16.

7 Minorsky, "Vīs u Rāmīn," 187; Rypka, *History of Iranian Literature*, 178.

8 Bürgel, "Die Liebesvorstellung," 75–6, 80–2; Bürgel, "The Romance," 165; Meisami, *Medieval Persian Court Poetry*, 139; Meisami, "Kings and Lovers," 4–5; Southgate, "Vīs and Rāmīn: An Anomaly," 46–7.

9 Kappler, "*Vîs et Râmîn*," 67–8; Kappler, "Présence du mazdéisme," 48–51; Shayegan, "Old Iranian Motifs," 34–8.

10 Propp, *Morphology of the Folktale*, 27–8; Hedāyat, "Chand nokta," 487; cf. Piri, "Gera-dāstāni," 70. The romance of *Varqa & Golshāh* offers two good examples of familiar Villain/Obstacle roles: Rabiᶜ b. ᶜAdnān, who abducts Golshāh against her parents' wishes, and the King of Damascus, who marries her with their blessing. Rabiᶜ is irredeemable and must eventually be killed (Golshāh does the deed), whereas the King, in his nobility, gets (literally) converted by the quality of the protagonists' love. The obstacle that these figures present, then, is removed either by death or by conversion.

11 Davis, "Vis o Rāmin"; see also Davis, "Introduction," xxx.

12 Van Ruymbeke, "Wretched King Mobad"; Cross, "A Tree Atop the Mountain."

13 Zumthor, *Toward a Medieval Poetics*, 4.

14 While admitting that my command of psychoanalytic theory is wholly amateur, I am often surprised by the sense of affinity I perceive when comparing Lacan's account of the mirror stage to the arguments I make about subject formation here and in the other chapters of this book: he points at the exact process of misunderstanding (*méconnaissance*) the mirror image *as* the self, and the subsequent self-alienation that arises from it, that I am trying to get at here, though naturally by a very different method. The ramifications of this misrecognition are equally apropos in both cases: if we take Lacan's descriptions of the specular image as an immobile and timeless "statue," the libidinous desire for which heralds the subject's entry into the symbolic order – or as "a 'double' that confers not truth, but 'illusion'" that forces the subject to confront the gap between these two visions, producing "fantasies of dismemberment, of dislocations

of the body, of castration" – and we can readily see how well this language applies to the case of Mobad in *Vis & Rāmin*. Quotes are from Murray, *Jacques Lacan*, 99–100, 116–17, which offers a novice-friendly overview of the mirror stage; for more technical discussions, see Evans, *An Introductory Dictionary of Lacanian Psychoanalysis*, 67–8, 117–19, 193; Fink, *The Lacanian Subject*, 36–7, 51–3; Grosz, *Jacques Lacan*, 32–43.

15 Minorsky speculates that "Manikān," which appears a few times in *V&R* (38/1, 40/30, 65/7), might be a matronym for Manizha, the Turanian wife of the Iranian hero Bizhan, making Mobad part of the Kārenid family line of Godarz-Giv-Bizhan; see Minorsky, "Vīs u Rāmīn," 182–6; cf. Pourshariati, "Kārin." While we must remain cautious of such historicizing identifications, this connection does offer an interesting intersection with Khaleghi-Motlagh's hypothesis that the romances of *Vis & Rāmin* and *Bizhan & Manizha* are part of the same Marv-Gorgan family of Parthian narratives; see Khaleghi-Motlagh, "Bīžan"; Khaleghi-Motlagh, "Bizhan-o Manizha," 286. An alternative reading for Manikān as "he who has authority" is offered by Shayegan, "Old Iranian Motifs," 40.

16 For the additional lines attesting to Mobad's power, preserved in the Istanbul manuscript, see *V&R* 32–3n5.

17 See Al-Azmeh, *Muslim Kingship*, 3. Other useful studies that explore, in a diachronic and art-historical fashion, the visual, literary, and ritual representation of the King of Kings in Middle Eastern contexts include Babaie and Grigor, *Persian Kingship and Architecture*; L'Orange, *Studies*; Soudavar, *The Aura of Kings*.

18 For studies on Achaemenid enunciations of world-kingship, see Briant, *From Cyrus to Alexander*, 217–54; Root, *The King and Kingship*; Root, "Defining the Devine"; Skjærvø, "The Achaemenids and the *Avesta*"; Waters, "To Be or Not to Be (Divine)." For the same topic in the Sasanian period, see Canepa, *The Two Eyes of the Earth*; Daryaee, "Kingship in Early Sasanian Iran."

19 For discussions of ritual enunciations of sacral-universal kingship in the late Umayyad and Abbasid contexts, particularly in connection with the performance of the qasida, see Ali, "Praise for Murder," 7–13; Ali, *Arabic Literary Salons*, 81–87; Crone, *God's Rule*, 40–2, 163–4; Sperl, "Islamic Kingship," 20–5; Sperl, *Mannerism*, 13–27; Stetkevych, *The Poetics of Islamic Legitimacy*.

20 For studies on the adoption and Islamicization of Sasanian-style titulature and ceremony by tenth-century Muslim rulers, see Busse, "The Revival of Persian Kingship"; Madelung, "The Assumption of the Title Shāhānshāh"; Richter-Bernburg, "Amīr-Malik-Shāhānshāh"; Tor, "The Long Shadow"; Treadwell, "*Shāhānshāh* and *al-Malik al-Mu'ayyad*." For the Seljuk context, see Durand-Guédy, "Ruling from the Outside"; Peacock, *The Great Seljuk Empire*, 136–8.

21 For more on the celebration of Nowruz in the Sasanian context, see
    Canepa, *The Two Eyes of the Earth*, 11–17. A survey of the sources that
    depict the celebration of Nowruz within Abbasid, Tahirid, Buyid,
    Samanid, and Ghaznavid courtly environments is provided in Shahbazi,
    "Nowruz ii. In the Islamic Period"; and for some specific examples of the
    latter context, see Bayhaqi, *History*, 1:98, 2:210, 2:303.

22 For detailed analyses of these friezes, see Briant, *From Cyrus to Alexander*, 174–
    8; Lincoln, "The Role of Religion"; Root, *The King and Kingship*, 86–95, 227–84.
    It should be stressed that in the Achaemenid case, there is no evidence that
    these reliefs depict an *actual* (Nowruz) ceremony of gift giving, and should
    rather be taken as an abstract representation of the king's relationship to his
    subject peoples; Lincoln's reading of the reliefs as an inverse tower of Babel,
    the "*con*-tributions of things that had been *dis*-tributed as a result of the Lie's
    assault" (232), is particularly interesting. Nonetheless, the Achaemenids were
    known for holding such ceremonies wherever they held court, as Herodotus,
    Xenophon, Aelian, and other classical sources inform us: "Is there any city or
    people of Asia that didn't send embassies to the king? Is there any produce or
    any fine and valuable product of their workshops that they did not bring as
    gifts to lay down before the king?" writes Theopompus of Chios. See Briant,
    From Cyrus to Alexander, 191–5.

23 The Achaemenids were largely known in medieval Islamic tradition
    through Jewish and some Zoroastrian accounts, which many
    contemporary historians tried to reconcile. Al-Ṭabarī, for example, situates
    one "Kay Ārish, son of Akhashwīrush" (> Heb. *Kerosh* > Per./Ar. *Kūrush*,
    Gr. Cyrus) in the reigns of Goshtāsp and Bahman Ardashir, as the father
    of Dārāb (= Darius I?) and grandfather of Dārā (= Darius III), though he
    claims he was never a king proper but rather the local ruler of Khuzestan
    on behalf of Bahman; see al-Ṭabarī, *The Ancient Kingdoms*, 51, 85–6. Ḥamza
    al-Iṣfahānī reports that some "Israelites" (*isrāʾīliyyūn*), perhaps also
    understood as transmitters of Jewish lore, identify Bahman and Cyrus as
    one and the same; see al-Iṣfahānī, *Tārīkh sanī mulūk al-arḍ*, 37 (Hoyland 53).

24 For more discussion of the Achaemenid solar crown, see Root, "Defining
    the Devine," 37–40. For more on the *farr*, see Al-Azmeh, *Muslim Kingship*,
    17; Gnoli, "Farr(ah)"; Soudavar, *The Aura of Kings*; Yarshater, "Iranian
    National History," 345; and finally Azarpay, "Crowns and Some Royal
    Insignia in Early Iran," 113–15, who, returning to the iconography of the
    crown, reminds us not to over-read these symbols "as the expression of
    an early Iranian theocracy headed by a god-king" but rather to attend to
    their historical and metaphorical functions in politics and court protocol (a
    position shared by Daryaee, "Kingship in Early Sasanian Iran," 60–1).

25 Yūsuf Khāṣṣ Ḥājib, *Wisdom of Royal Glory*, 1.

26 Ibid., 66.

27	For a discussion of the king-as-sun metaphor in the *Qābus-nāma*, see
	Amirsoleimani, "Of This World and the Next," 8–9. For more on justice as
	the "crowning, ultimate male virtue," see Ayubi, *Gendered Morality*, 96–103.

28	For more on the Sasanian legacy in medieval Islamic political theory, see
	Lambton, "Islamic Mirrors for Princes," esp. 421–3.

29	For a close reading of the phrase *čihr az yazdān*, see Daryaee, "Kingship
	in Early Sasanian Iran," 61. For further discussion of the significance of
	čihr as the "face" or "likeness" of the gods, establishing the kingly face as
	a reflection of the divine, see Soudavar, *The Aura of Kings*, 42–8; Canepa,
	The Two Eyes of the Earth, 101. For more on this concept's connection with
	the Achaemenid period, see Briant, *From Cyrus to Alexander*, 240–5, 551;
	Root, "Defining the Devine," 50–4. For a diachronic overview linking
	Zoroastrian, Achaemenid, and Sasanian enunciations of sacral kingship
	into the Islamic notion of the "shadow of God," as it was expressed under
	Abbasid, Buyid, Seljuk, and Mongol imperiums, see Arjomand, *The Shadow
	of God*, 89–100.

30	For the cited examples of this proverb, see: Ferdowsi, *Shāhnāma*, 6:231/552–
	3 (Davis 677), also 8:458/552; Tansar, Ibn al-Muqaffaᶜ, and Moḥammad b.
	al-Ḥasan b. Esfandiyār, *Nāma-ye Tansar*, 53 (Boyce 33–4); Ikhwān al-Ṣafāʾ,
	Rasāʾil, 2:368 (Goodman and McGregor 303); al-Ghazālī, *Iḥyāʾ ᶜulūm al-
	dīn*, 1:67; Neẓām al-Molk, *The Book of Government*, 63; Yūsuf Khāṣṣ Ḥājib,
	Wisdom of Royal Glory, 32, 226. So too will Gorgāni begin his encomium in
	V&R by listing three interconnected "commands" (*farmān*) that will ensure
	joy in this world and salvation in the next: the command of God, the
	command of the Prophet, and the command of the Seljuk sultan Ṭughrıl
	Beg, in whose sovereignty the splendour of God's religion is manifest (*be
	molk andar bahā-ye din-e dādār*, 10/7).

31	Some critics did not buy the association of Mobad's name with the
	Zoroastrian priesthood, believing the overlap between New Persian
	mobad and Middle Persian *mowbed* a mere coincidence. Sādeq Hedāyat
	argues that Gorgāni "made this name a substitute for another for the
	reason of poetic necessity" (i.e., metre) or as an allusion (*kenāya*), while
	Vladimir Minorsky suggests the etymology *marġu-pati-š*, "lord of Marġu
	(later Marv)"; see Hedāyat, "Chand nokta," 489, and Minorsky, "Vīs u
	Rāmīn," 185, respectively. Rahim Shayegan, however, offers the etymology
	magu-pati, "[chief] magus, priest," which to me seems more convincing;
	see Shayegan, "Old Iranian Motifs," 35. (Co-)incidentally, *rad* (Av.
	Ratu-), "religious reformer," was a title of Zoroaster and also of Kirdēr,
	the influential Sasanian high priest who consolidated Nowruz in state
	ceremony; see Arjomand, *The Shadow of God*, 90, Boyce, "Nowruz i. In the
	Pre-Islamic Period."

32	Humbach and Ichaporia, *Zamyād Yasht*, 103; Hinnells, *Persian Mythology*, 39.

33 Translation of Yasna (Hom Yašt) 9.4 in Müller, *The Zend-Avesta, Part III*,
    232. For further discussion of Yima/Jam's immortality, see Hinnells, *Persian
    Mythology*, 39; Boyce, *Textual Sources*, 10; Skjærvø, "Jamšid i. Myth of
    Jamšid." This deathless "golden age" imagery has interesting resonances
    with Hesiod ("No toil or misery was theirs; to them there never came
    / Wretched old age," 112–13) and the *Mahābhārata* ("It was Vishva·karman
    who built Yama's great hall ... In it there is no grief or aging, hunger or
    thirst, nor any affliction, weariness or ugliness," 2.8.1–5). See Hesiod,
    Theogony, 60; Vyasa, *Mahābhārata*, 87.
34 For accounts of Jamshid's deeds as king, see *Dēnkard* 7.1.20–4, translated
    in Müller, *Pahlavi Texts, Part V*, 9–10; al-Ṭabarī, *From the Creation to the
    Flood*, 350; al-Thaᶜālibī, *Histoire*, 10–13 (with an explicit comparison with
    Solomon, cf. Kisāʾī, *Tales of the Prophets*, 302–3); Ferdowsi, *Shāhnāma*,
    1:41/10–31 (Davis 6). An extensive compilation of other Avestan and
    Middle Persian writings on this topic is found in Humbach and Ichaporia,
    Zamyād Yasht, 103–9.
35 For similar stories of Jamshid's flight to heaven, see al-Bīrūnī, *The
    Chronology of Ancient Nations*, 200/29–35, 201/36, 202/13; al-Thaᶜālibī,
    Histoire, 13–14; al-Ṭabarī, *From the Creation to the Flood*, 349–50. The motif is
    discussed further in Abdullaeva, "Kingly Flight."
36 As Mary Boyce notes, this reference to Nowruz is, at least indirectly, the
    earliest literary record of the festival extant, given *V&R*'s roots in the
    Parthian era; see Boyce, "Nowruz i. In the Pre-Islamic Period."
37 Jamshid's fall is narrated in the *Shāhnāma*, 1:45/64–74 (Davis 7–8); it may
    be compared with Humbach and Ichaporia, *Zamyād Yasht*, 37/19.30–8. For
    a summary of other accounts, see Curtis, *Persian Myths*, 25–6; Hinnells,
    Persian Mythology, 39–43.
38 To be clear, I base the connections I see between the snake (*aži*), the
    demon(ess) Āz/Āzi, and the serpent-king Aži-Dahāka (> Żaḥḥāk)
    on thematic and not ontological grounds; the three are quite distinct
    and should not be conflated. However, when one compares how the
    snake is the first counter-creation of Ahriman and the harbinger of
    Winter (Wīdēwdād 1.3), how Āzi is associated with consumption and
    destruction (Wīdēwdād 18.19–22, Bundahishn 27.34), and how Aži-
    Dahāka seeks to empty the world of men (Abān Yašt 5.29–30, Rām Yašt
    15.19–20), it is easy to see how the three entities share a close thematic
    alignment; see Moazami, *Wrestling*, 30–1, 406–9; Müller, *The Zend-Avesta,
    Part I*, 3–4, 198; and Müller, *The Zend-Avesta, Part II*, 60–1, 253–4, for
    references. For more on the imbrication of desire and destruction in Āz/
    Āzi and Aži-Dahāka, see Asmussen, "Āz"; Choksy, *Evil, Good and Gender*,
    42–4; Cross, "If Death Is Just," 412–15; Lasman, "Dragons, Fairies, and
    Time," 241–2; Skjærvø, Khaleghi-Motlagh, and Russell, "Aždahā."

39 For a discussion of *barā‘at-e estehlāl*, see Kazzāzi, *Zibā-shenāsi*, 3:156–8.
   The classic example of this technique is Ferdowsi's famous prologue to
   the story of Rostam and Sohrāb in the *Shāhnāma*, 2:117/1–6 (Davis 187),
   with a brilliant analysis by Gabri, "Framing the Unframable in Ferdowsi's
   Shahnameh."

40 Hojviri, *Kashf al-maḥjub*, 575 (Nicholson 398).

41 For a comparable scene in the Greek novel tradition, cf. *Ephesiaka* 129/1.2,
   where a similar procession of maidens, "dressed as if to receive a lover,"
   precedes the introduction of the story's heroine, Anthia. For more on
   the erotics of the gaze in late antiquity, see Bartsch, *The Mirror of the Self*,
   67–83; and in the Islamic context, Bell, *Love Theory*, 125–47; Giffen, *Theory of
   Profane Love*, 117–32; and more recently, Ingenito, *Beholding Beauty*.

42 The erotic overtones of this banter, along with the possibility that Shahru is
   genuinely interested in Mobad as a sexual partner, are intensified in some
   manuscripts of *V&R*, when the narrator tells us in an aside that "whenever
   she joined with her impotent husband [Qāren], his 'cypress' grew as limp
   as a withered branch" (*cho bā joft-e ‘anin-e khwish payvast • cho shākh-e
   khoshk gashta sarv-e u past*, 41/48) – an interesting prefiguration of Mobad's
   own impotence later on. This line could also raise questions about the
   parentage of Shahru's many children (is Qāren impotent now, or has he
   always been so?), which could be further compared with Mobad's (angry?
   exaggerated?) claim that every one of Shahru's thirty-plus children were
   fathered by a different husband (179/46 [141]); but these are somewhat
   tangential questions to the present argument.

43 Hägg and Utas, *The Virgin and Her Lover*, 104/176 (the translation
   is unchanged except that I switched the order of the clauses); Kay-
   Kā’us, *Qābus-nāma* (ed. Yusofi), 83 (Levy 73). Other testaments to the
   relationship between love and youth are found across a wide spectrum of
   medieval and classical sources; in the *Symposium*, for example, Agathon
   says, "Love was born to hate old age and will come nowhere near it. Love
   always lives with young people and is one of them: the old story holds
   good that like is always drawn to like" (195b). See also Sa‘di, *Gulistan*,
   126/6.2, where a young woman declares she would rather take an arrow
   (*tir*) in her side (with obvious sexual implications) than an old man (*pir*).

44 Similar cases of noblewomen in public positions of authority who adopt
   and acquire a persona distinctly different from that of more typical
   female roles such as mother, wife, or beloved are seen in the characters
   Sindokht, Homāy, Qaydāfa, and Gordiya in the *Shāhnāma*: see pp. 83–96,
   549–60, 598–611, 870–917 in Davis's translation; also Davis, "Women in the
   Shahnameh." An interesting historical instance of this, relatively close to
   Gorgāni's time and milieu, is the Georgian Queen T'amar (r. 1184–1213),

who was typically heralded as "King" (*mep'e*) by writers such as Rust'aveli (see *The Knight in the Panther Skin*, 1/¶4).

45 We first learn of Shahru's descent from Jamshid from the Nurse as she tells Rāmin about Vis (125/202 [87]); it pops up again later as Mobad curses Shahru's "impious" (*bad-kish*) family (179/44–50 [142]), and again when Mobad's mother remarks that the only worthy thing about Vis is her lineage (190/31–2 [153]). The Georgian *Visramiani*, in contrast, makes the connection obvious from the outset; right after Shahru pledges the yet-unborn Vis to Mobad, the narrator adds, "Shahro's husband was Qaran. But Shahro was of nobler blood than Qaran; she was the offspring of king Djimshed, who was the fifth king after Adam." See T'mogveli, *Visramiani*, 7.

46 For more on the convergence of the roles of Priest and King to form the Perfect Man, see Meisami, *Medieval Persian Court Poetry*, 233, and the surrounding discussion.

47 For more on medieval Islamic embryology, see Musallam, "The Human Embryo in Arabic Scientific and Religious Thought," esp. 32–4 on Aristotle and Avicenna.

48 A seminal study of the "bond" as it pertains to kingship and friendship is Mottahedeh, *Loyalty and Leadership*; for some recent studies on the bonds and etiquette of friendship, especially as it spills over into the public sphere, see Babayan, *The City as Anthology*, esp. 112–17, 137–63, 177–95; Kia, *Persianate Selves*, esp. 57–62, 163–90; Mottahedeh, "Friendship in Islamic Ethical Philosophy"; Tobkin, "A Man of Our Times," esp. 303–8, 315–20.

49 Yūsuf Khāṣṣ Ḥājib, *Wisdom of Royal Glory*, 65–6.

50 For more on the tight imbrication of kingship and justice, see Ohlander, "Enacting Justice, Ensuring Salvation." A good example of an oath-breaking king in Persian literature is Goshtāsp, who repeatedly reneges on his promise to turn the throne over to his son Esfandiyār, leading to the latter's tragic encounter with Rostam. With his dying breath, Esfandiyār accuses his father of injustice (*bar man ze goshtāsp āmad setam*, 5:423/1501 [Davis 525]), a sin that not only undermines his own authority but seems to haunt his descendants down to their overthrow by Alexander.

51 For an interesting illustration of how a royal presence could be made manifest in a piece of paper, see Ibn Faḍlān, "Mission to the Volga," 217/§40, where the Abbasid ambassador insists to the Bulghar king that all must rise during the reading of the caliph's letter.

52 Yūsuf Khāṣṣ Ḥājib, *Wisdom of Royal Glory*, 166.

53 Kantorowicz, *The King's Two Bodies*, 39.

54 For a similar inversion of the imagery of springtime life and wartime destruction, see the famous prologue to the story of Rostam and Esfandiyār in Ferdowsi, *Shāhnāma*, 5:292/9–13 (Clinton 29–30).

55 Meisami, *Medieval Persian Court Poetry*, 100. For insightful discussions of this battle scene's imagery, see Meisami, ibid., 97–101; Davis, "Introduction," xxvii–xviii.

56 See Gabrieli, "Note sul *Vīs u Rāmīn*," 176; also his "Sul poema persiano *Vīs u Rāmīn*," 254.

57 Meisami, "Kings and Lovers," 5; cf. Meisami, *Medieval Persian Court Poetry*, 139.

58 T'mogveli, *Visramiani*, 59.

59 For further discussion of the talisman that "binds" Mobad, see Morrison, "Flowers and Witchcraft," 255, and Norozi, *Esordi del romanzo*, 182–90; the latter includes some intriguing notes about the Galenic properties of the materials used.

60 For a discussion of the parallels between Vis and Katāyun, Mobad and Bahman, see Norozi, "Il *Vis e Rāmin* di Gorgāni e il *Bahman-nāmé* di Irānshāh"; Ruyāni, "Tashābohāt," 76–7.

61 Though the common-sense taboo against kin killing need hardly be elaborated, there are numerous moments·in the *Shāhnāma* that testify just how serious an offence it is in this literary context. In addition to the death of Esfandiyār, discussed above, Ferdowsi writes passionately against Rostam's combat with his son Sohrāb (2:171/670–3 [Davis 204]) and Sām's abandonment of his son Zāl (1:167/75–9, 100–2 [Davis 64–5]); the latter can be compared with Irānshāh b. Abi al-Khayr, *Kush-nāma*, 228/1445–9, 249/1855–64. Notably, it is an act of patricide that announces the rise of the tyrannical Żaḥḥāk, and an act of fratricide that sets off the generations-long blood feud between Iran and Turan.

62 That Rāmin has designs on both Mobad's office and his life is hardly a secret. While hiding from Mobad after the ordeal by fire, he writes to inform his mother that if the king doesn't abdicate soon, "I'll throw him down from his throne, and sit upon it with my beloved; mark my words, it will be sooner than later!" (213/35–6 [175]). Later on, he announces to Vis, "My heart is now telling me: 'Pull your feet out of the mud! Go down and cast Mobad's head from his body; rid the world of his lowly nature! By my life, the blood of this brother is less to me than a cat's!'" (231/241–3 [194]).

63 Kantorowicz, *The King's Two Bodies*, 95–7.

64 For a more in-depth discussion of this 'backfiring' process, see Cross, "A Tree Atop the Mountain," xli–xliv.

65 The story of the chaste youth and the lustful stepmother is catalogued as motif K 2111 in Stith Thompson's *Motif-Index of Folk-Literature*. For a

comparative overview of prominent instances of this motif, see Yohannan, *Joseph and Potiphar's Wife in World Literature*.

66 Gottfried von Strassburg, *Tristan* (ed. Marold), 257/15250–70 (Hatto 242).

67 Žižek, *The Sublime Object of Ideology*, 15.

68 In translating this line, I am working from Gvakahria's 1995 emendation from *bedānestam ke bar bidād kardand*, "I knew they were committing injustice" to *nadānestam*, "I did *not* know ... "; see Gvaxaria, "Notes on the Persian Text," 59–60.

69 For a comparison of the ordeal by fire between *V&R* and the Tristan cycle, see Norozi, *Esordi del romanzo*, 389–92; Eslāmi-Nodushan, "Vis va Izut," 147–8. Dick Davis has frequently indicated this scene alongside a number of other shared motifs as evidence of a possible connection between the two narratives: see Davis, "Vis o Rāmin"; Davis, "Introduction," xxxv–xlii; Davis, "A Trout in the Milk," 48–9. For a recent survey of the *V&R-Tristan* debate, see Cross, "The Lives and Afterlives," 536–7, and associated endnotes; two studies not mentioned there (neither of which accept a "genetic" link between the two cycles) are Nagy, "The Celtic 'Love Triangle' Revisited"; Rowland, "Trystan and Esyllt." As Davis notes, the ordeal is a common topos in the Greek novels, such as a trial by water in *Leukippe & Kleitophon* (281/8.14) and others by fire in the *Aithiopika* (526/8.9) and *Rhodanthe & Dosikles* (Jeffreys 31/1.374–89); see Davis, *Panthea's Children*, 83–104. It also occurs in Genesis 38, again in connection with prostitution/adultery.

70 For the consequences of Bahrām Gur's withdrawal from political life, see Ferdowsi, *Shāhnāma*, 6:523/1423–36 (Davis 755). A much more striking version of this is found in Neẓāmi's *Haft paykar*, in which the plunder of Bahrām's kingdom during his seclusion forms one of the didactic centrepieces of the story: see Neẓāmi Ganjavi, *Heft Peiker*, 265/40.1–73 (Meisami 236–9), discussed in Meisami, *Medieval Persian Court Poetry*, 221–2 and 231–2.

71 In Lacanian terms, one might say that the body of Vis has taken on the position of becoming, rather than merely having, the object of the king's desire (the phallus); for more on this shift, see Grosz, *Jacques Lacan*, 71.

72 Ahmed, *What Is Islam?*, 11–12, 20–2, 349–52.

73 On the relationship between renunciation and sovereignty, we might again recall the example of Majnun, who – though not an old man – becomes king-like through his extreme asceticism; as his uncle tells him, "Anyone who contents himself with [eating] shrubs as you do becomes king of his world." See Neẓāmi Ganjavi, *Layli-o Majnun*, 217/46.31–45 (Gelpke 173, Davis 167). For more on Majnun's ascent to kingly status, see Seyed-Gohrab, *Laylī and Majnūn*, 115–25.

74 For one example of Avicenna's discussion of the animal soul, see
    Fackenheim, "A Treatise on Love," 216–18; cf. Ingenito, *Beholding Beauty*,
    313, 367–8. A broader survey of the concupiscent faculty in ethical (*akhlāq*)
    manuals is found in Ayubi, *Gendered Morality*, 90–6.

75 The mis-recognition of good things for the Good is an important theme
    in Neoplatonist metaphysics – e.g., Boethius's *Consolation of Philosophy*
    (20/1.6pr.21, 67/3.9pr.4–21, 76/3.10pr.28–39) – and it would later serve as
    one of the central objects of focus in Sufi thought and poetry. The famous
    frame tale of ʿAṭṭār's *Conference of the Birds*, for example, ends with thirty
    birds (*si morgh*) mis-/recognizing themselves as the divine Simorgh whom
    they sought; see O'Malley, "Poetry and Pedagogy," 167–71.

76 For a discussion of the internalization of *āz* in the *Shāhnāma*, see Cross, "If
    Death Is Just," 412–15.

77 While the parallels between Mobad and Ṭughrıl provide a useful contrast
    in modelling kingship, I would not take this coincidence as far as Marijan
    Molé, who argues that the presentation of Mobad's interactions with
    other political actors produces an allegory about the fortunes of the
    Seljukid state under Ṭughrıl Beg; see Molé, "«Vīs u Rāmīn» et l'histoire
    seldjoukide," 8–20. While I have no doubt that Gorgāni composed *V&R* as
    a didactic text, I don't think it was done in such a way as to be applicable
    only to Ṭughrıl's circumstances, especially since his primary patron was
    Abu al-Fatḥ, the governor of Isfahan. For another response to Molé's
    argument, see Minorsky, "Vis-u Rāmin (IV)," 282–5.

78 Gorgāni, *V&R* (tr. Massé), 16.

79 The full date, as the narrator provides it, is the day of Khordād (= the
    sixth day) of Ordibehesht (*mah-e ordibehesht-o ruz-e khordād*, 299/1). As the
    second month of the Iranian calendar, Ordibehesht is typically emblematic
    of high spring (e.g., Daqiqi's famous celebration of the month in his *Divān*,
    105/1221–32, translated in Lewis, "Shifting Allegiances," 366–7) and thus
    topologically connected with both political and amorous occasions; cf.
    Meisami, "Allegorical Gardens"; Sharlet, "A Garden of Possibilities." There
    has been some discussion about whether such calendrical references could
    be used for more precise datings of the poem, but this is a tricky business;
    for a survey of the complexities involved, see Minorsky, "Vis-u Rāmin
    (IV)," 280–2; Panaino, "Calendars i. Pre-Islamic Calendars."

80 For more on the minstrel (*gosān*) in pre-Islamic Iran, see Boyce, "The
    Parthian *Gōsān*"; Boyce, "Gōsān."

81 For comparative purposes, the dream of Nushin-Ravān is narrated as
    follows: "He saw in his dream that a kingly tree had sprouted up from
    before the throne. The king's heart was gladdened (*shahnshāh rā del
    biyārāsti*), and he called for wine, music, and singers. By his side, in that
    place of peace and delight, sat a sharp-tusked boar. When it sat and made

ready for wine-drinking, it requested the wine from Nushin-Ravān's cup!"
Ferdowsi, *Shāhnāma*, 7:167/986–9 (Davis 798–801).

82 In an interesting study of the minstrel scene, Claude-Claire Kappler
contends that the tree does not actually represent Mobad (contra the
gosān's own exposition, 301/32), but rather the primordial Tree of All
Seeds in Zoroastrian mythology, with possible connections with the
Islamic Tree of Ṭubā under whose shadow Rāmin's kingdom flourishes
(524/51); the appearance of the bull in this allegory may then figure
the cosmic sacrifice of the sacred ox that destroys Winter (Mobad) and
restores the Spring (Rāmin). See Kappler, "Présence du mazdéisme," 45–8;
cf. Boyce, *Textual Sources*, 11.

83 The notions of the carnival and the anti-rite are developed by Mikhail
Bakhtin and Mary Douglas, respectively; for a discussion of both elements
in the context of Menippean satire and the Greek novel, see Branham, "The
Poetics of Genre."

84 Kantorowicz, *The King's Two Bodies*, 30.

85 For a comparable discussion of how the interpenetration of dual "private"
and "public" personae instigates a process of self-alienation and self-defeat
in *Kallirhoe*'s Dionysios, see Whitmarsh, "Dialogues in Love," 119–24. An
even closer analogy, in terms of narrative structure, is found in King Mark
of the Tristan cycle, but his doom is spared by the premature deaths of
Tristan and Isolde.

86 Xenophon, *The Education of Cyrus*, 142/5.1.8–16; Kay-Kāʾus, *A Mirror for
Princes*, 73–4; Neẓām al-Molk, *The Book of Government*, 185–92.

87 Kay-Kāʾus, *Qābus-nāma* (ed. Yusofi), 85 (Levy 75); cf. Richter-Bernburg,
"Plato of Mind and Joseph of Countenance," 284.

88 For the variant readings of *moʾmen* versus *mardom*, compare Kay-Kāʾus,
Qābus-nāma (ed. Yusofi), 85; Kay-Kāʾus, *Qābus-nāma* (ed. Nafisi), 59. This
same proverb appears later in the poetry of Saᶜdi of Shiraz (*har ke ᶜāsheq
nabud mard nashod*): see Saᶜdi, *Ghazal-hā-ye Saᶜdi*, 112/240.2. I consider the
implications this line has for images of ideal manhood in Cross, "A Tree
Atop the Mountain," l–lv.

89 For Aristotle on *logos*, see *De anima*, 26/2.414a, and for its connection with
noṭq, see Gutas, *Avicenna and the Aristotelian Tradition*, 307–8.

90 For the deaths of Yazdgerd and Bahman, see Ferdowsi, *Shāhnāma*,
6:387/339–51 (Davis 718–19), and Irānshāh b. Abi al-Khayr, *Bahman-
nāma*, 600/10380–405 respectively. The latter scene is discussed in detail in
Lasman, "Dragons, Fairies, and Time," 331–41.

91 Müller, *The Zend-Avesta, Part II*, 137/18.70–2; see also 153/31.127 for a
similar image. In another interesting connection, Morrison notes the
dream-vision of a monstrous boar who ravages Mark's bed (but not the
king himself) in Gottfried von Strassburg, *Tristan* (tr. Hatto), 219–20; see

Gorgāni, *V&R* (tr. Morrison), 343n1. Kappler ("Présence du mazdéisme," 52–3) also suggests a comparison with the boar in the *Roman de Mélusine* by the fourteenth-century writer Jean d'Arras.

92 See Ferdowsi, *Shāhnāma*, 1:52/175 (Davis 13); al-Ṭabarī, *From the Creation to the Flood*, 352; al-Thaᶜālibī, *Histoire*, 17; Agostini and Thrope, *The Bundahišn*, 185/35.5.

93 For a comparative study of "illicit rage" in the *Shāhnāma*, specifically the story of Rostam and Sohrāb, see Cross, "If Death Is Just."

4 Affect: The Limits of Lyric

1 T'odua, "Yek do sokhan," xxv. The story of Samak has recently been translated into English by Freydoon Rassouli and Jordan Mechner; see Arrajāni, *Samak the Ayyar*.

2 Meisami, *Medieval Persian Court Poetry*, 141; cf. Meisami, "Kings and Lovers," 5.

3 For a discussion of the impact of the story of Laylā and Majnūn in Abbasid cultural production, see Khan, *Bedouin and 'Abbāsid Cultural Identities*. An important study laying out the connections between Abbasid, Andalusian, and Provençal lyric is Menocal, *The Arabic Role*, 27–38; see also Barry, "In the Worlds of Nizāmī," 99–107; Reynolds, "Arab Musical Influence on Medieval Europe"; Sells, "Love."

4 ᶜAbd-Allāhiyān, "Az farādast," 123; cf. T'odua, "Yek do sokhan," xxv.

5 Meisami, "Persona and Generic Conventions," 127–34; Bürgel, "Die Liebesvorstellung," 88. For more discussion of this "pious rogue" figure, see de Bruijn, *Persian Sufi Poetry*, 54–76; de Bruijn, "The *Qalandariyyāt*"; Graham, "Abū Saᶜīd"; Ilahi-Ghomshei, "The Principles," 90–94; Lewis, "Hafez viii. Hafez and Rendi"; Miller, "The Poetics of the Sufi Carnival"; Shafiᶜi-Kadkani, *Qalandariya dar tārikh*.

6 Gaunt, "Romance and Other Genres," 45.

7 Boulton, *The Song in the Story*, 274.

8 Parker, *Inescapable Romance*, 4–14; Fuchs, *Romance*, 31.

9 Bakhtin, *The Dialogic Imagination*, 49. For more on Bakhtin's distinction between "novel" and "novelistic," see Frow, *Genre*, 73; Holquist, "Introduction," xxxi. The applicability of Bakhtinian approaches to premodern narratives has been productively taken up in Branham, *The Bakhtin Circle*, and for an account of the ties between ancient, medieval, and modern "novelistic" texts (whether we call them novels or romances), see Doody, *The True Story*.

10 For discussions on the various functions and effects of lyric insertions in the Old French romance, see Gaunt, "Romance and Other Genres," 45–7;

Segre, "What Bakhtin Left Unsaid," 30–1; and especially Boulton, *The Song in the Story*.

11 "Floating timeline" is a phrase used in TV serials like *The Simpsons*, where the characters never age and there's a consistent *status quo* that each episode resets to, regardless of the outcome of the previous episode. In the same vein, Frye, *Anatomy of Criticism*, 186, invokes the "refrigerated deathlessness" of comic-strip characters.

12 Bakhtin, *The Dialogic Imagination*, 84, 89.

13 Ibid., 91.

14 In her debate with Rāmin in the snow storm, Vis complains, "Is it not enough, this ten-year hardship I have borne?" (*na bas timār-e dah-sāla ke bordam*, 459/17 [426]).

15 Gabrieli, "Note sul *Vīs u Rāmīn*," 174–5.

16 Frye, *The Secular Scripture*, 3–5 emphasizes the durability of the romance mythos, going so far as to call it "the structural core of all fiction" (ibid., 15).

17 Gabrieli, "Note sul *Vīs u Rāmīn*," 175 (though he does indicate some highlights from Rāmin's songs in 178–80). Many other critics have similarly complained of the story's prolixity (*eṭnāb*), most vociferously Pizzi, *Storia*, 2:87–90, but also Foruzānfar, *Sokhan*, 370; Maḥjub, "Moqaddema," 66–7.

18 Konstan, *Sexual Symmetry*, 15–26 gives numerous examples of the laments given by the "hapless heroes" of the Greek novel, a motif equally visible in the Byzantine revival in the mid-twelfth century, e.g., *Hysmine & Hysminias*, 220/6.6–7, 222/6.10, 230/7.9, or *Drosilla & Charikles*, 413/6.34–94, 421/6.331–558; Rhodanthe even apologizes for her "long speech" in *Rhodanthe & Dosikles*, 113/7.52. Chrétien's romance *Cligès* – perhaps intentionally, given the work's "Greek" setting and source – features a number of extended laments and inner monologues; see, e.g., 86/475–523, 94/625–872, 110/897–1046 (Staines 92–3, 95–7, 98–100). ʿOnṣori's *Vāmeq & ʿAẕrā* (another self-consciously "Greek" story) features similar passages in 94/105–11, 259–66, 276–88, 337–46, while in an interesting contrast the "monologues" of the Arabian story of *Varqa & Golshāh* are often delivered as monorhyme poems, reminiscent of the *ghazal*.

19 Boulton, *The Song in the Story*, 288. For an overview of the various voices assumed in *V&R* and their rhetorical function, see Meisami, *Medieval Persian Court Poetry*, 92–6.

20 Gabrieli, "Note sul *Vīs u Rāmīn*," 176.

21 Meisami, "Persona and Generic Conventions," 133–4.

22 Paul Zumthor makes similar claims about the implicit or "latent" narratives within medieval European lyric; see Zumthor, "Les Narrativités latentes," 39–45; also Zumthor, "The Text and the Voice," 88.

23 For an overview of the genealogy of this concept, see Genette, *The Architext*, 28–60; Jackson and Prins, *The Lyric Theory Reader*, 1–5.
24 See especially Jackson, *Dickinson's Misery*, 1–15.
25 Zumthor, *Toward a Medieval Poetics*, 143–4; cf. Segre, "What Bakhtin Left Unsaid," 33.
26 Haidu, *The Subject Medieval/Modern*, 89.
27 There are instances of embedded songs in the *Shāhnāma*, such as Rostam's song to himself (2:30/397–402 [Davis 156]) or Bārbad's lament (8:355/405–33 [Davis 931]), but they do not show the same formal distinctiveness that we see in ʿAyyuqi's *Varqa & Golshāh*.
28 Dankoff, "The Lyric in the Romance," 12.
29 Ibid., 13.
30 Lewis, "Reading, Writing, and Recitation," 48. In the first chapter of this dissertation, Lewis makes a strong case for situating the origins of the ghazal within the performative context of music and song; see esp. 99 for a discussion of the various ways context-specific meaning could be crafted through the kinetic and sonic cues of a given performance. Renate Jacobi brings a similar approach to her analysis of the Arabic ghazals of the Umayyad period in Jacobi, "Theme and Variations."
31 For more on the interplay of prose and verse in Persian narrative, see Meisami, "Mixed Prose and Verse"; Rubanovich, "Aspects of Medieval Intertextuality."
32 For *bā del goft*, see *V&R* 264/82, 269/190, 410/25, 250/58; for *sorud-i goft*, 219/18, 221/54, 230/218, 254/130; for *goft*, 257/178.
33 Bakhtin, *The Dialogic Imagination*, 47.
34 Panagiotis Roilos makes a similar case for considering these discrete discursive positions as "modulations" of genre in the Komnenian romances rather than alternative terms such as "mixture of genres" or "generic hybrid"; see Roilos, *Amphoteroglossia*, 16.
35 The scene of Vis and Rāmin's journey through the desert to Ray (203/92–102 [166]) is a good example of how the narrator utilizes landscape as a mirror into the psychology of lovers. A similar combination of address and commentary can be found at the end of the bed trick episode, where the narrator calls on the audience to behold (*negah kon*, 232/247 [195]) Vis's clever ruse, while simultaneously condemning her as a sinner (*gonahkār*, 233/268 [196]) for the way she fooled the king and commenting on the disastrous fruit love can bear for those who cultivate it (233/269–76). For comparable moments in Béroul's *Tristran*, see 26/519–20, 28/573–80, 32/643–8, 36/728, 44/909–1169/1437–9, 84/1783–92, 86/1816, among other examples.
36 To this day, many melodies, modes, and modal groupings in Iranian music are identified by names that suggest both mood and content; "agitation"

(*shur*), "flirtation" (*kereshma*), "burning and melting" (*suz-o godāz*), and "lovers" (*ʿoshshāq*) are some prominent examples (indeed, the latter term is simply the Arabic equivalent of the mode *delnavāzān* cited in this passage). See Barkechli, *La musique traditionnelle*, 39–56; During and Mirabdolbaghi, *The Art of Persian Music*, 72–8; Lewis, "Reading, Writing, and Recitation," 73–5; Lucas, *Music of a Thousand Years*, 141; Miller, *Music and Song in Persia*, 74–86.

37 For a discussion of the ghazal's typical length, see Lewis, "Reading, Writing, and Recitation," 43. It seems likely that song texts in performance were often culled from longer poems. For example, many of the song texts (identified as *ṣawt*) found in al-Iṣbahānī's *Kitāb al-aghānī* (*Book of Songs*) generally run from two to four lines; see also al-Jāḥiẓ, *Epistle on Singing-Girls*, 35. For a helpful discussion of the relationship between songs and poems in that work, see Kilpatrick, *Making the Great Book of Songs*, 63–6; in the early New Persian case, cf. Lewis, "The Transformation of the Persian Ghazal," 128.

38 The *kabg-e dari* is now the name of the caspian snowcock (*Tetraogallus caspius*), but Steingass describes it more broadly as "a beautiful kind of partridge." See Steingass, *A Comprehensive Persian-English Dictionary*, 1012.

39 We see similar references to a return to the *status quo* at the conclusion of the other three episodes. Episode 2 (The Bed Trick) ends with the narrator counselling the audience on the hazards of love, while episodes 3 and 4 (The Devils' Grotto and The Garden) both conclude with a "once again" (*degar rah, degar bāra*) passage as well as further narratorial advice to the audience; see *V&R* 233/269–76 [196], 279/151–61 [243], 298/170–9 [264].

40 Conte, *Genres and Readers*, 37.

41 Frow, *Genre*, 73.

42 Conte, *Genres and Readers*, 37.

43 For a force diagram of "narrative dynamism" against "lyric retardation," see Zumthor, *Toward a Medieval Poetics*, 273.

44 For a comparable discussion of the interaction between anecdote and ghazal in Saʿdi's *Golestān*, see Ingenito, *Beholding Beauty*, 124–7.

45 In addition to the famous *Symposium* by Plato, numerous examples of the symposium/*majlis* are found in Hellenistic and Islamic literature; see Ali, *Arabic Literary Salons*, 13–32. Such settings are also occasionally woven into romance narratives; for examples, see *Vameq & ʿAẕrā* (98/132–248); *Bayāḍ & Riyāḍ* (in Robinson, *Medieval Andalusian Courtly Culture*, 18–36); and *Hysmine & Hysminias*, which basically consists of a series of banquets, occurring in eight out of its eleven chapters (see Roilos, *Amphoteroglossia*, 242–51).

46 In my translation of this passage, I use "May" to gloss the month-name Ordibehesht, though a technically more precise term might be Taurus,

i.e., April 21 to May 20. I'm also taking a bit of a poetic licence in the last line; lacking gender markings, there is no grammatical indication that the sky would be masculine or the moon feminine, and the roles could easily be reversed or kept ambiguous using "it." However, in the context of the poem and its diegetic setting, the implied analogy between the moon and the sky and Vis and Mobad seems probable.

47 A similar case of a song revealing that which it purposed to hide is found in the interesting Andalusian story of *Bayāḍ & Riyāḍ* (w. early thirteenth c.); see Robinson, *Medieval Andalusian Courtly Culture*, 34.

48 Stetkevych, *The Zephyrs of Najd*, 125–36.

49 Unfortunately, I am not aware of any references that speak specifically about the performance of romantic masnavis at court, and can make only some general inferences by considering what we know about Ferdowsi's *Shāhnāma*. On this latter front, though, there are some helpful clues: Saʿdi, for example, relates in the *Golestān* how "someone was reading [to the king] from the *Shāhnāma*" (*bāri be majles-e u dar ketāb-e shāhnāma hami khwānand*), and Bayhaqi describes how storytellers would regale their sovereigns with tales of the bygone kings. See Saʿdi, *Gulistan*, 18/1.6; Bayhaqi, *History*, 1:189. The *Shāhnāma* itself, in a rather meta way, refers to its own recitation (or singing) during the reign of Bahrām Gur; see Ferdowsi, *Shāhnāma*, 6:442/319, 357, 452 (Davis 732, 734, 737). In discussing the embedded ghazals of *Varqa & Golshāh*, Lewis writes, "It is possible that these lyrics are also linked to a musical or cantillated style of delivery distinct from the declamatory style of the rest of the *masnavi*"; Lewis, "Reading, Writing, and Recitation," 48.

50 In the comparative spirit, we might consider Richard de Fournival's (d. 1260) statement that "when one hears a romance read, one *hears* adventures as if one had really *seen* them" (*Car quant on ot .i. romans lire, on entent les aventures aussi com l'on les veïst en present*); see Zumthor, *Toward a Medieval Poetics*, 84. For more on the fusion of the singer and the "I" in Provençal lyric, see Harvey, "Courtly Culture in Medieval Occitania," 22–3.

51 Conte, *Genres and Readers*, 37.

52 The comrade (*rafīq*) is another long-standing convention of ghazal poetry, hearkening back to Imruʾ al-Qays's famous call to his two friends to halt and weep over the traces of his beloved's abandoned camp: *qifā nabki min dhikrā ḥabībin wa-manzili* ● *bi-siqṭi al-liwā bayna al-dukhūli fa-ḥawmalī*, translated as "Halt, friends both! Let us weep, recalling a love and a lodging / by the rim of the twisted sands between Ed-Dakhool and Haumal" in Arberry, *The Seven Odes*, 61.

53 Cf. the discussion of "songs as monologues" in Boulton, *The Song in the Story*, 24–79.

54 On the stylistic affinities between al-ʿAbbās b. al-Aḥnaf and Rāmin, see
Meisami, *Medieval Persian Court Poetry*, 96n29, 141n15.

55 Some of the texts that deal with love in its "elegant" or "refined" (*ẓarīf*)
modality include Ibn Qutayba, *ʿUyūn al-akhbār*, 4:128–47; Ibn Dāwūd,
Zahra (cf. Tobkin, "A Man of Our Times"); al-Washshāʾ, *Muwashshā*; and
the *Maṣāriʿ al-ʿushshāq* of al-Sarrāj al-Qāriʾ (cf. Bell, "Al-Sarrāj's *Maṣariʿ
al-ʿushshāq*"; Vadet, *L'Esprit courtois*, 379–430); also, if one were to expand
the temporal and geographical boundaries somewhat, Ibn Ḥazm, *Ṭawq
al-ḥamāma*. For a comprehensive study of these texts and more, see Giffen,
Theory of Profane Love; von Grunebaum, *Medieval Islam*, 311–13; Vadet,
L'Esprit courtois. For a historical study of the *ẓurafāʾ* as a social group, see
Ghazi, "Un groupe social"; Irwin, *Night and Horses*, 112–13. Perhaps most
importantly, Avicenna discusses the "Love of the elegant [ones]" (*ʿishq
al-ẓurafāʾ*) in Avicenna, *Risāla fī al-ʿishq*, 65–76, translated by Fackenheim,
"A Treatise on Love," 218–22, and discussed in detail in Anwar, "Ibn Sīnā's
Philosophical Theology"; Bell, "Avicenna's Treatise"; von Grunebaum,
"Avicenna's *Risâla*."

56 Ingenito, *Beholding Beauty*, 81–2.

57 Bürgel, "The Romance," 162.

58 For a summary of the themes of al-ʿAbbās's poetry, see Jacobi, "al-ʿAbbās
ibn al-Aḥnaf." These themes can be productively compared against Bauer,
"Abū Tammām," 14–17, and also the Occitan poets discussed in Paterson,
"*Fin'amor*," 37. It should be noted that, in the Abbasid period of the Arabic
ghazal, the lover-poet is by no means necessarily male, nor the beloved
female, but since this is the default convention in the poetry of al-ʿAbbās, I
retain these genders here; see Bauer, "Male-Male Love in Classical Arabic
Poetry."

59 ʿAbbās b. al-Aḥnaf, *Dīwān*, 168–9, no. 331, lines 7–14 (see Wormhoudt no.
38 for a translation of the entire poem). A literal rendition of the final line
would be "What a giver, and what a one so inaccessible," but I loosened it
up a bit to avoid unnecessary translationese.

60 Girard, *Deceit, Desire, and the Novel*, 10, offers an insightful discussion of
this double-emotion through the concept of "triangular," or mediated,
desire: "The subject is torn between two opposite feelings toward his
model – the most submissive reverence and the most intense malice"; for
insights into how this manifests in troubadour poetry, see Kay, "Desire and
Subjectivity," 214–20.

61 Zumthor, *Toward a Medieval Poetics*, 160. Haidu, *The Subject Medieval/
Modern*, 79–94, and Kay, "Desire and Subjectivity," 220, similarly discuss
the incorporeal, female-gendered Other in medieval French love lyric.

62 It is worth noting that Vis's rival and double, Gol, also agrees to marry
Rāmin only on the promise of his fidelity; in return, she promises to be

"loyal, constant, and steadfast" (*vafā-varz-o vafā-juy-o vafā-dār*, 332/136) towards him.

63	Allen, *Intertextuality*, 29.

64	ᶜAyyuqi, *Varqa-vo Golshāh*, 36; Sturges, *Aucassin and Nicolette*, 30–1. For a discussion of the latter scene, see Pensom, *Aucassin et Nicolete*, 43–9.

65	Similarly, ᶜUmar b. Abi Rabīᶜa has a famous poem where he describes escaping his beloved's camp in women's clothing, related in Irwin, *Night and Horses*, 50–4. See also the scene where Khorshid Shāh infiltrates the witch's palace disguised as a singing girl in Arrajāni, *Samak the Ayyar*, 26–30.

66	On female warriors in Persian narratives, see Davis, *Panthea's Children*, 34, 50–1, 59; Gaillard, "Héroïnes d'exception"; Hanaway, "Anāhitā and Alexander," 286; Venetis, "Warlike Heroines." For an overview of the warrior women of the Arabic *sīra*, see Kruk, *The Warrior Women of Islam*. For an example of women-as-men marrying women, see the story of Qamar al-Zamān, Budūr, and Ḥayāt al-Nufūs in Lyons and Lyons, *The Arabian Nights*, 1:752–8 (discussed in Amer, "Cross-Dressing," 95–104), and of Burāndokht and Anṭuṭiya in Ṭarsusi, *Dārab-nāma*, 2:81–4. I thank Julia Rubanovich for pointing out the latter reference to me.

67	For discussions of voyeurism and scopophilia in the Greek novel, see Ballengee, "Below the Belt," 142–52; Elsom, "Callirhoe"; Egger, "Looking at Chariton's Callirhoe"; Morales, *Vision and Narrative*, 105–6, 165–99.

68	In addition to her famous "Ten Letters," which I discuss in chapter 5, Vis has a couple of full chapters dedicated to her lamentations (*zāri, muya*), which she recites to her Nurse (243–7 and 397–402), along with numerous shorter passages throughout the poem.

69	A similar example of Vis's shift into a ghazal-like mode of discourse is found in the seventh and eighth chapters of the "Ten Letters" sequence (382–7), which feature invocations of the springtime breeze and cover many of the motifs found in ghazal poems.

70	The closest thing to a "breakup" that I can think of in other romances I have studied is Béroul's *Tristran*, where the love between the protagonists is cut short, at least for a while. That tale, of course, offers an easy explanation for the change, for their love was engendered by a magic potion whose effects would last for only three years. That period having elapsed, both Tristan and Isolde "wake up" and amicably agree to end their affair and return to Mark's court. See Béroul, *Tristran*, 102/2147–2288. Ferdowsi's introduction to the tale of Khosrow and Shirin describes how the former was "separated" (*jodā bud*) from the latter for a period, but explains this by saying that the king's time was fully taken up with martial duties (*ke kār-ash hama razm bahrām bud*) and does not allude to any falling out of affection: see Ferdowsi, *Shāhnāma* 8:260/3405–6 (Davis 918).

71 Bakhtin, *The Dialogic Imagination*, 107.
72 Bakhtin discusses monology extensively in *Problems of Dostoevsky's Poetics*, 5–22, 51–2.
73 Many of these observations resonate in interesting ways with Gaunt's analysis of the "masculine discourse" of the troubadour *canso* in Gaunt, *Gender and Genre*, 125–35. Of particular note is the following: "The moment Arnaut privileges above all others in his songs is the moment when the lover's desire is at its most intense, but as yet unrequited. Rarely does he envisage shared love or allude to amorous encounters which are not fantasized. Poignant as this representation of desire may be, it is striking that this love poetry concentrates on the moment that precedes any possible union, the moment when the male lover is turned inwards, yet must articulate his desire. Arnaut's poetry, and the canso generally, is primarily concerned with its own utterance" (132).
74 For Tristan's attempts to satisfy his love for Isolde through Isolde of the White Hands, see Gottfried von Strassburg, *Tristan* (tr. Hatto), 290–6; for the version by Thomas, see ibid., 301–10.
75 This ideal "masculine" state can be compared with the troubadour ethos of *mezura*, discussed in Paterson, "*Fin'amor*," 35, alongside the Greek notion of *sophrosyne* or the Arabic *ḥilm*, often praised in Jāhiliyya-era poetry.
76 My reading of Behguy ("Speak-well") differs somewhat from that of Meisami, *Medieval Persian Court Poetry*, 185–7, who describes him as "ironically named" in that his take on love amounts to "the satisfaction of concupiscent passion." In the same vein as the "mirrors," however, the retention of male power and authority in the face of love seems to be the main order of business; see note 3 of chapter 3 for relevant references.
77 Bakhtin, *Problems of Dostoevsky's Poetics*, 53.
78 Rāmin's admixture of love and hate – or, thought differently, his flattening of them into one and the same thing – has a fascinating parallel in Thomas of Britain's *Tristran*, when the eponymous hero rages at himself for loving/hating Isolde of the White Hands; see Gottfried von Strassburg, *Tristan* (tr. Hatto), 305–6, 309.
79 For a review of the widespread practice of sport hunting among the elites of Islamicate societies, often on a massive and ecologically devastating scale, see Foltz, *Animals in Islamic Tradition*, 37–9; for the pre-Islamic Iranian context, see Shahbazi, "Hunting in Iran i. In the Pre-Islamic period."
80 Meisami, *Medieval Persian Court Poetry*, 140; Meisami, "Kings and Lovers," 5–6.
81 The figure of the estranged lover (*ʿāsheq-e gharib*), a minstrel who sings and tells love stories, went on to become a transcultural icon in the Caucasus and Anatolia, with both literary (textual) and historical (performative) actors taking on the role; witness the *Gharīb-nāma* ("Book

of the Stranger," w. 1330) by the fourteenth-century poet ᶜĀshık Pāshā
(see Pifer, *Kindred Voices*, 123–34), or the story of ᶜĀshık Gharīb, who dies
on the path of love to his beloved Shāh-Ṣanam and is then resurrected by
Kheżr (signalling strong resonances with *Varqa & Golshāh*), which was
eventually made into a film (*Ashik Kerib*, 1988) by the celebrated director
Sergei Parajanov. For more on this figure in its Anatolian, Armenian, Azeri,
Georgian, and Iranian contexts, see Başgöz, "Turkish Folk Stories about
the Livęs of Minstrels"; Başgöz, "The Structure of the Turkish Romances";
Nikaeen and Oldfield, "The Azerbaijani Ashiq"; Üstünyer, "Tradition of
the Ashugh Poetry and Ashughs in Georgia."
82 Pifer, "The Age of the *Gharīb*," 28; see 19–20 and 24–7 for further discussion
   of the dialogic and relational aspects of the *gharib*.

5 History: The Death of Romantic Love

1 Interestingly, even the "frame tale" of *Vis & Rāmin* – the parts of the
  poem set in Gorgāni's life – have the poet beginning his work in the
  spring (Nowruz) and offering it to his patron in the fall (Mehragān);
  see 27/14–15 and 540/102. This may suggest another level of allegorical
  synchronization between the diegetic time of the story and the historical
  time of the storyteller.
2 Bakhtin, *The Dialogic Imagination*, 90; Bakhtin, *Speech Genres and Other Late
  Essays*, 12.
3 Steven Smith notes that Bakhtin's claim about the absence of temporal
  change in the Greek novel is complicated by one of its earliest exemplars,
  Kallirhoe, whose eponymous protagonist does indeed age from a "girl" to a
  "mature woman" (61/3.8); time is certainly not reversible in this case. See
  Smith, "Bakhtin and Chariton," 168–73.
4 Eslāmi-Nodushan, "Vis-o Rāmin va Shāhnāma," 19: "*Hich ketāb-i dar
  zabān-e fārsi nist ke mānand-e vis-o rāmin ānqadr be shāhnāma nazdik-o ānqadr
  dur bāshad.*" An important study that demonstrates the considerable
  overlaps of world view between *V&R* and the *Shāhnāma* is Ringgren,
  Fatalism in Persian Epics.
5 For more on the reception and afterlife of the "Ten Letters," see Cross,
  "The Lives and Afterlives," 526–9; Gandjeï, "The Genesis and Definition."
6 For other examples of oaths and ordeals meant to confirm the heroine's
  immaculate state, see *Kallirhoe* 112/8.1, 123/8.8; *Leukippe & Kleitophon*
  280/8.13–14. See also the case of Fenice in Chrétien's *Cligès*, whose body
  suffers a gamut of horrible tortures that "leav[e] visible marks all the
  way down," only to be fully healed by her nurse's miraculous ointments,
  leaving her "healthier and livelier than she ever was before." See Chrétien
  de Troyes, *Cligès*, 380/5968, 398/6296–8 (Staines 159, 163).

7 Ballengee, "Below the Belt," 161. This entire chapter (130–61) offers invaluable insights into how the body in the Greek novels resists and complicates both Bakhtin's notion of adventure-time and Konstan's thesis on sexual symmetry.

8 See, e.g., Hādi and Naṣiri, "Sākhtār-e tashbih"; Rostami, "Barrasi-ye vizhegi-hā"; Tājbakhsh and Ḥasanpur, "Sabkshenāsi-ye dahnāma." The regular length of the compositions suggests that they were laid out according to a systematic framework: the exordium runs at a hundred lines, and each subsequent essay is 50, 51, 50, 50, 52, 50, 51, 50, and 47 lines, ending with a final letter and peroration clocking in at 72 lines.

9 Between these two bookends, the fourth letter contains another complex pattern that brings three phrases – "don't you see" (*nabini ke*), "in the hope of" (*be omid-e ān*), and "forever" (*hamisha*) – into compound anaphoric clusters. See *V&R* 373/13–32 (340–1); Morrison's more literal prose translation (249–50) makes the syntactic sequence a little more visible.

10 To be fair, whether these rhetorical techniques actually moved Gorgāni's audience the way they seem to have been intended is ultimately a matter of conjecture. Indeed, the eminent Iranian scholar Moḥammad Jaʿfar Maḥjub finds fault with these very lines for their repetitive nature; see Maḥjub, "Moqaddema," 67.

11 For the three uses of *allāh* in *V&R*, see 389/38–9 (cited in the body) and 382/9. In contrast – based on my searching of the digital text hosted by the TITUS project – *khodā* appears 141 times and *yazdān* 104 times.

12 For descriptions of Bilqis and her demonic/jinni ancestry, see Kisāʾī, *Tales of the Prophets*, 310–17; al-Rabghūzī, *The Stories of the Prophets*, 2:365–7; al-Thaʿlabī, *ʿArāʾis al-majālis*, 523, 534. In an interesting discussion, Bürgel observes how the shared rhyme between Vis, Bilqis, and Iblis is used to suggest further associations between Vis and the demonic on top of her already ambiguous descent from Jamshid; see Bürgel, "Die Liebesvorstellung," 79–80.

13 Kottman, *Love as Human Freedom*, 6.

14 Ferdowsi, *Shāhnāma*, 6:229/525–654, 7:456/4446–517 (Davis 677–681, 822–4). For further discussion and analysis of these testaments, see Fouchécour, *Moralia*, 38–58, 85–100; Askari, *The Medieval Reception*, 153–69.

15 Kottman, *Love as Human Freedom*, 154.

16 Askari, "A Mirror for Princesses," 124. For the Vis-Rāmin debate as a *monāẓara*, see Moḥammadi-Badr and Mahdizāda, "Taʾammol-i dar taḥavvol-e monāẓara," 182. For more on Asadi Ṭusi and the *monāẓara*, see Abdullaeva, "The Origins of the *Munāẓara* Genre"; Foruzānfar, *Sokhan*, 443; Khaleghi-Motlagh, "Asadī Ṭūsī"; Seyed-Gohrab, "A Treasury from Tabrīz," 141–3. A famous Middle Persian debate poem is the *Draxt ī Asūrīg*, on which see Brunner, "The Fable of the Babylonian Tree"; Shaked,

"Specimens of Middle Persian Verse"; Tavadia, "A Rhymed Ballad in
Pahlavi."

17 For a brief discussion of the *paraklausithyron* topos, see Cairns, *Generic
Composition*, 6. I thank Dick Davis for bringing this thematic connection to
my attention.

18 Text and translation from Tibullus, *Elegies*, 6–7.

19 I hesitate to suggest that the connection between the *paraklausithyron* and
this scene in *V&R* is anything more than the coincidence of a shared topos,
though there may be some history of addressing the locked building that
has yet to be fully traced in Persian and Arabic lyric poetry. For some
intriguing suggestions on what this shared poetic history might look like,
see von Grunebaum, *Medieval Islam*, 309–18.

20 Khaleghi-Motlagh, "Asadī Ṭūsī." For more examples of *monāzara* pairings,
including "rose and wine," "cypress and water," "wine and hashish,"
"sword and pen," "earth and sky," "sight and hearing," "poetry and
prose," etc., see Seyed-Gohrab, "A Treasury from Tabrīz," 142–3.

21 For Goethe's claim about the lack of drama in Islamicate literatures, see
Goethe, *The West-East Divan*, 228; its echoes can be heard centuries later
in overviews of Persian genre like ʿEbādiyān, *Anvāʿ-e adabi*, 20–3, 27–30,
and Shamisā, *Anvāʿ-e adabi*, 50–4, 157. Some examples of scholarship that
have challenged this view include Beeman, *Iranian Performance Traditions*;
Beeston, "The Genesis of the Maqāmāt Genre," 10–11; Chelkowski,
Taʿziyeh, Ritual and Drama in Iran; Guo, *The Performing Arts*.

22 For these elements of drama (specifically tragedy), see Aristotle, *Poetics*,
71/§19.1450a.

23 For descriptions of the use of platforms and curtains in giving audience,
see Neẓām al-Molk, *The Book of Government*, 14, 121–2; Bayhaqi, *History*,
1:113–14, 2:246; Ferdowsi, *Shāhnāma*, 7:478/161 (Davis 828).

24 For this and other proverbs used in the text, see Gorgāni, *V&R* (ed.
Rowshan), 501–10; Mahjub, "Moqaddema," 58–63.

25 Al-Masʿūdī, *Les prairies d'or*, 6:373 (Lunde and Stone 111).

26 Incidentally, Rāmin's response to Vis's ten-part letter similarly lurches
between apology and remonstrance, as though he cannot quite decide
on the account he wants to give of his actions. First he declares, "I am a
sinner" (*gonāhkār-am*, 420/10), then immediately backtracks, "Although
this sin isn't originally mine, it's also wrong to blame you for it" (*agar
che in gonāh az bon marā nist • gonah bar to nehādan ham ravā nist*, 420/11
[388]), then turns around the accusation: "The sin is yours, but I say you're
sinless" (*gonāh-e to-st-o guyam bigonāh-i*, 420/17). These inconsistencies
thus seem to be a consistent facet of his character.

27 Asa, Haug, and West, *The Book of Arda Viraf*, 184/§55. For further
discussions and references to the Zoroastrian vision of Hell as a cold, dark,

and malodorous place, see Gray, "Zoroastrian Elements," 173–4; Kłagisz, "An Iranian Vision of the Afterlife," 445.

28 The *zamharīr* is mentioned in the Qur'an as one of the torments from which the people of Paradise are shielded (76:13). For an overview of its broader treatment, see Tottoli, "The Qur'an, Qur'anic Exegesis and Muslim Traditions."

29 For two versions of Kay Khosrow's "occultation," see al-Ṭabarī, *The Ancient Kingdoms*, 19, and Ferdowsi, *Shāhnāma*, 4:367/3044–75 (Davis 471–5). The significance of this event in the Middle Persian literature of the medieval Zoroastrian community gets careful consideration in Vevaina, "The Ground Well Trodden," 172–82.

30 On the use of camphor in treating the dead, see Aʿlam, "Camphor"; Boyce, *Zoroastrians*, 120–1; van Ruymbeke, *Science and Poetry*, 127, 137.

31 Kottman, *Love as Human Freedom*, 151.

32 Not surprisingly for such an enigmatic passage, we find some significant textual divergences in the manuscript tradition. The second verse (*nagofti az gashi bā hich kas rāz*, 465/5) is especially prone to variations, including *nakardi bā kashi bā hich kas sāz* ("we [lit., our body] would never get along with anyone in joy") and *nakardi az kazhi bā hich damsāz* ("we [our body] would never get along with anyone out of [our/its] crookedness"). The Georgian *Visramiani* provides an instructive comparison: "If indeed it were not so with men, no one could caress with great appetite; none could become enamoured of anybody, nor give himself up to grief and death. And if they were not deceived in this thing, Fate could not have so turned as it did in the case of Vis and Ramin. After an unexampled affection there befell an equally unparalleled, merciless abandonment one of the other." T'mogveli, *Visramiani*, 342.

33 See Asmussen, "Āz." The demonic embodiment of *āz* continues in the *Shāhnāma*, 6:77/1110 (Davis 612), where Alexander is told that Greed (*āz*) and Need (*niyāz*) are two demons, "one emaciated and dry-lipped, the other sleepless at night out of [wanting] more."

34 For more discussion about the paradox of ennoblement through submission to love, see Barry, "In the Worlds of Nizāmī," 100–2, 106–8; Kappler, "La beauté," with a diagram on 328.

35 Kottman, *Love as Human Freedom*, 5–6.

36 Ibid., 27–70.

37 Kappler, "La beauté," 323.

38 Miller, "Embodying the Beloved," 5.

39 *Jahān-afruz* is one of Rāmin's main epithets, occurring some eleven times in the text (and twice for Shahru), with many of those occurrences clustered in the snowstorm episode. Kappler notes this association and suggests it establishes Rāmin as a "solar hero" with close ties to Mithra,

possibly with Buddhist overtones as well; see Kappler, "Présence du mazdéisme," 46; Kappler, "La beauté," 321, 324. For more on Avicenna's allegories of felicity, see Stroumsa, "Avicenna's Philosophical Stories"; Stroumsa, "'True Felicity'"; and for translations of the works mentioned, see Corbin, *Avicenna and the Visionary Recital*, 186–92; Faris, "Al-Ghazzali's Epistle of the Birds"; Sohravardi, *The Philosophical Allegories and Mystical Treatises*, 1–7; ʿAṭṭār, *The Conference of the Birds*. Matthew Keegan discusses the allegorical significance of the bird in Keegan, "'Elsewhere Lies Its Meaning,'" 31–4.

40 Kappler, "La beauté," 321.

41 I put "dragon" in scare quotes simply to avoid making too close an association between the Persian *azhdahā* and the dragon of medieval European literature or modern Euro-American fantasy, especially in light of Samuel Lasman's troubling of this equivalence; see Lasman, "Dragons, Fairies, and Time," 200–8.

42 The other highly visible interventions of fate in *V&R* include the boar that kills Mobad and the sudden flood that sweeps away the Nurse's talisman. For a thorough survey of the different names, manifestations, and attitudes towards fate in *V&R*, see Ringgren, *Fatalism in Persian Epics*, 20–3, 63–5, 69–72, 87–90, 102–6, 120–3.

43 For a study of silence in Rumi's poetry, see Keshavarz, *Reading Mystical Lyric*, 49–71.

44 For more discussion of this act of mutual submission, and the shift from external force to inner transformation, see Kappler, "La beauté," 322–4.

45 Ibid., 318, 325–6. Emphasis added.

46 Kottman, "Quid Non Sentit Amor," 522–3.

47 Smith, "Bakhtin and Chariton," 185.

48 Kappler, "La beauté," 305; Kottman, *Love as Human Freedom*, 10, 28–33.

49 To give a sense of scale, the conclusion of *V&R* takes up about 750 lines or 8 per cent of the poem, in comparison to the 2,000 lines or 20 per cent of the poem that is occupied by the letters and debates preceding it.

50 On the concept of poetry as "licit magic," see Bürgel, *The Feather of Simurgh*.

51 Vis does become the official sovereign over her ancestral home of Media, including the provinces of Azerbaijan, Arran, and Armenia (527/95–6), but this does not grant her much visibility in the story's conclusion.

52 Yūsuf Khāṣṣ Ḥājib, *Wisdom of Royal Glory*, 187–8; Neẓām al-Molk, *The Book of Government*, 185–92.

53 For a discussion of how the "taming" of Guenevere – who, like Vis, "refuses the knight" – "liberates" Lancelot in ways that correspond quite closely with *V&R*, see Krueger, *Women Readers*, 54–67.

54 Davis, "Women in the *Shahnameh*," 83.

55 Askari, "A Mirror for Princesses," 126. For examples of the prominent role
    that women played in the Seljuk court, see Peacock, *The Great Seljuk Empire*,
    178–81; and for further discussion of Neẓām al-Molk's bitter rivalries with
    some of the female members of the ruling family, see Bosworth, "Political
    and Dynastic History," 76–7; Safi, *The Politics of Knowledge*, 67–74. For
    some helpful examples of scholarship that engage with romance from
    the perspective of women readers, modelling approaches that might be
    productive in this case, see Egger, "Looking at Chariton's Callirhoe";
    Krueger, *Women Readers*.

56 For examples of "crown-holding" women in the *Shāhnāma*, I could suggest
    Māhāfarid, grandmother of Manuchehr; Farigis, mother of Kay Khosrow;
    and Homāy, mother of Dārāb. There are also two queens at the very end of
    the Sasanian period, Borāndokht and Āzarmdokht, who briefly rule Iran
    in the absence of any male relatives; for a discussion of these figures, see
    Khaleghi-Motlagh, *Women in the Shāhnāmeh*, 22–6, 45, 60–2, 73–8.

57 On the "crown-bestower" in the *Shāhnāma*, see Davidson, *Poet and Hero*,
    132. For discussions of Arnavāz, Shahrnavāz, and Farānak as they relate
    to institutions of sovereignty and good religion, see Lewis, "Shifting
    Allegiances," 392–408; Pierce, "Serpents and Sorcery," 361–2.

58 Meisami, *Medieval Persian Court Poetry*, 140; cf. Kappler, "*Vîs et Râmîn*," 77.

59 As noted in chapter 1, Marijan Molé even went so far as to claim that
    V&R was partially written in response to and as a commentary on
    the sometimes fraught relations between Ṭughrıl Beg and his male
    relatives, such as Chaghrı Beg and Ibrāhīm Yınāl. See Molé, "«Vīs u
    Rāmīn» et l'histoire seldjoukide," 12–17, 26, 28; and for more on the
    internecine politics of the early Seljuks, see Peacock, *The Great Seljuk
    Empire*, 50–1.

60 The word *ṭūbā* occurs only once in the Qur'an as a blessing given to the
    righteous (13:29), but many hadith, biographies, and exegeses give it a
    more concrete form as an immense and bountiful tree in Paradise. For
    more information, see Waines, "Tree(s)."

61 On the connections between history, politics, and ethics in the *Shāhnāma*,
    see Askari, *The Medieval Reception*; Meisami, "The Past in Service of the
    Present," 253–63.

62 Meisami, *Medieval Persian Court Poetry*, 187–92; Meisami, "Kings and
    Lovers," 6–7.

63 For a useful overview of the various ways truth could be verified in
    medieval Islamicate writing, see Zadeh, "The Wiles of Creation," 25–7,
    32–5. Lasman proposes "speculative fiction" as a way of theorizing the
    relationship between the past, the imagination, and the production of
    knowledge in Lasman, "Dragons, Fairies, and Time," 16–35; for more on
    this topic, see the epilogue.

64 For more on romance time and subjectivity in the western European context, see Knapp and Knapp, *Medieval Romance*, 6–12.

65 "Lived examples" comes from Meisami's translation of Mohammed Arkoun's discussion of the *Tajārib al-umam*, which he describes as "a collection of *lived examples* destined to illustrate the elucidation of [Miskawayh's] theoretical treatises"; in this way, we can imagine Gorgāni as expanding the parameters of what might count as exemplary material. See Meisami, "The Past in Service of the Present," 253n13.

66 Abbott, "A Ninth-Century Fragment," 155; for a discussion of this quote, see the section "Of Legends and Legerdemain" in chapter 1 of this book.

Epilogue

1 To compare the text of Gorgāni's exordium with Avicenna's "Sublime Sermon," see Gorgāni, *V&R* (tr. Morrison), 1–4; Akhtar, "A Tract of Avicenna," 220–2 (Arabic text in 232–3).

2 Fackenheim, "A Treatise on Love," 219. Fackenheim and von Grunebaum both comment on this "positive" reintegration of bodily desires into the process of spiritual perfection in Fackenheim, ibid., 211; von Grunebaum, "Avicenna's *Risâla*," 234 col. 2.

3 Ingenito, *Beholding Beauty*, 301–51.

4 Harb, *Arabic Poetics*, 30, 42, 52.

5 Meisami, "The Past in Service of the Present," 264, quoted also in chapter 1.

6 Harb, *Arabic Poetics*, 29.

7 Hämeen-Anttila, *Khwadāynāmag*, 145.

8 Lasman, "Dragons, Fairies, and Time," 227.

9 Zadeh, "The Wiles of Creation," 29–30.

10 On the interplay of pleasure and the imagination, phantasy and philosophy, time and subjectivity, "possible worlds" and the "posited world," and the "novel emergent" of perception and perspective, see Knapp and Knapp, *Medieval Romance*, 3–23, which theorizes romance in western Europe in ways that resonate strongly with the points made in this epilogue.

11 Nilsson, "Desire and God Have Always Been Around," 260, 251.

12 For some studies and introductions to this genre, see Ashtiany, "Al-Tanūkhī's *al-Faraj baʿd al-shidda* as a Literary Source"; Khalifa, *Hardship and Deliverance in the Islamic Tradition*; Weiner, "Die *Farağ baʿd aš-Šidda*-Literatur." Ulrich Marzolph has recently proposed that the *Faraj baʿd al-shidda* motif also provided an extraordinarily productive framework for the circulation of tales in the "middle literatures" in the premodern Muslim world; see Marzolph, *Relief after Hardship*, 42–6.

13 Bray, "Isnāds and Models of Heroes," 13.

14 Behzadi, "Standardizing Emotions," 817.
15 Hägg and Utas, *The Virgin and Her Lover*, 249–50.
16 Some examples of "mini-romances" used in the homiletic masnavis of ʿAṭṭār and Rumi include the story of Shaykh Ṣanʿān in ʿAṭṭār, *Manṭeq al-Ṭayr*, 286/1191–1601 (Darbandi and Davis 57–75); the tale of Marḥuma in ʿAṭṭār, *Elāhi-nāma*, 131/484–792, translated in Newman, "Attar's 'Tale of Marhuma:' The Woman with a Manly Heart"; and the King and the Slave-girl episode in Rumi, *Mathnawí*, 1:36–246 (Mojaddedi 1:6–17). As Austin O'Malley notes, ʿAṭṭār may well have composed an independent romance of his own as well, the *Khosrow-nāma*; see O'Malley, "An Unexpected Romance."
17 J.-C. Bürgel also notes the air of ambivalence that hangs about the ending of *V&R* in Bürgel, "Die Liebesvorstellung," 90. Tim Whitmarsh makes a similar case for the "uneasy settlement" of the ancient Greek novels, held in a state of tension "between two contradictory principles: one drives us relentlessly towards the end, the other threatens to maroon us in an endless state of narrative wandering"; see Whitmarsh, "Desire and the End of the Greek Novel," 140.
18 Keegan, "Commentarial Acts and Hermeneutical Dramas," 87.
19 For two landmark studies on the hermeneutics of ambiguity in Islamic intellectual history, see Bauer, *Die Kultur der Ambiguität*; Ahmed, *What Is Islam?*
20 Kinoshita, "Romance in/and the Medieval Mediterranean," 189.

Bibliography

ᶜAbbās b. al-Aḥnaf, al-. *Dīwān al-ᶜAbbās ibn al-Aḥnaf*. Edited by ᶜĀtika al-Khazrajī. Cairo: Dār al-Kutub al-Miṣrīya, 1954.

– *The Diwan of Abu Fadl 'Abbas ibn al Ahnaf*. Translated by Arthur Wormhoudt. Oskaloosa, IA: William Penn College, 1980.

Abbott, Nadia. "A Ninth-Century Fragment of the 'Thousand Nights': New Light on the Early History of the *Arabian Nights*." *Journal of Near Eastern Studies* 8, no. 3 (1949): 129–64.

ᶜAbd-Allāhiyān, Ḥamid. "Az farādast: Gerdāvarda-ye shesh mard-e dānā (nokāt-i dar bāb-e dāstān-e Vis-o Rāmin)." *Adabiyāt-e Dāstāni* 46 (1377 [1998]): 122–5.

ᶜAbdi, Laylā, and Akbar Ṣayyādkuh. "Barrasi-ye do shakhṣiyat-e aṣli-ye manẓuma-ye Vis-o Rāmin bar asās-e «safar-e qahremān»." *Adab-pazhuhi* 24 (1392 [2013]): 129–48.

Abdullaeva, Firuza. "Kingly Flight: Nimrūd, Kay Kāvūs, Alexander, or Why the Angel Has the Fish." *Persica* 23 (2009): 1–29.

– "The Origins of the *Munāẓara* Genre in New Persian Literature." In *Metaphor and Imagery in Persian Poetry*, edited by Ali Asghar Seyed-Gohrab, 249–73. Leiden; Boston: Brill, 2012.

Abu Nuwās, al-Ḥasan ibn Hānī. *Der Dīwān des Abū Nuwās: Teil V*. Edited by Ewald Wagner. Beirut; Berlin: Klaus Schwarz, 2003.

Abu Tammām, Ḥabīb ibn Aws al-Ṭāʾī. *al-Ḥamāsa*. Edited by ᶜAbd Allāh ibn ᶜAbd al-Raḥīm ᶜUsaylān. 2 vols. Riyadh: Jāmiᶜat al-Imām Muḥammad ibn Saᶜūd al-Islāmiyya, 1401 [1981].

Adamson, Peter. *The Arabic Plotinus: A Philosophical Study of the Theology of Aristotle*. London: Duckworth, 2002.

Afshār, Iraj, ed. *Eskandar-nāma: Revāyat-e fārsi-ye Kālistenes-e dorughin, pardākhta miyān-e qorun-e 6–8 hejri*. Tehran: Bongāh-e Tarjoma va Nashr-e Ketāb, 1343 [1964].

Āftābi. *Tarif-i-Husain Shah, Badshah Dakhan: Original Text, Translation and Critical Introduction*. Edited by G.T. Kulkarni and M.S. Mate. Pune: Bharata Itihasa Samshodhaka Mandala, 1987.

Agapitos, Panagiotis A. "Contesting Conceptual Boundaries: Byzantine Literature and Its History." *Interfaces: A Journal of Medieval European Literatures*, no. 1 (2015): 62–91.

– "Genre, Structure and Poetics in the Byzantine Vernacular Romances of Love." *Symbolae Osloenses* 79, no. 1 (2004): 7–101.

– "In Rhomaian, Persian and Frankish Lands: Fiction and Fictionality in Byzantium." In *Medieval Narratives between History and Fiction: From the Centre to the Periphery of Europe, c. 1100–1400*, edited by Panagiotis A. Agapitos and Lars Boje Mortensen, 235–367. Copenhagen: Museum Tusculanum Press, 2012.

– trans. *The Tale of Livistros and Rodamne: A Byzantine Love Romance of the 13th Century*. Liverpool University Press, 2021.

Agapitos, Panagiotis A., and Lars Boje Mortensen. "Introduction." In *Medieval Narratives between History and Fiction: From the Centre to the Periphery of Europe, c. 1100–1400*, edited by Panagiotis A. Agapitos and Lars Boje Mortensen, 1–24. Copenhagen: Museum Tusculanum Press, 2012.

Agostini, Domenico, and Samuel Thrope, eds. *The Bundahišn: The Zoroastrian Book of Creation*. Translated by Domenico Agostini and Samuel Thrope. Oxford University Press, 2020.

Ahmad, Aziz. "Epic and Counter-Epic in Medieval India." *Journal of the American Oriental Society* 83, no. 4 (1963): 470–6.

Ahmed, Shahab. *What Is Islam? The Importance of Being Islamic*. Princeton; Oxford: Princeton University Press, 2016.

Akbari, Suzanne Conklin. "Modeling Medieval World Literature." *Middle Eastern Literatures* 20, no. 1 (2017): 2–17.

Akhtar, Ahmedmian. "A Tract of Avicenna, Translated by 'Umar Khayyâm." *Islamic Culture* 9, no. 2 (1935): 218–33.

Aᶜlam, Hushang. "Camphor." *Encyclopædia Iranica* IV/7 (1990): 743–7. Available online at https://www.iranicaonline.org/articles/camphor-npers. Accessed 1 June 2022.

Alam, Muzaffar, and Sanjay Subrahmanyam. "Love, Passion and Reason: The Poet Fayzi and His *Nal-Daman*." *Studies on Persianate Societies* 2 (2004): 42–79.

Al-Azmeh, Aziz. *Muslim Kingship: Power and the Sacred in Muslim, Christian and Pagan Polities*. London; New York: I.B. Tauris, 1997.

Albin, Andrew, Mary Carpenter Erler, Thomas O'Donnell, Nicholas Paul, and Nina Rowe. *Whose Middle Ages?: Teachable Moments for an Ill-Used Past*. Fordham University Press, 2019.

ᶜAlī ibn Abi Ṭālib. *Nahj al-balāgha*. Edited by Ṣubhī al-Ṣāliḥ. 4th ed. Beirut; Cairo: Dār al-Kitāb al-Lubnānī; Dār al-Kitāb al-Miṣrī, 1425 [2004].

Ali, Samer M. *Arabic Literary Salons in the Islamic Middle Ages: Poetry, Public Performance, and the Presentation of the Past*. Notre Dame, IN: Notre Dame University Press, 2010.

– "Praise for Murder? Two Odes by al-Buḥturī Surrounding an Abbasid Patricide." In *Writers and Rulers: Perspectives on Their Relationship from Abbasid to Safavid Times*, edited by Beatrice Gruendler and Louise Marlow, 1–38. Wiesbaden: Reichart Verlag, 2004.

Allen, Graham. *Intertextuality*. London: Routledge, 2011.

Amer, Sahar. "Cross-Dressing and Female Same-Sex Marriage in Medieval French and Arabic Literatures." In *Islamicate Sexualities: Translations across Temporal Geographies of Desire*, edited by Kathryn Babayan and Afsaneh Najmabadi, 72–113. Cambridge, MA: Center for Middle Eastern Studies of Harvard University, 2008.

Amirsoleimani, Soheila. "Of This World and the Next: Metaphors and Meanings in the *Qābūs-nāmah*." *Iranian Studies* 35, no. 1/3 (2002): 1–22.

Andreas Capellanus. *The Art of Courtly Love*. Translated by John Jay Parry. New York: Columbia University Press, 1941.

Antrim, Zayde. "Qamarayn: The Erotics of Sameness in the 1001 Nights." *Al-ʿUsur al-Wusta* 28, no. 1 (2020): 1–44.

Anwar, Etin. "Ibn Sīnā's Philosophical Theology of Love." *Islamic Studies* 42, no. 2 (2003): 331–45.

Arberry, A. J., ed. *Homāy-nāma*. London: Luzac & Co., 1963.

– *The Seven Odes: The First Chapter in Arabic Literature*. London; New York: George Allen & Unwin; Macmillan, 1957.

Aristotle. *Aristotle's Poetics*. Translated by George Whalley. Montreal; Kingston: McGill-Queen's University Press, 1997.

– *De anima*. Translated by Christopher Shields. Oxford: Clarendon, 2016.

Arjomand, Said Amir. *The Shadow of God and the Hidden Imam: Religion, Political Order, and Societal Change in Shiʿite Iran from the Beginning to 1890*. University of Chicago Press, 1984.

Arrajāni, Farāmarz b. Khodādād. *Samak the Ayyar: A Tale of Ancient Persia*. Translated by Freydoon Rassouli and Jordan Mechner. New York: Columbia University Press, 2021.

Asa, Hoshangjī Jamaspjī, Martin Haug, and E.W. West, eds. *The Book of Arda Viraf*. Govt. Central Book Depot, 1872.

Asadi Ṭusi, ʿAli ibn Aḥmad. *Garshāsb-nāma*. Edited by Ḥabib Yaghmāʾi. Tehran: Ṭahuri, 1354 [1975].

Ashtiany, Julia. "Al-Tanūkhī's *al-Faraj baʿd al-shidda* as a Literary Source." In *Arabicus Felix, Luminosus Britannicus: Essays in Honour of A.F.L. Beeston on His Eightieth Birthday*, edited by Alan Jones, 108–15. Reading, UK: Ithaca Press, 1991.

ʿAskarī, Abū Hilāl al-. *Risāla fī al-tafḍīl bayn balāghatay al-ʿArab wa-l-ʿAjam*. Edited by ʿAbbās Arḥīla. Ḥawliyāt al-ādāb wa-l-ʿulūm al-ijtimāʿiyya 27. Qism al-Lugha al-ʿArabiyya, Jāmiʿat al-Qāḍī ʿAyyāḍ, 1427 [2006].

Askari, Nasrin. *The Medieval Reception of the Shāhnāma as a Mirror for Princes*. Leiden; Boston: Brill, 2016.

– "A Mirror for Princesses: *Mūnis-nāma*, a Twelfth-Century Collection of Persian Tales Corresponding to the Ottoman Turkish Tales of the *Faraj baᶜd al-shidda*." *Narrative Culture* 5, no. 1 (2018): 121–40.

Asmussen, J.P. "Āz." *Encyclopædia Iranica* III/2 (1987): 168–9. An updated version is available online at https://www.iranicaonline.org/articles/az-iranian-demon. Accessed 1 June 2022.

Athamina, Khalil. "*Lafẓ* in Classical Poetry." In *Israel Oriental Studies XI: Studies in Medieval Arabic and Hebrew Poetics*, edited by Sasson Somekh, 47–55. Leiden: Brill, 1991.

Athenaeus. *The Learned Banqueters*. Edited and translated by S. Douglas Olson. Cambridge, MA: Harvard University Press, 2006–12.

ᶜAṭṭār, Farid al-Din. *The Conference of the Birds*. Translated by Afkham Darbandi and Dick Davis. London; New York: Penguin, 1984.

– *Elāhi-nāma*. Edited by Moḥammad-Reża Shafiᶜi-Kadkani. Tehran: Sokhan, 1385 [2006].

– *Mokhtār-nāma*. Edited by Moḥammad-Reża Shafiᶜi-Kadkani. Tehran: Tus, 1358 [1979].

– *Manṭeq al-ṭayr*. Edited by Moḥammad-Reża Shafiᶜi-Kadkani. Tehran: Sokhan, 1389 [2010].

Avicenna. *al-Risāla fī al-ᶜishq*. Edited by Ḥusayn al-Ṣiddīq and Rāwiya Jāmūs. Damascus: Dār al-Fikr, 1426 [2005].

Ayubi, Zahra. *Gendered Morality: Classical Islamic Ethics of the Self, Family, and Society*. New York: Columbia University Press, 2019.

ᶜAyyuqi. *Varqa-vo Golshāh-e ᶜAyyuqi*. Edited by Ẕabiḥ-Allāh Ṣafā. Tehran: Dāneshgāh-e Tehrān, 1343 [1964].

Azarpay, Guitty. "Crowns and Some Royal Insignia in Early Iran." *Iranica Antiqua* 9 (1972): 108–19.

Babaie, Sussan, and Talinn Grigor, eds. *Persian Kingship and Architecture: Strategies of Power in Iran from the Achaemenids to the Pahlavis*. London; New York: I.B. Tauris, 2015.

Babayan, Kathryn. *The City as Anthology: Eroticism and Urbanity in Early Modern Isfahan*. Stanford University Press, 2021.

Bakhtin, Mikhail. *The Dialogic Imagination: Four Essays*. Edited by Michael Holquist. Translated by Caryl Emerson and Michael Holquist. Austin: University of Texas Press, 1981.

– *Problems of Dostoevsky's Poetics*. Edited and translated by Caryl Emerson. Minneapolis: University of Minnesota Press, 1984.

– *Speech Genres and Other Late Essays*. Edited by Caryl Emerson and Michael Holquist. Translated by Vern W. McGee. Austin: University of Texas Press, 1986.

Ballengee, Jennifer R. "Below the Belt: Looking into the Matter of Adventure-Time." In *The Bakhtin Circle and Ancient Narrative*, edited by R. Bracht

Branham, 130–63. Groningen: Barkhuis Publishing & Groningen University Library, 2005.

Barkechli, Mehdi. *La musique traditionnelle de l'Iran*. Tehran: Secrétariat d'État aux Beaux-Arts, 1963.

Barry, Michael. "In the Worlds of Nizāmī of Ganjeh: Layli and Majnūn and the Riddle of Courtly Love." In *The Routledge Companion to World Literature and World History*, edited by May Hawas, 93–110. Routledge, 2018.

Bartsch, Shadi. *The Mirror of the Self: Sexuality, Self-Knowledge, and the Gaze in the Early Roman Empire*. University of Chicago Press, 2006.

Başgöz, İlhan. "The Structure of the Turkish Romances." In *Folk Groups and Folklore Genres Reader: A Reader*, edited by Elliott Oring, 197–208. Logan, UT: Utah State University Press, 1989.

– "Turkish Folk Stories about the Lives of Minstrels." *The Journal of American Folklore* 65, no. 258 (1952): 331–9.

Bauer, Thomas. "Abū Tammām's Contribution to 'Abbāsid 'Ġazal' Poetry." *Journal of Arabic Literature* 27, no. 1 (1996): 13–21.

– *Die Kultur der Ambiguität: Eine andere Geschichte des Islams*. Berlin: Verlag der Weltreligionen, 2011.

– "In Search of 'Post-Classical Literature': A Review Article." *Mamlūk Studies Review* 11, no. 2 (2007): 137–67.

– "Male-Male Love in Classical Arabic Poetry." In *The Cambridge History of Gay and Lesbian Literature*, edited by E.L. McCallum and Mikko Tuhkanen, 107–24. Cambridge University Press, 2014.

Bausani, Alessandro. "Muhammad or Darius? The Elements and Basis of Iranian Culture." In *Giorgio Levi della Vida Biennial Conference Publications*, edited by Speros Vryonis, 4:43–57. Wiesbaden: Harrassowitz, 1975.

Bayhaqi, Abu al-Fażl. *The History of Beyhaqi*. Translated by C.E. Bosworth and Mohsen Ashtiany. 3 vols. Cambridge, MA; London: Harvard University Press, 2011.

– *Tārikh-e Bayhaqi*. Edited by Moḥammad Jaᶜfar Yāḥaqqi and Mahdi Sayyedi. 2 vols. Tehran: Sokhan, 1388 [2009].

Beecroft, Alexander. *An Ecology of World Literature: From Antiquity to the Present Day*. Brooklyn, NY: Verso, 2015.

Beeman, William O. *Iranian Performance Traditions*. Costa Mesa, CA: Mazda, 2011.

Beeston, A.F.L. "The Genesis of the Maqāmāt Genre." *Journal of Arabic Literature* 2 (1971): 1–12.

Behzadi, Lale. "Standardizing Emotions: Aspects of Classification and Arrangement in Tales with a Good Ending." *Asiatische Studien – Études Asiatiques* 71, no. 3 (2017): 811–31.

Bell, Joseph Norment. "Al-Sarrāj's *Maṣariᶜ al-ᶜushshāq*: A Ḥanbalite Work?" *Journal of the American Oriental Society* 99, no. 2 (1979): 235–48.

– "Avicenna's Treatise on Love and the Nonphilosophical Muslim Tradition." *Der Islam* 63, no. 1 (1986): 73–89.

– *Love Theory in Later Hanbalite Islam*. Albany, NY: State University of New York Press, 1979.

Bernard, Paul. "The Greek Kingdoms of Central Asia." In *History of Civilizations of Central Asia, Vol. 2: The Development of Sedentary and Nomadic Civilizations, 700 B.C. to A.D. 250*, edited by G.F. Etemadi, János Harmatta, and Baij Nath Puri, 99–129. Delhi: Motilal Banarsidass, 1999.

Béroul. *The Romance of Tristran*. Edited and translated by Norris J. Lacy. New York: Garland, 1989.

Bīrūnī, Abu al-Rayḥān al-. *Al-Biruni's Book on Pharmacy and Materia Medica*. Edited and translated by Hakim Muhammad Said. 2 vols. Karachi: Hamdard National Foundation, 1973.

– *Chronologie orientalischer Völker* [= al-Āthār al-bāqiya ʿan al-qurūn al-khāliya]. Edited by C. Eduard Sachau. Leipzig: Brockhaus, 1878.

– *The Chronology of Ancient Nations: An English Version of the Arabic Text of the Athâr-ul-Bâkiya of Albîrûnî, or "Vestiges of the Past."* Translated by C. Eduard Sachau. London: W.H. Allen & Co., 1879.

Bladel, Kevin van. *The Arabic Hermes: From Pagan Sage to Prophet of Science*. Oxford University Press, 2009.

Bloch, R. Howard. *Medieval Misogyny and the Invention of Western Romantic Love*. University of Chicago Press, 1991.

– "The Arthurian Fabliau and the Poetics of Virginity." In *Continuations: Essays on Medieval French Literature and Language in Honor of John l. Grigsby*, edited by Norris J. Lacy and Gloria Torrini-Roblin, 231–49. Birmingham, AL: Summa Publications, 1989.

Blois, François de. *Burzōy's Voyage to India and the Origin of the Book of Kalīlah wa Dimnah*. London: Royal Asiatic Society, 1990.

– *Persian Literature: A Bio-Bibliographical Survey. Volume V: Poetry of the Pre-Mongol Period*. 2nd ed. London: RoutledgeCurzon in association with the Royal Asiatic Society of Great Britain; Ireland, 2004.

– "Pre-Islamic Iranian and Indian Influences on Persian Literature." In *General Introduction to Persian Literature*, edited by J.T.P. de Bruijn, 333–44. London: I.B. Tauris, 2009.

Boethius. *Consolation of Philosophy*. Translated by Joel C. Relihan. Indianapolis: Hackett, 2001.

Bonebakker, Seeger A. "Some Medieval Views on Fantastic Stories." *Quaderni Di Studi Arabi* 10 (1992): 21–43.

Bosworth, C.E., ed. *Historic Cities of the Islamic World*. Leiden: Brill, 2007.

– "The Early Ghaznavids." In *The Cambridge History of Iran, Volume 4: The Period from the Arab Invasion to the Saljuqs*, edited by Richard N. Frye, 162–97. Cambridge University Press, 1975.

– "The Political and Dynastic History of the Iranian World (A.D. 1000–1217)."
In *The Cambridge History of Iran, Volume 5: The Saljuq and Mongol Periods*,
edited by J.A. Boyle, 1–202. Cambridge University Press, 1968.

Boulton, Maureen Barry McCann. *The Song in the Story: Lyric Insertions in
French Narrative Fiction, 1200–1400*. Philadelphia: University of Pennsylvania
Press, 1993.

Bowersock, G.W., D.C. Innes, E.L. Bowie, and P.E. Easterling. "The Literature
of the Empire." In *The Cambridge History of Classical Literature, Volume 1:
Greek Literature*, edited by Bernard M.W. Knox and P.E. Easterling, 642–713.
Cambridge University Press, 1985.

Boyce, Mary. "Ayādgār ī Jāmāspīg." *Encyclopædia Iranica* III/2 (1987): 126–7.
An updated version is available online at https://iranicaonline.org
/articles/ayadgar-i-jamaspig-memorial-of-jamasp-a-short-but-important
-zoroastrian-work-in-middle-persian-also-known-as-the-. Accessed 1 June
2022.

– "Gōsān." *Encyclopædia Iranica* XI/2 (2002): 167–70. An updated version is
available online at https://www.iranicaonline.org/articles/gosan. Accessed
1 June 2022.

– "Nowruz i. In the Pre-Islamic Period." *Encyclopædia Iranica, Online Edition*,
2009. Available at https://www.iranicaonline.org/articles/nowruz-i.
Accessed 1 June 2022.

– "The Parthian *Gōsān* and Iranian Minstrel Tradition." *Journal of the Royal
Asiatic Society*, no. 1/2 (1957): 10–45.

– ed. *Textual Sources for the Study of Zoroastrianism*. University of Chicago
Press, 1990.

– *Zoroastrians: Their Religious Beliefs and Practices*. London: Routledge & Kegan
Paul, 1979.

Branham, R. Bracht, ed. *The Bakhtin Circle and Ancient Narrative*. Barkhuis
Publishing & Groningen University Library, 2005.

– "The Poetics of Genre: Bakhtin, Menippus, Petronius." In *The Bakhtin
Circle and Ancient Narrative*, edited by R. Bracht Branham, 3–31. Barkhuis
Publishing & Groningen University Library, 2005.

Bray, Julia Ashtiany. "Isnāds and Models of Heroes: Abū Zubayd al-Ta'i,
Tanūkhī's Sundered Lovers and Abū 'l-'Anbas al-Saymarī." *Arabic & Middle
Eastern Literature* 1, no. 1 (1998): 7–30.

Briant, Pierre. *From Cyrus to Alexander: A History of the Persian Empire*. Winona
Lake, IN: Eisenbraun, 2002.

Browne, Edward G. *A Literary History of Persia*. 4 vols. London: T. Fisher
Unwin, 1902–24.

Bruckner, Matilda Tomaryn. "The Shape of Romance in Medieval France." In
The Cambridge Companion to Medieval Romance, edited by Robert L. Krueger,
13–28. Cambridge University Press, 2000.

Bruijn, J.T.P. de. "Classical Persian Literature as a Tradition." In *General Introduction to Persian Literature*, edited by J.T.P. de Bruijn, 1–42. London: I.B. Tauris, 2009.

– "Fiction i. Traditional Forms." *Encyclopædia Iranica* IX/6 (1999): 572–9. An updated version is available online at https://iranicaonline.org/articles/fiction-i-traditional. Accessed 1 June 2022.

– "Ḵᵛāju Kermāni." *Encyclopædia Iranica, Online Edition*, 2009. Available at https://iranicaonline.org/articles/kvaju-kerman-poet-and-mystic. Accessed 1 June 2022.

– *Persian Sufi Poetry: An Introduction to the Mystical Use of Classical Persian Poems*. Richmond, Surrey: Curzon, 1997.

– "Poets and Minstrels in Early Persian Literature." In *Transition Periods in Iranian History*, 15–23. Leuven: E. Peeters, 1987.

– "The *Qalandariyyāt* in Mystical Poetry, from Sanā'ī Onwards." In *The Legacy of Mediaeval Persian Sufism*, edited by Leonard Lewisohn, 75–86. London; New York: Ergon, 2006.

Bruijn, J.T.P. de, B. Flemming, and Munibur Rahman. "Mathnawī." In *Encyclopaedia of Islam, Second Edition*, edited by P. Bearman et al., 2012. doi:10.1163/1573-3912_islam_COM_0709. Accessed 1 June 2022.

Brunner, Christopher J. "The Fable of the Babylonian Tree." *Journal of Near Eastern Studies* 39, nos. 3–4 (1980): 191–202, 291–302.

Buḥturī, al-Walīd ibn ʿUbayd al-. *Kitāb al-ḥamāsa*. Edited by Louis Cheikho. Beirut: Imprimerie Catholique, 1910.

Bulliet, Richard W. *The Case for Islamo-Christian Civilization*. New York: Columbia University Press, 2006.

– "Naw Bahār and the Survival of Iranian Buddhism." *Iran* 14 (1976): 140–5.

Bürgel, J.C. "Die Liebesvorstellung im persischen Epos Wis und Ramin." *Asiatische Studien – Études Asiatiques* 33 (1979): 65–98.

– *The Feather of Simurgh: The "Licit Magic" of the Arts in Medieval Islam*. New York University Press, 1988.

– "The Romance." In *Persian Literature*, edited by Ehsan Yarshater, 161–78. Albany, NY: Bibliotheca Persica, 1988.

Busse, Heribert. "The Revival of Persian Kingship under the Būyids." In *Islamic Civilisation 950–1150*, edited by D.S. Richards, 47–69. Oxford University Press, 1973.

Cairns, Francis. *Generic Composition in Greek and Roman Poetry*. Edinburgh University Press, 1972.

Canepa, Matthew P. *The Two Eyes of the Earth: Art and Ritual of Kingship between Rome and Sasanian Iran*. Berkeley: University of California Press, 2009.

Cereti, Carlo. "Gayōmard." *Encyclopædia Iranica, Online Edition*, 2015. Available at https://iranicaonline.org/articles/gayomard. Accessed 1 June 2022.

Chaucer, Geoffrey. *The Riverside Chaucer*. Edited by Larry Dean Benson. Boston: Houghton Mifflin, 1987.

Chelkowski, Peter J. *Mirror of the Invisible World: Tales from the Khamseh of Nizami*. New York: The Metropolitan Museum of Art, 1975.

– *Ta'ziyeh, Ritual and Drama in Iran*. New York University Press, 1979.

Chittick, William. "Love in Islamic Thought." *Religion Compass* 8, no. 7 (2014): 229–38.

Choksy, Jamsheed K. *Evil, Good and Gender: Facets of the Feminine in Zoroastrian Religious History*. New York: Peter Lang, 2002.

Chrétien de Troyes. *Cligès: Édition bilingue*. Edited by Laurence Harf-Lancner. Paris: H. Champion, 2006.

– *The Complete Romances of Chrétien de Troyes*. Translated by David Staines. Bloomington: Indiana University Press, 1990.

Classen, Albrecht. "Introduction." In *Paradigm Shifts during the Global Middle Ages and the Renaissance*, edited by Albrecht Classen, vii–xlvi. Turnhout, Belgium: Brepols, 2019.

Conte, Gian Biagio. *Genres and Readers: Lucretius, Love Elegy, Pliny's Encyclopedia*. Translated by Glenn W. Most. Baltimore: Johns Hopkins University Press, 1994.

Corbin, Henry. *Avicenna and the Visionary Recital*. Translated by Willard R. Trask. New York: Pantheon Books, 1960.

Crone, Patricia. *God's Rule: Government and Islam*. New York: Columbia University Press, 2004.

Cross, Cameron. "'If Death Is Just, What Is Injustice?': Illicit Rage in 'Rostam and Sohrab' and 'The Knight's Tale.'" *Iranian Studies* 48, no. 3 (2015): 395–422.

– "The Lives and Afterlives of *Vis and Rāmin*." *Iranian Studies* 51, no. 4 (2018): 517–56.

– "The Many Colors of Love in Niẓāmī's *Haft Paykar*: Beyond the Spectrum." *Interfaces: A Journal of Medieval European Literatures*, no. 2 (2016): 52–96.

– "Poetic Alchemy: The Rise of Romance from a Persian Perspective." *Medieval Encounters*, forthcoming.

– "The Poetics of Romantic Love in *Vis & Rāmin*." PhD thesis, University of Chicago, 2015.

– "A Tree Atop the Mountain: Mobad Manikan and the Elusive Promises of Masculinity." *Iran Namag* 3, no. 1 (2018): xxvi–lxiii.

Curtis, Vesta Sarkhosh. *Persian Myths*. London: British Museum, 1993.

Curtius, Ernst Robert. *European Literature and the Latin Middle Ages*. Translated by Willard R. Trask. 1953. Reprint, Princeton University Press, 2013.

D'Orbigny, Robert. *Le conte de Floire et Blanchefleur: nouvelle édition critique du texte du manuscrit A (Paris, BNF, fr. 375)*. Edited by Jean-Luc Leclanche. Paris: Champion, 2003.

Dabashi, Hamid. *The Shahnameh: The Persian Epic as World Literature*. New York: Columbia University Press, 2019.

Dankoff, Robert. "The Lyric in the Romance: The Use of Ghazal in Persian and Turkish Maṣnavīs." *Journal of Near Eastern Studies* 43, no. 1 (1984): 9–25.

Daqiqi, Abu Manṣur. *Divān-e Abu Manṣur Moḥammad b. Aḥmad Daqiqi Ṭusi*. Edited by Moḥammad Javād Shariᶜat. Tehran: Asāṭir, 1368 [1989].

Daryaee, Touraj. "Kingship in Early Sasanian Iran." In *The Sasanian Era*, edited by Vesta Sarkhosh Curtis and Sarah Stewart, 60–70. London: I.B. Tauris, 2008.

Davidson, Olga M. *Poet and Hero in the Persian Book of Kings*. Ithaca, NY: Cornell University Press, 1994.

Davis, Dick. "Introduction." In *Vis and Ramin*, ix–xlvi. London: Penguin, 2009.

– *Panthea's Children: Hellenistic Novels and Medieval Persian Romances*. New York: Bibliotheca Persica, 2002.

– "The Problem of Ferdowsi's Sources." *Journal of the American Oriental Society* 116, no. 1 (1996): 48–57.

– "A Trout in the Milk: *Vis and Ramin* and *Tristan and Isolde*." In *Erin and Iran: Cultural Encounters between the Irish and the Iranians*, edited by Houchang Chehabi and Grace Neville, 44–53. Cambridge, MA: Harvard University Press, 2015.

– "Vis o Rāmin." *Encyclopædia Iranica, Online Edition*, 2005. Available at https://www.iranicaonline.org/articles/vis-o-ramin. Accessed 1 June 2022.

– "Women in the *Shahnameh*: Exotics and Natives, Rebellious Legends, and Dutiful Daughters." In *Women and Medieval Epic: Gender, Genre, and the Limits of Epic Masculinity*, edited by Sara S. Poor and Jana K. Schulman, 67–90. New York: Palgrave Macmillan, 2008.

Davis, Kathleen, and Michael Puett. "Periodization and 'the Medieval Globe': A Conversation." *The Medieval Globe* 2, no. 1 (2015).

Dehkhoda Lexicon Institute. "Loghat-nāma." Accessed 1 June 2022. https://dehkhoda.ut.ac.ir/fa/dictionary/.

Delcourt, Denyse. "Swords and Flowers: Conversion in La Chanson de Roland and Floire et Blanchefleur." *Modern Language Notes* 127, no. 5 (2012): S34–53.

Derrida, Jacques. "The Law of Genre." Translated by Avital Ronell. *Critical Inquiry* 7, no. 1 (1980): 55–81.

Doniger, Wendy. "The Rings of Budur and Qamar al-Zaman." In *Scheherazade's Children: Global Encounters with the Arabian Nights*, edited by Philip F. Kennedy, 108–26. New York University Press, 2013.

Doody, Margaret Anne. *The True Story of the Novel*. New Brunswick, NJ: Rutgers University Press, 1996.

Dowlatshāh Samarqandi. *The Tadhkiratu 'sh-Shuᶜará* ("Memoirs of the Poets"). Edited by Edward Granville Browne. London: Luzac & Co.; Brill, 1901.

Durand-Guédy, David. *Iranian Elites and Turkish Rulers: A History of Iṣfahān in the Saljūq Period*. London; New York: Routledge, 2010.

– "Ruling from the Outside: A New Perspective on Early Turkish Kingship in Iran." In *Every Inch a King: Comparative Studies on Kings and Kingship in the Ancient and Medieval Worlds*, edited by Lynette Mitchell and Charles Melville, 325–42. Leiden: Brill, 2013.

During, Jean, and Zia Mirabdolbaghi. *The Art of Persian Music*. Washington, DC: Mage, 1991.

ᶜEbādiyān, Maḥmud. *Anvāᶜ-e adabi*. Tehran: Ḥowza-ye Honari, 1379 [2000].

Egger, Brigitte. "Looking at Chariton's Callirhoe." In *Greek Fiction: The Greek Novel in Context*, edited by Richard Stoneman and John Robert Morgan, 31–48. London: Routledge, 1994.

Eksell, Kerstin. "Genre in Early Arabic Poetry." In *Literary Genres: An Intercultural Approach*, edited by Gunilla Lindberg-Wada, 156–98. Berlin: De Gruyter, 2006.

El-Hibri, Tayeb. *Reinterpreting Islamic Historiography: Hārūn al-Rashīd and the Narrative of the 'Abbāsid Caliphate*. Cambridge University Press, 1999.

El-Rouayheb, Khaled. *Before Homosexuality in the Arab-Islamic World, 1500–1800*. University of Chicago Press, 2005.

Elsom, Helen E. "Callirhoe: Displaying the Phallic Woman." In *Pornography and Representation in Greece and Rome*, edited by Amy Richlin, 212–30. New York; Oxford: Oxford University Press, 1992.

Ephrat, Daphna. *A Learned Society in a Period of Transition: The Sunni ᶜUlamaᵓ of Eleventh-Century Baghdad*. Albany, NY: State University of New York Press, 2000.

Epps, Brad. "Comparison, Competition, and Cross-Dressing: Cross-Cultural Analysis in a Contested World." In *Islamicate Sexualities: Translations across Temporal Geographies of Desire*, edited by Kathryn Babayan and Afsaneh Najmabadi, 114–60. Cambridge, MA: Center for Middle Eastern Studies of Harvard University, 2008.

Ernst, Carl W. "The Stages of Love in Early Persian Sufism, from Rābi'a to Rūzbihān." In *The Heritage of Sufism, Vol. 1: Classical Persian Sufism from Its Origins to Rumi (700–1300)*, edited by Leonard Lewisohn, 435–56. Oxford: Oneworld, 1999.

ᶜEshqi-Sardehi, ᶜAli, Abu al-Qāsim Amir-Aḥmadi, and Iraj Kiyāni. "Naqd-e shakhṣiyat-e Vis az manẓar-e amniyat-e ᶜāṭefi." *Moṭāleᶜāt-e Naqd-e Adabi* 38 (1394 [2015]): 111–28.

Eslāmi-Nodushan, Moḥammad-ᶜAli. "Āyā 'Vis-o Rāmin' yek manẓuma-ye żedd-e akhlāq ast?" In *Jām-e jahānbin dar zamina-ye naqd-e adabi va adabiyāt-e taṭbiqi*, 346–83. Tehran: Ebn-e Sinā, 1349 [1970].

– "Vis va Izut." In *Jām-e jahānbin dar zamina-ye naqd-e adabi va adabiyāt-e taṭbiqi*, 143–67. Tehran: Ebn-e Sinā, 1349 [1970].

– "Vis-o Rāmin va Shāhnāma." In *Nāma-ye Minovi*, edited by Ḥabib Yaghmāᵓi, Iraj Afshār, and Moḥammad Rowshan, 18–37. Tehran: Kāviyān, 1350 [1971].

Ethé, Hermann. "Neupersische Litteratur." In *Grundriss der iranischen Philologie*, edited by Wilhelm Geiger and Ernst Kuhn, 2:212–368. Strasbourg: K. J. Trübner, 1895–1904.

Evans, Dylan. *An Introductory Dictionary of Lacanian Psychoanalysis*. London; New York: Routledge, 1996.

Fackenheim, Emil L. "A Treatise on Love by Ibn Sina." *Mediaeval Studies* 7 (1945): 208–28.

Farghadani, Shahla. "A History of Style and a Style of History: The Hermeneutic of *Tarz* in Persian Literary Criticism." *Iranian Studies* 55, no. 2 (2021): 1–19.

Faris, Nabih Amin. "Al-Ghazzali's Epistle of the Birds: A Translation of the *Risālat al-Ṭayr*." *The Muslim World* 34, no. 1 (1944): 46–53.

Ferdowsi, Abu al-Qāsem. *In the Dragon's Claws: The Story of Rostam & Esfandiyar*. Translated by Jerome W. Clinton. Washington, DC: Mage, 1999.

– *Shāhnāma*. Edited by Djalal Khaleghi-Motlagh, Mahmoud Omidsalar, and Abolfazl Khatibi. 8 vols. New York: Bibliotheca Persica, 1987–2008.

– *Shahnameh: The Persian Book of Kings*. Translated by Dick Davis. 2nd ed. New York: Penguin, 2016.

Fink, Bruce. *The Lacanian Subject: Between Language and Jouissance*. Princeton University Press, 1995.

Flatt, Emma J. "Martial Skills." In *The Courts of the Deccan Sultanates: Living Well in the Persian Cosmopolis*, 268–302. Cambridge University Press, 2019.

Foltz, Richard C. *Animals in Islamic Tradition and Muslim Cultures*. Oxford: Oneworld, 2006.

Foruzānfar, Badiᶜ al-Zamān. *Sokhan va sokhanvarān*. Zavvār, 1387 [2009].

Foucault, Michel. *The History of Sexuality*. Translated by Robert Hurley. 3 vols. New York: Pantheon Books, 1978–86.

Fouchécour, Charles-Henri de. *Moralia: Les notions morales dans la littérature persane du 3e/9e au 7e/13e siècle*. Paris: Editions Recherche sur les civilisations, 1986.

Fromherz, Allen James. *The Near West: Medieval North Africa, Latin Europe and the Mediterranean in the Second Axial Age*. Edinburgh University Press, 2016.

Frow, John. *Genre*. 2nd ed. New York: Routledge, 2015.

Frye, Northrop. *Anatomy of Criticism: Four Essays*. Princeton University Press, 1957.

– *The Secular Scripture: A Study of the Structure of the Romance*. Cambridge, MA: Harvard University Press, 1976.

Frye, Richard N. "Development of Persian Literature under the Samanids and Qarakhanids." In *Yádnáme-ye Jan Rypka: Collection of Articles on Persian and Tajik Literature*, 69–74. Academia, 1967.

Fuchs, Barbara. *Romance*. New York: Routledge, 2004.

Fusillo, Massimo. *Il romanzo greco: Polifonia ed eros*. Venice: Marsilio Editori, 1989.

Gabbay, Alyssa. "Love Gone Wrong, Then Right Again: Male/Female Dynamics in the Bahrām Gūr-Slave Girl Story." *Iranian Studies* 42, no. 5 (2009): 677–92.

Gabri, Richard. "Framing the Unframable in Ferdowsi's *Shahnameh*." *Iranian Studies* 48, no. 3 (2015): 423–41.

Gabrieli, Francesco. "Note sul *Vīs u Rāmīn* di Faḫr ad-Dīn Gurgānī." *Rendiconti della R. Accademia Nazionale dei Lincei, Classe di scienzi morali, storichi e filologiche, ser. 6* 15 (1939): 168–88.

– "Sul poema persiano *Vīs u Rāmīn*." *Annali, Istituto Orientale di Napoli N.S.* 1 (1940): 253–8.

Gaillard, Marina. "Héroïnes d'exception: Les femmes *'ayyār* dans la prose romanesque de l'Iran médiéval." *Studia Iranica* 34, no. 2 (2005): 163–98.

Gandjeï, Tourkhan. "The Genesis and Definition of a Literary Composition: The Dah-Nāma ('Ten Love Letters')." *Der Islam* 47 (1971): 59–66.

Gaunt, Simon. "French Literature Abroad: Towards an Alternative History of French Literature." *Interfaces: A Journal of Medieval European Literatures*, no. 1 (2015): 25–61.

– *Gender and Genre in Medieval French Literature*. Cambridge University Press, 1995.

– "Romance and Other Genres." In *The Cambridge Companion to Medieval Romance*, edited by Robert L. Krueger, 45–59. Cambridge University Press, 2000.

Gazerani, Saghi. *The Sistani Cycle of Epics and Iran's National History*. Leiden: Brill, 2016.

Gelder, Geert Jan van. *Close Relationships: Incest and Inbreeding in Classical Arabic Literature*. London: I.B. Tauris, 2005.

Gelder, Geert Jan van, and Marlé Hammond, eds. *Takhyil: The Imaginary in Classical Arabic Poetics*. Cambridge, UK: Gibb Memorial Trust, 2008.

Genette, Gerard. *The Architext: An Introduction*. Translated by Jane E. Lewin. 1979. Reprint, Berkeley; Los Angeles: University of California Press, 1992.

Gerhardt, Mia I. *The Art of Story-Telling: A Literary Study of the Thousand and One Nights*. Leiden: Brill, 1963.

Ghazālī, Abu Ḥāmid Muḥammad al-. *Iḥyāʾ ʿulūm al-dīn*. 10 vols. Jeddah: Dār al-Minhāj, 1432 [2011].

Ghazi, Mohammed Ferid. "Un groupe social: 'Les raffinés' (ẓurafāʾ)." *Studia Islamica* 11 (1959): 39–71.

Ghazoul, Ferial Jabouri. *The Arabian Nights: A Structural Analysis*. Cairo: Cairo Associated Institution for the Study and Presentation of Arab Cultural Values, 1980.

Giffen, Lois Anita. *Theory of Profane Love among the Arabs: The Development of the Genre*. New York University Press, 1971.

Girard, René. *Deceit, Desire, and the Novel*. Translated by Yvonne Freccero. Baltimore: Johns Hopkins University Press, 1965.

Gnoli, Gerardo. "Farr(ah)." *Encyclopædia Iranica, Online Edition*, 1999. Available at https://www.iranicaonline.org/articles/farrah. Accessed 1 June 2022.

Goethe, Johann Wolfgang von. *The West-East Divan: The Poems, with "Notes and Essays"; Goethe's Intercultural Dialogues*. Translated by Martin Bidney and Peter Anton von Arnim. Albany, NY: State University of New York Press, 2010.

Goldhill, Simon. *Foucault's Virginity: Ancient Erotic Fiction and the History of Sexuality*. Cambridge University Press, 1995.

– "Genre." In *The Cambridge Companion to the Greek and Roman Novel*, edited by Tim Whitmarsh, 185–200. Cambridge University Press, 2008.

Gorgāni, Fakhr al-Din. *Le Roman de Wîs et Râmîn*. Translated by Henri Massé. Paris: Société d'Édition «Les Belles Lettres», 1959.

– *Vis and Ramin*. Translated by George Morrison. New York: Columbia University Press, 1972.

– *Vis and Ramin*. Translated by Dick Davis. London: Penguin, 2008.

– *Vis and Rāmin: A Romance of Ancient Iran Originally Written in Pahlavi and Rendered into Persian Verse by Fakhroddin Gorgānī c. 1054 A.D.* Edited by Mojtabā Minovi. Tehran: Beroukhim, 1314 [1935].

– *Vīs va Rāmīn of Fakhr al-Dīn Gorgānī: Persian Critical Text Composed from the Persian and Georgian Oldest Manuscripts*. Edited by Magali T'odua, Alek'sandre Gvaxaria, and Kamāl ᶜAyni. Tehran: Iranian Culture Foundation, 1349 [1970].

– *Vis-o Rāmin*. Edited by Moḥammad Rowshan. Tehran: Ṣedā-ye Moᶜāṣer, 1377 [1998].

– *Vis-o Rāmin: Ba moqaddema-ye mabsuṭ va ḥavāshi va taᶜliqāt va farhang-e vāzhahā va fehresthā-ye se-gāna*. Edited by Moḥammad Jaᶜfar Maḥjub. Tehran: Ebn-e Sinā, 1337 [1959].

– *Wís o Rámín: A Romance of Ancient Persia, Translated from the Pahlawi and Rendered into Verse*. Edited by William Nassau Lees and Munshi Ahmad Ali. Calcutta: Printed at the College Press, 1865.

Gottfried von Strassburg. *Tristan; With the "Tristan" of Thomas*. Translated by Arthur Thomas Hatto. 2nd ed. 1967. Reprint, London: Penguin, 2004.

– *Tristan: Band 1, Text*. Edited by Karl Marold. Berlin; New York: De Gruyter, 2004.

Graf, Karl Heinrich. "Wîs und Râmîn." *Zeitschrift der Deutschen Morgenländischen Gesellschaft* 23 (1869): 375–433.

Graham, Terry. "Abū Saʿīd ibn Abī'l-Khayr and the School of Khurāsān." In *Classical Persian Sufism: From Its Origins to Rumi*, edited by Leonard Lewisohn, 83–135. Oneworld, 1999.

Gray, Louis H. "Zoroastrian Elements in Muhammedan Eschatology." *Le Muséon* 21 (1902): 153–84.

Green, Dennis H. *The Beginnings of Medieval Romance: Fact and Fiction, 1150–1220*. Cambridge University Press, 2002.

– "The Rise of Medieval Fiction in the Twelfth Century." In *Medieval Narratives between History and Fiction: From the Centre to the Periphery of Europe, c. 1100–1400*, edited by Panagiotis A. Agapitos and Lars Boje Mortensen, 49–61. Copenhagen: Museum Tusculanum Press, 2012.

Greene, Robin J. "(Un)happily Ever After: Literary and Religious Tensions in the Endings of the *Apocryphal Acts of Paul and Thecla*." In *The Ancient Novel and Early Christian and Jewish Narrative: Fictional Intersections*, 21–33. Groningen: Barkhuis Publishing & Groningen University Library, 2012.

Grosz, Elizabeth. *Jacques Lacan: A Feminist Introduction*. London; New York: Routledge, 1990.

Gruendler, Beatrice. "Motif vs. Genre: Reflections on the *Dīwān al-Maʿānī* of Abū Hilāl al-ʿAskarī." In *Ghazal as World Literature: Transformations of a Literary Genre*, edited by Thomas Bauer and Angelika Neuwirth, 1:57–85. Beirut: Ergon, 2005.

Grunebaum, Gustave E. von. "Avicenna's *Risâla fî ʾl-ʿišq* and Courtly Love." *Journal of Near Eastern Studies* 11, no. 4 (1952): 233–8.

– "Greek Form Elements in the Arabian Nights." *Journal of the American Oriental Society* 62, no. 4 (1942): 277–92.

– *Medieval Islam: A Study in Cultural Orientation*. 2nd ed. University of Chicago Press, 1954.

Guo, Li. *The Performing Arts in Medieval Islam: Shadow Play and Popular Poetry in Ibn Daniyal's Mamluk Cairo*. Leiden; Boston: Brill, 2012.

Gutas, Dimitri. *Avicenna and the Aristotelian Tradition: Introduction to Reading Avicenna's Philosophical Works*. Leiden; Boston: Brill, 2014.

– *Greek Thought, Arabic Culture: The Graeco-Arabic Translation Movement in Baghdad and Early ʿAbbāsid Society (2nd–4th/8th–10th Centuries)*. London: Routledge, 1998.

– "Plato's *Symposion* in the Arabic Tradition." *Oriens* 31 (1988): 36–60.

Gvaxaria, Alek'sandre. "Notes on the Persian Text of Gorgani's Vis o Ramin." In *Ex Oriente: Collected Papers in Honour of Jiří Bečka*, edited by Adéla Křikavová and Luděk Hřebíček, 53–62. Prague: Czech Academy of Sciences, Oriental Institute, 1995.

Hādi, Ruḥ-Allāh, and Zaynab Naṣiri. "Sākhtār-e tashbih dar Khosrow-o Shirin va Vis-o Rāmin." *Adab-e Fārsi* 12 (1392 [2013]): 115–32.

Hägg, Tomas. "Metiochus at Polycrates' Court." *Eranos* 83 (1985): 92–102.

– *The Novel in Antiquity*. Berkeley: University of California Press, 1983.

– "The Oriental Reception of Greek Novels: A Survey with Some Preliminary Considerations." *Symbolae Osloenses* 61 (1986): 99–131.

– "The *Parthenope Romance* Decapitated?" *Symbolae Osloenses* 59 (1984): 61–92.

Hägg, Tomas, and Bo Utas. "Eros Goes East: Parthenope the Virgin Meets Vāmiq the Ardent Lover." In *Plotting with Eros: Essays on the Poetics of Love and the Erotics of Reading*, edited by Ingela Nilsson, 153–86. Copenhagen: Museum Tusculanum Press, 2009.

– *The Virgin and Her Lover: Fragments of an Ancient Greek Novel and a Persian Epic Poem*. Leiden: Brill, 2003.

Haidu, Peter. *The Subject Medieval/Modern: Text and Governance in the Middle Ages*. Stanford University Press, 2004.

Hākemi, Ismāᶜil, and Rāziya Zavāriyān. "Barrasi-ye jāygāh-e zan va ᶜeshq dar Vis-o Rāmin-e Fakhr al-Din-e Asᶜad-e Gorgāni." *Faṣlnāma-ye Takhaṣṣoṣi-ye Zabān va Adabiyāt-e Fārsi* 3, no. 10 (1390 [2012]): 91–107.

Halperin, David M. *One Hundred Years of Homosexuality: And Other Essays on Greek Love*. New York: Routledge, 1990.

Hämeen-Anttila, Jaakko. *Khwadāynāmag: The Middle Persian Book of Kings*. Leiden: Brill, 2018.

– *Maqama: A History of the Genre*. Wiesbaden: Harrassowitz, 2002.

Hanaway, William L. "Anāhitā and Alexander." *Journal of the American Oriental Society* 101, no. 2 (1982): 285–95.

Hansen, Valerie. *The Year 1000: When Explorers Connected the World – and Globalization Began*. New York: Scribner, 2021.

Harb, Lara. *Arabic Poetics: Aesthetic Experience in Classical Arabic Literature*. Cambridge University Press, 2020.

Harvey, Ruth. "Courtly Culture in Medieval Occitania." In *The Troubadours: An Introduction*, edited by Simon Gaunt and Sarah Kay, 8–27. Cambridge University Press, 1999.

Heath, Peter. "Romance as Genre in 'The Thousand and One Nights': Part I." *Journal of Arabic Literature* 18 (1987): 1–21.

– "Romance as Genre in 'The Thousand and One Nights': Part II." *Journal of Arabic Literature* 19 (1988): 3–26.

– *The Thirsty Sword: Sīrat ᶜAntar and the Arabic Popular Epic*. Salt Lake City: University of Utah Press, 1996.

Hedāyat, Sādeq. "Chand nokta dar bāra-ye Vis-o Rāmin." In *Majmuᶜa-ye neveshta-hā-ye parākanda-ye Sādeq-e Hedāyat*, 486–523. Tehran: Amir Kabir, 1334 [1955].

Hemmat, Kaveh. "Completing the Persianate Turn." *Iranian Studies* 54, no. 3–4 (2021): 633–46.

Heng, Geraldine. *Empire of Magic: Medieval Romance and the Politics of Cultural Fantasy*. New York: Columbia University Press, 2003.

– "A Global Middle Ages." In *A Handbook of Middle English Studies*, edited by Marion Turner, 413–29. Chichester: John Wiley & Sons, 2013.

– *The Invention of Race in the European Middle Ages*. Cambridge University Press, 2018.

Heng, Geraldine, and Lynn Ramey. "Early Globalities, Global Literatures: Introducing a Special Issue on the Global Middle Ages." *Literature Compass* 11, no. 7 (2014): 389–94.

Herzog, Thomas. "'What They Saw with Their Own Eyes ... ': Fictionalization and 'Narrativization' of History in Arab Popular Epics and Learned Historiography." In *Fictionalizing the Past: Historical Characters in Arabic Popular Epic*, edited by Sabine Dorpmueller, 25–43. Leuven: Peeters, 2012.

Hesiod. *Theogony and Works and Days*. Translated by Catherine M. Schlegel and Henry Weinfield. Ann Arbor, MI: University of Michigan Press, 2006.

Hinnells, John R. *Persian Mythology*. London: Hamlyn, 1973.

Hodgson, Marshall G.S. *The Venture of Islam: Conscience and History in a World Civilization*. 3 vols. University of Chicago Press, 1977.

Hoffmann, Alexandra. "Cats and Dogs, Manliness, and Misogyny: On the *Sindbad-Nameh* as World Literature." In *Persian Literature as World Literature*, edited by Mostafa Abedinifard, Omid Azadibougar, and Amirhossein Vafa, 137–52. New York: Bloomsbury Academic, 2021.

Høgel, Christian. "World Literature Is Trans-Imperial: A Medieval and a Modern Approach." *Medieval Worlds* 8 (2018): 3–21.

Hojviri, Abu al-Ḥasan ʿAli b. ʿOsmān. *Kashf al-maḥjub*. Edited by Moḥammad Ḥosayn Tasbiḥi. Islamabad: Markaz-e Taḥqiqāt Fārsi-ye Irān va Pākestān, 1374 [1995].

– *The Kashf al-Maḥjúb: The Oldest Persian Treatise on Ṣúfiism*. London; Leiden: Luzac & Co.; Brill, 1911.

Holquist, Michael. "Introduction." In *The Dialogic Imagination: Four Essays*, edited by Michael Holquist, xv–xxxiii. Austin: University of Texas Press, 1981.

Holzberg, Niklas. *The Ancient Novel: An Introduction*. London: Routledge, 1995.

– "The Genre: Novels Proper and the Fringe." In *The Novel in the Ancient World*, edited by Gareth Schmeling, 11–28. Leiden: Brill, 2003.

Honarmand, Saeed. "Between the Water and the Wall: The Power of Love in Medieval Persian Romance." In *The Layered Heart: Essays on Persian Poetry*, edited by Ali Asghar Seyed-Gohrab, 55–80. Washington, DC: Mage, 2019.

Hoyland, Robert G. *The "History of the Kings of the Persians" in Three Arabic Chronicles: The Transmission of the Iranian Past from Late Antiquity to Early Islam*. Liverpool University Press, 2018.

Hubert, Merton Jerome, trans. *The Romance of Floire and Blanchefleur: A French Idyllic Poem of the Twelfth Century*. Chapel Hill: University of North Carolina Press, 1966.

Humbach, Helmut, and Pallan R. Ichaporia. *Zamyād Yasht: Yasht 19 of the Younger Avesta: Text, Translation, Commentary*. Wiesbaden: Harrassowitz, 1998.

Huot, Sylvia. *From Song to Book: The Poetics of Writing in Old French Lyric and Lyrical Narrative Poetry*. Ithaca: Cornell University Press, 1987.

Ibn al-Muqaffaʿ, Abu Muḥammad Rūzbih. *Kalila and Dimna: Or the Fables of Bidpai*. Translated by Wyndham Knatchbull. Oxford: W. Baxter, 1819.

– *Kitāb Kalīla wa-Dimna*. Cairo: Maṭbaʿ al-Amīriyya bi-Būlāq, 1937.

Ibn Dāwūd, Abū Bakr Muḥammad al-Iṣbahānī. *al-Niṣf al-awwal min kitāb al-zahra*. Edited by Alois Richard Nykl and Ibrāhīm ʿAbd al-Fattāḥ Ṭūqān. Beirut: Maṭbaʿ al-Ābāʾ al-Yasūʿiyīn, 1351 [1932].

Ibn Faḍlān, Aḥmad. "Mission to the Volga." In *Two Arabic Travel Books*, edited by James E. Montgomery, Philip F. Kennedy, and Shawkat M. Toorawa, translated by James E. Montgomery, 163–297. New York University Press, 2014.

Ibn Ḥazm, ʿAlī ibn Aḥmad. *Ṭawq al-ḥamāma fī al-ulfah wa-l-ullāf*. Edited by Ṭāhir Aḥmad Makkī. Cairo: Dār al-Maʿārif, 1993.

Ibn Qutayba. *al-Shiʿr wa-al-shuʿarāʾ*. Edited by Aḥmad Muḥammad Shākir. Cairo: Dār al-Maʿārif, 1486 [1967].

– *ʿUyūn al-akhbār*. 4 vols. Cairo: Dār al-Kutub al-Miṣrīya, 1996.

Ikhwān al-Ṣafāʾ. *The Case of the Animals versus Man before the King of the Jinn: A Translation from the Epistles of the Brethren of Purity*. Translated by Lenn E. Goodman and Richard McGregor. Oxford University Press, 2009.

– *Rasāʾil Ikhwān al-ṣafāʾ wa-khullān al-wafāʾ*. 4 vols. Beirut: Dār Bayrūt, 1957.

Ilahi-Ghomshei, Husayn. "The Principles of the Religion of Love in Classical Persian Poetry." In *Hafiz and the Religion of Love in Classical Persian Poetry*, edited by Leonard Lewisohn, 77–106. London: I.B. Tauris, 2010.

Ingenito, Domenico. *Beholding Beauty: Saʿdi of Shiraz and the Aesthetics of Desire in Medieval Persian Poetry*. Leiden; Boston: Brill, 2021.

Irānshāh b. Abi al-Khayr. *Bahman-nāma*. Edited by Rahim ʿAfifi. Tehran: Enteshārāt-e ʿElmi va Farhangi, 1370 [1991].

– *Kush-nāma*. Edited by Jalāl Matini. Tehran: ʿElmi, 1377 [1998].

Irwin, Robert. "Futuwwa: Chivalry and Gangsterism in Medieval Cairo." *Muqarnas* 21 (2004): 161–70.

– *Night and Horses and the Desert: An Anthology of Classical Arabian Literature*. London: Allen Lane; The Penguin Press, 1999.

– "The Arabic Beast Fable." *Journal of the Warburg and Courtauld Institutes* 55 (1992): 36–50.

Iṣbahānī, Abu al-Faraj al-. *Kitāb al-aghānī*. Edited by Iḥsān ʿAbbās. 25 vols. Beirut: Dār Ṣādir, 1423 [2002].

Iṣfahānī, Ḥamza al-. *Tārīkh sanī mulūk al-arḍ wa-l-anbiyāʾ*. Edited by Yūsuf Yaʿqūb Maskūnī. 3rd ed. Beirut: Dār Maktabat al-Ḥayāh, 1961.

Jackson, Virginia. *Dickinson's Misery: A Theory of Lyric Reading*. Princeton University Press, 2005.

Jackson, Virginia, and Yopie Prins, eds. *The Lyric Theory Reader: A Critical Anthology*. Baltimore: Johns Hopkins University Press, 2014.

Jacobi, Renate. "al-ʿAbbās ibn al-Aḥnaf." In *Encyclopedia of Arabic Literature*, edited by Julie Scott Meisami and Paul Starkey, 2–3. London; New York: Routledge, 1998.

– "Theme and Variations in Umayyad Ghazal Poetry." *Journal of Arabic Literature* 23, no. 2 (1992): 109–19.

Jāḥiẓ, Abū ʿUthmān ʿAmr b. Baḥr al-. *The Epistle on Singing-Girls of Jāḥiẓ*. Edited and translated by A.F.L. Beeston. Warminster, Eng.: Aris & Phillips, 1980.

– *Rasāʾil al-Jāḥiẓ*. Edited by ʿAbd al-Salām Muḥammad Hārūn. Cairo: Maktabat al-Khanjī, 1384 [1964].

Jakobson, Roman. "The Dominant." In *Readings in Russian Poetics: Formalist and Structuralist Views*, edited by Ladislav Matejka and Krystyna Pomorska, 82–7. Ann Arbor, MI: Michigan Slavic Publications, 1978.

Jameson, Fredric. "Magical Narratives: Romance as Genre." *New Literary History* 7, no. 1 (1975): 135–63.

– *The Political Unconscious: Narrative as a Socially Symbolic Act*. Ithaca, NY: Cornell University Press, 1981.

Jāmi, ʿAbd al-Raḥmān. *Maśnavi-ye haft owrang*. Edited by Aʿlākhān Afṣaḥzād, Jābelqā Dād ʿAlishāh, Aṣghar Jānfedā, Ẓāher Aḥrāri, and Ḥosayn Aḥmad Tarbiyat. 2 vols. Tehran: Markaz-e Moṭālaʿāt-e Irāni, Daftar-e Nashr-e Mirāś-e Maktub, 1378 [1999].

Jauss, Hans Robert. *Toward an Aesthetic of Reception*. Translated by Timothy Bahti. Minneapolis: University of Minnesota Press, 1982.

Jayyusi, Salma K. "Umayyad Poetry." In *Arabic Literature to the End of the Umayyad Period*, edited by A.F.L. Beeston, T.M. Johnstone, R.B. Serjeant, and G.R. Smith, 378–432. Cambridge History of Arabic Literature. Cambridge University Press, 1983.

Jeffreys, Elizabeth, ed. *Digenes Akritis: The Grottaferrata and Escorial Versions*. Translated by Elizabeth Jeffreys. Cambridge University Press, 1998.

– trans. *Four Byzantine Novels*. Liverpool University Press, 2012.

Jeffreys, Elizabeth, and Michael Jeffreys. "The Oral Background of Byzantine Popular Poetry." *Oral Tradition* 1, no. 3 (1986): 504–47.

Julian, Emperor of Rome. "Fragment of a Letter to a Priest." In *The Works of the Emperor Julian*, translated by Wilmer Cave Wright, 2:297–339. London: W. Weinemann; New York: Macmillan, 1913. doi:10.4159/DLCL.emperor_julian-fragment_letter_priest.1913.

Kahane, Ahuvia. "Epic, Novel, Genre: Bakhtin and the Question of History." In *The Bakhtin Circle and Ancient Narrative*, edited by R. Bracht Branham, 51–73. Groningen: Barkhuis Publishing & Groningen University Library, 2005.

Kahduni, Moḥammad-Kāẓem, and Maryam Bohrani. "Taḥlil-e shakhṣiyat-e Mobad dar Vis-o Rāmin bar asās-e naẓariyāt-e Yung." *Moṭāleʿāt-e Irāni* 15 (1388 [2009]): 223–38.

Kaladze, Inga. "The Georgian Translation of *Vis and Rāmin*: An Old Specimen of Hermeneutics." *Journal of Persianate Studies* 2, no. 2 (2009): 137–42.

Kanazi, George. "The Literary Theory of Abū Hilāl al-ʿAskarī." In *Israel Oriental Studies XI: Studies in Medieval Arabic and Hebrew Poetics*, edited by Sasson Somekh, 21–36. Leiden: Brill, 1991.

Kantorowicz, Ernst H. *The King's Two Bodies: A Study in Mediaeval Political Theology*. Princeton University Press, 2016.

Kappler, Claude-Claire. "La beauté dans 'Vîs et Râmîn': puissance transformatrice, appel à l'eveil." In *Gott ist schön und er liebt die Schönheit / God Is Beautiful and He Loves Beauty*, edited by Alma Giese and J.C. Bürgel, 305–29. Bern: P. Lang, 1994.

– "Présence du mazdéisme dans le roman de Gorgâni, *Vîs o Râmîn*." *Dabireh* 1 (1991): 39–54.

– "*Vîs et Râmîn*, ou comment aimer un autre que son frère … ?" *Luqmân* 7, no. 2 (1991): 55–80.

Kay, Sarah. "Desire and Subjectivity." In *The Troubadours: An Introduction*, edited by Simon Gaunt and Sarah Kay, 212–27. Cambridge University Press, 1999.

– "Genre, Parody, and Spectacle in Aucassin et Nicolette and Other Short Comic Tales." In *The Cambridge Companion to Medieval French Literature*, edited by Simon Gaunt and Sarah Kay, 167–80. Cambridge; New York: Cambridge University Press, 2008.

Kay-Kāʾus, ʿOnṣor al-Maʿāli b. Eskandar b. Qābus. *A Mirror for Princes: The Qābūs Nāma*. Translated by Reuben Levy. London: Cresset Press, 1951.

– *Qābus-nāma*. Edited by Saʿid Nafisi. Tehran: Maṭbaʿ-e Majles, 1312 [1933].

– *Qābus-nāma*. Edited by Gholam-Ḥosayn Yusofi. Tehran: Enteshārāt-e ʿElmi va Farhangi, 1390 [2011].

Kazzāzi, Mir Jalāl al-Din. *Zibā-shenāsi-ye sokhan-e pārsi*. 3 vols. Tehran: Nashr-e Markaz, 1368–73 [1989–94].

Keegan, Matthew L. "Commentarial Acts and Hermeneutical Dramas: The Ethics of Reading al-Harīrī's 'Maqāmāt.'" PhD thesis, New York University, 2017.

– "'Elsewhere Lies Its Meaning': The Vagaries of Kalīla and Dimna's Reception." *Poetica* 52, no. 1–2 (2021): 13–40.

Keene, Bryan C. "Introduction: Manuscripts and Their Outlook on the World." In *Toward a Global Middle Ages: Encountering the World through Illuminated Manuscripts*, edited by Bryan C. Keene, 5–34. Los Angeles: The J. Paul Getty Museum, 2019.

Ker, W. P. *Epic and Romance: Essays on Medieval Literature*. London: Macmillan and Co., 1897.

Keshavarz, Fatemeh. *Reading Mystical Lyric: The Case of Jalal al-Din Rumi*. Columbia: University of South Carolina Press, 1998.

Key, Alexander. *Language between God and the Poets: Maʿnā in the Eleventh Century*. Oakland, CA: University of California Press, 2018.

Khaleghi-Motlagh, Djalal. "Asadī Ṭūsī." *Encyclopædia Iranica* II/7 (1987): 699–700. An updated version is available online at https://iranicaonline .org/articles/asadi-tusi. Accessed 1 June 2022.

– "ʿAyyūqī." *Encyclopædia Iranica* III/2 (1987): 167–8. An updated version is available online at https://www.iranicaonline.org/articles/ayyuqi-a-poet. Accessed 1 June 2022.

– "Bīžan." *Encyclopædia Iranica* IV/3 (1989): 309–10. An updated version is available online at https://iranicaonline.org/articles/bizan-son-of-giv. Accessed 1 June 2022.

– "Bizhan-o Manizha va Vis-o Rāmin (moqaddema-i bar adabiyāt-e pārti va sāsāni)." *Irānshenāsi* 2, no. 2 (1369 [1990]): 273–98.

– "Ferdowsi, Abu'l-Qāsem i. Life." *Encyclopædia Iranica* IX/5 (1999): 514–23. An updated version is available online at https://www.iranicaonline.org /articles/ferdowsi-i. Accessed 1 June 2022.

– "Gošasb Bānu." *Encyclopædia Iranica* XI/2 (2002): 170–1. An updated version is available online at https://www.iranicaonline.org/articles/gosasb-banu. Accessed 1 June 2022.

– *Women in the Shāhnāmeh: Their History and Social Status within the Framework of Ancient and Medieval Sources.* Edited by Nahid Pirnazar. Translated by Brigitte Neuenschwander. Costa Mesa, CA: Mazda, 2012.

Khalidi, Tarif. *Arabic Historical Thought in the Classical Period.* Cambridge University Press, 1996.

Khalifa, Nouha. *Hardship and Deliverance in the Islamic Tradition: Theology and Spirituality in the Works of al-Tanūkhī.* London; New York: I.B. Tauris, 2010.

Khan, Pasha M. *The Broken Spell: Indian Storytelling and the Romance Genre in Persian and Urdu.* Detroit: Wayne State University Press, 2019.

Khan, Ruqayya Yasmine. *Bedouin and 'Abbāsid Cultural Identities: The Arabic Majnūn Laylā Story.* London; New York: Routledge, 2020.

Khāqāni, Afżal al-Din. *Divān-e Khāqāni-ye Shirvāni.* Edited by Mir Jalāl al-Din Kazzāzi. 2 vols. Tehran: Nashr-e Markaz, 1375 [1997].

Khaṭīb al-Baghdādī, al-. *Selections from the Art of Party-Crashing in Medieval Iraq.* Translated by Emily Selove. Syracuse, NY: Syracuse University Press, 2012.

Khorāsāni, Maḥbuba, and Farida Dāvudi-Moqaddam. "Taḥlil-e dahnāma-hā-ye adab-e fārsi az didgāh-e anvāᶜ-e adabi." *Matn-pazhuhi-ye Adabi* 50 (1390 [2011]): 9–36.

Kia, Mana. *Persianate Selves: Memories of Place and Origin before Nationalism.* Stanford University Press, 2020.

Kilpatrick, Hilary. *Making the Great Book of Songs: Compilation and the Author's Craft in Abū I-Faraj al-Iṣbahānī's Kitāb al-aghānī.* London: Routledge, 2003.

Kinoshita, Sharon. *Medieval Boundaries: Rethinking Difference in Old French Literature.* Philadelphia: University of Pennsylvania Press, 2006.

– "Romance in/and the Medieval Mediterranean." In *Thinking Medieval Romance*, edited by Katherine C. Little and Nicola McDonald, 187–202. Oxford University Press, 2018.

Kisāʾī, Muḥammad ibn ʿAbd-Allāh al-. *Tales of the Prophets = Qiṣaṣ al-anbiyāʾ*. Translated by Wheeler M. Thackston. Chicago: Great Books of the Islamic World; KAZI Publications, 1997.

Kłagisz, Mateusz M. "An Iranian Vision of the Afterlife According to the Middle Persian 'Ardā Wīrāz-Nāmag.'" *ARAM Periodical* 32 (2020): 421–61.

Knapp, James F, and Peggy Ann Knapp. *Medieval Romance: The Aesthetics of Possibility*. University of Toronto Press, 2017.

Kobidze, David. "On the Antecedents of Vis-u-Ramin." In *Yádnáme-ye Jan Rypka: Collection of Articles on Persian and Tajik Literature*, 89–93. Prague; The Hague; Paris: Academia; Mouton & Co., 1967.

Konstan, David. *Sexual Symmetry: Love in the Ancient Novel and Related Genres*. Princeton University Press, 1994.

Konstan, David, and Kurt A. Raaflaub, eds. *Epic and History*. Chichester, West Sussex, UK; Malden, MA: Wiley-Blackwell, 2010.

Kottman, Paul A. *Love as Human Freedom*. Stanford University Press, 2017.

– "Quid Non Sentit Amor: Romantic Love as the Struggle for Freedom in Ovid's 'Pyramus and Thisbe.'" *Constellations* 19, no. 3 (2012): 509–25.

Krasnowolska, Anna. "Ferdowsi's *Dastan*: An Autonomous Narrative Unit?" In *Ferdowsi's Shāhnāma: Millennial Perspectives*, edited by Olga M. Davidson and Marianna Shreve Simpson. Boston: Ilex Foundation, 2013.

Krause, Kathy M. "Gender and Paradigm Shift in Old French Narrative, or What Happens When the Heroine Becomes a Hero." In *Paradigm Shifts during the Global Middle Ages and the Renaissance*, edited by Albrecht Classen, 65–79. Turnhout, Belgium: Brepols, 2019.

Krueger, Roberta L. "Introduction." In *The Cambridge Companion to Medieval Romance*, edited by Robert L. Krueger, 1–9. Cambridge University Press, 2000.

– *Women Readers and the Ideology of Gender in Old French Verse Romance*. Cambridge University Press, 1993.

Kruk, Remke. *The Warrior Women of Islam: Female Empowerment in Arabic Popular Literature*. New York: I.B. Tauris, 2014.

Kunitzsch, Paul. "The 'Description of the Night' in Gurgānī's *Vīs u Rāmīn*." *Der Islam* 59, no. 1 (1982): 93–110.

L'Orange, Hans Peter. *Studies on the Iconography of Cosmic Kingship in the Ancient World*. Oslo: H. Aschehoug, 1953.

Lambton, Ann K.S. "Islamic Mirrors for Princes." Rome: Accademia Nazionale dei Lincei, 1971.

Landau, Justine. "Naṣīr al-Dīn Ṭūsī and Poetic Imagination in the Arabic and Persian Philosophical Tradition." In *Metaphor and Imagery in Persian Poetry*, edited by Ali Asghar Seyed-Gohrab, 15–65. Leiden; Boston: Brill, 2012.

Lane, Edward William. *Arabic-English Lexicon*. 8 vols. London: Williams and
    Norgate, 1863–93.

Lasman, Samuel. "Dragons, Fairies, and Time: Imagining the Past in Medieval
    Welsh, Persian, and French Narratives." PhD thesis, University of Chicago, 2020.

Latham, J. Derek. "Ebn al-Moqaffaᶜ, Abū Moḥammad ᶜAbd-Allāh Rōzbeh."
    Encyclopædia Iranica VIII/1 (1997): 39–43. An updated version is available
    online at https://www.iranicaonline.org/articles/ebn-al-moqaffa. Accessed
    1 June 2022.

Lazard, Gilbert. "Dari." *Encyclopædia Iranica* VII/1 (1994): 34–5. An updated
    version is available online at https://www.iranicaonline.org/articles/dari.
    Accessed 1 June 2022.

– "La source en 'farsi' de 'Vis-o-Ramin.'" *Šromebi* (*T'bilisis saxelmcip'o
    universiteti = Proceedings of Tbilisi University*) 241 (1983): 34–9.

– "Pahlavi, Pârsi, Dari: Les Langues de l'Iran d'Après Ibn al-Muqaffa'." In *Iran
    and Islam*, edited by C.E. Bosworth, 361–91. Edinburgh University Press, 1971.

– "The Rise of the New Persian Language." In *The Cambridge History of Iran,
    Volume 4: The Period from the Arab Invasion to the Saljuqs*, edited by Richard N.
    Frye, 595–632. Cambridge University Press, 1975.

Lewis, Franklin D. "Hafez viii. Hafez and Rendi." *Encyclopædia Iranica* XI/5
    (2002): 483–91. An updated version is available online at https://www
    .iranicaonline.org/articles/hafez-viii. Accessed 1 June 2022.

– "One Chaste Muslim Maiden and a Persian in a Pear Tree: Analogues
    of Boccaccio and Chaucer in Four Earlier Arabic and Persian Tales." In
    Metaphor and Imagery in Persian Poetry, edited by Ali Asghar Seyed-Gohrab,
    137–203. Leiden: Brill, 2012.

– "Reading, Writing, and Recitation: Sanāᵓi and the Origins of the Persian
    Ghazal." PhD thesis, University of Chicago, 1995.

– *Rumi: Past and Present, East and West*. 2nd ed. Oxford: Oneworld, 2008.

– "Shifting Allegiances: Primordial Relationships and How They Change in
    the Shahnameh." In *The Layered Heart: Essays on Persian Poetry*, edited by Ali
    Asghar Seyed-Gohrab, 363–409. Washington, DC: Mage, 2019.

– "The Transformation of the Persian Ghazal: From Amatory Mood to
    Fixed Form." In *Ghazal as World Literature II: From a Literary Genre to a Great
    Tradition*, edited by Angelika Neuwirth, Michael Hess, Judith Pfeiffer, and
    Börte Sagaster, 121–39. Wurzburg: Ergon Verlag in Kommission, 2006.

Lincoln, Bruce. "The Role of Religion in Achaemenian Imperialism." In
    Religion and Power: Divine Kingship in the Ancient World and Beyond, edited by
    Nicole Brisch, 221–41. Oriental Institute of the University of Chicago, 2008.

Little, Katherine C., and Nicola McDonald. "Introduction." In *Thinking
    Medieval Romance*, edited by Katherine C. Little and Nicola McDonald, 1–9.
    Oxford University Press, 2018.

Lomuto, Sierra. "Becoming Postmedieval: The Stakes of the Global Middle Ages." *postmedieval* 11, no. 4 (2020): 503–12.

London, Jennifer. "How to Do Things with Fables: Ibn al-Muqaffa's Frank Speech in Stories from *Kalīla wa Dimna*." *History of Political Thought* 29, no. 2 (2008): 189–212.

Lopez, Donald S. Jr., and Peggy McCracken. *In Search of the Christian Buddha: How an Asian Sage Became a Medieval Saint.* New York; London: W.W. Norton & Company, 2014.

Lorris, Guillaume de, and Jean De Meun. *The Romance of the Rose.* Translated by Charles Dahlberg. Princeton University Press, 1995.

Lucas, Ann E. *Music of a Thousand Years: A New History of Persian Musical Traditions.* Oakland, CA: University of California Press, 2019.

Lumbard, Joseph E.B. "From Ḥubb to ʿIshq: The Development of Love in Early Sufism." *Journal of Islamic Studies* 18, no. 3 (2007): 345–85.

Lyons, Malcolm C. *The Arabian Epic: Heroic and Oral Story-Telling.* 3 vols. Cambridge University Press, 1995.

Lyons, Malcolm C., and Ursula Lyons, trans. *The Arabian Nights: Tales of 1001 Nights.* 3 vols. London: Penguin, 2010.

MacDonald, D.B. "The Earlier History of the Arabian Nights." *Journal of the Royal Asiatic Society of Great Britain and Ireland* 56, no. 3 (1924): 353–97.

MacKenzie, D.N. *A Concise Pahlavi Dictionary.* London: Oxford University Press, 1971.

Macnaghten, William Hay, ed. *Alf layla wa-layla.* 4 vols. Calcutta: W. Thacker, 1839–1842.

Macrobius. *Commentaire au Songe de Scipion: texte établi, traduit et commenté.* Edited and translated by Mireille Armisen-Marchetti. Paris: Les Belles Lettres, 2001.

– *Commentary on the Dream of Scipio.* Translated by William Harris Stahl. New York: Columbia University Press, 1990.

Macuch, Maria. "Pahlavi Literature." In *The Literature of Pre-Islamic Iran*, edited by Ronald E. Emmerick and Maria Macuch, 116–96. London; New York: I.B. Tauris, 2009.

Madelung, Wilferd. "The Assumption of the Title Shāhānshāh by the Būyids and 'The Reign of the Daylam (*Dawlat al-Daylam*).'" *Journal of Near Eastern Studies* 28, nos. 2–3 (1969): 84–108, 168–83.

Magidow, Melanie. *The Tale of Princess Fatima, Warrior Woman: The Arabic Epic of Dhat al-Himma.* New York: Penguin, 2021.

Mahjub, Moḥammad Jaʿfar. "Chivalry and Early Persian Sufism." In *Classical Persian Sufism: From Its Origins to Rumi*, edited by Leonard Lewisohn, 549–81. Oneworld, 1999.

– "Moqaddema dar bāra-ye Vis-o Rāmin va sorāyanda-ye ān." In *Vis-o Rāmin*, 7–105. Tehran: Ebn-e Sinā, 1337 [1959].

Mallette, Karla. *Lives of the Great Languages: Arabic and Latin in the Medieval Mediterranean*. University of Chicago Press, 2021.

– "Translation in the Pre-Modern World." *Middle Eastern Literatures* 20, no. 1 (2017): 18–30.

Malti-Douglas, Fedwa. *Woman's Body, Woman's Word: Gender and Discourse in Arabo-Islamic Writing*. Princeton University Press, 1991.

Manāqibī, ʿAli ibn Mūsā al-. *Sīrat al-amīra Dhāt al-Himma wa-waladihā ʿAbd al-Wahhāb*. 7 vols. Beirut: Al-Maktaba al-Thaqāfiyya, 1400 [1980].

Marzolph, Ulrich. *Relief after Hardship: The Ottoman Turkish Model for the Thousand and One Days*. Detroit: Wayne State University Press, 2017.

Masʿūdī, Abu al-Ḥasan al-. *The Meadows of Gold: The Abbasids*. Edited and translated by Paul Lunde and Caroline Stone. London: Kegan Paul, 1989.

– *Murūj al-dhahab wa-maʿādin al-jawhar*. Edited by Charles Pellat. 5 vols. Beirut: Manshūrāt al-Jāmiʿa al-Lubnāniyya, 1966.

– *Les prairies d'or*. Edited by C. Barbarier de Meynard. 9 vols. Paris: L'Imprimerie Nationale, 1873

Massé, Henri. "Gurgānī." In *Encyclopaedia of Islam, Second Edition*, edited by P. Bearman et al., 2012. doi:10.1163/1573-3912_islam_SIM_2567. Accessed 1 June 2022.

– "Introduction." In *Le roman de Wîs et Râmîn*, 5–24. Paris: Société d'Édition «Les Belles Lettres», 1959.

McCracken, Peggy. *The Romance of Adultery: Queenship and Sexual Transgression in Old French Literature*. Philadelphia: University of Pennsylvania Press, 1998.

Meisami, Julie Scott. "Allegorical Gardens in the Persian Poetic Tradition: Nezami, Rumi, Hafez." *International Journal of Middle East Studies* 17, no. 2 (1985): 229–60.

– "Fitnah or Azadah? Nizami's Ethical Poetic." *Edebiyât N.S.* 1, no. 2 (1989): 41–75.

– "Genres of Court Literature." In *General Introduction to Persian Literature*, edited by J.T.P. de Bruijn, 233–69. London: I.B. Tauris, 2009.

– "Kings and Lovers: Ethical Dimensions of Medieval Persian Romance." *Edebiyât N.S.* 1, no. 1 (1987): 1–27.

– *Medieval Persian Court Poetry*. Princeton University Press, 1987.

– "Mixed Prose and Verse in Medieval Persian Literature." In *Prosimetrum: Crosscultural Perspectives on Narrative in Prose and Verse*, edited by Joseph Harris and Karl Reichl, 295–319. Cambridge, UK: D.S. Brewer, 1997.

– "The Past in Service of the Present: Two Views of History in Medieval Persia." *Poetics Today* 14, no. 2 (1993): 247–75.

– "Persona and Generic Conventions in Medieval Persian Lyric." *Comparative Criticism* 12 (1990): 125–51.

– "The Theme of the Journey in Niẓāmī's *Haft Paykar*." *Edebiyât N.S.* 4, no. 2 (1993): 155–72.

Meisami, Julie Scott, and Paul Starkey, eds. *Encyclopedia of Arabic Literature*. London: Routledge, 2010.

Melikian-Chirvani, Assadullah Souren. "Le roman de Varqe et Golšâh: Essai sur les rapports de l'esthétique littéraire et de l'esthétique plastique dans l'Iran pré-mongol, suivi de la traduction du poème." *Artes Asiatiques* 22 (1970): 1–262.

Melvin-Koushki, Matthew. "Imperial Talismanic Love: Ibn Turka's *Debate of Feast and Fight* (1426) as Philosophical Romance and Lettrist Mirror for Timurid Princes." *Der Islam* 96, no. 1 (2019): 42–86.

Menocal, María Rosa. *The Arabic Role in Medieval Literary History: A Forgotten Heritage*. Philadelphia: University of Pennsylvania Press, 1987.

Merguerian, Gayane Karen, and Afsaneh Najmabadi. "Zulaykha and Yusuf: Whose 'Best Story'?" *International Journal of Middle East Studies* 29, no. 4 (1997): 485–508.

Milani, Farzaneh. "The Mediatory Guile of the Nanny in Persian Romance." *Iranian Studies* 32, no. 2 (1999): 181–201.

Miller, Lloyd Clifton. *Music and Song in Persia: The Art of Āvāz*. Surrey, UK: Curzon, 1999.

Miller, Matthew Thomas. "Embodying the Beloved: Embodiment, (Homo)eroticism, and the Straightening of Desire in the Hagiographic Tradition of Fakhr al-Dīn ʿIrāqī." *Middle Eastern Literatures* 21, no. 1 (2018): 1–27.

– "Poetics of the Sufi Carnival: The 'Rogue Lyrics' (*Qalandariyât*) of Sanâ'i, 'Attâr, and 'Erâqi." PhD thesis, Washington University in St. Louis, 2016.

– "The Poetics of the Sufi Carnival: The Rogue Lyrics (*Qalandariyyāt*) as Heterotopic Countergenre(s)." *Al-ʿUsur al-Wusta* 30 (2022): 1–46.

Minorsky, Vladimir. "The Older Preface to the *Shāh-Nāma*." In *Studi orientalistici in onore di Giorgio Levi Della Vida*, 2:159–79. Rome: Istituto per l'Oriente, 1956.

– "Vis u Rāmin: A Parthian Romance (Continued)." *Bulletin of the School of Oriental and African Studies* 11, no. 4 (1946): 741–63.

– "Vis u Rāmin: A Parthian Romance (Conclusion)." *Bulletin of the School of Oriental and African Studies* 12, no. 1 (1947): 20–35.

– "Vis-u-Rāmin (III)." *Bulletin of the School of Oriental and African Studies* 16, no. 1 (1954): 91–2.

– "Vis-u Rāmin (IV)." *Bulletin of the School of Oriental and African Studies* 25, no. 1/3 (1962): 275–86.

– "Vīs u Rāmīn: A Parthian Romance." In *Iranica: Twenty Articles*, 151–99. Hertford, Eng.: S. Austin, 1964.

Minovi, Mojtabā. "Vis-o Rāmin." *Sokhan* 6, no. 1, 2 (1333 [1954]): 13–21, 129–37.

– "Yek-i az fāresiyāt-e Abu Novās." *Majalla-ye Dāneshkada-ye Adabiyāt, Dāneshgāh-e Tehrān* [*Revue de la Faculté des Lettres, Université de Téhéran*] 1, no. 3 (1332 [1953]): 62–77.

Moazami, Mahnaz. *Wrestling with the Demons of the Pahlavi Wīdēwdād: Transcription, Translation, and Commentary*. Leiden; Boston: Brill, 2014.

Mohammadi-Badr, Narges, and Hāshem Mahdizāda. "Taᵓammol-i dar tahavvol-e monāẓara az derakht-e āsurik tā ashᶜār-e nimāyi." *Fonun-e adabi* 15 (1395 [2016]): 179–90.

Mohaqqeq, Mahdi. "Yāddāsht-hā-i dar bāra-ye manẓuma-ye Vis-o Rāmin." *Yaghmā* 10, no. 9, 10 (1336 [1957]): 417–21, 461–4.

Molé, Marijan. "«Vīs u Rāmīn» et l'histoire seldjoukide." *Annali, Istituto Universitario Orientale di Napoli N.S.* 9 (1959): 1–30.

Montiglio, Silvia. *Love & Providence: Recognition in the Ancient Novel*. Oxford University Press, 2013.

Morales, Helen. "The History of Sexuality." In *The Cambridge Companion to the Greek and Roman Novel*, edited by Tim Whitmarsh, 39–55. Cambridge University Press, 2008.

– *Vision and Narrative in Achilles Tatius' Leucippe and Clitophon*. Cambridge University Press, 2004.

Morgan, J.R. "Make-Believe and Make Believe: The Fictionality of the Greek Novels." In *Lies and Fiction in the Ancient World*, edited by Christopher Gill and T.P. Wiseman, 175–229. University of Exeter Press, 1993.

Morrison, George. "Flowers and Witchcraft in the 'Vīs o Rāmīn' of Fakhr ud-Dīn Gurgānī." In *Commémoration Cyrus: actes du Congrès de Shiraz 1971 et autres études rédigées à l'occasion du 2500e anniversaire de la fondation de l'Empire perse*, 249–59. Tehran; Leiden: Bibliothèque Pahlavi; diffusion, E.J. Brill, 1974.

Morson, Gary Saul, and Caryl Emerson. *Mikhail Bakhtin: Creation of a Prosaics*. Stanford University Press, 1990.

Mostowfi Qazvini, Hamd-Allāh. *Tārikh-e gozida*. Edited by ᶜAbd al-Hosayn Navāᵓi. Tehran: Amir Kabir, 1362 [1983].

Mottahedeh, Roy P. "Friendship in Islamic Ethical Philosophy." In *Essays in Islamic Philology, History, and Philosophy*, edited by Alireza Korangi, Wheeler M. Thakston, Roy P. Mottahedeh, and William Granara, 229–39. Berlin; Boston: De Gruyter, 2016.

– *Loyalty and Leadership in an Early Islamic Society*. Princeton University Press, 1980.

Muchow, Michael David. "Passionate Love and Respectable Society in Three Greek Novels." PhD thesis, Johns Hopkins University, 1988.

Müller, F. Max, ed. *Pahlavi Texts, Part V: Marvels of Zoroastrianism*. Translated by E.W. West. The Sacred Books of the East 47. Oxford: Clarendon Press, 1897.

– ed. *The Zend-Avesta, Part I: The Vendîdâd*. Translated by James Darmesteter. The Sacred Books of the East 4. Oxford: Clarendon Press, 1895.

– ed. *The Zend-Avesta, Part II: The Sîrôzahs, Yasts, and Nyâyis*. Translated by James Darmesteter. The Sacred Books of the East 23. Oxford: Clarendon Press, 1883.

– ed. *The Zend-Avesta, Part III: The Yasna, Visparad, Âfrînagân, Gâhs, and Miscellaneous Fragments*. Translated by L.H. Mills. The Sacred Books of the East 31. Oxford: Clarendon Press, 1887.

Mullett, Margaret. "No Drama, No Poetry, No Fiction, No Readership, No Literature." In *A Companion to Byzantium*, edited by Liz James, 227–38. Chichester: Wiley-Blackwell, 2010.

Murray, Martin. *Jacques Lacan: A Critical Introduction*. London: Pluto Press, 2016.

Musallam, Basim F. "The Human Embryo in Arabic Scientific and Religious Thought." In *The Human Embryo: Aristotle and the Arabic and European Traditions*, edited by G.R. Dunstan, 32–46. University of Exeter Press, 1990.

Nadīm, Muḥammad ibn Isḥāq al-. *al-Fihrist lil-Nadīm*. Edited by Ayman Fuʾād Sayyid. 2 vols. London: Al-Furqan Islamic Heritage Foundation, 1430 [2009].

– *The Fihrist of al-Nadīm: A Tenth-Century Survey of Muslim Culture*. Edited and translated by Bayard Dodge. New York: Columbia University Press, 1970.

Nagy, Joseph Falaky. "The Celtic 'Love Triangle' Revisited." In *Proceedings of the XIV International Congress of Celtic Studies*, edited by Liam Breatnach, Ruairí Ó hUiginn, Damian McManus, and Katharine Simms, 221–44. Maynooth: Dublin Institute of Advanced Studies, 2015.

Najmabadi, Afsaneh. "Reading – and Enjoying – 'Wiles of Women' Stories as a Feminist." *Iranian Studies* 32, no. 2 (1999): 203–22.

Najmābādi, Sayf al-Din, and Siegfried Weber, eds. *Mujmal al-tavārīkh va al-qiṣaṣ: Eine persische Weltgeschichte aus dem 12. Jahrhundert*. Neckharhausen: Deux Mondes, 2000.

Nallino, Carlo A. "Tracce di opere greche giunte agli arabi per trafila pehlevica." In *A Volume of Oriental Studies Presented to E.G. Browne*, edited by T.W. Arnold and R.A. Nicholson, 345–63. Cambridge University Press, 1922.

Nāṣer-e Khosrow, Abu Moʿin. *Nasir-i Khusraw's Book of Travels [Safarnama]: A Parallel Persian-English Text*. Edited and translated by Wheeler M. Thackston. Costa Mesa, CA: Mazda, 2001.

– *Safarnāma-ye Ḥakim Nāṣer-e Khosrow Qobādiyāni Marvazi*. Edited by Moḥammad Dabir Siyāqi. Tehran: Zavvār, 1389 [2010].

Neugebauer, Otto. "The Date of the 'Horoscope' in Gurgānī's Poem." *Der Islam* 60, no. 2 (1983): 297–301.

Newman, Richard Jeffrey. "Attar's 'Tale of Marhuma:' The Woman with a Manly Heart." *Modern Language Studies* 46, no. 2 (2017): 52–81.

Neẓām al-Molk. *The Book of Government, or, Rules for Kings: The Siyāsat-nāma or Siyar al-Mulūk*. Translated by Hubert Darke. New Haven: Yale University Press, 1960.

Neẓāmi Ganjavi. *The Haft Paykar: A Medieval Persian Romance*. Translated by Julie Scott Meisami. Oxford University Press, 1995. Reprint, Indianapolis: Hackett, 2015.

– *Heft Peiker: ein romantisches Epos des Niẓāmī Genǧe'ī*. Edited by Hellmut Ritter and Jan Rypka. Prague: Orientální Ústav, 1934.
– *Khosrow-o Shirin*. Edited by Behruz Ṡarvatiyān. Tehran: Amir Kabir, 1392 [2013].
– *Layli & Majnun*. Translated by Dick Davis. Odenton, MD: Mage, 2020.
– *Layli-o Majnun*. Edited by Behruz Ṡarvatiyān. Tehran: Enteshārāt-e Tus, 1364 [1986].
– *The Story of Layla and Majnun*. Translated by R. Gelpke, E. Mattin, and G. Hill. Oxford: Cassirer, 1966.

Nikaeen, Behrang, and Anna Oldfield. "The Azerbaijani Ashiq: Musical Change, Transmission, and the Future of a Bardic Art." *Journal of Folklore Research* 57, no. 3 (2020): 1–25.

Nilsson, Ingela. "Desire and God Have Always Been Around, in Life and Romance Alike." In *Plotting with Eros: Essays on the Poetics of Love and the Erotics of Reading*, edited by Ingela Nilsson, 235–60. Copenhagen: Museum Tusculanum Press, 2009.

Norozi, Nahid. *Esordi del romanzo persiano: Dal Vis e Rāmin di Gorgāni (XI sec.) al ciclo di Tristano*. Alessandria: Edizioni dell'Orso, 2021.
– "The Verse Romance *Homāy o Homāyūn* of Ḫwājū Kermānī: A 'Love and Adventure Story' or an Allegory of a Spiritual Quest?" *Eurasian Studies* 17, no. 1 (2019): 23–48.
– "Il *Vis e Rāmin* di Gorgāni e il *Bahman-nāmé* di Irānshāh: Aspetti intertestuali anche in relazione con il *Khosrow e Shirin* di Neẓāmi." In *Come la freccia di Ārash: Il lungo viaggio della narrazione in Iran*, edited by Nahid Norozi, 197–219. Milan; Udine: Mimesis, 2021.

Norris, H.T. "Fables and Legends." In *ᶜAbbasid Belles-Lettres*, edited by Julia Ashtiany, T.M. Johnstone, J.D. Latham, R.B. Serjeant, and G. Rex Smith, 136–45. The Cambridge History of Arabic Literature. Cambridge University Press, 1990.

O'Malley, Austin. Poetry and Pedagogy: The Homiletic Verse of Farid al-Din ᶜAṭṭâr." PhD thesis, University of Chicago, 2017.
– "An Unexpected Romance: Reevaluating the Authorship of the *Khosrow-nāma*." *Al-ᶜUṣūr al-Wusṭā: The Journal of Middle East Medievalists* 27, no. 1 (2019): 201–32.

Ohlander, Erik. "Enacting Justice, Ensuring Salvation: The Trope of the 'Just Ruler' in Some Medieval Islamic Mirrors for Princes." *Muslim World* 99, no. 2 (2009): 237–52.

Omidsalar, Mahmoud. *Poetics and Politics of Iran's National Epic, the Shahnameh*. New York: Palgrave Macmillan, 2011.
– "Unburdening Ferdowsi." *Journal of the American Oriental Society* 116, no. 2 (1996): 235–42.

Orlemanski, Julie. "Genre." In *A Handbook of Middle English Studies*, edited by Marion Turner, 207–21. Chichester, West Sussex: Wiley-Blackwell, 2013.

Orsatti, Paola. "Ḵosrow o Širin." *Encyclopædia Iranica, Online Edition*, 2006. Available at https://www.iranicaonline.org/articles/kosrow-o-sirin. Accessed 1 June 2022.

Ouyang, Wen-chin. "The Epical Turn of Romance: Love in the Narrative of ʿUmar al-Nuʿmān." *Oriente Moderno* 22 (83), no. 2 (2003): 485–504.

– "Romancing the Epic: ʿUmar al-Nuʿmān as Narrative of Empowerment." *Arabic & Middle Eastern Literature* 3, no. 1 (2000): 5–18.

– "War and the Worlding of Story." In *A Companion to World Literature, Vol. 2: 601 CE to 1450 CE*, edited by Christine Chism, 1–7. John Wiley & Sons, Ltd., 2019. doi:10.1002/9781118635193.ctwl0071. Accessed 1 June 2022.

Overtoom, Nikolaus Leo. *Reign of Arrows: The Rise of the Parthian Empire in the Hellenistic Middle East*. New York: Oxford University Press, 2020.

Ovid. *Metamorphoses*. Translated by Frank Justus Miller. 2 vols. Cambridge, MA: Harvard University Press, 1951.

ʿOwfi, Moḥammad. *The Lubábu 'l-albáb of Muḥammed 'Awfi*. Edited by Edward G. Browne and Moḥammad Qazvini. 2 vols. London; Leiden: Luzac & Co.; Brill, 1903.

Panaino, Antonio. "Calendars i. Pre-Islamic Calendars." *Encyclopædia Iranica* IV/6–7 (1990): 658–77. Available online at https://www.iranicaonline.org/articles/calendars. Accessed 1 June 2022.

Parker, Patricia A. *Inescapable Romance: Studies in the Poetics of a Mode*. Princeton University Press, 1979.

Paterson, Linda. "*Fin'amor* and the Development of the Courtly *Canso*." In *The Troubadours: An Introduction*, edited by Simon Gaunt and Sarah Kay, 28–46. Cambridge University Press, 1999.

Pavel, Thomas. "Literary Genres as Norms and Good Habits." *New Literary History* 34, no. 2 (2003): 201–10.

Peacock, A.C.S. *Early Seljūq History: A New Interpretation*. London; New York: Routledge, 2010.

– ed. *The Great Seljuk Empire*. Edinburgh University Press, 2015.

Pellat, Charles. *The Life and Works of Jāḥiẓ*. Translated by D.M. Hawke. Berkeley: University of California Press, 1969.

Pensom, Roger. *Aucassin et Nicolete: The Poetry of Gender and Growing up in the French Middle Ages*. Bern: Peter Lang, 1999.

Perez, Gilberto. *The Material Ghost: Films and Their Medium*. Baltimore; London: Johns Hopkins University Press, 1998.

Perkins, Judith. *The Suffering Self: Pain and Narrative Representation in the Early Christian Era*. London: Routledge, 1995.

Perry, John. "The Origin and Development of Literary Persian." In *General Introduction to Persian Literature*, edited by J.T.P. de Bruijn, 43–70. London: I.B. Tauris, 2009.

Phillips, Noëlle. *Craft Beer Culture and Modern Medievalism: Brewing Dissent.* Leeds: Arc Humanities Press, 2019.

Pierce, Laurie. "Serpents and Sorcery: Humanity, Gender, and the Demonic in Ferdowsi's *Shahnameh.*" *Iranian Studies* 48, no. 3 (2015): 349–67.

Pifer, Michael. "The Age of the *Gharīb*: Strangers in the Medieval Mediterranean." In *An Armenian Mediterranean*, edited by Kathryn Babayan and Michael Pifer, 13–37. Cham: Springer International Publishing, 2018.

− *Kindred Voices: A Literary History of Medieval Anatolia.* New Haven: Yale University Press, 2021.

Pingree, David. "Classical and Byzantine Astrology in Sasanian Persia." *Dumbarton Oaks Papers* 43 (1989): 227–39.

Piri, Musā. "Gera-dāstāni dar Khosrow-o Shirin va Vis-o Rāmin." *Kayhān-e Farhangi*, no. 195 (1381 [2003]): 70–3.

Pizzi, Italo. *Storia della poesia persiana.* 2 vols. Turin: Unione tipografico-editrice, 1894.

Plato. *Plato on Love: Lysis, Symposium, Phaedrus, Alcibiades, with Selections from Republic and Laws.* Edited by C.D.C. Reeve. Indianapolis: Hackett, 2006.

Plotinus. *Ennead, Volume III.* Translated by A.H. Armstrong. Loeb Classical Library 442. Cambridge, MA: Harvard University Press, 1967. doi:10.4159/DLCL.plotinus-enneas.1969.

Pollock, Sheldon I. *The Language of the Gods in the World of Men: Sanskrit, Culture and Power in Premodern India.* Berkeley: University of California Press, 2009.

Pourshariati, Parvaneh. "Kārin." *Encyclopædia Iranica, Online Edition*, 2017. Available at https://iranicaonline.org/articles/karin. Accessed 1 June 2022.

− "The Parthians and the Production of the Canonical Shāhnāmas: Of Pahlavī, Pahlavānī and the Pahlav." In *Commutatio et Contentio: Studies in the Late Roman, Sasanian, and Early Islamic Near East in Memory of Zeev Rubin*, 347–92. Düsseldorf: Wellem, 2010.

Propp, Vladimir. *Morphology of the Folktale.* Translated by Laurence Scott. 2nd ed. Austin: University of Texas Press, 1968.

Rabghūzī, Nāṣir al-Dīn al-. *The Stories of the Prophets.* Edited by H.E. Boeschoten and J. O'Kane. 2nd ed. 2 vols. Leiden; Boston: Brill, 2015.

Rādfar, Abu al-Qāsem. *Ketābshenāsī-ye Neẓāmi Ganjavi.* Tehran: Pazhueshgāh, 1371 [1992].

Rāghib al-Iṣfahānī, al-. *Muḥāḍarāt al-udabāʾ wa-muḥāwarāt al-shuʿarāʾ wa-al-bulaghāʾ.* Edited by ʿUmar Ṭabbāʿ. Beirut: Dār al-Arqam, 1999.

Reardon, Bryan P., ed. *Collected Ancient Greek Novels.* Berkeley; Los Angeles: University of California Press, 1989.

− *The Form of Greek Romance.* Princeton University Press, 1991.

Reddy, William M. *The Making of Romantic Love: Longing and Sexuality in Europe, South Asia, and Japan, 900–1200 CE.* Chicago; London: University of Chicago Press, 2012.

Reichel, Michael. "Xenophon's Cyropaedia and the Hellenistic Novel." In *Xenophon*, edited by Vivienne J. Gray, 418–38. Oxford University Press, 2011.

Reynolds, Dwight F. "Arab Musical Influence on Medieval Europe: A Reassessment." In *A Sea of Languages: Rethinking the Arabic Role in Medieval Literary History*, edited by Suzanne Conklin Akbari and Karla Mallette, 182–98. University of Toronto Press, 2013.

– "Epic and History in the Arabic Tradition." In *Epic and History*, edited by David Konstan and Kurt A. Raaflaub, 392–410. Chichester, West Sussex, UK; Malden, MA: Wiley-Blackwell, 2010.

Rezakhani, Khodadad. *ReOrienting the Sasanians: East Iran in Late Antiquity*. Edinburgh University Press, 2017.

Richter-Bernburg, Lutz. "Amīr-Malik-Shāhānshāh: ʿAḍud ad-Daula's Titulature Re-Examined." *Iran* 18 (1980): 83–102.

– "Plato of Mind and Joseph of Countenance: The Notion of Love and the Ideal Beloved in Kay Kāʾūs b. Iskandar's *Andarznāme*." *Oriens* 36 (2001): 276–87.

Ridgeon, Lloyd V.J., ed. *Javanmardi: The Ethics and Practice of Persianate Perfection*. London: Gingko Library, 2018.

Ringgren, Helmer. *Fatalism in Persian Epics*. Uppsala: Lundequistska Bokhandeln, 1952.

Robinson, Cynthia. "Going Between: The Ḥadīth Bayāḍ wa Riyāḍ and the Contested Identity of the ʿAjouz in 13th-Century Iberia." In *Under the Influence: Questioning the Comparative in Medieval Castile*, edited by Cynthia Robinson and Leyla Rouhi, 199–230. Leiden: Brill, 2005.

– *Medieval Andalusian Courtly Culture: Ḥadīth Bayāḍ wa-Riyāḍ*. London: Routledge, 2007.

Roilos, Panagiotis. *Amphoteroglossia: A Poetics of the Twelfth-Century Medieval Greek Novel*. Washington, DC; Cambridge, MA: Center for Hellenic Studies, Trustees for Harvard University; Distributed by Harvard University Press, 2005.

Root, Margaret Cool. "Defining the Devine in Achaemenid Persian Kingship: The View from Bisitun." In *Every Inch a King: Comparative Studies on Kings and Kingship in the Ancient and Medieval Worlds*, edited by Lynette Mitchell and Charles Melville, 23–65. Leiden: Brill, 2013.

– *The King and Kingship in Achaemenid Art: Essays on the Creation of an Iconography of Empire*. Leiden: Brill, 1979.

Rostami, Roqiya. "Barrasi-ye vizhegi-hā-ye adabi dar nāma-hā-ye ʿāsheqāna-ye Vis-o Rāmin-e Asʿad-e Gorgāni." *Hafez*, no. 85 (1390 [2011]): 27–35.

Rouhi, Leyla. *Mediation and Love: A Study of the Medieval Go-between in Key Romance and Near-Eastern Texts*. Leiden: Brill, 1999.

Rowland, Jenny. "Trystan and Esyllt." In *Arthur in the Celtic Languages: The Arthurian Legend in Celtic Literatures and Traditions*, edited by Ceridwen

Lloyd-Morgan and Erich Poppe, 51–64. Cardiff: University of Wales Press, 2019.

Rubanovich, Julia. "Aspects of Medieval Intertextuality: Verse Insertions in Persian Prose *Dāstāns*." *Jerusalem Studies in Arabic and Islam* 32 (2006): 247–68.

– "In the Mood of Love: Love Romances in Medieval Persian Poetry and Their Sources." In *Fictional Storytelling in the Medieval Eastern Mediterranean and Beyond*, edited by Carolina Cupane and Bettina Krönung, 67–94. Leiden: Brill, 2016.

Ruiz-Montero, Consuelo. "The Rise of the Greek Novel." In *The Novel in the Ancient World*, edited by Gareth Schmeling, 29–86. Leiden: Brill, 2003.

Rumi, Jalāl al-Din. *The Masnavi*. Translated by Jawid Mojaddedi. Oxford University Press, 2004.

– *The Mathnawí of Jalálu'ddín Rúmí*. Edited and translated by R.A. Nicholson. 8 vols. London: Luzac & Co., 1925–40.

Rust'aveli, Shot'a. *The Lord of the Panther-Skin*. Translated by R.H. Stevenson. Albany: State University of New York Press, 1977.

– *The Man in the Panther's Skin*. Translated by Marjory Scott Wardrop. London: Royal Asiatic Society, 1912.

Ruyāni, Vahid. "Tashābohāt-e Vis-o Rāmin va Bahman-nāma." *Jostār-hā-ye Adabi*, no. 176 (1391 [2012]): 75–94.

Ruymbeke, Christine van. "Hellenistic Influences in Classical Persian Literature." In *General Introduction to Persian Literature*, edited by J.T.P. de Bruijn, 345–68. London: I.B. Tauris, 2009.

– *Science and Poetry in Medieval Persia: The Botany of Nizami's Khamsa*. Cambridge University Press, 2007.

– "Wretched King Mobad Loses the War of Love." In *The Layered Heart: Essays on Persian Poetry*, edited by Ali Asghar Seyed-Gohrab, 81–97. Washington, DC: Mage, 2019.

Rypka, Jan. *History of Iranian Literature*. Edited by Karl Jahn. 1956. Reprint, Dordrecht: D. Reidel, 1968.

Saʿdi. *Bustān-e Saʿdi: Saʿdi-nāma*. Edited by Gholām-Ḥosayn Yusofi. Tehran: Anjoman-e Ostādān-e Zabān va Adabiyāt-e Fārsi, 1359 [1981].

– *Ghazal-hā-ye Saʿdi*. Edited by Gholam-Ḥosayn Yusofi. Sokhan, 1385 [2006].

– *The Gulistan (Rose Garden) of Sa'di*. Edited and translated by Wheeler M. Thackston. Bethesda, MD: Ibex Publishers, 2008.

– *Kolliyāt-e Saʿdi*. Edited by Moḥammad-ʿAli Forughi. Tehran: Hermes, 1385 [1996].

– *Morals Pointed and Tales Adorned: The Būstān of Saʿdī*. Translated by G.M. Wickens. University of Toronto Press, 1974.

Sadan, Joseph. "Maidens' Hair and Starry Skies." In *Israel Oriental Studies XI: Studies in Medieval Arabic and Hebrew Poetics*, edited by Sasson Somekh, 57–88. Leiden: Brill, 1991.

Sadeghi, Fatemeh. *The Sin of the Woman: Interrelations of Religious Judgments in Zoroastrianism and Islam*. Islamkundliche Untersuchungen, Band 336. Berlin: Klaus Schwarz Verlag, 2018.

Ṣafā, Ẕabih-Allāh. "Sharāyeṭ-e ejtemāᶜi va siyāsi-ye Irān baᶜd az soquṭ-e shāhanshāhi-ye Sāsāni va aṡar-e ān dar tarjoma va tadvin-e revāyat-hā-ye melli tā naẓm-e shāhnāma-hā va dāstān-hā-ye qahremāni." *Irānshenāsi* 2, no. 2 (1369 [1990]): 239–47.

Safi, Omid. *The Politics of Knowledge in Premodern Islam: Negotiating Ideology and Religious Inquiry*. Chapel Hill: University of North Carolina Press, 2006.

Schine, Rachel Nicole. "On Blackness in Arabic Popular Literature: The Black Heroes of the *Siyar Shaʿbiyya*, Their Conceptions, Contests, and Contexts." PhD thesis, University of Chicago, 2019.

Scott, Walter. *Essays on Chivalry, Romance, and the Drama*. The Miscellaneous Prose Works of Sir Walter Scott 6. Edinburgh: Robert Cadell, 1834.

Segre, Cesare. "What Bakhtin Left Unsaid: The Case of Medieval Romance." In *Romance: Generic Transformations from Chrétien de Troyes to Cervantes*, edited by Kevin Brownlee and Marina Scordilis Brownlee, 23–46. Hanover; London: University Press of New England, 1985.

Selden, Daniel. "Mapping the Alexander Romance." In *The Alexander Romance in Persia and the East*, edited by Richard Stoneman, Kyle Erickson, and Ian Netton, 19–60. Barkhuis Publishing & Groningen University Library, 2012.

Sells, Michael. "Love." In *The Literature of al-Andalus*, 126–58. The Cambridge History of Arabic Literature. Cambridge University Press, 2000.

– *Mystical Languages of Unsaying*. University of Chicago Press, 1994.

Seyed-Gohrab, Ali Asghar. *Laylī and Majnūn: Love, Madness and Mystic Longing in Niẓāmī's Epic Romance*. Leiden: Brill, 2003.

– "A Treasury from Tabrīz: A Fourteenth-Century Manuscript Containing 209 Works in Persian and Arabic." *Persica* 19 (2003): 125–64.

Shafiᶜi-Kadkani, Moḥammad-Reża. *Qalandariya dar tārikh*. Tehran: Sokhan, 1386 [2007].

Shahbazi, A. Shapur. *Ferdowsī: A Critical Biography*. Costa Mesa, CA: Mazda, 1991.

– "Hunting in Iran i. In the pre-Islamic period." *Encyclopædia Iranica* XII/6 (2004): 577–80. An updated version is available online at https://www.iranicaonline.org/articles/hunting-in-iran. Accessed 1 June 2022.

– "Nowruz ii. In the Islamic Period." *Encyclopædia Iranica, Online Edition*, 2009. Available at https://www.iranicaonline.org/articles/nowruz-ii. Accessed 1 June 2022.

Shaked, Saul. "Specimens of Middle Persian Verse." In *W.B. Henning Memorial Volume*, edited by Mary Boyce and Ilya Gershevitch, 395–405. London: Lund Humphries, 1970.

Shaked, Shaul, and Ẕabiḥ-Allāh Ṣafā. "Andarz." *Encyclopædia Iranica* II/1
(1985): 11–22. An updated version is available online at https://www
.iranicaonline.org/articles/andarz-precept-instruction-advice. Accessed
1 June 2022.

Shamisā, Sirus. *Anvāᶜ-e adabi*. Tehran: Bāgh-e Āyina, 1370 [1992].

Shams-e Qays. *Al-Moᶜjam fi maᶜāyir ashᶜār al-aᶜjam*. Edited by Moḥammad
Qazvini and Moḥammad-Taqi Modarres Rażavi. Tehran: Khāvar, 1314 [1935].

Sharlet, Jocelyn. "A Garden of Possibilities in Manuchehri's Spring
Panegyrics." *Journal of Persianate Studies* 3, no. 1 (2010): 1–25.

Shayegan, M. Rahim. "Old Iranian Motifs in Vīs o Rāmīn." In *Essays in Islamic
Philology, History, and Philosophy*, edited by Alireza Korangi, Wheeler M.
Thakston, Roy P. Mottahedeh, and William Granara, 29–50. Berlin; Boston:
De Gruyter, 2016.

Skjærvø, Prods Oktor. "The Achaemenids and the *Avesta*." In *Birth of the
Persian Empire*, edited by Vesta Sarkhosh Curtis and Sarah Stewart, 52–84.
London; New York: I.B. Tauris, 2005

– "Jamšid i. Myth of Jamšid." *Encyclopædia Iranica* XIV/5 (2012): 501–22.
An updated version is available online at https://www.iranicaonline.org
/articles/jamsid-i. Accessed 1 June 2022.

– "Marriage ii. Next of Kin Marriage in Zoroastrianism." *Encyclopædia Iranica,
Online Edition*, 2013. Available at https://www.iranicaonline.org/articles
/marriage-next-of-kin. Accessed 1 June 2022.

Skjærvø, Prods Oktor, Djalal Khaleghi-Motlagh, and James R. Russell.
"Aždahā." *Encyclopædia Iranica* III/2 (1987): 191–205. An updated version is
available online at https://www.iranicaonline.org/articles/azdaha-dragon
-various-kinds. Accessed 1 June 2022.

Smith, Steven D. "Bakhtin and Chariton: A Revisionist Reading." In *The
Bakhtin Circle and Ancient Narrative*, edited by R. Bracht Branham, 164–92.
Groningen: Barkhuis Publishing & Groningen University Library, 2005.

Sohravardi, Shehāb al-Din Yahyā. *The Philosophical Allegories and Mystical
Treatises*. Edited and translated by Wheeler M. Thackston. Costa Mesa, CA:
Mazda, 1999.

Soudavar, Abolala. *The Aura of Kings: Legitimacy and Divine Sanction in Iranian
Kingship*. Costa Mesa, CA: Mazda, 2003.

Southgate, Minoo S. "Conflict between Islamic Mores and the Courtly
Romance of Vīs and Rāmīn." *The Muslim World* 75, no. 1 (1985): 17–28.

– "Vīs and Rāmīn: An Anomaly among Iranian Courtly Romances." *Journal of
the Royal Asiatic Society*, no. 1 (1986): 40–52.

Sperl, Stefan. "Islamic Kingship and Arabic Panegyric Poetry in the Early 9th
Century." *Journal of Arabic Literature* 8 (1977): 20–35.

– *Mannerism in Arabic Poetry: A Structural Analysis of Selected Texts*. Cambridge
University Press, 1989.

Sperl, Stefan, and Christopher Shackle, eds. *Qasida Poetry in Islamic Asia and Africa*. 2 vols. Leiden; New York: E.J. Brill, 1996.

Sprenger, Alois. "Bibliographische Anzeigen: Literarische Notizen." *Zeitschrift der Deutschen Morgenländischen Gesellschaft* 8 (1854): 608–10.

Stackelberg, Baron R. von. "Neskol'ko slov o persidskom epose 'Visa i Ramin'." *Drevnosti Vostochnye* 2, no. 1 (1896): 10–23.

Steingass, Francis. *A Comprehensive Persian-English Dictionary: Including the Arabic Words and Phrases to Be Met with in Persian Literature*. London: Routledge & Kegan Paul, 1963. First published in 1892.

Stetkevych, Jaroslav. *The Zephyrs of Najd: The Poetics of Nostalgia in the Classical Arabic Nasīb*. University of Chicago Press, 1993.

Stetkevych, Suzanne Pinckney. *The Poetics of Islamic Legitimacy: Myth, Gender, and Ceremony in the Classical Arabic Ode*. Bloomington: Indiana University Press, 2002.

Stoneman, Richard. "Persian Aspects of the Romance Tradition." In *The Alexander Romance in Persia and the East*, edited by Richard Stoneman, Kyle Erickson, and Ian Netton, 3–18. Barkhuis Publishing & Groningen University Library, 2012.

Stoneman, Richard, Krzysztof Nawotka, and Agnieszka Wojciechowska, eds. *The Alexander Romance: History and Literature*. Groningen: Barkhuis Publishing & Groningen University Library, 2018.

Stroumsa, Sarah. "Avicenna's Philosophical Stories: Aristotle's Poetics Reinterpreted." *Arabica* 39, no. 2 (1992): 183–206.

– "'True Felicity': Paradise in the Thought of Avicenna and Maimonides." *Medieval Encounters* 4, no. 1 (1998): 51–77.

Sturges, Robert S., ed. *Aucassin and Nicolette: A Facing-Page Edition and Translation*. Translated by Robert S. Sturges. East Lansing, MI: Michigan State University Press, 2015.

Sullivan, Karen. *The Danger of Romance: Truth, Fantasy, and Arthurian Fictions*. Chicago: University of Chicago Press, 2018.

Sunjana, Peshotun Dustoor Behramjee, ed. *The Dinkard: The Original Péhlwi Text; the Same Transliterated in Zend Characters; Translations of the Text in the Gujrati and English Languages; A Commentary and a Glossary of Select Terms*. 19 vols. Bombay: Duftur Ashkara Press, 1874–1928.

Ṭabarī, Abu Jaʿfar Muḥammad ibn Jarīr al-. *The Ancient Kingdoms*. Translated by Moshe Perlmann. Albany: State University of New York Press, 1987.

– *General Introduction and From the Creation to the Flood*. Translated by Franz Rosenthal. Albany: State University of New York Press, 1989.

Tafażżoli, Aḥmad. "Fahlavīyāt." *Encyclopædia Iranica* IX/2 (1999): 158–62. An updated version is available online at https://www.iranicaonline.org /articles/fahlaviyat. Accessed 1 June 2022.

Tājbakhsh, Esmāᶜil, and Hivā Ḥasanpur. "Sabkshenāsi-ye dahnāma-ye Vis-o Rāmin-e Fakhr al-Din Asᶜad Gorgāni." *Sabkshenāsi-ye Naẓm-o Naṣr-e Fārsi* 13 (1390 [2011]): 183–200.

Talattof, Kamran. "Niẓāmī Ganjavī, the Wordsmith: The Concept of *Sakhun* in Classical Persian Poetry." In *A Key to the Treasure of the Hakīm: Artistic and Humanistic Aspects of Niẓāmī Ganjavī's Khamsa*, edited by J.C. Bürgel and Christine van Ruymbeke, 211–44. Leiden University Press, 2011.

– "Nizami's Unlikely Heroines: A Study of the Characterizations of Women in Classical Persian Literature." In *The Poetry of Nizami Ganjavi: Knowledge, Love, and Rhetoric*, edited by Kamran Talattof and Jerome W. Clinton, 51–81. New York: Houndmills, Balsingstoke, Hampshire, 2000.

– "The Wordsmith: Further Reflection on the Source of Nezami Ganjavi's Creativity." In *The Interpretation of Nizami's Cultural Heritage in the Contemporary Period*, edited by Rahilya Geybullayeva and Christine van Ruymbeke, 135–49. Berlin: Peter Lang, 2020.

Talib, Adam. "Qasida Poetry: A World Unto Itself." In *A Companion to World Literature, Vol. 2: 601 CE to 1450 CE*, edited by Christine Chism, 1–10. John Wiley & Sons, Ltd., 2019. doi:10.1002/9781118635193.ctwl0318. Accessed 1 June 2022.

Tansar, Ibn al-Muqaffaᶜ, and Moḥammad b. al-Ḥasan b. Esfandiyār. *The Letter of Tansar*. Translated by Mary Boyce. Rome: Istituto Italiano per il Medio ed Estremo Oriente, 1968.

– *Nāma-ye Tansar be Goshnasp*. Edited by Mojtabā Minovi. Tehran: Khwārazmi, 1354 [1975].

Tarbiyat, Moḥammad-ᶜAli. "Maṡnavi va maṡnavi-guyān-e Irāni." *Mehr* 5 (1316 [1937]): 225–31, 313–20, 433–42, 539–44, 654–61, 757–67, 844–52, 941–51, 1061–8.

Ṭarsusi, Moḥammad b. Ḥasan Abu Ṭāher. *Dārāb-nāma-ye Ṭarsusi*. Edited by Ẕabiḥ-Allāh Ṣafā. 2 vols. Tehran: Bongāh-e Tarjoma va Nashr-e Ketāb, 1344–6 [1965–8].

Tavadia, J.C. "A Rhymed Ballad in Pahlavi." *Journal of the Royal Asiatic Society*, no. 1/2 (1955): 29–36.

Tawḥīdī, Abu Ḥayyān al-. *Kitāb al-imtāᶜ wa-l-muʾānasa*. Edited by Aḥmad Amīn and Aḥmad al-Zayn. Beirut: Manshūrāt Dār Maktabat al-Ḥayāh, 1965.

Tawḥīdī, Abu Ḥayyān al-, and Abu ᶜAlī Miskawayh. "On Why People Take Pleasure in Contemplating Beautiful Forms." In *The Philosopher Responds: An Intellectual Correspondence from the Tenth Century, Volume One*, edited by Bilal Orfali and Maurice A. Pomerantz, translated by Sophia Vasalou and James E. Montgomery, 212–17. New York University Press, 2019.

Tayyib, Abdulla el. "Pre-Islamic Poetry." In *Arabic Literature to the End of the Umayyad Period*, edited by A.F.L. Beeston, T.M. Johnstone, R.B. Serjeant, and G.R. Smith, 27–113. Cambridge History of Arabic Literature. Cambridge University Press, 1983.

Thaʿālibī, Abu Manṣūr al-. *Histoire des rois des perses / Tārīkh ghurar al-siyar.* Edited and translated by H. Zotenberg. Paris: Imprimerie Nationale, 1900.

Thaʿlabī, Aḥmad ibn Muḥammad al-. *ʿArāʾis al-majālis fī qiṣaṣ al-anbiyāʾ, or, Lives of the Prophets.* Translated by William M. Brinner. Leiden; Boston: Brill, 2002.

Thomas of Britain. *Tristran.* Edited by Stewart Gregory. New York: Garland, 1991.

Thompson, Stith. *Motif-Index of Folk-Literature: A Classification of Narrative Elements in Folktales, Ballads, Myths, Fables, Medieval Romances, Exempla, Fabliaux, Jest-Books, and Local Legends.* Charlottesville, VA: InteLex Corporation, 2000.

Tibullus. *Elegies.* Edited and translated by Guy Lee. 3rd ed. Leeds: Francis Cairns, 1990.

T'mogveli, Sargis. *Visramiani: The Story of the Loves of Vis and Ramin.* Translated by Oliver Wardrop. London: Royal Asiatic Society, 1914.

Tobkin, Jennifer. "A Man of Our Times: Muḥammad ibn Dāwūd al-Iṣbahānī's Pioneering Vision of Male Love." *Journal of Arabic Literature* 52, no. 3–4 (2021): 295–320.

Todorov, Tzvetan. "The Origin of Genres." *New Literary History* 8, no. 1 (1976): 159–70.

T'odua, Magali. "Yek do sokhan dar bāra-ye vizhegi-hā-ye suzha-ye dāstān-e Gorgāni." In *Vīs va Rāmīn of Fakhr al-Dīn Gorgānī: Persian Critical Text Composed from the Persian and Georgian Oldest Manuscripts,* edited by Magali T'odua, Alek'sandre Gvaxaria, and Kamāl ʿAyni, xxi–xxvi. Tehran: Iranian Culture Foundation, 1349 [1970].

Tolan, John. "Forging New Paradigms: Towards a History of Islamo-Christian Civilization." In *A Sea of Languages: Rethinking the Arabic Role in Medieval Literary History,* edited by Suzanne Conklin Akbari and Karla Mallette, 62–70. University of Toronto Press, 2013.

Toorawa, Shawkat M. *Ibn Abī Ṭāhir Ṭayfūr and Arabic Writerly Culture: A Ninth-Century Bookman in Baghdad.* London; New York: RoutledgeCurzon, 2005.

Tor, D.G. "The Long Shadow of Pre-Islamic Iranian Rulership: Antagonism or Assimilation?" In *Late Antiquity: Eastern Perspectives,* edited by Teresa Bernheimer and Adam Silverstein, 145–63. Exeter: Gibb Memorial Trust, 2012.

– *Violent Order: Religious Warfare, Chivalry, and the ʿAyyār Phenomenon in the Medieval Islamic World.* Würzburg: Ergon, 2007.

Tottoli, Roberto. "Hārūt and Mārūt." In *Encyclopaedia of Islam, THREE,* edited by Kate Fleet, Gudrun Krämer, Denis Matringe, John Nawas, and Everett Rowson, 2017. doi: http://dx.doi.org/10.1163/1573-3912_ei3_COM_30337. Accessed 1 June 2022.

– "The Qur'an, Qur'anic Exegesis and Muslim Traditions: The Case of *zamharīr* (Q. 76:13) among Hell's Punishments." *Journal of Qur'anic Studies* 10, no. 1 (2008): 142–52.

Treadwell, Luke. "*Shāhānshāh* and *al-Malik al-Muʾayyad*: The Legitimation of Power in Sāmānid and Būyid Iran." In *Culture and Memory in Medieval Islam: Essays in Honour of Wilferd Madelung*, edited by Farhad Daftary and Josef W. Meri, 318–37. London; New York: I.B. Tauris, 2003.

Trzaskoma, Stephen, trans. *Two Novels from Ancient Greece: Chariton's Callirhoe and Xenophon of Ephesos' An Ephesian Story: Anthia and Habrocomes.* Indianapolis: Hackett, 2010.

Ṭusi, Naṣir al-Dīn. *Akhlāq-e nāṣeri.* Tehran: Enteshārāt-e Khwārazmi, 1356 [1978].

– *The Nasirean Ethics.* Translated by G.M. Wickens. London: George Allen & Unwin, 1964.

Üstünyer, Ilyas. "Tradition of the Ashugh Poetry and Ashughs in Georgia." *Scientific Journal of International Black Sea University* 3, no. 1 (2009): 137–49.

Utas, Bo. "The Aesthetic Use of New Persian." *Edebiyât N.S.* 9 (1998): 1–16.

– "The Ardent Lover and the Virgin: A Greek Romance in Muslim Lands." *Acta Orientalia Academiae Scientiarum Hungaricae* 48, no. 1–2 (1995): 229–39.

– "Did ʿAdhrā Remain a Virgin?" *Orientalia Suecana* 33–5 (1984–6): 429–41.

– "'Genres' in Persian Literature 900–1900." In *Literary Genres: An Intercultural Approach*, edited by Gunilla Lindberg-Wada, 199–241. Berlin: De Gruyter, 2006.

Vadet, Jean-Claude. *L'Esprit courtois en Orient dan les cinq premiers siècles de l'Hégire.* Paris: G.-P. Maisonneuve et Larose, 1968.

Venetis, Evangelos. "Warlike Heroines in the Persian Alexander Tradition: The Cases of Arāqīt and Burāndukht." *Iran* 45 (2007): 227–32.

Vevaina, Yuhan Sohrab-Dinshaw. "'The Ground Well Trodden but the Shah Not Found … ': Orality and Textuality in the 'Book of Kings' and the Zoroastrian Mythoepic Tradition." In *Orality and Textuality in the Iranian World: Patterns of Interaction across the Centuries*, edited by Julia Rubanovich, 169–90. Leiden; Boston: Brill, 2015.

Vyasa. *Mahābhārata: Book 2: The Great Hall.* Translated by Paul Wilmot. New York University Press, 2006.

Waines, David. "Tree(s)." In *Encyclopaedia of the Qurʾān*, edited by Jane Dammen McAuliffe, n.d. doi:10.1163/1875-3922_q3_EQSIM_00425. Accessed 1 June 2022.

Washshāʾ, Muḥammad ibn Aḥmad al-. *al-Muwashshā, aw al-ẓarf wa-l-ẓurafāʾ.* Edited by Kamāl Muṣṭafā. Cairo: Maktabat al-Khanjī, 1372 [1953].

Waters, Matt. "To Be or Not to Be (Divine): The Achaemenid King and Essential Ambiguity in Image, Text, and Historical Context." In *Art/Ifacts and ArtWorks in the Ancient World*, edited by Karen Sonik, 159–81. Philadelphia: University of Pennsylvania Museum of Archaeology; Anthropology, 2021.

Weiner, Alfred. "Die *Faraǧ baʿd aš-Šidda*-Literatur. Von Madāʾinī (†225 h) bis Tanūḫī (†384h). Ein Beitrag zur arabischen Literaturgeschichte." *Der Islam* 4 (1913): 278–98, 387–420.

Whitmarsh, Tim. "Desire and the End of the Greek Novel." In *Plotting with Eros: Essays on the Poetics of Love and the Erotics of Reading*, edited by Ingela Nilsson, 135–52. Copenhagen: Museum Tusculanum Press, 2009.

– "Dialogues in Love: Bakhtin and His Critics on the Greek Novel." In *The Bakhtin Circle and Ancient Narrative*, edited by R. Bracht Branham, 107–29. Groningen: Barkhuis Publishing & Groningen University Library, 2005.

– *Dirty Love: The Genealogy of the Ancient Greek Novel*. Oxford University Press, 2018.

– "The Greek Novel: Titles and Genre." *The American Journal of Philology* 126, no. 4 (2005): 587–611.

– *Narrative and Identity in the Ancient Greek Novel: Returning Romance*. Cambridge University Press, 2011.

Whitmarsh, Tim, and Stuart Thompson, eds. *The Romance between Greece and the East*. Cambridge University Press, 2013.

Wiersma, S. "The Ancient Greek Novel and Its Heroines: A Female Paradox." *Mnemosyne, Fourth Series* 43, no. 1/2 (1990): 109–23.

Xenophon. *The Education of Cyrus*. Translated by Wayne Ambler. Ithaca; London: Cornell University Press, 2001.

Yarshater, Ehsan. "The Indian or Safavid Style: Progress or Decline?" In *Persian Literature*, edited by Ehsan Yarshater, 249–88. New York: Bibliotheca Persica, 1988.

– "Iranian National History." In *The Cambridge History of Iran, Volume 3(1): The Seleucid, Parthian and Sasanian Periods*, edited by Ehsan Yarshater, 359–477. Cambridge University Press, 1983.

Yohannan, John D., ed. *Joseph and Potiphar's Wife in World Literature: An Anthology of the Story of the Chaste Youth and the Lustful Stepmother*. New York: New Directions, 1968.

Yūsuf Khāṣṣ Ḥājib. *Wisdom of Royal Glory: A Turco-Islamic Mirror for Princes*. Translated by Robert Dankoff. University of Chicago Press, 1983.

Zadeh, Travis. "The Wiles of Creation: Philosophy, Fiction, and the 'Ajā'ib Tradition." *Middle Eastern Literatures* 13, no. 1 (2010): 21–48.

Zakeri, Mohsen. "ʿAlī ibn ʿUbaida ar-Raiḥānī: A Forgotten Belletrist (*adīb*) and Pahlavi Translator." *Oriens* 34 (1994): 76–102.

– "Javānmardi." *Encyclopædia Iranica* XIV/6 (2008): 594–601. An updated version is available online at https://www.iranicaonline.org/articles/javanmardi. Accessed 1 June 2022.

Zeitlin, Froma I. "Gendered Ambiguities, Hybrid Formations, and the Imaginary of the Body." In *Narrating Desire: Eros, Sex, and Gender in the Ancient Novel*, edited by Marília P. Futre Pinheiro, Marilyn B. Skinner, and Froma I. Zeitlin, 105–26. Berlin: de Gruyter, 2012.

Zenker, Rudolf. "Die Tristansage und das persische Epos von Wîs und Râmîn." *Romanische Forschungen* 29, no. 2 (1911): 321–69.

Žižek, Slavoj. *The Sublime Object of Ideology*. London: Verso, 1989.

Zolfaqāri, Ḥasan. *Yekṣad manẓuma-ye ᶜāsheqāna-ye fārsi*. Tehran: Nashr-e Charkh, 1394 [2014].

Zumthor, Paul. "Les Narrativités latentes dans le discours lyrique médiéval." In *The Nature of Medieval Narrative*, edited by Minnette Grunmann-Gaudet and Robin F. Jones, 39–55. Lexington, KY: French Forum, 1980.

– *Speaking of the Middle Ages*. Translated by Sarah White. Lincon; London: University of Nebraska Press, 1986.

– "The Text and the Voice." Translated by Marilyn C. Engelhardt. *New Literary History* 16, no. 1 (1984): 67–92.

– *Toward a Medieval Poetics*. Translated by Philip Bennett. Minneapolis, MN: University of Minnesota Press, 1991.

Zutphen, Marjolijn van. *Farāmarz, the Sistāni Hero: Texts and Traditions of the Farāmarznāme and the Persian Epic Cycle*. Leiden: Brill, 2014.

Index

Note: Page numbers in *italic* indicate an illustration or a table.